Sir Walter Raleigh

SIR
WALTER
RALEIGH

RALEIGH TREVELYAN

A JOHN MACRAE BOOK

HENRY HOLT AND COMPANY

NEW YORK

Henry Holt and Company, LLC
Publishers since 1866
115 West 18th Street
New York, New York 10011

Library of Congress Cataloging-in-Publication Data
Trevelyan, Raleigh.
  Sir Water Raleigh / Raleigh Trevelyan.—1st American ed.
    p. cm.
  Originally published: London : Allen Lane, 2002.
  Includes bibliographical references and index.
  ISBN 0-8050-7502-X
    1. Raleigh, Walter, Sir, 1552?–1618. 2. Great Britain—Court and
courtiers—History—16th century. 3. Great Britain—History—Elizabeth,
1558–1603—Biography. 4. Explorers—Great Britain—Biography. 5. Soldiers—Great
Britain—Biography. 6. Scholars—Great Britain—Biography. I. Title.
  DA86.22.R2T88 2004
  942.05'5'092—dc21
  [B]   2003051120

FIRST AMERICAN EDITION 2004
PRINTED IN THE UNITED STATES OF AMERICA

1   3   5   7   9   10   8   6   4   2

FOR RAÚL
at long last

Contents

List of Illustrations

1. Kat Astley
2. Hayes Barton
3. The Duke of Alba spears his enemies
4. Sir Humphrey Gilbert
5. Raleigh, the 'dear minion'
6. Queen Elizabeth, the Ermine Portrait
7. Philip II
8. Sir Richard Grenville
9. Sir Francis Drake
10. Raleigh as Captain of the Guard
11. Bess when young
12. Wife of the chief of Pomeioc
13. Pomeioc Village
14. The gateway at Sherborne Castle
15. Sherborne Castle
16. An Indian house
17. The *tepuy* Auyán
18. Panning for gold at Payepal
19. Lake Guatavita
20. The headless man (detail from 22.)
21. Effigy at San Augustín
22. Hariot's map of Guiana
23. The Earl of Essex
24. Raleigh, after Cadiz
25. Robert Cecil as Earl of Salisbury
26. Lord Henry Howard
27. James I
28. Bess in later years
29. The Conde de Gondomar
30. Gondomar's coffin

Within the Text

The text decorations and those at chapter headings are taken from the first edition of the *History of the World*.

List of Maps

A Preface

'He was a liar.'

These were nearly the last words that A. L. Rowse said to me. I was back from the Azores, and had told him that I had reread his *Grenville of the Revenge*, and that I had been to the island of Fayal, which had been captured by Sir Walter Raleigh on the famous Islands Voyage (and had nearly cost him his head). I watched for a reaction, as he lay there so quietly. He opened his eyes, and there was a gleam in them as he spoke.

'But', I ventured, 'don't you feel more sympathetic towards him when he was in the Tower?'

'Best place for him. Served him right'.

I never saw him again, and he died three weeks later.

Over the years whenever I happened to mention Raleigh's name to Rowse, he tended to be vehement, though always scornful of anyone who attempted to 'glamourize' Raleigh. He often repeated that Raleigh's *History of the World* was magnificent and that he was certainly a genius, but would generally add that he was an 'egoist first and last,' an 'equivocator'. 'I got him right,' he would say, and that was the end of it.

Well, I was not always to find myself in agreement. I was amused on coming across a comment by the distinguished French authority on Raleigh's writings, Pierre Lefranc, when he went to discuss Raleigh with Rowse, evidently with some contrary views; the conversations had been '*enflammées et souvent éclairantes*', different it would seem from meetings with the more pacific British *autorités raleghennes* Agnes Latham and Walter Oakeshott. Rowse did, however, agree with Lefranc about that much quoted contemporary verdict on Raleigh's trial in 1603: that it had 'injured and degraded the justice of England'.

Having been baptized Walter Raleigh because of a tenuous family connection, I shall have to admit occasional embarrassments when introducing myself as Raleigh in gatherings where everyone else was called Bill, Liz, Bob or Mary. Nevertheless, I was made to grow up with a romantic idea of a hero who was held out as a symbol of the Elizabethan Renaissance, and the virtual founder of the British Empire. My father owned a first edition copy of the *History of the World* and a locket supposed to contain a piece of Raleigh's hair. He also liked to recite Raleigh's reputed last poem 'Even such is time'.

As a boy I was taken to see tomb effigies of two Raleigh knights at Nettlecombe in Somerset, poor crumbling things, each beside his wife, with hounds at their feet: still dignified, and to me then as now moving. The future Sir Walter's ancestors came from that deep sleepy valley, once filled with deer and where ancient oaks had been drastically felled for building ships at the time of the Armada. Raleigh was born, probably in 1554, near East Budleigh in South Devon. The famous red cliffs of Devon and the not always blue sea were only three miles away across wooded hills. I thought it a magic place. The then owner showed me the room in which he said Raleigh had been born and told me that it was in the central porch that Raleigh's servant had seen him smoking a pipe of tobacco and, thinking he was on fire, had thrown a bucketful of water or spiced ale over him. If such a thing ever happened, it could never – as I subsequently discovered – have been at Hayes Barton.

All my life I have had to contend not only with the spelling of the name Raleigh as against Ralegh, but with its pronunciation: 'Rawley' as against 'Rahley' or 'Rally'. The spelling is more difficult to justify, because having signed himself Rauley and even Rauleygh, after 1584 when he was knighted he preferred Ralegh. His wife and younger son used that spelling too. However, Raleigh or Raleighe was more common among contemporaries; in fact over seventy variations have been counted, and these include Raghley, Rawleghe, Raulie, Raleh, Raughley, Rawlley, Wrawley, but more frequently Rawley or Rawly. To the Spaniards he could be Guaterral, Ralé or Gualtero. In the patent of 1584 that led to the discovering of Virginia his name is spelt both Raleighe and Raleigh. Raleigh is used as a first name by Gilberts, Chichesters, Trevelyans, Kerrs and others who have family connections. There is a great number of places in Devon that end in -eigh not -egh, and not just Colaton Raleigh and Withycombe Raleigh. To America's North Carolinans he is always spelt Raleigh, which is not surprising, their state capital being Raleigh. The result is that whereas British academics now hardly dare to use the -eigh version, that is and always will be the popular spelling. To my prejudiced eye Ralegh looks awkward and ugly. And if Robert Cecil nearly always signed himself Cecyll, why shouldn't we . . . ?

As for pronunciation, there is absolutely no argument that 'Rawley' is correct. The majority of variations in the spelling again prove it, and those who are of Raleigh descent use it. There were many puns on his name, based on *raw* and *lie*. At the height of his unpopularity there was for instance the riddle

> The foe to the stomach [raw] and the world of disgrace [lie]
> Shows the gent's name with the bold face.

When he was accused of atheism we also have

> *Raw* is the reason that *lie* within the atheist's head
> Which saith the soul of man doth die when the body's dead.

Most famous of all is James I's pun on first meeting Raleigh, against whom he was already prejudiced: 'Raleigh, Raleigh, I have heard but rawly of thee'.

What did he look like? He was about six foot, dark haired with lighter beard and moustache, and light brown eyes. Aubrey* described him as 'tall, handsome and bold, with a graceful presence', adding that his voice was 'small' and that he spoke with a strong Devonshire accent until his dying day, in spite of mixing with the greatest in the land, the 'learnedst and politest persons'. Which was to his credit.

A character in Anthony Powell's *A Dance to the Music of Time* is made to say: 'I thought of the portraits of Raleigh, stylised in ruff, short cloak, pointed beard, fierce look. "All the pride, cruelty, ambition of man"'. Powell was no doubt thinking of the best-known portrait, which is in the National Portrait Gallery. It was painted in 1588, the year of the Armada, when he was about thirty-four and at the height of his favour with Elizabeth. In this he sports an ear-ring of two large pearls, and his silken doublet, breeches and fur-lined cloak are intricately sewn with pearls, large and small. There is nothing effeminate about him. The extravagance and richness of his clothes vastly annoyed his contemporaries, but were part of his attraction for the Queen, who of course could dress far more bizarrely. His armour might be of silver, studded with pearls, diamonds and rubies. That he looked cruel in the 1588 portrait is maybe an over-exaggeration. He had certainly committed some terrible cruelties in the past, but mostly under orders. He was a byword for vanity and ambition, and was accused of being 'damnably proud'. After his death it was written that he had that 'awfulness

---

* John Aubrey (1626–97), antiquary, folklorist, gossip. His famous *Brief Lives*, selected from 426 entries, was first published in 1898 from mss. in the Bodleian.

and ascendancy in his aspect over other mortals', and it was this superior manner that upset people, especially if the mortals happened to be aristocrats. He did not care what others thought of him so long as he kept the affection and trust of the Queen, from whom all power and wealth derived.

Aubrey added that his moustache curled up naturally, evidently regarded as something to be envied, and that he had 'a most remarkable aspect, an exceedingly high forehead, long-faced and sour eye-lidded, a kind of pig-eye'. In the 1588 portrait the forehead is certainly high and the moustache does curl, though the eyes are made to look fairly large. But the 'pig-eye' does appear in some other portraits. Raleigh was painted many times, and as in the case of the innumerable portraits of Elizabeth we sometimes wonder if we are looking at the same person. At Longleat there is a full-length portrait by Zuccaro which makes him look a crazy fop, with a large bow on his arm, other bows on his legs, ostrich feather in his hat, baggy doublet like a skirt. The 'pig-eye' is there, but there is not so much 'pride, cruelty, ambition'. It has been suggested that this picture could really be of his brother Carew (who married the widow of the builder of Longleat) and this does seem a strong possibility.

As in many Elizabethan portraits, especially of Elizabeth herself, there is a symbolism in the 1588 picture which shows that it was painted to please the Queen: in the top left-hand corner there is a half moon symbolizing the chaste goddess Diana, as the Virgin Queen liked to be known. His earliest portrait is the well-known Nicholas Hilliard miniature painted in about 1585 when he was the Queen's 'dear minion'. Here there is no symbolism, and we recognize someone who has style and elegance, wearing a huge wheel-ruff edged with lace, and on his carefully arranged hair a 'Henri Trois' bonnet decorated with pearls and feathers, surmounting a face that is resolute, intelligent, confident of sexual attraction, although the 'pig-eye' is also there. His habitual show of finery would seem to have been due more to sheer extravagance and for the sake of the Queen rather than a desire to outdo noble rivals at Court.

There is no portrait of him as a frontispiece to the first edition of the *History of the World* – James had not allowed it. But it did appear in subsequent editions: he is still finely dressed, with a deliberate show of confidence, but there is a depth in those sad eyes. The strong intelligence is certainly there.

'I have been', he said on his scaffold, 'a seafaring man, a soldier and a courtier, and in the temptations of the least of these there is enough to overthrow a good mind and a good man.' He did have many temptations in the sharkpool of Elizabeth's court and he succumbed to some of them.

At the same time he was an outstanding poet, and a patron of poets; he was a chemist and scientist, and a patron of scientists; he was a ship designer, an explorer and empire builder; he was a naval and military strategist; he was a parliamentarian, and became recognized as a great historian. He introduced the potato to Ireland, and tobacco to England. He was accused of atheism, and was the victim of a scandalous trial.

Until his trial he was the most unpopular man in the country, but after his execution the most popular, becoming a hero to the republicans in the next decades. He was a man of almost supernatural energy, with huge ambition, and a patriot. He could be magnanimous and exceedingly brave, but at times embarrassingly cringing. His performance on the scaffold was a great piece of theatre but it is impossible not to be won over by it, as indeed were all, or nearly all, his spectators.

Gibbon thought of writing a biography of him, but was worried about dealing with Elizabethan politics – into which I have not attempted to delve overmuch here. New discoveries and new assessments of Raleigh's life and works continue to appear, and since Gibbon's day there have been many biographies, two of which, by Edward Edwards (1868) and William Stebbing (1899), are among the essential sources for any writer on Raleigh. T. N. Brushfield's 'Raleghana' series in the *Transactions of the Devonshire Association* (1868–1909) and V. T. Harlow's two books (1928 and 1932) on Raleigh's journeys to Guiana are also indispensable, while the work of the great scholar David Beers Quinn in more recent years is humbling to anyone aspiring to write on the early North American voyages and settlements.

For an obvious reason (my first name) I have retained the spelling Raleigh in this book, though on occasions I quote other versions. Mostly I have modernized the chaotic Elizabethan and Jacobean spellings in letters and documents that are hard to decipher for the non-specialist; and the same applies to manuscripts in Spanish. Where I have not modernized spellings I have done so for special reasons.

I am of course aware that some of the poems by Raleigh that I quote come in the category of 'attributed'. By and large I have followed Agnes Latham and more especially Walter Oakeshott, and I have consulted Michael Rudick's important work; but I have come to my own conclusions.

In the case of Raleigh's letters, some exist only in transcripts, which vary in small details. I have been greatly indebted to the invaluable volume of collected letters edited by Agnes Latham and Joyce Youings, but there have been occasions when I have decided to use different versions.

I am fortunate to have close Spanish relations, some being directly descended from the Conde de Gondomar, regarded by many non-Spaniards as the arch-villain in the story. This for all of us has been a joke, and when young we used to play card games, Raleighs versus Gondomars. It has been impossible not to take sides in writing this book, but I hope I have said enough for readers to appreciate the Spanish point of view and the reasons for the Spanish attitude towards Raleigh and other *corsarios* such as Drake, Hawkins and even Essex. I also hope that I have shown at least some of my sincere admiration for Gondomar's qualities as a diplomat, patriot, and a *Gallego*.

Family and Childhood

'He hath been as a star at which the world has gazed; but stars may fall . . .' These were the words of the Attorney-General when the final order was given for Raleigh's execution in 1618.

Sir Robert Naunton,* who was Secretary of State at that time, used a different metaphor as he looked back at the span of Raleigh's career in the time of Queen Elizabeth. He called him 'Fortune's tennis-ball' – 'She tossed him up of nothing, and to and fro to greatness, and from thence down to little more than to that wherein she found him, a bare gentleman. Not that he was less, for he was well descended and of good alliance; but poor in his beginnings.'[1] Raleigh descended from an old Devon family, and liked to claim that he could count on the support of 'more than a hundred gentlemen of my kindred', chiefly through his nearest relatives, the Champernownes, Carews and Grenvilles. As so little is known about his childhood, it is important to single out a few of those who had an influence on his upbringing. It must also be said that by no means all his supporters and relatives were from such backgrounds.

The reason for his own family's decline can be traced to the Cornish rising of 1497, in which his grandfather was somehow involved. This had meant not only a heavy fine but having to let the ancestral home Fardel Manor, that still stands in the lee of Dartmoor near Ivybridge and Cornwood.

His father, also called Walter, was married three times, and Raleigh was his youngest child. The first wife was Joan Drake, a step down socially maybe, though she was related to Francis Drake and was the daughter of a merchant with large shipping interests at Exmouth, sending tin and cloth to northern Spain and France, and in return bringing back wine, iron and glass. The Raleighs had manorial rights in the parish of Colaton Raleigh, not far from Exmouth and where the Drakes had land. For this reason Walter and Joan,

---

* Naunton (1563–1635), author of *Fragmenta Regalia* (1641), written however before he became Secretary in 1618, the year of Raleigh's execution.

I

no doubt with help from her father, acquired a lease on the farmhouse or barton of Hayes in the neighbouring parish of East Budleigh.

The future Sir Walter Raleigh loved Hayes Barton, as it became known, and in his years of affluence tried to buy it. The house – large, thatched with gabled wings, and mullioned windows – stands in rolling country and is well watered with a stream and pool. To the north is Woodbury Common, these days mostly covered with bracken and gorse. Possibly the original medieval building was modernized after his parents left – the windows for instance being glazed instead of shuttered. The red stone walls have now been mostly cemented over, and there is a general air of prosperity with several recent farm buildings. Pigs are bred here, or were in the 1990s. Perhaps the garden gnomes are not quite in character, but the flowerbeds appear weedless and the lawn is immaculate. A long narrow lane leads to East Budleigh, a traffic problem for the many pilgrims, who in any case obviously are a burden to the present owners.

There was not much land attached to Hayes Barton in Walter's and Joan's day, so presumably the family had grazing rights over part of Woodbury Common. Perhaps they were also able to farm some land at Colaton. Be that as it may, Walter was soon to join the Drakes in privateering, a sea-going activity little short of piracy – at any rate it was all very lucrative.

The modern village of East Budleigh, kept scrupulously tidy, has an unspoilt charm, and the massive sandstone tower of St Mary's rises above it like a castle keep. Walter senior must have been regarded as the squire, for in 1543 he was called upon to raise men for the French war and in 1547 he was made Justice of the Peace. At St Mary's he occupied the front left-hand pew, at the end of which his arms used to be carved, supported by two foxes and with an antlered helmet above, indicating no doubt a love of the chase. There is also a date, 1537. But the panel which contained the coat of arms has been cut away by some vandal or souvenir-seeker. There are many curiously carved bench-ends in the church, some grotesque and including the Green Man wreathed in leaves; and one does still have the Raleigh arms (five diamonds diagonally) impaled with those of Grenville, in deference to Walter senior's mother, who was a Grenville. As the family grew in size this is where the younger members would have sat.*

Walter was an ardent supporter of the reformed religion, as was a new vicar who presided over the removal of the rood loft. Its not especially pleasant to

---

* Joan is buried in the centre of the nave next to the Raleigh pew, under a large slab of grey stone. The lettering is strange because it has been reversed – through the looking-glass as it were. One theory is that it is the work of an illiterate who copied it from a pattern wrong way round.

record that in 1546 Walter was responsible for carrying off a cross of gold and silver, and that he refused to give it up, grinding it to pieces.

Walter and Joan had two sons, George born in 1527 and John about two years younger. Both boys seem to have grown into pretty rough characters and took up privateering with zest, sometimes in alliance with their father and the Drakes. We get the impression that Sir Walter Raleigh was not particularly close to these half-brothers, and was even ashamed of them, especially George. On the other hand his expert knowledge of shipbuilding and his love for the sea obviously had much to do with his connection with the Drakes of Exmouth.

Joan died in the late 1530s. There have been two theories about Walter's second marriage. One was that his wife was Italian, Elizabeth the daughter of Giacomo di Ponte of Genoa, the other – generally favoured and more likely – that she was Isabel Dorrell, daughter of a London merchant. Whoever she was, she died giving birth to a daughter named Mary, eventually to marry Hugh Snedall of Exeter, also a merchant. The Snedalls had a daughter, Margaret, who married the very rich William Sanderson, yet again a merchant, also a financier. Dorrells and Snedalls appear in the ups and downs of Raleigh's fortunes. Sanderson became Raleigh's financial agent and an important investor in his overseas ventures.

In 1548 or 1549, Walter married again, this time certainly a love match, and into the gentry. His third wife was Katherine, daughter of Sir Philip Champernowne of Modbury and Katherine Carew. Like Walter she was a strong Protestant, 'with a hatred of bigotry and the Spanish',[2] and the widow of Otho Gilbert, owner of Compton Castle, a fortified manor house in a wooded valley near Newton Abbot. They had three children: a son called Carew, a daughter variously known as Margaret or Margery, and Walter the subject of this book.

The Champernownes were a leading Devon family, of Norman descent (like the Gilberts), from Cambernon (Campo Arnulfi), and one ancestor had married the daughter of an illegitimate son of Henry I. In Tudor times widows of the gentry and nobility were much sought after, and thus soon remarried. The Gilberts were well off, their money coming from ships and shipbuilding; in the 14th century, for instance, they had provided ships for conveying pilgrims to Santiago de Compostela. However, Katherine had three sons by Otho Gilbert, so it is unlikely that she would have wished to deprive them of any inheritance from their father, and thus she would not have brought her new husband much financial benefit.

These three Gilbert sons were all remarkable people. They had been born at Greenway, overlooking the river Dart, its tall dense woods reflected in the river.* The eldest, John, later Sir John, went to live at Compton Castle, which still has a strong atmosphere of the period, with its portcullis, solar (drawing room), and chapel. He became Sheriff and a Vice-Admiral of Devon, with responsibilities for local defences against the Armada. The second, Humphrey, born in 1537, the great navigator and would-be colonizer, has a secure place in Elizabethan history; a brilliant and courageous man, though hot-tempered and at times cruel, he was also knighted, and was a great influence on the young Walter Raleigh. The third was Adrian, less extrovert, an astrologer and chemist, closely allied to the mysterious and controversial 'magus' Dr Dee. Adrian was also a garden designer and had mining interests. According to Aubrey he was 'very sarcastic, and the greatest buffoon [mocker] in the nation'; a suggestion has been made that he was a model for Falstaff in *The Merry Wives of Windsor*.[3]

It has often been regretted that no portrait exists of Katherine Champernowne, who as Raleigh's mother and the mother of these Gilberts injected genius into this 'fighting clan'. A portrait does however exist of one of her aunts, which could have had some resemblance. This aunt was also called Katherine: 'Kat' Astley,† who was the much loved governess and confidante of Elizabeth when she was a princess. Her face in this portrait is not especially handsome, but pleasant and calm, with dark eyes and dark straight hair parted at the middle. 'She bringeth me up from the cradle to the grave', Elizabeth once said.‡[4]

Another of Raleigh's great-aunts was Joan Champernowne. She married Sir Anthony Denny, who had been Chief Gentleman of the Privy Chamber to Henry VIII and was also related to the Boleyns. At periods of particular stress in her youth Elizabeth stayed with the Dennys.

Whether Raleigh actually met these two great-aunts is unlikely, but their relationship with the Queen was to stand him in good stead. He certainly was close to his uncle, his mother's brother, Sir Arthur Champernowne of Dartington Hall, a powerful figure in the county who for a while was a Vice-Admiral of Devon.§

*

* For many years Agatha Christie lived in a house on this site.
† Sometimes spelt Ashley, and written as such in a letter from Sir Walter Raleigh on 11 November 1601: 'My aunt Ashley'.
‡ Kat was not the most discreet of women, but her unwitting part in the sordid manoeuvres and treason of Lord Thomas Seymour belongs to another story. On Elizabeth's accession, she became First Lady to the Bedchamber and her husband Keeper of the Queen's Jewels.
§ Arthur's wife was the widow of the Sir George Carew who was drowned when the *Mary Rose* famously sank off Southsea in 1545.

There are two anecdotes worth telling about Raleigh's parents, both from before he was born. The first shows how Walter senior could behave in that thick-skinned way that so infuriated his son's enemies – and in his case leading to a nearly fatal result.

The year was 1549. There was serious unrest in Devon and Cornwall, where the old faith was still strong. The government of Edward VI had decreed that Cranmer's new prayer book should be used from Whit Sunday. In the ensuing explosion of fury, known afterwards as the Commotion but now as the Prayer Book Rebellion, barns were set on fire, trees were felled to block roads, and local grandees were threatened or went into hiding. A band of Cornishmen crossed the upper Tamar, where they were joined by Devonians. It was at this stage that Walter, riding to Exeter, came across an old woman telling her beads, on the way to Clyst St Mary outside the city. He scolded her, saying that telling beads was now illegal and she had better watch out. This put her into a fury, and off she dashed into the church crying out to the congregation that the gentry were getting ready to burn down their homes, adding 'many other speeches very false and untrue'. 'All in haste and like a sort of wasps', the people 'flung' themselves out of the church. 'They overtook Master Raleigh and were in such a choler, and so full of rage with him, that, if he had not shifted himself into the chapel there, and had been rescued by certain mariners [employees of his Drake father-in-law?] he had been in great danger of being murdered.' Barricades were put up and the bridge was fortified. Meanwhile Walter had tried to escape, but they caught him again and had him imprisoned in the tower of St Sidwell at Exeter, where he was 'many times threatened with death'.[5]

Clyst St Mary became a focus for the rebels. Exeter was besieged, and food became scarce, which made it even more unpleasant for Master Raleigh. But there was not much hope for the rebels against the troops under Lord Grey of Wilton. 'The fighting was fierce and cruel and bloody.' Some of the rebels were put to the sword, some burnt alive in their houses, others drowned as they tried to escape across the river: all rather hard to visualize in respectable, present-day, Clyst St Mary, virtually a suburb of Exeter.*

The story has a postscript. The repercussions of the Rebellion were felt in the next reign, on the accession of Queen Mary. Katherine Raleigh's cousin Sir Peter Carew was also a strong Protestant and had been a leading figure in quelling the revolt. Now, in 1553, he was one of those actively

---

* When Walter was released, he took away with him several church objects, including its best cope, valued at twenty marks. On being told that the people wanted it back, he said: 'If it were not already cut for a sparmer of a bed, they should have it.'[6]

campaigning against Mary's marriage to Philip II of Spain.[7] His arrest was ordered, and it was Walter who provided the bark to convey him, 'apparelled like a servant', to Weymouth with other dissidents. From there they crossed the Channel and were enthusiastically welcomed by Henri II of France. Afterwards Walter was locked up for three weeks in the Fleet prison in London, we assume for his part in Carew's escape.

The second, very different, anecdote concerns Katherine, and indeed is the only one we have concerning her. It appears in Foxe's *Book of Martyrs* and also occurred in the reign of Mary.

Agnes Prest of Launceston, 'a worthy gentlewoman,' though illiterate, was arrested for heresy and utterly refused to heed the views of her husband and children, who remained Catholic. She was taken to Exeter Castle and sentenced to be burnt. Many tried to reason with her, including her husband. Then Katherine Raleigh came – as Foxe tells us, a 'woman of noble wit, and of a good and godly opinion'. She said the creed to Agnes, but when she came to the words 'He ascended' told Agnes that 'God dwelleth not in temples made with hands; and that Sacrament to be nothing else but a remembrance of His blessed Passion'. On her return home Katherine told her husband that she had never heard a woman of such simplicity 'talk so godly, so sincerely, and so earnestly; insomuch that, if God were not with her, she could not speak such things. To which I am not able to answer her, who can read, and she cannot.' Soon afterwards Agnes went to the stake, determined on her martyrdom.

Here, it must be admitted, Katherine showed a humility rather different from that associated with any of her sons. Her visit to Agnes Prest, in the climate of those times, was certainly courageous.

Sir Walter Raleigh's age given on his portraits is by no means constant. As a result some biographies favour 1552 as his year of birth, and others, more usually, 1554. But then it could have been just as easily 1553. For this book it is taken as 1554.

His brother Carew was born in 1550. Aubrey tells us that he was musical and had a 'delicate clear voice and played singularly well on the olpharion (which was the instrument in fashion in those days) to which he did sing'. Like Walter he was tactless and quick-tempered. Carew's finances were enormously improved by his marriage to Dorothy Wroughton, daughter of a Mayor of London and widow of John Thynne of Longleat, to whom he had been 'gentleman of the horse'. Eventually knighted, he was not nearly so gifted as his brother, nor as handsome (if we assume that he is the subject of the ridiculously garbed portrait on the stairs at Longleat).

Not much is known of their sister Margaret/Margery, except that she married twice, first Lawrence Radford, second George Hall of Exeter. The latter was to hold a position of trust in the family, especially in the darkest days of her younger brother's life.

Nearly all is speculation about young Walter Raleigh's early years. We have for instance Charles Kingsley writing about this daring boy, fishing in the trout brooks, or going up with his father to the Dartmoor hills to hunt with hound or horse. If he did hunt deer, more likely it would have been on Woodbury Common. Certainly he would on occasions have accompanied his father and half-brothers on journeys by sea from Exmouth and Budleigh Salterton, and helped in the shipbuilding. No doubt he also listened to the yarns of ancient, and not so ancient, mariners/privateers/pirates about the Spanish Main and exotic lands full of strange beasts and fabulous treasure. The exploits of the Hawkins family of Plymouth certainly would have been a tremendous inspiration for boys such as the Raleighs; in 1562 and 1564 John Hawkins went on his two voyages to the Caribbean, trading in slaves and ivory acquired in Portuguese Guinea, 'partly by the sword and partly by other means'.[8]

Then of course there would have been visits to Compton Castle. John Gilbert, his eldest half-brother on his mother's side, was nineteen years older than young Walter, and was knighted in 1571. Humphrey Gilbert was seventeen years older and regarded as a great hero in the family. In 1562 he was at the siege of Le Havre where he served with 'great commendation' and was wounded. With him were cousins, Nicholas and Andrew Tremayne, identical twins; they were killed at Le Havre, and there were stories of their bravery. Other close relatives – Richard Grenville, Henry Champernowne, Philip Budockshide and William Gorges – went to Hungary to join in the war against the Turks. All of this would have stirred the imagination and ambitions of the younger members of their families.

The first recorded mention of Carew and young Walter is in 1560, when there was a lease of tithes of fish and larks (a great delicacy) at Sidmouth granted to 'Walter Rawlegh the elder esquire and Carow Raleye and Walter Rauleigh the younger sons of the said Walter'. This lease was disposed of by them in 1578, when young Walter gave his surname as both Rauleygh and Rawlygh, and Carew's was Raullgh and Raulligh.[9]

The tradition at East Budleigh is that the vicar John Ford had been the boys' tutor. Ford was a zealous Protestant; during his time the church's ornate altar was swept away, and the extravagant use of candles much reduced. It is also very possible that the boys attended the school of Ottery

St Mary, opened in 1545.* (Ottery St Mary is one of the many places where it is claimed that Raleigh had a house.) At all events it is perfectly acceptable to visualize them trudging with their satchels along that muddy lane from Hayes Barton.

Towards the end of the 1560s his parents left Hayes Barton and went to live in Exeter, where in 1569 Walter senior is listed as a man of property. This could have been one reason why young Walter decided to go to fight in France. The lease of Hayes Barton had been jointly in the names of his father and John Raleigh, whose wife appears to have felt that such an old-fashioned building was not up to her standards. So now it had been broken.

* Two and half centuries later Samuel Taylor Coleridge also went to school at Ottery, where his father was vicar.

With the Huguenots
1568–72

According to Anthony à Wood in his *Athenae Oxonienses* young Walter Raleigh became a commoner at Oriel College, Oxford, in 1568 'or thereabouts' – the age of fourteen would have been no barrier to his going to university. But *Athenae Oxonienses* was compiled in the next century, and Raleigh's name only appears in the Register of Oriel for 1572. This is one of the many question marks in mapping out his early life, especially as there is also a possibility that he went to France to fight for the Huguenots in 1568. John Hooker, a friend of Raleigh and Chamberlain of Exeter, in his supplement to Holinshed's *Chronicles*, tells us that he spent a good deal of his youth in 'wars and martial services'.

In Raleigh's *History of the World* there is a reference to the battle of Jarnac, which occurred on 13 March 1569.[1] What he said in that book may have been hearsay, but much more likely he was writing from experience, having taken part in the fighting in a troop led by his relative Henry Champernowne. There have also been suggestions that he was in France for several years on and off, returning at times to his studies at Oxford. At any rate the chance had come to prove himself, belonging as he did, as Hooker said, to that squirearchy which 'according to their innate fortitude thought themselves born to arms'. His other cousins were back from the Continent and would have been full of exciting tales. He needed the pay too, and in France there were prospects of good plunder. Having been brought up a strong Protestant, there was also for him an element of crusade in the venture.

The old pattern of Europe was collapsing, the religious upheavals breaking into hatreds and rivalries. For Elizabeth 1568 was a crucial year. The Queen of Scots had fled to England and had begun her long years of castle prisons, to become the centre of Catholic plots. The Papacy had also begun a new aggressive policy, with Elizabeth declared excommunicate. The Protestant Netherlanders had rebelled against their Spanish overlords, and thousands had been mercilessly executed at the order of the Governor-General, the

Duke of Alba. Ships bringing pay for Alba's troops had been driven by storms and privateers into the harbours of Fowey and Plymouth, and had their cargoes confiscated. In retaliation for this Alba had seized all English ships in Netherlands ports. Stories of the treachery of Spaniards at San Juan de Ulloa in Central America, and the seizure of some hundred men from John Hawkins' and Francis Drake's fleet, had stirred up a frenzy of anti-Spanish and anti-Catholic feeling in England, especially in the South-West, and that certainly would have included Raleigh. At the same time the third war of religion had begun in France, inaugurating a period of gruesome atrocities.

La Rochelle was the Huguenot capital, and Admiral Gaspard de Coligny's fleet, which included several English ships, was out to catch any Catholic vessel, large or small. One of these English ships was the *New Bark*, owned by a consortium including Raleigh's Cornish cousin Philip Budockshide, his uncle Sir Arthur Champernowne of Dartington, and William Hawkins of Plymouth. Captured goods were in this way pouring into the ports of Devon and Cornwall, especially Plymouth, ostensibly for safe keeping.

It was Elizabeth's policy to give covert aid to the Huguenots, with little cost to herself. When the French ambassador pointed out that bands of English were helping the rebels, she typically insisted that they had gone without her backing or permission. This meant that there would be serious consequences for Henry Champernowne and his followers, such as Raleigh, if they were caught: they would be hanged with a placard round their necks saying that they had come against the will of the Queen of England. But they were quite prepared for such a risk. As Raleigh was to write in another context, the mercies of God are not infinite.

So at last something of Raleigh's life begins to open up for us. His ancestors, some of them Crusaders, might have smiled encouragement, or they might have given a warning. Young men go to war as if starting on a game, maybe to prove themselves, but it has been reckoned that even two months of unremitting battle can be enough to break you. Either that, or you become hardened to the killing, immune to guilt, and perhaps even hailed as a hero. In Raleigh's case, assuming that he was at Jarnac, his first involvement in warfare was brief and disastrous, a defeat for the Huguenots. He returned to England for a while, perhaps to Oxford, still with his ideals, and by no means broken, ready to go back and no doubt still anxious to build up a fortune.

We realize from bitter references in the *History of the World* that Raleigh was never a hero in the French wars, but they did change him. His scepticism remained with him all his life, as his other writings, especially his poetry, make clear: death the inevitable and final leveller is a constant theme. Because of his experiences in France he was made to question religious doctrines – which led ultimately to the accusations of atheism that were flung at him towards the end of Elizabeth's reign. Take for instance this quotation from the *History of the World*: 'It is plain that Admiral Coligny advised the Prince of Condé to sign with the Huguenots not only out of love to their persuasion but to gain a party.' Or again: 'The greatest and most grievous calamity that can come to any state is civil war . . . a misery more lamentable than can be described, barbarous murders, devastations and other calamities . . . began and carried on by some few great men of ambitions and turbulent spirits, deluding the people with the cloak and mask only of religion, to gain their assistance to what they did more especially aim at.'

He himself did learn to be ruthless and inured to killings, as will be shown later. His experiences in France give many clues to the enigma of his character. He also learnt to understand the French to some degree and to speak their language, and this was to stand him in very good stead.

In 1568 Henry Champernowne was aged thirty and had seen plenty of active service, not only in Hungary. He had become friendly with the Comte de Montgomerie, a convert to Protestantism during his exile in England, and was now off to join him in France under the aegis of the Huguenot leaders, Admiral Coligny and Louis de Bourbon, the famous Prince of Condé. Montgomerie had fled from France after accidentally killing Henri II of France, husband of Mary Queen of Scots, in a jousting duel. Historians have tended to point out that his daughter, variously known as Robarda and Gabrielle, was married to Gawen Champernowne (a name straight from *Morte d'Arthur*?), son of Arthur Champernowne.[2] In fact they did not marry until 1572. Montgomerie flew a black banner with a defiant motto, *Finem det mihi virtus* (Let virtue end my days); it also showed a severed head, an unlucky symbol as it happened, for his own head was destined to be chopped off.

Champernowne is recorded as having been four leagues from Poitiers on 28 November 1568. On 6 February 1569, he wrote to the Earl of Leicester from La Rochelle to tell him that 'many of our footmen' had died during the winter, and that several more were sick. But he was still confident, he said. 'Our army without them liveth, but in small fear of the French king, so long as we hope that God is with us.'[3] In the approaching battle he reckoned that 100,000 men would be involved, and he was about right.

Raleigh would have been with the cavalry, attached to Montgomerie like the rest of the English contingent. The battle of Jarnac should more properly be called the battle of Bassac, for it was this small town or village that was at the centre. These days Bassac is a place of much charm, dominated by its huge fortress-like Benedictine monastery, founded in 1000 and with a superb Romanesque portal, still showing the marks of the cannon balls of 1569; it had also suffered greatly in 1434 when it had been pillaged by '*les Anglo-gascons*'.

Coligny made Bassac his headquarters, protected by the river Charente to the west and on other side by smaller streams. The countryside is very fertile, with vineyards that produce the grape that makes Jarnac famous for its cognac. Some defensive errors were made by the Huguenots, but the royalist army was in any case stronger, sweeping up from Vibrac and capturing Bassac, leaving it in ruins. A withdrawal by the Huguenots was made towards the next town, Triac. All this is easily visualized today. The fiery-tempered Condé, like England's Richard I also known as *Coeur de Lion*, took the lead against the enemy with his three hundred horsemen. Montgomerie's cavalry was to his right, Coligny's to the left, but both were beaten back. Condé fearlessly galloped ahead, crying out '*Doux est le péril pour Christ*'. His horse was wounded and fell. He was surrounded, recognized and when about to surrender shot in cold blood through the head. His body was carried into Jarnac on the back of a donkey.

The defeat was a severe blow to the Huguenots, even though they had lost only 400 men. This is Raleigh's comment in his *History of the World*: 'I remember it well that when the Prince of Condé was slain after the battle of Jarnac, the Protestants did greatly bewail his loss, in respect of his religion, person, and birth; yet that comforting themselves; they thought of rather an advancement than hindrance to that affair, for so much did the valour of the one [Condé] outreach the advisedness of the other [Coligny], that whatsoever the admiral intended to win by waiting the advantage, the prince adventured to lose by being over-confident in his own courage.'[4] A small pyramid was erected in the 19th century to commemorate the place where Condé died. It still stands, its top snapped off, with privet hedges on either side: a place of memories always.

Henry Champernowne and his men returned to rest and refit in England. After Jarnac Elizabeth sent an expedition to La Rochelle, with supplies of food and ammunition. This time the English volunteers had included fifty engineers, perhaps Cornish miners, to help with the defences. Her ships returned with a cargo of wine, salt and some booty from the Caribbean. Champernowne, with the blessing of the Queen, organized another and more ambitious troop, a hundred volunteer horsemen from the West Country gentry. They arrived in France, says William Camden in his

Annales, in October 1569, and among them were 'Philip Budockshide, Francis Berkeley and Walter Raleigh, a very young man who now began to be of any note.' According to De Thou in his *Mémoires*, they were a 'gallant company, nobly mounted and accoutred'. Both Champernowne and Budockshide were to die in France.*

Camden must have meant September; if we are to assume that the troop was plunged into yet another bloody battle, at Moncontour in Poitou, on 3 October. In any case Champernowne wrote an encouraging letter on 28 September to Elizabeth, saying that the hope was to march on Paris or Normandy. Since July the Huguenots had been besieging Poitiers, where the situation was dire and rats and mice were being eaten. Coligny's army, although numerically less than the Catholics', was so strong that the Duke of Anjou (later Henri III) was unable to dislodge them. Instead Anjou decided to make a feint attack on the Huguenot town of Châtellerault to the north of Poitiers, and this successfully drew away Coligny, who was afraid that he might be cut off from Moncontour and Airvault on his west flank. We are told that on both sides the mercenaries – who made up a large proportion of both armies – were clamouring for battle, although Coligny would have preferred to wait.

An attempt to reach Airvault was prevented by Anjou swinging north across the plain of Moncontour. At first it seemed as if the Huguenots might win. The English troop was only a small part of the cavalry, but in the vanguard of the charge. Suddenly all was confusion and the German mercenaries began to panic. Champernowne reckoned afterwards that 12,000 footmen had been lost, but it could have been more, as several of the captured survivors had their throats cut. Coligny himself was wounded in the face, and collapsed from loss of blood.

Those on horseback were luckier. As Raleigh was to write in the *History of the World*, the retreat of Ludwig of Nassau, brother of the Prince of Orange, at Moncontour was made 'with so great resolution as he saved one half of the Protestant army, then broken and disbanded, of which myself was an eye-witness, and was one of them that had cause to thank him for it.'[5] He also commented on 'a sure rule of war': 'It is less dishonour to dislodge in the dark than to be beaten in the light.' It must also have been farewell to the fine accoutrements.

---

* Cornish surnames can be confusing. Budockshide appears elsewhere not only as Butshead, but Budocushyde and Butshed. In the church of Lansallos, on the steep cliffs near Polperro, the elaborately carved slate coffin slab of Philip's widow is fixed to the wall, complete with farthingale, stomacher and ruff. Before her death (in 1577) she had settled on an easier version of the name: Buttonhead.

The battlefield of Moncontour can still be clearly visualized from the ramparts of the great Romanesque church at Saint Jourin-de-Marnes which was sacked by the Protestants. Across the flat wheatfields and clumps of poplars is the line of Moncontour's houses with their little red roofs and its *donjon*. To the right is the lake which in 1569 the Huguenots fondly hoped would give them protection.

Coligny, accompanied by Prince Henry of Navarre and the young Prince of Condé, now began the long retreat south, romantically known as the 'Voyage of the Princes'. But it must have been a hellish experience. Most of the infantry was left at Saint Jean d'Angely, where nearly all the inhabitants were slaughtered. We are told that Champernowne's troop – including therefore young Raleigh – continued with the cavalry, 'trumpets sounding'. However, such bravado did not last and after two months they arrived at Montauban, exhausted, even their horses barely able to walk. Henry Champernowne became ill and was sent to La Rochelle, where he died; the Queen of Navarre sent a letter of condolence to Queen Elizabeth, praising him for his *'pieté, prudence, vertu et vaillance'*.[6]

Revived by local wine, Coligny's men and the English remnant were joined by Montgomerie, in contrast full of energy and enthusiasm after beating the Catholics at Béarn. But by all accounts there was not much discipline. The voyage continued along the river Garonne, ravaging the countryside, torturing, sacking and raping. Toulouse was besieged, houses of the rich were looted and then burnt. Remembering all this, Raleigh made a sour comment in the *History of the World*, when writing about Alexander the Great's march on India: 'They [Alexander's soldiers] were pestered with the spoils of so many cities as the whole army seemed but the guard of their carriages (not much unlike the warfare of the French)'.[7] At Navarrens the entire garrison was massacred by Montgomerie. In retribution the royalist Catholics under Montluc put the population of Mont-de-Marson to the sword, and that included the women who had been throwing stones from the walls.

Raleigh's only other comment arising from his experiences at that time seems relatively mild in context: 'I saw in the third civil war in France certain caves in Languedoc which had but one entrance, cut out in the midway of high rocks which we knew not how to enter to by any ladder or engine; till at last by certain bundles of lighted straw, let down by an iron chain, and a weighty stone in the midst, those that defended it were so smothered that they rendered themselves, with their plate, money, and other goods therein hidden, or they must have died like bees that are smoked out of their hives.'[8] He did not say so, but no doubt emerging from the caves they had their throats cut.

Most of Provence and much of Languedoc were now under the control of the Huguenots. The Voyagers swung east, pillaging all the way, to the Rhone and then up the Loire. With Paris in danger, the Queen Mother, Catherine de' Medici, was obliged on 8 August 1570 to sign the Peace of St Germain. This would have been the sign for Raleigh and other survivors of the Champernowne troop to return to England. But it would not have been for long, if Richard Hakluyt is correct in a dedicatory epistle to Raleigh he published in 1587, 'Calling to mind that you had spent more years in France than I, and understand the French much better than myself...'[9] That would also have meant that altogether Raleigh was in France five years; or perhaps part of the time he was in Flanders with Humphrey Gilbert. Certainly, he might well have been tempted on occasions to return to La Rochelle, looking for opportunities for some lucrative privateering.

There has also been speculation as to whether he was in Paris during the St Bartholomew's Day Massacre on 24 August 1572, and that he was one of the English residents, along with Philip Sidney, who took refuge in the house of the ambassador, Sir Francis Walsingham. On the other hand in none of his writings does Raleigh give any indication of having been a witness to those ghastly events. He might well have been with his uncle Sir Arthur Champernowne who went to Paris in May that year, when the Earl of Leicester was attempting to negotiate a treaty, and could have decided to stay on for the marriage of the king's sister, Marguerite de Valois, to Henry of Navarre, designed to cement the alliance between Catholics and Protestants. As Champernowne was related to Walsingham, Raleigh might even have been staying at the English embassy.

Huguenot leaders had gathered for the marriage celebrations. Whereupon the Queen Mother ordered that they should all be slaughtered with their families and adherents. In any case few people were more hated in Paris than Coligny. He was the first to be murdered, his body thrown from the window. The mob rampaged through the city, slaughtering the heretics, and over the next weeks thousands more Protestants throughout France were killed. But the news brought rejoicing throughout Catholic Europe, and the Pope issued a special medal as a celebration.

'There are no such things', Raleigh was to write, 'as wars of religion, only civil wars. The condition of man was never bettered by them.'[10]

Desirous of Honour
1572–9

In whatever years Raleigh was at Oriel, he did not stay long enough to take a degree. In 1594, when he was in trouble over his supposed atheism, it was reported by the commission that he had been 'a scholler some tyme in Oxford under a Bachelor of Arte'. There are only few references or anecdotes about his 'tyme' there, and not many, though rather more, about his appearance at the Inns of Court, where in the register of the Middle Temple for 27 February 1575 he features as 'Walter Rawley, late of Lyons Inn, Gentleman, Son of Walter Rawley of Budleigh, County Devon, Esquire'.[1] Lyons Inn was one of the Inns of Chancery attached to the Inner Temple, and Raleigh had moved on to the livelier and more exciting Middle Temple.

It seems reasonable to assume that he was finally settled at Oxford after his various exploits in France, in which case 1572, the year in which he features as W. Rawley in Oriel's list of members, would be perfectly valid. Anthony à Wood tells us that Raleigh was at Oriel with 'C. Champernowne, his kinsman', and Charles Champernowne does also appear on that list. The two Unton brothers were friends of Raleigh – Henry Unton became twice ambassador in France, and Edward Unton was with him in Ireland in 1586–7 – and they certainly were at Oriel in the early 1570s.

Sir Robert Naunton, Secretary of State to James I, was to write: 'His approaches to the University and Inns of Court were the grounds of his improvement, but they were rather excursions than sieges or sitting down, for he stayed not long in a place, and being the younger brother and the house diminished in its patrimony, he foresaw his own destiny that he was first to roll through want and disability before he could come to a repose and as the stone doth by lying long gather moss.' This rolling stone must have found it hard to settle down to university life. Presumably he was living on his gains, fair or foul, earned in France. But he was not one for wasting time. He knew that to achieve his ambitions he not only had to work hard, but to pull strings – and in this way the Champernowne connection was at first especially useful. Naunton describing him also said: 'He had in the outward man a good presence in a handsome and well-compacted person, a strong natural wit [intelligence] and a better judgement, with a bold and plausible tongue whereby he could set out his parts to the best advantage, and to these he had the adjunct of some general learning which by diligence he enforced to a great augmentation and perfection, for he was an indefatigable reader whether by sea or land, and none of the least observers both of the men and the times . . . If ever a man drew venture out of necessity, it was he, and therein he was the greatest example of industry.'

Raleigh became famous, or notorious, for his love of extravagant clothes, but at this stage of life he certainly could not have afforded them. Aubrey says that in his youth he was for several years 'under straits for want of money', and goes on to tell a story about his sharing chambers with a Mr Child of Worcestershire, and then borrowing a gown from him or his father, which he never returned or paid for. He being a hardened warrior other students were in awe of him, judging from another story, this time by Francis Bacon (a Cambridge man) in his *Apophthegms*: 'There was at Oxford a cowardly fellow that was a very good archer. He was abused greatly by another, and moaned himself to Walter Raleigh, then a scholar, and asked his advice what he should do to repair the wrong that had been offered him'. Raleigh's impatient reply was, 'Why, challenge him to a match of "shooting".'

Anthony à Wood again wrote: 'His natural parts being strangely advanced by academical learning, under the care of an excellent tutor, he became the ornament of the juniors, and was worthily esteemed a proficient in oratory and philosophy.' This tutor could have been Henry Pigot, who was Henry Unton's tutor. Pigot was Principal of St Mary Hall, closely connected with Oriel. Thomas Hariot, the brilliant mathematician and scientist, entered St Mary Hall in 1577 and obtained his degree in 1580. Because of their joint interest in navigation and exploration he was to become one of Raleigh's most loyal friends and allies. It thus seems very probable that Pigot had introduced Hariot to Raleigh. Hariot, as will be seen, became part of Raleigh's household in 1582. Among others more or less contemporary with Raleigh at Oxford were his cousins Arthur Gorges and George Carew, as were Richard Hakluyt the younger and Lawrence Keymis, all important and trusted friends. Hakluyt went into the Church, but again his interest in navigation and exploration made him a key supporter and propagandist for Raleigh's future territorial ambitions. His uncle, also called Richard Hakluyt, was at the Middle Temple, and gave geographical advice to the Muscovy Company, a group of English merchants trading with Russia; Raleigh would have got to know him well, especially as his half-brother Adrian Gilbert had been the elder Hakluyt's neighbour.

Raleigh was to say at his trial in 1603 that he had never 'read a word of law or statutes' before he became a prisoner in the Tower. This may have been true, as scions of the landed gentry and the rising merchant class at that period did not necessarily expect to take a degree at their university or to learn to practise as barristers at the Inns of Court. It was like joining a club or a finishing school, where one hoped to make influential friendships, preferably in royal circles, and to learn about politics and current events.

According to Sir Stephen Powle, in the next century an eminent member of the Virginia Company, 'my bedfellow at the Inns of Court and many years' companion was riotous, lascivious, and incontinent Raleigh.'[2] Students at the Middle Temple were expected to live in, but some had to live out, or preferred to do so as it gave them more freedom. So the bed that Raleigh shared with Stephen Powle may not have been in constant use. Sharing a bed, it must be hurriedly added, was common then, often for reasons of economy.

Aubrey reported that Raleigh's friends in his youth were 'boisterous blades', though generally those who had 'wit'. He also seems to have chosen rowdy characters as servants, for in 1577 he had to bail out two of them on a couple of occasions for riotous behaviour and defying the watch. In one instance he is described as 'Walter Rawley, of Islington, Esq.', and in the other 'Walter Rawley, Esq *de Curia*', that is, of the Court.[3] Nowadays a public house in Islington, the Old Queen's Head, on the corner of Raleigh Street and Essex Street, is sometimes said to be on the site of Raleigh's house but if it still has some Elizabethan features, they are extremely hard to detect. Another contender is the Finnock and Firkin in Upper Street. What is certain is that his original house, 'a bow's shot from the church', did turn into an inn, but traditionally it became the Pied Bull, pulled down in 1827.[4]

'*De Curia*' shows that he was already looking for preferment at Court, and had even acquired some sort of minor post there.

When many years later Raleigh's elder son got into trouble with hard-drinking friends, in particular Ben Jonson, his mother laughed and admitted that his father had also been 'so inclined'.[5] We are given another example of Raleigh's boisterous behaviour when in a tavern he became tired of a 'bold impertinent fellow' named Charles Chester, who was an incessant talker, making a noise like a drum in the room.[6] Raleigh grabbed him, beat him, and sealed up his moustache and beard with wax. Charles Chester never forgave him, for there is another anecdote of a much later period. Chester became one of the Queen's jesters and was forever 'girding' at Lord Knollys and Raleigh. So one day the two of them decided to invite him to dinner. After the meal Raleigh said: 'Come, sirrah, we'll be revenged on you for all your roguery.' He called the servants, tied Chester up hand and foot, stuck him in a corner, and then 'called a mason or two, built him presently to the chin and so close he could not move, and threatened to cover him in, but that he begged hard and swore that he would abuse them no more; so they let him stand till night.'[7] Aubrey claimed that this Chester was the original of Carlo Buffone in Ben Jonson's *Every Man Out of His Humour*.

It was in 1576 that Raleigh appeared first in print, as 'Walter Rawely of the Middle Temple', in the form of commendatory verses prefixed to *The Steele Glas* by the soldier-poet George Gascoigne. *The Steele Glas* was a satire in blank verse of fashionable society, the title referring to the fact that the usual mirror for those times was made of polished steel, while the new Venetian crystal mirror gave a reflection that was more flattering. Raleigh's contribution was suitably sardonic, though strangely he almost seemed to have a foreknowledge of his own fate. His style was also epigrammatic, as so often in his later poetry.

In the poem he attacked the envious and those people who delighted to see the worst in what is actually the best. 'Sweet were the sauce', he began, 'that would please each kind of taste'. Then he moved on, rather mixing up his anatomy, to 'spiteful tongues' in 'cankered stomachs'. Perhaps he was already conscious that his superior ways and too-blatant ambition were making enemies:

> But curious brains do naught, or light, esteem
> Such stately steps as they cannot attain:
> For whoso reaps renown above the rest
> With heaps of hate shall surely be oppressed.

Mottoes were important in those days. Gascoigne's was a double dedication, to Mars and Mercury, *Tam Marti Quam Mercurio*, which Raleigh, probably still restless and longing for action, thought suited him too, and in due course he adopted it. Gascoigne had been in Flanders with Humphrey Gilbert, and most importantly had the Earl of Leicester as patron. So it may have been he who introduced Raleigh to Leicester. In that same year, 1576, Gascoigne published, apparently without permission, Gilbert's *Discourse to prove a Passage by the North-West to Cathaia [Cathay] and the East Indies*, which had been written ten years before, and dedicated to the 'Queen's most excellent Majesty'. This enthusiastic and patriotic piece caused a certain stir, and contained a phrase that was remembered after Gilbert's heroic death in 1583: 'He is not worthy to live at all, that for fear, or danger of death, shunneth his country's service, and his own honour.'[8]

Humphrey Gilbert was not only Raleigh's half-brother but also very much his mentor, and after his death it was said that Raleigh saw himself as heir to his 'originating spirit'. Gilbert had been educated at Eton and Oxford. At the age of seventeen he had been a page to Princess Elizabeth, thanks both to his aunt Kat Astley and Elizabeth's tutor Roger Ascham, under whom he had also studied. Elizabeth liked him and according to Hooker when she became Queen would often 'familiarly discourse with him'. It is therefore very likely that he had been instrumental in getting Raleigh his first foothold at Court.

He was tall and dark, like Raleigh, but with a 'choleric complexion'.[9] Judging from the portrait at Compton Castle, there could have been a certain family likeness between him and Raleigh: those eyes are rather 'piggy', the moustache does curl up and the forehead is fairly high. There were certain similarities in character too. By now Gilbert had a high reputation for courage, indeed ferocity. He was vain, outspoken, ambitious, and impulsive, with a quick temper and an 'excellent and ready wit'. His motto was *Quid non?* (Why not?). Some people were attracted by him, others quite the opposite.

For three years Humphrey Gilbert had been in Ireland, first in Ulster, then in Munster, where he had crushed a rebellion with, according to modern standards, terrible savagery – the most notorious incident being lining the path to his tent with heads of captives when receiving their relatives.[10] He had been knighted, and it was after this he had gone to Flanders, where Raleigh may or may not have joined him. This last enterprise had ended in humiliating failure, and Gilbert was anxious to redeem himself.

The *Discourse* in its original version had caught the attention of that puzzling character, the Welsh 'magus' Dr John Dee, Queen Elizabeth's astrologer (he had been asked to choose the date for her coronation) and not surprisingly regarded by some of his contemporaries as a sorcerer. Reading Dee's later diaries, with their references to angels, wife-swapping and the spirits, one might find it hard to appreciate his importance, which was indeed very real, especially in early English maritime history; or how great an effect he had on Raleigh's sceptical mind. The Gilberts consulted him, Adrian Gilbert was especially fond of him. As a geographer and mathematician of international fame this handsome man with his long white pointed beard had an immense range of knowledge including navigational science and metallurgy, and a huge library. He is also credited with being the first to coin the phrase British Empire, and to propagate the theory that Elizabeth had the rightful title to the whole of North America, based on the voyage of the Cabots nearly a century before. In his preface to Euclid's *Elements* he gave an accolade to the *Discourse*, agreeing that the fabled land of Cathay was 'far passing in all riches and worldly treasure'.

Dee's writings, his influence at Court, and Humphrey Gilbert's *Discourse* were useful propaganda for the Muscovy Company, which had been forced to recognize the futility of reaching Cathay along the north coast of Siberia. Then in 1576 the newly formed Company of Cathay despatched Martin Frobisher across the Atlantic in search of a north-west passage. Encouraged by Dr Dee, the Queen had given her blessing to this venture, and had waved farewell to Frobisher's ships as they sailed past her palace at Greenwich.

And so England belatedly had entered the imperial competition for the New World. Frobisher's voyages, though ultimately disappointing, provided vital lessons not only for future explorers and navigators, but for Gilbert's and Raleigh's colonial attempts.

Frobisher reached Baffin Island, believing that the bay was part of the Pacific Ocean. There was excitement when he brought back to England an Eskimo with suitably Oriental features, and almost frenzy when he produced a piece of black rock that glinted like gold. There was no difficulty now in raising money from the Court and the City, a major investor being Sir Thomas Gresham, Founder of the Royal Exchange. Again Dee's opinion was sought, and in May 1577 a second expedition sailed to the land which Elizabeth named Meta Incognita, the unknown boundary. The aim was not so much to establish the passage, but to bring back a quantity of this black ore for further investigation. The Queen put up £1,000. At last there was a chance of challenging the riches of Spain and Portugal.[11]

The expedition sailed in 1577, bringing back 140 tons of the ore, also drawings of Eskimos and kayaks by John White, who was to be important later to Raleigh. Assays were made by a Venetian, Baptisto Agnello, but notably by one Burchard Kranich, a German mining expert and a highly suspect individual. Both declared a good yield of gold, in spite of some growing doubts by Dee and others. A large furnace was prepared at Deptford. Thus in the following year Frobisher set forth once more, this time also with the intention of establishing some sort of permanent base in those Arctic waters. He left with fifteen ships, one being the Queen's flagship, and with 150 Cornish miners and 250 other men.

Gilbert had turned to different schemes. He yearned for more overt action against the great enemy, and had meanwhile produced another pamphlet, *How Her Majesty May Annoy the King of Spain*, the three main recommendations being the rounding up of all fishing vessels off the Newfoundland coast, the sending of ships to Bermuda to lie in wait for the Spanish treasure fleet, and – much more risky – the dispatching of some five or six thousand men to capture Cuba and Hispaniola, which he believed to be undefended.

As before he ended his pamphlet with a splendid literary flourish, to prove his patriotism and loyalty: 'The wings of man's life are plumed with the feathers of Death.'[12] But Elizabeth was by no means ready for this kind of confrontation. In greatest secrecy, she had in fact already given permission for Drake's famous voyage through the Magellan Straits and up the Pacific coast of South and North America that was to result in his circumnavigation of the globe. Quite what the original purpose of his daring voyage was is still vague, but it had distinguished backers, including the Secretary of State Walsingham, the Earl of Leicester, Sir Christopher Hatton the Vice-Chamberlain, and Sir John Hawkins, Comptroller of the Navy.

Frobisher's proposed settlement on Baffin Island came to nought, because part of the prefabricated building was lost at sea. His expedition returned with the amazing load of 1,200 tons of black ore. There had been great storms, and one ship, the *Emanuel*, was driven ashore with its cargo and wrecked at Smerwick on the Dingle Peninsula in Ireland. Smerwick: a desolate place that over the centuries was a slur on Raleigh's reputation, especially in Ireland, as will later be clear.

Kranich, the suspect mining expert, had meanwhile died. The new assayers could find no gold in that ore, and the awful truth dawned that it was mere iron pyrites, 'fool's gold'. Then it transpired that both Agnello and Kranich had cheated.* Agnello admitted that he had inserted real gold into the furnace, in order to 'coax nature'. Kranich had secretly added two gold

---

* The shady history of Burchard Kranich, or Cranach, is full of obscurities. There is no doubt that he had a considerable reputation as a mining engineer. By coincidence around 1560 he erected a smelting house for silver on the site of a house in south-east Cornwall, now owned by the author of this book; here he also kept a 'hoor or two'. Such a remote spot may have been chosen for practising alchemy, as he was generally believed to have a 'familiar' or attendant spirit. The bailiffs were soon after him, and he was arrested, though meanwhile he had cured Sir William Mohun of Boconnoc of a dangerous sickness. When sent to the Marshalsea prison in London he became known as Dr Burcot, but was called out to cure Lord Hunsdon, with success. When the Queen became ill, he again was summoned, only to pronounce that she had the smallpox. Elizabeth was furious and would not believe it. 'Have away the knave out of my sight,' she cried. She became worse, and again Cranach/Burcot was sent for. As he had been so insulted by her, he refused to come, saying: 'By God's pestilence, if she be sick, then let her die. Call me a knave for my good will.' He remained in deep umbrage and had to be forced to see her at the point of a poniard. 'Almost too late, my liege,' he told her encouragingly. ''Tis the pox.' Still she would not believe it. 'By God's pestilence,' he cried, 'which is the better, to have the pox in the hands, in the face and in the arse, or to have them in the heart and kill the whole body?' He gave her a cordial, wrapped her in a scarlet cloth, and put her on a pallet in front of the fire. She of course survived, and is said to have presented him with a pair of gold spurs that had belonged to her grandfather Henry VII, as well as land in Cornwall worth £100. Whether Cranach/Burcot was related to the great artist Lucas Cranach is yet to be proved.[13]

coins, so as to be sure that he would be employed as assayer for all future loads of this black ore.

Recriminations, law suits, financial ruin followed. Frobisher had to return to privateering to recoup his losses. In a back street at Deptford, there is a wall containing a few of his black blocks that glitter in the sun. Others were used for roadmaking.

Gilbert had been having discussions with Walsingham following his last pamphlet, and already had ships in preparation for some sort of 'sea voyage' – the borderline between private enterprise and national commitment as always being vague. Then at last there was royal assent for a quite different and momentous project, which Gilbert acknowledged had been pushed through by Walsingham. The Spanish ambassador in London, Bernardino de Mendoza, reported to Philip II that down in the south-west his spies had reported that Humphrey Gilbert (oddly transmuted in Spanish as either Ongiberto or Fregilberto) and Henry Knollys (Conois), son of the Queen's Treasurer, were secretly assembling ships, probably for the West Indies. Worse, they were employing a traitorous Portuguese, by name Simon (Simão) Fernandez, 'a thorough-paced scoundrel', well experienced in those waters.[14]

On 11 June 1578, the Queen signed letters patent, valid for six years, giving her 'trusty and well-beloved servant Sir Humphrey Gilbert of Compton' the 'free liberty and licence from time to time and at all times for ever hereafter, to discover, find, search out, and view such remote, heathen and barbarous lands, counties and territories not actually possessed by any Christian prince or people'. No specific destination was given, but the document gave legality to any colonizing enterprise. It was assumed that he would probably head for the area in North America known as Norumbega, roughly between the present Cape Cod and Cape Breton Island, though there was a rumour that it might be to that yet unexplored and almost mythical continent in the South Seas known as Terra Australis Incognita. Gilbert had thus the distinction of being the forerunner in all the English colonizing enterprises, apart from Ireland. All land that he discovered could be disposed of 'in fee simple or otherwise according to the laws of England' and anyone who chose to live in the colony would be subject to the same rights and privileges as in England.

In the excitement of this new phase of English sea policy there was much speculation about this Terra Australis and its possible riches. Richard Grenville had put up a project for an ambitious expedition there in 1574, but the Queen had finally revoked his licence.[15] When Francis Drake sailed from Plymouth in November 1577 on what was to be his epic journey round the world, his original intention seems to have been to reach Terra Australis through the Magellan Straits, and then on to the Moluccas. But Drake and Grenville were out for plunder, and Gilbert looked to wealth from founding colonies.

According to Edward Hayes in Hakluyt's *Principall Navigations*, 'Very many gentlemen of good estimation drew into him [Gilbert] in so commendable an enterprise, so that the preparation was expected to grow with a puissant fleet able to encounter a king's power by sea'. Even so there was not enough money. Gilbert had married a moderately well off heiress, Anne Aucher, and had been forced to sell some of his and her properties.

Naunton tells us that Raleigh's 'new chance' had arrived, and that this included an interlude in the Low Countries and a 'voyage to sea'. So he may have been briefly in Flanders under Sir John Norris, but had hurried back when he had heard of the letters patent. He could have taken part in the battle of Rimenant, where famously 'the English being more sensible of a little heat of the sun than any cold fear of death threw off their armour and clothes and gained victory in their shirts'.[16] In any case he was certainly in Devon on 11 April 1578 when with his father and elder brother Carew, he signed the document renouncing the tithe of fish and larks at Sidmouth.

Gilbert's puissant fleet only numbered seven vessels, and Raleigh was to be captain of the *Falcon*, 100 tons. In fact the *Falcon* belonged to the Queen, which might have meant that she had by now heard of this pushing young man. The ship was about seventy foot long, and in it were crammed seventy people, including soldiers and Raleigh's cousin Charles Champernowne, who had been with him at Oriel, as well as six other gentlemen. As always there had to be a motto, and for this journey Raleigh had chosen *Nec mortem peto, nec finem fugio* (I neither seek death nor flee my end).

Carew Raleigh agreed to be captain of the *Hope of Greenway*, and a cousin Edward Denny was to be captain of the *Bark Denny*. Altogether there were to be 409 men, and as another cousin George Carew was among them, it was quite a family affair. The second-in-command was Henry Knollys, on board the *Elephant*. Gilbert's ship was the *Anne Aucher*.

At this stage there were no would-be settlers in any of the ships. Indeed the Privy Council was alarmed by the reputations of some of the crews, who included pirates: Knollys's captain was a well-known pirate, John Cullis. Two attempts were made to set sail in September and October, but on each occasion there were storms and the ships were driven back. Then early in November Gilbert and Knollys quarrelled, and on the 18th Knollys deserted him, taking three ships. Gilbert with the remainder sailed the next day from Dartmouth, heading first for Ireland, but once more there was a gale, and the *Hope of Greenway* sprang a leak. So back they went to Dartmouth. Only the *Falcon* did not return.

Hooker says that Raleigh had been 'desirous to do something worthy of honour'. He disappeared for six months. The only information we have about this obviously disastrous adventure is in two slightly conflicting accounts in Holinshed's *Chronicles*: in one, written by Hooker, he merely sets off on his own; in the other he gave up waiting for the rest of the fleet. According to Hooker: 'He took his course for the West Indies, but for want of victuals and other necessaries (needful in so long a voyage), when he had sailed so far as the islands of Cape Verde, upon the coast of Africa, was enforced to set sail and return to England. In this voyage he passed many dangerous adventures, as well by tempests as fights by sea; but lastly he arrived at Plymouth in the West Country in May next following.' We also learn that the ship was 'sore battered and disabled', and that 'many of his company were killed'.

He may have proved his courage, but the whole affair sounds foolhardy and must have been a hellish experience. Very likely the Portuguese pilot Simon Fernandez, from his past experiences, had lured Raleigh on with the hope of good booty. Fernandez had been born on the island of Terceira in the Azores; he claimed to have been in the Spanish service in the West Indies, but was suspected of various piratical activities. Because of the north-east trade winds, the Cape Verde islands, on a latitude with Senegal, were an important calling point for ships sailing across the Atlantic. John Hawkins had landed at Ribeira Grande on the island of Santiago with slaves from Guinea in 1562, and in 1567 Drake and John Lovell had captured Portuguese ships loaded with slaves, ivory, gold dust and pepper off Santiago and another island, Maio. Although the islands were of volcanic origin and desolate-looking, there were some lush enclaves worth plundering, including one inhabited by Jewish refugees on the north coast of São Antão.* If Fernandez had indeed headed the *Falcon* for the Cape Verde islands, it would have meant arriving at a period when strong winds sweep across from the Sahara and make visibility extremely difficult. And this may have resulted in one of the 'dangerous adventures'.

By the time of Raleigh's return Gilbert had again been to Ireland and back. In April Gilbert was at Dartmouth preparing to set out again, when on the 26th there was an order from the Privy Council forbidding him to leave because of piracies by his associates – in connection it would seem with Henry Knollys – and with reports about Raleigh's activities at sea. On

---

* The place is still known as Sinagoga.

28 May 1579 there were two letters from the Privy Council, one to Sir John Gilbert as Vice-Admiral, and the other to the sheriff of Devonshire. Both concerned the despoiling of a Spanish ship with a cargo of oranges and lemons at Dartmouth by Humphrey Gilbert's men, to 'Her Majesty's indignation'. Sir John Gilbert was asked 'friendly to advise' his brother to 'surcease from proceeding any further and to remain at home', and the same was also to apply to Walter Raleigh who had been reported as arriving at Dartmouth.[17]

This was the first time that Raleigh's name appeared on the Council's books. The Queen could not have been pleased with the condition of the *Falcon*. He now had to retrieve his reputation at Court, and also to set about ways of earning an income.

Foothold at Court
1580

Raleigh lost no time in looking for ways to get himself established at Court. Such a tall, handsome, self-assured young man, already well seasoned as a soldier and sailor, could hardly be ignored. Through Gascoigne he already had a tenuous link with Leicester, and through Humphrey Gilbert another with Sir Francis Walsingham, now principal Secretary of State and organizer of Elizabeth's secret service. Possibly the Queen had heard of the existence of this great-nephew of her beloved Kat Astley, again through Humphrey Gilbert. At all events, in 1580 he was able to secure a position as an Esquire of the Body Extraordinary, part of a group of personable young men who would be available, virtually unpaid, for minor duties at Court.[1]

This was a time when, after reigning for twenty-one years as England's Virgin Queen, Elizabeth had been splitting the country over the possibility of her marriage to the Duke of Alençon, brother of Henri III of France and a Catholic, her 'Frog Prince'. Throughout his career Raleigh was to show himself an adept at intrigue, and was ready to play any sort of double game if it suited his career. Now he eagerly plunged into the Court's hothouse of gossip, backbiting and quarrels. For a short while he joined a circle of wild aristocratic young courtiers, mostly Catholics or crypto-Catholics, including Charles Arundell, Francis Southwell, the Earl of Sussex and Edward de Vere, seventeenth Earl of Oxford and premier earl of England; also on its fringe was Lord Henry Howard, son of the poet Earl of Surrey and brother of the Duke of Norfok, both executed. Raleigh's cousin Arthur Gorges, who in turn was a cousin of Charles Arundell, may have been responsible for the original introduction. There were of course social advantages to being welcomed into such a group of promiscuous hard drinkers, for good measure also interested in literary matters and fashionably capable of turning out a poem or two. Raleigh may also have been considered a decorative and amusing asset, with his Devon accent and his gift for repartee. The suggestion (which does seem likely) has been made that, having been brought up a strong Protestant, he had been planted there by Walsingham, who like

27

Leicester and Hatton was against the French marriage – the Catholics being in favour. Oxford was married to the daughter of the great Lord Treasurer Burghley (in favour of the royal marriage), but temporarily separated from her.

At one time Oxford had been a special favourite of the Queen, who still had an affection for him and a respect for his ancient lineage. He was also a poet, and has even been put forward as the 'real' author of Shakespeare's early plays (Oxford died in 1604). He may have contributed some of the lyrics in Gascoigne's *A Hundredth Sundrie Flowers* (1573). Brilliant in some ways he may have been, but he was immensely arrogant and vindictive, indeed at times appearing mentally unbalanced. It also seems that he was bisexual. His relationship with Raleigh, blowing hot and finally very cold, is hard to disentangle. He loathed Sir Philip Sidney.

One of Aubrey's classic stories concerns Oxford: 'This Earl of Oxford, making his low obeisance to Queen Elizabeth, happened to let a fart, at which he was so abashed and ashamed that he went to travel, seven years. On his return the Queen welcomed him home, and said "My Lord, I had forgot the fart".'*[2]

In February 1580, Raleigh fought a duel with Sir Thomas Perrot, an important figure at Court, and both were sent to the Fleet prison for six days, being released after they had given sureties to keep the peace.[4] Nevertheless, only a month later Raleigh became involved in a fight with a man called Wingfield outside a tennis court at Whitehall. This time they were sent to the Marshalsea, normally used as a prison for offenders on the high seas. In fact both stays in prison could not have been all that arduous. Gentlemen were allowed to have their own food brought in and even to receive visitors. At the Marshalsea there was for Raleigh a special consolation as he

---

* He had been in Italy, and had returned a Catholic, but soon abandoned the faith. Raleigh was one of those dining with him at his rooms at Greenwich Palace when he drunkenly announced that the Virgin Mary was a whore and Joseph a wittol (cuckold). A while before this episode Oxford had quarrelled with Philip Sidney, a greater poet, as he well knew, but just as hot-tempered. Sidney's friend Fulke Greville told the story.[3] Oxford had called Sidney a 'puppy' for refusing to give up a tennis court on which he wanted to play, and this in front of a number of spectators, including important French visitors. Sidney had thereupon given him the 'lie direct', challenging him to a duel, and the 'gentleman of worth' who delivered the letter to Oxford to that effect is thought to have been Raleigh, though another theory is that Raleigh brought the reply to Sidney. The Queen had to intervene, and reminded Sidney that it was wrong for a mere gentleman to challenge an earl of such high rank. But Oxford was certainly not in a forgiving frame and was soon rumoured to be plotting Sidney's murder. Aubrey says that Raleigh had been a second to Oxford in a duel, but this may be a confusion over the tennis court affair.

was joined by Arthur Gorges who had committed the offence of 'giving the lie' to a nobleman in the Presence Chamber. Gorges was always particularly close to Raleigh and became involved in some of his exploits overseas. He was also a poet, stylistically similar to Raleigh, and especially remembered for his anthology, *The Phoenix Nest*, published in 1594. On occasion claims (not always convincing) have been made for Gorges as being the author of some of the best-known poems attributed to Raleigh.

The 'riotous, lascivious and incontinent' Raleigh had now been able to meet, or at least observe, some of the Queen's vestals, her Maids-of-Honour. One of them, Elizabeth Leighton, found a poem, written anonymously but known to have been written by him, in her pocket. She was the sister of Lettice Knollys, the widowed Lady Essex, whom Leicester had secretly married (and had thus incurred the fury of the Queen). Usually the Maids-of-Honour were unmarried, but in this case Elizabeth was the wife of the Governor of the Channel Islands who was often away. So Raleigh was running a risk with this poem, unless of course it was meant as a joke, or mere flattery. It begins:

> Lady, farewell, whom I in silence serve!
>   Would God thou knews't the depth of my desire!
> Then might I hope, through nought I can deserve,
>   Some drop of grace would quench my scalding fire . . .

Then there was Anne Vavasour, another vestal. This poem is entitled *The Advice*, and it is indeed surprising to find Raleigh of all people giving a young woman advice against losing her virginity.

> Many desire, but few or none deserve
> To win the fort of thy most constant will:
> Therefore take heed, yet fancy never swerve
> But unto him that will deserve thee still.
>   For this be sure, the fort of fame once won,
>   Farewell the rest, thy happy days are done.

The man he was warning her against in this roundabout way was none other than the Earl of Oxford. It was to no avail. Anne was in love with Oxford, and they wrote poems to one another. When she had a child by him, the furious Elizabeth invoked her usual penalty: she sent both to the Tower. Anne's uncle, Sir Thomas Knivet, also a courtier, challenged Oxford to a duel.

Oxford's attitude towards Raleigh suddenly changed, and Raleigh became one of his bitterest enemies. It could well have been because of this foolish poem, or that Oxford had found out that Raleigh was spying for Walsingham. Perhaps, like many another, he had taken against the arrogance of this handsome upstart, parading himself in expensive clothes that he could not afford. Or had Raleigh behind his back laughed at the 'little apish hat' he loved to wear and thought so fashionable? As for the fascinating Anne Vavasour, she caused further scandal by becoming the 'dearest dear' of Sir Henry Lee, a Knight of the Garter and the Queen's Champion.*[5]

The Queen's skittish behaviour towards Jean de Simier, the Duke of Alençon's envoy, caused real alarm: a man 'exquisite in the delights of love',[6] he had once crept into the royal bedroom to steal a night cap as a love token for his master. When the Puritan John Stubbs dared to publish a protest against the unpopular French marriage, Elizabeth not only had his hand chopped off but that of his printer too. This was a shocking and unusual barbarity. But nobody knew what was really going on in Elizabeth's 'deep and inscrutable' mind, as Anthony Bacon called it.[7] How serious was she about the marriage? After all, she was in her late forties, and Alençon was fifteen years younger, ugly, pockmarked and with a bulbous nose. Was it all just a political charade, to keep the French at bay in case they decided to ally themselves with Spain? Likewise the Spaniards would hesitate over any action that might mean Elizabeth calling for help from France. There were strong rumours of a 'Holy League' between the Pope, the King of Spain and the Duke of Florence to overthrow Protestantism in England and dethrone Elizabeth, replacing her with Mary Queen of Scots. Did Elizabeth even want to share her power with a husband? For years she had been urged to marry so as to produce an heir. Contrary to her doctors' opinion, was she not too old to bear a child?

When at last Simier went back to France, Raleigh being fluent in French was one of those deputed to accompany him. Pirates tried to attack the ship on that journey, instigated, some said, by Leicester.[8]

Meanwhile, Oxford's hate campaign against Sidney was unabated, and the venom was now directed just as much against Raleigh, whom he also proposed to have murdered. A vicious poem in a manuscript, sarcastically entitled 'A pleasant conceit of Vere, Earl of Oxford, discontented at the rising of a mean gentleman at the English Court, circa 1580', could have been directed at either of them.

* Before he died in 1611 Lee built his own tomb with his effigy on it, and with Anne kneeling at his feet. His heirs had her effigy erased.

Oxford had also quarrelled with Arundell and Southwell, accusing them of Catholic plots against the Queen. Then he attacked Lord Henry Howard, another who had developed an intense and even more dangerous hatred against Raleigh, for reasons unknown but no doubt connected with his Catholicism; a secret homosexual and an embittered Iago figure, this 'Harry' lived under the shadow of the fact that both his father and brother had been attainted. Arundell retaliated with wild accusations about Oxford's 'detestable vices' and 'unpure life', sometimes invoking Raleigh as a witness. He also claimed that Oxford had urged both him and Raleigh to murder Sidney.

All this was one good reason for Raleigh accepting a troop of men to take to Ireland; a task which had suddenly been offered him, possibly as a reward from Walsingham.

Ireland
1580–81

The history of Ireland in the reign of Elizabeth is a maze of hatreds, betrayals, rivalries and atrocities, and regrettably it must be said that Humphrey Gilbert and Walter Raleigh are still remembered as the perpetrators of some of the worst horrors.

Nevertheless, for a gentleman adventurer such as Raleigh, Ireland was an opportunity to prove himself, and with luck build a fortune – as India was to be for younger sons three centuries later. To revisionist historians such people are usually branded as greedy and ruthless speculators, intent on grabbing a handsome estate and then selling it later; and it is difficult by modern lights to make a defence. The English were shocked by the backwardness and primitive ways of the Celtic Irish, and this meant that they had little compunction in clearing out its barbarous inhabitants from what they saw as a potentially fertile land, and then recolonizing it with hardworking Anglo-Saxons, or even Celtic Cornishmen. Any resistance needed to be mercilessly crushed.

The poet Edmund Spenser, who was to become a close friend and admirer of Raleigh, said: 'It is the fatal destiny of that land that no purposes whatever which are meant for her good will prosper'.[1] For the Irish it depended on what was meant by 'good'. Again there is a comparison with 19th-century India. Sir Thomas Munro, Governor of Madras, wrote in 1818: 'Englishmen suppose that no country can be saved without English institutions'.[2] The Irish certainly were not convinced by such a doctrine, and English settlers soon discovered that the peasant 'kerns', armed only with bows, darts and swords or spears, excelled in guerrilla-type warfare. These men would creep out of the forests and bogs to lay ambushes, raid and burn English settlements, and then as mysteriously melt away. In pitched battles they let out alarming war-cries. One of Raleigh's earliest biographers compared them to nettles, which sting even if gently handled; the only solution, he considered, had been to scythe them down.[3]

At this stage a few preliminary comments are necessary. Setting aside

Ireland's strategic importance for the English, the wars were in fact mainly provoked by the ambitions of the Irish and Anglo-Irish aristocracy, most of Norman descent and nearly all hating one another, in spite of intermarriages. Religion, needless to say, played a considerable part. In Munster the two great rival families were the FitzGeralds, familiarly known as Geraldines, headed by the Earl of Desmond, a Catholic, and the Butlers, headed by the Earl of Ormond, a Protestant. Ormond had a certain brilliance; known as Black Thomas, he was close to the Queen, to whom he was related through the Boleyns, and their relationship had once provoked some gossip. Desmond was proud and stubborn, with reason suspected of having dealings with agents of the Papacy – the bulk of the Irish population being also Catholic. It is a surprise to discover that he was married to Ormond's widowed mother, but that apparently made no difference to the two men's enmity. Available to the nobles throughout Ireland were the 'gallowglasses', ex-Scottish mercenaries who had settled with their families in the country; they wore armour, wielded battle-axes, and had a kind of discipline.

Humphrey Gilbert was knighted for his part in the so-called FitzMaurice rebellion that began in 1569. Relations between England and Spain had become strained as a result of Spanish ships being detained at English ports. The Spanish ambassador in London had advised Philip II that now was the opportunity to drive the English out of Ireland, and that aid should be sent to James FitzMaurice, a cousin of Desmond who at that time was imprisoned in the Tower. The revolt led to devastation in Munster and the threat of famine. Some English settlers were murdered. Close relatives of both Gilbert and Raleigh – Richard Grenville, Sir Peter Carew and Sir Warham St Leger, who had attempted to colonize large tracts of land near Cork – were among those also in danger.

Gilbert, after a spell in Ulster, came as colonel to Munster, and was thus in effect its military governor. He heavily defeated FitzMaurice, and had followed this by capturing twenty-three castles, massacring all who resisted, including as he blithely admitted women and children. His habit of making an avenue to his tent with severed heads has already been mentioned; prisoners had to walk along this path and kneel before him. He was also liable to break into alarming explosions of rage. Such a reign of terror was certainly successful in keeping the inhabitants of Munster subdued, and as he said: 'No conquering nation will ever yield willingly their obedience for love but rather for fear'.[4] The Lord Deputy of Ireland, Sir Henry Sidney, was delighted with Gilbert's success, and wrote to Burghley: 'I cannot say enough. The highways are made free, where no man [once] might travel unspoiled . . . Yet this is not the most, nor the best he hath done; for the estimation that he hath won to the name of Englishman here, before almost not known, exceedeth all the rest, he himself admitted, without compunction.'[5]

Raleigh at this time wholeheartedly admired his half-brother's strong-arm behaviour. Many years later, immured indefinitely in the Tower, he evidently had second thoughts about the benefits of terror, judging from passages in his *History of the World*: how the Romans when they captured a town would deliberately commit atrocities, so as to terrify the inhabitants, often killing 'the very dogs that ran athwart them in the streets, hewing their bodies asunder, as men delighted in the shedding of blood'.[6] To believe that it was possible 'by cruelty to change hatred with fear' was not only misguided but fatal. Even more damning of the tactics of Gilbert would seem to be this remark about Alexander the Great: 'His carefulness to destroy those women and children whose lives hindered his progress, argues him to have been rather skilful in matters of arms than a valiant man, such cruelty being the true mark of cowardice.'[7]

Gilbert's successor in Munster was the rough-mannered and foul-mouthed Sir John Perrot, father of the Sir Thomas Perrot with whom Raleigh had fought a duel, and for good measure thought by some to be the bastard son of Henry VIII, whom he did resemble (Perrot in fact was believed to have been responsible for the summary execution of eight hundred rebels). Perhaps the cause of the duel had been to do with insulting words relayed back about Gilbert. At any rate support for the revolt dwindled, and in 1573 FitzMaurice had to make his 'humble submission' to the Queen, having being told that if he did this mercy would be accorded to him – and so it was. Five years of a sort of peace followed.

FitzMaurice went to Rome, where he was received with much enthusiasm. The Pope, Gregory XIII, had already published a Bull excommunicating Elizabeth and freeing her subjects from 'all manner of duty, fidelity and obedience'.[8] In the spring of 1579 rumours reached her that he was prepared to consider Philip II as rightful heir to Ireland and therefore send an invasion force. In June she heard that FitzMaurice was at Bilbao, ready to sail for Ireland.

Humphrey Gilbert, in spite of being under grave suspicion of having committed some piratical acts, was hurriedly given permission to send ships to intercept FitzMaurice. The result, however, was a failure. He did not find FitzMaurice's 'fleet', but in compensation was able to bag a Portuguese vessel with some useful and lucrative cargo. In fact FitzMaurice, accompanied by an English Jesuit, Nicholas Sanders, as Papal Nuncio, had sailed with only three ships and possibly not more than a hundred men – Spanish, Italian and expatriate Irish – though with enough weapons, it was later said, for many more. He landed at St Mary's Wick, garbled into Smerwick, on the Dingle peninsula in the far south-west of Ireland: a bleak, windswept spot, but on a vast bay, great bare mountains rising behind. It had been a dangerous journey, with the uncertainty of Atlantic weather, not to mention fogs, past the Blasket Islands and the jagged cliffs of Clogher Head. It had been here, almost on the identical spot, that one of Frobisher's ships had been wrecked with its cargo of mock gold. So when FitzMaurice built some earthworks on a headland he sarcastically called it Fort Del Oro, Fort of Gold. Sanders also consecrated the place.

According to Hooker, Thomas Courtney, 'a Devonshire gentleman and a man of war', in other words a privateer, happened to be at Kinsale in the south. He heard of FitzMaurice's landings, and so he sailed round the peninsula and captured the three ships, which he took away with him. Meanwhile two of Desmond's brothers rose in revolt, raiding English settlements and burning their crops. Sanders went about the land distributing the Bull against the 'tyrant' Elizabeth. But FitzMaurice made for the north of the country, and on the way became involved in a skirmish and was shot in the head, and killed. The Italians and Spanish, isolated at Smerwick, were experiencing the wintry blasts of Irish weather and decided to abandon Fort Del Oro. Most in consequence were captured by the English and slaughtered.

As for the Earl of Desmond, he was at last proclaimed a traitor. He might have been shown mercy had he not with his relative the Seneschal of Imokilly attacked and burnt the walled town of Youghal on the south-east corner of Ireland. There were now fresh rumours of a Papally-inspired invasion. Sir Warham St Leger at Cork wrote urgently for reinforcements. Now it was the turn of Lord Grey of Wilton to be appointed Lord Deputy of Ireland; a staunch Puritan, he was the son of the Lord Grey who had subdued the Devon and Cornish peasants in 1549.

Raleigh was aged twenty-six, ready and eager for glory. In the Acts of the Privy Council for 11 July 1580, it is recorded that 'Walter Raleigh, gentleman, by the appointment of the Lord Grey is to have charge of one hundred of those men presently levied within the City of London to be transported for her Majesty's service into Ireland'. Ned Denny, a cousin, also threatened with death by Oxford, was to bring another hundred men. He was also related to Grey on his father's side. Their pay as captains was four shillings a day, and for their soldiers it was eight pence a day. In due course Raleigh arrived at Cork, where there were already 850 soldiers under the command of St Leger. Raleigh's first surviving letter (at that time he was signing himself W. Rauley) is from Cork to Lord Treasurer Burghley, complaining about inadequate pay and rations. Any hope of building up a fortune was already beginning to look thin.

Grey had accepted appointment to 'that unlucky place' Ireland with misgivings, and had no option but to obey the Queen's order. He had a literary bent, having been a patron of Gascoigne and having chosen Edmund Spenser as his secretary. No doubt he had also been impressed by Raleigh's talents as a poet, and this, apart from a slight family connection, may have had some influence in his applying for the already battle-experienced young man to join him. He was to regret it.

St Leger had a FitzGerald in custody, a younger brother of Desmond. Although reputedly wounded unto death, this James FitzGerald was tried for treason and condemned to be strung up with the usual gruesome aftermath. It has always been assumed that Raleigh's men took a part in the drawing and quartering. 'He was cut in little pieces while still alive and died a fervent Catholic'.[9] The head was set up as a spectacle on the main gate of the city and thus became 'the prey of fowls'. Hooker dismissed the affair with 'and thus the pestilent hydra lost another of its heads'. Not surprisingly the death of James 'did marvellously dismay the Earl himself'.

Lord Grey arrived at Dublin on 12 August. At once he found himself having to deal with a revolt in the Wicklows headed by Viscount Baltinglass, and the result, at the battle of Glenmalure, was humiliating for the English. One of those killed was Sir Peter Carew; he had found himself encumbered by his heavy armour, and in what he thought was a quiet moment had taken it off, lying down for a rest.

In October news arrived of the expected Spanish landing under Papal auspices. Once again it was at Smerwick, and FitzMaurice's Fort Del Oro was being strengthened with a timber palisade and a moat. Grey had been alerted some while before that enemy ships had left the port of La Coruña in northern Spain, and was therefore fully prepared. Immediately he ordered the entire reserve of the English army to be directed to Kerry and the Dingle peninsula, including Raleigh's contingent at Cork and troops gathered by the Earl of Ormond. In fact Ormond had already sent a column for a preliminary inspection, and after a skirmish had discovered that the Spaniards were in fact mostly Italians, reputedly extracted from Papal gaols and thus ill trained. There were about seven hundred all told, though apparently they had arms enough for 5,000 soldiers, so reinforcements were evidently to be expected. They also had made contact with the Jesuit Sanders, who had sent them another priest, William Walsh, now in the fort. Banners displayed the keys of St Peter, and the commander was a man from Bologna, Sebastiano di San Giuseppe.

English soldiers on the march, from The Image of Irelande *by John Derricke, 1581. The foremost carries a head, and the two behind have heads on sword points. Cattle are driven away, and other Irish await their fate.*

There is an anecdote about Raleigh on his march to Smerwick that is characteristic of his behaviour in Ireland. He had come to realize that as soon as the English left an encampment the Irish kerns would come swarming in to glean whatever was left behind. So one day he decided to lay an ambush after moving out of camp. Predictably the kerns appeared, and were rounded up. One of the prisoners was carrying a large bundle of withies on his back. Raleigh asked him what they were for. 'To hang up the English churls with,' the man said. 'Is it so?' Raleigh replied. 'Well, they shall now serve for an Irish kern'. And he arranged for the man to be hanged with his own withies. 'The residue [of the kerns],' Hooker enigmatically tells us, 'he handled according to their deserts.'[10]

Grey's army numbered 3,000, one third from Cork. He is said to have driven his men relentlessly cross-country through exceptionally heavy rain. Various sergeants and soldiers were executed on the way for looting and pillaging. Spenser has described the general devastation and misery of the disrupted villages. 'At this time,' he said, 'not the lowing of a cow, or the voice of a ploughman, could be heard from Dunqueen in Kerry to Cashel in Munster.'[11]

Smerwick is one of Ireland's famous battlegrounds. It lies at the west entrance of the bay, and at the far end there is a long sandy beach suitable for an invasion force. Mount Brandon looks down on it, and in that period

37

the only way to approach the bay by land was through the mountain pass from the town of Dingle. The land being treeless, it would have been easy to see an enemy approaching. The area also has religious associations, for a mile across the bay is the strange little oratory of St Galarus, built in the 9th century with stone blocks and in the shape of an upturned boat, a relic of early Celtic Christianity. And on the other side of the peninsula groups of 'beehive' huts are to be found, primitive settlements. Some of the trenches at Fort Del Oro (also now known as Dun-an-oir) can still be traced beneath the brambles. The site, which would also have been used in prehistoric times, is only about 100 yards by 30, which makes the existence inside of so many people all the more amazing, taking into account the fierce bombardment that they suffered and the lack of water.*

Grey had to wait for the arrival of English ships, which came on 5 November under the command of Admiral Winter. The remaining foreign ships were easily taken, and under the screen of darkness eight culverins were unloaded, and bulwarks were dug. On the 7th the bombardment began, with the support of musketry. The defendants fired back, and from time to time attempted sallies, but with losses. The only English casualty was that 'lusty young gentleman' John Cheke, yet another on the Earl of Oxford's death list.

According to some versions the bombardment continued for four days. On the first day it was under the command of Captain Raleigh. Trenches were pushed up nearer the fort, almost to pistol range so it has been said – though anyone looking at the causeway leading to the fort today would be surprised by this. Now it had become clear to the defendants that they could not expect help by sea or land, even though a small force of Irish was known to be up in the hills. So a white flag was raised, and a truce party was allowed out for a parley. It was admitted that they had not been sent by the King of Spain, but by the Pope 'to defend the Catholic faith'. The zealous Puritan Grey was the last person to be impressed by such an admission, and replied that under the circumstances no condition of surrender could be given, since to the English the Pope was a 'detestable shaveling, the right Antichrist, patron of the *diabolica fede*'. They would have to surrender, and there were to be no guarantees or conditions.

The next morning San Giuseppe himself appeared with an Irish priest, Oliver Plunkett, as interpreter. There are many contradictory reports about this meeting. Spenser claimed afterwards that he had been 'as near to them as any' and that no guarantees were given: the garrison was to surrender 'at discretion', and that was that. If the expedition had not been commissioned

---

* A plan of the fort is in the Vatican archives.

by the King of Spain then it was an act of piratical lawlessness, the Pope's involvement being neither here nor there. The standard Irish version, backed by the report of the Spanish ambassador in London, Bernardino de Mendoza, to Philip II, is that Grey promised quarter, but went back on his word. San Giuseppe is said to have embraced Grey's knees.

The English renewed the bombardment the next morning. If the Italians had been confident of mercy, it can be fairly pointed out, they would presumably have surrendered at once, and there would be no need of another bombardment. In any case after a while the white flag was once more raised, and the defendants came streaming out, crying '*Misericordia, misericordia*' (Mercy, mercy) and begging for water.[12] They had not been able to drink for forty-eight hours. For a start they were all stripped of any armour and made to lay down their arms. Then they were herded back into the fort, presumably without water. The fort was searched and a number of Irish women were dragged out, along with the priests Plunkett and Walsh and a friar named Moore; also a member of the FitzGerald family. Gallows were erected for the women, who were immediately hanged, their pleas of pregnancy being ignored. The FitzGerald was sent for ransom to England. The priests were taken into Smerwick village where their arms and legs were smashed on an anvil by the local blacksmith. They were then put in a shed without food or water for two days, and afterwards brought to the gallows where they were hanged, drawn and quartered.

According to Camden in his *Annales* a reason for refusing *misericordia* to the other defendants was that the English soldiers might have mutinied if they did not get the loot, which included clothes. Camden also says, 'It was resolved against the Deputy's will, who full of mercy and compassion wept for it, that all strangers, the commanders excluded, should be put to the sword.' Whether he wept or not, he sent in two hundred soldiers to do the deed under the command of the duty officers, Captains Mackworth and Raleigh. It has also been said that Admiral Winter's sailors, afraid that the soldiers would get all the plunder, climbed over the walls and joined in the massacre. The system used for the slaughter, we are told, was 'hewing and punching', slashing at the neck followed by a stab in the belly. The work was over in an hour. The corpses were then stripped and thrown onto the beach below. Grey in his official letter to Walsingham made this dry comment: 'And then I put in certain bands, who straight fell to execution. There were 600 slain.' He is supposed to have walked past those gruesome naked bodies, their stomachs gashed open, and to have made this strange remark: 'Here lay as gallant and goodly personages ever I have seen'.[13]

San Giuseppe and the other officers, spared and kept for ransom, would have heard the fearful screams. Camden says: 'The Queen who from her heart detested to use cruelty to those that yielded, wished that the slaughter had not been, and was with much difficulty appeased and satisfied with it'.

The massacre at Smerwick caused as much horror in Catholic Europe as had the St Bartholomew's Day Massacre in Paris among Protestants. Its significance can be compared to later horrors such as the Black Hole of Calcutta in 1756 or the Ardeatine Caves massacre in Rome during the Second World War. Grey's name became an anathema, *Fides Graiae*, the Faith of Grey, being synonymous with betrayal and perfidy. Spenser defended him as a man 'most just, sincere and Godly and right noble', and pointed out that to Grey the invaders were no better than 'rogues and renegades', who if released would merely have joined the forces of the rebel Desmond.[14] What is supposed to be true is that Grey told the defendants they must yield themselves 'for life and death'.

Worse things had happened in Ireland and were to happen. It was also pointed out that, not many years before, in 1565, the Spaniards had slaughtered a French settlement in Florida with equal brutality. A. L. Rowse briefly dismissed the Smerwick episode with 'They should not have come'.[15] Well, that was true. Even in the 18th century Raleigh's biographer Oldys was able to write: 'The country was thus weeded of noxious foreigners'. Nevertheless, Smerwick had, and will always have, a symbolic significance.

Of the two English captains concerned, Mackworth may be forgotten, but Raleigh is forever linked with this atrocity. It was an episode to which he never referred in writing, but in his *History of the World* cruelty in battle is a recurrent theme. In those pages he may have been thinking of Smerwick, but he must also have been remembering the Huguenot wars, where very likely he took part in many horrific scenes.

Smerwick may be a renowned battlefield, but for present-day visitors unable to read the signs in Gaelic it is difficult to find. Fuchsia hedges give way to bristling brambles on stone walls, and the narrow lane is badly potholed. Black-faced sheep impassively stare. A monument in grey stone has been erected, with faces on it rather in the style of Epstein. On a clear day the otherwise desolate landscape could be said to be beautiful, especially when the sun turns the sea to silver. But what a place to have your throat cut, or to swing from gallows and be disembowelled.

It was a miserable winter, with near famine, but the war continued. As Spenser pointed out, winter was the best time for subduing the Irish, who would be close to starving. Raleigh, back in Cork, found his soldiers restless, and it was then that he wrote to Burghley for more money. He too was impatient. Francis Drake's return in the previous autumn, with enormous booty and acclaim and knighted by the Queen, had stirred the ambitions of men like himself. He considered that Grey was being too lenient with the rebels. In particular he was suspicious about the activities of David Barry, son of Lord Barry who was already in prison in Dublin, and other young Anglo-Irish aristocrats. The Barrys owned a castle called Barryscourt in a strategic position near Cork harbour. Raleigh had his eye on this castle, particularly as it might have been acquired illegally (possibly through a murder) by the father. So he rode to Dublin declaring that David Barry and his friends must be named as traitors.

Although Lord Grey had taken a dislike to this bumptious young man, Raleigh got his way and he returned with a commission to seize castle and lands for himself. But he did not know that David Barry had got to hear of this and had burnt down Barryscourt and laid waste all the country around it.

On his way back to Cork, Raleigh passed Youghal and reached a river ford at Ballinacura in Barry country. The Seneschal of Imokilly, John FitzEdmund FitzGerald, had been alerted by David Barry and was lying in ambush for him, with six horsemen and some kerns – Hooker points out that Raleigh was travelling in this dangerous area with far too small a force. He was also riding ahead, along with a guide. The Seneschal's men attacked as Raleigh approached the ford. The guide ran away, but Raleigh managed to ride across. He was followed by a fellow Devonian, Henry Moyle, whose horse foundered in the middle of the ford and threw him. Moyle called for help and Raleigh plunged in and recovered the horse. But Moyle in his haste overleapt the horse and fell into the mire on the other side, at which the horse bolted and was captured by the enemy. Raleigh boldly remained on horseback with Moyle beside him, his staff in one hand and a loaded pistol in the other, until the rest of the party arrived, including his man Jenkin carrying £200. The Seneschal, although he had been reinforced with more horsemen and kerns, outnumbering Raleigh's force by twenty to one, merely 'railed and used hard speeches', thus allowing Raleigh to ride off unscathed.[16]

Today's visitor to Ballinacurra ford, now surrounded by many houses, will be struck by the high banks on each side and the fact that the water is tidal. If the sea had been coming in at that time, it would have been all the more dangerous, and this probably inhibited the Seneschal. (Later, according to Hooker, Ormond called a parley at which the Seneschal was taunted with cowardice by Raleigh, and a challenge was issued. But this does seem unlikely.)

The story of Raleigh's courage and reckless indifference to danger soon spread around Ireland. Never a one for modesty, he wanted London to know about it too. Walsingham had written to him on some matter, and on 23 February Raleigh replied thanking him for expressing a 'disposition and opinion more favourable than I can any way deserve'. He told him about David Barry and others 'linked together in rebellion', that he had coveted to recover a 'little old castle' belonging to Barry, and that on his way there he had a 'hard escape'. 'The manner of mine own behaviour I leave to the report of others, but the escape was strong [strange?] to all men.' He also wrote about the need for more men. The last contingent sent over from England were such 'poor and miserable creatures' that their captain did not dare lead them into battle.

He had not by then heard that Barryscourt had been burnt down, and this most unwelcome news prompted another and longer letter to Walsingham on 25 February. Even more galling for Raleigh was the fact that Ormond, as Governor of Munster and General of the Forces, was refusing to let him have either the ruins of Barryscourt, or the adjoining island (on which Cóbh now stands) that had been promised him by Grey. This may have been due to snobbery or personal dislike. Raleigh now took it upon himself to criticize Ormond who, he pointed out, although related to the traitorous Geraldines, was so loathed by them that they would 'rather die a thousand deaths, enter into a million of mischiefs and seek succour of all nations rather than they will ever be subdued by a Butler [Ormond]'.[17]

In this somewhat presumptuous outpouring he urged that the Queen must send an Englishman to take Ormond's place. 'Would God your Honour and Her Majesty, as well as my poor self, understood how pitifully the service here goeth forward.' And what man would be better for this appointment than Raleigh's own half-brother, Sir Humphrey Gilbert, who 'with the third part of the garrison now in Ireland, ended a rebellion not much inferior to this, in two months?' Now the Almighty was invoked: 'I take God to witness I speak it not for affection, but to discharge my duty to Her Majesty; for I never heard nor read of any man more feared than he is among the Irish nation. And I do assuredly know the best about the Earl of Desmond, yea, and all the unbridled traitors of these parts, would come into him, and yield themselves to the Queen's mercy, were it but known that he were come among them.' The letter ended with a protestation of loyalty to the Queen, and a promise to keep Walsingham informed of all developments; also a request that his letter should be kept private. And finally and most importantly: 'I beseech your honour that I may by your means enjoy the keeping of this Barryscourt and the island, or that it will please your honour but to write to my Lord Deputy [Grey] that he will confirm it to me.'

On 1 May Raleigh wrote to Grey, once more complaining about Ormond's slackness and muddling; also the shortage of food for his men at Cork. 'No day passeth', he wrote, 'without some traitorous villainies by the Barrys committed.' One of these Barrys had recently attacked the garrison at Youghal. Then, not only Lady Barry but the Countess of Desmond had been allowed into Cork, with a considerable entourage, to obtain supplies, but they had been permitted to leave without their luggage being searched. Raleigh was obsessed by Barryscourt. If Walsingham had written to Grey there had been no response. 'If it shall please your Honour to think me worthy of the keeping and custody thereof, I will at mine own cost build it up again and defend it for her Majesty.'

How could he afford to rebuild Barryscourt? His father had died in February, so it is conceivable that he had come into a little money, though not nearly enough. What, however, is interesting about the letter is a marginal note written by Grey himself, from which it is clear that Raleigh had submitted a paper on Munster to the Queen, a document which has not survived.

There had already been considerable disagreements between Grey and Ormond. When summer came, Elizabeth gave orders for Ormond to be recalled. His replacement as Governor and General of Munster was to be John Zouch, who as a captain had been at Smerwick. Meanwhile, until Zouch's arrival, there would be a triumvirate in charge, and one of these would be Raleigh; the others were Sir William Morgan, a colleague of Raleigh's in France, and Captain Piers, who had also been at Smerwick.

So Raleigh really had made a mark. His headquarters were at Lismore and we are told 'in the country and the woods thereabouts [he] spent all this summer in continual action against the rebels.'[18] On 26 August he wrote to Leicester in his own hand, a tactful letter reminding him of their acquaintance and protesting that 'Your Honour, having no use of such poor fellows, hath utterly forgotten me.' Referring to his own discontent, he in a backhanded way now criticized Grey. 'I have spent some time here under the Deputy [Grey] in such poor place and charge as were it not for that I know him to be one of yours, I would disdain it as much as to keep sheep.' He also took it upon himself to introduce Warham St Leger evidently returning to London and who he obviously hoped – as his cousin – would put in a good word for him: 'a wise, faithful and valiant gentleman' who would tell Leicester of the good, the bad, the mischiefs of 'this common wealth, or rather common woe.'

Returning in due course to Cork, Raleigh had two encounters with the 'archtraitor' David Barry, who had been waiting for him with a 'a great troop of sundry hundreds of men.' Undaunted, Raleigh 'with a lusty courage gave the onset on him', and Barry fled. Later he spied a group of foot soldiers and charged them. This time the enemy fought back 'very valiantly,' and killed various horses. Raleigh's horse was struck by a dart and started bucking and plunging. Raleigh was now in real danger for his life, and was saved by his devoted servant Nicholas Wright and an Irishman 'Patrike Fagaw'.

The new General, Zouch, had decided that it was time that Lord Roche, who had a son supposed to be a supporter of David Barry, should be arrested, and ordered Raleigh to bring him and his wife to Cork. The episode that followed, although 'particularly remembered and applauded' at the time, now makes uneasy reading.[19] Roche lived in the castle of Bally-in-Harsh some twenty miles from Cork. David Barry and the Seneschal (though not Lord Roche) had got wind of this plan and had arranged an ambush. Raleigh, however, was aware of the danger and astutely led his band of ninety men at night, arriving at the castle gates at dawn. The people of the village of Bally were alarmed and armed themselves, but Raleigh arranged for his men to be placed in strategic spots around the village. He then marched back to the castle and knocked at the gate. When asked why he had come he merely said that he wished to speak to his lordship. So he was invited inside with six companions (one of whom was graced with the peculiar name of Pinking Huish). In the words of the chronicler: 'He so handled the matter by devices and means that little by little, and by some and some, he had gotten in within the iron door or gate of the courtlodge all his men.' He then put guards on the gate, and 'likewise charged every man to come into the hall with his piece prepared with two bullets.'

Not surprisingly Lord Roche was 'suddenly amazed and stricken at the heart with fear.' Nevertheless he received Raleigh with courtesy, introduced him to his lady and invited him and his companions to join them at breakfast. After the meal Raleigh revealed the cause of his visit, and told Roche that he had been accused of being a traitor, and that he and his wife would have to accompany him to Cork. Roche protested but was firmly told that if he did not agree he would be taken there by force. So there was no alternative, and preparations were made for the departure.

The party left that evening, and it was a dreadful journey, 'tempestuous and foul', so dark that they were spared any ambush. The way was so full of 'balks, hillocks, pits and rocks' that the soldiers were 'marvellously troubled and encumbered.' Weapons were lost and people were hurt. One man hurt his foot so badly that it never recovered; 'it did in the end consume and rot away'. At Cork there was 'no little admiration' that Raleigh had survived such a journey, 'being verily supposed of all men that he could not have escaped.'

Roche was examined and acquitted, but after such an unpleasant experience he took care to serve the Queen loyally thereafter. Three of his sons were killed fighting on her behalf.

Raleigh, having been thwarted over Barryscourt, was now sick of Ireland. Grey also had made requests to be recalled, and there were rumours that this might happen in the spring. Meanwhile, Desmond's men were said to have burnt down thirty-six 'towns' or settlements. And as always the English troops were discontented, crying out for more money. To make matters worse for Grey, the Queen decided that the army in Ireland should be reduced, and between November and January 3,000 men had been discharged. Early in December, Raleigh returned to England, carrying Grey's despatches, only a short while before the capture and death of John of Desmond, brother of the Earl – his body was hung by the heels at the north gate of Cork, and his head was sent to Dublin. Raleigh had acquired neither land nor fortune, but he had consolidated his reputation as a fearless man of action. He was also determined now to establish himself as an experienced military thinker and strategist.

He left at the beginning of a terrible famine, made worse by plague. Over six months 30,000 people were said to have died in Munster. Edmund Spenser was to write: 'Out of every corner of the woods and glens they came creeping forth upon their hands, for their legs could not bear them; they looked like anatomies of death, they spake like ghosts crying out of their graves; they did eat of the dead carrions, happy were they if they could find them, yea, and one another seen after, insomuch as the very carcasses they spared not to scrape out of the graves; and if they found a plot of watercresses or shamrocks, there they flocked as to a feast.'[20]

The Earl of Desmond was eventually caught and killed in 1583. His head was sent to London and put on a pole on London Bridge; it is thought that his body was left to be eaten by wild animals. 'And thus,' said Hooker, 'a noble and ancient family, descended from out of the loins of princes, is now for treasons and rebellions utterly extinguished and overthrown.' Since he had been a traitor, all his vast domains became the property of the Crown.

A Kind of Oracle
1582–3

Setting aside the famous story of the cloak, it has been generally agreed that Raleigh first impressed the Queen (and her advisers) through his forceful views on Ireland. Naunton said that his 'variance' with Lord Grey drew both men to the Council table, and that Raleigh had 'much the better in telling of his tale'; but if correct this could only have happened after Grey's dismissal in August 1582 and his return to London. In January, Grey had already complained to Walsingham about misrepresentation and the 'plots' emerging from Raleigh. And in March, when warned that Raleigh might be returning to Ireland, he said: 'I must be plain: I neither like his carriage nor his company.'[1]

A further comment on the effect of Raleigh's appearance at Court and his meteoric rise is without doubt true: 'He had gotten the Queen's ear at a trice; and she began to be taken with his elocution, and loved to hear his reasons to her demands. And the truth is, she took him for a kind of oracle, which nettled them all; yea those that he relied on began to take this sudden favour for an alarm, and to be sensible of their own supplantation.'[2] Soon there were many more who found themselves not liking his carriage or his company.

Elizabeth might even have read some of his poetry. If the ageing Leicester, whom he had so assiduously courted, had played a part in bringing Raleigh to her notice it would have been because he knew that this brash and virile young man was just the type, and of the right age, to appeal to her. It was said that 'she had in her time four principal favourites: namely the Earl of Leicester, Sir Christopher Hatton, Sir Walter Raleigh, and the Earl of Essex. All these successively enjoyed her grace in the highest measure, being men of very comely personage, and adorned with all outward gifts of nature, but much differing from one another in their minds.'[3] And to quote Aubrey: 'Queen Elizabeth loved to have all the servants of her Court proper men.'

It had been a relief to nearly everybody, including Elizabeth, when William of Orange (William the Silent) demanded Alençon's urgent presence in the Netherlands, where he had been offered the crown. For Dutch Protestants this was a political manoeuvre, ensuring an alliance with France against Spain.

The charade of Elizabeth's behaviour towards Alençon is a story on its own. On his first visit she really did seem to have been aroused by his 'frenzied wooing'[4] and at his departure it had been observed, to general alarm, that the farewells were 'tender on both sides'. On the second visit she had gone so far, in November 1581, as to announce publicly that she intended to marry him. But very soon she showed signs of wavering, especially when faced with Henri III's terms, which involved subsidizing an army. She became desperate to be rid of her Frog. Nevertheless she saw him off to Antwerp early in February with tears in her eyes, real or false. How much had all this been make-believe? Was it true, as has since been said, that she devoted her wiles to the purpose for which most English battles in Europe were fought, from Crécy to Waterloo? She could lose her temper, and she could weep, but as always she had to wear a mask, not to show her true emotions.

Alençon was accompanied by an appropriate retinue of ladies and gentlemen, including Leicester, Philip Sidney, Fulke Greville and Raleigh. Raleigh could have been chosen because of his fluency in French, but by then the impression he had made on the Queen was common knowledge. Leicester had to return to England soon after the safe delivery of Alençon, after a pageant held in his honour, so it was to Raleigh that William gave letters for Elizabeth, including a verbal message, *Sub umbra alarum tuarum protegimur*, We are protected under the shadow of your wings.[5] From all this it is clear that Raleigh had caught Elizabeth's eye at the right moment (maybe as Leicester had intended) when the pretence – or otherwise – of her romance with Alençon was fading.

The cloak episode, said to have happened at Greenwich and usually regarded as a fairy story, could easily have been true, being perfectly in keeping with Raleigh's character – an extravagant gamble on his part. Fortuitously, the seals he adopted in 1584, as Captain of the Queen's Guard and Governor of the Colony of Virginia, show the heraldic image of a cloak 'mantling' his coat of arms like wings, above his new and tactfully chosen motto, *Amore et Virtute*. The story is found in Fuller's *Worthies*, and it has to be admitted that no other contemporary comment has been found on such a fascinating piece of gossip: 'This captain Raleigh coming out of Ireland to the English Court in good habit (his clothes then being a considerable part of his estate) found the Queen walking, till, meeting with a plashy place, she seemed to scruple going thereon. Presently Raleigh cast and spread his new plush cloak on the ground, whereon the Queen trod gently, rewarding him afterwards with many suits, for his so free and seasonable tender of so fair a footcloth.'

It was not just his dark good looks and up-curling moustache that made him the 'darling of the English Cleopatra', a phrase invented by a Flemish Jesuit.[6] His boldness, his blatant ambition, his tremendous self-confidence, his vanity, all appealed to her: in other words it was that 'damnable pride', or 'awfulness and ascendancy in his aspect over other mortals', so much resented by rivals and people of higher social standing in the Charybdis pool of the English Court. In fact she enjoyed the resentment of his rivals, and even encouraged it. She recognized that here was an extraordinary intelligence, a quickness of mind and reaction, that Elizabethans called wit, and a flicker of literary genius that might burst into a flame. He was also a well-seasoned man of action, both by land and sea, and had experienced the full horror and dangers of war, and this too gave him an advantage over most other courtiers. And he was a very hard worker. She was also amused by his West Country burr, and called him 'Water', which was near to the way he pronounced his own name, Watar. She was a great one for nicknames. Leicester was her 'Eyes', Burghley her 'Spirit', Archbishop Whitgift her 'Little Black Husband'. Hatton was her 'Mutton', 'Lids', or 'Bell-wether' (leader of the flock). They were names Hatton did not like, but he had to put up with them, just as the undersized Robert Cecil, Lord Burghley's son, disliked being 'Pygmy'.

Then there was his love of extravagant clothes and jewels, which in another age would have raised eyebrows. As the formidable antiquarian George Eland, who had no love for Raleigh, once put it, 'The Elizabethan age was the age of Swank';[7] and others in the Court also wore rich and colourful clothes. But Raleigh outdid everybody, and the more unpopular he became the more this was resented and despised as *nouveau riche* showing off. He especially loved pearls, and they appear in his hair in Nicholas Hilliard's miniature of this period. Such gorgeously fashionable clothes are quite a contrast to that unsmiling, almost glowering face in the picture. That same Flemish Jesuit spread the rumour that the jewels on his shoes were worth more than 6,600 gold pieces, but this need not of course be believed.

Elizabeth's own passion for elaborate finery is of course well known, often with symbolic motifs as for instance in the portrait by William Segar at Hatfield House, where she has an ermine on her arm, the symbol of chastity. This portrait, no doubt idealized, shows her in full majesty and command, still handsome and well preserved, with auburn hair (possibly a wig) and her dress studded with pearls and rubies, and was painted in 1585. It is not altogether surprising that Raleigh was flattered when the Queen showed that she was attracted by him, and that he was ready to imagine himself in love.

Fuller is the source for another well-known anecdote. With Elizabeth evidently watching him, Raleigh scratched these words with a diamond on a window-pane: 'Fain would I climb, yet I fear to fall'. The Queen went to see what he had written, and then wrote underneath: 'If thy heart fails thee, climb not at all'.

Raleigh may have had jokes with the Queen, but he was essentially a cynic, whereas she loved to tease. He does not seem to have been especially musical, as she certainly was. She played the virginals, and loved dancing. One does not hear of Raleigh dancing. Nor did he much go in for jousting, which the Queen loved to watch. His wide reading, his knowledge of languages, his spirited conversation, his imagination and originality of mind, his multiplicity of interests; all these appealed to her. As a poet, he knew better than anyone how to woo her with words. His wit matched hers. She too was vain and wanted not only admiration but devotion, something more than chivalry. She created around her a great game of love, surrounding herself with courtiers who had to pretend that they were hopelessly and endlessly in love with this inaccessible Virgin Queen. She enjoyed provoking jealousies, and playing one against another. She was their ageless Gloriana. Raleigh called her his Diana, goddess of the moon, a symbol of chastity, the virgin huntress. She was also Cynthia, who came down to earth to kiss the sleeping Endymion, and was thus capable of mortal love. This game of praising her enduring beauty was kept up to an absurd extent until the end of her life, when she was nearing seventy. As Francis Bacon was to say, she 'suffered herself to be honoured and caressed, and celebrated, and extolled with the name of love; and wished it and continued it, beyond the suitability of her age'.[8]

A poetic dialogue has been attributed to Raleigh and Elizabeth, and if genuinely written by them must belong to this early period in their relationship. The lover, Raleigh, makes his complaint in a long and rather weak poem:

> Fortune hath taken thee away my love,
> My life's joy, and my soul's heaven above.
> Fortune hath taken thee away my princess
> My only light and my true fancy's mystery . . .

To which his lady, Elizabeth, makes reply in a light-hearted, affectionate but more non-committal way.

> Ah silly pug wert thou so sore afraid?
> Mourn not (my Wat) nor be thou so dismayed,
> It passeth fickle fortune's power and skill,
> To force my heart to think thee any ill . . .

Foreign ambassadors were quick to assume that there was much more than platonic love between the Queen and her favourites. Mary Queen of Scots actually wrote to Elizabeth accusing her of having Sir Christopher Hatton as a paramour (among others). There was plenty of gossip about her relationship with Leicester, but such talk was dangerous, not to say highly treasonable, and the pillory was the usual punishment. It was, however, said that in 1566 they spent the night of New Year's Eve together; Elizabeth Jenkins in her biography considered this to have been possible though penetration as always would have been unlikely. Rowse, though he never said it on paper, was sure that some sort of 'touching' went on between her and her lovers.

Even now it is almost heretical to suggest that there was any sexual contact with Elizabeth. In the 19th century, Stebbing, one of Raleigh's foremost biographers, angrily dismissed suggestions of 'sensual love' between Elizabeth and her favourites. 'There is not a tittle of evidence', he wrote, 'which will be accepted by any who do not start by presuming in her the mark of a courtesan.' Various theories have been advanced about her wish to remain a virgin, beginning with her shame as a girl over Lord Thomas Seymour's horseplay, which led indirectly to his execution for treason. Her mother was executed when she was three; her stepmother, Katherine Howard, of whom she was fond, when she was eight. And Jane Seymour had died in childbirth. All these 'emotional blocks' are of course mere supposition, though again to quote from Elizabeth Jenkins, Leicester, who knew her from childhood, said that at the age of eight she told him that she would never marry. Nor is there any proof in the rumour, propagated by Ben Jonson, that she had a 'membrane which made her incapable of man', even if 'for her delight she tried many'. Her jealous rages whenever a courtier or lady-in-waiting got married, usually secretly because they knew the consequence, do on the face of it seem both unreasonable and spinsterish. She wanted undivided loyalties, and much of this she would lose if she had a husband, or submitted herself to a man.

With the departure of Alençon there was no further need to look for a husband. Tall, muscular, intelligent, in his late twenties, Raleigh arrived at the right moment. In 1582 he was still one of her Esquires and as such travelled with her from court to court, from Whitehall to Greenwich (her favourite), to Richmond, to Nonsuch in Surrey, to Windsor, to Hampton Court, and on her progresses he would be given accommodation with other courtiers. At Whitehall the Esquires took charge of the Presence Chamber at night and slept there. The Privy Chamber was the room where the Queen would breakfast and sup, and be attended and entertained by her ladies and Maids-of-Honour, all expected to remain maids. Beyond the Privy Chamber were the Privy Lodgings, the Queen's private rooms including her bedroom and bathroom. Maids-of-Honour took turns to sleep in a room in the Privy Lodgings. As Raleigh was to say, these young ladies were like witches. 'They could do hurt, but they could do no good',[9] and thus would gleefully report any untoward behaviour. And Elizabeth herself said: 'I do not live in a corner – a thousand eyes see all I do'.[10] Which must have been mostly true and have made opportunities for Rowse's 'touching' difficult. It was to be a very different situation with James I, when a Gentleman of the Bedchamber was expected to sleep on a pallet by his bedside: an unpleasant ordeal, as the king disliked washing or changing his clothes (Elizabeth kept herself scrupulously clean).

Despite his position at Court, Raleigh still needed to earn money, and it was not long before his charms began to be rewarded. The first real indication of royal support is in a minute of the Privy Council on 1 February 1582, authorizing a backdated payment of £200 to Walter Rawley and Edward Denny 'upon the entertainment due to them' in Ireland. In April the Queen issued a curiously worded warrant allowing Raleigh to take over the company of footmen in Ireland that had been under the command of a Captain Appesley, 'lately deceased'. This starts with the words 'Our pleasure is to have Our servant Walter Rawley trained some time longer in that Our realm [Ireland] for his better experience in martial affairs'. But then she goes on to say that 'He is, for some consideration, by this excused to stay here'. She did not want him out of her sight; a lieutenant would take his place, and Raleigh would be paid regardless.

A further document concerning Ireland was written jointly by Raleigh and Burghley and entitled 'The Opinion of Mr. Rawley upon motions made to him for the means of subduing the Rebellion in Monster [sic].'[11] This was in reality a summary of his ideas put forward earlier in the year and which had been repeated in the presence of Grey. He had pointed out that the Irish chieftains had disliked Desmond, following him 'less from love than fear'. They were afraid that the Queen might pardon Desmond and that he would be reinstated after the rebellion was over. It would also, he pointed out, save much expense if the chieftains could be persuaded to police their own territories under the protection of the Crown. Thus we have the beginnings of the time-honoured British imperial policy of divide and rule.

By 1583 there was no doubt that Raleigh was Elizabeth's chief favourite. Throughout the year he was steadily promoted in influence and there was an evergrowing alarm among those who considered themselves closest to her. If Leicester had indeed been responsible for introducing him, by now he had begun to regret it. None of Raleigh's rivals could compete with his sycophantic versifying.

> Those eyes which set my fancy on a fire,
> Those crispèd hairs which hold my heart in chains,
> Those dainty hands which conquered my desire,*
> That wit which of my thought does hold the reins!
>
> Those eyes for clearness do the stars surpass,
> Those hairs obscure the brightness of the sun,
> Those hands more white than ever ivory was,
> That wit even to the skies hath glory won.

And again:

> Praised be Diana's fair and harmless light,
> Praised be the dews, wherewith she moists the ground;
> Praise be her beams, the glory of the night,
>   Praise be her power, by which all powers abound . . .

These and other poems, known as the 'Poems to Cynthia', were written for her alone, but somehow went into circulation. Some years later they were published without permission, and others appeared anonymously in the *Phoenix Nest*. It is also thought a good many have been lost. It was the fashion to write poetry, and people of 'quality' did so for private pleasure, not for publication. Nevertheless in 1589 George Puttenham wrote in *The Art of English Poesie*: 'For dittie and amorous ode I finde Sir Walter Rawlegh's vayne most loftie, condolent [in some versions insolent, meaning powerful] and passionate.'

More attractive is another early poem.

---

* Elizabeth was proud of her hands and liked to be complimented on them. Rowse however saw this line as proof of 'touching'.

Calling to mind mine eye went long about
T'entice my heart to seek to leave my breast;
All in a rage I thought to pull it out,
By whose device I lived in such unrest . . .

And told myself, myself now slay I will:
   But when I saw myself to you was true,
   I loved myself, because myself loved you.

Sir Christopher Hatton, who was Captain of the Queen's Guard and her Vice-Chamberlain, a Privy Councillor and soon to be Chancellor of the University of Oxford, became so jealous of Raleigh that he left the Court, shamming illness. This was not the first time that he had behaved in such a way. Nearly ten years before he had been in a huff about the Earl of Oxford becoming too close to the Queen, and had written a childishly indignant letter of complaint.

The Queen had spotted Hatton as a young man aged twenty-two at a masque at the Inns of Court, and had been much taken by his 'activity and person which was tall and proportional'. He danced well and loved pageantry, which were other attributes that appealed to her. She also recognized that he had the quality of a statesman, and that she could rely on him. Soon she began to load him with lands and offices. He was a patron of artists and writers, also of the great Dr Dee (who dedicated to him the first of his projected volumes on the British Empire, a book on navigation), and had been one of the promoters of Drake's great voyage – Drake named his ship the *Golden Hind* in Hatton's honour, because his crest included a golden deer. He certainly could not compete with Raleigh's poetic gifts. Instead he wrote long and extravagant letters, as if from an ardent suitor, now tedious to read.*

On one occasion, instead of complaining direct to the Queen about Raleigh, he sent a message with 'tokens' through the medium of his friend, Sir Thomas Heneage, her Treasurer of the Chamber. The tokens consisted of a diminutive bucket, a book, and a small dagger-shaped bodkin to be worn in the hair – as Hatton's biographer has said, suggesting the contents of a modern Christmas stocking. The bucket was meant to symbolize water, in other words Raleigh. The bodkin presumably meant that the 'bell-wether'

---

* Sheridan in *The Critic* makes Mr Puff say: 'You'll know Sir Christopher by his turning out of toes – famous, you know, for his dancing.' Lytton Strachey's flippant comment 'Hatton danced, and that is all we know of him', quoted in St John Brooks's biography, evoked A. L. Rowse's remark pencilled alongside: 'B. F. All *he* knew.'

would kill himself unless the bucket was emptied. The significance of the book is not known.

In any case it was all very petty. Heneage caught up with the Queen just as she was about to ride in Windsor Park to catch a doe. She seemed at first pleased, then irritated, sending back a cryptic message about bounding banks to keep out the flood and how she loved her sheep.

Hatton continued to sulk. Naunton said of him: 'He had a large proportion of gifts and endownments, but too much of the season of envy'. And Hatton continued to hate Raleigh.

Grandeur at Durham House
1583

For a while Raleigh appears to have acted not only as the Queen's companion, but as her personal secretary. The royal exchequer could not afford large salaries for those whom she favoured, so instead Elizabeth would appoint them to profitable posts which could earn them big subsidies. Her chosen favourites might be given Church properties, estates forfeited by traitors, or lucrative monopolies. In return such people would be expected to be on hand whenever required, perhaps entertain her and her courtiers at their country houses on her very expensive progresses; or they might build ships that would be available in emergencies, or be used for privateering, in which case a proportion of the plunder would to be paid into her coffers.

Raleigh's rapid rise in favour was matched by his rapid rise in wealth. Two leases were extracted from All Souls College, Oxford and these Elizabeth bestowed on him. Far more important was a wine monopoly, 'the farm of wines' which became one of the reasons for his increasing unpopularity. This monopoly gave him the authority to charge every vintner in the country £1 a year to retail wines; import permits had also first to be obtained from him. Thus he received an income of about £1,000 a year, although £400 of this went to his agent. Some while later he was given large and exceedingly profitable grants in connection with the export of woollens, renewed over several years.[1]

One example of Raleigh's closeness to the Queen and her reliance on him occurred on 18 April 1583. They were riding together from Richmond to Greenwich, and were about to pass to Dr Dee's house at Mortlake. Dee's reputation had not been damaged by the fiasco of Frobisher's black rocks. He was still held much in awe, and visitors flocked to see or consult his famous library. He was an automatic choice to be entrusted with checking the proposed new calendar of Pope Gregory XIII, a formidable task. At times he would be summoned to Court to give advice on matters of the royal health. So Raleigh reminded Elizabeth that she had once promised to call on her astrologer. She stopped her horse, and the 'magus' was summoned. 'Being new up', she did not dismount, but put out her right hand for him to kiss, saying '*Quod defertur non aufertur*' (What is deferred is not put off).[2]

In fact there would have been other reasons for Raleigh's reminder. He would certainly have wanted to slip in a few words with Dee on behalf of his half-brothers, Adrian and Humphrey Gilbert, both of whom were planning expeditions and who relied on Dee's support and expert knowledge. Adrian was particularly close to Dee, and was planning a new attempt to find a north-west passage to Cathay in conjunction with the Muscovy Company. Humphrey's ships were in fact ready to sail, and Dee had a very large investment in Humphrey's later attempt to found a colony in North America before his charter of 1578 expired.

A letter from Raleigh on 12 May 1583 to Lord Burghley also illustrates how it was now accepted that he had the ear of the monarch. Burghley had asked him to intercede with her over a delicate family matter, in connection with his erratic son-in-law the Earl of Oxford, who had been in disgrace ever since his duel with Sir Thomas Knivet. Oxford had been banned from Court, whereas Knivet had been forgiven. Not only that, but Oxford was still refusing to take back his wife, Burghley's daughter. Burghley's request is all the more surprising given that Oxford and Raleigh were such enemies. For his part, Raleigh was only too willing to oblige the most influential man in the land: 'The evening after the receipt of your lordship's letter I spake with Her Majesty; and ministering some occasion touching the Earl of Oxford, I told Her Majesty how grievously your lordship received her late discomfortable answer.' She had answered that Oxford's behaviour was not to be lightly passed over, but Raleigh – so he said – had told her how important it was that the Lord Treasurer should have peace of mind. And so she had relented. Raleigh then pointed out to Burghley that he himself was now likely to be the one to suffer. 'I am content, for your sake, to lay the serpent [Oxford] before the fire, as much as in me lieth, that [he] having recovered strength myself may be most in danger of his poison and sting.'

A few days later when the Queen was staying at Burghley's house, Theobalds in Hertfordshire, she told her host that she would receive Oxford. Raleigh was right, however; there was never to be peace between him and that serpent. The old quarrel was not to be forgotten.* Oxford continued to regard him with contempt, as an insolent commoner, who had wormed his way into his circle and had then betrayed him.

When in London and free from official duties Raleigh was living in very

* p. 30.

grand quarters, Durham House, also known as Duresme Place, on the banks of the Thames next to the Strand and where the Adelphi now is. This had been passed to him by the Queen either at the end of 1582 or early 1583. In actual fact it belonged to the See of Durham and had been held by the Crown since the time of Henry VIII. The Bishop would have liked it back, but Elizabeth overruled him; there could be no argument about this, especially after the experience of the Bishop of Ely, who had been forced to give up his London palace (where Hatton Garden now is) to Christopher Hatton, after receiving this peremptory letter from the Queen: 'Proud prelate, you know that I who made you what you are can unmake you; and if you do not forthwith fulfil your engagement by God I will immediately unfrock you.'[3] She was no doubt half joking, for she graciously conceded that the Bishop of Ely could visit his garden occasionally, and pick twenty bunches of roses every year. Durham House had gardens and an orchard, but whether its Bishop had similar privileges we know not.

Aubrey wrote: 'Durham House was a noble palace; after he [Raleigh] came to his greatness he lived there, or in some apartment of it. I well remember his study, which was a little turret that looked into and over the Thames, and had the prospect which is pleasant perhaps as any in the world, and which not only refreshes the eye-sight, but cheers the spirits, and (to speak my mind) enlarges an ingenious man's thoughts.'

There were many large mansions, palaces or 'inns' between the Fleet river and Westminster. Nine of them were said to have been owned by bishops. Streets to this day commemorate the names of noble families who lived there – Arundel, Norfolk, Surrey, Essex. There is also a Durham House Street. Somerset House had been started by Protector Somerset in 1549, but the famous Savoy Palace had already been demolished and the area around it had become notorious, a 'chief misery of rogues',[4] according to Lord Burghley whose great turreted house was across the way.

Durham House was one of the oldest mansions, and had a long frontage above the Thames with a watergate. York House was to its west, and Russell House to its east. Built originally in the time of Edward I, it was rebuilt in the 14th century, and was probably somewhat cold and damp, though the entire front ground floor, most susceptible to the damp, was inhabited by Sir Edward Darcy and his family. In engravings of the 1590s Raleigh's turret is visible, as is the watergate and other towers. Evidently there was an addition at the back, with a higher roof, as well as stables for twenty horses along the Strand. There were two courtyards, one with a spring of water, also outhouses for up to forty servants. Catherine of Aragon, Anne Boleyn and Elizabeth herself had all lodged at Durham House. Lady Jane Grey had

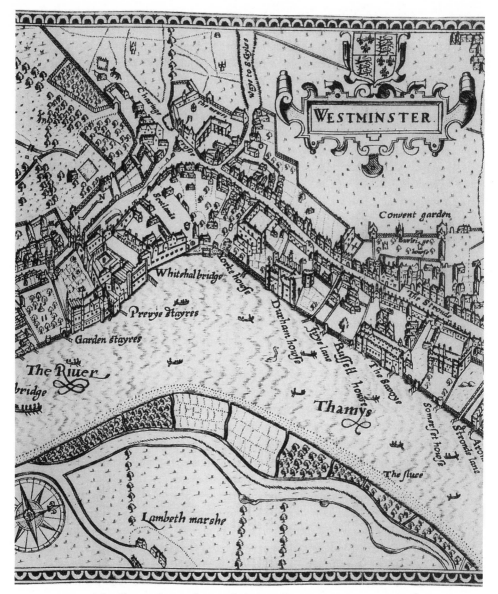

Part of the Thames from John Norden's Speculum Britanniae, *1593. Durham House is right of centre, the Strand behind.*

been married there. There are mentions of a stately hall with lofty marble pillars. Across the river were the Lambeth marshes and meadows. Being on the curve of the Thames Raleigh from his turret would have been able to see on one side Southwark Cathedral, and on the other Whitehall Palace and Westminster Abbey. A wherry boat or ferry, usually for grander people, operated nearby which would have made for constant activity below – for some reason it was said that Raleigh did not like using wherry boats and preferred crossing the Thames by London Bridge. The Strand had recently been paved, which would have made access to Whitehall easier and quicker. Always crowded, it had many taverns; the Black Bull, very noisy, was opposite Durham House.

Raleigh loved Durham House and used it as a London base or even as a home for his team of advisers in planning expeditions across the seas, including among many others Philip Amadas, Arthur Barlow, Charles Thynne, Jacob Whiddon and, especially, Richard Hakluyt the younger* and Thomas Hariot. Hakluyt is one of the great remembered Elizabethans, a man of vision, to become one of the chief propagandists for an English settlement in North America, and the first of the English naval historians. About the same age as Raleigh, he had been fired with the excitement of exploration when visiting his uncle and namesake at the Middle Temple, and being shown all the maps, charts and books laid before him. After the failure of Frobisher's three expeditions, followed by the triumphant return of Francis Drake in 1580, he became convinced of the need of a lectureship on the theory of navigation, going far beyond the standard works of, say, William Bourne, whose *Inventions or Devices* was in effect a war manual; more serious and systematic navigational training was required.

Drake was interested in this idea of a lectureship and offered to endow it. Young Thomas Hariot, fresh from Oxford, undertook the task. Born in 1560, he was soon to be regarded as the country's most profound mathematician. He was also an astronomer, mineralogist and physicist, and set up a twelve-foot telescope on the roof of Durham House, the first telescope in England. Whether his lectures actually began at Durham House is not clear, but they certainly were eventually held there, and in the winter of 1582–3 were of supreme importance to Humphrey Gilbert's preparations for his voyage. As geographers, Richard Hakluyt and Thomas Hariot had advanced beyond the speculations of Dr Dee. Hakluyt was already planning his epoch-making work, a complete collection of all English travels and exploration since earliest times, the *Principall Navigations*, the first volume of which was published in 1589. Compared to Dee Hariot was a modern scientist, and soon became Raleigh's most important adviser.

One of Hariot's students was Maurice Browne, a friend of John Thynne

* p. 17.

59

of Longleat, stepson of Carew Raleigh. He had been several weeks in the Azores on the periphery of a rebellion against the Spaniards by the Portuguese inhabitants who were in favour of the priestly pretender to the throne of Portugal, Dom Antonio, prior of Crato. Browne had returned in July 1582 and was enthused with the idea of overseas possessions for England. He wrote to Thynne that he was planning to study cosmography and the art of navigation under an 'excellent fellow who dwelleth here in London' – who surely must have been Hariot.[5] Another student of Hariot, who became a friend of Browne, was a Hungarian poet, Stephen Parmenius, obviously a person of great charm and intellect. He had been a protégé of Hakluyt at Christ Church, and indeed had shared his bed. He wrote a poem 'De Navigatione', which was well received. Both he and Browne volunteered to join Gilbert.

Browne's letter to Thynne also gives a picture of the new splendours at Durham House: the silver plate engraved with the Raleigh coat of arms, liveried servants with chains of gold, walls lined with tapestries. Raleigh's bed was covered with green velvet edged with broad silver lace and surmounted by white plumes and a spangle. According to Browne it had been credibly reported that 'Master Rawley hath spent within the half year alone three thousand pounds.' Browne like many another was amazed by Raleigh's sumptuous clothes. As an example of this, in the year following, we read of a 'Welsh gentleman', Hugh Pugh, who was charged at Westminster with stealing a jewel worth £80, a hatband of pearls worth £30, five yards of damask worth £3, 'all the goods and chattels of Walter Rawley, esq of Westminster, Co. Midd.'[6]

In April 1583 Nicholas Faunt, purveyor of court gossip to Anthony Bacon,[7] who was still gathering intelligence for Walsingham in France, wrote about Humphrey Gilbert's plan for a voyage to 'a part of America not yet discovered', and how his half-brother 'Mr. Rawley our new favourite had put the great sum of £2000 in a ship and furniture.' All of which was true. The impecunious Gilbert was indeed set for his new expedition – still under his charter of 1578, which was close to expiring – and Raleigh had invested this sum in a ship to sail with Gilbert, which he had named *Bark Raleigh*. In March there had been a hiatus, when Walsingham relayed a shattering message from the Queen, forbidding Gilbert to leave because he was not 'of good hap by sea'.[8] This could have been a reference to his reputation for being unlucky or possibly because he was prone to seasickness (as was Raleigh). Gilbert was outraged, pointing out that he had put all he owned into the expedition, almost being forced to 'sell my wife's clothes off her back'. He also utterly repudiated some malicious slurs about delaying his departure; he had not been able to sail earlier because of the exceptional force of the south-westerly gales.

We may wonder just how much this so-called message had to do with the fact that at the same time Walsingham was promoting a rival expedition, backed by the merchant adventurers of Bristol, that was being organized by his stepson Christopher Carleill. At any rate Raleigh hastened to intervene with the Queen, and was able to calm Gilbert with another message from her, very affectionate even though written in such a way as if she and Raleigh both had a premonition that they would never see him again:[9]

Brother, I have sent you a token from her Majesty, an anchor guided by a lady, as you see; and farther her Highness willed me to send you word that she wished as great good hap and safety to your ship, as if she were there in person; desiring you to have care of yourself, as of that which she tendereth; and therefore, for her sake, must provide for it accordingly.

Farther she commendeth that you leave your picture with me. For the rest, I leave till our meeting, or to the report of this bearer, who would needs be the messenger of this good news. So I commit you to the will and protection of God, who send us such life or death as he shall please, or hath appointed.

Your true brother W. Rauley

The token is described in one of Maurice Browne's letters. The lady was a queen wearing a crown, and all was set with rubies and diamonds; on the back of the anchor was engraved, *Tuemur sub sacra ancora*, we are safe under the sacred anchor.

Soon Raleigh would sign himself in letters not as Rauley but Ralegh. From then onwards it was always such, apart from a document (now in the Raleigh Collection in the University of North Carolina at Chapel Hill) related to his 'farm of wines' dated 4 December 1583, when he authorizes Philip Haywood and his daughter to keep a tavern in Lyme Regis. In this document Raleigh's name is spelt throughout with an i.

Gilbert's expedition, although ultimately doomed, was to lead to the first attempt at founding a colony in Virginia a year later. The failure of the 1579 expedition had not deterred him from his dream of a settlement across the Atlantic, probably in Norumbega (roughly from Nova Scotia south to Cape Cod). In 1580 he had dispatched Simon Fernandez in the pinnace *Squirrel*, carrying only eleven men, on a preliminary investigation of that part of the North American coastline. The *Squirrel* returned after three months. For

Raleigh's signature on the wine licence of December 1583, with facsimiles of autographs 26 July 1584 and 8 October 1587. If, as has been suggested, it was a stamp, the document would not have had legality.[10]

such a small ship the journey was a memorable feat of seamanship, and the reports were encouraging, duly relayed to Dr Dee.

In Dee's diary for 28 August 1580, it is revealed that he had begun negotiations with Gilbert for a 'grant of discovery', in return for cash and expert advice.[11] Gilbert in his desperate attempts to raise money had been selling grants of land in advance, and Dee was able to obtain a very good bargain indeed: he was to have all rights north of 50° latitude, which would have made him lord of all Canada north of the St Lawrence river.

Privateering would have been another way of subsidizing an expedition, but that plan had to be abandoned. The Spanish ambassador, Bernardino de Mendoza, was by now highly suspicious and wrote to Philip II saying that he was demanding to see Elizabeth. 'There could be no better way of putting a stop to these activities', he wrote, 'than for your Majesty to order that if any of their ships is captured on the Indies route, or put into any port, not a man is to be left alive – but all sent to the bottom.'[12] In this and other letters he mentioned both Martin Frobisher and Humphrey Gilbert, whose names were now delightfully Spanishified into Jorbirger and Onxiginberto. The Queen's eventual answer to Mendoza was that she would see him only when she had satisfaction for the piratical interventions in Ireland.

By the spring of 1582 Gilbert had worked out an elaborate project for the governing of the proposed new territories, which would in effect be a colonial utopia, virtually independent of England. Villages, churches, tithes, rents, schools were all plotted out. Documentary material was gathered for him by Hakluyt, then still at Oxford. He was also assisted by Sir George Peckham and Sir Thomas Gerrard, both Catholics who had spent some time in prison for their beliefs. On 19 April 1582, a certain PH wrote to Burghley warning him that this association had given rise to a 'muttering among ye Papists'.[13] Gilbert had indeed realized that one way of raising money could be from dissatisfied Catholic gentry suffering from fines and penalties, and that they would welcome grants of estates in Norumbega. We are told that between 6 June 1582 and 28 February 1583 he actually assigned over 8,500,000 acres and seven islands to Catholics. Sir Philip Sidney was also assigned 3,000,000 acres; apart from his sympathy towards some Catholic gentry, a link was the fact that he had been a pupil of Dee. However, by June 1583, the month of Gilbert's eventual sailing, it was decided that the Catholic associates of Peckham would make their own way to America, on the presumption that they would retain their rights in these enormous lands for which Gilbert had been paid. These Catholics seem to have had some encouragement from Walsingham: possibly a shrewd device for getting suspect Papists out of reach, and into the wilds, when otherwise they might be tempted to defect to an enemy country.[14]

When Mendoza got to hear of the Catholics' plans he was aghast. At his instigation stern warnings were issued to them by priests pointing out that what was known as Florida, which included all territories up the east coast, belonged to Spain and that they would risk having their throats cut if caught there, as had been the fate of some French Protestants and would-be colonists in 1565. The other danger for Spain, as Mendoza was well aware, was that any English settlement, Protestant or Catholic, would act as a base for attacks on Spanish treasure fleets returning from the West Indies. Partly because of this pressure, the Catholic venture came to naught.

Gilbert's fleet eventually sailed from Devon on 11 June.[15] It comprised five ships, including the *Squirrel*, 10 tons only, presumably the same that Fernandez had piloted. The others were the *Swallow*, 40 tons, at one time owned by the notorious pirate John Cullis; the *Golden Hind* (not Drake's), 40 tons, belonging to Edward Hayes and once also involved in piracy; the *Delight*, 120 tons, partly owned by Gilbert and captained by Maurice Browne, with the poet Parmenius on board (Thynne sent Browne 'butter and cheeses and marmylade' for the journey); and the *Bark Raleigh*, three-masted and 200 tons, equipped for sixty men and acting as flagship. There were about 200 men in the other ships, including shipwrights, masons, carpenters. Presents and goods for bartering had been brought for 'savages'. Sidney had wanted to join the expedition, but Elizabeth would not let him go.

The *Bark Raleigh* soon returned to port, the excuse being that a contagious disease had broken out on board, though later an alternative reason was given: complaints by the crew that there were insufficient victuals. Gilbert was furious and wrote to Peckham asking him to 'solicit my brother Rawley to make them an example to all knaves'. In fact, as it turned out, the survival of the *Bark Raleigh* was to prove a backhanded benefit for Raleigh when he began planning his expedition at the end of the year. It is to Edward Hayes that we owe the account of the disastrous story that followed.

Victuals were also to be a problem on the other ships, as Hayes makes clear. The whole affair had been arranged on the cheap. The *Swallow*, which in any case was manned by an ex-pirate crew, slipped away in a fog to rob a ship of food and clothing, and rejoined the others at Newfoundland, of which Gilbert had already taken possession for the Queen, 'to behoof of Sir Humphrey Gilbert, his heirs and assigns for ever' – hence Newfoundland's claim to be the first of British colonies. Plots for the drying of fish were rented out to English, Spanish, Portuguese and French fishermen who were already there. Gilbert wrote home full of enthusiasm. Parmenius was less impressed: 'What shall I say, my good Hakluyt, when I see nothing but a very wilderness'. But, he added: 'Of fish there is an incredible abundance.'

Many of the men refused to accompany Gilbert any further, some of them being ill, so it was decided to leave the *Swallow* behind to take them back to England. Then the *Delight* was wrecked on shoals off Sable Island. Eighty men were drowned, including Maurice Browne and Stephen Parmenius. Most of the provisions were lost, as well as Gilbert's notes and charts.

Now the remaining men, because of the desperate shortage of supplies, insisted on returning home. It had all been a great disappointment, but Gilbert said that he was determined to send out another fleet the following spring – he would borrow £10,000 from the Queen. The weather became stormy, but Gilbert refused to leave the little *Squirrel*. North of the Azores he came aboard the *Golden Hind* 'to make merry, but lamenting the loss of his great ship and men'. Before the *Delight* sank he had despatched a boy aboard to collect certain things, including a piece of ore which presumably he had thought might contain gold. On the *Golden Hind* he sent for the boy only to find that he had forgotten the ore. 'The remembrance touched him so deep, as he beat the boy in a great rage.'

The *Squirrel* was dangerously overloaded. In spite of the terrible seas, 'breaking short and pyramid wise', and in spite of St Elmo's fire* having been seen on the mast, always considered a bad omen by sailors, he insisted on returning. On 9 September he came alongside the *Golden Hind* and was seen sitting on the deck with a book in his hand. He shouted out words that became famous: 'We are as near to heaven by sea as by land'. That night, towards midnight, in the unremitting storm, the watch on the *Golden Hind* saw the lantern on the *Squirrel* go out; ship and Humphrey Gilbert were never seen again, 'devoured by the seas'.

And so 'in great torment of weather, and peril of drowning' the *Golden Hind* reached Falmouth, and the sad news was brought to John Gilbert and Raleigh. In all the tributes to Humphrey Gilbert's initiative and bravery, his pioneering spirit and optimism, there is a discernible note of criticism about his rashness and obstinacy. Sir John Gilbert attempted to exploit Humphrey's claim to Newfoundland, without success. Raleigh immediately applied for the transference of the patent to himself before it ran out in a few months. In its stead Elizabeth granted him a six-year patent.

* An electric phenomenon that appears on a mast or steeple before a storm.

The First Virginia Voyage
1584

Sir George Peckham,* in collaboration with Sir Philip Sidney, was making another plan to form a colony in North America, but without any particular association with Catholics. After the death of Humphrey Gilbert, he had written 'A True Reporte' for Walsingham, who had been impressed, and Frobisher was interested in heading the expedition.[1] All this foundered, partly because Peckham went to prison for Catholic activities, partly because the Queen still refused to let Sidney out of the country. Likewise another project by Christopher Carleill petered out. A further expedition to New-foundland was planned by Bernard Drake of Ash, a connection of Raleigh's through his father's first marriage, and was supported by Sir John Gilbert and Raleigh. As this was to be chiefly privateering it went ahead without any special difficulties, and the result was a good haul from Spanish ships which Drake brought back to England.

Raleigh was determined to carry on with Humphrey Gilbert's dream, and for a while contemplated associating with Adrian Gilbert and John Davis in yet another attempt to find the North-West Passage to Cathay, on the basis of Dr Dee's 'grant of discovery' from Humphrey Gilbert.[2] Early in 1583 Walsingham had visited Dee's house and found Adrian Gilbert there, when the talk had been all about the plan. Contracts were made with the Muscovy Company.

Meanwhile, we learn from Dee's 'spirits' diary that in his search, through his medium Edward Kelley, for direct communication with the Almighty, he had been consulting an angel known as Medicina Dei as to whether Adrian Gilbert should be given his full support. It is hard for the reader of the diary today to associate this nonsense with such a revered and brilliant polymath, whose fame had spread to the continent and who was known to men such as the geographer and map maker Mercator, and to understand why he should have been bamboozled by Kelley (whose ears had been

---

* p. 63.

cropped because of committing forgery, though Dee might not then have known it); one has to accept that Dee's hermetic and occult beliefs were in the mainstream of the magical tradition of the Renaissance. Sir Philip Sidney and the poet-diplomat Edward Dyer had been pupils of Dee, and Dyer fell under the spell of Kelley. Mary Herbert, Lady Pembroke, Sidney's sister, was a patroness not only of Dee, but of Adrian Gilbert, and was herself a 'great chymist' or alchemist. Raleigh certainly would have had great respect for Dee, but one cannot imagine him being interested in crystal balls. He may have been accused of dabbling in magic, but this had other implications which will be touched on later. He was certainly not as close to Dee as was his half-brother Adrian.

Medicina Dei confirmed that Adrian should be 'privy to the mysteries'[3], and this meant that Dee must join with him and Davis in the plan to colonize Atlantis, as Dee called America, if only to 'carry the name of Jesus among the infidels' who would otherwise be doomed to hellfire. Unfortunately the angels were distinctly unhelpful over practical matters. Everything suddenly changed when a Polish nobleman, Prince (or Count) Albert Laski, came up the river to Mortlake to call on Dee. This strange bombastic character, a gourmand with a long white forked beard, was a devotee of alchemy and the occult. He invited Dee and Kelley to travel back with him to Cracow, the bait being a possible audience with the Emperor Rudolf II, whose court at Prague was the great centre of learning and culture in Europe. The invitation was accepted, clearly encouraged by Walsingham who saw the possibility of valuable intelligence on Rudolf being relayed back by Dee.

So Dee sold his assignment from Humphrey Gilbert to Adrian Gilbert and John Davis. The permit, for the North-West Passage, was issued in Adrian's name on 6 February, but was too limited in scope for Raleigh who was already preparing ships to explore the north American mainland under Humphrey Gilbert's patent. In the event Elizabeth gave Raleigh a new patent for himself, and this was signed on 25 March 1584 and addressed to her 'well beloved servant'.

Some while after Dee's departure for Cracow anti-magic rioters attacked and ransacked his house. His famous library was burnt and a great deal of his chemical equipment destroyed.* It was a great disaster, but at least Dee had taken with him his indispensable crystal ball and his precious magic 'skrying' mirror (made of obsidian, possibly Aztec in origin, and now in the British Museum).

It has been thought that Davis was responsible for appropriating some of

---

* Another theory is that the library was ransacked by pupils and associates.

Dee's equipment, but if so he made good use of it. As a result of Adrian's patent he undertook the series of remarkable voyages, beginning in 1585, to latitudes further north than ventured by any navigator hitherto. The Davis Strait is named after him, believed at the time to be the entrance, at long last, to the North-West Passage.*

Raleigh was rewarded with yet another monopoly by Elizabeth, even more lucrative, but a very unpopular one. He was given the licence to export undyed woollen broadcloths, on payment of rent recovered to the Crown. This was renewed or extended over the next years until Burghley complained that the profits were excessive, calculating that in the first year Raleigh had received the immense sum of £3,500. The Company of Merchant Adventurers at Exeter was particularly outspoken in complaint, which ought to have been embarrassing for a native son. But he appeared not to mind. Much was due to spite and envy, but a great deal of his new wealth went towards preparing an expedition across the Atlantic.

Elizabeth seemed actually to enjoy the unpopularity of her latest favourite, knowing that by promoting rivalries in her inner circle it had the effect of binding each member more closely to her. In earlier times Leicester had been much disliked, and there had been similar grumblings about Hatton's riches.

Raleigh was also to have trouble with his 'farm of wines' monopoly. The Vice-Chancellor and Senate of the University of Cambridge continued to issue wine licences in Cambridge, and had not been pleased about this particular gift to Raleigh – neither were the undergraduates, who nearly lynched one of the wives of Raleigh's five licensed vintners in the town. Raleigh wrote what he considered a polite letter to the Vice-Chancellor, addressing him as 'my loving friend', asking him to take appropriate action over 'such unseemly outrages'.[4] There was no reply either to this or to a subsequent letter; and the Vice-Chancellor proceeded to put the offending vintner in prison. So Raleigh had to write more strongly, no longer to a 'loving friend': 'I cannot a little marvel at your peremptory and proud manner of dealing. I was content to use all manner of courtesy towards you ... but I perceive that my reasonable, or rather too submiss dealing hath bred in you a proceeding unsufferable.'[5]

'This was not the way to win the love of dons', A. L. Rowse once rightly remarked. The Vice-Chancellor wrote sharply back, reproving Raleigh as a gentleman, scholar and courtier for using such language. The matter was referred to Burghley and the Privy Council, and as a result it was decided

---

* Davis was a tenant of the Gilberts in Devon, in the parish of Stoke Gabriel, and would have been well known to Raleigh as a boy, being of about the same age.

that the university did in fact have the power to issue its own wine licences. Raleigh's vintner was to remain in prison for another two years. Trouble continued with Raleigh's 'knavish deputy' Richard Browne, whose behaviour did much to increase resentment over the monopoly. This resulted in Browne being suspended by the Council and Raleigh having to pay out £1,100. The patent was revoked but then renewed, with special provisos in favour of the Universities of Cambridge and Oxford.

Very different was Raleigh's relationship with William Sanderson, who was the husband of Margaret Snedall, Raleigh's niece by his father's second wife, and soon to be recognized – perhaps was already – as one of the leading merchant adventurers in the City of London. If her mother, as some maintained, was of Genoese descent, the connection would have been of quite some use to Sanderson. He now became Raleigh's chief man of business, which included managing the broadcloth monopoly, and no doubt eventually the 'farm of wines' in place of Browne.

According to a document written for James I 'by a friend' after Raleigh's death, Sanderson had trading links all over Europe and had financed expeditions to China, the Spice Islands and to the North-West Passage. Referring to his family connections with Raleigh this writer added: 'He did manage his affairs all the time of his [Raleigh's] prosperity, and did at several times stand bound for the said Sir Walter Raleigh for more than one hundred thousand pounds, and also for mere debt more than sixteen thousand pounds at a time, taken up in London most part thereof at usury upon his own bonds, such was his credit and reputation in those days.' In particular it was said that he backed 'several adventures into Virginia with Sir Walter Raleigh at the first discovery thereof.'[6] All of which was true.

By the time Raleigh received his letters patent, he already had his two ships ready for a reconnaissance voyage to the New World. Thus they were able to set out on 27 April under the command of Philip Amadas and Arthur Barlow. It would seem extremely probable that Dr Dee's giant chart on vellum, now in the British Library, would have been consulted.[7] This endeavoured to map out the North American coastline from Norumbega to Cape Florida and as far as the Gulf of Mexico. Right in the centre, somewhere north of what is now North Carolina and its string of islands, is marked the Bahia (Bay) de Santa Maria, obviously the equivalent of Chesapeake Bay; this must have seemed to Raleigh an ideal possibility for a fortified harbour. The chart, dated 1580, may have been partly made from information given by Simon Fernandez, the Portuguese pilot who in that year visited Dee after his voyage of reconnaissance on behalf of Humphrey Gilbert. Fernandez also accompanied Amadas and Barlow in 1584.

It was in 1580 that Dee was also recorded as having said that the problems of navigation were best solved by a mathematician. This may have been a reference to Thomas Hariot, and it has also been suggested that Hariot could have travelled with Amadas and Barlow – records of the voyage are very sparse, apart from Barlow's report or *Discourse* written after his return. John White, famed painter of the first Virginia colony, was to comment much later that the voyage he made in 1590 was his fifth. If so, then he too must have been with Amadas and Barlow. And if so, any comments, maps or paintings by either White or Hariot on that particular expedition have, alas, been lost.

Likewise we know little about other investors in the expedition, besides Sanderson. Captain John Smith was to say in the next century that Richard Grenville was one, as well as 'eleven gentlemen and merchants'. It is thought that Sir George Carey, George Carew and William Camden might have been subscribers. On this journey no revenue was necessarily expected, though the ships were well equipped with objects likely to be useful for bartering with primitive people. It was purely exploratory, an investment for the future.

Hariot in 1584 published his Durham House lectures in his pamphlet *Arctica*, now also lost. It became an essential textbook for navigators. Until the discovery of longitude nearly two hundred years later,[8] navigation at sea was a perilous business, especially when out of sight of land. Knowledge of the trade winds was essential for crossing the Atlantic, and latitude was usually calculated by measuring the angle of the sun or pole star above the horizon. The astrolabe, ancestor of the sextant, was difficult to use in rough seas, and was being supplemented by the cross- (or Jacob's-) staff. Timepieces were still not fully developed, and sometimes hour-glasses were used. Hariot devised tables for what he liked to call the three marriages: astrolabe and cross-staff, sun and stars, compass and chart. He also recalculated the table of the sun's declination, and developed a system for working out the variations of the compass.

Raleigh's patent was wider in scope than Humphrey Gilbert's, but carefully worded. It would be unlimited in its rights to territories newly discovered, giving him total power over settlers, though excepting the Newfoundland fishery and limited to the equivalent of 600 miles from any place where his settlers had made their 'dwelling or abiding'.

Elizabeth, by the grace of God, of England, France and Ireland Queen, Defender of the Faith etc. Know ye that of our especial grace . . . we have given and granted . . .

Thomas Hariot, engraved by Francis Delaram, 1620.

to our trusty and well-beloved servant Walter Raleighe Esquire, and to his heirs and assigns for ever free liberty from time to time and at all times to discover search find out and view such remote heathen and barbarous lands countries and territories not actually possessed by any Christian prince nor inhabited by Christian people . . . the same to have hold occupy and enjoy to him his heirs and assigns forever with all prerogatives commodities jurisdictions and royalties privileges franchises and permanencies thereto and thereabouts both by sea and land whatsoever we by over letters patent may grant . . .[9]

The Queen reserved for herself and her heirs and successors one fifth of any gold and silver ore that might be 'gotten or obtained'. If Raleigh and his associates did anything to 'rob or spoil by sea and land' the property of Christian states 'in amity with us', then full retribution would have to be made. At the same time he had the right to expel or resist anybody attempting without permission to inhabit his domains or to 'annoy' him by sea or land. All this was in great secrecy.

Amadas and Barlow were both of Raleigh's household, so we are told in Holinshed. Amadas was also related to Raleigh, hailing from Plymouth, and aged about twenty.* He was captain of the flagship, thought to have been the *Bark Raleigh*, with Fernandez as his pilot. Barlow had been in Ireland with Raleigh; from his *Discourse* he seems to have been a good deal older and to have travelled widely in Europe and around the Mediterranean. He was in command of the pinnace, probably the *Dorothy*. Very likely there were about a hundred men aboard both ships, including soldiers.

Barlow's *Discourse* on the voyage is vividly written, a real traveller's tale, full of enthusiasm, though from the historical point of view in some ways rather too concise.[10] Essentially it was a piece of propaganda to be read by the Queen, depicting a land full of charms and possibilities for settlers, and inhabited by delightful friendly natives. Very likely it was compiled with the help of Raleigh, as there are definite similarities in style with Raleigh's future book *The Discoverie of Guiana*. It is also obvious that anything untoward has been left out.

They had sailed past the Canaries to the West Indies, and had then followed the coastline of Florida to what they hoped would be Dr Dee's Bahia de Santa Maria. At last on 2 July they found shoal water, 'which smelt so sweetly, and was so strong a smell, as if we had been in the midst of some delicate garden, abounding with all kinds of odoriferous flowers, by which we were assured that the land could not be far distant.' Finally they found a place to land, 'very sandy, and low towards the water side, but so full of grapes, as the very beating and surge of the sea overflowed them. We found such plenty, as well there, as in all places else, both on the sand and on the green soil on the hills, as in the plains, as well on every little shrub, as also climbing towards the tops of high cedars, that I think in all the world the like abundance is not to be found.'

This spot has been identified as Hatarask, at the north end of the island of Hatteras, and near the centre of the long chain of islands about 200 miles long, known as the Outer Banks, and at this point about thirty miles from the North Carolinan mainland across Pamlico Sound. The inlet here was probably the one that was later christened Port Ferdinando, no doubt in

* He may have been the son of John Amadas, who married Elizabeth Budockshide, the sister of Philip Budockshide who was killed in France (p. 13).

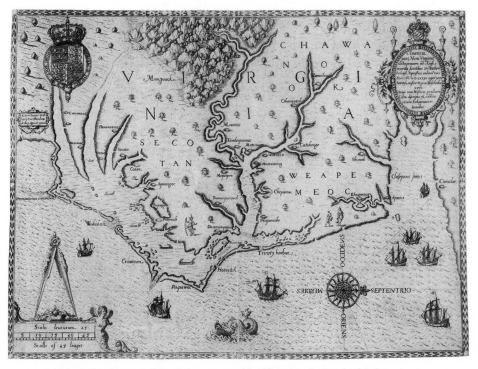

John White's map of Virginia, engraved by Theodor de Bry for his America.

honour of Simon Fernandez. The island was formally taken possession of 'in the right of the Queen's most excellent majesty'. A member of the crew let off an arquebus, at which 'such a flock of cranes (the most part white) arose under us, with such a cry redoubled by many echoes, as if an army of men had shouted all together.'

On the third day natives appeared, completely fearless, curious about such extraordinary newcomers and eager to do some bartering of animal skins in return for knives, hatchets, and especially tin dishes and a copper kettle. But the English would not part with their swords. They met the king who was called Wingina and understood that the country was known as Wingandacoa. The king's brother offered a large box of pearls for a suit of armour, but this the English refused because they wanted to know first where the pearls came from. Later they met his wife and three little children; she was 'very well favoured, of mean stature, and very bashful', and on her ears were 'bracelets of pearls, hanging down to her middle'.

Every day the English were sent a 'brace or two of fat bucks, conies [rabbits], hares, fish, the best of the world', also 'divers kinds of fruits, melons, walnuts,

73

cucumbers, gourds, peas'. 'The soil is the most plentiful, sweet, fruitful, and wholesome of all the world . . . we found the people gentle, loving, and faithful, void of all guile and treason, and such as live after the manner of the golden age.' They crossed to an island which they learnt was called by the natives Roanoke, at the end of which there was a village. Here the king's brother lived, and his wife came running to meet them and took them to her house. 'She caused us to sit down by a great fire, and after took off our clothes, and washed them, and dried them again. Some of the women plucked off our stockings and washed them, some washed our feet in warm water. She herself took great pains to see all things ordered in the best manner she could, making great haste to dress some meat for us to eat.'

Barlow also said that there were wars with neighbouring tribes on the mainland, 'very cruel and bloody', and that there were kings with a 'mortal malice' against Wingina. He had at least to be honest about such possible drawbacks. More encouragingly there appeared to be a large town due south-west, about four days' journey, called Secoton, where the people were known to be friendly. Some years back, he said, white people had been shipwrecked near Secoton and had been cared for by the inhabitants. He was not able to hold up prospects of gold and precious stones on the mainland, but at least he and Amadas brought back with them two 'lusty savages' called Wanchese and Manteo.

Present-day visitors to Hatteras might be surprised by this description of a land apparently flowing with milk and honey. A first impression is of waves crashing on the wide beach and dunes covered with stunted marsh-elder and bayberry, with patches of bristly grasses: exhilarating for those who love wide open spaces. Gulls swirl overhead, battling against the wind. It depends on the time of year of course.

The expedition seems to have been fortunate with the weather, for the hurricane season would have been to hand. In fact this is a very dangerous coast, famous for wrecks, known as the 'graveyard of the Atlantic' not just because of the storms and water spouts, but also because of the shifting submerged sandbanks. It is true, though, that in Barlow's time the island was very much wider, and on the west side more forested.*

A rather more domestic side of Raleigh's character is revealed in a letter of 26 July to Richard Duke at Otterton, written while he was waiting for the

---

* Professor David Quinn visited Hatteras soon after the Second World War, and counted the wrecks of forty torpedoed ships. The island is now designated 'National Seashore' and has a wildlife refuge. Here loggerhead turtles are to be seen, and on the salt marshes there are herons, snow geese and whistling swans. Deer are still in the remnants of the maritime forest.

return of Amadas and Barlow. He needed, indeed longed for, a base in Devon, so where better than the place of his birth, Hayes Barton? Richard Duke was its owner. 'I will most willingly, give whatsoever in your conscience you shall deem it worth,' Raleigh wrote, 'for I had rather seat myself there than anywhere else.' If this were not possible, he said, he might consider building at Colaton Raleigh nearby. As an extra inducement he added, 'If at any time you shall have occasion to use me, you shall find me a thankful friend to you and yours.'[11]

Unfortunately, in spite of this prospect of influence in high places, Duke was not interested. Raleigh no doubt would have rebuilt the modest Hayes Barton on a much grander scale. The only freehold property he owned was at Colaton Raleigh, a small ancestral estate, and at this period when signing wine licences he would describe himself as 'of Colaton Raleigh'. If on the other hand it had been a question of combining family sentiment with prestige in the South-West, it is perhaps surprising that he did not think of trying to establish himself at Fardel Manor.* But Fardel belonged to his half-brother George and it would have meant interfering with the time-honoured system of primogeniture. Very likely too the house was let on a long tenancy. He did not build at Colaton. The time would come when the Queen would reward him with something much more splendid.

Amadas and Barlow reached England in September. One source says that Amadas had made a diversion to the Azores in the hope of picking up some plunder, but returned empty-handed. Barlow's *Discourse* would seem to have been presented to Elizabeth in October, at about the same time as Wanchese and Manteo were put on view at Court – more useful publicity. They had been installed at Durham House under Hariot, who was teaching them English and at the same time attempting to learn something of their Algonquin language. Leopold von Wedel, a traveller from Pomerania, wrote in his journal on 18 October: 'He [Raleigh] allowed us to see them. In face and figure they were like white Moors. Normally they wear no shirt, just a wild animal skin across the shoulders and a piece of fur over the privies, but now they were dressed in brown taffeta. No one could understand what they said, and altogether they looked very childish and uncouth.'[12]

Meanwhile Richard Hakluyt the younger returned to London from Paris, and Raleigh set him to work on a piece of promotional literature for his transatlantic plans. This was for the eyes of Elizabeth and the Privy Council only, the aim being to persuade them, and especially the Queen, that the

* p. 1. Raleigh's father had died in 1581.

establishment of a colony needed government backing and was not just a matter for private enterprise. The title was *A Discourse on Western Planting*.

The epistle dedicatory, written at the 'request and direction' of the 'right worshipful Mr. Walter Raghley', and addressed to Walsingham, included an attractive little description of calling at the Middle Temple on Hakluyt's elder namesake, who had shown him a great map of the known world and had then opened his Bible at Psalm 107, verses 23 and 24, where he read those beautiful words: 'They that go down to the sea in ships and occupy their business in great waters; these see the works of the Lord, and his wonders in the deep.' The pamphlet was very much to the point, listing all the benefits of such a colony as Wingandacoa (presumaby including the mainland). First there was the opportunity of spreading the 'glad tidings of the Gospel'. Then there were twice-yearly harvests, and vegetation such as vines, palm trees, cedars, cypresses and sassafras (used as a cure for venereal diseases). It would produce 'manifold enjoyment for idle men', and almost above all it would be a base that would act as a 'bridle to Spanish ambitions'; in other words by depriving Philip of his West Indian treasure 'his power and strength would be diminished, his pride abated, and his tyranny utterly suppressed'.

On 23 November Parliament assembled, for the first time in twelve years, and under the non-elective system of the time Raleigh was nominated one of the two members for Devon. This was a time of great alarm for the safety of the Queen, who was regarded by the Holy See as 'that guilty woman of England'. The Papal Secretary of State is recorded as having written to the Nuncio in Madrid: 'If those English [Catholic] gentlemen decide actually to undertake so glorious a work [the murder of Elizabeth], your Lordship can assure them that they do not commit any sin.'[13] Following the Throckmorton conspiracy for the restoration of Roman Catholicism in England, in which her cousin Mary Queen of Scots had been implicated, Mendoza the Spanish ambassador had been ordered to leave the country. On the very day that Throckmorton was executed, 10 July 1584, William of Orange was assassinated, after several earlier attempts on his life. Then news came of another plot by the Guise family to replace Elizabeth with the Queen of Scots. This resulted in the Earls of Northumberland and Arundel being sent to the Tower. Behind all this there was the perennial anxiety over Elizabeth's reluctance to name her successor – the Queen of Scots being the nearest in consanguinity.

Raleigh took the opportunity of introducing a Private Bill for the confirmation of his patent for founding a colony in North America. A committee was formed including Sidney, Grenville, Walsingham and Francis Drake, all people to be trusted – and as a result a foregone conclusion for acceptance. Provisos were however produced: that he was not to press (requisition) ships, or send criminals or debtors to the colony. In fact the whole affair was a waste of time, in that the Queen had already given her assent and would never admit that Parliament had the right to countermand her prerogative, or even to make provisos. More to the point historically was the decision by Parliament to introduce the death penalty for harbouring Jesuits.

Von Wedel's diary gives a good description of the splendour of Elizabeth's Court, and the reverence she commanded, in an account of a dinner at Greenwich palace on 27 December 1584.[14] He was among the great crowd in the Presence Chamber watching her eat. To her right stood Leicester, Burghley, Oxford, Lord Charles Howard and Christopher Hatton, 'the captain of the bodyguard, who is said to have been the Queen's lover after Leicester.' 'If she summoned one of them, as often happened – as a rule, she talks with scarcely a break – he had to kneel until she commanded him to rise. Then he made a low bow and retired, and when he came to the centre of the room he bowed again.'

When the Queen rose two bishops said grace and five noblemen advanced with a silver gilt bowl and a napkin for her to wash her fingers, again kneeling before her. After a while, she took a cushion and sat on the floor, to watch the dancing, first by the highest in rank, and then by the young men who 'laid aside their rapiers and cloaks, and in doublet and hose invited the ladies to the galliard.' During the dancing the Queen summoned various people to come and talk to her. They all had to kneel, and she chatted and joked with them. 'She said to a captain named Raleigh, pointing with a finger at his face, that there was a smut on it, and was going to wipe it off with her handkerchief; but before she could he wiped it off himself. She was said to love this gentleman above all others; and this may be true, because two years ago he could scarcely keep a servant, and now with her bounty he can keep five hundred.'

As Thomas Morgan, Mary Queen of Scots' agent, wrote to Mary: 'Master Rawley is the Queen's dear minion, who daily groweth in credit'.[15] It was not surprising that Elizabeth would not allow Raleigh to sail with his fleet to the New World, which would mean some months out of her sight. His cousin Sir Richard Grenville was therefore chosen to take his place. Possibly it was Elizabeth herself who chose the name Virginia instead of the tongue-twisting Wingandacoa, but more likely it was Raleigh's tactful invention. What more appropriate name for a colony of which he was proprietor? In any case Hariot, having mastered some Algonquin, had discovered that

Wingandacoa was not the name of the country, but simply meant 'You have fine clothes'.[16]

On 6 January, the twelfth day of Christmas, Elizabeth knighted Raleigh. It was now that he devised his grand seal, with a cloak enveloping the coat of arms, and the tactful motto, *Amore et Virtute*. A roebuck surmounted the coat of arms, a family emblem which he was to use as the name for one of his ships. The supporters were two foxes, as at the end of the pew at East Budleigh, and round the seal were these proud words, in Latin: 'Arms of Walter Raleigh Knight Lord and Governor of Virginia'.

The Roanoke Fort
1585

Raleigh may have been the professed lover of the Queen, but he was also the obsessed planner of the Virginia colony. She must have complained that he was not being attentive or demonstrative enough to her, and he therefore had to excuse himself with a poem:

> Our passions are most like to floods and streams;
> The shallows murmur; but the deeps are dumb.
> So when affections yield discourse, it seems
> The bottom is but shallow whence they come.
>   They that are rich in words must needs discover
>   That they are poor in that which makes a lover.

And he continued:

> Wrong not, dear Empress of my heart,
>   The merit of true passion
> With thinking that he feels no smart
>   That sues for no compassion;
> Since if my plaints serve not to prove
>   The conquest of your beauty
> It comes not from defect of love
>   But from excess of duty . . .
>
> Silence in love bewrays more woe
>   Than words, though ne'er so witty;
> A beggar that is dumb, ye know,
>   Deserveth double pity.
> Then misconceive not, dearest heart,
>   My true though secret passion,
> He smarteth most that hides his smart
>   And sues for no compassion.

This poem was for Elizabeth's eyes only, even if it was to find its way into print a few years later. Raleigh's enemies at Court would not have been surprised at his daring to address the Queen as his 'dearest heart'. Sir John Harington, her godson, renowned for his witty epigrams, wrote thus (his name for Raleigh was Paulus):

> No man more servile, no man more submiss
> Than to our Sovereign Lady Paulus is.
> He doth extol her speech, admire her features
> He calls himself her vassal, and her creature.
> Thus while he deals his speech with flattering plaster
> And calls himself her slave, he grows our Master.

Her slave maybe, but he was also a shooting star, and like any royal favourite able to make himself seem indispensable. Added to which he had that immense capacity for hard work. And like any royal favourite from a relatively obscure background he was hated by the old nobility and by all who were so desperately jostling for power, wealth and status.

Hatton was again upset. The Court had temporarily moved to the Archbishop of Canterbury's palace at Croydon, and Raleigh was allocated a room which should by rights have been his. Two years before, when Raleigh had a lowlier status, he would have had to share a room, as for instance when the Court had been at Theobalds, Lord Burghley's house. Therefore, as when he last took umbrage, Hatton despatched Heneage with a letter of complaint to the Queen, sending as a token a 'true lover's knot'. The message that Heneage brought back was surprising. The Queen, he told Hatton, had spoken bitterly against Raleigh, saying that she would rather 'see him hanged than equal to you, or that the world would think him so'.[1] All this was part of her game to set jealous courtiers against one another, forcing them to play the parts of ardent lovers. On New Year's Day it was the custom for her to receive gifts, and from Hatton they were always expensive. She would give presents in return. It is interesting to discover that Raleigh did not appear in any of those lists, either as giver or receiver.

There is no doubt that Raleigh intended to lead the expedition to Virginia, but the Queen could not part with him for so long. Thus it was decided that his place would be taken by Sir Richard Grenville.

Grenville was some twelve years older than Raleigh and related to him on both his father's and mother's side and had been knighted after becoming

High Sheriff of Cornwall. In spite of his involvement in the Terra Australis project, and in spite of some privateering, this was his first major voyage; Drake, who had been on the committee approving the patent, supported him. Like Raleigh, Grenville appeared to have become on reasonably friendly terms with Drake even after the disappointment of long ago.*

Most of the money was raised by Raleigh with the help of Sanderson. It is a pity that we have so little information about the immense amount of work in these preparations: finding volunteer settlers, impounding sailors and shipping, collecting supplies and armaments. Sir Francis Walsingham was a prominent 'adventurer', and various members of his household accompanied Grenville. Sir George Carey, a Member of Parliament, was certainly closely connected with supporting the venture. Thomas Cavendish, later famous as circumnavigator of the world, and Anthony Rowse, both also MPs, were to accompany Grenville.

The Queen empowered Raleigh to order £400 worth of gunpowder from the Tower, and put at his disposal one of her ships, the *Tyger*, possibly even a gift; as always, she preferred to make gifts in kind rather subscribe large sums of money. She gave orders for Ralph Lane, a seasoned soldier and an authority on fortifications (also a relation of Catherine Parr, Henry VIII's last Queen), to be released from service in Ireland; he was to be in charge of the colonists after Grenville had returned. Raleigh's authority to impound shipping was limited to Devon, Cornwall and Bristol – but the captains of the ships he acquired did not scruple to confiscate foreign vessels, presumably with his connivance. A Dutch ship, carrying wine, was intercepted, and the master and pilot found themselves having to go on the voyage to Virginia.

Thomas Cavendish, on Raleigh's behalf, applied to a friend for military advice, and a rough draft (quaintly headed 'For master Rauley's Viage: notes geven to Master Candishe') has been discovered, with suggestions for numbers of troops, types of weapons and armour, the sort of fort that ought to be built, the duties of officers and the importance of treating natives with courtesy. It was also recommended that a 'good geographer' and an 'excellent painter' should accompany the expedition, advice certainly taken, for these were to be Thomas Hariot and John White.

The Spaniards were aware that preparations were being made by Raleigh for a voyage to America, and that Francis Drake was arranging another. Hakluyt, now in Paris, relayed back their alarm. Charles Thynne wrote to Walsingham, also from Paris, that the Spanish ambassador's Jesuit confessor

---

* p. 23. Some two months after Drake's sensational return from around the world in 1580 Grenville had sold him his Buckland Abbey estate for £3,400.

'marvelled' that 'whereas the King of Spain was said shortly to take possession of England, Sir Walter Raleigh . . . doth nevertheless undertake to seek to hinder the Spaniards.'[2] It was important to keep them guessing.

Grenville was also to be accompanied by his half-brother John Arundell and his brother-in-law John Stukeley (father of the Sir Lewis or 'Judas' Stukeley, to be regarded at the end of Raleigh's life as his great betrayer). Many well-known West Country names were on the expedition: Kendall, Prideaux, Rowse, Bonythan, Courtney. Ralph Lane was designated Grenville's lieutenant and eventual Governor of the new colony. Philip Amadas would be Admiral, Francis Brooke Treasurer, and Cavendish 'High Marshal', responsible for enforcing discipline and settling disputes.

Five vessels, with two small pinnaces, left Plymouth on 9 April 1585, everyone full of hope and with six hundred men 'or thereabouts' aboard, as is recorded in the Plymouth City records. About half of these men were soldiers and sailors, the rest potential colonists. Grenville's flagship was the *Tyger*, 160 tons, three-masted and square rigged, with Lane and the Portuguese pilot Fernandez on board. Raleigh's flyboat, the *Roebuck*, so named because of the beast on his coat of arms, a medium-sized cargo carrier of 140 tons, was commanded by John Clarke. The *Lion*, 100 tons, was commanded by George Raymond, and the *Elizabeth*, 50 tons, by Thomas Cavendish who was probably her owner. Then there was the *Dorothy*, evidently the same vessel presumed to have gone to Virginia the year before and thus appropriately commanded by Arthur Barlow. The two Indians Manteo and Wanchese were also returning to Virginia, no doubt on the same ship as Hariot, who had learnt some of their language. It seems that Manteo had taken up English ways, but Wanchese had not.

Five days out of Plymouth the fleet was scattered by a storm off Portugal so Grenville and the *Tyger*, which had lost her pinnace, had to proceed alone.[3] Passing Lanzarote and Fuerteventura in the Canaries, he eventually reached Dominica and then sailed on to Puerto Rico, where he landed at what is now Tallaboa Bay, five kilometres wide and dotted with several islets, between two peninsulas, not far from the present town of Ponce. He chose a spot, 'within a fawlcon shot of the shoare', well protected on one side by a mangrove swamp behind which was a lush forest, and on the other by a river.[4] Here elaborate fortifications were immediately set up, a forge was built, and work begun on building a new pinnace, vital for exploring the shallow waters off Virginia. Marine fireflies and the phosphorescence in the sea at night were a spectacular (and now famous) feature of the area. Iguanas were found to be 'very delicate meat'. Pineapples grew there too. White was busy painting much of this.

In due course Cavendish and the *Elizabeth* appeared, this place having been fixed as a rendezvous from reports following the Amadas–Barlow journey. Their arrival was a relief for Grenville, as it increased his complement of men to about two hundred. Trees were being felled up to three miles inland, and not surprisingly bands of Spanish horsemen duly appeared, hovering in the distance. There were two Spanish garrisons in the vicinity, one at Guayanilla and the other further inland, at San Germán, founded in 1573, where one of the great glories of Spanish colonial architecture was to be built. There were parleys, amicable enough, and after a month the English left, having flattened their encampment and burnt the huts and the woods around it. A wooden post was erected, inscribed with a message for the three still-missing ships, should they arrive later. Not surprisingly, the Spaniards at once dug up the post and in great excitement sent it to Spain for deciphering. But it proved a great disappointment. All it said was: 'We are about to leave on the 23rd in good health, glory be to God, 1585'.

In the Mona channel two frigates were captured by Grenville. The smaller had been abandoned by its crew and was found empty. The other was much larger, with some lucrative booty, and the crew was kept for ransoming. Grenville ordered Lane to take the smaller frigate back to Puerto Rico to collect salt at Cabo Rojo, at its south-western corner. Lane found two convenient piles of salt waiting for him, and with the help of prisoners began removing them, until a threatening-looking Spanish troop appeared. In a bad temper he returned to the ship and had the first of his many quarrels with Grenville. Nevertheless, some bargaining took place between Grenville and the Spaniards, using the prisoners as payment, or at least some of it. By fair means or foul – it is not clear which – cattle, pigs, horses and plants were taken on board, some of them loaded into the two captured vessels. Grenville then sailed on to Hispaniola.

Here they were met with great hospitality by the local governor, who entertained them with a bull fight. Perhaps it was realized that this was the safest way of dealing with such a heavily armed and potentially hostile force. More animals were purchased, also hides, sugar, tobacco and pearls. Then on 7 June off the English sailed. The weather was hot, and it was not pleasant having to live on board at such close quarters with the farm animals. They needed to keep going.

They passed the Caicos islands, anchored briefly at Eleuthera in the Bahamas, then at last on the 24th reached a harbour now identified as the modern Beaufort, North Carolina. On the 26th they anchored at an inlet through the Outer Banks at the south end of the island of Wococon, where Amadas and Barlow had landed the previous year. There, as Lane

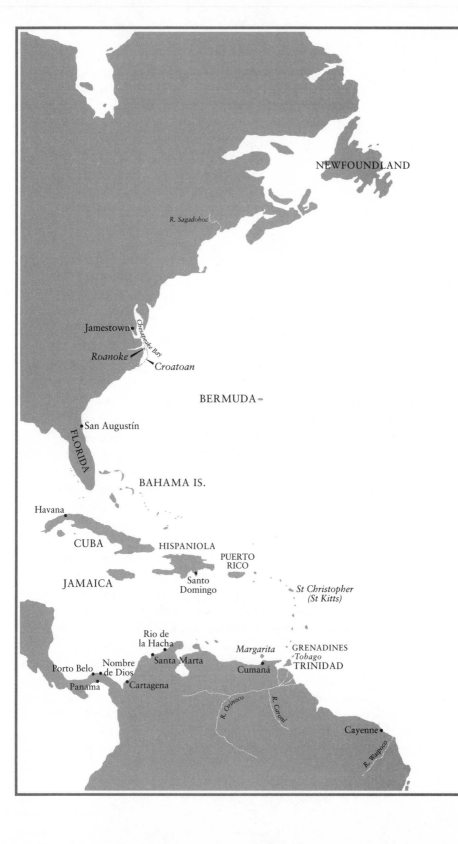

NEWFOUNDLAND

R. Sagadohoc

Jamestown•

Chesapeake Bay

Roanoke•←
└•*Croatoan*

BERMUDA -

•San Augustín

FLORIDA

BAHAMA IS.

Havana•

CUBA

HISPANIOLA

PUERTO RICO

JAMAICA

Santo Domingo

St Christopher (St Kitts)

Rio de la Hacha
•Santa Marta

Margarita

GRENADINES
Tobago
TRINIDAD

Porto Belo• Nombre •de Dios

Cumaná•

Panama•   •Cartagena

R. Orinoco

R. Caroni

Cayenne•

R. Warpoco

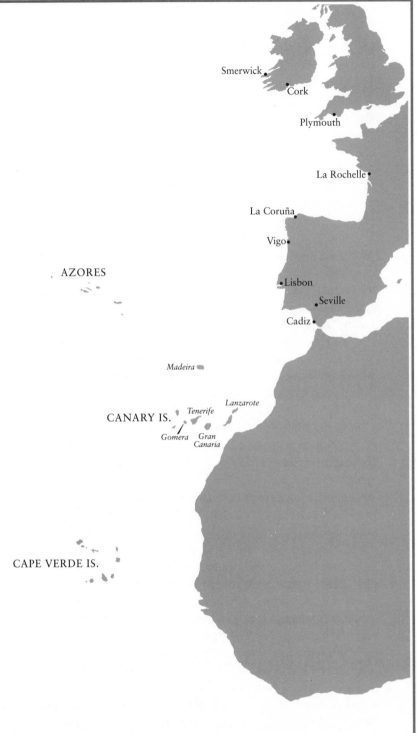

Smerwick
Cork
Plymouth
La Rochelle
La Coruña
Vigo
AZORES
Lisbon
Seville
Cadiz
Madeira
Lanzarote
Tenerife
CANARY IS.
Gomera   Gran
          Canaria
CAPE VERDE IS.

THE NORTH ATLANTIC

was to write, all the ships went aground, but were refloated with the exception of the *Tyger*, due according to the ship's journal to the carelessness of Fernandez – which was not the view of Lane, who was to be full of praise for the pilot. Indeed the *Tyger* was nearly swept away, but after two hours she was finally beached. Particularly distressing was the loss of all the provisions stored on board, including corn, salt, meat, rice and biscuit.

Exploring parties were immediately sent out, and soon on the island of Croatoan, a little north of Wococon, two Englishmen were found; they were from the *Lion* and had been left there earlier with thirty others by her captain George Raymond in the middle of June. Remarkably the *Lion*, possibly also the *Dorothy*, were later discovered at some unnamed spot, as Holinshed speaks of a general reunion of the fleet. Presumably too the remaining thirty men were also found, though there is no mention of this in the journal. The *Roebuck* must also have joined the main party at this time, as Captain Clarke and Amadas were with those who accompanied Grenville across Pamlico Sound.

What had happened to the four ships scattered in the storm off Portugal is extremely hazy, and maybe deliberately kept so. The *Lion* appears to have become involved in a fight with a French vessel off Jamaica, and then to have been driven ashore by bad weather. She had been refloated, but as the company was extremely short of food Raymond had dumped some twenty soldiers on shore, leaving them to fend for themselves in this uninhabited place. Only two survived and were rescued by Spaniards, who were thus able to obtain information about the main expedition and relay it back to Spain.

Grenville crossed Pamlico Sound with about sixty men. First they visited the palisaded village of Pomeioc, consisting of eighteen huts, near Mattamuskeet Lake. This White sketched. In the centre of his picture a crowd is shown round a bonfire, and one hut is possibly a temple. At the estuary of the Pungo river they found another village, Aquascogoc, and on the 15th they reached Socoton, evidently unenclosed, again sketched by White: a composite picture, showing cocoon-shaped huts, a ritual dance, people eating, a communal fire, sunflowers, and three stages in the growing of maize – this being of special interest, as confirming that Algonquian Indians had three harvests a year. The English were hospitably received at Secoton. It was then discovered that a silver cup must have been stolen by an Indian at Aquascogoc. A boat under Amadas was sent back, and the village was found deserted. His reaction was to prove disastrous: he burnt down the village and the surrounding cornfield. Grenville may have thought he had taught these savages a lesson, but the English were to pay for it dearly later on.

By the 18th all were back at Wococon where the *Tyger* had been caulked and refloated. So they sailed on, past the sand bars and scrubby dunes, to the so-called Port Ferdinando or Hatarask, an inlet opposite Roanoke Island. The Indian chief Wingina had heard of their arrival and his brother Granganimo came with Manteo to meet them, and there was a discussion about the location for an English fort: eventually the north-western tip of Roanoke was chosen. It was also probably here at Port Ferdinando that they were reunited with the *Lion* and the *Dorothy*.

Amadas now went to explore Albemarle Sound, around the mouth of the Roanoke and Chowan rivers, and on 5 August John Arundell left for England to hasten the sending of supplies. Lane gave him letters to Walsingham, Sidney and Hakluyt, revealing that great ill-feeling had developed between him and Grenville. It was in any case now time that Grenville, his task completed, should also return home, and charge of the settlement was handed over to Governor Lane. The building of the fort was well under way, and the hurricane season was imminent.

The *Tyger*, with Grenville on board, left on 25 August. Off Bermuda he had some unexpected luck. The flagship of the Santo Domingo squadron had become separated from the main treasure *flota*. This was the *Santa Maria de San Vicente*, possibly 400 tons. Grenville opened fire and went in with a boarding party of about thirty men on an improvised small boat (his own having been left at Roanoke), which sank soon after his boarding and the Spanish captain's surrender. According to a subsequent estimate by a Portuguese merchant who was on board, the loot included 40,000 ducats worth of gold, silver and pearls, and more valuables were taken from the passengers. If this were true, Grenville played down the value on his return. In addition the cargo included ivory, sugar, cochineal and ginger, worth double that amount.

Grenville transferred to the *Santa Maria*, to be sure of keeping a watch on its load of riches, but he became separated from the *Tyger*, which sailed home on her own. He meanwhile found himself forced to look for water and provisions at Flores, the furthest west of the islands of the Azores, a place with which his name was to be famously remembered after his epic fight in the *Revenge* in 1591. The Spaniards he had on board were abandoned there, probably in lieu of ransom, and Grenville reached Plymouth on 18 October to find Raleigh and other 'worshipful friends' waiting for him.

There were question marks about the fate of the plunder, which included profits from the West Indies. It was said that the Queen had taken for herself

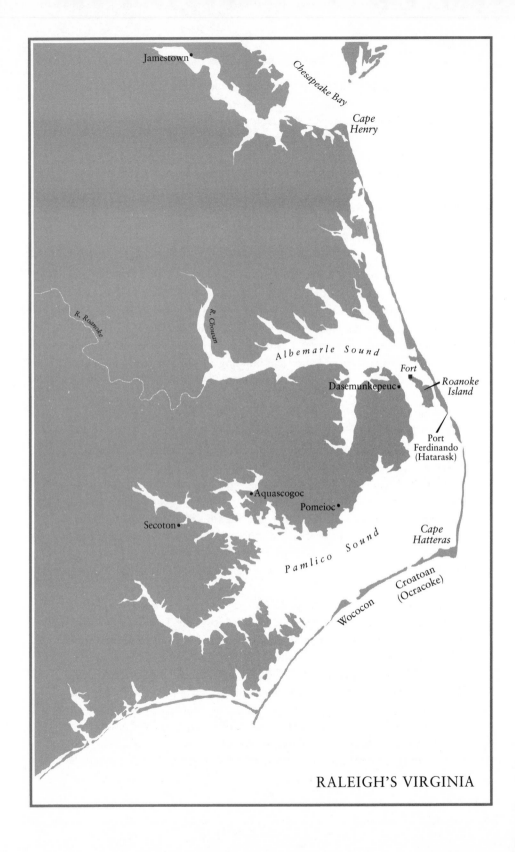

Jamestown

Chesapeake Bay

Cape
Henry

R. Roanoke

R. Chowan

Albemarle Sound

Fort

Roanoke
Island

Dasemunkepeuc

Port
Ferdinando
(Hatarask)

Aquascogoc

Pomeioc

Secoton

Cape
Hatteras

Pamlico Sound

Croatoan
(Ocracoke)

Wococon

RALEIGH'S VIRGINIA

a whole casketful of pearls (without sparing a single one for Raleigh). Officially the value of the prize was given as about £15,000, but this could have been only a third of the total; Grenville maintained that the sailors had embezzled whatever had been taken off the passengers of the *Santa Maria*. Dividends worth £10,000 were paid to investors, but Grenville kept back the ivory which was divided between himself, Raleigh, Sir John Gilbert and Adrian Gilbert. It was now realized that successful privateering could underwrite the cost of colonization.

Grenville had also brought back an Indian, who was baptized 'Raleigh' at Bideford and described in the parish register as a native of Wynganditora. But the Devon climate did not suit the poor fellow, who died a year later.

Meanwhile Ralph Lane had been writing more letters from Virginia, full of praise for its inhabitants and its potentialities.[5] At first he wrote from Port Ferdinando, but later it was from 'New Fort'. The letters had further complaints about Grenville, who he said had 'demeaned himself' from the very first day. Words like 'tyrannous', 'untrue', 'intolerable pride' and 'insatiable ambition' were used. He asked Walsingham if in future he could be freed 'from any place where Sir Richard Grenville [spelt Greenefeld] is to carry any authority in chief.'

Grenville had also been greeted with the news – if he had not already heard it from the commander of the *Santa Maria* – that in May the King of Spain had ordered an embargo on English shipping. All English ships in Spanish harbours had been seized and their contents confiscated, most of the crews being sent to the galleys. Elizabeth had at once ordered Raleigh to send a ship or ships to Newfoundland with a warning not to put in at Spanish ports and at the same time if possible to round up and capture any Spanish vessels found there. War had not been officially declared, but in reality that was what it was. Raleigh had planned to send Bernard Drake in the *Golden Royal* with supplies for Virginia, but now he had no choice but to divert him to Newfoundland.

Drake sailed on 20 June, accompanied by Amyas Preston, whose father was the owner of the *Golden Royal*. On the way they captured a Portuguese ship from Brazil, with a cargo so important that Preston needed to accompany it back to England. No less than seventeen Spanish ships were rounded up near Newfoundland. Then George Raymond turned up, sailing from Virginia. Forces were joined, and they continued together to the Azores, where four more ships were taken.

In July 1585 the Earl of Bedford died, and Raleigh was immediately appointed to take his place as Lord Warden of the Stannaries, a position of huge prestige in the West Country, further enhanced in September when he became Lord Lieutenant of Cornwall, and in November Vice-Admiral of Cornwall and Devon. At a time when war threatened this was a clear sign of the Queen's confidence in his ability and enthusiasm, for the southern coasts of both counties were now in the front line for possible enemy attacks. It was the first time that a commoner had become Lord Lieutenant, the Queen's deputy. Elizabeth recognized Raleigh's administrative talents but it soon became clear that she did not entirely trust him in matter of higher policy. Such, as Anthony Bacon said, was the 'deep and inscrutable centre of the Court, which is Her Majesty's mind'.[6]

The Stannaries were the tin-mining districts of Cornwall and Devon, kingdoms within kingdoms, with their own laws, parliaments and privileges, also their own taxes which were known as coinage. The revenue was important to the Crown; in previous reigns it would have been paid to the Prince of Wales, who was also (as now) the Duke of Cornwall. The Warden had the power to levy troops in time of war and was their titular commander. In disagreements or disputes with the Crown, especially over fiscal or military matters, he could refer to the Lord Lieutenant, representing the Privy Council. Now Raleigh held both positions. As Vice-Admiral he also had the responsibility of building up fortifications along the coast, and supervising the availability of ships and armaments.

Raleigh's half-brother Sir John Gilbert became his deputy as Vice-Admiral in Devon. A landowner, William Carnsew, was his quartermaster in Cornwall.[7] His sub-warden for the Cornish Stannaries was Sir Francis Godolphin, who was also a Deputy Lieutenant, and for the Devon Stannaries Richard Carew. He had also been granted two minor posts in Dorset, the governorship of Portland Bill and the rangership of Gillingham Forest, but he made over the administration and profits of these to his elder brother Carew Raleigh, recently married to the wealthy widow of Sir John Thynne, builder of Longleat.* Carew had been Thynne's Master of the Horse, and was no doubt glad to have some independent means of his own. On occasions he also acted as sub-warden for the Devon Stannaries.

The Cornish and Devon Stannaries had been separated since 1305, probably for racial reasons, since the Cornish were Celts and the Devonians mostly of Anglo-Saxon stock. Both were on an equal footing in relation to the Crown, but Cornwall was the more important in the tin industry, even

---

* This formidable lady had been born Dorothy Wroughton, daughter of Sir William Wroughton, a Lord Mayor of London, and was the second wife of Sir John Thynne, by whom she had eight children. At the time she was in deep conflict with her stepson, the heir to Longleat, and on one occasion so terrified his young wife that she fled in the middle of the night.

though there had been a short boom in Dartmoor tin early in the century. Most of the administration of the Stannaries was the responsibility of the sub-wardens, under whom were stewards, foresters and bailiffs. The four Stannary towns in Cornwall were Lostwithiel, Truro, Launceston and Helford, and in Devon Chagford, Tavistock, Ashburton and Plympton. In Cornwall the remains of the great palace and the coinage* hall, also the Stannary gaol, are still to be seen at Lostwithiel, and here in 1588 a parliament was held, particularly important because of the threat of Spanish invasion and the need to raise troops.

The Devon Stannary parliament met in a quite different place, in the centre of Dartmoor at Crockern Tor, near Two Bridges and Princeton, a wild and windswept spot, in ancient times a tribal meeting place, as evocative and mysterious as the ancient clapper bridges and the primeval oak forest of Wistman's Wood up the valley. The fallen granite slabs that were used as seats can be seen lying in haphazard abandon. The Devon tinners had their own gaol at Lydford, still standing, an awesome building. Raleigh attended a parliament at Crockern Tor in 1600. His 'Judge's chair' and the granite table were stolen, perhaps in the 18th century, after meetings were transferred to the greater comfort of an inn parlour. Hummocks from the open-cast mining and the blowing-houses are still visible.

Raleigh's appointment as Lord Warden inspired a vicious letter from 'A. B.' (Sir Anthony Bagot) to Lord Burghley, written on 7 July 1585, from Exeter.[8]

Her Majesty and you have placed Sir Walter Raleigh as Lord Warden of the Stannaries, but amongst so rough and mutinous a multitude, 10,000 or 12,000, the most strong men in England, it were meet their governor were one whom the most part well acquainted of, using some familiarity, and abiding amongst them. Whereas no man is more hated than him; none cursed more daily by the poor, of whom infinite numbers are brought to extreme poverty through the gift of cloth to him. His pride is intolerable, without regard to any, as the world knows; and as for dwelling amongst them, he neither does nor means it, having no place of abode; so that in time of service, this head must fight without a body, or else the members will cut off such a head.

This piece of venom, not entirely fair, is one of the first recorded references to the hatred that had been engendered by his 'intolerable pride' (that phrase

---

* The word coinage derived from the French *coign*. After weighing each block of tin the assay master chiselled off a small piece from a corner (*coign*) and assayed it before stamping it.

also used against Grenville). Not that Raleigh cared much about what people thought of him, provided he kept the Queen's favour. He was not one to seek popularity, and at times seemed to enjoy attacks. He was reported to have said: 'If any man accuseth me to my face, I will answer him with my mouth, but my tail is good enough to return an answer to such who traduceth me behind my back.'[9]

The accusation about the cloth monopoly was a pure distortion. The monopoly referred to the export of cloth and not to preventing it. The industry was going through a bad period, partly because of Spanish reprisals and hostility in Europe. Hence complaints at Exeter. A scapegoat needed to be found.

Raleigh had tried hard enough to regain a foothold in Devon at Hayes Barton. His extensive cousinage, particularly among the Gilberts, Champernownes, Edgcumbes and Grenvilles, was certainly enough to prove his suitability as Lord Warden. Although he was always to be more popular in the West Country, it was true that at this period his name was hardly known among the ordinary tinners, whether hirelings or labourers – and they were indeed a notoriously hard-drinking and turbulent lot, living in primitive conditions. By the mid 1590s the tin industry was in decline, at a time of general depression and a rise in the cost of living.* Nevertheless, he worked hard for them in Parliament and elsewhere, in spite of some accusations of profiteering. Richard Carew, in his dedication to Raleigh in his *Survey of Cornwall*, published in 1602, wrote: 'Your ears and mouth have ever been open to hear and deliver our grievances, and your feet and hands ready to go and work their redress, and that, not only as a magistrate, or yourself, but also very often as a suitor and solicitor of others of the highest place.'

There are times when Sir Walter Raleigh does deserve to be defended.

---

* The last tin mine (in Cornwall) closed in 1999.

El Draque
1586

That Raleigh had daring and vision could not be denied, but his ascent to power and his haughty manner were resented ever more bitterly at Court. In one of his epigrams Sir John Harington called him a pike, a 'greedy fish'. In another he accused Raleigh of speaking 'in mock' – he would 'lose a friend to coin a jest', and he had a 'scoffing fashion'. There may have been an element of literary rivalry between the two; Harington was also riled when 'proud Paulus' sneered at him for plagiarizing classical poets.

Still, neither he nor most others at Court could deny Raleigh's poetic gifts. Harington was appalled, like the rest, by the way these gifts were so blatantly used to grab yet more honour and preferments. Raleigh was getting 'what he list without control' and through flattery, 'singing the old song, *re mi fa sol*' (the king makes my sun).

William Byrd, the organist at the Chapel Royal, set some of Raleigh's poems to music. One believed to be by him, and which became well known, begins

> See those sweet eyes, those more than sweetest eyes,
> Eyes whom the stars exceed not in their grace.
> See love at gaze, Love that would fair devise
> But cannot speak to plead his wondrous case . . .

Elizabeth was still Raleigh's Cynthia, the virgin moon-goddess who was also Diana, born with her brother Apollo on the hill Cynthus on the island of Delos. In a poem *To Cynthia* he seemed to be seeking assurance that his love was reciprocated. His new commitments in Devon and Cornwall began to keep him away from Court for long periods, and there was always the danger of out of sight out of mind:

> My thoughts are winged with hopes, my hopes with love,
> Mount love unto the Moon in clearest night;

And say, as she doth in the heavens move,
On earth so wanes and waxeth my delight.
And whisper this, but softly in her ears,
Hope oft doth hang the head, and trust shed tears . . .

Reactions to the ups and downs of lovers' tiffs, true or imagined, were favourite themes of his poems. One beginning 'Wounded I am, but dare not seek relief' was also set to music by Byrd. Another, more explicitly, is a reaction to what Raleigh considered a 'wound':

A secret murder hath been done of late;
Unkindness found to be the bloody knife;
And she that did the deed a dame of state,
Fair, gracious, wise as any beareth life . . .

Yet another has a more unsettling theme – the disastrous consequence of an untrue love, a 'poisoned serpent':

Farewell, false love, the oracle of lies,
A mortal foe and enemy to rest;
An envious boy, from whom all cares arise,
A bastard vile, a beast with rage possessed.
A way of error, temple fall of treason,
In all effects contrary unto reason . . .

Perhaps Elizabeth was aware of the Paulus epigrams. Not that she would have minded. Rivalries among courtiers were a reflection of the power she held. Sometimes there would be a daring and more explicit attempt at criticism, as in an anecdote recorded by Edmund Bohun:[1] 'Tarleton, the best comedian of these times in England . . . when a pleasant play he had made was acting before her Majesty, he pointed at Sir Walter Raleigh and said: "See the Knave commands the Queen!" For which she corrected him with a frown. Yet he had the confidence to add that he [Raleigh] was of too much and too intolerable a power.'

Then again in Francis Bacon's *Apophthegms*: 'When Queen Elizabeth had advanced Raleigh, she was one day playing on the virginals, and my Lord of Oxford and another nobleman stood by. It fell out so, that the ledge before the jacks* was taken away, so the jacks were seen. My Lord of

* The mechanism that plucked the strings.

Oxford and the other nobleman smiled, and a little whispered. The Queen marked it, and would needs know what the matter was. My Lord of Oxford answered that they smiled to see that when jacks [common fellows] went up heads went down.'

It was the fashion among the gentry to hire genealogists who could search out some noble, or better still, royal, ancestry. Even the aristocracy was not immune from such stunts. The Howards once claimed that they were descended from Hereward the Wake. Raleigh employed John Hooker, as a fellow Westcountryman, to dig for his family's past glories. And so eureka! he found that Raleigh was descended from a Sir John de Raleigh who had married the daughter of D'Amerie (or Damerei) Clare, who was descended from Henry I. Thus Raleigh could claim Plantagenet blood. Unfortunately, nothing has since been found to substantiate such a happy discovery. All the same Raleigh duly devised a coat of arms for himself, with sixteen quarterings (always considered the grandest).

Francis Drake had long been hatching ways of 'annoying' the King of Spain. One had been to capture the island of Terceira in the Azores, which had the best harbour in the archipelago and where the inhabitants were still said to be supporters of the pretender to the Portuguese throne, Dom Antonio of Crato. If successful this would be an almost impregnable base for intercepting the Spanish fleets from the West Indies. But Elizabeth lost interest, not being very impressed by Dom Antonio, and the Spaniards themselves sent a force to keep the island occupied.

Another plan was to send ships to Calicut on the Malabar coast of India, where there could be a trading post with the Moluccas, nominally under Portuguese control. In 1584 Drake had been plotting a major expedition to the Moluccas, and a large fleet was being prepared. The Queen had agreed to invest £10,000 and Drake was ready to put in £7,000 of his own. Other major investors included Leicester and John and William Hawkins. Raleigh was putting up £400, somewhat less than most but then his main resources were about to be devoted to the Virginian enterprise. Drake's standing was still at its height: the great patriot, fearless, confident. As Hooker said, his exploits 'inflamed the whole country with a desire to adventure unto the sea, in the hope of like success'.

This was not just 'annoyance'. It was the blatant first round of open sea-war with Spain. By February 1585 the plan was much more ambitious. Mendoza's spies reported, accurately enough, that there were to be some twenty-four vessels and many pinnaces, and that the Queen had raised her contribution to £20,000.[2] There were delays, and in April Grenville sailed for the New World and Virginia, and Elizabeth changed her mind. Then in May came the Spanish embargo on English ships in Spanish ports, and Elizabeth had to decide how to deal with this new crisis.

Most of these embargoed English ships were at the port of Vigo in Galicia, north-west Spain. Elizabeth now ordered that Drake's fleet should proceed to Vigo and negotiate for their release. Soon afterwards the Privy Council issued letters of marque whereby permissions for reprisal against Spanish ships would be granted to merchants who had suffered losses: which meant that privateering was now legal, if under licence. As we have seen, Bernard Drake was sent to Newfoundland, and for various obscure reasons Francis Drake's departure was delayed. As a result the chance of regaining the ships at Vigo was lost. The project therefore changed to one of straight revenge, not just at Vigo, but in the West Indies, perhaps occupying and burning Havana, Cartagena or Panama. Whether or not at that stage there was an intention of calling on the Virginia colony as well is not clear, though it does seem likely that Raleigh would have discussed it with Francis Drake and that half-promises were given. Drake certainly knew all about Grenville's intentions.

Next there were problems about command. Sir Philip Sidney arrived in Plymouth, announcing that he would accompany Drake. Given Sidney's importance and his high rank, it would inevitably mean that he expected to share the command.* Drake was not at all pleased by the appearance of this renowned courtier poet and the Queen had to give orders for Sidney to be recalled. On the other hand it seems that Lane was actually expecting Sidney to come out to Virginia.

Christopher Carleill arrived from Ireland as Drake's military commander designate. The flagship was the 600 ton *Elizabeth Bonaventura*. Drake's vice-admiral was Martin Frobisher, in the *Primrose*, and his rear-admiral Francis Knollys was in the *Leicester*. Knollys was brother-in-law of the Earl of Leicester, and an unfortunate choice as it turned out. The fleet, eventually numbering some thirty-three vessels, with about 2,300 soldiers and sailors, sailed from Plymouth on 14 September, in spite of not yet being adequately provisioned; it had been decided to take the advantage of fine weather.

Two ships from Newfoundland with cargoes of salted cod were encountered and one was sunk. Then a small French ship was commandeered. On 27 September the fleet anchored in the bay of Bayona near Vigo, dodging the great castle of Monte Real at its entrance. The governor of Bayona wanted a parley, but instead received this terse message, typical of Francis

---

* Sidney's mother, born Lady Mary Dudley, was the sister of the Earl of Leicester. Sidney was now working on his *New Arcadia*.

Drake: 'We are men of war and seek nothing but what we can win by force'. The English duly came ashore and set about looting the most sacred building at Bayona, the chapel of the Ermita de la Misericordia.[3]

Bayona was where *La Pinta* had landed, the first of Columbus's ships to reach Spain from the New World – not that the English would have cared. From Raleigh's point of view, much more serious was the fact that nearby at Gondomar was the family house of his future most deadly enemy, Don Diego Sarmiento de Acuña, later Conde de Gondomar. The youthful Diego himself on that day not only witnessed the devastation and terror caused by these English pirates, but took part in the fighting himself – an experience never to be forgiven or forgotten.

A storm caused a delay in departure from Galicia. Also Drake needed to make good the shortage of supplies. News came of some caravels attempting to escape up the Vigo river. They were caught, but their cargoes were disappointing, including 'copes and such other church trash' from the church at Vigo and only worthy to be tipped into the sea. Another foray resulted in four Englishmen being caught and beheaded. The weather still being bad, Drake established himself at Cangas on the other side of that great, deep and beautiful bay, and during the succeeding week Vigo and the villages around were duly plundered and burnt. Drake left an indelible reputation behind him. The women of Cangas became so crazed with grief at the slaughter of their men, after a succession of piratical attacks, that they were thought to be bewitched.* To this day at Cangas when children misbehave they are warned that El Draque will come and get them.

Waiting at Vigo meant that Drake had missed the return of the Spanish treasure fleet, some of which had even been without an armed escort. This was a shameful blow. He sailed on, pausing at the Canaries, and then to the Cape Verde Islands, about 600 kilometres out in the Atlantic. On 17 November the fleet reached the island of São Tiago, Santiago in Spanish, where Carleill disembarked 1,000 men on the beach of the small town of Praia, easily securing the fortress on a plateau above. From there he marched across the weird volcanic landscape to Ribeira Grande, ten kilometres away. This was the place which Raleigh must have attempted to attack in 1579. Much more importantly for Drake was the fact that William Hawkins came here in 1582; a promise by the locals had on that occasion been deliberately broken, and many English had in consequence been murdered – some of them had been Drake's men.

---

* Cangas is known for *Las Lloronas*, professional women mourners who can be hired to wail at funerals.

Inhabitants of Ribeira had been frightened off in advance, and Carleill found the town empty except for a few unfortunate patients in hospital, suffering from a 'fowle and fylthie disease'.[4] The town* of some 600 or 700 houses and a cathedral (whose ruins are still to be seen), was in a deep fertile canyon, so fresh food was to be had.

The English stayed two weeks at Santiago. Drake found the need to impose more discipline, and two men were hanged. In his typically authoritarian and tactless way he also demanded oaths of loyalty and obedience from all the officers. Knollys took offence, refusing to sign, and the enmity between the two men continued for the rest of the expedition. Praia was burnt down as Drake's parting gesture. Out to sea the great number of whales would have caused alarm. Then a nemesis struck the fleet. That 'fowle disease' was infecting the crew. 'We were not many days at sea, but there began amongst our people such mortality, as in a few days there were dead above two or three hundred men.' A burning fever and plague-like spots were part of the symptoms. The sickness continued for several weeks and had a disastrous effect on Drake's plans.

On reaching the West Indies, on 3 January 1586 Carleill captured the much more important town of Santo Domingo at Hispaniola. The harbour had been blocked, so he approached the town by a land route. Everything was looted that could be looted, and Drake stayed a whole month, waiting for a ransom to be paid. Eleven slaves were taken on board for possible use by the colonists at Virginia, if Drake decided to call there on his way back to England. Some friars were hanged. Quarrels flared up again, especially with Knollys.

The capture of Cartagena, which was largely unfortified, was in some ways easier, though the fighting was fierce. Another ransom was paid, and more slaves were gathered in – largely females, causing problems about prostitution; there were also some Moors. The Cape Verde sickness continued with more deaths, so Drake had to give up his plan for capturing Panama. Morale was flagging, and the time had come to return home. Yes, he decided, they would call at Virginia. He had heard that there were Spanish plans to 'root out' the English colony before it became established.

Drake's bloodthirsty reputation was now widely spread in the West Indies, and there was relief at Cuba when Havana was bypassed. Instead he continued up the Florida coast, reaching the main Spanish outpost of San

* Ribeira Grande is said to have been the first European 'city' to be founded in the tropics. In the main square there is a pillar to which runaway slaves or recalcitrant foreigners were chained and flogged.

Augustín on 27 May. The fort was obliterated, everything of value having been first removed, including all the doors, locks and 'equipment', which he thought could be useful for the settlers. Even the maize fields were set on fire.[5]

He may not have had the success he had hoped for but his actions at Santo Domingo, Cartagena and San Augustin compelled the Spaniards to reconsider the defence of their American empire, and led them finally to decide on the 'enterprise of England'.

Drake reached Roanoke on 10 June 1586, finding a very different situation from that which he had expected.

More Riches
1586–7

Raleigh's mind may have drifted from Ireland as a result of the Roanoke venture, but in 1585 his interest had been quickly revived when plans began for the establishment of a plantation of English settlers in Munster. If in the history of the British Empire he is remembered for his attempts to establish bases in the New World – Virginia and eventually Guiana – it was Ireland where he was to make his first substantial contribution to colonization, if not a very happy one.

Now that the Earl of Desmond's lands in Munster had been forfeited to the Crown, a scheme of plantation had been scrupulously worked out by Burghley, Francis Walsingham, Christopher Hatton and Thomas Egerton the Solicitor-General. Raleigh could well have been consulted, because of the paper he had written in 1581 and his two years' experience in the country. In the division of spoils he naturally wanted to be sure that the best would come his way.

There were to be twenty-three seignories or blocks of land, each of 12,000 acres, and the plan was that the grants should be made to men of wealth and enterprise, known as 'undertakers', able to support themselves with sufficient capital for developing their properties. Each seignory would have six freeholders, in addition to farmers, copyholders and cottagers. Rents would be from £200 a year downwards, and the Irish would of course be excluded. Buildings had to be strong for defence. It was also recognized that an immense amount of clearance would be needed, as the potentially rich countryside had been reduced to a wilderness overrun by wolves and foxes. Virtually the whole native population had disappeared, either killed, dead from starvation or disease, or had fled.

A special effort was made to interest younger sons, particularly from the west and north-west of England, although it became clear that those who benefited most were closest to the Queen. In the Letters Patent of 27 June 1586 Raleigh headed the list of undertakers from Devon, Somerset and Dorset, along with Sir John Clifton and Sir John Stowell. Hatton was another undertaker, and among the rest were Sir William Courtney, Sir John Popham, Edward Unton, Francis Berkeley, James Gould and Edmund Spenser; also Sir Warham St Leger, who was later joined by Sir Richard Grenville – though these two, to their annoyance, were forced to surrender lands that had earlier been leased from Desmond.

Raleigh was indeed able to secure for himself particularly fertile land, also woods, in a beautiful stretch along the river Blackwater that ran down to Youghal, once one of the most important ports in Ireland in view of its closeness to England. Remarkably, at Raleigh's suggestion, and in order to further his own plans, Hatton was given lands on the other side of the river. Then on 27 February 1587, with the consent of the Queen, and to the disgust of numerous ill-wishers, Raleigh was awarded three and a half seignories, 42,000 acres. This was in direct contravention to the original rules, but it is possible that he had persuaded the Queen to let him take over the seignories of Sir John Clifton and Sir John Stowell, who had visited Munster and had been disillusioned by what they had found. The Lord Deputy, Sir John Perrot, had raised a dissenting murmur, only to find himself slapped down as 'impertinent'. Burghley had to warn him that Raleigh was 'able to do you more harm in one hour than we are able to do you good in a year'.[1]

Perrot's successor as Deputy, Sir William Fitzwilliam, was more than unhappy about Raleigh's new status, which he saw in some ways competing with his own. Raleigh's domain stretched from White's Island in County Cork, and the Barony of Inchiquin, to the town of Tallow and various ruined castles in County Wexford. He also set about acquiring some outlying ecclesiastical properties, one being Lismore Castle, romantically perched above the Blackwater and which he leased from the Bishop of Lismore, Mylor McGrath. In the same way he obtained Molana Abbey and additional houses at Youghal. But he planned to make Lismore his seat. In spite of his many other commitments, including the defences of Devon and Cornwall, and the launching of another and more ambitious expedition to Virginia, he did manage to pay visits to Ireland, and he is listed as having been resident at Youghal. He is also supposed to have been elected its mayor. His energy was truly extraordinary.

In April 1586 Raleigh despatched a relief squadron with supplies for Virginia under Sir Richard Grenville. It consisted perhaps of seven ships and 400 men. Shortly after this he sent two pinnaces, the *Serpent* and the *Mary Spark*, on a privateering expedition to the Azores. A little later he sent the pinnace *Dorothy* to join the Earl of Cumberland on his proposed voyage to the South Seas.

The *Serpent* and the *Mary Spark* had a successful time in the Azores, bringing back some worthwhile prizes, including sugar, ivory, brasilwood and rice. On the way home they encountered a large Spanish fleet – to be exact twenty-four sail, two carracks of about 1,000 tons, ten galleons, and some other small ships. They made for the carracks, battering at them for thirty-two hours, until they ran out of powder. A courageous but not very profitable affair, so it would seem. Why, we may well wonder, did the rest of the Spanish fleet not try to interfere? At any rate they had some prizes, and 'Sir Walter Raleigh, being our owner, rewarded us with our shares'. They also acquired an eminent prisoner, Don Pedro Sarmiento de Gamboa, Governor of Patagonia, who was brought back to England. It was claimed that the crew of Don Pedro's ship had been tortured with fire, and that they had their knuckles and tips of their fingers crushed in order to make them reveal where any gold or silver might be hidden. The ordnance and small shot had already been thrown into the sea, along with most of Don Pedro's papers and maps concerning Patagonia.

Don Pedro was taken in charge by Raleigh and brought to Durham House, with the hope of a fat ransom. They appear to have got on well. Raleigh said that he found his guest a 'worthy gentleman', and in the *History of the World* he mentions a 'pretty jest'.[2] The two of them had been studying a map of the Magellan Straits and Raleigh asked the name of an island. To which Don Pedro 'merrily' replied that it was to be called the 'Painter's Wife Island', the reason being that the man who drew the map had his wife sitting beside him, and she 'desired him to put in one country for her'.

Don Pedro was from Galicia, where Sarmiento is a fairly well-known surname. It was to be an odd twist that Raleigh's eventual arch-enemy, the Conde de Gondomar, was Don Pedro's relative. More importantly at the time, it was Don Pedro who was responsible for exciting Raleigh with tales of the fabled El Dorado. He was an authority on the Incas and had written a book about them. A highly experienced navigator, he had led an expedition to the Solomon Islands and had chased after Drake in the Pacific. Here was a very special political prisoner. Raleigh was able to winkle out of him some of the problems encountered by the Spanish in establishing a colony in the New World. He took him to see the Queen and Burghley. A deal was made: Don Pedro was to be released without ransom, and in return would tell his king that if the embargo was lifted on English shipping Elizabeth would do her best to stop the privateering.

So Raleigh had to forgo his ransom money. But by way of compensation he devised an ingenious plot. He fooled Don Pedro into believing that he was willing to act as a spy on Spain's behalf, and among other things pretended to offer to sell one of his warships for 5,000 crowns, with the prospect of perhaps even two more. He said he would also do his best to stop English support for the Portuguese pretender Dom Antonio.[3]

This extraordinary ploy, which now sounds crazy, was in fact typical of the Elizabethan hothouse world of spies and counterspies masterminded by Sir Francis Walsingham, who no doubt must have been completely aware of Raleigh's efforts. It is also a tribute to Raleigh's ability to charm if he felt like it. An equivalent piece of double-dealing had been carried on for several years by John Hawkins, who had managed to convince the Spaniards that he was fed up with serving Queen Elizabeth. In return he had been substantially recompensed. This had been with the consent of the Queen and the Privy Council, to whom Hawkins would duly pass on snippets of Spanish information.

Don Pedro was captured by Huguenots in France on his way back to Spain, and as an earnest of good faith Raleigh arranged for his release, when even Bernardino de Mendoza, the Spanish ambassador who had been exiled to Paris, had been quite unable to help him.

Mendoza was also duped into believing that Raleigh's offer to Don Pedro was sincere. 'I am assured', he wrote to Madrid, 'that he [Raleigh] is very cold about [England's] naval preparations, and is secretly trying to dissuade the Queen from them. He is much more anxious to sell his ships in Spain than to use them for robbery.'[4] Raleigh had cleverly brought up another reason for wanting support from Spain; he had told Don Pedro that he knew his favour with Elizabeth could not last forever, and he needed security for the future.

But in Spain Raleigh was by now well known as a bloodthirsty pirate, in a bracket with Drake and Grenville. Philip and his councillors were not so easily bamboozled by his promises. They were rightly suspicious, and at once refused, bringing to an end Raleigh's first attempt at international intrigue.

Perhaps the Spaniards already knew that John Davis was back from investigating the North-West passage, under Adrian Gilbert's patent. Davis had reported that he had given the name of 'Mount Raleigh' to a 'brave mountain, cliffs orient as gold', on the east coast of Greenland and near what is now Lindenows Fjord. And on 17 August the debonair Earl of Cumberland had set off privateering with a fleet including Raleigh's pinnace, as the Spaniards must have known: a not very profitable voyage as it turned out – the main loot was a store of marmalade.

Yet more potential wealth and power were in store for Raleigh. On 14 August 1586 church bells were rung and bonfires lit in London to celebrate the capture of Anthony Babington and some other Catholic gentle-men who had been plotting the assassination of Elizabeth. Even more seriously Mary Stuart – the Queen of Scots – was heavily implicated. The plan had been to release Mary from prison, after a general uprising, and to proclaim her Queen, with the help of Spanish troops from the Netherlands. For the past months Walsingham's spies had been mingling with the con-spirators, Mary's correspondence having been smuggled in and out of her prison in false bottoms of beer barrels. Mary was tried for treason and found guilty. Parliament therefore petitioned for her execution, but only after much agonizing did Elizabeth sign the death warrant. She was beheaded at Fotheringay Castle on 8 February 1587.

This is a simplification of the tortuous and bungled affair. Its importance for Raleigh was his own personal enrichment. Babington was an exceedingly wealthy young man, and his estates were forfeited to the Crown. Raleigh was awarded a great clutch of his properties in the Midlands, including Babington Hall in Lincolnshire, 'together with all goods, personals, and moveables', with the exception of a 'certain curious clock, reserved to Her Majesty's personal use.' Possibly this great gift to Raleigh was meant in some way to compensate for the expenses involved in preparations for the next expedition to Virginia.

It would seem that Raleigh had been privy to Walsingham's secret manoeuvres, and that he had even been attempting to play a double role, as in the case of Don Pedro Sarmiento. His secretary William Langherne was a Catholic, and through him he had attempted to obtain some of Mary's secrets by making an approach to her agent Thomas Morgan.[5] On the day before his execution Babington had actually offered Raleigh £1,000 if he could arrange a pardon from the Queen. Again, it is perfectly possible that Raleigh had already put in a plea to Elizabeth that he might acquire some of the estates. In Paris Mendoza wrote to Philip that Raleigh had known all about the plot before its discovery.

Babington and his fellow conspirators were executed on 20 and 21 September at St Giles's Fields, with the maximum cruelty, at any rate on the first day. Having been dragged on sleds through the streets, the first group was left to hang for a few minutes before the carts were drawn away. They were then cut down, still alive, and their 'privities' sliced off. After that they were disembowelled and quartered. On the second day, at the Queen's special request, the remainder were allowed to hang until they were dead before being disembowelled.

Elizabeth changed her mind and tried – too late – to stop Mary's death warrant. She wept, not so much for Mary as a woman but as a Queen, remembering no doubt the horrors of her own mother's execution and that of Katherine Howard, both on the order of her father Henry VIII, and how close she herself had been to death during her half-sister Mary I's reign. She also knew that outright war with Catholic Spain was now inevitable.

In the previous year, Antwerp had fallen into Spanish hands, causing real alarm in England. A treaty was made with the Dutch states whereby Elizabeth agreed to send an army which she would maintain at her own cost. The English would be allowed to garrison Flushing and some other ports, and in December 7,000 men were sent over under the command of Leicester, who brought with him his young stepson the Earl of Essex. His nephew Philip Sidney was already at Flushing as its new Governor.

It was a delicate situation. Elizabeth was hoping that the English presence would result in some sort of peaceful gesture from the Spaniards. Leicester had been expressly forbidden to take on any administrative role. He was showing his age, which no doubt accounted for the muddles over wasted supplies and leaving the tattered troops unpaid, while increasing his own salary and those of the officers. He wrote to Raleigh asking for a 1,000 pioneers, or sappers, of whom a hundred should be miners, out of his 'jurisdiction in Devon and Cornwall'. Within weeks of his arrival he also accepted from the Dutch the title of Governor-General of the United Provinces, and this made Elizabeth explode with rage.[6] She sent him a fierce letter, reminding him that he was merely her 'creature', 'a man raised by ourself, and extraordinarily favoured by us above any subject of this land'. He was treating her with contempt. He must retract at once, in public. What was worse, she had heard that Lady Leicester, whom she loathed, was joining him with a retinue of ladies and grand coaches. Finances were also worrying her; the maintenance of the army, she learnt, would cost £126,000 per annum.

Leicester was the man whom she may once have thought of marrying. At last she was mollified when she heard that he was ill, and she gave orders that the affairs of the Netherlands were not to be discussed by the Privy Council without her permission. They would be entirely under her control.

Word was getting around that Raleigh had been fuelling her anger. He became alarmed by the dangerous rumour, and asked if he could be allowed to take the Queen's despatches to the Netherlands so that he could scotch such malicious gossip in person. Instead the Queen sent Walsingham bearing a special letter written by himself to Leicester defending Raleigh,[7] 'to signify unto your Lordship, and to assure you upon her honour, that the gentleman hath done good offices for you and that, in the time of her displeasure, he dealt as earnestly for you as any other in this world that professeth the most good will towards your Lordship. This I write by her Majesty's commandment.'

Raleigh himself now wrote to Leicester, on 29 March, referring to the pioneers and insisting that the delay in sending them was not his fault. He also said: 'I have been of late very pestilent reported in this place [the Court] to be rather a drawer back than a furtherer of the action where you govern. Your Lordship doth well understand my affection [feelings] towards Spain, and how I have consumed the best part of my fortune, hating the tyrannous prosperity of that estate [i.e. Spain], and it were now strange and monstrous that I should become an enemy to my country and conscience.' He asked Leicester in future always to deal direct with him 'in all matters of suspect doubleness', so that he could prove his good faith. 'In the meantime I humbly beseech you, let no poetical scribe work your Lordship by any device to doubt that I am a hollow or cold servant to the action.' Then he added a postscript: 'The Queen is on very good terms with you and, thank be to God, you are again her "Sweet Robyn".'

How did this mighty nobleman take such a reassurance from a younger rival in her affection, much inferior in social status? And who was the 'poetical scribe'? Oxford? At any event on 11 May the Council was permitted to give orders for a hundred miners to be sent to the Netherlands.

Leicester's venture brought no positive results, but it has lived in history because of the mortal wounding of Sir Philip Sidney at Zutphen in September. He is said to have been wounded because he had lent his thigh armour to another officer, and to have spoken the famous words to a dying common soldier to whom he had given his water bottle, 'Thy necessity is yet greater than mine.' This legend was in the account by his friend Fulke Greville. Needless to say doubts have been cast on it, and it is certainly very like Plutarch's story about Alexander the Great. But does it matter? He developed gangrene and was reported to be smiling when his leg was amputated. Do we have to dismiss this too? In his lifetime Sidney was regarded with a certain awe, as the gilded aristocrat with stunning good looks and manners, and regarded as a potential genius – though his writings were not published until after his death.

He was embalmed and buried at St Paul's Cathedral on 19 February 1587. There was a huge funeral procession, numbering 344 persons, in which Raleigh took part, along with all the great officers of the Court, judges, the Mayor and Aldermen of London, generals, admirals. Sidney's *Arcadia* and *Astrophel and Stella* were not long after published by his sister the Countess of Pembroke, and came to be regarded as initiating the golden age of English poetry.

Raleigh, like many another, wrote an elegy on Sidney's death (according to Aubrey there were some 'roguish verses' published too). In it he seems to admit jealousy of Sidney's contemporary fame, when he writes of 'love that envy in thy life suppressed', and how 'I, that in thy time and living state – did only praise thy virtues in my thought'. He did however include all the right things in the poem: Sidney's ancestry, godson of a king (Philip II) who gave him his name, his great gifts, his valour, the 'Scipio, Cicero and Plutarch of our time'. He had watched Sidney, he said, like the rising sun.

Leicester returned to England in November 1586, and it was noted by some with a certain glee that on the day before he came to Court Raleigh left for the West Country.

On 27 July 1586 Drake had arrived at Plymouth. To general dismay he brought with him, not just the loot he had acquired in the West Indies, which was considerable, but the settlers from Virginia, many of them thoroughly disgruntled. He also had with him a hundred Moorish galley slaves and some Spanish prisoners. There was no news of Grenville. What had happened?

It was nearly a year since Ralph Lane and his 107 companions had been left to set about establishing the first English colony on American soil. Lane's account on his return to England, written for Raleigh, is of course a vital record, but it is Hariot's *Briefe and True Report*, completed in February 1587, and his notes to John White's marvellously evocative drawings that illuminate this strange new land for us. Hariot previously wrote his *Report* to encourage fresh settlers and investors after adverse and damaging rumours.

A few of John White's drawings became known to his contemporaries as the basis for engravings in Theodor de Bry's massive book *America*, published in 1590, so it is only in recent years that they have been fully appreciated. His maps of Raleigh's Virginia, along what are now the Carolina Sounds as far as Chesapeake Bay, are amazingly exact, making one long for more details about how he and Hariot set about surveying the territory and gathering information about its flora and fauna.

The foundations of the Roanoke fort have been excavated, star-shaped and only forty yards square with a wide trench surrounding them. Beyond would have been the huts, protected by an outer palisade. Presumably all this would have been built with the Indians' consent or at least connivance. There was little ground available for cultivation. Apart from hunting and fishing the settlers had to rely on the Indians for food.

Lane in his written account was frank about the problems in exploiting the country, in spite of the good climate and potentially fertile soil.[8] He did not believe that the climate was right for Mediterranean-type fruits, and felt that it would be hard for a colony to be self-supporting. The discovery of a mine or a passage to the Pacific would certainly be inducements for future settlers and investors. A good harbour was vital, and such a possibility had been discovered, a four-day journey away – Chesapeake Bay in fact.

Lane had at once set about sending expeditions to the mainland. Hariot and White went north to Chesapeake Bay and spent the winter there. Hariot's *Report* about this 'paradise of the world' is full of enthusiastic details about probable 'merchantable commodities' and edible fruits, fowls and animals, including the 'multitude of bears being an excellent good victual'; also fish, timber, *openauk* (potatoes), and the much prized *uppowoc* (tobacco) – recommended especially for purging 'superfluous phlegm and other gross humours', and opening 'all the pores and passages of the body'. The English were visited by natives from what came to be known as the Powhatan Confederacy, both Algonquins and Iroquois, who were friendly and impressed by Hariot's knowledge of their language. He even tried to proselytize them, with some success.

Among White's best-known portraits is of the wife of Chief Herowan of Pomeioc with her daughter. The wife is tattooed or painted, with strings of pearls and carrying a large gourd. The rather ugly but endearing child, naked except for a string over her pubis, is holding a present of a doll, fully clothed, which obviously delights her. Another picture is evidently of the chief Wingina of Roanoke, painted before things went stale, with a cock's comb hair style and a copper tablet hanging round his neck as a sign of authority. At first, we learn, Wingina 'would be glad many times to be with us at our prayers, and many time call upon us in our town as also in others, whither he sometimes accompanied us to pray and sing psalms'. At Secoton the charnel-house shows the desiccated bodies of dead chiefs laid in a row, while below on a platform a priest 'mumbleth'. The ritual dance shows a circle of totem poles carved with human heads.

On his journey up the Chowan river near Roanoke, Lane got into grave trouble. For by this time Wingina, who now called himself Pemisapan, had turned against the English, partly because of being pressed for maize which he was unable to supply, partly because there was alarm over a strange disease (influenza?) which was causing many deaths and was believed to be some sort of secret weapon of the English. Very likely too there had been 'cruelty and outrages' against the native inhabitants, as an anonymous source later alleged. Wingina/Pemisapan was organizing an alliance of chieftains; and Lane, whose suspicions had been aroused, came across a conference at the large village of Chawanoac. Lane entered the village and seized its chief, Menatonon, a cripple, whom he kept prisoner for two days, and then exchanged for his son, who was sent down to Roanoke for safekeeping. Menatonon, 'a very wise and grave man', turned out to be cooperative and gave hopes of finding goldmines further inland.

Lane now set off up river with a large company of men and taking Manteo (apparently Wanchese had turned against the English and had gone back to his tribe).* But Pemisapan had sent warning messages ahead, and as a result the villages were found to be completely deserted. Voices were heard from the undergrowth lining the river, which Manteo translated as threatening. Sure enough, volleys of arrows were fired at the boats, but without any casualties. The English fired back, and the 'savages betook themselves to flight'. Food had become so short that they were reduced to killing and eating the two mastiff dogs they had brought with them. Being now 160 miles from home, they decided to return to the fort.

On their arrival at Roanoke they found that Pemisapan had been alarming the sixty or so settlers left behind with a report that Lane and all his companions were dead, and that he himself was preparing to leave Roanoke without planting any maize. Lane also learnt from a friendly Indian that Pemisapan was preparing a massacre of the English, with the help of neighbouring tribes. So he decided on action. Making an excuse to enter Pemisapan's village, Lane suddenly attacked and killed Pemisapan. 'Thus plot was met with counterplot and treachery with treachery.' Although it had the temporary effect of quietening the Indians, nobody could feel safe thereafter. With the threat of famine plans had to be made in case Raleigh's and Grenville's relief ships did not arrive.

On 1 June word came that a fleet of over twenty ships had been sighted by Captain Stafford's watch on the island of Croatoan to the south. It was not known whether they were friends or enemy. Then on the 9th Stafford himself appeared with the news that the great Sir Francis Drake was on his way.

Drake was appreciative of the settlers' unhappy state and promised help, not only food and clothing, but pinnaces and small boats. He had also brought slaves and the furniture taken from San Augustín. Lane asked if he would take back to England a number of weak and unfit men, and replace them with oarsmen and craftsmen. He also needed more weapons and tools. Then he requested a ship that could be used for searching for a more suitable harbour, and which would be available for taking them all back to England if necessary. Drake, obviously having realized that Roanoke was totally

---

* pp. 74, 82.

unsuitable as a privateering base against the Spaniards, agreed to all this and allotted him 'a very proper bark', the *Francis*, 70 tons, and gave orders for her to be provisioned with enough food for a hundred men for four months.

Lane sent some of his chief officers aboard the *Francis* to supervise the loading. On the very next day, 13 June, a tremendous storm blew up, lasting four days. Anchors and cables were broken and some ships were blown out to sea, including the *Francis*. When the lull came the *Francis* was last seen sailing off for England, with Lane's officers and all the provisions still on board.

Drake now generously offered Lane the 170-ton *Bark Bonner*, but this was too large for coastal exploration. The settlers were beginning to despair and agitated to be sent back to England at once, abandoning Roanoke altogether. They had been promised that Grenville would arrive with the relief and supplies before Easter, and now they had given up hope of ever seeing him. Once again Drake was helpful and considerate. As it was not possible to bring the *Bark Bonner* close to land, small boats would have to be sent to pick them up. Agreement having been reached, there was suddenly a great rush, a panic, especially as the weather was still 'boisterous'. There was not even time to dismantle the fort. The sailors became impatient with the luggage, pitching everything overboard, not only pearls (a present from Menatonon) but most of White's and Hariot's precious notes, journals, pictures and books. They also refused to wait for three men who were still up country.

Grenville's relief squadron, ironically, arrived just too late, only a fortnight later. As usual, chasing after prizes had caused a delay. It must have been obvious that the settlers had only recently left. Searches were made, and Indians kept themselves well out of sight (no sign either of those three unfortunates who had been left behind). Grenville now guessed that the settlers must have left with Drake. He decided, rashly, to leave a holding party of fifteen men at Roanoke with supplies for two years. The result was inevitable: they were never seen again.

On his way home Grenville was hoping to encounter the Spanish treasure fleet, but had no success, managing only to capture a couple of barks off the Azores. He was in no hurry, and it was December when he reached England, with a modest haul of sugar, ginger and spices.

In his *Briefe and True Report* Hariot attacked the grumblers and slanderers among the company who had returned, some of whom had actually been punished for their 'misdemeanour and ill dealing'. Such people had not attempted to pull their weight, he said, and some had not even ventured

A briefe and true report
of the new found land of Virginia.
of the commodities and of the nature and man
ners of the naturall inhabitants. Difcouered by
the Englifh Colony there feated by Sir Richard
Greinuile Knight In the yeere 1585.Which Rema
=ined Vnder the gouernement of twelue monethes,
At the fpeciall charge and direction of the Honou=
rable SIR WALTER RALEIGH Knight lord Wardten
of the ftanneries Who therein hath beene fauoured
and authorifed by her MAIESTIE
:and her letters patents:
This fore booke Is made in Englifh
By Thomas Hariot feruant to the abouenamed
Sir WALTER, a member of the Colony, and there
imployed in difcouering

CVM GRATIA ET PRIVILEGIO CÆS.MA.TIS SPECIA.LD

FRANCOFORTI AD MOENVM
TYPIS IOANNIS WECHELI, SVMTIBVS VERO THEODORI
DE BRY ANNO CD D XC.
VENALES REPERIVNTVR IN OFFICINA .SIGISMVNDI FEIRABENDII

The frontispiece of Hariot's Briefe and True Report, *1588,
reissued by de Bry in 1599.*

III

to leave the island. After discovering that there was no gold or silver to be found, they had 'little or no care for any thing than to pamper their bellies.' 'Some also were of nice bringing up, only in cities and towns, as such as never seen the world before. Because there were not to be found any English cities, nor such fair houses, nor any of their old accustomed dainty food, nor any soft beds of down and feathers, the country was to them miserable, and their reports according.' He pointed out that in contrast he and his colleagues, during their three months near Chesapeake Bay, were not averse to sleeping on the ground.

No word was ever given about the fate of the 300 Indians and hundred Negro slaves whom Drake had brought with him from the West Indies. Were they simply dumped at Roanoke and left to the mercy of local inhabitants? Grenville apparently saw no trace of them. At least there is a record that the Moorish prisoners and galley slaves were returned to Turkish dominions.

A Competition of Love
1587

On 7 January 1587, within a fortnight of Grenville's return, a charter had been drawn up naming John White as Governor of the proposed 'Cittie of Raleigh in Virginia', with twelve 'Assistants'.[1] The Cittie was to have its own coat of arms, as would White and each of the Assistants, one of whom was Simon Fernandez the Portuguese pilot and another Ananias Dare, White's son-in-law. This new expedition was to be different from that of 1585, which had been largely military in conception. It was to be permanent and self-supporting, and the settlers would include women and children, perhaps numbering 200 in all. Naturally a quick profit for investors was hoped for.

There was no doubt now that the colony ought to be established in the vicinity of Chesapeake Bay, and in a place where there would be a deep-water harbour. Hakluyt the younger had been studying the reports from Virginia and from Paris had written to Raleigh, reaffirming that the 'best planting will be about the bay of the Chesapians'. In February his translation of Peter Martyr's *De Orbe Novo* was published, and in his dedication praises were heaped on Raleigh, describing how he had spent the huge sum of 10,000 ducats in equipping the fleet. At the same time he castigated detractors of this great enterprise. And there was praise for Hariot:

By your [Raleigh's] experience in navigation you clearly saw that our highest glory as an insular kingdom would be built up to greatest splendour on the firm foundation of the mathematical sciences, and so for a long time you have nourished in your household, with a most liberal salary, a young man well trained in those studies, Thomas Hariot; so that under his guidance you might in spare hours learn those noble sciences and your collaborating sea captains, who are many, might very profitably unite theory with practice, not without almost incredible results.

Once again we wonder at the immense amount of preparation and organization under the aegis of Raleigh and his Durham House team, and regret that we have such few details. Sanderson as usual must certainly have been involved in the raising of funds, and it has also been assumed that Sir George Carey, Vice-Admiral of Hampshire and an enthusiastic privateer, was involved – indeed Carey was already preparing an expedition of his own to the West Indies. It seems possible that Raleigh had in mind a separate privateering expedition, in order to recoup some of the expenses, and this could have been in conjunction with Carey. He was also determined to keep control of Roanoke, the idea being to make Manteo a kind of feudal sub-tenant as chief of the Roanoke and Croatoan Indians.

All this was set against the realization in England that Spain was intent on an invasion. The fact that the highly respected and formidable Marqués de Santa Cruz had been named as Captain-General of what he termed the 'Felicisima Armada' was another cause for alarm in England. Thus Drake easily convinced the Queen and her Council that it was essential to attack as soon as possible the ports where the enemy ships were being assembled. Consequently on 2 April he set sail from Plymouth with a substantial fleet that included four royal warships on what was to become the famous episode of 'singeing the King of Spain's beard'. As usual his crews were a turbulent lot, and there had been trouble over desertions. Some were Raleigh's tinners, others had been pressganged or had come from prisons.*

Finding Lisbon too heavily fortified Drake continued to Cadiz, sailing right into the inner harbour. His arrival was totally unexpected, and he found the Spanish ships packed tightly together. They were easy prey, and he acted with amazing fearlessness. Over thirty ships were looted or burnt, including Santa Cruz's galleon of 1,500 tons and a Biscayan galleon of 1,200 tons. It would have been dangerous to attempt a landing on the narrow neck of the isthmus at the end of which were the fortified town and castle. In any case Drake had no intention of doing so, and he sailed out without the loss of a man or boat.

He moved on to Sagres in southern Portugal, where there was yet more pillage, this time on land. It was commonly said that for Drake no such raid was complete unless a church could be destroyed, and this was duly done. On he went to the Azores, where he captured an East Indian carrack loaded with spices, silk and calico, valued at £114,000.

The result of this expedition had been exactly as hoped, making it impossible for Spain to launch her Armada that year, thus leaving more time for

---

* One of those who sailed with Drake was a William Trevelyan, brother of an ancestor of the author of this book. He was paying the price for revenging himself against a neighbour in Somerset by driving off a flock of sheep.[2]

preparing the defences of England. Not surprisingly, the shock caused a severe crisis of confidence in Spain; but it was only temporary.

That same April Sir Christopher Hatton was created Lord Chancellor, a much criticized appointment, since he had no legal training – as Camden said, 'the great lawyers of England took it very offensively'. But the move was political, and a reward for Hatton's constant loyalty and service as a Privy Councillor and Vice-Chamberlain over many years. His position as Captain of the Guard, which he had held since 1572, now went to Raleigh, an important sinecure. Raleigh longed also to be elected to the Privy Council, but Elizabeth never allowed this. He might still have been her 'oracle' but she knew the limitations to his passionately expressed ideas; and there was the matter of his unpopularity at Court.

In effect, as Captain of the Guard Raleigh was now responsible for the safety and protection of the Queen's person. Under his command were the famous Yeomen of the Guard as well as the more privileged Gentlemen Pensioners, recruited from the gentry, usually handsome, well-built and tall young men, who served the Queen at meals and took personal messages and errands for her. It also meant that Raleigh was more often in her company, at a time when her spirits were low after the execution of the Queen of Scots. This was an honorary position, with no salary, but with great prestige. He did however get an uniform allowance: six yards of tawney medley (yarn), so we read, at 13 shillings and 4 pence a yard, with a fur of black budge (lambskin), rated at £10.[3] No doubt at his own expense he was allowed to decorate his uniform with a few of his favourite pearls.

There is a story told by Aubrey about a man coming to see Raleigh in this new role, offering his young son as a Pensioner, and Raleigh answering, 'I put in no boys'. The father insisted on producing his son, who turned out to be a six-foot Adonis, just the type that appealed to Elizabeth. And so, Aubrey continued: 'Sir Walter Raleigh swears him immediately, and ordered him to carry the first dish at dinner, where the Queen held him with admiration, as if a beautiful young giant stalked in with the service.'

New tensions, however, had arisen at Court. The Queen, at the age of fifty-four, had become besotted by a fresh arrival, the nineteen-year-old Robert Devereux, second Earl of Essex, Leicester's stepson, tall, dark-eyed, at present without a beard and with dark auburn hair, elegant, intelligent, and – which Raleigh lacked – impeccable aristocratic descent, having Edward III as an ancestor; further, Anne Boleyn was his great-aunt. He took an immediate and violent dislike to Raleigh.

Essex had actually been introduced at Court by Leicester two years before, and dangled before the Queen as a way of diverting the ambitions of Raleigh, who was already into his thirties and losing his physical attraction for her. The young man had conducted himself well in the recent Low Countries campaign and had been close to Sidney, who had included him in his will: 'I give to my beloved and much honoured Lord, the Earl of Essex, my best sword.' In some ways Essex was considered to have inherited the mantle of Sidney's chivalry. As Naunton said: 'There was in this young lord, together with a most goodly person, a kind of urbanity or innate courtesy, which both won the Queen, and too much took upon the people.'

His mother, born Lettice Knollys, had secretly married Leicester in 1578, and had thus never regained the Queen's favour or been forgiven – admittedly a drawback. He had the quick temper of a redhead, given to passionate outbursts and tantrums. In David Lloyd's *State Worthies* we read how 'he always carried on his brow either love or hatred and did not understand concealment.' He was a 'great resenter'; and his greatest resentment of all was against Raleigh, partly for snobbish reasons but chiefly through jealousy, not just because of his closeness to the Queen, but because of his literary prestige and his spectacular enterprises overseas.

Another young man developed into a rival for the Queen's ear, but not because of his looks or lineage. This was Burghley's son, Robert Cecil, now aged twenty-four. She had already realized that this prudent, peaceful young man was of the right stock, and it was not long before he was knighted and admitted to the Privy Council. Small and slightly hunchbacked, she called him her 'Elf' or 'Pygmy', which he hated.

Both Burghley and Robert Cecil realized that Elizabeth needed someone to rejuvenate her, and there was no doubt that she found Essex an exhilarating companion. In some ways she treated him like a son, and she allowed him a freedom of speech that had not been the case with Hatton or Raleigh. He undoubtedly had the qualities of a leader, but as the years went by there was alarm about his interference in affairs of state. He also was popular in London in a way that Raleigh never had been. Hence Naunton's words: 'He too much took upon the people.' Anthony Bagot wrote: 'When she [the Queen] is abroad, nobody near her, but my Lord of Essex, and, at night, my Lord is at cards, or one game and other, with her, that he cometh not to his own lodgings till the birds sing in the morning'.[4] She also enjoyed watching him at the tiltyards. For his part he was of course flattered by the attentions of an older woman, especially when she was his Queen and one of the cleverest women in Europe. He was moreover ready to play up to all elaborate performances required by Gloriana. He tried to write poems, sometimes quite successfully and sometimes a little quaint.

Raleigh's enemies were watching the situation with glee, noting a certain change in his behaviour. Evidently he was kept in the background when the twelve-year-old Lady Arabella Stuart (known as Arbell) was introduced at Court and dined in the presence of the Queen as her near cousin and possible heir to the throne. He was, however, invited to another dinner party for Arbell, given by Burghley. Sir Charles Cavendish was there too, and sent a letter full of gossip to the formidable Lady Shrewsbury, 'Bess of Hardwick', the girl's grandmother and with whom she was living. 'Sir Walter Raleigh', he wrote, 'is in wonderful declination, yet labours to underprop himself by my Lord Treasurer [Burghley] and his friends. I see he is courteously used by my Lord and friends, but I doubt the end, considering how be hath handled himself in his former pride, and surely now groweth so humble towards everyone, as considering his former insolency he commiteth over-great baseness, and is thought will never rise again.'[5]

This was an exaggeration, indeed wishful thinking. Raleigh's position was still secure in the Queen's trust, as she continued to make clear. He was no longer her lover, and he obviously missed those delicious days of flirtation. But he could still enchant her with his poetry. A poem, set to music by Alfonso Ferrabosco and becoming a popular song, could well have been written at this time, and begins:

> Like to a hermit poor in place obscure,
> I mean to spend my days of endless doubt,
> To wail such woes as time cannot recure,
> Where none but Love shall ever find me out.
>
> My food shall be of care and sorrow made,
> My drink nought else but tears fall'n from mine eyes,
> And for my light in such obscurèd shade,
> The flames shall serve, from which my heart arise . . .

It was just the sort of poem that enraged Essex, and with which he could not compete. However, in June Elizabeth made him her Master of the Horse, with a welcome salary of £1,500 a year and some other advantages. Then came a row. Elizabeth was on one of her progresses, staying with Lord and Lady Warwick on her way to Burghley's house, Theobalds. On arrival she discovered that another guest was Dorothy Devereux, one of Essex's sisters. Dorothy had committed the grave crime of making a runaway marriage with Sir Thomas Perrot (the same man with whom Raleigh had had a 'fray' in 1580), without of course the consent of the Queen. Although some years had passed, she was still very much *non grata*, like her mother, and Elizabeth was furious that she should be under the same roof. She gave orders for Dorothy to stay in her room and not to leave it. Essex took umbrage and accused Elizabeth of having done this merely to please 'that knave Raleigh'.

Essex wrote to his friend Edward Dyer on 21 July:[6]

It seemed she could not well endure anything to be spoken against him [Raleigh]; and taking hold of one word 'disdain', she said there was no such cause why I should disdain him. This speech troubled me so much that as near as I could I described unto her what he had been, and what he was, and then I did let her see whether I had cause to disdain his competition of love, or whether I could have comfort to give myself over to the service of a mistress that was in awe of such a man. I spake, what of grief and choler, as much against him as I could, and I think he standing at the door might well have heard the worse that I spoke of himself. In the end I saw she was resolved to defend him, and to cross me. For myself, I told her, I had no joy to be in any place but loath to be near about her when I knew my affection so much thrown down, and such a wretch as Raleigh highly esteemed of her. To this she made no answer, but turned away to my Lady of Warwick

In the deepest of sulks Essex stormed out of the house and rode to Sandwich, intending to sail to the Low Countries with the Earl of Cumberland who was then preparing to leave – there he would prove himself a hero; and if he was killed, what would the Queen then think? But the Queen sent Robert Carey to tell the bad boy that he was forgiven and must return.

If Raleigh had been standing at the door, he would not have been much disturbed by such a tirade. For him the episode had been a victory. Only later was he forced to recognize Essex as a danger. He still had security and power, and was more free to act on his own, not having to concentrate on the time-consuming love-game with Elizabeth.

Raleigh had also acquired an important new friend, with a mind and character far more interesting than this petulant youth's, and for that matter with a grander pedigree. This was Henry Percy, ninth Earl of Northumberland, some ten years younger than Raleigh, born in 1564. Northumberland had come into his great estates and two magnificent houses, Syon House and Petworth, on the suicide (or murder) of his father, a Catholic, in the Tower. He was not so handsome as Essex and temperamentally the opposite: reserved, with a stutter, absorbed by all that was new in philosophy, mathematics and science, subjects which some in the outside world regarded as 'magick'. Hence his nickname the Wizard Earl. The miniature by Nicholas Hilliard shows him in a fashionably melancholic attitude, lying on the ground, head in hand, doublet unbuttoned and with an impressive tome nearby. It was not surprising that he should be drawn to the coterie of intellectuals at Durham House. Expensive gifts were exchanged between him and Raleigh, and they played cards together, rode together. He gave Raleigh a straw-coloured saddle, and Raleigh sent him a bed made of 'cedar or cypress'. At Petworth Northumberland had an enormous library, which Raleigh consulted. He also had a great admiration for Hariot, to whom in later years he gave an annual subsidy and a house on the Syon House estate.

Northumberland did not necessarily share Raleigh's enthusiasm for the arts of war. According to John Shirley, 'no expert soldier or mariner escaped his [Raleigh's] acquaintance or enquiries'.[7] It was also said that Raleigh needed only five hours' sleep. He spent four hours a day 'in reading and mastering the best authors,' and two 'in select conversation and inquisitive discourse, the rest in business'.[8]

In the circle were William Warner, who was working on the circulation of the blood, and the mathematician Robert Hues, who accompanied Thomas Cavendish round the world. They with Hariot came to be known as Northumberland's 'three magi'. Then there were the scientist Nathaniel Torporley, Emery Molyneux the geographer who later (subsidized by William Sanderson) made cartographical globes, and Thomas Allen a leading astrologer and mathematician, feared by the 'vulgar' as a magician (his servant put it about that he conjured up spirits that would be met 'coming up the stairs like a swarm of bees'). The renowned Dr Dee was in a sense a godfather to them all; he did not return from abroad until 1589, and Hariot visited him soon after. Obviously Raleigh respected the old man for his pioneer work, but by this time his influence was only peripheral to Raleigh's interests.

Giordano Bruno, the fiery Italian occultist, had been in London between 1583 and 1585 and Hariot certainly met him – some of his own ideas can be traced back to him. Raleigh also met him at the house of the French ambassador, the Marquis de Mauvissière, where Bruno was often to be seen. Northumberland was a collector of Bruno's writings, regarded generally as highly controversial if not subversive and blasphemous.

Hariot seems to have been a friend of Christopher Marlowe, who was about the same age as Northumberland. By 1587 Marlowe had already become famous for his lyric poetry and plays. In that year his *Tamburlaine* was first performed, and it is possible that *Doctor Faustus* had also been written by then. Aspects of Faustus's character were obviously drawn from Bruno, also perhaps the Swiss alchemist and occultist Paracelsus and even Dr Dee and Hariot.

Northumberland was among 'Kit' Marlowe's patrons, but whether

Raleigh was one too is not proven. Marlowe does not seem to have belonged to the Durham House circle, in spite of having friends there. In 1593, just before his death, the scandal having grown about his heretical views, it was claimed that he had read an 'atheist lecture' to Raleigh at Durham House. Raleigh may in fact have decided to keep his distance from Marlowe, given rumours of his links with the homosexual underworld.

Raleigh's chief literary ally was his cousin Arthur Gorges, who like Raleigh wrote poetry in the Petrarchian tradition ostensibly for private circulation. At this stage Raleigh was writing light-hearted verse unconnected with the Queen, some of which might even have been in collaboration with Gorges. It was not considered gentlemanly to publish poems commercially, so when in 1593 contributions by both Raleigh and Gorges appeared in *The Phoenix Nest*, an anthology of courtiers' poems, they did not bear either of their names. In any case there have always been arguments about whether or not some of the unsigned poems were actually written by Raleigh.

Marlowe's ballad *The Passionate Shepherd to his Love* had become immensely popular and was set to music.

> Come live with me, and be my love,
> And we will all the pleasures prove,
> That valleys, groves, hills and fields,
> Woods or steepy mountains yields . . .
>
> And I will make thee beds of roses,
> And a thousand fragrant posies,
> A cap of flowers, and a kirtle,
> Embroidered all with leaves of myrtle . . .

Raleigh wrote a half facetious response, *The Nymph's Reply to the Shepherd*, which also became well known, although as usual written for private amusement.

> If all the world and love were young,
> And truth in every shepherd's tongue,
> These pretty pleasures might me move
> To live with thee and be thy love . . .
>
> Thy gowns, thy shoes, thy beds of roses,
> Thy cap, thy kirtle, and thy posies
> Soon break, soon wither, soon forgotten,
> In folly ripe, in reason rotten . . .

But could youth last, and love still breed,
Had joys no date, nor age no need,
Then these delights my mind might move,
To live with thee, and be thy love.

This poem is as typical of Raleigh as the other is of Marlowe. All things, Raleigh is saying, lack permanence. Desire and dreams of idyllic love are fulfilled only in poetry – or in religion (another form of poetry?). Time and mutability are constant themes in Raleigh's poetry and prose. Marlowe's poem is of loneliness and nostalgia, and must have been inspired by Virgil's second *Eclogue*. Raleigh had written this poem to amuse his friends, but in later years it was held to have a much more sinister significance, and as Walter Oakeshott has said the verses do suggest a direct and personal response to Marlowe.

A poem which Raleigh and Gorges could well have written together was in the form of a riddle, almost like a crossword, that could be read vertically and horizontally.

Her face,	Her tongue,	Her wit,
So fair,	So sweet,	So sharp,
First bent,	Then drew,	Then hit,
Mine eye,	Mine ear,	My heart,
Mine eye,	Mine ear,	My heart,
To like,	To learn,	To love,
Her face,	Her tongue,	Her wit,
Doth lead,	Doth teach,	Doth move,
Oh face,	Oh tongue,	Oh wit,
With frowns,	With check,	With smart,
Wrong not,	Vex not,	Wound not,
Mine eyes,	Mine ear,	My heart,
Mine eyes,	Mine ear,	My heart,
To learn,	To know,	To fear,
Her face,	Her tongue,	Her wit,
Doth lead,	Doth teach,	Doth swear.

Raleigh's 'Walsingham' poem, referring to the shrine in Norfolk, and written in the form of question and answer, is regarded as a masterpiece, remembered especially for the first two lines in the last verse. Obviously it was written for the Queen, and might have been composed a little later than 1587 when the rift between them had begun. Or it might have been composed as a gentle reminder of his devotion after the rudeness of Essex. The first verses were based on a popular song (there is also a later echo in the second verse of Ophelia's song in Act IV, Scene v of *Hamlet*).

As you came from the holy land,
　Of Walsingham,
Met you not with my true love
　By the way as you came?

How shall I know your true love
　That have met many one
As I went to the holy land
　That have come, that have gone?

She is neither white nor brown
　But as the heavens fair,
There is none hath a form so divine
　In the earth or the air.

Such an one I did meet, good sir,
　Such an angelic face
Who like a queen, like a nymph did appear
　By her gait, by her grace.

She hath left me here all alone,
　All alone as unknown,
Who sometimes did lead me with herself
　And me loved as her own.

What's the cause that she leaves you alone
　And a new way doth take,
Who loved you once as her own,
　And her joy did you make?

I have loved her all my youth,
　But now old as you see,
Love likes not the falling fruit
　From the withered tree.

Know that love is a careless child
　And forgets promise past,

He is blind, he is deaf when he list
And in faith never fast . . .

But true love is a durable fire
In the mind ever burning;
Never sick, never old, never dead,
From itself never turning.

It is not very likely that Raleigh remained virginal during the years of the Queen's favour. There is a poem, attributed posthumously to him, entitled *Sir Walter Raleigh and a Lady:*[9]

Ra: Say not you love, unless you do,
          For lying will not profit you.

Ladie: Sir, I do love with love most true:
          I will not love, unless't be you.

Ra: You say I lie, I say you lie, choose you whether,
          But if we both lie, let's lie both together.

This could have been written a year or two later. As Captain of the Guard he had plenty of opportunities of meeting the Queen's Maids-of-Honour, expressly chosen not just because of their looks and lineage, but because they were virgins. Each girl knew that if she fell from grace the terrible wrath of the Queen would mean banishment from the Court for evermore, perhaps even a temporary sojourn in the Tower of London. Nevertheless, Raleigh must have felt a kind of liberation at this stage, judging from one of Aubrey's more famous passages – from which one also deduces that hitherto he had contented himself with less well-born women.

He loved a wench well; and one time getting up one of the Maids of Honour against a tree in a wood ('twas his first Lady) who seemed at first boarding to be something fearful of her honour, and modest, she cried, 'Sweet Sir Walter, what do you me ask? Will you undo me? Nay, Sweet Sir Walter! Sweet Sir Walter! Sweet Sir Walter!' At last, as the danger and the pleasure at the same time grew higher, she cried in the ecstasy, 'Swisser Swatter! Swisser Swatter!'. She proved with child, and I doubt not, but this hero took care of them both, as also the product was more than an ordinary mortal.

How did this rather implausible, but wonderful, story get about? Were they being spied on, or did Raleigh brag about it later?

To return to the journey to the 'Cittie of Raleigh' under John White. When White published his *Narrative* he gave a list of the colonists who left England, now reduced to 117, including seventeen women and nine young boys, and accompanied by two 'savages', Manteo and another called Towaye who could have been Manteo's servant. At least two of the women were pregnant. Among the colonists were two ex-prisoners, a former sheriff, a lawyer, a tailor, a goldsmith, and someone from a Cambridge college. Nearly all were from London or the eastern counties. The three ships, into which they were packed, along with supplies, animals and poultry, were the *Lion* (probably the same as the *Red Lion* of 1585 and therefore 120 tons), a flyboat and a pinnace for navigating the shoals. Fernandez was master of the *Lion*, Edward Spicer and Edward Stafford were masters of the other two.

The little fleet sailed from Plymouth on 8 May. From the start in White's *Narrative*[10] there are complaints about Fernandez, who had obviously hardened into a ruthless self-seeker, looking for profit and in a hurry to get to Virginia, so that on his return journey to England he might catch a vessel or two from the Spanish treasure *flota*. Rumours had long been circulating about his early experience as a pirate before he settled in England, and he was also held to have been in part responsible for the grounding of the *Tyger* in 1585. As for White, he gives the impression of having been a weak leader, unable to stand up to Fernandez. We read how Fernandez 'lewdly forsook our flyboat, leaving her distressed in the Bay of Portugal'; the assumption was that they would never see it again.

White had wanted to collect fresh fruit and tropical plants in the West Indies, but was constantly being harried by Fernandez, anxious not to waste time. There was a plan to pick up salt at Puerto Rico, but Fernandez would not allow it. 'He suddenly began to swear, and tear God in pieces, dissembling great danger, crying to him at the helm, "Bear up hard, bear up hard"; so off we went, and were disappointed of our salt, by his means'.

After a near wreck (again Fernandez's fault, according to White) they finally dropped anchor at Hatarask on 22 July. Raleigh had given specific orders for this, so that a search could be made for the fifteen men left behind by Grenville. White therefore embarked for Roanoke island in the pinnace, taking with him forty of his best men – it being impossible for the larger ship to negotiate the shallow passage. At once he was hailed by Fernandez, who said that the men were to be left on the island, and only White and two or three others were to return. He gave as his excuse that the summer was coming to an end, but he was really meaning that it was getting close to the time when treasure ships could be intercepted. What was more, he said, the colonists would have to stay at Roanoke, instead of going on to Chesapeake Bay. Amazingly White gave in, because the sailors were all for Fernandez. 'Therefore it booted not for the Governor to contend with them.'

Some human bones were found on Roanoke, but otherwise there was no sign of Grenville's men. The earthworks of the fort had been flattened, but huts were still standing, overgrown with 'melons of divers sorts, which were being eaten by deer'. Then on the 25th the flyboat miraculously appeared, to the delight of everybody except Fernandez, 'who grieved greatly at their safe coming', having 'purposely left them . . . and stole away from them in the night', hoping that its master Spicer would never be able to find his way to Virginia. It may have been that Fernandez had a personal dislike for Spicer, and that to try to help him was a waste of privateering time.

The Indians had left their village near the camp, but they were still lurking in the undergrowth. One of the Assistants, George Howe, was attacked while wading in the surf searching for crabs. He was shot with arrows and his head battered in. Two days later Stafford and a group of his men took Manteo to Croatoan, where Manteo had relatives, and they were received with friendliness. Now the fate of Grenville's men was revealed. They had been set upon by the tribe of which Wingina/Pemisapan had been chief; some had managed to escape but had never been seen again. The 'savages' had come from a village called Dasamunkepeuc, and were the same people who had killed George Howe. It was decided that there would have to be a reprisal, and Dasamunkepeuc was attacked, one Indian being killed. Then it was discovered that the Indians who were in the village at that time were mainly from Croatoan, and therefore friends, and had simply come to gather corn and tobacco. This of course 'somewhat grieved' Manteo, but all was eventually forgiven.

A great symbolic day for the settlers came on 13 August 1587 when Manteo was christened and dubbed Lord of Roanoke and Dasamunkepeuc, in the name of Sir Walter Raleigh. Five days later White's daughter Eleonora, wife of Ananias Dare, gave birth to a daughter, who was christened Virginia, famous now as the first English child to have been born in America. In fact, within a few days, another child was born, sex unknown, with the family name of Haruye, presumably Harvie.

By the 21st the unloading had finished, including the cannons and heavy equipment. Now there were more controversies. Quite clearly there was not going to be sufficient food for the winter, especially since a promise had been given to the Croatoans not to take their food. There was also a shortage of salt, and more livestock was needed. Fernandez was preparing to leave in the *Lion*, taking the flyboat but leaving the pinnace. He was impatient to get away to the Azores, for soon the treasure fleet would be due – indeed he would already have left but for a storm that had lasted for five days. It was decided that two of the Assistants should go with him, in order to persuade Raleigh to send urgent help. But none of the Assistants wanted to leave, arguing that they had already sacrificed too much in order to build this new life.

It was realized that Fernandez could not be trusted to explain the situation satisfactorily in England. So it was decided that the only person who could do this was White, even though he was Governor. It all involved a great deal of heart-searching. White was even more reluctant to go when he learnt that the settlers were intending to move north. What would happen to all his valuable equipment and his drawings? Would not people in England assume that he had never intended to stay in Virginia, and would they not blame him for abandoning his own daughter and new-born grandchild? In the end he gave in, after being given a testimonial proving that he was leaving at the general request of all. The document was signed on 25 August, confirming that 'We, all of one mind and consent have most earnestly entreated, and incessantly requested, John White, Governor of the planters of Virginia, to pass into England, for the better and more assured help'. A stronger man acting as Governor would surely have *ordered* the two Assistants to leave.

The ships left for England on 27 August, White in the flyboat, Fernandez in the *Lion*. On weighing anchor there was a disaster with the capstan on the flyboat which injured twelve of the fifteen-man crew. It must have been an unpleasant and dangerous journey across the Atlantic in that almost flat-bottomed boat. They did manage to reach the Azores safely however, Fernandez thereupon announcing that he would 'linger about the island of Terceira', where the treasure ships habitually docked in the safe-harbour of the town of Angra. It has been suggested by Quinn that he may also have been hoping to join forces with privateers from England. If so, none were to be seen, and White sailed home alone, bringing with him letters from the settlers.

It was a terrible journey, stormy, and with drinking water running out. Two of the sailors died and others were very sick. Blown hither and thither for thirteen days, White thought that they would all die of thirst and starvation. At last land was sighted, and they found that they had reached Smerwick on the Dingle Peninsula in Ireland, the spot where the Papal invaders had been massacred in 1580. Three more of the crew died, and the rest were now too weak to continue. White at least managed to find another ship which brought them to Southampton on 8 November. There he found that the *Lion* had already arrived, after an equally dreadful voyage, and without any prizes. Indeed its crew had been 'in such weakness by sickness, and death of their chiefest men, that they were scarce able to bring the ship into the harbour, but were forced to let fall anchor without', where they were rescued just in time, otherwise they 'might all have perished there'.

No more has been discovered about the fate of that equivocal character Simon Fernandez. And for Raleigh there was a large debt to pay off. At least White was able to report to him that the colonists were still full of determination and hope, and that they were preparing to move on to Chesapeake Bay.

Sir George Carey had meanwhile set out on his expedition, but information about it is unfortunately vague. It seems likely that he had a group of would-be colonists on board, and that he may have called at Chesapeake Bay, hoping to find a settlement – there is a hint of this in Spanish documents. At least he did manage to take a prize worth about £2,000, before deductions of customs fee.

White found England preparing to meet the Spanish Armada. In October there had been a general stay on shipping from English ports. Nevertheless Raleigh promised that he would send a pinnace to Virginia with supplies as soon as he could. He would also arrange for Grenville to follow this up with a much larger fleet, to be assembled at Bideford.

Armada
1588

There was little time now for the writing of poetry, either for the amusement of friends or in the 'competition of love'. Because of the stay on shipping there was no possibility for Raleigh – officially at least – of sending out privateering expeditions, which would have helped to offset losses from the Virginian venture, though money still somehow had to be raised for equipping Grenville's supply ships at Bideford, now awaiting official permission to leave.

In the previous June Raleigh's magnificent new warship, the *Ark Raleigh*, had been launched. She was about 1,100 tons, with a keel length of 100 feet and a hold 37 feet in breadth. There were said to be many innovations, though precisely what they were is obscure; she did have four masts instead of the usual three, topgallant sails and three banks of guns. Raleigh had designed the ship himself, but she had been built by the Queen's master shipwright Richard Chapman. It must always have been understood, or hoped, that the ship would become part of the royal fleet. Raleigh agreed therefore to sell her to the Queen for a nominal £500, though in fact he was not given the money, because of financial worries at such a critical time. However Elizabeth did not forget, and she wiped the equivalent sum off his debts when he fell into disgrace: a generous gesture under the circumstances.

The name *Ark Raleigh* was changed to *Ark Royal*, the first of a long line of famous ships. She was given as flagship to the Lord High Admiral, Charles Lord Howard of Effingham. He was delighted with her. 'I pray tell her Majesty from me', he wrote to Burghley, 'that her money was well given for the *Ark Royal*, for I think her the odd ship in the world for all conditions; and truly I think there can be no great ship make me change and go out of her.'[1] He was ready for the fight. 'I protest before God, as my sail shall answer for it, that I think there were never in any place in the world worthier ships than these are, for so many. And as few as we are, if this King of Spain's forces be not hundreds we will make good sport with them.'

The Ark Raleigh, *renamed* Ark Royal.

In November 1587 Raleigh had been appointed to the Council of War. Among the ten others present were two seasoned veterans, Sir John ('Black John') Norris and Sir Roger Williams, Sir Richard Grenville, and Ralph Lane who was designated Muster General of the Forces. The chief danger points were considered to be Milford Haven, the Isle of Wight, Portland, the Downs, Margate and the Thames estuary, with Plymouth having one of the most vulnerable harbours. Raleigh's specific job was to levy troops and improve defences in the South-West. As he was to comment later in his *History of the World*, it would be madness for an invader to land without securing a deep-water harbour. 'For to invade by sea upon a perilous coast, being rather in possession of any port, may better fit a prince presuming on his fortune than enriched with understanding.'[2] This was written with hindsight, of course. Raleigh attributed Philip's strategic failures to dogma and over-confidence.

Raleigh's energy during the winter months was as usual prodigious, and his tours were not confined to the South-West, but as far as Kent and East Anglia. He was particularly anxious about the weakness of Portland and Weymouth, and put his brother Carew as supervisor of their defences, at the same time lobbying for more heavy cannon for them. A system of beacons were prepared from Cornwall along to the south coast. On 7 December, as Lord Warden of the Stannaries, he received the order to hold musters of trained men, 2,000 foot and 200 light horse, from Devon and Cornwall, 'to be placed in form of camp . . . against sudden invasion.'

Unfortunately, two weeks later he had to report an unpatriotic lack of enthusiasm at Exeter, where the civic authorities (unlike most of the gentry in the South-West), were still not friendly towards him. They felt that they were being unfairly burdened with too large a part of the country's war effort, when they had already been made to pay big levies for protection against Barbary and other pirates. Raleigh insisted however that he was confident that his deputies and sub-wardens would persuade their 'inferiors' to make preparations 'for her Majesty's safety and their own defence.'[3]

The welcome at Plymouth was very different and Raleigh was presented with a valuable silver cup. In the city records there is mention of a dinner which could have been at this time. We read that Mr Hawkins had £4 and Master White £8 11s 4d for Sir Walter Raleigh's diet, while the Mayor had £5 for the diet of Drake and 'my lady and other justices.'[4] Sir John Gilbert was also at the party. All in all an extravagant affair. There is no mention anywhere of Raleigh actually having a pied-à-terre in Plymouth, but every now and then there are references to his staying with his friend Christopher Harris in the parish of Plymstock nearby.

In January 1588 there was a meeting of the Stannary parliament at Lostwithiel, over which he surely must have presided.* The result was successful, with a suitably loyal and generous response: 5,560 Cornishmen are recorded as having been furnished with 1,395 shot, 633 corselets, 1,956 bills and halberds, 1,528 bows, four lances and ninety-six light horse.[5]

There is no record of a parliament at Crockern Tor or at some other spot less exposed to the January winds. The Devon tinners, however, were also won over. All this was a credit to Raleigh, proof of his popularity in the Stannaries. On receiving the good news the Council decided that 6,000 trained men – 4,000 from Devon, 2,000 from Cornwall – should be held ready to converge on Plymouth if it were attacked; and if Falmouth were to be the Spaniards' choice (and this in 1587 for a while had been Philip's plan), 4,000 men from Devon and 4,000 from Cornwall should be available.

Raleigh was worried about sending supplies to Virginia, but the ban on shipping leaving England was still in force. John White was also desperate about the fate of his family. At last permission was given for two small ships to 'steal away' from Bideford, one being the *Brave*, commanded by a dubious character called Arthur Facy, and the other the *Roe*, a pinnace, both owned

---

* It has been suggested that his place could have been taken by his sub-warden, Sir Francis Godolphin.

by Grenville. White went with the *Brave*, and there was even a handful of would-be settlers in each ship. As might have been expected, Facy was only interested in privateering, in other words piracy, and the same applied to his 'evil-disposed mariners'. It was to be a nightmare experience for White. Only a few days out, Facy gave chase to two ships and boarded them. The English were then pursued by a French man o' war from La Rochelle which attacked them, resulting in many casualties, including White, and some deaths. So back they limped to Bideford and as a result there could be no more attempts that year to relieve Virginia.

Raleigh's name, to his regret, hardly appeared in contemporary descriptions of the defeat of the Armada, as indeed was to be the case in subsequent histories. This was because of his being in charge of land defences; if the Spaniards had been able to attempt a landing, his role would certainly have been a vital one. He was at least able to take pride in the performance of the *Ark Royal*. His own heavily armed merchantman, the *Roebuck*, also took part in the battle.

Philip's preparations for the invasion of England were reckoned the worst-kept secret in Europe. Various plans had been mooted over the past couple of years. Land first in Ireland? Or at Milford Haven? Falmouth geographically had one of the nearest harbours, but the river Tamar would be too much of a barrier for foot soldiers marching up from Cornwall. Plymouth? Or should the Duke of Parma, commander-in-chief in the Nether-lands, first send a contingent across the Channel to Kent, and wait for the arrival of the Armada? Finally it was agreed that the best plan would be for the Armada to sail direct to the Low Countries, and there to combine its military force with Parma's for a joint invasion.

Santa Cruz had brought his fleet to Lisbon in September 1587. But he was in poor health, and the situation was chaotic, with provisions rotting and men dying of typhus. On 7 February he died. In his place the King appointed the extremely reluctant Duke of Medina Sidonia, admired for his organizational abilities, but who had never been to sea.

There was a slight atmosphere of relaxation in England at the news of Santa Cruz's death. Raleigh is actually believed to have rushed over to Ireland to deal with the administration of his new empire. Lord Admiral Howard became alarmed by the Queen's unhurried attitude. 'For the love of Jesus Christ, Madam', he wrote to her, 'awake and see the villainous treasons around you, against your Majesty and the realm.'[6] And indeed by the end of March it was clear that Medina Sidonia's preparations were nearly ready. Pope Sixtus V promised Philip a million *scudi* if the 'Enterprise of England' were to be successful. He sent priests to bless each Spanish soldier and mariner, and decreed that Elizabeth should not be killed, but taken prisoner and sent to Rome.

Like Raleigh, Drake was convinced that Plymouth was especially at risk. There were already rumours that Medina Sidonia intended to install himself at Mount Edgcumbe on the headland across the Sound. Drake also insisted that the main English naval force should be based at Plymouth, and accordingly in early June he was joined by Howard, bringing their combined fleet to sixty fighting vessels. The total English defence force numbered 76,000, of which about 17,000 were at Tilbury at the mouth of the Thames. Morale was high, but it was realized that English soldiers were ill-trained compared to Parma's seasoned troops.

Then at last the Armada, numbering 130 ships, with nearly 19,000 troops on board, and carrying 2,500 guns, sailed from Lisbon. There was a storm, and they were forced to take shelter at La Coruña.

To a certain degree the English and Spaniards were evenly matched. The English had mobilized about 150 ships, of which all except thirty-four were privately owned. Their ships were much smaller, with no troops on board, and therefore more mobile and faster; they were also better armed, and their guns had a longer range. This mobility was recognized as being the great advantage. Raleigh, looking back in the *History of the World*, wrote of the importance of having ships ready to meet and harass an approaching invasion fleet. Soldiers were ready in case of a landing in the South-West, but if the enemy went sailing past to a point further up to the coast it might mean a six days' march to get there.

On 29 July 1588, after so many weeks of tension, so many months of preparation, the great Spanish Armada approached the Lizard in Cornwall. A pirate, Thomas Flemying, acting as a scout for Howard, had spotted the enemy ships out to sea, and had hurried back to Plymouth to alert Howard and Drake. Thus overnight the greater part of the English ships were able to warp out of the harbour, and in the afternoon the closely packed Armada was sighted. It was an awesome sight, the tall ships with their many flags like a swarm of hornets in crescent shape. Raleigh's beacons flared along the coast, from cliff to cliff (in tradition, the first to be lit was by a member of the Trefusis family); his hitherto demonic efforts seemed now about to be put to the test.

During darkness the English were able to manoeuvre themselves up-wind from the west, and with daylight they at once began discharging broadsides at the two corners of the Spanish crescent. Raleigh had hurried to Plymouth, but realizing that the Spaniards were moving on, gave orders for his Stannary men to begin their march east, flying the red cross of St George of England.

Howard in the *Ark Royal* knew that if he closed with the Spaniards and there were boarding parties, the English would be the losers so he relied on his long-range cannons. Two other large English ships were the *Galleon Leicester*, 600 tons with forty-two guns, and Oxford's *Edward Bonaventura*, 450 tons with thirty guns. Watchers from the shore saw the Spaniards still in perfect crescent formation as they passed the red cliffs of the Devon coast. Small boats were pushed out to sea, ready to assist in attacks on stragglers. The Spaniards had two disasters on the 31st. Some powder barrels exploded on the *San Salvador*, which had to be abandoned, then the great *Nuestra Señora del Rosario*, commanded by Don Pedro de Valdés, collided with another galleon and also had to be abandoned. Valdés surrendered to Drake, who arranged for the treasure and pay-chests to be transferred to his own ship, the *Revenge*, before the *Rosario* was towed into Torbay by Raleigh's *Roebuck*, under the command of Jacob Whiddon. The *San Salvador* was taken to Weymouth.

Several coffers containing 'clothes of gold and other furniture' were discovered on the *Rosario* and appropriated by the crew of the *Roebuck*. Enquiries were held about this some months later, but to no avail. However, a good quantity of the ship's treasure did reach the Queen's exchequer.

As for Drake's whereabouts over the next couple of days there was a big mystery, and he was later strongly attacked about this by Frobisher, who accused him of cowardice. The Queen took no notice of such slanders, and indeed allowed Drake to keep the ransom for Valdés and two other officers.

According to Hakluyt, Raleigh took part in the battle off Portland Bill on 2 August, like the smart young courtiers who rushed down from London, but there is no hint of this in Raleigh's own writings. He would certainly have felt frustrated, cooped up on shore. But more credibly, and according to a Spanish source, he was sent by the Queen with a message to Howard as he neared the French coast. She told Howard that he should now grapple, but it is not likely that Raleigh would have backed her on this. He was an admirer of Howard's tactics, and did not accept later criticisms that the Lord Admiral should not have allowed the enemy to drift so close to the French coast. He wrote: 'There is a great difference between fighting loose, or at large, and grappling. The guns of a slow ship pierce as well and make as great a hole as swift. To clap ships together without consideration belongs rather to a madman than to a man of war . . . The Lord Charles Howard, Admiral of England, [had] been lost in the year 1588 if he had not been better advised, than a great many malignant fools that were that found fault with his demeanour. The Spaniards had an army aboard them, and he had none; they had more ships than he had, and of higher building and charging; so that, had he entangled himself with those great and powerful vessels, he had greatly endangered this kingdom of England.'[7] He compared the situation with the battle at the Azores in 1582, when the Spaniards were fighting the Portuguese rebels and the Spanish victory was not certain until one ship managed to grapple and board the Portuguese flagship.

Medina Sidonia had been despatching pinnaces to warn Parma of his approach and asking for details of his plans. There had been no response. It was not possible for such huge ships to anchor off the Flanders coast because of the danger of sandbanks. In any case a Dutch squadron was guarding this shoal water. On 6 August the Armada anchored off Calais, and it was only on the next morning that Medina Sidonia received the dire news that Parma would not be able to join forces for an invasion for some days. Meanwhile the English had decided to make a fire-ship attack, and eight privately owned vessels, 'hell-burners', were prepared for this.

The attack came at night, causing panic. In the confusion the Spanish galleons cut their cables and headed out to sea. It was on the next day that the major battle was fought off Gravelines. It lasted nine hours and there were casualties on both sides. Two of Medina Sidonia's ships were sunk, and two more were driven onto the shoals. According to one biographer, Stebbing, Raleigh was among the 'many gallant captains', but there is no confirmation of this; if he had been there it would have been without authority. The wind was blowing stronger and visibility was poor. With the danger of yet more ships being driven onto the shoals, Medina Sidonia realized that it was impossible to wait for Parma. Up to this point he could leave with honour. The great Armada had fought and failed but had not been defeated. So he decided that there was no option but to sail towards Scotland, where there might be friendly help. The English, their ammunition nearly exhausted, followed for a while, but when the wind ferociously changed to gales they turned back; also a contagious disease was decimating the crews. The Spaniards were forced to continue round Scotland and the west coast of Ireland, with the well-known disastrous consequences. 'God [the Protestant God] blew with his winds and they were scattered.' The Catholic God had done his best with the contagious disease.

In all some two thirds of the Armada reached Spain, and some 11,000 Spanish lives had been lost. Fourteen ships, possibly even twenty-three, were wrecked. One was the *Santa Maria della Rosa*, a huge Basque merchantman, which was swept onto the great craggy flakes of rock off the Dingle Peninsula

– near Smerwick, adding to its terrible associations. Only one member of the crew reached the shore. Some artefacts from the wreck have been salvaged in recent years and are in Irish museums. Another ship, the *San Juan de Fernando Horra*, was also sunk off the Dingle Peninsula.

Two other Spanish warships, the *San Juan de Portugal* and the *San Juan Bautista*, nearly met the same fate. The former was commanded by Juan Martinez de Recalde, Vice-Admiral of the Armada and a veteran of high standing. There was irony in his having to face danger in this place, because it was he who had brought the flotilla carrying men and armaments to Smerwick in 1580. He knew the treacherous conditions only too well, how the Atlantic weather could change from calm to storm without warning. But he also knew that there was a broad stretch of sheltered water between Great Blasket Island and Beginish, and it was here that he guided the two ships to safety.

In the great epic of 1588 Raleigh's endeavours had never been put to the test, and he could not thus match the heroic reputations of Howard, Hawkins and Drake. The Spaniards, he wrote, in spite of their 'so great and terrible ostentation', did not 'in all their sailing round about England so much as sink or take one ship, bark, pinnace or cockboat of ours or even burned so much as one sheepcote of this land.'[8] He praised the magnanimity of Elizabeth in the aftermath of victory. While not denying that many shipwrecked Spaniards had been slaughtered by the Irish, whom they had expected to be friendly, there were some, he said, who were 'sent from village to village, coupled in halters to be shipped to England, where her Majesty, of her princely and invincible disposition, disdaining to put them to death, and scorning either to retain or entertain them, they were all sent back to their countries, to witness and recount the worthy and invisible achievements of their invincible and dreadful navy.'

The sarcasm was typical, but in fact it was also a backhanded compliment to himself, if we are to believe Stebbing, who tells us that several of the noble prisoners were committed to Raleigh's charge. Presumably these nobles were extracted from the miserable castaways reputed to have been mercilessly slaughtered by the Governor of Connaught, Sir Richard Bingham, and the Lord Deputy, Sir William Fitzwilliam. And according to Camden, some Spaniards were also 'slain by the Irish dwelling in the woods'.

There had been a plan to send Raleigh and Grenville to Ireland in case there should be some organized body of armed fugitives, but this was soon abandoned. Nevertheless there was still a fear that the Spaniards might attempt a landing in Ireland, in the hope of stirring up a revolt. So on 14 September, the Queen wrote to Grenville ordering him to make a stay of shipping along the north coasts of the south-west, and to be ready to transfer 700 men to Ireland, with the assistance of Raleigh.*

On the next day the Council wrote to Raleigh telling him to make sure that the hundred Cornishmen he was to supply were 'well chosen' and with good officers. (Had there been complaints in the last muster?) Three of the Queen's ships, the *Foresight*, the *Aid*, and the *Tyger*, would be at his disposal. Thus for much of the autumn Grenville and Raleigh were patrolling the stormy Irish Sea – not a pleasant experience for Raleigh, who always admitted that he was a bad sailor. When the crisis was considered to be over, both he and Grenville took the opportunity of visiting their lands across the water.

Raleigh's headquarters were still at Youghal, until such time as Lismore Castle was repaired. He also bought more houses at Youghal, one being Myrtle Grove, where traditionally he made his home. His duties as mayor would have been mainly carried out by his agent William Magner. Otherwise, the principal agents for the rest of his properties were Andrew Colthurst and Robert Mawle, who supervised arrangements for the arrival of settlers. Raleigh was too preoccupied with his Irish problems to be able to stand for Parliament in 1589.

Also on his mind were the poor abandoned settlers in Virginia.

* The fear of Spanish invasion brought out the 'hobby-horse' at Minehead in Somerset, and Padstow in Cornwall. This ancient May Day custom of the hobby-horse (a kind of pantomime horse decked with rags and ribbons and accompanied by melodeons and drums) dates back at least to the ninth century and was for scaring away Danes and evil spirits; it continues to this day. In 1588, to be on the safe side, Padstow also mobilized pikemen and musketeers.

Two Shepherds Meet
1589

In December 1588 Essex challenged Raleigh to a duel. He was just twenty-one, thirteen years younger than Raleigh, who by Elizabethan standards was already middle-aged. The reason for the quarrel is unknown, but jealousy would inevitably have been at the root of it. At this distance, if we have to take sides, it must be remembered that in Court circles Raleigh was still greatly disliked. Even so, it is not always easy now to appreciate Essex's aristocratic charm and ingenuousness that was so much admired by his contemporaries of every class. If Raleigh was supercilious, so was Essex. They were both prima donnas, but because of their intimacy with the Queen they were having to see too much of one another. On another occasion Essex had boxed Raleigh's ears, and the Council had to forbid a duel. To Londoners Essex already was a kind of hero. When he had accompanied the Queen on her white gelding to Tilbury in August 1588 – and she made that famous rousing speech: 'I know I have the body but of a weak and feeble woman, but I have the heart and stomach of a King' – he had been hailed by nobles, common people and soldiers as England's paladin *sans peur et sans reproche*, taking on the mantle of Sir Philip Sidney. For all that, he could be wilful, overbearing, rash and petty-minded.

Tilbury was also a confirmation of the worship that Elizabeth expected from her subjects. She was still the intangible goddess of everlasting beauty; for her, time had stood still. But a goddess can fall in love, and she was in love with this handsome, exhilarating, fiery young man, less than half her age. The old affection for Raleigh remained, but time had not stood still for him, and as a result he was more free to deal with his now myriad responsibilities. He was also rich, while Essex was in debt and desperately needing the benefits of royal patronage.

Elizabeth had given Essex his stepfather's apartments at Court, and in accordance with Leicester's wishes in his will she created him Knight of the Garter, the ribbon of which he was proud to display on his shapely leg. She also gave him the right to the customs on the import of sweet wines, which provided him with some income. She almost seemed determined to encourage his rivalry with Raleigh.

Raleigh was as enthusiastic a privateer as ever, and fetching in good profits. In February his *Roebuck* captured a Flemish ship, the *Angel Gabriel*, on her way to Cadiz. The owner brought a suit against him, but Raleigh was able to claim that either the man was a Spaniard in disguise or else he was guilty of trading with the enemy. Then two French ships were taken, and the Council was constrained to send Raleigh and his captains a warning that they must 'offer no further cause of grief to the subjects of the French King'.[1]

Commercial interest in Virginia was by no means dead. Hariot's *Brief and True Report*, published in 1588, remained an important document of propaganda and was to make Raleigh's name famous on the Continent, being translated into Latin, French and German. But Raleigh reckoned he had already spent £40,000 on the venture, and now there were further calls on his resources for his Irish estates. The delay must have been agonizing for White. So a company was formed, including White, Richard Hakluyt, Raleigh's nephew-in-law and manager William Sanderson, and nineteen others, giving them trading rights in Virginia over seven years, Raleigh retaining a fifth share of any gold or silver that might be discovered. He did, however, give £100 towards helping the settlers and for teaching Christianity to the native Indians.

Once again grand strategy intervened and this meant yet another postponement. The Spanish coasts were at present virtually undefended, and the crippled remnants of the Armada were being repaired and refurbished, mainly at Santander and Lisbon. Portugal had been occupied by Spain since 1581, in view of Philip II's perfectly legitimate claim to the throne; the Azores, being Portuguese, had been the last territory to hold out, and were now the vital staging point for ships from South America – in particular the island of Terceira where there was a virtually impregnable harbour. The pretender to the Portuguese throne, Dom Antonio, was still in England and had been friendly with Drake, convincing him that Portugal was seething with unrest and only waiting for his return to rise up and expel the hated Spaniards. This time the Queen was interested, though she still had her suspicions about Dom Antonio. In general but somewhat hazy terms the plan was to smash Philip's navy wherever possible, landing a force in Portugal that would bring in some pillage, and afterwards, almost more importantly, seize the treasure ships as soon as they reached the Azores.

Excitement grew, and with the prospect of good booty, Elizabeth invested £20,000 and supplied six ships 'of the second sort', two pinnaces and the captured ships the *Nuestra Señora del Rosario* and the *San Salvador*. Over £40,000 came from private adventurers, including Drake and 'Black John' Norris, who were to lead the expedition. Even Raleigh, in spite of his financial anxieties after Virginia, subscribed a sum and made ships available.

A chance seizure of some sixty Dutch flyboats on their way to France to collect salt increased the fleet to about 180 ships. Including 4,000 mariners, the total complement of men was about 23,000: a pretty rough collection, most of them, by all accounts, even including gaolbirds. There were grumbles about overcrowding and food shortages. Then, a week before the fleet sailed, there was more trouble with Essex. It seems that the Queen had given permission for Raleigh to take part in the expedition, but had said that Essex must stay behind. Indignant, and in his impulsive way, Essex left London in disguise, galloped off to Plymouth and boarded the *Swiftsure*, commanded by Sir Roger Williams, Norris's second-in-command; the ship then sailed on its own. The Queen was enraged and threatened Williams with execution. She also sent a ship in pursuit, but to no avail. Essex was determined to be the hero of this expedition, come what may; he also hoped for enough treasure to get him out of debt.

The assumption is that Raleigh did not go. If he did, he would have taken only an uncharacteristically minor role, and he would not have wanted that.

Drake and Norris, instead of sailing to Santander, wasted ten days attacking and pillaging La Coruña. They found the port almost empty, and the only loot to be had in the lower town, which they destroyed, was a certain quantity of wine, oil and dried foods. Some inhabitants were killed, and villages round about were set on fire, but it proved impossible to scale the well-fortified upper town. The whole episode was a humiliating failure.

The *Swiftsure*, after rounding Cape Finisterre and having explored to no avail some of the *rias*, or estuaries, of the gnarled and jagged Galician coast, joined them at Bayona. The Queen was already annoyed about La Coruña and would have been even more furious if she had known that Essex had meanwhile landed at Cangas opposite Vigo (only to find that all the locals had fled, taking their valuables with them). The Vigueses, the people of Vigo, were by now resigned to their great bay being a favourite target for English expeditionary forces.

Essex insisted that he must lead the landing party in Portugal. This turned out to be at Peniche, about fifty miles north of Lisbon. He marched as far as the outskirts of the city, without any signs whatever of a general uprising in favour of Dom Antonio. Worse, Drake had decided that it was too dangerous to sail up the river Tagus – if the winds failed he would be trapped. In any case soldiers were dying from some unspecified disease, and morale was low. So it was decided to sail for the Azores, in the hope at least of some small remuneration. But the winds were all wrong, and the sickness was worsening. So it was back to Vigo, and the usual story: a fierce bombardment, only to find on entering that the town was deserted. The surrounding countryside was laid waste, and the town torched, before they returned to face the displeasure of the Queen.

Raleigh was one of the few who did fairly well financially out of the affair. His ships had taken prizes off Portugal and Sir Roger Williams had lent men to bring them home. Sir Roger had thereupon claimed that the whole of the prizes should be his. The matter went to the Privy Council, which decided in favour of Raleigh, to whom Elizabeth, no doubt as a slap at Essex, now gave him a gold chain as a sign of appreciation and affection. But as usual Essex was soon forgiven, which was not to be the case with Norris and, especially, Drake, who was forced to rusticate for a long while. The English casualties had been enormous, perhaps 11,000, nearly all from the sickness. On top of that there was great resentment among the survivors when it was found that there was not enough money for them to be paid. Riots broke out in London, and some of the men took to highway robbery.

On 17 August, Sir Francis Allen wrote gleefully to Anthony Bacon, still in France, with a nice piece of gossip, namely that 'My Lord of Essex hath chased Mr. Raleigh from the Court, and hath confined him to Ireland.'[2]

Raleigh certainly was in Ireland by August, and he stayed there for some time, but it is barely conceivable that he would have allowed himself to be 'chased' by Essex. It is of course possible that he would have needed time to organize his estates, and as a result could have been granted leave of absence. Yet his 19th-century biographer Edwards does mention a 'passing cloud' between him and the Queen, and Naunton talks of Raleigh 'falling into a recess' and wisely deciding to leave the *terra infirma* of the Court. We can certainly sympathize with his wanting to have a rest from the snaps and snarls of fellow courtiers, if indeed that was only the reason for his departure – which does appear very unlikely.

During this time in Ireland in 1589 Raleigh developed a close friendship with the English poet Edmund Spenser who was in government service there, and as will be seen there are very definite suggestions in both *The Faerie Queene* and *Colin Clout's Come Home Again* that Raleigh confided in him about a rift with Elizabeth, and the agony of being rejected.

Love can also include desire. A clue to Raleigh's disgrace and his exile to Ireland may lie in a poem discovered in a collection of manuscripts belonging to Arthur Gorges. Possibly Gorges did make some corrections, but Raleigh's authorship seems pretty clear. If addressed to the Virgin Queen, as it surely must have been, it is not surprising that she was affronted by the poem's eroticism, and at being compared no longer to the celestial Diana, but to Danae and Leda of Greek mythology. Could it be that Raleigh had written it after Elizabeth had seemed to give him encouragement at some indiscreet moment, an encouragement which she afterwards regretted? Or was it a gamble on his part, an attempt to show that his desire for her was something with which Essex could not possibly compete?

> Would I were chang'd into that golden shower
> That so divinely streamèd from the skies
> To fall in drops upon my dainty flower,
> Where in her bed she solitary lies;
>   There would I hope such shower as richly shine
>   Would pierce more deep than those waste tears of mine.
>
> Else would I were that plumèd swan, snow white,
> Under whose form was hidden heavenly power;
> Then in that river would I most delight
> Whose waves do beat against her stately bower,
> And in those banks so tune my dying song
> That her deaf ears would think my plaints too long . . .

Walter Oakeshott has pointed out that the poem appears in Gorges's collection immediately before his own sonnet in praise of Elizabeth's chastity:[3]

> . . . A mind reposed whence the vain fancies rise;
> Desires that tend unto the heavenly throne
> The world beloved whom love cannot surprise . . .

This, Oakeshott says, is as if Gorges were saying 'Here is Raleigh's disastrous poem, and here mine which smoothed things down.' He also points out that in *The Faerie Queene* Spenser actually (deliberately?) introduced the phrase 'golden shower' when referring to the poems addressed by Raleigh to Elizabeth:

> . . . the streams that, like a golden shower
> Flow from thy fruitful head, of thy love's praise . . .

A draft written by Elizabeth in June 1589 does appear to underline the seriousness of her displeasure, if not rage. It is addressed to the Lord Deputy Sir William Fitzwilliam, and in it she decrees that Raleigh should surrender his 42,000 acres and revert to a single seignory of 12,000 acres, bringing him into line with all other Undertakers in Ireland. But this drastic letter was not sent. One fact, however, remained constant: the friction between Raleigh and Fitzwilliam, which was to develop into real enmity.

In the previous month Raleigh had produced what should have been regarded as a satisfactory report, listing 144 men, including craftsmen, who had settled on his Irish estates, about half of them bringing their families. These were mainly from the south-west of England. But there were also some 'old English' (Anglo-Irish) tenants, and even some purely Irish ones. Ploughs and cattle had been brought over. Thus he was half way towards completing his contract for settling 320 families. Among his tenants then and in future were several people who had been connected with his and Humphrey Gilbert's New World enterprises, including Thomas Hariot who was established at Molana Abbey – a sublimely beautiful spot, on an island near Ballinatra with dense woods around (though Hariot does not seem to have spent much time at it). John White also was given land, and settled there after 1590.

By May 1589 Grenville had brought over ninety-nine settlers, many from his family circle (though they too may not have spent much time there), such as his future son-in-law Christopher Harris. Warham St Leger had brought over forty-six settlers. Both had introduced English cattle.

Raleigh also formed a partnership for exporting timber, to be made into pipe- and hogshead-staves for vineyards in the Canaries and Madeira. These were floated down the Blackwater river and loaded on to ships at Youghal. He also explored the potentialities of fisheries off Youghal, and experimented with growing hops. Later iron ore was discovered, so mills were set up at Mogeely. Thus in two years, as David Quinn has pointed out, Raleigh achieved in Ireland what had been hoped for by White's Virginia colonists in 1587. Some of this may have decided Elizabeth not to send that angry letter after all.

Raleigh obviously became attached to the walled town of Youghal, and especially to the house known as Myrtle Grove. Within the town there is not much left from his day, apart from Tynte's Castle and, possibly, a clothes shop that bears the brave insignia 'established 1580'. He is also now commemorated by a Walter Raleigh Hotel.

On 14 March 1587 he had been allotted 'four messuages or tofts in the town of Youghal, with the patronage or gift of the wardenship of Our

Lady's College of the same.'[4] It has been assumed that Myrtle Grove was the warden's house, but there are arguments against this. Maybe it was one of the tofts. The house has been altered over the centuries, but still has an Elizabethan appearance, with three front gables and tall chimneys. Here Raleigh is supposed to have planted Ireland's first potatoes, and even to have tried to grow tobacco. Myrtle Grove is also another of the contenders for the place where Raleigh was dowsed with a bucket of water or a tankard of ale when smoking in the porch.* The myrtles have gone; but the great yews, needless to say, are supposed to have been planted by Raleigh; and there are arbutus bushes also associated with him. Somewhere in Youghal there are affane cherries, reckoned to be descended from trees brought from the Canaries. Raleigh is also said to have introduced a sweet-smelling yellow wallflower from the Azores.

Close by Myrtle Grove is St Mary's Collegiate church, 13th century, where lie Richard Boyle, the great Earl of Cork, to whom Raleigh eventually sold his Irish estates, and the Countess of Desmond, who died in 1604 allegedly aged 140, after falling from an apple tree. High above the church are the fragmented remains of the medieval walls that once encircled Youghal.

Raleigh could well have been the first to grow potatoes in Ireland. Hariot in his *Report* had described 'openhauks' as being 'roots of round form, some of the bigness of walnuts, some far greater' – and very likely it was he who brought tubers back for Raleigh. In fairness it must be said that other candidates for bringing back potatoes to England were John Hawkins and Francis Drake.

Both Hawkins and Drake have also been credited with bringing back tobacco plants, 'uppowoc' in the *Report* – 'the Spaniards generally call it Tobacco'. Hariot described how when the leaves were dried and powdered the Indians set the result alight and smoked it in pipes. Certainly Raleigh was responsible for making tobacco smoking fashionable in England, which happened very rapidly. He even, it was said, in happier days made the Queen take a puff from his silver pipe, but she said it gave her nausea. Nevertheless she did force the Countess of Nottingham and her Maids to give it a try.[5] (The most common form of pipe, in the early stages, was a straw attached to a walnut shell.)

---

* Successive owners of South Wraxall Manor in Wiltshire, the house owned by Raleigh's friend Sir Walter Long, have always been convinced that they have this honour, and the story still sticks at Hayes Barton. A piece of Devon folklore concerns a rock in the river Dart below Greenway. This is pointed out to tourists as the spot 'where Sir Walter Raleigh first smoked tobacco'. (When the tide was low?)

Raleigh also at that time made a bet with Elizabeth that he could weigh tobacco smoke, and won it by subtracting the weight of the ash from the original tobacco leaves. Elizabeth retaliated by saying that she had heard of many who had turned gold into smoke, but that he was the first to turn smoke into gold.

There may not have been gold mines for the settlers in Virginia, but in the long run its tobacco was to be almost more profitable. At first tobacco was regarded, as Hariot had suggested, as medicinal, but it soon became widely popular. In England the best known tobacco plantation was at Winchcombe in the Cotswolds. In France it was known as *nicotiana*, after Jean Nicot, the French ambassador to Portugal who sent seeds to France in 1559–61. The Old Queen's Head in Islington, where Raleigh may or may not have lived, became known as the smokers' tavern.

Harington was inspired to write another Paulus epigram:

> I see it clearly
> Why Paulus takes Tobacco, buys it dearly,
> At Tippling-houses, where he eats and drinks
> That every room straight of Tobacco stinks.
>
> He swears 'tis salve for all diseases bred,
> It strengthens one's weak back, comforts the head,
> Dulls much flesh-appetite, 'tis cordial durable
> It cures that ill which some thought incurable.

On the first floor of Myrtle Grove there is some fine wainscoting of dark oak, and in the main room over the fireplace are carved mermaids blowing trumpets. Both of these would have been there in Raleigh's time. Sir John Pope Hennessy inhabited the house in the 1880s and wrote a cynical monograph about Raleigh. There is a curious passage at the beginning of the book, possibly a fantasy though it has been claimed to be true, in which it appears that there were still relics of Raleigh in the study: an oak chest, deeds with his seal, vellum-bound books.*[6]

According to Stebbing, Pope Hennessy had found remnants of a 'monastic library' in a recess behind the wainscot of Raleigh's bedroom, and one book

---

* After Pope Hennessy's death his books were sold at Sotheby's. In the Raleigh Collection at the University of North Carolinia at Chapel Hill there is a book entitled *De Naturae Philosophia seu de Platonis et Aristotelis Consensione Liber* by Sebastiani Foxi Marzilli and published in 1560. It came from that sale at Sotheby's and has a bookplate 'Sir Walter's Study'. This is certainly very much the type of book that Raleigh would have been likely to possess.

was Peter Comestor's *Scholastica Historia*, which is quoted in the *History of the World*.

The view over the churchyard wall of the house, somewhat dank and overgrown with ivy, is a little melancholy, and Raleigh was certainly in a melancholy mood when he arrived there in the summer of 1589. Dating his poems is a notorious problem, but there is one which is usually assumed to be connected with this period of his retreat. It is among his best and deserves to be quoted in full. He called it 'Farewell to Court'.

Like truthless dreams, so are my joys expired,
And past return are all my dandled days;
My love misled, and fancy quite retired,
Of all which past, the sorrow only stays.

My lost delights now clean from sight of land,*
Have left me all alone in unknown ways;
My mind to woe, my life in fortune's hand
Of all which past the sorrow only stays.

As in a country strange without companion,
I only wail the wrong of death's delays,
Whose sweet spring spent, whose summer well nigh done,
Of all which past, the sorrow only stays.
   Whom care forewarns, ere age and winter cold
   To haste me hence, to find my fortune's fold.

It has also been suggested that the popular poem 'Like to a hermit poor'†
could have been written at Myrtle Grove.

No doubt Raleigh paid various visits to Ireland over the years that are not recorded in documents that survive. They would only have been brief, and he did not stay long at Youghal in 1589. It was in September that he went to see Spenser at Kilcolman, further inland on an adjoining estate. By the end of the month he was at Lismore with his cousin Sir George Carew, Master of Ordnance in Ireland, in order to discuss repairs. In Carew's presence he granted his 'servant' Robert Maple the stewardship of the castle and grounds, and very shortly afterwards departed for England, taking Spenser with him.

In spite of his great show of unrequited love, Raleigh also needed consolation. And this he did find, as has at last been revealed in an appendix to

---

* This line could mean that he wrote the poem while crossing the Irish sea.   † p. 117.

his collected letters recently published and edited by Joyce Youings and the late Agnes Latham.

There had long been speculations among historians as to whether or not Raleigh had an illegitimate daughter, on account of a reference in what he thought could have been his farewell letter to his wife, on 27 July 1603. In this he begged her to be 'charitable' to his 'poor daughter' and to teach her son to 'love her for his father's sake'. That was all that was known about this mysterious girl, until in 1971 Raleigh's will, signed on 10 July 1597, was discovered at Sherborne Castle, Dorset. In this we read of 'my reputed daughter begotten on the body of Alice Goold, now in Ireland.' She was to get 500 marks out of the sale of his ship the *Roebuck*. It was thereupon assumed by biographers that the affair would have taken place when Raleigh was first in Ireland in 1580–1, which was obviously not the case. Searches were made for possible Alice Goolds, Golds or Goulds, but without much success.

Then a letter was found, as a transcript only, among Miss Latham's papers, with a note saying that it originated from a book or booklet published by J. P. Collier, who was a notorious Victorian forger. However, as Professor Youings is inclined to agree, there are details which make clear that it was *not* a forgery.[7]

It was addressed to 'Master Gould' and dated 10 October 1589. This Gould was James Gould of Cork, the Attorney-General of Munster. Not only was he an Undertaker but he had been commissioned by the Crown to make a survey of some of the Earl of Desmond's lands. Raleigh was certainly back in England by that date. The letter ran:

I have it from my cousin Sir George Carew that you have harkened to a malicious knave, Nebucodunozer Jewell, who saith that I have been too forward with your daughter. He is one of my undertakers, a fellow that oweth me much, and this he saith, I know not for what reason, but it is false and I pray you to suppress it as much as you are able, for your sake and for your daughter's, a gentlewoman I swear before the living God whom I have ever held in true honour and respect.

If you desire a lease of Castle [illegible word] in my seignory as I have heard you would, I will have the papers drawn for you this Michaelmas. I have written to my Lord Deputy [Fitzwilliam] for your suit against Donogh McCormac and the others and will put an end to their cavillations. I come not into Ireland, for my nearness to Her Majesty makes me much business here. I pray you look not for me.

Your friend as I shall find you W. Ralegh

From the Court this 10th day of October.

Commend me to the gentlewoman your daughter.

'Nearness to Her Majesty' meant that Raleigh was busy patching up the summer's tiff with Elizabeth. In any case he was lying, and Judge Gould's daughter was to be delivered of a girl. 'Now in Ireland' in the will could have referred to the daughter, not the mother, for if Alice Gould or Goold were still alive in 1597 she had remained remarkably discreet. The existence of an illegitimate child would have been a choice bit of scandal for the Court. So did Alice die in childbirth, or soon after? At any rate the lease of the castle and help over McCormac may have helped to quieten the Judge.

When, later in his career, Raleigh became Governor of the Channel Island of Jersey, it was recorded in the journal of Elie Bevint of Sark that Raleigh had married off his daughter to a wellborn young man, his ward and page, Daniel Dumaresq, son of the Seigneur de Saumarez. There is no record of children, but according to the journal she died 'in London or Kingston', of the plague. It is also said that Dumaresq disowned the marriage after her death.

Raleigh's visit to Edmund Spenser appears to have been unexpected. Spenser's estate was small compared to most other Undertakers', about 3000 acres. He and Raleigh would have met when Spenser was secretary to Lord Grey, the Lord Deputy of Ireland, perhaps even at Smerwick, but up to now their acquaintanceship was slight. Raleigh had obviously admired Spenser's *Shepheardes Calendar* published in 1579 and dedicated to Philip Sidney. Recently Spenser had also written *Astrophel*, a lament on the death of Sidney. Raleigh for his part needed some kindred mind on whom to unburden himself.

Spenser was living in Kilcolman Castle, or nearby. Only the lower floor of the castle remains, although there is a staircase up the tower. Originally there were three rooms. The land slopes down to a small lake and nearby is a forest park. Across the fields there is a view of the Ballyhoura hills, to which the dispossessed tribesmen had been driven and from which in due course they would return, with terrible consequences for Spenser. He was writing *The Faerie Queene* which he had begun under Sidney's patronage. Apart from the annoyance of a 'choir of frogs' the beautiful Irish landscape gave him inspiration for his long allegorical poem. Nevertheless his reputation in Ireland is somewhat equivocal, mainly because of his defence of Grey whom he accompanied on many of his ruthless expeditions.

Spenser was born in 1552. Aubrey described him as 'a little man, wore short hair, little band and little cuffs'. The meeting with Raleigh was the start of a great literary friendship, and is described by Spenser in his typically Arcadian style in *Colin Clout's Come Home Again*.

One day . . . I sat (as was my trade)
Under the foot of Mole, that mountain hoar,
Keeping my sheep amongst the cooling shade
Of the green alders by Mulla's shore.
There a strange shepherd chanced to find me out,
Whether allured with my pipe's delight,
Whose pleasing sound yshrillèd far about,
Or thither led by chance, I know not right.
Whom when I asked from what place he came
And how he hight, himself he did yclepe
The Shepherd of the Ocean by name
And said he came from the main-sea deep.

If the phrase 'Shepherd of the Ocean' was not Raleigh's invention he delighted in it, and seized on it – the reference being derived from the Queen's nickname for him, 'Water'. Evidently he had set out to flatter Spenser:

He, sitting beside me in that same shade,
Provok'd me to play some pleasant fit;
And when he heard the music which I made
He found himself full greatly pleased with it.

But Raleigh had another reason for wanting to meet Spenser. He had verses of his own on which he needed an opinion, and he lost no time in unburdening himself about the Queen's coolness towards him.

His song was all a lamentable lay
Of great unkindness and of usage hard,
Of Cynthia, the Lady of the Sea,
Which from her presence faultless him debarred,
And ever and anon, with singults [sighs] rife,
He crièd out, to make his undersong;
'Ah, my love's queen and goddess of my life!
Who shall me pity, when thou dost me wrong?'

It is possible that Raleigh was meditating or had even begun his own huge poem, designed to be in twelve parts, in honour of the Queen, and of which only a fragment in draft remains – and this written two or three years later. Perhaps because of *Colin Clout* he decided to call the poem *The Book of the Ocean to Cynthia*. At any rate when Spenser read whatever Raleigh had written he said that it lulled his senses 'in slumber of delight' (which could, surely, be double-edged?).

When Raleigh read part of *The Faerie Queene*, an Arthurian allegory, at Kilcolman, he had no doubt that it was a masterpiece and insisted that Spenser should accompany him to England and present it to the Queen. The first three books were published together, the third being completed in England, probably at Durham House, and introducing not only Elizabeth, this time under the name of Belphoebe, but Raleigh whom Spenser called Timias, a squire.

The fact that Timias was a squire and not a knight was a subtle point, obviously a reference to Raleigh's social handicap at Court when compared to grandees like Essex, Leicester and Oxford. As a 'meek and lowly' squire he could not aspire to win the love of someone 'heavenly born' (though 'meek' one might think was hardly a word to apply to Raleigh). In the poem he has been badly wounded, and Belphoebe takes pity, using costly cordials to cure him, including the 'divine tobacco'.

The Faerie Queene was dedicated to Elizabeth, and the work was preceded by a long preamble. First, in the form of a letter and addressed in quaint spelling to 'The Right noble, and Valorous Sir Walter Raleigh, knight, Lo. Wardern of the Stannerys, and her Maiesties Liefetenant of the County of Cornwyll', there is an explanation of the allegory, linking Spenser's Belphoebe to Raleigh's 'excellent conceit' of Cynthia – Phoebe, Cynthia being yet another alternative name for Diana. Then came 'Verses addressed to the Author' written by his admirers, the first of which is by Raleigh himself and one of his most admired sonnets:

> Methought I saw the grave where Laura lay
> Within that temple where the vestal flame
> Was wont to burn; and passing by that way
> To see the buried dust of living fame,
> Whose tomb fair love, and fairer virtue kept,
> All suddenly I saw the Fairy Queen:
> At whose approach the soul of Petrarch wept
> And from henceforth those graces were not seen;
> For they this Queen attended, in whose stead
> Oblivion laid him down on Laura's hearse.
> Hereat the hardest stones were seen to bleed
> And groans of buried ghosts the heavens did pierce:
>> Where Homer's spright did tremble all for grief
>> And cursed the access of that celestial thief.

Another poem is by 'Hobynoll', alias Gabriel Harvey,* urging Spenser in effect to cherish his Muse and not to be spoiled by 'envy and disdain' in the grand world (the Court) which he was about to enter. Raleigh's humour in his poetry, such as it is, is usually sardonic, but in the case of his sonnet it has been suggested unfairly that he was writing tongue in cheek. Petrarch's love for Laura was the great model for Renaissance poets, and Homer was held the greatest poet of all – hence Raleigh's device of Homer's ghost trembling at the appearance of this new rival.

Next in the book is a service of dedicatory sonnets by Spenser addressed to the most powerful individuals in the land, such as Burghley, Walsingham, Oxford, Hatton, Essex, Lord Grey of Wilton, Sir John Norris, Ormond. But to Raleigh there was the best poem of all, and the compliment is returned:

> To thee, that art the summer's Nightingale
> Thy sovereign Goddess's most dear delight
> Why do I send this rustic Madrigal
> That may thy tuneful ear unseason quote . . .

The second line makes it clear that Raleigh had been forgiven by his 'Goddess' (one wonders what Oxford and Essex thought about this poem).

In the parlance of 21st-century publishing *The Faerie Queene* was therefore well packaged; and it worked, for Spenser was indeed immediately recognized as a major poet. Cynthia was generous and granted him a pension of £50 a year, to the dismay of Lord Treasurer Burghley ('All this for a song?'). The book had done his friend Raleigh a service too.

But life at Court and the emptiness of worldly success soon began to pall on Spenser. He had hoped for some official advancement, and now he saw the corrupting influence of power and wealth. In spite of the miseries and dangers in Ireland, he returned in 1591, in some ways reluctantly, to his 'exile' at Kilcolman and his 'pastoral' life. *Colin Clout* was not published until 1595. Hobynoll reappears in the poem, relieved that Colin the shepherd has heeded his warnings, but nevertheless alarmed by his bitterness over the artificiality of Cynthia's court (needless to say without casting aspersions on Cynthia herself who had been so generous to him – 'her words were like a stream of honey . . . her deeds were like great clusters of rich grapes').

By the time *Colin Clout* appeared Raleigh had fallen into much deeper

---

* Academic Cambridge poet and Spenser's mentor, in spite of having once advised him not to continue with *The Faerie Queene*.

disgrace with Elizabeth, and had every reason himself to feel thwarted by the insincerity and fickleness of Court. All this must have been discussed with Spenser. Nevertheless Hobynoll was at pains to tell Colin that there were plenty of persons at Court who were of 'rightworthy parts' and 'spotless honesty'. Yet it was also true, as Spenser said:

> . . . either they be puffed up with pride
> or fraught with envy that their galls do swell,
> Or they their days in idleness divide,
> Or drownèd lie in pleasures wasteful well,
> In which like Moldwarps [moles] nousling still they lurk,
> Unmindful of chief parts of manliness.

Perhaps he was thinking of Lord Oxford.

But Spenser had fallen in love, and this was to make his life, and the simpler surroundings of Kilcolman, much easier – or so he hoped. The lady was Elizabeth Boyle, celebrated in his *Amoretti* sonnets and with family connections with the future Earl of Cork.

The Lost Colonists
1590

On 12 November 1589 Raleigh had written an ingratiating letter from London to Sir William Fitzwilliam in Ireland, recommending his cousin Sir George Carew* to the Irish Council, signing himself 'Your lordship's assured loving kinsman to command W R'. Such overtures were not to last. Carew wrote back to Raleigh with disturbing news and warnings of Fitzwilliam's continued hostility: 'Old English' and Irish landowners were returning to put in claims for properties that had been allocated to Undertakers, and a number of lawsuits were looming which would affect Raleigh. Evidently in Ireland it was still assumed that he was in the Queen's disfavour, and that advantages could now be seized.

Raleigh wrote back angrily on 28 December: 'If in Ireland they think I am not worth the respecting they shall much deceive themselves.' He was ready to do battle with anyone, including Fitzwilliam. The letter makes it clear that he was back in 'nearness' to the Queen; and indeed he was again fulfilling his duties as Captain of the Guard.

In the same letter he raised the subject of Lismore and the restoration of the Castle. His lease from the Bishop was being challenged. This certainly was on an exceedingly flimsy excuse, and an order was soon obtained from the Queen dismissing such 'cavillations'. Nothing more was heard of the suit, and the lease remained Raleigh's.

It turned out that he was never able to finish the alterations to Lismore Castle. As so often in his life competing preoccupations arose, involving huge expenses. Indeed there is little now left of the castle he knew, apart from a round tower and the outer gatehouse, known as the Riding House. The dimensions of the great courtyard must however be as they were then, and it would have been surrounded by cottages and stables, since of course disappeared.†

---

* Carew was the brother of Sir Peter Carew who was killed in Ireland in 1579. In the time of James I he became Lord Carew of Totnes.

† Lismore Castle was entirely rebuilt by the 6th Duke of Devonshire, the 'Bachelor Duke', using dressing stone from Derbyshire. Work began in 1811 with William Atkinson as architect. The

Fitzwilliam was to be impressed by Carew, who was duly appointed to the Council in Dublin. This did not stop him from harrying Raleigh on other matters, which were difficult for Raleigh to combat when he fell into yet deeper disgrace with Elizabeth in 1592. At the end of that year Raleigh sent a list of complaints to Robert Cecil. For instance, Fitzwilliam was demanding rents of £400 when Raleigh claimed that only £33 6s 8d was due. He had also forced Raleigh's agents to relinquish a castle that had been rebuilt at considerable expense. Raleigh even claimed that he had to withdraw some of his settlers because he had not been allowed troops to defend them from Irish guerrillas.

Far more worrying for Raleigh was a matter arising from his exporting of staves, which had been a very successful business – 340,000 were claimed to have been sent to the Canaries and Madeira in one year. Suddenly Fitzwilliam ordered that there should be no more exporting of staves.[1] The charges were that some of these had gone to the Spanish mainland, and that planking for ships had also been included in the cargoes. Then there was the highly dangerous charge that Raleigh's agent for the staves was being used as a channel of communication for Catholic refugees and recusants in Ireland and England. Fitzwilliam was also (rightly) worried by the reduction of forests around Mogeely, the main centre of the enterprise. Two years were to pass before exports to the islands could be resumed.

It was not surprising, now that Raleigh was back and active in London, that John White should once more agitate for the relief of the benighted colonists in Virginia. Because of a renewed possibility of a Spanish naval attack, the Privy Council on 1 February 1590 once more put a ban on all ships leaving English ports. As a result three ships belonging to Alderman John Watts, all set for a major privateering expedition to the Caribbean, had been held up in the Thames.

This John Watts, later a Lord Mayor of London, was a crafty operator and has been described as the greatest privateering promoter of his time:[2] Raleigh occasionally was in partnership with him. White now had the idea of getting Raleigh to approach the Queen for a licence to free these three ships, on condition that they called at Virginia, taking White with them, as well as stores, weapons and additional settlers.

The Spanish threat was a false alarm. Even before Drake's unsuccessful

designing of interiors and of furniture was largely undertaken by Pugin, the most splendid room being the banqueting hall. Joseph Paxton, who as a young man worked as the Duke's under-gardener, added to the south and east wings.

raid on Galicia and Portugal a new and modernized Spanish high seas fleet was on order. The galleons would be more manoeuverable, on the English model, with twenty-two guns broadside capable of firing both long distance and short range. At present twelve were being built, known as the 'Twelve Apostles', and nine more were to be on the Portuguese model: all to be ready for service in 1591. In addition there would be *gallizebras*, small fast-moving vessels heavily armed. Maybe the Privy Council's alarm in 1590 had been caused by a spy's report that Philip II was for a while contemplating the seizure of the Isle of Wight.

But Spain was far more preoccupied at this period with dangers from France, following the murders first of Philip's protégé the Duke of Guise and then of the King, Henri III. In July the Duke of Parma invaded France from the Netherlands and advanced on Paris.

Elizabeth approved White's suggestion about releasing the three ships, and on Raleigh's behalf William Sanderson managed to obtain a bond of £5,000 from Watts towards the venture.[3] Why, it could be asked, had nothing more been done about sending relief to Virginia in 1589, at what must have been a time of tremendous urgency for the colonists? That tripartite agreement arranged with respected and wealthy traders in May had not resulted in any action. It is all a mystery. Was it to do with Raleigh's sudden disgrace, and the consequent impossibility of getting the Queen's sanction?

By the end of February the ships were ready to leave for Plymouth and on to the Caribbean, but the crews were so eager to get on with privateering that they now refused to take on any supplies or settlers for Virginia. The three ships were the *Hopewell*, 140–160 tons, with Abraham Cocks captain, the *Little John* 100–120 tons, and the *John Evangelist*, a pinnace. Sanderson persuaded Watts to allow his own ship, the *Moonlight*, Edmond Spicer captain, to join them, presumably with some supplies on board – but it does not seem likely that Raleigh had any investment on this occasion. By the time the *Moonlight* had reached Plymouth, the others had left, taking White with them.

The *Moonlight* was delayed, because of a decision to join forces with the *Conclude*, a pinnace, and they did not catch up with the rest until 2 July off Hispaniola. White must have been in despair as the ships he was with rushed hither and thither looking for prizes, from Santo Domingo to Puerto Rico and back. All five ships were present off Jamaica when the *Buen Jesus* of Seville, 300–350 tons, was captured. The captain and owner was Vice-Admiral of the Spanish squadron, and thus worth a goodly ransom. Precisely which of the English ships were the most involved became later a matter of dispute, affecting the amount of plunder claimed by the various crews. Full of encouragement, the *Little John* and *John Evangelist* tackled a much larger galleon, the *Nuestra Señora del Rosario*, which sank with all its cargo, apart from some sacks of cochineal. In the fight the captain of the *Little John*, Christopher Newport, lost an arm and four men were killed.

The hurricane season was approaching, so it was decided that the *Hopewell* and *Moonlight* should sail for Virginia. What had happened to the *Conclude* at this stage is obscure, because only the *Little John* and the *John Evangelist* set out for the Azores and then for England, taking the *Buen Jesus* with them.

The Carolina Banks, as the line of islands are now known, were reached on the 3 August, in stormy weather. It was not until the 15th that the ships were able to anchor three leagues from the harbour of Port Ferdinando. The first view was encouraging, for smoke was sighted near where the old colony had been on Roanoke island. After a night full of anticipation, White with Captains Cock and Spicer set off, every now and then firing shots in the hope that they would be heard on shore. Then they saw more smoke, further south and closer to hand, on the dunes. White in his *Narrative*, based on his diary, wrote:[4]

We therefore thought good to go to that second smoke first. But it was much further from the harbour where we landed than we supposed it to be, so that we were very sore tired when we came to the smoke. But that which grieved us more was that when we came to the smoke we found no man nor sign that any had been there lately, nor yet any fresh water in all this way to drink. Being thus wearied with this journey we returned to the harbour where we left our boats.

On the 17th the bad weather returned. Fresh water was badly needed, and this was at last found, though it had meant a delay. A party set off once more. Captain Cocks's boat, carrying White, managed to get safely over the bar, but a great wave broke over the other. White continued in his matter of fact style.

The men kept [to] the boat, some in it and some hanging on it: but the next sea set the boat on ground, where it beat so, that some of them were forced to let go their hold, hoping to wade ashore. But the sea still beat them down, so that they could neither stand nor swim. The boat twice or thrice was turned keel upward; whereupon Captain Spicer and Skinner [his mate] hung until they sunk and [were] seen no more.

Five others were drowned. It took some persuading to get the rest of the party to continue to Roanoke, and by the time they reached the island darkness was descending and they could not attempt a landing. Then once more they saw through the trees the light of a fire, which they felt must be a signal from the colonists, as it was from the northern end of the island. 'We let fall our grapnel near the shore and sounded with a trumpet a call, and afterwards many familiar English tunes of songs, and called to them friendly. But we had no answer.' When dawn came they made their way to where the light had been, but once more they were disappointed, for 'coming to the fire, we found the grass and sundry rotten trees burning about the place'. Evidently it was the result of lightning during a thunderstorm, as they now had to assume had been the case with the other fire. Again no sign of life.

They walked on to where the settlers had been. In the sand they saw the fresh imprints of Indian feet, 'trodden that night'. So they must have been under observation. They climbed the scrubby dune, 'upon a tree in the very brow thereof were curiously carved these fair Roman letters CRO. Which letters presently we knew to signify the place, where I should find the planters seated, according to a secret token agreed upon between them and me at my last departure from them, which was that in any ways they should not fail to write or carve on the trees or posts of the doors the name of the place where they should be seated.' The settlers had indicated to White that they might move to a place fifty miles inland, and had promised to leave signs showing where they had gone. It had been agreed that if there had been any distress or trouble, they would carve a Maltese cross. There was no cross, but the name was unfinished. Could that be a bad omen?

Having well considered of this, we passed toward the place where they were left in sundry houses. But we found the houses taken down, and the place very strongly enclosed with a high palisade of great trees, with curtains and flankers very fortlike. And one of the chief trees or posts at the right side of the entrance had the bark taken off, and five foot from the ground in fair capital letters was graven CROATOAN without any cross or sign of distress.

Inside the palisade they found some iron bars, pigs of lead, four cannon, some shot 'and such like heavy things, thrown here and there, almost overgrown with grass and weeds'; all of it material that would have been too heavy to carry. And Croatoan was not on the mainland. White and Cocks went to the creek, but could find no sign of boats. On their return the sailors told them that five chests had been found, which had been hidden in a trench and had evidently been unearthed by Indians a long while back and the contents scattered – this trench had originally been dug by Captain Amadas in 1585, evidently as part of the defences. Three of the chests had belonged to White: 'About the place many of my things spoiled and broken, and my books torn from the covers, the frames of some of my pictures and maps rotten and spoiled with rain, and my armour almost eaten through with rust.'

He realized that the Indians must have watched the departure of the colonists and had then rushed in to dig up anything that might have been hidden. In spite of his distress over the loss of his possessions, the wretched man felt that there was still hope of survivors at Croatoan, 'which is the place where Manteo was born, and the savages of the island our friends'. The weather was getting worse, so they had to hurry to get back to the ships.

It was a 'foul and stormy' night. Even so, an attempt was made to continue with the search, but it was not possible. A cable broke and two anchors were lost, 'and the weather grew to be fouler and fouler, our victuals scarce, and our cask and fresh water lost'. It was suggested that they might winter in the Caribbean, at Trinidad perhaps, and then return for a further search. The idea did not appeal to the new captain of the *Moonlight*, which was already leaking, and he insisted on returning home. The *Hopewell* therefore set course alone for Trinidad, but the winds blew so strongly that it was decided to run for the Azores, which they reached on 20 September. Off the island of Flores they found Sir John Hawkins and the Queen's fleet lying in wait for the Spanish treasure ships (but they had arrived too late). It took another three weeks to reach England, and on 24 October they came 'in safety, God be thanked, to anchor at Plymouth'. The other four ships had by then also reached England, but at different times.

The squabbles over the spoils of the *Buen Jesus* began at once. The cargo had been valued at £5,806 10s 4d, and after the Queen's customs duty and the percentage to Lord High Admiral Howard, some £3,300 would be due to Watts and the investors. There was a libel case, and Watts attacked Sanderson, claiming that the *Moonlight* and the *Conclude* had no active part in the taking of the *Buen Jesus*. It is possible that some private offer was made to Sanderson, who lost the case. Raleigh was nevertheless quite prepared to join Watts' privateering syndicate in 1591. There were some worthwhile prizes, but so many investors meant a small return for each. As Raleigh commented: 'We might have gotten more to have sent them fishing'.[5] Nevertheless it by no means deflected him from further privateering expeditions, which continued until the end of Elizabeth's reign.

White retired to Ireland, and his last documentary appearance is in a letter written to Hakluyt from his house at Newtown in County Cork, on 4 February 1593. Hakluyt had asked him for a report on what White said had been his fifth voyage to Virginia, to appear in the third Volume of the *Principal Navigations*, eventually published in 1600. White wrote his report, accompanying it with a scornful letter about the behaviour of the crews of John Watts' ships, who had ignored the plight of their fellow countrymen in Virginia and had instead been obsessed by chasing after 'prizes and spoils'. He had finally given up hope, he said, and had decided to be content with his present lot, 'thus committing the relief of my discomfortable company, the planters in Virginia, to the merciful help of the Almighty, whom I most humbly beseech to help and comfort them, according to his most holy will and their good desire.'

The behaviour of Watts' men had indeed been unforgivable, but we must also regrettably come to the conclusion that White was a better artist and cartographer than he was a leader of men.

The fate of the lost colonists of Virginia is one of the abiding and haunting mysteries. None of them were seen again by white men after John White's departure in 1587. Courage, privation, horror all lie unrecorded and can only be imagined. There is, however, strong evidence (though not accepted by all North Carolinans) that at least some of them migrated to near Cape Henry at the north of Chesapeake Bay. It had after all been the original plan that the 'Cittie of Raleigh' should be somewhere there, and it would have made sense to have aimed for the area visited by Hariot and White, so glowingly described. There is a possibility that a Captain William Irish landed near Chesapeake Bay in 1587 and found not only traces of cattle (which the Indians did not possess) but a stray mule. The theory is that a group of the colonists intermingled with and perhaps married local people, for the whole of the Indian hinterland was far more thickly populated than originally realized.[6]

There is also a belief that these colonists, and the Indians they were living with, were massacred by the Algonquin chief Powhatan in 1607, a few days before the arrival of Christopher Newport of the Virginia Company, that resulted in the first permanent settlement at Jamestown. Seven of the colonists are said to have escaped and taken refuge with the Chowan tribe, who enslaved them. The main authority for this story is William Strachey in his *Historie of Travell into Virginia Britania*; he was secretary to the Jamestown colony in 1610. In 1623 Samuel Purchas also wrote that Powhatan had confessed to the massacre to Captain John Smith, when he captured him in December 1607.

The Indians inland from Chesapeake Bay were more warlike than those further south. Powhatan, David Quinn considers, could have been first alerted to danger from these white foreigners when a Spanish ship from San Augustín entered the Bay looking for the rumoured English settlement. Accounts of the behaviour of the Roanoke settlers and the murder of Chief Wingina would inevitably have reached Powhatan. Simon Fernandez, if he is to be believed, also claimed that he had been on various Spanish expeditions to Chesapeake Bay between 1565 and 1572 before he became a turncoat. All this would certainly have had an unsettling effect on the Indians. In 1570 a party of Jesuits was supposed to have been massacred there.

Raleigh's patent had been due to expire in 1591, so it was in his interest to keep alive the possibility that the colonists had survived. Even so it was only in 1602 that he despatched any serious search party, in spite of his claim to have already sent four others. Presumably he was referring to the expeditions of 1588 and 1590, though he may have sent some in 1600 and 1601, most probably in search of medicinal herbs and roots such as sassafras.

An expedition in 1603 was under the command of Samuel Mace. But this Mace had enticed some of Powhatan's men on board his ships and had then kidnapped them. So there would have been a very strong reason in April 1607 for Powhatan giving an order for the slaughter at Cape Henry as soon as Newport's ships were sighted. Indeed on the very night that Newport landed, his encampment was attacked and some of the English were killed.

Quinn also thinks it likely that some of the younger men from Roanoke would have gone to Croatoan. Those carved letters CRO were certainly a clue, and Manteo could indeed have promised protection. The Spaniards who had been to Chesapeake Bay in 1587 are recorded as having located Roanoke; they found it deserted, though the debris had seemed to show recent occupation – all of which could have indicated a sudden flight, and not long after White's departure.

Rumours persist that Indians on Hatteras Island (Croatoan) later claimed to have had white blood, and a lighter colouring was noted in them. John Lawson on a visit there in 1701 believed this to be true, and saw that some of them had grey eyes. But by that time these Indians could just as easily have been descended from pirates or crews of shipwrecks on this notoriously dangerous coast. In recent years various small objects have been excavated at Hatteras Island, including recently, three metres down, a clay pipe and a gold signet ring with a prancing lion with one paw lifted (the lion of Cornwall?).

So faded the dream of the Cittie of Raleigh – for the time being. The mistake had been to look upon these colonies as a means for quick profit; and the failure to send out search parties was certainly shocking. It was all very well Raleigh saying to Robert Cecil in 1602, twelve years after John White's last voyage: 'I shall yet live to see it an English nation'. At least he died knowing that England had achieved a permanent foothold in North America. Roanoke had shown the way to Jamestown.

Grenville of the *Revenge*
1591

After the humiliating failure of Drake's expedition to Lisbon a new strategy was devised. The plan now was to send a series of small squadrons to patrol the Azores and the western coast of Spain and Portugal, in the hope of catching the *flotas* or Spanish treasure ships from the West Indies. Hence that meeting of the *Hopewell* off the Azores with John Hawkins, who had recently taken over from Martin Frobisher's squadron. Their presence, like John Watts' ships off Hispaniola, had caused much alarm in Spain during 1590. A Dutch merchant, Linschoten, who happened to be in the Azores at the time, wrote that the English were now 'lords and masters of the sea, and need care for no man'.[1] In fact Philip had given orders that no treasure fleets should sail from the West Indies that year.

Nevertheless, thanks in part to the capture of the *Buen Jesus*, 1590 had been another extremely successful year for privateering. But the English were becoming over-confident and had not realized how quickly the Spaniards were rebuilding their naval forces, under the formidable Alonso Pardo de Bazán, brother of the late Marqués de Santa Cruz. In September Pardo de Bazán had set out for the Azores with forty ships, which would have put Hawkins in serious trouble had not bad weather driven him back.

The seesaw of Court influence was now back temporarily with Raleigh. As his 19th-century biographer Edwards was to write: 'The Queen's smiles were being freely bestowed on him'.[2] Essex had committed the heinous crime of marrying Frances Sidney, widow of Sir Philip Sidney and daughter of Walsingham, and this had not been revealed to the Queen until she had noticed Frances's pregnancy. She considered that Frances was 'beneath his degree', which made it even worse. So Essex was for the time being in disgrace. From Raleigh's point of view there was perhaps for a while a faint advantage in this marriage, in that Philip Sidney's brother Robert had married Barbara Gamage, Raleigh's first cousin and a considerable heiress.* Walsingham had died in April 1590 (heavily in debt, so much so that he had been buried secretly in case the creditors tried to snatch his body). Hatton was ailing, indeed soon to die. Thus, apart from old Burghley, Raleigh was now in the position of being one of the last of Elizabeth's close companions of old.

Raleigh's ascendancy was such that, when in January 1591 a new and larger expedition of twenty ships to the Azores was planned, she appointed him Vice-Admiral under Lord Thomas Howard, a cousin of the Lord High Admiral Howard, and nephew of one of Raleigh's arch enemies, Lord Henry Howard. Five of the ships were the Queen's own, and Raleigh undertook the victualling of the *Revenge* and the *Crane*. Howard's flagship was the *Defiance*, about 500 tons. Also included in the squadron was a new ship called the *Bark Raleigh* (not of course to be confused with the *Ark Royal*).

Almost at the last moment the Queen decreed that Raleigh must stay by her side and should not go, which must have been a disappointment for him. Perhaps it had been decided that there might be too much friction between him and Howard. As in 1585, when the voyage to Virginia was planned, Raleigh was able to arrange that his place should be taken by Sir Richard Grenville.

Grenville's last fight on the *Revenge* is one of the great remembered Elizabethan episodes in Our Island Story, like Drake playing bowls on Plymouth Hoe and the singeing of the King of Spain's beard, and indeed like Raleigh's cloak and his first smoking tobacco. It had in effect very little strategic importance, but its immortality is due to Raleigh's pamphlet of that same year, *Report of the Truth of the Fight about the Isles of Azores*, a vigorous piece of journalism, written obviously at speed, rushed out within a few weeks of the news of the disaster, though at first anonymously. It was his first effort in prose and unlike his poetry very much for the public, being also intended as anti-Spanish propaganda and not just a piece of family loyalty. Indeed the pamphlet is sometimes regarded as a forerunner of modern English prose, comparable to Francis Bacon's essays.

After four months of cruising round the Azores to no particular effect, at the end of August Howard and Grenville anchored at the island of Flores. There had been a fear of sickness, especially on the *Revenge*, where ninety men were ill and had to be taken ashore. Some ships needed recaulking, and all had to be 'rummaged', which meant cleaning out the foul-smelling

---

* This family connection did not help Raleigh, as Robert Sidney became closely allied to Essex.

ballast, mixed with vomit, sewage and other waste, and scrubbing out the interior with vinegar before loading it up again with fresh shingle.

'At Flores in the Azores Sir Richard Grenville lay', runs the well-known opening of Tennyson's poem, which was inspired by Raleigh's account. The islands of the Azores, all of volcanic origin, are spread over 600 kilometres, divided into four groups of which Flores and its tiny neighbour Corvo are the furthest west. As its name in translation, 'Flowers', denotes, Flores is very beautiful in the spring and summer; its cliffs are of basalt and lava, striated in fantastic patterns. Undoubtedly the English fleet would have been on the east side of the island, at Santa Cruz which has the only harbour.

The presence of the English had been relayed back to Portugal. At Flores they were now keeping a watch on the west, waiting for the *flota*, usually due early in September. But unknown to them Pardo de Bazán was approaching with his fleet from the east. On 30 August he had reached the main island of Terceira. Here he met a pilot who had for a while been a prisoner on the English flagship, and was able to get some exact information about the number of ships and personnel. Lord Thomas Howard, he was told, was '*un hombre moço y no marinero*', a young man and not a sailor, whereas Grenville, described as 'Almirante Ricardo de Villa Verde', was '*un gran corsario e de mucha estimación entrellos*', a great pirate and of high esteem among them.[3]

The Earl of Cumberland had been cruising along the Portuguese coast and had observed Pardo de Bazán's departure. He immediately sent a pinnace, the *Moonshine* – the same that had made the Virginian voyage – to warn Howard. She arrived on 9 September only a short while before Pardon de Bazán's ships were sighted. The English were unprepared, still at their rummaging, and Howard ordered the ships to put out to sea. But Grenville was delayed with bringing his sick aboard, 'disdaining' to leave them to the Spaniards. There was still a chance for him to escape, but he refused to do so. He was ready to stand alone against the might of Spain, 'alleging that he would rather choose to die, than to dishonour himself, his country and her Majesty's ship'. Raleigh's fast-moving report of what followed reads like a first-hand account, being based on interviews with survivors and a captured Spanish captain.

The massive galleon *San Felipe*, 1,500 tons, after attempting to board Howard's flagship, turned her attention on the *Revenge*, only 500 tons, 92 foot long and 32 in beam, which according to a Spanish account came '*gallardeando*', swaggering, along towards it, as though full of confidence. Other enemy ships closed in. The *San Felipe* was the first to bombard the *Revenge* with a broadside of thirty-three guns, 'three tiers of ordnance on a side and eleven pieces in every tier'. During the night the galleon *Ascensión* and another ship went to the bottom. The bombardments continued until the next morning, and included an attempt at boarding.

All the powder of the *Revenge* to the last barrel was now spent, all her pikes broken, forty of her best men slain, and the most part of the rest hurt. In the beginning of the fight she had but one hundred free of sickness, and fourscore and ten sick, laid in hold upon the ballast. A small troop to man such a ship, and a weak garrison to resist so mighty an army. By those hundred all was sustained, the volleys, the boardings, and enterings of fifteen ships of war, beside those which beat her at large. On the contrary the Spanish were always supplied with soldiers brought up from every squadron, all manner of arms and powder at will. Unto ours there remained no comfort at all, no hope, no supply either of ships, men or weapon; the masts all beaten overboard, all her tackle cut asunder, her upper deck altogether razed and in effect evened, she was with the water, but the very foundation or bottom of a ship, nothing being left overhead for flight or defence . . .

The deck, said Raleigh, was like a slaughterhouse, 'the ship being marvellous unsavoury, filled with blood and bodies of dead and wounded men'. Grenville had been wounded by a musket-shot, and while being dressed he was hit again in the head. The surgeon was killed beside him.

They had been fighting for fifteen hours. Now came the last gesture. On the face of it there was no alternative but to surrender, but Grenville with his 'daemoniac will' thought otherwise. He commanded the master gunner, whom 'he knew to be a most resolute man, to split and sink the ship' – evidently there was enough gunpowder left for that – 'so that nothing might remain of glory or victory to the Spaniards'. But his crew, including the ninety sick who were lying below, were not quite so ready to die for their country in this way and to 'yield themselves to the mercy of God'. So the ship's master disobeyed the order of the helpless Grenville, and went across to Pardo de Bazán to arrange a truce. He was assured that those who were able would pay a ransom, and that the rest would not be imprisoned or put to the galleys.

Grenville was carried to the Spanish flagship, where he was well treated, though Pardo de Bazán would not see him. He lived on for two or three days, his captors watching in awe as this strange creature lay dying, crunching wine glasses with his teeth and swallowing the fragments, blood running out of his mouth. The Dutch merchant Linschoten reported the gist of his last words:[4]

'Here die I, Richard Grenville, with a joyful and quiet mind, for that I have ended my life as a true soldier ought to do, that hath fought for his country, Queen, religion and honour, whereby my soul most joyful departeth out of this body, and shall always leave behind it an everlasting fame of a valiant and true soldier that hath done his duty, as he was bound to do.'

A long speech for a man on his death-bed?

Thanks to Raleigh he achieved his everlasting fame, but those who sailed and fought with him were not always so impressed by his daredevil attitude, finding him 'very unquiet in his mind and greatly affected to war'.

His final words concluded: 'But the others of my company have done as traitors and dogs, for which they shall be reproached all their lives and leave a shameful name forever.' The assumption was that he was referring to those of his crew who preferred surrender to suicide. But he could have just as well have been referring to Howard, who had not come to his aid.

Indeed, rumours abounded about Lord Thomas's 'craven' behaviour; ridiculous of course, for if he had stayed on to fight, the Queen would have lost more of her ships. Thomas Phelippes, decipherer of codes for the government's intelligence service, wrote to Charles Paget, an English agent in Paris:[5] 'Here they condemn Lord Thomas infinitely for a coward, and some say he is for the King of Spain'. He also said that there were rumours of a possible duel with Raleigh. Whether this was true or not, Raleigh went out of his way to praise Howard in the *Report*.

There were several reasons for the Spaniards to be pleased with the capture of the *Revenge*; she had been Drake's flagship in 1588 and had sailed with Frobisher to the Azores in 1590, and was also a middle-sized ship, of the type that the Spaniards were trying to emulate. Pardo de Bazán, however, came in for criticism in Spain, where it was thought that with such superiority it would have been easy to destroy many more English ships.

Pardo de Bazán's fleet was later joined by treasure ships from the West Indies and thus increased to 140. At the end of September a tremendous storm blew up, continuing for seven or eight days, the worst in living memory according to Linschoten, waves beating over the cliffs. Twelve ships were destroyed off the island of Terceira, and among them was the shot-battered *Revenge* with seventy men on board, including some of the captured Englishmen. Only one man escaped to shore, but he died later. For Raleigh it was a sign that it 'pleased God to fight for us and to defend the justice of our cause against the ambitious and bloody pretences of the Spaniard who, seeking to devour all nations, are themselves devoured.' People on Terceira, Linschoten said, believed that the storm was caused because Grenville's corpse had been thrown overboard and he was raising devils from the depths.

In the *Report* Raleigh had made his kinsman a national hero. But he also attacked the Spaniards for their perfidy in breaking their promise to send prisoners home; a member of the Desmond family, he wrote, was trying to persuade these prisoners to serve under the Spanish King and convert to Catholicism. There then followed a diatribe about Spanish greed and tyranny in Sicily, Naples, Milan and the Low Countries; while on the island of Hispaniola, he claimed, 30,000 natives had been killed, a 'poor and harmless people created by God'. Under the pretence of religion, Spain only wanted to 'bewitch us from our Prince, thereby hoping in time to bring us to slavery and subjection'.

Raleigh had succeeded in making himself into a symbol of resistance to Spain. In a great paean of patriotism and loyalty to the Queen he wrote how the English were ready to repel 'whatsoever attempts against her sacred person or kingdom'. 'Let the Spaniard and traitor [Desmond] vaunt of their success, and we her true and obedient vassals, guided by the shining light of her virtues, shall always love her, serve her, and obey her to the end of our lives.'

For a short period in 1591 there was a curious alliance between Essex and Raleigh. It concerned the Puritans, growing in popularity, much to the ire of the bishops. They interested Essex not only for theological reasons, but because he saw them as a possible means of political support. For all that, their attacks on Church abuses and in particular on the 'Martin Marprelate' tracts* were held by the bishops as an indirect attack on the Queen herself as supreme governor of the Church in England. Thus in February 1589 she had issued a proclamation against the Puritans as subversives threatening the security of the state. There were arrests including that of John Udall, a very distinguished scholar and compiler of the first Hebrew dictionary in English, who was sentenced to death for high treason, having said among other things that the bishops 'cared for nothing but the maintenance of their dignities, be it damnation of their own souls, and infinite millions more'. The sentence shocked many people, including both Essex and Raleigh.

Raleigh's support for the Puritans had its roots in his experiences during the French wars of religion, when he had seen how men were willing to slaughter one another because of doctrinal differences. He continued to denounce Catholics and especially Jesuits as symbols of bigotry and intoler-

---

* Witty satires by a pseudonymous author trouncing bishops and their assistants.

ance – even though, as his biographer Edwards rightly said, it is not easy to 'ascertain Raleigh's precise views, in regard to theological matters, at any epoch'.

On 22 March 1591 Thomas Phelippes noted: 'The Puritans hope well of the Earl of Essex, who makes Raleigh join him as an instrument from them to the Queen, upon any particular occasion of relieving them'. He was referring to the case of Udall, whose bearing at his trial had impressed Raleigh. In due course Udall received a letter suggesting that he should send Raleigh a statement showing how his beliefs had been misconstrued, so that it could be shown to the Queen. This was done, and in it Udall confirmed his devotion to her, at the same time begging that his sentence should be changed to banishment. The Queen did relent, though the bishops continued to press hard for his execution. Udall was to be sent to Guinea, as chaplain to the Company of Turkey Merchants. Now it was he who put up objections over the terms, and while the quibbling continued he died in his cell in the Marshalsea, probably from gaol fever or typhus.[6]

Raleigh also took up the case of a brave army officer named Spring, to whom the government owed a large sum, which in his opinion was being unjustly withheld, although the man had received many wounds in her Majesty's service. It is said that Elizabeth was becoming a little irritated by so many similar applications from Raleigh. So much so that on telling her one day he had a favour to ask, she exclaimed with some impatience: 'When, Sir Walter, will you cease to be a beggar?' To which he replied: 'When your gracious Majesty ceases to be a benefactor'.[7]

There were occasions when Raleigh showed a surprising humanity in religious matters. If those whom he considered bigots wanted to expound their views, he was interested enough to listen. As Captain of the Guard his duty was to attend certain executions at Tyburn. A young Jesuit, Oliver Plasden, had been sentenced to be hanged, drawn and quartered, and Raleigh arrived at Tyburn when Plasden was already standing on the cart below the gallows with the rope round his neck. The usual mob was pressing around, looking forward to the horrid spectacle. Raleigh heard him praying for the Queen and 'the whole' realm. So he called a halt.[8]

'Then thou dost acknowledge her for thy lawful Queen?' said Raleigh.

'I do sincerely.'

'Wouldst thou defend her,' quoth Raleigh, 'against all her foreign and domesticable enemies, if so thou were able?'

'I would,' said Plasden, 'to the uttermost of my power, and so I would counsel all men who would be persuaded by me.'

This was not the sort of talk that the spectators had come to hear, but there were some who were impressed by Plasden's sincerity.

'I know, good people,' said Raleigh, 'Her Majesty desireth no more at these men's hands than that which this man has now confessed. Mr Sheriff,' said he, 'I will presently go to the Court. Let him be stayed. He sayeth marvellous well. I will presently post to the Queen. I know she will be glad of this plain dealing.'

Standing by was Richard Topcliffe, government interrogator and arch-torturer, fanatically Protestant: one of the most odious characters in Elizabethan London.* He was not impressed by all this rigmarole.

'I pray you,' saith he, 'suffer me to offer him one question, and anon you shall hear that I will convince him to be a traitor . . . Thou sayest, Plasden,' quoth he, 'that thou wouldst counsel all to defend the Queen's right, but tell me, dost thou think that the Queen hath any right to maintain this religion and forbid yours?'

'No,' said the priest.

'Then thou thinkest not,' quoth he, 'to defend the Queen against the Pope, if he would come to establish thy religion. Speak, what sayeth thou to this? I charge thee before God.'

'I am a Catholic priest,' quoth he, 'therefore I would never fight nor counsel others to fight against my religion, for that were to deny my faith. Oh Christ!' saith he, looking up to heaven and kissing the rope, 'I will never deny thee for a thousand lives.'

Then, lo! They cried, he was a traitor, and the cart was drawn away, and he, by the word of Raleigh, was suffered to hang until he was dead; then he was drawn and quartered after their custom.

For Raleigh intellectual inquiry was one thing, but this refusal to deny the Pope was enough. So on hearing those last words he had no hesitation in ordering the execution to go ahead; but at least he had allowed him to die before the ritual of disembowelling.

---

* Topcliffe was a man of 'birth and education' and had been an MP. One of his most notorious victims was the Jesuit Robert Southwell, who under interrogation told him: 'It is neither priest nor treason that you seek, only blood'. As Rowse has said, Southwell's death at Tyburn was 'horribly mangled'. Rowse in a certain way defends Topcliffe, in that he was acting under orders from the Government, which had appointed him to pursue Catholics who had defied the law, such as refusing to go to church or sending children abroad to be educated. He was especially required to hunt down Jesuits.[9]

Scandal and the Tower
1592

For some months in 1591 Essex had been in Normandy, in command of a small English force sent by Elizabeth to assist Henri IV against Spanish invaders allied to the Catholic League in France. It had been a dispiriting affair, and she was annoyed by the bungling. She had also been annoyed by Essex taking upon himself to bestow twenty-four knighthoods. So he was now recalled, even though he felt he had acquitted himself well at the siege of Rouen.

He was eager not only for military glory, but for power, real power, political power. He believed in his own genius, and there was a charm in such naivety combined with his aristocratic grace and good looks. His success with ladies was legendary, and be appeared also to attract his own sex. In spite of his immaturity he was recognized as the coming man. But secure as he was in her affection, the Queen knew his limitations. Although she let him take charge of an army in the field, when Sir Christopher Hatton died in November 1591 she was certainly not going to let him replace Hatton as Chancellor of the University of Oxford.

A faction gathered round him, opposed to Burghley's promotion of his son Robert Cecil. It was fortunate for young Essex that the group included the brilliant Bacon brothers, Francis and Anthony, both highly ambitious and well connected, closely related to Burghley (his wife was their aunt) but resenting his complete lack of interest in their careers, and both disliking Raleigh. Anthony was well versed in intelligence work, and Francis, trained as a lawyer and twice a Member of Parliament, was destined for a fame, as a philosopher and statesman, far greater than Essex ever could aspire to.

For the time being Raleigh was still in high favour, all the more so because of his pamphlet on the *Revenge* with its stirring patriotism and compliments to the Queen. In January she gave him the two great rewards for which he had long hankered.

The first was the command of an ambitious new expedition. There were fresh rumours of an imminent Spanish invasion, and it had been decided

that a strong counter-blast was necessary, namely an attack on the treasure
fleet off Panama, and the sacking of Panama itself. As Admiral, Raleigh was
given a very wide scope, with authorization to act on sea and land, 'on
continents and islands'. And as usual this was to be a privately organized
enterprise, though the Queen would be investing £1,800 and would provide
two ships, the *Foresight* and the *Garland*, the latter of which would be
Raleigh's flagship. He was providing his own faithful *Roebuck*, and this
would have his Vice-Admiral Sir John Borough on board. His financial
contribution would be almost double the Queen's, in fact nearly all his
spare capital – so much so that not only did he have to borrow £11,000,
presumably through or from William Sanderson, but he had to ask the
government to pay him for the *Ark Royal* which he had sold to the Queen
before the Armada. Carew Raleigh was to provide the *Galleon Raleigh*, 250
tons, and the swashbuckling Earl of Cumberland, ace privateer, no less than
six ships, including the *Dainty*, the *Foresight* and the *Dragon*. The London
merchants equipped six more. So altogether there would be at least sixteen
ships in Raleigh's fleet.

Essex must have been grinding his teeth in annoyance and envy.

The second reward was the gift of a ninety-nine-year lease of Sherborne
Castle in Dorset. Raleigh had coveted it for a long while, and usually passed
through the town when riding backwards and forwards between London
and the South-West. This massive building, complete with four three-storey
towers, a banqueting hall, drawbridge and moat, had been built in the 12th
century by Bishop Roger of Sarum, and stood in the shallow valley of the
river Yeo surrounded by a large and beautiful deer park. All very much
grander than Barryscourt Castle which Raleigh had tried to get for himself
in Ireland so many years before. It still belonged to the Bishop of Salisbury,
but Raleigh saw the chance of acquiring it when the see became vacant. The
Queen had no objection, but needed to find a new bishop who would be
compliant enough to relinquish the prize. Sir John Harington, who had a
house nearby, called it Raleigh's Naboth's Vineyard, and told how once
when Raleigh and some friends were riding past, and Raleigh 'above the
rest began talking of it, of the commodiousness of the place, and how easily
it might be got from the bishopric', his horse suddenly fell down, 'over and
over'. Raleigh's face went flat into the mud.[1]

This could have been considered a bad omen, and would certainly have
been hurtful to that famous pride. But then it has also been said that
Harington was more famous for his wit than his veracity. If true, Raleigh
would have known how eagerly his enemies would seize on the story at
Court. Luckily – we are told – Adrian Gilbert was with him, and Gilbert

being an astrologer was able to assure him that his contact with good Sherborne earth meant possession not misfortune.

To speed things along Raleigh gave Elizabeth a jewel worth £250, 'to make the bishop'. But it took three years before she found someone – Dr John Coldwell – flattered enough to relinquish Sherborne Castle in return for a bishopric. The lease was taken up by the Crown, and then transferred to Raleigh at £200 6s 1d payable yearly to the bishop. For good measure, a manorial property belonging to the Bishop of Bath and Wells was also added. This bishop in his old age had made the great mistake not only of getting married, which Elizabeth disliked in clerics, but of choosing a very young wife.

Bishop Coldwell later resented criticisms of his 'weakness'. He began to complain of Raleigh's 'wily intrigues' and made many unsuccessful attempts to reclaim the castle and its estates. And indeed we have this comment on Raleigh, and a slightly different story, in a mid 19th-century history of Dorset.[2]

In 1592 he obtained by his merit and the royal favour a grant of the manor and castle of Sherborne and many other lands belonging to the See of Sarum; but he seems to have effected his design not without some fraudulent, or perhaps violent means, being charged with having persuaded Bishop Coldwell to pass it to the Crown on his election to the See of Salisbury; after which Sir Walter obtained a grant of it. This was one of the greatest blemishes to his character, and was probably the cause of his misfortunes. Those rich possessions raised the envy and avarice of his fellow courtiers, who waited for, and soon after found, an opportunity to deprive him of it.

There were many frustrating delays, chiefly due to bad weather, over the departure of Raleigh's fleet. Sir John Gilbert was Vice-Admiral of Devon, and urgent letters exist from Raleigh to him about preparations for the expedition. First Raleigh asked him to set aside fifty tons of cider 'in good casks with iron hoops' and 10,000 dried Newfoundland fish, to be sent to Plymouth (though perhaps some of this was destined for the troops in Brittany in the continuing fight with Spain).[3] Not long afterwards there was another order for sixty tons of cider, which were to go to Falmouth, the port from which Raleigh was eventually to sail.[4]

Sir John was asked to put a stay on all shipping at Dartmouth and Exmouth so that any prospective sailors could be rounded up for Raleigh's own fleet. Above all, and most importantly, Sir John must make sure that these men came from places least infected with plague.

The fleet was being assembled at Chatham. The Queen was becoming impatient and 'began to call the proceeding of this preparation into question'. Raleigh was alarmed to hear this, in case she reneged over her promise to pay part of the men's wages. He wrote to Robert Cecil from Chatham on 10 March, saying that he would be ruined if such a thing were to happen. The letter also revealed that Elizabeth had changed her mind about his role in the expedition. Now it seemed that he was to go only part of the way and then hand over to Martin Frobisher.

If Raleigh was disliked by the grandees at Court, it was not the case with his sailors; whatever his other failings he was a natural and inspiring leader. Frobisher had the reputation of a martinet and was consequently unpopular in the maritime world. So the ruse becomes clear. Raleigh was to transfer the command in mid-ocean, when it was too late for crews to object. He was then to return in the *Disdain*, especially loaned for the purpose by Lord Admiral Howard.

The letter to Cecil ended on a quite different note, and on the face of it a shock.

I mean not to come away, as they say I will, for fear of a marriage [i.e. Raleigh's own] and I know not what. If any such thing were I would have imparted it unto yourself before any man living. And therefore I pray believe it not, and I beseech you to suppress what you can any such malicious report. For I protest before God there is none on the face of the earth that I would be fastened unto.

This toadying paragraph was an out-and-out lie, for not only had Raleigh been secretly married some months back, but a child was about to be born. Clever Cecil was not so easily deceived, or likely to forget. His father Lord Burghley had said when he was starting on his career: 'Seek not to be Essex, shun to be Raleigh'.[5] Gossip about this scandal must surely have reached him. Obviously Raleigh's hope had been to get out of the country much earlier in the year, and with luck return a great hero with some spectacular prize that would offset the inevitable royal rage when the truth of the marriage was officially known. The Queen's decision to supplant him with Frobisher must therefore have been a bitter setback.

His wife was Elizabeth, or Bess, Throckmorton, about twelve years younger and a Maid-of-Honour since 1584. She was the daughter of Sir Nicholas Throckmorton, long dead, who had been the Queen's first ambassador to Paris and had been acquitted of treason during Mary's reign. A strong Protestant and considered to have been a 'master of intrigue', Sir Nicholas had been sent to Scotland to try to prevent the marriage of Mary

Stuart and Lord Darnley.* Bess had six brothers, the second eldest, Sir Arthur Throckmorton, acting as her guardian and the one who had introduced her to Court life. Her mother, also dead, had been a Carew, and another of Bess's brothers, Nicholas, was to inherit Carew estates in Surrey and change his name to Carew. So for Raleigh the Carew connection had now become even stronger. Francis Throckmorton, the Catholic perpetrator of the so-called Throckmorton plot, had been a cousin, but this was never held against Bess's immediate family.

Bess owned a farm at Mitcham, Surrey, but otherwise her inheritance from her father had been only £500, which her mother had lent to the Earl of Huntingdon and had never been able to retrieve. The Queen would have been aware of Bess's lack of dowry and therefore have been glad that there was less likelihood of her being sought for marriage. As Stebbing was to write, in Elizabeth's view 'love-making, except to herself, was so criminal at Court that it had to be done by stealth'. Leicester and Essex had both discovered this, and Southampton was to do so. It was never any use asking her permission to marry, especially if it were to be to a Maid-of-Honour, because refusal would be a foregone conclusion. By and large for Elizabeth the women would be the worst sinners in these clandestine marriages, and usually would be banned from Court forever afterwards.

Raleigh's early biographer Oldys recalled seeing a portrait of Bess in 1730 owned by the Elwes family, connected to descendants of Raleigh. From his description of her elaborate dress, covered in seed pearls, and her jewels, this must be the portrait now in the National Gallery of Ireland: not particularly beautiful, but commanding, with light brown eyes and a well-scrubbed look, certainly a 'noble presence'. Another portrait, said to be of Bess and now in the Colonial Williamsburg collection in present-day Virginia, has a much sweeter and prettier face and is obviously much younger. If they are of the same person it is not surprising, taking into consideration the stresses and strains of living and coping with Raleigh, that there was such a startling change in Bess's features. Her letters are a delight to read, showing that she was ready to be a fighter on his behalf, with a sharp tongue to boot; the spelling, however, is unashamedly phonetic.

With the extraordinary discovery of Arthur Throckmorton's diary around 1950, by a carpenter in an outhouse, we learn that the marriage had taken

---

* Sir Nicholas's fine Renaissance tomb is in the church of St Katherine Cree, Leadenhall Street in London, having survived the Great Fire and the Blitz. Throgmorton Street is named after him.

place on 19 November 1591, about four months before the birth of the child.[6] Alice Goold's baby had presumably been born the year before in Ireland, but Alice was not important enough to be made into an 'honest' woman – unless of course she had died in childbirth. It is possible of course that the 'Swisser Swasser' joke applied to Bess.* Certainly falling in love with her brought about a change and a new lightness in Raleigh's poetic style, very different from the generally platonic lines addressed to his royal mistress. In his poem Bess was his Serena, as was to be confirmed in a later book of Spenser's *Faerie Queene*.

This poem by Raleigh is headed 'SWR on his Mistress Serena'.

> Nature that washed her hands in milk
>   And had forgot to dry them,
> Instead of earth took snow and silk
>   At Love's request to try them,
> If she a mistress could compose
>   To please Love's fancy out of those.
>
> Her eyes he would should be of light,
>   A violet breath, and lips of jelly,
> Her hair not black, nor over bright,
>   And of the softest down her belly,
> As for her inside he'd have it
>   Only of wantonness and wit . . .

He goes on to say that such delights must be seized upon and enjoyed before they faded: that unavoidable theme which he famously used in his reply to Marlowe's *Passionate Shepherd*. So the poem ends:

> Oh cruel Time, which takes in trust
>   Our youth, our joys and all we have,
> And pays us but with age and dust,
>   Who in the dark and silent grave
> When we have wandered all our ways
>   Shuts up the story of our days.

On the day before his execution, as will be seen, he adapted this verse and added an extra couplet, which made it one of his best known and most quoted.

* p. 123.

Another poem to Bess has the title 'To his love when he had obtained her'.*

> Now, Serena, be not coy,
> Since we freely may enjoy
> Sweet embraces; such delights,
> As will shorten tedious nights . . .
> Nature her bounties did bestow
> On us that we might use them. And
> 'Tis coldness not to understand
> What she and youth and form persuade
> With opportunity, that's made
> As we could wish it. Let's then meet
> Often with amorous lips, and greet
> Each other till our wanton kisses
> In number pass the days Ulysses
> Consumed in travel . . .

On 24 February, while Raleigh was at Chatham making preparations for the expedition, Arthur Throckmorton sent him an urgent message. Four days later Bess came to stay at his house at Mile End. Either there was a danger of a premature birth, or Bess's farthingale was no longer concealing her pregnancy. Spelling was not one of the Throckmortons' strongest points, and Arthur was never sure how to spell his brother-in-law's name. Sometimes it was Really, sometimes Rayley or Rawley. On 29 March he wrote: 'My sister was delyvered of a boye between 2 and 3 in the afternowne. I wryte to Syr Walter Rayley, and sent Dycke the footsmand to whom I gave hym 10s.' Then on 10 April there was the even more sensational entry: 'Damerei Raelly was baptzied by Robert Earle of Essexes and Ar. Throkemorton and Anna Throkemorton'.[7]

Essex a godfather? Raleigh's great enemy, who never lost a chance of blackening him to Elizabeth? Perhaps it was felt that this religious bond might help. Perhaps by letting him into the secret, it was a way of compromising him. Only two years before Essex himself had incurred the Queen's ire by his secret marriage. It was all very odd.

Anna Throckmorton was Arthur's wife. The choice of Damerei apparently referred to the so-called discovery of Raleigh's royal Plantagenet descent. The sneers of the Essex, Oxford and Henry Howard factions can

---

* Possibly a loose translation of Catullus's *Vivamus mea Lesbia* . . .

be imagined. On the other hand the fact that the Cornish Carews had property in Stoke Damerel (now submerged into Plymouth) may also have a bearing on the choice of name.* Bess went back to wait on the Queen: a brazen insult when discovered, and never to be forgiven.

On 6 May, in Arthur Throckmorton's words Raleigh 'set himself under sail at Falmouth towards the Indies'. A day or so later he was overtaken by Frobisher with an order to return. This has often been taken as the moment when he knew of Elizabeth's displeasure, but judging from that letter of his on 10 March to Cecil, Frobisher's appearance had been prearranged; and Raleigh did not go back at once. He sailed on to Cape Finisterre. There, having captured a Spanish ship with an Englishman on board, he learnt that there were to be no treasure *flotas* that year. He therefore decided to drop the Panama plan, and to divide the fleet into two. Frobisher would remain off the Galician coast, cruising up and down to 'annoy' the Spaniards, while the others, under Admiral Borough, would make for the Azores and there lie in wait for any stray carracks that might arrive from the East or West Indies. So by the middle of the month, after having endured 'a tempest of strange and uncouth violence', he was back in England.

Meanwhile Arthur Throckmorton had been summoned to a meeting with Lord Hunsdon who had a responsibility for the Maids-of-Honour. On the 19th Arthur paid the expenses of the nurse, and 'Browne and Sir George Carew came to have me seal the writings between Sir W. Raelly and Eliz', evidently the marriage settlement.

It was a period of waiting, limbo. The nurse and child arrived at Mile End, where perhaps by now Bess was too. According to Adrian Gilbert some years later, most of Raleigh's friends were avoiding him. On the 28th the child and nurse went to Durham House. This could have been regarded as the last visit, and in any case it fuelled the gossip. Indeed it is the last known mention of little Damerei. We never hear of him again. He must have died soon afterwards. London was by now agog with gossip and ribald innuendoes.

Arthur's wife had to make a statement to the Lord Chamberlain. Then on the 30th Raleigh was committed to Sir Robert Cecil's custody. Still no attempt was made to see the Queen, and no comment was made by her, at least publicly. There was no explosion of great wrath, as when Essex's marriage had been discovered. She was waiting, making up her mind. It was a measure of her feeling for a man who had been close to her for so many

* It is worth noting that the first sheriff of Devon in the reign of Richard II was John Damerell. So maybe Damerei was just another misspelling.

years. Raleigh may have felt that a gesture should come from her; or he may have felt that to apologize would serve no purpose. He misjudged the situation, whatever it was. The suspicion is that for once he should have dropped his pride and asked for pardon. In that way the inevitable punishment might not have been so drastic.

On 2 June Raleigh was back at Durham House, a form of house arrest under the supervision of his cousin and confidant Sir George Carew. Bess was committed to the custody of Sir Thomas Heneage, the Vice-Chamberlain. Raleigh wrote to Lord Burghley full of his usual confidence and self-assurance and defending the behaviour of his crews off Finisterre after receiving letters of complaint from owners of Flemish ships returning from Cadiz. Then on 27 June the gift of the lease of Sherborne Castle and its estates was confirmed, giving hope of continuing favour. Could this have been the Queen's gesture – generous enough? Was she waiting for some message in return from a man whom she had loved and trusted? Still there was silence, on both sides.

Raleigh wrote to Robert Cecil, asking for help over the attitude of Sir William Fitzwilliam, who was related to the Cecils and who had been taking advantage of Raleigh's absence by allowing appropriation of some of his estates in Munster.* But in his next letter one sees that he had at last begun to understand the consequences of what he had done.[8]

The letter opened on a practical matter, the need for the authorization of payment for the liveries of the Queen's guards, Raleigh being their captain. He then launched out into a great theatrical outpouring that he obviously hoped would be shown to Elizabeth. He had heard that she was preparing her summer progress, and this would be the first time that he would be left behind.

My heart was never broken till this day that I hear the Queen goes away so far off, whom I have followed so many years with so great love and desire, in so many journeys, and am now left behind her and in a dark prison all alone . . . I that was wont to behold her riding like Alexander hunting like Diana, walking like Venus, the gentle wind blowing her fair hair about her pure cheeks, like a nymph, sometime sitting in the shade like a goddess, sometimes singing like an angel, sometime playing like Orpheus. Behold the sorrow of this world, once amiss hath bereaved me of all . . . All those times past, the loves, the sighs, the sorrows, the desires, can they not weigh down one frail misfortune. Cannot one drop of gall be hidden in so great heaps of sweetness . . .

* p. 153.

The nymph was now aged sixty. Describing Durham House as a dark prison was a typical Petrarchian conceit: the eyes of one's loved one being the source of all illumination. Probably Elizabeth was never shown this letter, but if she did read it even she, so used to hyperbole about her divine beauty, must have recognized the insincerity. The letter ended on a death wish, one of many to come.

She is gone in whom I trusted, and of me hath not one thought of mercy nor any respect of that that was. Do with me therefore what you list. I am more weary of life than they are desirous that I should perish, which if it had been for her, as it is by her, I had been too happily born.

Yours not worthy any name or title, W R

Great rhetoric. Great drama. No sign of any anxiety for his wife and child, but that would have been even more tactless. What he cared for most was loss of prestige.

He wrote again to Cecil about Ireland,[9] having heard about a revolt and prophesying a greater rebellion – which actually came to pass six years later. In this he referred to another letter he had written on the same subject, which, surprisingly, the Queen had actually read and 'made a scorn at my conceit'. He could not resist another swipe at Fitzwilliam: 'Your cousin the doting deputy has dispeopled me, of which I have written to your father. It is a sign how my disgraces have passed the seas and have been highly commended to that wise governor who hath used me accordingly.' Evidently he was also affecting illnesses as a result of his shock, and he ended with a bag of mixed metaphors: 'So I leave you at this time, being become like a fish cast on dry land, gasping for breath, with lame legs and lamer lungs.'

An even greater piece of play acting was to follow.

The account of it appears in a letter to Cecil by Raleigh's poet cousin Arthur Gorges who had called at Durham House.[10] On hearing that Elizabeth was to land at the Blackfriars Stairs, Raleigh went up to his turret to watch from his study window, gazing and sighing at the sight of boats and barges. Suddenly he got into a frenzy, crying out that his enemies had deliberately brought her there 'to break his gall asunder with Tantalus' torment'.

And as a man transported with passion, he swore to Sir George Carew that he would disguise himself and get into a pair of oars to ease his mind but with a sight of the Queen; or else, he protested, his heart would break.

Sir George naturally refused to let him do any such thing. At which they 'fell out to choleric outrageous words, with stirring and struggling at the doors'.

And in the fury of the conflict, the jailor had his new periwig torn off his crown . . . At last they had gotten out their daggers, which when I saw I played the stickler between them, and so purchased such a rap on the knuckles as I wished both their pates broken. And so with much ado they stayed their brawl to see my bloodied fingers.

Then they went on with their 'malice and snarling'. Gorges added that he told Cecil all this because 'I fear Sir. W. Raleigh will shortly grow up to Orlando Furioso if the bright Angelica persevere against him a little longer'. He added a postscript, 'All lameness is forgotten', which really deserved an exclamation mark.

This manic outburst showed precious little remorse. The gossip had reached a pitch, and on 30 July, Sir Edward Stafford, once ambassador in Paris, wrote to Anthony Bacon with malicious glee:[11] 'If you have anything to do with Sir Walter Raleigh or any love to make to Mrs Throckmorton, at the Tower tomorrow you may speak to them, if the countermand comes not tonight, which some think will not be'. And on 7 August Arthur Throckmorton decided to write in French: 'Ma Soeur s'en alla a la tour, et Sr W Raelly'.

There have been suggestions that there were darker reasons for Raleigh's imprisonment, partly because of a letter from Anthony Bacon to his agent Anthony Standen in 1593,[12] in which he speaks of Raleigh being in disgrace 'for several occasions', and not just because of having 'debauched the lady' (words he used in an earlier letter). Raleigh himself when later writing to Lord High Admiral Howard used the words 'my great treasons', but more likely he was then trying to be sarcastic. The final blow may have come when Elizabeth discovered, no doubt thanks to Essex, that it had not just been a case of Raleigh marrying a Maid-of-Honour, but doing so when she was four months pregnant, and then never having had a word of apology from either of them.

It was a time of bad plague in London. Streets were strewn with rosemary. Abandoned dogs howled. There were so many deaths that the tolling of church bells was forbidden. Raleigh was in the Brick Tower, still under the surveillance of George Carew. Bess was put elsewhere, and although both were allowed servants and visitors, they would have been kept apart. He wrote a despairing poem, considered to be among his best.

My body in the walls captived
Feels not the wounds of spiteful envy,
But my thrallèd mind, of liberty deprived,
Fast fetter'd in her ancient memory,
Doth naught behold but sorrow's dying face.
Such prison erst was so delightful
As it desired no other dwelling place,
But time's effects, and destinies despiteful,
Have changèd both my keeper and my fare,
Love's fire and beauty's light I then had store,
But now, close kept, as captives wonted are,
That food, that heat, that light I find no more.
    Despair bolts up my doors, and I alone
    Speak to dead walls, but those hear not my moan.

'Spiteful envy' shows that he put blame on his enemies. He still continued writing business letters to the Lord High Admiral, whom he regarded as an ally, and who did seem to stand by him. Just before leaving Durham House for the Tower he ended one such letter:[13]

I must humbly thank your Lordship for your honourable care of me in this unfortunate accident. But I see this is a determination to disgrace me and ruin me, and therefore I beseech your Lordship not to offend Her Majesty by any further by suing for me. I am now resolved of the matter. I only desire that I may be stayed not one hour from all the extremity that either law or precedent can avow, and of that be too little would God it were withal concluded, that I might feed the lions* as I go by to save labour. For the torment of my mind cannot be greater, and for the body, would others did respect themselves as much as I value it at little. And so much my humble duty and thanks which I cannot express I leave your Lordship to God.

Your Lordship's poor kinsman† to do you service for ever, W. Raleigh

We now come to one of the great mysteries in Raleigh's life. At Hatfield House, where Raleigh's correspondence with Robert Cecil is kept, there is a long poem, carefully transcribed but obviously in draft, though neatly written, of over 500 lines and headed *The 21st (and last) Book of the Ocean to Cynthia*.[14] There is no doubt that it was written at this period. Rambling, inconclusive, written with such intensity it gives the impression that it all

---

* Some half dozen wretched caged lions were a special attraction for visitors at the Tower.
† The relationship was evidently through the Gamage family.

came pouring out of his head without interruption. Whether or not there were ever twenty other books is not known, nor is it certain whether they could have been begun when Raleigh visited Spenser at Kilcolman. From this Hatfield poem it is clear that by now he had lost hope of ever regaining Elisabeth's (Cynthia's) affection, and with it had gone all his chances of furthering his ambitions. It is a poem of despair and disillusion, a lover's lament. As so often in his poetry it is full of epigrammatic lines.

He begins with the death of love.

> Sufficeth it to you, my joys interred
> In simple words that I my woes complain,
> You that then died when first my fancy erred,
> Joys under dust that never live again.

'You' in the third line refers to the joys. He goes on to write of fallen blossoms, sapless trees, broken monuments, cinders of extinguished fires. He then seems to refer to the events just before his imprisonment:

> The honour of her love, love still devising,
> Wounding my mind with contrary conceit,
> Transferred itself sometime to her aspiring,
> Sometime the trumpet of her thought's retreat;
> To seek new worlds, for gold, for praise, for glory,
> To try desire, to try love severed far,
> When I was gone she sent her memory
> More strong than were ten thousand ships of war
> To call me back, to leave great honour's thought,
> To leave my friends, my fortune, my attempt,
> To leave the purpose I so long had sought
> And hold both cares and comforts in contempt

Then comes one of the best-known passages:

> Twelve years entire I wasted in this war,
> Twelve years of my most happy younger days,
> But I in them, and they now wasted are,
> Of all which past, the sorrow only stays,
> So wrote I once,* and my mishap foretold,

* In his poem 'Like truthless dreams', written in Ireland.

My mind still feeling sorrowful excess,
Even as before a storm the marble cold
Doth by moist tears tempestuous times express.

He had been one of the few who had dared to stand up to Elizabeth, and she had enjoyed it, and had rewarded him for it.

It has been suggested that there are erotic allusions in these next lines:

Such is of women's love the careful charge
Held and maintained with multitude of woes;
Of long erections such the sudden fall:
One hour diverts, one instant overthrows,
For which our lives, for which our fortunes' thrall
So many years those joys have dearly bought,
Of which when our fond hopes do most assure,
All is dissolved, our labours come to nought . . .

And, near the end of the poem, despair:

She is gone, she is lost, she is found, she is ever fair:
Sorrow draws weakly, where love draws not too.
Woe's cries sound nothing but only in love's ear.
Do then, by dying, what life cannot do.

Perhaps when he is dead she will remember those last happy years together:

Her love hath end: my woe must ever last.

This was the last line of the poem. What about Bess? Did she ever read *The Ocean to Cynthia*? Certainly in later years the marriage proved strong and devoted. Bess's concern for him is shown in a letter from the Tower to Heneage's son-in-law, Sir Moyle Finch. She thanks Sir Moyle for his kindness and for the advice that she should write to the Vice-Chamberlain in such a way that he could show her letter to the Queen. (Could this at last have been an attempt at an apology?)

She then continues in her wonderfully phonetic spelling. We can almost hear her voice.[15]

I am dayly put in hope of my delivery: I assur you truely I never desaired nor ever wolde desiar my lebbarti, with out the good liking of Sur WR: hit tis not this in prisonment if I bought hit with my life that should make me thinke hit long if hit shuld doo him harme to speke of my delivery . . . who knooeth what will be com of me when I am out: the plage is gretly sesid and ever hath bin cliar heer a bout: and wee ar trew in ourselfes I can assur you. Towar, ever assuredly in frinship. E.R.

If Elizabeth ever read the letter, which she probably refused to do, it was unlikely to soften her heart. Bess, after all, for her was most to blame. Her return to Court would never be allowed. Nor would Elizabeth have been amused by Bess signing herself ER, the Queen's own initials.

At Hatfield there is another manuscript in Raleigh's handwriting, headed *The beginning of the 22nd Book of the Ocean to Cynthia, entreating of Sorrow*. It consists only of twenty-two lines and breaks off in mid-sentence (and was to have relevance to another poem that he was to write many years later). It begins:

> My day's delight, my springtime joys foredone,
> Which in the dawn and rising sun of youth
> Had their creation and were first begun,
> Do in the evening and winter sad
> Present my mind, which takes my time's account,
> The grief remaining of the joy it had . . .

And it ends:

> Leaving as only woe, which, like the moss,
> Having compassion of unburied bones,
> Cleaves to mischance and unrepairèd loss
> For tender stalks –

The reason for this break has been thought to have been due to Raleigh's sudden release from the Tower, to cope with urgent business.

Such a turn of events was not perhaps altogether unexpected. At the end of August Raleigh was visited in the Tower by Sir John Hawkins, who brought him news of a huge carrack from the East Indies, with the largest prize ever, that was being escorted to Plymouth by Sir John Borough from the Azores. This was the *Madre de Dios*, a floating castle, 1,600 tons, with seven decks and manned by 600 men, and with a cargo estimated at half a million pounds.

Raleigh's hope had of course been that some valuable prize would counteract his offence, but this far exceeded anything that he – and everyone else – had ever dreamed of. He and Hawkins wrote to the Lord High Admiral warning him that the Spaniards would be desperate to recover the carrack, and might even try to set fire to it, as had been done to another great ship in the same fleet, the *Santa Cruz*. Spanish men o' war were lurking off the Brittany coast, so it was essential that Howard should send out extra ships to join the convoy escorting the *Madre de Dios*.

Borough in the *Roebuck* had been off Flores in the Azores when one of Cumberland's ships, the *Foresight*, appeared in hot chase of the *Santa Cruz*. This Portuguese vessel, probably about 900 tons, had for weeks been sailing with her precious cargo across the Indian Ocean and round the Cape of Good Hope, then up the African coast, only to be confronted by these English pirates. The *Foresight* and the *Roebuck* were getting ready to attack when there was a sudden storm, and all three were scattered. The commander of the *Santa Cruz* realized that escape was impossible, so he gave orders for her to be beached and set on fire. But Borough learnt from one of its crew that an even larger ship was on its way, the *Madre de Dios*.

Frobisher's presence off the Spanish coast had prevented the expected armed escort from leaving. So Raleigh's strategy of splitting the fleet into two had paid off. The *Foresight* and the *Roebuck* went into attack at ten o'clock at night, and the fight lasted until the small hours when the *Madre de Dios* surrendered. Then Cumberland's men boarded the carrack and the pillaging of the upper decks began. It was the customary right for seamen to take the personal effects of passengers, and fires broke out because candles were being used by the rampaging searchers. It is not known how much other pillage was taken. The cargo was immense, reckoned to include 537 tons of spices and 8,500 hundredweight of pepper, not to mention quantities of cloves, cinnamon, nutmeg, ambergris, pearls, silk, ivory, silver, rubies, gold, and much else. Of special mention in the final list were two enormous crosses of gold and a large piece of jewellery studded with diamonds, that had been meant for the King.[16]

The *Madre de Dios* docked at Dartmouth, not Plymouth, on 7 September. At once there was a fresh orgy of plundering. An eyewitness said it was like St Bartholomew's Fair, only much more dangerous. If you dared to intervene, you might be stabbed. Drunken sailors were exchanging pieces of ambergris for tankards of ale, and jewellers and merchants were hurrying from London to grab the bargains. In the end it was reckoned that only £141,000, in addition to the precious stones, was left to be divided among investors. Hawkins, who was Controller and Treasurer of the Navy, therefore wrote to Burghley that Raleigh was the 'especial man' to bring order to the situation, and tactfully suggested that Her Majesty might conditionally release him. He pointed out that Raleigh was indispensable because of his knowledge of the respective shares due to investors and the claims of mariners, and various individuals who had been employed before sailing, such as coopers, carpenters and armourers. He also said that Raleigh would know what were the rights of the Crown. So Sir George Carew was sent to visit Raleigh in order to discover 'how much in particular Her Majesty might be profited'.

Raleigh replied in a letter addressed to Burghley in some detail, with the no doubt disappointing news that Her Majesty's share in the profits amounted to only one tenth, about £20,000 (for at first it was thought that £200,000 was available).[17] He pointed out that he had been the largest adventurer, and had borne the cost of provisioning the fleet. Being worried (or suspicious) that the Queen would try to commandeer more than her due, he also warily added: 'I know Her Majesty will not take the rights of her subjects from them contrary to her hand and seal'. And he ended: 'If my imprisonment or my life might do Her Majesty more good I protest before God I would never desire either liberty or further respect of breathing, and if Her Majesty cannot beat me from my affection I hope her sweet nature will think it no conquest to afflict me. What her will shall be I shall as willingly obey. And so I humbly take my leave of your Lordship from this unsavoury dungeon.' Such fine words were unlikely to soften her heart.

The Privy Council had already sent Robert Cecil to Dartmouth hoping that he would restore order. The scent of spices and perfumes was so great that he told his father that he could smell it from afar. 'My Lord, there never was such spoil.' He thought that there were 2,000 buyers at work. 'Fouler ways, desperate ways, no more obstinate people did I ever meet with.' In fact very little notice was taken at Dartmouth of this puny townsman.

The Queen finally agreed on 14 September to Raleigh's provisional release from the Tower. Time was getting very short. On the journey down the 'especial man' suggested to Burghley that he might find out which goldsmiths and jewellers had been to Devon, and that their premises should be searched and the owners examined on oath. Then with a typical show of panache he said: 'If I meet any of them coming up, if it be upon the wildest heath, in all the way I mean to strip them as naked as ever they were born, for it is infinite [definite] that Her Majesty hath been robbed and that of the most rare things.'

When finally he arrived at Dartmouth, still with a keeper in charge, Cecil was amazed by the enthusiasm with which he was greeted.[18] 'I assure you, Sir,' he wrote to Sir Thomas Heneage, 'his poor servants, the number of

140 goodly men, and all the mariners came to him with such shouts of joy as I never saw a man more troubled to quiet them in my life.' Raleigh was back among his own folk. Nevertheless, Cecil realized that his shame hung heavily on him. 'His heart is broken,' he wrote, 'for he is very extremely pensive, longer than he is busier.' And it was then that Cecil used the often quoted words, 'He can toil terribly.' He also said: 'But if you did hear his rage at the spoils . . . you would laugh as I do, which I cannot choose.' Cecil knew when Raleigh could put on an act, but could not help being impressed by his reception which 'I do voice before God is greater than I thought for'. Sir John Gilbert wept when he met his half-brother. When friends came to congratulate Raleigh he kept replying, 'No, I am still the Queen's poor captive'. Cecil went on: 'I do grace him as much as I may, for I find him marvellous greedy to do anything to recover the conceit of his brutish offence' – which was hardly surprising. As Raleigh was later to write, life is a play of passion.

The two worked hard together. Cecil's comments were characteristically ironic, Raleigh's characteristically exaggerated, telling Lord Burghley: 'I dare give the Queen ten thousand pounds sterling for that which is gained by Sir Robert Cecil's coming down; which I protest before the living God I speak of truth, without all affection or partiality, for (God is my judge) he hath more rifled my ship [the *Roebuck*] than all the rest'. This was in part meant as a joke, since the shareholders looked to their profit from Raleigh.

Raleigh was sent back to the Tower, and the Government, or rather the Queen, came to a decision about the division of spoils. The Earl of Cumberland, whom Raleigh had more or less accused of appropriating for himself a quantity of the jewels, was awarded a profit of £17,000 on an investment of £19,000. Raleigh, his brother Carew and other associates had invested £34,000 and received a profit of only £2,000, which really meant a loss for them because interest was due on the money he had borrowed (£11,000). This, he complained, was after all his work at Dartmouth, snatching back loot from the profiteers for the common pool. He was understandably bitter.[19]

The Earl of Cumberland is allowed also £36,000, and his account came but to £19,000; so he hath £17,000 who adventured for himself; and we that served the Queen, and assisted her service, have not our own again. Besides I gave up my ship's sails and cables to furnish the carrack, and bring her home, or else she had perished. My ship first boarded her and only [alone] stayed with her; and brought her into harbour, or else she had also perished upon Scilly . . .

The London merchants received £12,000 on their investment of only £6,000.

And I that adventured all my estate lose of my principle and they have double. I took all the care and pains, carried the ships from hence to Falmouth, and from thence to the north cape of Spain; and they only sat still, and did but disburse £6000 out of the common store, for which double is given to them and less than mine own to me . . .

A retort could have been that 'all my estate' had come from the Queen. He had never been fined for his misdemeanour. She could easily have cancelled the gift of Sherborne. But it was Elizabeth who did best of all. Before leaving for Dartmouth, Raleigh had said to Burghley: 'Four score thousand pounds is more than ever any man presented Her Majesty as yet. If God have sent it for my ransom I hope Her Majesty of her abundant goodness will accept it.' He never imagined that she would actually take £80,000, on her investment of £1,800.

His complaints were ignored. From Arthur Throckmorton's diary we learn that on 22 December 'My sister was delivered out of the Tower'. So Raleigh must have left at about the same time. At least they could spend Christmas together at Sherborne. This was one mercy granted by the Queen in her capricious old age.

The School of Night
1593

Raleigh and his Bess had been debarred from Court; the ban on Raleigh was not to be lifted until 1597, but hers was permanent. In his exile a new Raleigh emerges. He was obviously looking forward to playing the squire at Sherborne, and there was the excitement of moving into such grandeur, and in such a beautiful setting. At last he could put down roots, found a family. His brother Carew with his rich wife lived nearby in Wiltshire, as most likely did Carew's numerous Thynne stepsons, including the second Sir John Thynne at Longleat. It was also much more convenient at Sherborne for dealing with his many commitments in the South-West, and that included his sponsoring of privateering expeditions. Adrian Gilbert was called in to give advice on landscaping the park.

Not every neighbour was ready to welcome him, and there were some who took advantage of his disgrace. Lawsuits and quarrels over land lay ahead, and the see of Sarum was the perpetual enemy. While still in the Tower Raleigh had appointed John Meere as his agent. They might have met at the Inns of Court, and Meere's father was a Sherborne man. Even so it was an unfortunate choice, and Raleigh evidently had not delved deeply enough into Meere's history, which included two spells in prison and, almost worse, being employed once as a reeve or administrator for the Bishop of Salisbury. By 1596 Raleigh was attempting to get rid of him.

Perhaps Edmund Spenser was trying to ease the shame of Raleigh's predicament in Book IV of *The Faerie Queene*, though it was not published until 1596. It certainly gives an intriguing sidelight on Raleigh's fall from grace. Here again we have the squire Timias and Belphoebe. Timias has rescued the lovely Amoret from a 'wild and savage man', representing lust. Belphoebe appears and chases away this 'carle', whom she slays with an arrow; she returns to find Amoret in a swoon and Timias wiping away the tears and kissing her. Belphoebe's 'noble heart' was filled with 'deep disdain and great indignity' at such a sight. She almost shot her arrows at them both.

'Is this the faith?' she said – and said no more,
But turned her face, and fled away for evermore.

Then

He, seeing her depart, arose up light,
Right sore aggrievèd at her sharp reproof,
And followed fast: but when he came in sight,
He durst not nigh approach, but kept aloof,
For dread of her displeasure's utmost proof.

However, in the poem reconciliation does come, through the medium of a dove to which Timias gives a jewel, a ruby like a bleeding heart, to take back to its mistress. But this poem appeared in 1596, and Raleigh was no nearer to a reconciliation by then. Could Spenser himself have been the dove, and his poem the bleeding heart which would pacify the affronted Elizabeth?

Shakespeare's sonnet 25 is sometimes thought to be a comment on Raleigh at this time:

Great princes' favourites their fair leave spread
But as the marigold at the sun's eye,
And in themselves their pride lies buriéd,
For at a frown they in glory die . . .

Raleigh may have sought peace of mind at Sherborne, but the bitterness had by no means gone. Loyal Bess had to live with his damnable pride and accept whatever explanation he gave for the 'twelve years' war' with Elizabeth. He wrote a poem that was published unsigned that year in the *Phoenix Nest*. If Elizabeth read it and recognized him as the author it could hardly have been a help.

My first-born love unhappily conceived,
Brought forth in pain, and christened with a curse,
Die in your infancy, of life bereaved
    By your cruel nurse.

Restless desire, from my love that proceeded,
Leave it to be, and seek heaven by dying,
Since you, O you?, your own hope have exceeded
    By too high flying . . .

And you careless of me, that without feeling,
With dry eyes behold my tragedy smiling,
Deck your proud triumphs with your poor slave's yielding
  To his own spoiling.

But if that wrong, or holy truth despised
To just revenge the heavens ever moved,
So let her love, and so he still denied
  Who she so loved.

This may of course have been written in the Tower. The last two lines seem to mean that if the heavens take revenge, let her suffer as he has suffered. Other older poems of his also appeared in the anthology, 'Like to a hermit poor' and 'Like truthless dreams'.

None of these poems were more savage than *The Lie*, which was believed to be by him, although other attributions have been suggested, and it has been said that it was not by him but about him. It was deeply shocking at the time, and as Oakeshott has said a superb act of defiance.[1]

Go soul the body's guest
  upon a thankless errand,
Fear not to trouble the best
  the truth shall be thy warrant:
Go since I needs must die,
  and give the world the lie.

Say to the Court it glows
  and shines like rotten wood,
Say to the Church it shows
  what's good, and doth no good.
If Church and Court reply,
  then give them both the lie.

Tell Potentates they live
  acting by others' action,
Not loved unless they give,
  not strong but by affection;
If Potentates reply,
  give Potentates the lie.

Tell men of high condition
  that manage the estate,

Their purpose is ambition,
　　their practice only hate:
And if they once reply,
　　then give them all the lie . . .

Tell age it daily wasteth,
　　tell honour how it alters,
Tell beauty how she blasteth,
　　tell favour how it falters;
And as they shall reply,
　　give every one the lie.

So Diana and Cynthia, once Empress of his Heart, had become a mere potentate. He had toiled for her, and this was his reward. The men around her were driven only by ambition and hate for one another. Beauty and good looks were blasted by age, and thus favour from on high was ended.

The Lie provoked puns and ripostes, playing with Raleigh's name – one already quoted, from Aubrey:

The enemy to the stomach [raw], and the word of disgrace [lie],
Is the name of the gentleman with the bold face.

The lines on the Church were to prove dangerous for him. And there were some vicious counterattacks.

On 18 October 1591 Elizabeth had issued a strongly worded proclamation against the Jesuits 'working treason under a false pretence of religion', and among other things claiming that the Pope was the King of Spain's creature. This brought immediate and vehement reactions on the Continent, one of which was the *Responsio* by Robert Parsons, a Jesuit, under the pseudonym of Andreas Philopater, written in Latin but which was translated into English in an abbreviated form as *An Advertisement*.[2]

It was chiefly an attack on Lord Burghley, a 'malignant worm' and 'ambitious serpent', and accused him not only of atheism but of opening the way to atheist teaching in the universities. Raleigh was also accused of conducting a school of atheism, which would result in grave dangers should he ever be promoted to the Council, as had been generally expected before he fell into disgrace.

Certainly if the school of atheism of Sir Walter Raleigh flourishes a little longer which he is well known to hold in his house, with a certain necromantic astrologer as teacher, in order that considerable numbers of noble youths may spend their time in making fun of both the old law of Moses and the new of the Lord Christ, with brilliant witticisms and jokes . . . And if Raleigh be chosen for the Council then there will be an edict denying the immortality of the Soul* . . .

What was more, thanks to Raleigh and his 'conjuror' assistant, scholars were being taught to spell the word God backwards.

The ridiculous attack on Burghley was disregarded, but that on Raleigh stuck. The booklet was widely read and reprinted, and rumours of his 'atheism' spread rapidly. Possibly Parsons had heard of Raleigh's tolerant attitude towards the Puritan preacher John Udall – the Puritans in particular being regarded as responsible for such stringent measures against Catholics.[3]

The 'necromantic astrologer' must certainly have been Hariot, whose association with Raleigh was well known. All the same, Dr Dee was alarmed that it was he who was being slandered. Although favoured by the Queen and well known to her advisers, he had found his influence at Court diminished since his return from the Continent. He was still under shock from the depredations to his priceless library, and knew well enough that many people regarded him as a sorcerer or wizard. The fact that Dee was so much afraid does seem to mean that there was a closer link between him and Raleigh than has been generally supposed. He was agitating about this possible slur in 1604 after James I's accession, in view of the new statute against black magic and witchcraft – the penalties being either to be burned alive or to be stoned to death.

Father Parsons' diatribe was the first document to accuse Raleigh directly of atheism, a charge which stuck to him for many years to come, and has been taken as historical evidence of the existence of a 'School of Night'.

The time had come for Elizabeth to recall Parliament, for there was urgent need to raise more money for the war. Raleigh saw the chance of bringing himself back into public view. Unfortunately such was the prejudice against him that he was unable to secure a nomination as important as in the previous Parliament. Instead he was elected for the small borough of Mitchell in north Cornwall, evidently by arrangement with his relative Richard Carew, who was also his deputy lieutenant of the county, and was to be member for Mitchell in the next Parliament. The borough also belonged to the Arundells of Trerice, only a few miles away, and Carew's wife was an Arundell.

Parliament opened on 19 February. Raleigh, no longer fettered by connec-

---

* The last sentence is a reduced version of this dire warning.

tions at Court, was able to speak openly and as such was one of the most conspicuous and sometimes provocative speakers – though his voice being 'small', he was on occasion asked to speak up. Hatred of Spain and all its works was a constant theme of most of his utterances.[4] He was also on a number of committees.

His time in London – Parliament was not dissolved until 10 April – meant that he could not be in Sherborne as much as he would have wished. Bess was left in charge of turning the castle into a family home. What was more, she was again pregnant.

Raleigh, needless to say, when in London was living at Durham House. A letter dated 15 February written from there is about the rights of Devon tinners. On 23 February he actually wrote a memorandum, with a letter to the Queen, on the succession to the throne. This was a sensitive subject, one that she would not allow to be discussed in Parliament – indeed on that very day a Member, Peter Wentworth, was sent to the Tower because he said he was intending to speak about it.

Raleigh's letter was sent to Robert Cecil and was probably never shown to Elizabeth. The style is ingratiating, whining even, but still unrepentant: how she had left him 'all alone in the world', how he was 'forgotten in all rights', and his enemies had their 'wills and desires' over him. But there are some sarcastic stings at the end of the letter:*

I have already presumed too much, which love stronger than reason hath encouraged, for my errors are eternal, and these of others mortal [meaning that the crimes of others were just as bad as his, but he will never be forgiven] and my labours thankless – I mean unacceptable, for thanks belongeth not to vassals. If your Majesty pardon it, it is more than too great a reward. And so most humbly embracing and admiring the memory of those celestial beauties (which with the people is denied me to renew) I pray God your Majesty may be eternal in joy and happiness.

Your Majesty's most humble slave, W R

In Parliament, it is recorded that he spoke strongly in favour of increasing taxation for the war, 'not only, as he protested, to please the Queen, to whom he was infinitely bound above his deserts, but for the necessity he saw and knew'. He considered that the situation was worse than in 1588, now that Spain was sending ships to Brittany and looking for a landing place in Scotland. As for Ireland, the people there were 'so addicted to

---

* Lefranc describes them as '*quelques gouttes d'acide*'.

Papistry that they are ready to join any foreign forces against us. I think there are not six gentlemen of that country of our religion'.

He argued in favour of those with an annual taxable income assessed at £3 being exempted, and that the deficit to the State should be recouped from people who were better off; 'The £3 men should be spared, and the sum which came from them to be levied upon those of £10 and upward.' This was a consistent theme of his: lightening the burden on the poorest, and more tax for those able to pay. He spoke on the number of beggars in London, many of whom were soldiers who had been wounded and had not gone back to their home towns; the situation was also partly due, he said, to the number of clothiers who had taken the spinning of wool into their own hands and were thereby causing unemployment.

He was also in favour of an open declaration of war against Spain, which would put privateering on a proper basis. He pointed out that since Parliament had begun £44,000 had been seized from West Countrymen, while Newcastle colliers were actually afraid to put out to sea. In the case of the former he spoke with authority, as the defences of the South-West were in his charge.

He was eloquent in attacking Dutch and other immigrant traders who were flooding the country. There were other dangers too from these people, who after all were co-religionists. He did not trust the Dutch. 'The nature of the Dutchman is to fly to no man but for his profit, and they will obey no man living . . . The Dutchman by his policy hath gotten trading with all the world in his hands . . . they are the people who maintain the King of Spain in his greatness'. (Sentiments which were to be echoed during the Dutch trade wars in Cromwellian times.)

There was danger here for Raleigh, his views being regarded as an incitement to racist violence, in a roundabout way linked to his tolerant views towards free-thinkers in religion. Archbishop Whitgift, the Queen's 'little black husband', was promoting a bill which would penalize Protestant extremists as well as Catholics. This bill was chiefly designed to strengthen the Act against Catholic recusants (those who would not go to church) of 1581. It was proposed among other things that children should be removed from their parents and given a Protestant education, at their parents' expense, and that recusants should be restricted to within five miles from their homes. As for Protestant extremists such as the Brownists (followers of Robert Browne, brilliant preacher and pamphleteer, with congregationalist views), the proposals were that for a first offence there would be three months in gaol, for a second offence an ear would be cut off, and a third offence would mean permanent banishment from the country.

Raleigh spoke vehemently against the bill. He by no means supported the Brownists, he said, and wished that they could be 'rooted out of the commonwealth', but legislation against an individual's beliefs was extremely dangerous. 'What danger may grow to ourselves if this law pass, it were fit to be considered. For it is to be feared that men not guilty will be included in it. And the law is hard that taketh life and sendeth into banishment, where men's intentions shall be judged by a jury and they shall be judged what another means.' In the case of the Brownists it would mean banishing 20,000 people, including women and children. Where would they go? Who would pay for them? He did not want 'windows into men's souls' to be created.

He won the day and several of the more severe points in the bill were withdrawn. Nevertheless he was soon to pay the price, through popular misinterpretation of his stance.

The 'revolting' Archbishop Whitgift, as J. E. Neale unfairly called him,[5] was defeated. But he had a kind of revenge. Henry Barrow, one of the leading Brownists, was already in prison for sedition and under sentence of death. Within a day of the committee's decision about the bill he had him executed at Tyburn.

Elizabeth was voted a treble subsidy for the war. In her speech she gave a 'great thanks as ever prince gave to loving subjects'.

Raleigh's exertions in Parliament had affected his health, so he went to Bath, which was already becoming fashionable as a spa. It did him no good, as he told Cecil on 10 May when writing about Irish affairs. Throughout this period of rustication he kept up a continual correspondence with Cecil, sometimes with unsolicited opinions.

In one of his letters he makes a reference to Sherborne which is always quoted when describing his love for the place: 'my fortune's fold'. Deciphering both his handwriting and his spelling can be baffling, and in this case it has been suggested that the words were 'my fortress fold', meaning the fortress or castle of Sherborne which he was attempting to make habitable.[6]*

He was also back on the theme of his constant feud with the Lord Deputy Fitzwilliam in Ireland, that 'accursed kingdom'. He had been forced to withdraw settlers because he had not been allowed to raise troops to defend them. Trouble was expected in Ulster, and indeed soon large parts of it would be in revolt. The Earl of Tyrone had now allied himself with the Lord

---

* But see the last line of the poem 'Like truthless dreams', p. 145.

of Tyrconnell. 'There be others in Ireland that lie in wait.'[7] As always he criticized the bungling of defences. 'We are so busied and dandled with these French wars, which are endless, as we forget the defence next the heart.' Here he was referring to the campaign in Brittany against Spain led by Sir John Norris. Huge sums had been wasted in Ireland, he wrote to Cecil. 'A better kingdom might have been purchased at less price . . . if good order had been taken'. The King of Spain was not interested in sending arms and troops to Ireland just for Ireland's sake.

In due course his worries about his estates in Ireland brought him back to London, in the hope of persuading Burghley to intercede over the ban on exporting staves to the Canary Islands for the making of wine barrels. Later, in 1594, the ban was lifted, after he had pointed out that he had made a considerable investment in sawmills at Mogeely, which had provided work for two hundred men, mostly English, and that the wood had been cut and was rotting on the ground.[8] After all this was just the sort of enterprise that Burghley and Walsingham had originally envisaged. Also in 1594 Raleigh sent out fifty Cornish miners to set up iron mills, which were designed to use local timber as fuel. All this was to be lost in the 1598 rebellion. In fact by that time Raleigh had been negotiating to sell these mills, but the deal had come too late.

Another letter to Robert Cecil was written from Gillingham Forest, of which he was Warden jointly with his brother Carew.[9] Raleigh had developed an enthusiasm for breeding horses and for falconry, both of which appealed to Cecil. Thus we read in a postscript that the 'Indian falcon is sick of the buckworm and therefore if you would be so bountiful to give another falcon I would provide you with a roan gelding'. On one occasion he offered to pay the reversion of an Irish leasehold for the price of a goshawk. In Munster he particularly prized his entitlement to half the produce of an eyrie of hawks in the wood at Mogeely.

Raleigh was always uneasy about his hold on the lease of Sherborne, and this involved him in a series of lawsuits and complicated manoeuvres over leases, not to mention bribes. The Bishop of Salisbury remained his staunch enemy, writing to Cecil about Raleigh not honouring the terms of his lease and not paying rent on time. 'The evil reports that I bear for him', he wrote to Cecil, 'and his evil usage of me, do make me in good faith weary of all'.[10] A neighbour, John Fitzjames of Laverton, became exceedingly troublesome, making private deals with the Bishop. 'This Fitzjames', the exasperated Raleigh was eventually to write, 'is as smooth a knave as any liveth, and false.'[11]

Finally, however, he and Bess had to agree that it was just not possible to convert the castle into a comfortable, warm, damp-free home. Instead they decided to move across the river Yeo and build a new house on the site of the old hunting lodge. The result was a brilliant success, universally admired, and still standing with the wings that were added in the next century, forming the letter H. A local historian was to write: 'Sir Walter Raleigh began very fairly to repair the castle; but altering his purpose, he built in the park adjoining it from the ground a most fine house, which he beautified with orchards, gardens and groves of such variety and delight, that whether you consider the goodness of the soil, the pleasantness of the seat, and other delicacies belonging to it, it is unparalleled by any in these parts'.[12] And Aubrey said: 'Sir Walter Raleigh begged it [Sherborne] as a *bôn* from Queen Elizabeth: where he built a delicate lodge in the park not big, but very convenient for the bigness, a place to retire from the Court in summer time, and to contemplate etc. In short and indeed 'tis a sweet and pleasant place and site on any in the West, perhaps none like it.' It is still a lovely creation, with sweeping views across a landscaped deer park and across the meandering Yeo.

The house is said to be one of the earliest examples of exterior plastered walls. Originally worked over with brown lime, it is now biscuit-coloured. There are three upper storeys, with hexagonal towers at each corner. The windows are mullioned and the façade has ogee arches at roof level. Heraldic beasts (put there later?) and a series of tall chimneys give an impression, as has been often remarked, of both fantasy and fortress.

The architect was Simon Basyl. On his visits to his constituency of Mitchell in Cornwall Raleigh would have visited Trerice, only about seven miles away, and may have been inspired to copy, or at least adapt, the decorative scrolled gables on the façade, admittedly fairly typical of the period. Trerice was built twenty years earlier, and is much lower, and less grand, but there is certainly a similarity. At the other end of Bodmin Moor at St Clether is a late Elizabethan mansion, somewhat plainer, called Basil or Basyl, built for Humphrey Trevelyan. So here there could be another connection.

Inside the house there are still many exciting features in the kitchen, base-ment rooms and attics dating from Raleigh's time – doors, window frames, well-worn staircases, fireplaces, panelling. Judging by the size of the hinges, security was considered important. What is now known as Lady Bristol's bedroom was Raleigh's bedroom; in his recently discovered will his bed is described as hung with china silk. In his day the Green Drawing-Room was blue. Its ceiling, moulded with rosettes and lozenges, and with his coat of arms, is intact; and in the bedroom there is his roebuck, of which he was so proud. Tudor roses decorate the ceiling of the solarium on the ground floor.

Nearly two centuries later Capability Brown was called in to create the lake, and it was Alexander Pope's suggestion that Jerusalem Hill should be planted with trees. There is a group of beech trees where once were stables. Otherwise the prospect is essentially as the Raleighs knew and loved. The cedar trees, brought as seedlings from Virginia, are still standing, a bit battered by centuries of English weather. A stone seat near the cascade is said to be where Raleigh sat enjoying his pipe, overlooking the main road to Dorchester. Adrian Gilbert, we are told, laid out the water gardens and walks, as he did at Burghley's house, Theobalds.[13] There was also a bowling green. The view of the old castle is still a romantic feature, but is now a shell, having been blasted by General Fairfax in 1645 – though some of Raleigh's attempts at improvements are still visible.

One of the only recorded carping comments (and there were many) on Raleigh's efforts at Sherborne came, typically, from his then constant critic, Sir John Harington, who had a house near by: 'With less money than he has bestowed on Sherborne (in building, and buying out leases, and in drawing the river through rocks in his garden) he might very justly, and without offence to either church or state, have compassed a much better purchase.'[14]

During the summer of 1593 Sir George Trenchard, a Deputy Lieutenant of Dorset, gave a large supper party at Wolveton near Dorchester. Those present included Raleigh, his brother Carew, John Fitzjames (still presumably on reasonably good terms with Raleigh), Sir Ralph Horsey who was another Deputy Lieutenant, the Revd Ralph Ironside, Vicar of Winterbourne Abbas, the Revd Whittle of Fordington, and some other local dignitaries. Part of the conversation at this gathering was recorded in some detail, and gives a vivid glimpse of that questing sceptical mind of Raleigh which people were finding so alarming.[15]

It must have been a convivial party, for Sir Ralph Horsey had to reproach Carew for his 'loose talk' with the words *colloquia prava corrumpunt bones mores* (evil talk corrupts good manners). Carew Raleigh must have said something about the Church, for he now asked Ironside what he thought, the assumption being that the reverend gentleman had a reputation as a theologian. 'The wages of sin is death,' was the trite reply.

Carew would not let this go, pointing out that death is common to all, saint or sinner. To which Ironside 'inferred further' that life which is properly the gift of God through Jesus Christ is life eternal, 'so that death which is properly the wages of sin is death eternal, both of the body and soul also.'

Ironside must have hoped that this answer was the end of it, but Carew insisted: 'Soul. What is that?' Patiently Ironside replied: 'Better it were that we would be careful how the souls might be saved than to be curious about finding out their essence.'

Sir Walter Raleigh, obviously irritated by such evasiveness, insisted that Ironside should answer his brother's question, adding: 'I have been a scholar some time at Oxford, I have answered under a Bachelor of Arts, and had talk with divers; yet hitherto in this point (to wit what the reasonable soul of man is) have I not by any been resolved. They tell us it is *primus motor*, the first mover in a man.' Ironside replied with a stream of Latin tags, also quoting Aristotle, which Raleigh quite rightly dismissed as 'obscure and intricate'.

And so the argument continued. Ironside said that it could not be obscure to Raleigh, as a learned man, but might seem so to others at the table. 'Plainly,' he now said, 'the reasonable soul is a spiritual and immortal substance breathed into man by God, whereby he lives and moves and understandeth, and so distinguished from other creatures.'

'Yes,' said Raleigh, 'but what is that spiritual and immortal substance?'

'The soul,' replied Ironside, bringing the argument back full circle.

'Nay, then,' insisted Raleigh, 'you do not answer like a scholar.' There followed more Latin tags, and Ironside ended with what he must have hoped would settle the matter: 'Nothing more certain in the world than that there is a God, yet being a spirit, to subject him to the sense otherwise than perfected it is impossible.' What he was trying to say was that material things could only be discussed in a material way, and spiritual things in a spiritual way.

'Marry,' said Raleigh, 'there two be alike, for neither could I learn hitherto what God is.' Now Fitzjames interposed with a definition from Aristotle: God was *ens entium*, the being of beings. Ironside welcomed this, declaring that God was indeed *ens entium*, 'having being of Himself, and giving being to all creatures, it was most certain, and confirmed by God Himself to Moses.'

Raleigh had a contempt for such references to Aristotle,* and the 'school-men', medieval fathers. He continued the attack. 'Yes, but what is this *ens entium*?' Ironside simply answered, 'It is God.'

Raleigh, exasperated, requested that grace might be said, 'For that is better than this disputation.' The outraged and humiliated Ironside departed for Dorchester, 'with my fellow minister', Mr Whittle. He decided that he must write down a full record of this dangerous conversation, which in due

---

* Raleigh was to write later: 'I shall never be persuaded that God hath shut up all light of learning within the lanthorn of Aristotle's brains.'[16]

course reached the Privy Council where Raleigh's enemy Essex, at the age of twenty-seven, was now a member (and had made a good impression on his fellow councillors, it was said, for his 'honourable gravity' and judgement).

All this was grist to the gathering rumours about the iniquities of Raleigh's School of Atheism, supposedly at Durham House, promulgated first by the Jesuit Parsons and about which Thomas Nashe, satirist, poet and enemy of Gabriel Harvey, had made some pointed remarks in his *Pierce Peniless*.[17] The reputation of Hariot, not only as a scientist and mathematician, but as an exponent of 'true knowledge' was now to many people decidedly sinister. Then there was Raleigh's ally, the 'wizard earl', Northumberland, suspected of being influenced by the occult pronouncements of Giordano Bruno. Other members of this 'School', as friends and supporters of Raleigh, were literary figures such as George Chapman and Matthew Roydon, and scientists such as Robert Hues and Walter Warner,* who later transferred to Northumberland's protection after Raleigh's final fall. Hariot was also to be given an annual subsidy by Northumberland and lodgings at Syon House. Lawrence Keymis, a Fellow of Balliol, was also about to be drawn into Raleigh's circle.

'Atheism' broadly included any form of blasphemy or deviation from orthodoxy, and this meant that mathematics, astrology and alchemy were all under suspicion. Then there was the couplet about the Church in *The Lie*† – which in fact had not been meant as an attack on religion itself but on the Church's failure to obtain its spiritual goals. Raleigh's interventions in Parliament on the freedom of thought, in connection with the bill penalizing the Brownists, had come to be regarded as 'Machiavellian'. Even more alarming was believed to be his attack on Dutch traders, for very soon after his speech a racist libel was pinned outside the Dutch churchyard, signed 'Tamburlaine', after an anti-aliens demonstration. The libel was certainly not the work of Christopher Marlowe, whose play *Tamburlaine the Great* had been such a success when first performed in 1587. Nevertheless he was immediately under suspicion. Was Marlowe also part of the Durham House set? This was considered to be a possibility.

Arrests followed. An ant-heap of spies and counterspies has in recent years been dug out, in particular by Charles Nicholl.[18] Marlowe himself appears to have worked as a spy for Walsingham at one stage. A secret document by an informer concerning a Richard Cholmeley circulated in government circles in what was to be the fateful month of May. It included the allegation that Cholmeley had said that 'one Marlowe is able to show

* p. 119.   † p. 190.

more sound reasons for atheism than any divine in England is able to give to prove divinity, and that Marlowe told him that he hath read the atheist lecture to Sir Walter Raleigh and others.'[19]

Other accusations made against Cholmeley were that he had been putting it about that Jesus Christ was a bastard and his mother Mary a whore. When Thomas Kyd, author of the very successful play *The Spanish Tragedy*, was arrested, he accused Marlowe of 'monstrous opinions', such as St Paul being a 'juggler' and that Christ loved St John 'with extraordinary love'; but this was under torture. The testimony of Richard Baines, possibly a follower of Essex, contained alarming items on the 'opinions of one Christopher Marlowe concurring his damnable judgement of Religion':

That the Indians and many others of antiquity have assuredly written of above sixteen thousand years ago whereas Adam is proved to have lived within six thousand years . . . He affirmeth that Moses was but a juggler, and that one Hariot being Sir W. Raleigh's man can do more than he. That Moses made his Jews travel forty years in the wilderness, which journey might have been made in one year ere they came to the promised land.[20]

(When the testimony was shown to the Queen the sentence about Hariot and Raleigh was omitted.)

The assertion that Marlowe read the atheist lecture to Raleigh, if true, is the only evidence that they ever met. Raleigh's well-known reply to the *Passionate Shepherd* does not necessarily prove that they had known one another. Another reference to Raleigh's set could be read into the charge that Marlowe had said that 'all that love not tobacco and boys are fools'. Tobacco-smoking was of course very much a feature of life at Durham House. There seems no doubt that Marlowe was homosexual, which Raleigh emphatically was not, though it is of course conceivable that some of Raleigh's friends were, Hariot for instance.* The homosexual theme recurs constantly in Marlowe's work, not only in *Edward II*. 'Come live with me' would appear to be based on Virgil: Corydon's invitation to Alexis.

On 18 May Marlowe was apprehended. He was put on bail, but on

---

* A 'Paulus' epigram by Harington could be relevant.

> This Christmas Paulus for his reputation
> To keep an open house makes proclamation;
> To which (to make it noted) he annexes
> These general words: for all of both the sexes.
> If Paulus' meaning be as he writes,
> He keeps house only for Hermaphrodites.

30 May he was stabbed to death in a hired room at Deptford, where he had been spending the day with three others. There was a quarrel with one of the men, Ingram Frizer, over the bill. Marlowe drew a dagger, wounding Frizer, who wrested it from him and fatally stabbed him above the eyes. That was the official and accepted story. Frizer was pardoned.

Over the centuries there have been other theories about Marlowe's murder. Was there some political motive? A literary rivalry? A drunken homosexual squabble? We shall never know the real truth. What is certain, as Charles Nicholl has discovered, is that of the other two men present, one – Nicholas Skenes – was the servant of the Earl of Essex, whilst the other – Robert Poley – was a government agent working for Robert Cecil. Ingram Frizer remains vague, evidently connected with Walsingham, and as Nicholl suggests, a property speculator. It has been said that it was he who invited Marlowe to the party at Deptford. Was it an attempt to blacken Raleigh in some way? It is hardly possible that either Essex or Cecil would have ordered the killing. There has even been an idea, put forward by Dr Samuel Tannenbaum in 1926, that Raleigh actually ordered Marlowe's death.[21] This, he said, was to prevent Marlowe from giving evidence about his atheism to the Privy Council.

In Nicholl's opinion, which is certainly more credible, Raleigh was a key figure in the drama, but he was the target, not the perpetrator. A lot of wine had been taken. There could have been threats in connection with Marlowe's imminent appearance before the Council. Marlowe, drunk, had lost his temper. A less exciting solution, but surely the most probable.

The tragedy was that a great poet died, aged only twenty-nine.

Plague raged in London, worse than ever, during the winter of 1593–4. The theatres were closed, so Shakespeare's latest play, *Love's Labour's Lost*, was first performed privately, most likely at the house of his young patron the Earl of Southampton. Guests would have included Essex and others in the anti-Raleigh circle, such as the Earl of Rutland.

The play was intensely topical, full of references, jokes and images that are now mostly lost to us, though some are recognizable or can be guessed at.[22] It was obviously a kind of pantomime and must have seemed uproarious from beginning to end – well-known characters muddled up together and made to speak absurdities. There was or had been a real King of Navarre, and there had been much gossip about his court; but his name was Henri not Ferdinand, and he was now King of France. Among his most faithful supporters were the Ducs de Brion, Langueville and Mayenne; in the play we have Berowne, Longaville and Dumain. One topical reference could be in Act III when Armado and Moth speak of the 'French brawl'. This could refer to the anti-alien demonstrations in May, involving Huguenot refugees as well as Dutch traders.

Raleigh has sometimes been identified with Don Adriano de Armado, and Hariot with Holofernes. The King of Navarre in the play could have been intended for the Earl of Northumberland, and the Lords attending him could have been seen as the Earl of Derby and Sir George Carey, later Lord Hunsdon. It is because of *Love's Labour's Lost* that Raleigh's so-called School of Atheism has been equated with Navarre's reference to the School of Night. When Berowne says that 'No face is fair that is not full so black', the King replies:

> O paradox! Black is the badge of hell,
> The hue of dungeons and the school of night.

It has been argued that 'school' was a misprint. When the play was first published the world could have been 'suit' or 'shroud'. But comparisons have been made with George Chapman's poem 'Shadow of Night', which eulogizes study and contemplation over worldly frivolities. *Love's Labour's Lost* ridicules the academic pretensions of a group of noblemen who take themselves too seriously and have denied themselves the pleasure of female company for three years. When Berowne at last announces the dissolution of the 'academy' and a return to reality, he says

> Never durst poet touch a pen to write
> Until the ink was temper'd with Love's sighs.

This has been held to be the answer to Chapman's

> No pen can anything eternal write
> That is not steep'd in honour of the Night.

If Shakespeare did have his prototypes, they would have only been pegs on which to elaborate. In the 1930s Frances Yates discovered an essay written by Northumberland which does seem significant to the theme of *Love's Labour's Lost*.[23] In this Northumberland extols the attractions of learning, and refers to the fact that his passion for a lady had dwindled owing to his enthusiasm for mathematical studies. His marriage was indeed known to be under strain, and his wife was none other than Dorothy Devereux, sister of Essex, and like her sister Penelope (Sidney's 'Stella') a famous beauty, which would have been all the more insulting. In fact Shakespeare ends the play by turning the situation upside down. North-umberland rejects love for learning, whereas Navarre rejects learning for love.

To present the Spanish-hating Raleigh as Don Armado, 'a fantastical Spaniard', would have been a good joke, and certainly suits the portrait supposed to be of him on the Longleat staircase. It also could be significant that Don Armado professes to address the Princess of France in such ridiculous and extravagant language – 'I do adore thy sweet grace's slipper' – when he is really courting the country wench Jaquenetta. Another significant remark could be the King's 'I do love to hear him lie'. (Poor Bess, if she was the 'country wench'!)

On the other hand there *was* a fantastical Spaniard very much around in London: Antonio Pérez, who early in 1593 had defected to England from Spain, where he was (and still is) regarded as the arch-traitor, having been secretary to Philip II. The character of Don Armado points much more strongly to Pérez. He dressed flamboyantly and his mispronunciations were a joke in the Essex circle, and especially to the Bacon brothers. He hated Robert Cecil, calling him 'Roberto il diavolo', and this became a private joke. In the play Armado pronounces 'Sirrah' as 'Chirrah', and must have caused a great laugh. Then again, Pérez bored everyone with his claim to have been the confidant of Princess Catherine of France. He was also a homosexual, which must have made the dialogue between Armado and his page Moth all the more comic:

ARMADO Who was Samson's love, my dear Moth?
MOTH   A woman, master.

Holofernes may well have had an element of Hariot in him, also of Giordano Bruno. But he does point strongly to John Florio, of Italian Jewish descent, a famous teacher and translator of Montaigne. The title of the play had quite obviously been taken from Florio's well-known remark about the over-prevalence of 'lewd' literature: 'It were labour lost to speak of love'. Then in Act III we have a direct quotation from Florio's book *First Fruits*: '*Venetia, chi non te vede, non to prese*'.

Florio was certainly friendly with Raleigh, or knew him fairly well. When Michel de Mauvissière was French ambassador and had Giordano Bruno staying with him, he asked Florio to take a letter to 'Monsieur de Raglay' inviting him to sup or dine in order to meet a Signor Gizi, an Italian businessman connected with the bankers Pallavicino. On the other hand

THE SCHOOL OF NIGHT

Florio had his foot very much in the opposing camp, in that he had been tutor to Southampton and Rutland. Perhaps Southampton had become bored with Florio and did not mind his being made into a pedant and figure of ridicule.

Running through the play would inevitably be references to the long drawn-out quarrel between Thomas Nashe and Gabriel Harvey: a great joke in the literary world. It has been suggested that Moth was meant to be Nashe, but this seems improbable. Harvey, being a friend of Spenser, was in Raleigh's camp. He had also been a protégé of Leicester and Sidney, and was supposed to have made fun of the Earl of Oxford at the time of the tennis court row.* Nashe was particularly well known for his attacks on the Puritan Martin Marprelate tracts. So Nashe can be safely rejected for Moth. But Shakespeare's audience could have recognized both him and Harvey in the play, though the clues are lost to us, except perhaps in one case. There is an obscure reference in Act III to the 'fox, the ape and the humble-bee'. The fox could possibly be Raleigh, who had foxes as his supporters on his coat of arms. Martin was synonymous with an ape for Elizabethans. The humble-bee remains a mystery. Hariot? Moth says:

> The fox, the ape, and the humble-bee
> Were still at odds, being but three.

and Armado replies

> Until the goose came out of the door,
>   Staying the odds by adding four.

Could this goose be Harvey? Nashe in his *Have With You to Saffron Walden* wrote:

> Gabriel Harvey, fame's duckling,
>   hey noddie, noddie, noddie,
> Is made a gosling and a suckling,
>   hey noddie, hey noddie.

This was all gentle fun. But revenge was on its way.

* Footnote, p. 28.

The Mind in Searching
1594

As usual there were masques and entertainments for Elizabeth at the New Year, and the account of them was relayed back to Raleigh, languishing in his Dorset castle. She had her 'wild horse' Essex by her side, and was observed often to be caressing him in a 'sweet and favourable manner'. It was remarked that since becoming a Privy Councillor he was a 'new man, clean forsaking youthful tricks, carrying himself with honourable gravity, and singularly liked for his speech and judgement'.[1] It was he who had been able to reveal that Elizabeth's chief physician, Rodrigo Lopez, in origin a Portuguese Jew, was plotting to poison her. This was the great excitement of the moment and not necessarily true. Indeed, very likely it was a fabrication, simply to consolidate Essex's position as a leader of the anti-Spanish and pro-war faction, a position that Raleigh had considered to be his. At any rate Lopez was taken to Tyburn, and there hanged, drawn and quartered.

Raleigh was a father once more. A son had been born in October and christened Walter, but known as Wat. Raleigh still seemed to have imagined that his disgrace was a passing phase. From two letters we deduce that he now rushed up to London to put forward two dramatic proposals to Cecil, one being that he should be admitted to the Privy Council. Nicholas Faunt was referring to this when he told Anthony Bacon that it was 'now feared by all honest men that he shall presently come to Court', adding, 'God grant him further resistance'.[2] Needless to say, although Raleigh was officially still Captain of the Guard (his duties were being performed by John Best, 'Champion of England') it was out of the question that Elizabeth should contemplate such a thing.

The other letter is from Raleigh's wife Bess to Cecil, dated 8 February 1594. Evidently Raleigh had returned from London, full of plans to lead an expedition to Guiana, in order to search for the fabled city of El Dorado and break the Spanish monopoly in South American treasure. This project had been in his mind for several years, and may have been inspired by his conversations with Sarmiento de Gamboa, back in 1586. Transparently it was a desperate ploy to regain royal favour, and as such it had become an obsession. Bess was alarmed, not only because of the huge expense but also because of the dangers involved, Raleigh being no longer a young man. After thanking Cecil for the gift of a book, she continued in her special phonetic style: 'Now, sur, for the rest I hope for my sake you will rather draw Sur Watar towardes the est than healp hymne forward toward the soonsett, if ani respecke to me or love to him be not forgotten'. And then (in modern translation) she continued, with all due tact:[3]

But every month hath his flower and every season his contentment, and you great councillors are so full of new councils, as you are steady in nothing; but we poor souls that hath bought sorrows at a high price desire and can be pleased with, the same misfortune we hold, fearing alterations will but multiply misery, of which we have already had sufficient. I know only your persuasions are of effect to him, and held as oracles tied to them by love; therefore I humbly beseech you rather stay him than further him. By the which you will bind me forever.

A preliminary reconnaissance voyage along the Spanish Main (the north coast of South America) had been made by Sir John Borough in Raleigh's *Roebuck* with three other ships. Although he had been repulsed after an attack on the Spanish garrison on the island of Margarita, with the loss of sixteen men, he would have brought back useful information about the deployment of Spanish forces. It may have been he who recommended Trinidad for its strategic importance, opposite the delta of the Orinoco, as the most suitable point of entry into Guiana.

Raleigh also sent out an expedition under his trusty captain Jacob Whiddon. It had been Whiddon who had captured Sarmiento de Gamboa off the Azores, and he had been on many a privateering adventure on behalf of Raleigh: a tough old sea-dog. This time he was to investigate Trinidad, and to make friends with the native Indians. He was also, apparently, hoping to meet the *Edward Bonaventure*, commanded by James Lancaster, but this does seem a tall story. If true, it would point to the expedition taking place very early in 1594.*[4]

The Spanish governor of Trinidad, Whiddon was to report, was Antonio

---

* The indefatigible Lancaster had set off for the East Indies in 1591. In April 1592 he had crossed the Atlantic and had tried to call at Trinidad, desperately needing food and water – only to find that Spaniards had preceded him. Storms and mutiny followed. The *Edward Bonaventure* was captured by Spaniards, and Lancaster and his remaining companions reached England only in May 1594. Investors, who might well have included Raleigh, could have asked Whiddon to look out for the ship, of which nothing had been heard for so long.

de Berrío. He had been welcoming at first, but later got some Indians to lure a few of the English on to the shore, where they were ambushed and eight were killed. At least Whiddon was able to give Raleigh the encouraging news that the Indians there hated Berrío and all Spaniards, and that the same appeared to be the case on the mainland around the Orinoco. Like Hariot at Virginia, he also brought back an Indian to be trained as an interpreter.

Money had to be raised on a large scale, since there was no hope of contributions from the Queen, who in any case was committed to underwriting a major expedition by Drake and Hawkins – in effect a revival of Drake's abortive plan of 1585–6.* The fortune that Raleigh had received from the Babington estate was no doubt being poured into the building works at Sherborne, and on these preliminary expeditions. As always Sanderson was the figure behind the finances, and it is clear that by the time of Raleigh's return from London the underwriting was well under way, though complicated by the need for secrecy. Bess was even not to know that Robert Cecil was an investor, as was Lord Admiral Howard.

Meanwhile, the scandal about that provocative argument with the Revd Ironside at Sir George Trenchard's dinner party had reached London, and there were more stories about suspicious atheist goings-on among Raleigh's associates in Dorset. It was decided, no doubt instigated by the Bishop of Salisbury, that there should be an official enquiry by an ecclesiastical commission. For Essex and his friends this was going to be a wonderful opportunity to have Raleigh finally impeached.

The enquiry began on 21 March at Cerne Abbas in Dorset, a strange choice of venue it might now be thought, with the great apparently pagan priapic giant cut from the chalk in the downs above.†[5] A sworn statement by Ironside was produced and a number of local witnesses were summoned, nearly all connected with the Church and inevitably biased. Sir Ralph Horsey, who had been at the dinner, was on the commission. The other members were Thomas Lord Howard of Binden, Francis James Chancellor of the diocese of Bristol, Francis Hawley of Corfe Castle and Vice-Admiral for Dorset (the equivalent post that Raleigh held for Devon), John FitzJames, Raleigh's neighbour at Sherborne and with whom he was still on reasonable terms, and John Williams Sheriff of Dorset and neighbour of Sir George Trenchard. A formidable group of local worthies. Neither Raleigh nor his brother Carew were called.

---

* p. 95 et seq.

† Whether the giant was then in existence is debatable. There is an amazing absence of any reference to him until the late 18th century.

The result was a fiasco, a medley of gossip and hearsay. A list of 'interrogatories' was produced, the first one being: '*In primis*, whom do you know, or have heard to be suspected of atheism; or apostasy? And in what manner do you know or have heard the same? And what notice can you give thereof?' A typical reply by most witnesses to this was that he could say 'nothing of his own knowledge', but he 'had been told that . . .'

Hariot's name, not surprisingly, was bandied around. John Jessop, minister of Gillingham, Dorset, said that he had heard that 'one Herryott of Sr Walter Rawleigh his howse hath brought the godhead into question'. He had heard the equivalent said of Carew Raleigh and Thomas Allen, Raleigh's lieutenant at Portland Castle whom he had got to know in Ireland. John Davis, curate of Motcombe, implicated a Mr Thynne of Wiltshire (Francis Thynne perhaps, or Charles), because of what he had been told by a barber living in a by-lane at Warminster. Davis then said something that was the key to the whole absurdity of this three-day hearing, that Ironside's report was 'not as the voice of the country reported thereof' – in other words not the same as the general gossip.

Nicholas Jeffries, parson of Wyke Regis, claimed that Hariot had been brought before the Lords of Council for denying the Resurrection of the Body. He then said that three years before, on his way to Blandford, Sir Walter Raleigh and Carew Raleigh had commandeered his horse for a post-horse; when he had begged them not to take it as he was giving a sermon the next day, Carew had said that the horse would preach for him. Thomas Norman, minister for Melcombe Regis, had been told that Thomas Allen had torn out two leaves from his Bible to dry his tobacco. John Dench, churchwarden of Wyke Regis, had been told that Allen had said that when he died he would carry his soul to the top of a hill, and that God or the Devil could have it, whoever got there first. This same Allen was supposed to have cursed God when out hawking, because on that day it was raining.

Francis Scarlett was vicar of Sherborne and reported that Allen's servant Oliver, on coming out of church had told two local ladies that the preacher had never said in his sermon that Moses had fifty-two whores, at which the ladies' ears 'did glow'. He also said that a shoemaker in the town had told him that there was a 'company' about the town who said that hell meant poverty and penury, and that heaven meant riches and having fun. Finally the ladies of the glowing ears were called, and they confirmed what Oliver had said, but had told him to go to bed and have a sleep because they realized that he was 'gone with drink'. They also knew that it was Solomon who had fifty-two whores, not Moses.

Not surprisingly there were no charges, and no action could be taken;

even Allen was not called. It did not mean, however, that Raleigh was absolved from the stigma of atheism, which hung on his reputation to the end of his life. How much he really cared about this is as usual hard to say. Truth was more important to him than accusations by bigots, and to say that he was a deist is probably correct. He certainly did have faith. Later in his essay *A Treatise on the Soul* he wrote: 'As the fire mounteth of itself upward and is carried round the heavens, so is the soul of man led upwards ... The mind in searching causes is never quiet until it comes to God, and the will is never satisfied with any good until it comes to the immortal goodness' – which is as good a clue to his beliefs as any.

Only three weeks after the Cerne Abbas enquiry he was off riding with Sir Ralph Horsey and Sir George Trenchard in order to round up recusants, and was proudly reporting to Cecil that at Lady Stourton's house, Chideock Castle, they had arrested a 'notable knave', a Jesuit known as Father Cornelius. In a postscript he added: 'He calls himself John Mooney but he is an Irishman and a notable stout villain, and I think can say much.'[6]

In fact the man was half Cornish and half Irish, and his original name appears to have been Mohun. He had lived quietly at Lady Stourton's for several years without being disturbed, though he expected martyrdom. He also had a reputation for casting out devils. Old Lady Stourton's second husband had been Sir John Arundell of Lanherne in Cornwall, but she had reverted to her first husband's name on returning to Chideock – the Arundells being in the category of kinsmen to Raleigh makes his motives for the arrest and breaking into her house all the more strange. Mohuns were also important in Cornwall.

Father Cornelius was taken to Sir George Trenchard's house and kept there for two weeks.[7] In that same panelled room where the notorious dinner party had been held he was cross-questioned by local clerics including the Revd Ironside and in the presence of Horsey, Trenchard, Raleigh and some others. There was no hope of his renunciation, as he refused to say grace at a Protestant table. Raleigh was talking to Cornelius one evening and was so intrigued that

he passed the whole night with him alone that he might have certain doubts resolved; nor would such a man [Raleigh] rest contented with mere questions and doubts, but would go into matters more deeply. He was so pleased with the Father's conviction and reasoning and his modest and courteous manner that he offered to do all he could in London for his liberation, and this although the Father had gently reproved him for his mode of life and conversation.

Lady Trenchard also spent some time with Cornelius, and she too 'promised her aid for the Father's liberation'.

This account, from the records of the Society of Jesus, rings true. Once again Raleigh was ready to listen to the views and opinions of someone with profound convictions. It had been very different with that old buffer Ironside. One is reminded of Raleigh's mother visiting Agnes Prest in the 1550s on the night before Agnes was to be burnt.

On the other hand there is no clue as to whether Raleigh made any effort to have the priest freed. It appears unlikely. Cornelius was sent to London where he was tortured, probably racked, and then sent back to Dorchester for execution on 4 July. Raleigh was in charge, and as Cornelius stood on the scaffold with the rope round his neck he was ready to let him speak. But what he had to say was politically so dangerous that Raleigh was afraid that there might be violence among the onlookers, so he gave orders for the cart to be pulled away; the priest was hanged until half dead, then cut down, disembowelled and quartered. His head was stuck on St Peter's church at Dorchester, and the four quarters of the body were put on display at the entrances to the town.

Love's Labour's Lost was followed by Shakespeare's long and rather gloomy poem *The Rape of Lucrece*, published in 1594 and dedicated to Henry Wriothesley, Earl of Southampton. Very probably there were various inner meanings which would have been appreciated by Essex's set, one being that 'Tarquin the Proud' referred to Raleigh the Proud. Later that year another poem, *Willobie his Avisa*, was published anonymously, and has been seen as a response to *Lucrece* and other more obvious attacks on the Raleigh–Northumberland group.[8] 'Avisa' was the beautiful and unassailably chaste wife of the owner of an inn, identified as The George at Sherborne, where travellers to the south-west of England would be likely to call. She had many admirers of high birth, one being H. W. who had a close friend W. S. So could H. W. have been Henry Wriothesley and W. S. William Shakespeare? The poem was held so scandalous that in 1599 it was in the category of books to be burned. 'Willobie' was possibly an invented character, though Willoughbys were a well-established family at Payhembury in Devon, and it may be significant that a copy of the *Poem* was in possession of a descendant until very recently. A possible candidate as author has also been Matthew Roydon, one of Raleigh's followers and to whom Chapman's *The Shadow of Night* was dedicated.

Into the fray comes Sir John Harington with another of his epigrams 'Proud Paulus, led by the Sadducees' infection', etc. – the Sadducees having believed that the soul died within the body. However, as a neighbour of Raleigh in Dorset, he soon came to know him in a different light, as a local squire. Later, when Raleigh's life was at stake, Harington wrote a testament that deserved wider circulation, in a letter to Dr Still, Bishop of Bath and Wells: 'He hath often discussed to me with much learning, wisdom, and freedom, I know he doth somewhat differ in opinion from some others; but I think also his heart is well fixed in every honest thing, as far as I can look into him ... In religion, he hath shown (in private talk) great depth and good reading, as I once experienced at his own house, before many learned men.'

There arose a somewhat complicated affair known in Cornwall as the Duchy Suit, and judging from it Raleigh's position as Lord Lieutenant was now on hold and recognized as such in Cornwall itself. For Raleigh this new trouble was hardly a welcome distraction, for in the county discontent was boiling up, and in a very unsettled time – what with the threat of invasion, deaths from plague and the closure of some tin mines.[9]

The Suit concerned a number of manors belonging to the Duchy with leases that had been regularly renewed for the best part of 300 years. As a result they had come to be regarded as heritable estates. Now the Exchequer was allowing non-Cornish 'foreigners' to move in and buy leases. A deputation to London was being prepared, under the leadership of Sir John Trelawny and Richard Carew of Antony. A letter of complaint had been sent to Raleigh, but to be on the safe side other letters had been dispatched not only to Lord Burghley, Sir John Fortescue the Chancellor of the Exchequer, and Lord Justice Anderson, but to the Queen and Essex.

The deputies left Exeter on 30 April and reached Sherborne two days later, whereupon they 'made repair to Sir Walter Raleigh', 'where they were entertained by Mr Adrian Gilbert, his half-brother, with viewing the new buildings, and had their access delayed upon pretence of sickness (but more indeed upon a report that they meant either not to visit him at all, or else only to do it for fashion's sake).' Raleigh may of course have been unwell, though clearly the suspicion was that he simply wanted to avoid them.* Evidently the new house was not yet finished, and he was still living in the castle.

---

* His mother seems to have died in 1594; if this was before their arrival, it could have been a good reason for such behaviour. Her will, addressed to her 'deare sonnes', is touching, mostly concerned with the payment of debts, and making sure that her servants were cared for, so that 'I may end my days towards God with a pure heart and conscience.' She owed the considerable sum of £8 to the butcher and £4 15s to the apothecary. To be divided between two young relatives she left her bed and its furnishings, a pair of Holland sheets, her saddle and its cloth, a small salt, two spoons and a small table with a green cover.[10]

They were about to leave when suddenly 'admittance was given' to the great man, 'whom they found lying upon a pallet in his little chamber; received a courteous welcome, and delivered their letters [presumably not the one addressed to Essex]. Which after he had read, he alleged his indisposition of health and gave his advice which cause was fittest to be taken following the Suit'. He told them to concentrate on Burghley, and not to be put off by any 'sharp terms'; they must persist with him. He waved aside some obligatory flattery and promised to write letters on their behalf.

The Court was at Greenwich. Burghley's reaction was stiff as Raleigh predicted, but they did manage to get an audience with the Queen who was entirely sympathetic. She even said to them: 'I would they were hanged who have been the doers thereof.' All the same the deputies were kept waiting for an official document – over several weeks in fact, in a wet and cold summer. On their return to Cornwall they found that those foreigners were back again. One of them, Edwards, was particularly difficult, demanding £250 in compensation. The whole affair dragged on until February 1595. Then at last the leases to the foreigners were revoked, and the tenancies reverted to the original customs.

Edwards got his money too. Carew did not forget or forgive him. In 1602, when his *Survey of Cornwall* was published, he wrote in an unusually forthright manner: 'Since which time this barking dog has been muzzled. May it please God to reward him an utter choking, that he may never have the power to bite again.'

If Raleigh did write his promised letters, they are no longer to be found, which is a little surprising, especially in the case of Robert Cecil, who appears to have kept all Raleigh's correspondence addressed to himself and his father. On the other hand a letter on a different matter does still exist, written to Sir Thomas Egerton, Keeper of the Great Seal, on 2 May, the very day that Raleigh was visited by the deputies, that shows that he was still conscious of his duties as Lord Warden of the Stannaries. But did he realize that all this time the odious Earl of Oxford, taking advantage of his disgrace, was trying to get Burghley (who was of course Oxford's father-in-law) to persuade the Queen to let him have a concession on Cornish tin? Very likely. At any rate it was not allowed.

Other letters written by Raleigh in 1594 concerned Ireland, where the rebellious activities of the Earl of Tyrone in Ulster were becoming serious. It is odd to find him actually writing in favour of his old enemy, David Barry, who had been pardoned after the death of Desmond and was now described by Raleigh as a 'noble gentlemen [who] hath to my knowledge lived a long time civilly and conformable to all Her Majesty's directories and commandments.'[11] *O tempora, o mores*. So there were no more regrets about losing Barryscourt, which he had once so much coveted – after all, it was small compared to Sherborne. Raleigh also defended another past enemy, Patrick Condon, who he felt was worthy to repossess his lands. But he warned against pardoning Florence MacCarthy, 'a man reconciled to the Pope' and dangerous. In this he was justified: MacCarthy had already been in the Tower and was due to return there in a few years' time.

There had been a great deal of buying and selling of leases in Raleigh's seignory between London merchants and settlers. Several of these investors never visited their properties and sold out quickly, and had taken the land 'in the spirit of playing the stock exchange'. One such case was that of Robert Reeve, who was granted one ploughland and 400 acres, that he immediately sold for £127. Raleigh himself had invested at least £1,000 in the seignory, but from 1594 all had been leased to Englishmen. Maybe in some way these Irish transactions helped towards raising money for the Guiana project, which was fast gathering momentum. James Gould, who was now Second Justice in Munster, was attempting to expand his properties and became an Undertaker in Kerry.* The Goulds were another reason for Raleigh, in his newly found domestic happiness, for not wanting to revisit Ireland at present.

In spite of Guiana, and in spite of worries about Ireland, Raleigh was ready to participate in any dramatic gesture that might help to restore him to royal favour.

By autumn preparations for Guiana were well advanced. All was still in the utmost secrecy, as is clear from a letter to Cecil dated 20 September. Raleigh was writing from Durham House, as for the time being he was forced to keep away from Sherborne. 'The plague in the town is very hot. My Bess is one way sent, her son another way, and I am in very great trouble therewith.'

---

* T. E Lawrence's father Thomas Chapman maintained that the family had been granted land in Kerry because of a family relationship with Raleigh.

Arrival at Trinidad
1595

Preparations for Raleigh's departure for Guiana were nearly complete by November 1594. He still waited for the Queen's permission to leave, the Letters Patent. Five ships carrying about 150 men, including officers, gentlemen volunteers and soldiers, in addition to mariners, were being equipped and provisioned for a year.

'Spurn not the immortal fame which is offered you', Hakluyt had written in 1587, 'but let the doughty deeds of Ferdinand [*sic*, Hernán] Cortés, stout conqueror of New Spain . . . resound for ever in your ears'.[1] It is by no means clear from Raleigh's famous account of his adventures, *The Discoverie of the large and bewtiful Empire of Guiana*, how much he had already gleaned about the fabled land of El Dorado, with its supposedly fantastic wealth and Inca civilization, perhaps even greater than that of Cuzco in Peru, the City of the Sun. Under the circumstances, his inspiration should rather have been the deeds of Pizarro than of Cortés.

It was widely known that this territory of Guiana – now mostly the equivalent of Venezuela and what was British Guiana – was still unexplored; its name was thought to have been derived from an Indian greeting, *Uyana! Uyana!* And there had been further encouragement from Hakluyt. 'All that part eastward from Cumaná,' he had written, 'in length along the seaside 1200 miles, in which compass and tract there is neither Spanish, Portingale nor any Christian man, but only Caribs, Indians and savages. In which place is great plenty of gold, pearl and precious stones.' The situation had slightly changed as Raleigh knew, because of the Spanish garrison established at Trinidad.

The discussions with Sarmiento de Gamboa would inevitably have ranged over the feats of the early Conquistadors. He was not mentioned by Raleigh in the *Discoverie*, though Raleigh does say in it that he had knowledge of Guiana 'by relation'. It is possible that Sarmiento de Gamboa may have spoken of the early expeditions of Antonio de Berrío in the jungles of Guiana, and he certainly believed in the existence of a lake sacred to the Incas connected with the El Dorado legend.

Rumours about Guiana gold were already seeping out, and Raleigh, as he waited for his official sanction, was getting nervous about competitors, as no doubt were William Sanderson and other investors, including Cecil and Lord Admiral Howard, who was providing a ship, the *Lion's Whelp*. As usual several of the gentlemen volunteers were relatives or trusted friends of Raleigh; they included Humphrey Gilbert's son John, Butshead Gorges, Richard Grenville's son John, and one of the Thynnes, possibly Henry.

Raleigh's policy was to win the confidence of the Indians and treat them as allies, while at the same time convincing them of the power of the great Queen of England, under whose protection they would be safe. In this way information might also be coaxed out of them about locations of gold mines. It was vital therefore not to allow any rival privateers who might be operating at the eastern end of the Spanish Main to antagonize the Indians against the English. So he was greatly alarmed by the news that the mayor of Southampton, Thomas Heaton, was preparing ships for sending out to the West Indies, in case – as he put it – they might 'attempt the chiefest places of my enterprise'.[2]

Then there was the case of Robert Dudley, illegitimate son of the Earl of Leicester, and in this the role of Elizabeth was decidedly equivocal. She was certainly privy to Raleigh's scheme, and knew the importance of secrecy. Yet it was her suggestion that the young man should head for Trinidad in November 1594, and presumably investigate the possibility of finding El Dorado. It had been his original intention to sail to the South Seas, which Elizabeth had considered much too dangerous, with his lack of experience, and this could have been her reason for diverting him to the West Indies. He was, however, taking with him as pilot the very experienced Abraham Kendall, who had served under Francis Drake and who knew something of the waters around Trinidad.[3]

The great worry for Raleigh was whether Dudley and his men would mal-treat the natives. Dudley's ships were the *Bear*, 200 tons, with its pinnace the *Bear's Whelp*, and two other pinnaces graced with names imaginative even by Elizabethan standards, the *Frisking* and the *Earwig*. In fact they were all driven back to port by bad weather, and were not able to leave until December, by which time Raleigh's Letters Patent were ready. There was another storm and the three pinnaces were lost, though the crews must have been saved because 140 men are recorded as having been crammed into the *Bear*.

The legend of El Dorado had been through various transformations, and had already cost hundreds of lives on many desperate and heroic expeditions, which had also involved treachery, massacres and fearful atrocities. The

Spaniards became aware of the legend around 1540, either at Quito or at Bogotá, after it had been reached by the great *Adelantado*, Gonzalo Jiménes de Quesada, the founder of the province of New Granada, now Colombia. Quantities of gold had already been acquired, and stories were circulating about sacred lakes where sacrifices of gold and emeralds were made. But where were the gold mines? Could it be possible that yet another Inca civilization was flourishing somewhere in the interior of the continent, with temples, palaces and tombs just waiting to be ransacked? At Quito Indians talked of a priest-king who went about naked, having been smeared with resin and then covered with gold dust blown on him daily by minions through special pipes. Hence his name *El Dorado*, the Golden One.

Soon a connection was revealed with lakes, and especially Guatavita north of Santa Fé de Bogotá, as it then was, and in the territory of the Muiscas, 10,000 feet up. Every year, it was said, there had been a special day of sacrifice, probably connected with the worship of the sun. Joaquín Acosta's description in his *Descubrimiento de la Nueva Granada* is often quoted: how on that appointed day the king 'gilded and resplendent, entered the canoe, surrounded by nobles, whilst an immense multitude of people, with music and songs, crowded round the shores of the lake. Having reached the centre, the chief deposited his offerings of gold, emeralds and other precious things, and then jumped in himself to bathe. At this moment the surrounding hills echoed with the applause of the people, and, when the religious ceremony concluded, singing and drinking began.'[4] Another account, by the friar Pedro Simón, mentions the king being on a raft with perhaps three officers and drawn across the lake by ropes.

Raleigh of course in 1595 was unaware of the Guatavita legend, though he must have learnt of it later. The existence of such a ceremony is confirmed by the discovery of a miniature gold model of a raft, complete with a chieftain and his assistants, now in the gold museum at Bogotá – though this was found in another lake in the same area. Guatavita still has a strange and silent beauty, perfectly circular, two and half miles in circumference, its water peridot-coloured rather than emerald green, and with tall banks rising up steeply, covered with scrub. On one side there is a deep trench made by a succession of treasure-seekers attempting to drain the lake, using as labour Muesca Indians whose ancestors had worshipped there.* The lake could

* The first attempt to drain Guatavita was by royal licence in 1562, but hardly any gold was found. Other efforts were made without success, until 1904 when a few gold objects and some Muescan ceramics were discovered – this after eight years' work. The mud when dried became hard as cement. An American diver in 1953 attempted to use a scouring machine, but without luck. The Colombian authorities later put a ban on further excavations.

have been a volcanic crater or, some think, made by a meteorite. The search for El Dorado moved on from Guatavita, but a lake was always part of the quest.

At first it was hoped to find the gold dust at Timaná, near the mysterious tombs at San Augustín, by the source of the river Magdalena. There were certainly small gold deposits between the western Colombian Andes and the Pacific. Several expeditions were made along the jungle tributaries in the basin of the upper Amazon, where the warlike Omaguas lived. As Charles V of Spain was also Holy Roman Emperor, some of the expeditions were subsidized by the German bankers Fugger and Welser. A German explorer, Philip von Hutten, claimed to have glimpsed the city, which in the imagination of the Conquistadors became more and more magnificent. There was also talk of a great mountain range full of gold further to the east.

It was of course perfectly possible that Indians, to appease their persecutors, were only too ready to invent stories about mines and fabulous cities – the further away the better.

Some accounts of the ordeals of the explorers are almost incredible. The remnants of one group returned looking as if a 'charnel house had given up its dead'. So the search for a golden king called El Dorado turned into a search for a golden city, which the Indians called Manoa and the Spaniards El Dorado, and this city was always said to be situated on the edge of a great lake, as big, it was later claimed, as the Caspian Sea. Diego de Ordaz was the first to be convinced that the site must be somewhere near the source of the Orinoco. Francisco de Orellano fought against female warriors – hence the name of the river Amazon. Lopez de Aguirre was the most notorious of the seekers for El Dorado, a psychopathic monster, leaving a trail of misery and destruction among both Indians and Spaniards.

Antonio de Berrío had more amiable qualities than most other Conquistadors, and it was he who finally decided that El Dorado must be in Guiana. His story has to be told at a certain length, because of its eventual bearing on Raleigh. An experienced soldier, who had fought in Italy for Charles V and against the Moriscos in Spain and the Barbary pirates, he had married the niece of the *Adelantado* Quesada. Raleigh was to describe him as a 'gent well descended of great assuredness and of very great heart'. When Quesada died Berrío found, at the age of nearly sixty, that he and his wife were the heirs. So off they went to Bogotá with their five daughters and two sons. On arrival in 1580 it was discovered that the will stipulated that the Berríos should devote their inheritance to the continuance of the search for El Dorado.

Berrío was ready to honour the old man's bequest. He struck out east towards what he believed was Guiana, across plains and swamps, and was thrilled at last to glimpse the distant peaks of a great *cordillera* or mountain range, which as he put it had been 'so ardently desired and sought for seventy years past, and which has cost the lives of so many Spaniards'. Indians confirmed that up there were powerful tribes and a 'vast population with gold and precious stones', also a very great *laguna* or lake. Thus was born the belief that Manoa, El Dorado, was somewhere in Guiana. Berrío continued down the whole length of the Orinoco as far as its mouth, the Boca Grande. When at last he returned to Bogotá, he had been away seventeen months and the journey had cost 30,000 ducats out of his inheritance.

The second journey was even longer, from 1585 to 1588. As a result of this he realized that the best way to reach the Orinoco from the open sea was through one of the channels that formed its delta opposite Trinidad, and that Trinidad was thus the essential base for any operations to find this rich empire. There was trouble with cannibals, and finally a mutiny. On returning to Bogotá, Berrío found that Madrid had officially appointed him governor of the province of El Dorado, otherwise known as Guiana or Nueva Andalucía.

The last journey, begun in 1590, was the one most relevant to Raleigh, and described in the *Discoverie*. During the first year there were some truly desperate experiences, and many deaths from disease and attacks by Indians. There were also desertions. Starvation loomed. But Berrío sailed on to where the river Caroní joined the Orinoco, in the province of the *cacique* or chief Morequito, and here he stayed some months. He now learnt that the land of El Dorado began a hundred leagues inland, but the way up the Caroní was blocked by a great waterfall – which Raleigh himself was to encounter. There was a quarrel with Morequito, and he was obliged to continue to the territory of another *cacique*, called Carapana, who seemed ready to submit to Spain. Fever was decimating his soldiers, so he made his way up the delta to Trinidad, arriving on 1 September 1591. Here he spent three weeks reconnoitring the island, and then continued to the island of Margarita, where there was a Spanish governor, Don Juan Sarmiento de Villandrando.

All this is covered in voluminous correspondence from and to Philip II, and confirms the accuracy of Raleigh's own later account.[5] Unfortunately Sarmiento de Villandrando was unimpressed by the seventy-year-old, but excited by the prospect of fabulous riches; so he wrote to the King that Berrío was far too old and an incompetent, and that he, Villandrando, was proposing to take over the quest for El Dorado.[6] Even worse for Berrío was the information that one Lucas Fajardo, who had been sent with thirty arquebusiers to meet him, had met some of his original companions who had taken him back to the province of Morequito, and had proceeded to plunder the area, taking away 300 people as slaves. Berrío, by now suspicious of the Governor's behaviour, was outraged about Fajardo. All this was on top of the news that his wife had died at Bogotá.

Possibly while at Margarita Berrío met or heard of Juan Martín de Albujar, who features in the *Discoverie* as Johannes Martines. Let us hope that Raleigh did not really believe Albujar's ridiculous story, which he nevertheless put into the *Discoverie*. The beginning seems credible enough. Albujar was the sole survivor of an expedition led by an earlier conquistador, Pedro de Silva; he was captured by Caribs, and instead of being eaten, settled down with the Caribs and had several wives. But on his return to civilization, his story took wing. He claimed that after his capture he had been blindfolded and had travelled for fifteen days seeing nothing. At last he found himself before a great and marvellous city, Manoa no less. He walked for a whole day through the streets until he reached the palace of the Inca emperor, where he lived for seven months. At least, unlike Voltaire's Candide, who found himself in El Dorado, he was not given a robe of humming-bird down. And when the time came for him to leave, again unlike Candide his presents were not loaded on a hundred red sheep.

One ambitious character, whom Berrío met at Margarita, and who in effect became his lieutenant, was Domingo de Vera Ybarguen. He was entrusted by Berrío to take formal occupation of Trinidad on his behalf, and to found a 'city' there, San José de Oruña, so named in honour of Berrío's wife, whose maiden name was Oruña. To complicate matters further, Berrío acquired a new deadly rival. This was Francisco de Vidés, who arrived on Christmas Eve 1592 at Cumaná – on the mainland, nearly opposite the island of Margarita – with a royal commission appointing him both as its governor and of Nueva Andalucia/Guiana, provided he established a colony at Trinidad within six months. This sent Berrío hurrying off to Trinidad with twenty soldiers, and Vera was despatched to the Orinoco in order to establish once and for all the exact location of Manoa.

Vera had trouble with Morequito, but from other *caciques* he obtained information about what seemed to be the exact distance to this golden city, situated he was assured on a vast salt lake near the source of the river Caroní. In this area he was told lived a population of clothed people who had arrived only some twenty years before, and who were great traders though in a state of feud with neighbouring Indian tribes. Such information was to be duly repeated in Raleigh's *Discoverie*.

Berrío was delighted with all this, and especially with the fact that Vera had brought back some golden 'ornaments'. His troubles were by no means over, however. He continued to be harassed by Vidés, Villandrando and more recently by the governor of Caracas, Don Diego Osorio. Ten of his men and a friar were killed by Morequito when returning from the Orinoco. There were Carib raids, and then came the unwelcome appearance of an English ship, Raleigh's reconnaissance party under Jacob Whiddon, which was driven off, but only after eight of Whiddon's men had been killed. Reinforcements at Trinidad were now therefore urgent. Vidés refused any aid, and forbade Berrío to look for recruits on pain of death.

Berrío came to two decisions. First Vera must go to Spain, with an appeal to the King himself. Then Berrío's elder son, Fernando, who had been with him on the last journey, should return to Bogotá and organize a relief expedition. In October 1594, when Vera was preparing to depart, Vidés suddenly appeared at Trinidad, demanding that Berrío should leave the island immediately. After a great confrontation Vidés was obliged to return to Cumaná, and added a furious letter of complaint for Vera to take to the King.[7]

Now aged nearly seventy-five, Berrío was anxiously waiting for Vera's and his son's return when an entirely new, and even worse, disaster struck him: the arrival of Sir Walter Raleigh.

When at last Raleigh received the Letters Patent he found that he was no longer termed 'trusty' or 'well-beloved' as when he was planning to colonize Virginia. Now he was simply 'Our servant.'[8] At least he was still entitled to 'discover and subdue heathen lands not in possession of any Christian prince, or inhabited by any Christian people'. He was also authorized to 'offend and enfeeble the King of Spain' and to 'resist and expel' any who tried to settle within two hundred leagues of the place chosen for the colony.

There were still financial worries. He had raised money the previous year by selling revenues from two episcopal manors to Fitzjames. A certain 'widow Smith,' with connections at Court, was causing him alarm in case she took action against him while he was abroad. All this is revealed in a letter to Robert Cecil, though the details are vague.[9] It seems that it had to do with Raleigh having stood security for a merchant in London. If action were taken by this woman, there might be an attempt to seize his property, and then it would be revealed that he had made a conveyance to his baby son, Wat.

'You must esteem me for your evil spirit that haunts you with so many tedious businesses,' he wrote apologetically. He went on: 'All the interest is in my son, yet the discredit will be great if I am driven to show that conveyance. And besides by that means my wife will know that she can have no interest in my living, and so complain.'

This conveyance had therefore been made without the knowledge of Bess. Was Raleigh in awe of his wife, or of her brother, Arthur Throckmorton? Did he assume that if he died Bess might remarry, and that Wat would somehow be deprived of what should have been his inheritance? Later, in 1609, Raleigh claimed that he had conveyed the lease of Sherborne to Wat in 1598, 'without power of revocation', subject to a payment of £200 a year to Bess. There may have been a muddle about dates – some letter may have been (conveniently?) lost. Or the 1594 conveyance could have been cancelled on his safe return from Guiana, and a new one made in 1598.

In all this Cecil was completely in his confidence, and the matter of the conveyance would have been kept secret from the Queen. At present Cecil and Raleigh were in alliance, as a defence against the Essex clique. Yet, as it turned out, Cecil was ready to betray Raleigh, and did so some years hence, when it suited his career. In the letter about Widow Smith, Raleigh signed it 'From Alresford, this Saturday, after I left you with a broken heart'. He could have been worrying about the language of the Letters Patent, or about rival voyages such as Dudley's. Or was it just a deliberately exaggerated farewell?

In January 1595 Raleigh, accompanied by Hariot and his new friend from Balliol, Lawrence Keymis, now a great enthusiast for Guiana, arrived in Devon, almost certainly Plymouth, for the final preparations for the voyage. They were followed by the bailiff John Meere and William Sanderson, and a little later by Bess.

It is a shock to discover that years afterwards, in February 1611, Raleigh's representatives brought a suit against Sanderson, claiming that he had been fraudulent in his management of the accounts for this voyage. The amount for which Sanderson was held accountable was the huge sum of £60,000. Sanderson brought a counter-suit, denying fraud but claiming that he was owed over £700 personally loaned to Raleigh, as well as several thousands of pounds' interest on letters of credit for which he stood bound. The case later went to the Star Chamber, with accusations even of forgery, but there is no record of the final judgement. Hariot acted as Raleigh's accountant, and in his will he directed that all his papers concerning Raleigh's affairs should be burnt.[10]

A salient point in this affair is that Sanderson makes clear that the whole success of the expedition depended on the money he had raised, about 80 per cent of the total cost. He had come to Devon to obtain a legal safeguard in case Raleigh did not return alive from South America. Bess, for her part, wanted protection against possible suits in this eventuality. A memorandum was drawn up on 3 February which seemed to satisfy everybody, Bess being liable only for about £1,000 which included Sanderson's personal loan. Two evenings later, 'in the very instant of his departure', Raleigh asked Sanderson if he could have another look at the documents, and when he got hold of them gave them to Hariot, telling him only to give them back to Sanderson if he failed to return; if Raleigh did return safely then Hariot must pass them on to him not Sanderson. At this Sanderson fell into 'great discontent' at such 'wicked doings'. So much so that he refused to say goodbye to Raleigh before his departure early the next morning.

Raleigh sailed off in style, as usual with a quantity of books. The name of his ship is not known. It could have been the *Roebuck* or the *Bark Raleigh*. The faithful Jacob Whiddon, 'most honest and valiant', was its captain, and the master was John Douglas. He also had with him his secretary Edward Hancock and Captain Robert Calfield, who had been on the *Roebuck* at the time of the capture of the *Madre de Dios*. Two other ships sailed with him. One was a '*gallego*', presumably a vessel once captured from the Spaniards, commanded by Lawrence Keymis. The other was 'a small bark of Captain Cross'. Evidently this Captain Cross was not the same as Robert Cross, later knighted, who had been involved with the *Madre de Dios* affair and had annoyed Raleigh, describing him as 'insolent'. Then there were Amyas Preston and George Somers, who had a fleet of four ships which was expected to join the expedition, but were not ready to leave. In any case Amyas Preston obviously had other priorities on his mind, namely privateering. He was not on good terms with Raleigh, who he considered had swindled him over some prizes in 1589.

The *Lion's Whelp* was also not ready to leave. It was commanded by George Gifford, a dubious character and a Catholic, possibly once acting as a double spy in connection with Mary Stuart, and who had been in the Tower a short while.* He was related to the Throckmortons, which may have been why Raleigh chose him as his Vice-Admiral.

Raleigh wrote that he lost sight of the *gallego* off the Spanish coast. The two remaining ships reached the Canaries on 17 February. For over a week, he said, he waited in vain off Tenerife for Preston and the *Lion's Whelp* to arrive. So he decided to sail on, arriving near the southernmost tip of Trinidad known to the Indians as Curiapan, and which is now Icaros Point, on 22 March. He may have hoped to have met a good friend there, George Popham. He missed him by ten days.

Bess meanwhile was anxiously waiting for news. It is hard to resist quoting

---

* His graffiti are still visible in the Beauchamp Tower: *Dolor Patientia Vincitur*, Patience Conquers Grief.[11]

her first sentence of a letter to Cecil in its original spelling: 'Sir Waltar's remembrans of me to you at his last departur shall ad and incres, if itt weer possibell, more love and dew respect to him.' She went on to say that as soon as she heard anything. 'I shall fly to you in all my cumbers as the surest staff I trust to in Sir Walter's absence'. At the same time she asked for help in recovering her £500 from the Earl of Huntingdon. 'I would rather choose this time to follow it in Sir Walter's absence, that myself may bear the unkindness and not he; the money being long due to me.'[12] (If Cecil did bother to intervene, nothing transpired, and she did not get her money.)

Very soon afterwards some news did reach Bess about Raleigh's progress. Before reaching the Canaries he had come across six Portuguese ships laden with fish. He had taken a little fish, wine and water from each and then had let them go. One of the vessels a little later had been taken as a prize to Plymouth, and its coxswain had reported that Raleigh had seemed 'merry and bright'; by coincidence this man had once been a servant of Dom Antonio, the Portuguese pretender, and had seen Raleigh often. Then again there was another report, in a letter from a Captain Martin White to Bess, dated 10 May. He told her that off the Canaries her husband had taken a Spanish ship laden with firearms, also a Flemish ship from which he had taken twenty butts of wine. All in good privateering tradition.

Raleigh would have been sorry to have missed Popham, but not so pleased if he had known that Dudley had been at Trinidad for six weeks, and that Popham and he had left together.

A certain charm, different from the enthusiastic bravura of the *Discoverie*, shines through accounts of Dudley's adventures. He struck variable weather, but Christmas was a hot calm day, so his men jumped into the sea and swam from ship to ship, 'and made great cheer to each other'. The flying fish were like flocks of frightened larks. There were also dolphins. On the other hand a storm seemed like 'a second inundation of the whole world', the work of 'devilish witches' or 'sea devils'. The bay at which he landed at Trinidad was full of pelicans.

Berrío knew about his presence, but kept his distance. He had only a few soldiers, not more than fifty, but Dudley feared that he had many more. In fact Dudley could have captured the island if he had wished, but he did not want a confrontation. Nevertheless, he did put up a plaque claiming Trinidad for Queen Elizabeth. He cruised round in a barge, looking for gold, but false trails only led to his collecting bags of sand and marcasite. A Spanish-speaking Indian told him stories about El Dorado, which so enthused him that he wanted to lead an expedition up the delta. There were problems because it would mean leaving his pilot Abraham Kendall in charge and the men 'feared his villainy.'*

When Popham reached Trinidad he was appalled to discover that Dudley had been ill-treating the natives. He therefore told him how Raleigh's plans depended absolutely on Indian support; not only that, Robert Cecil had invested in Raleigh's project and would not be pleased. Dudley took alarm, and made off in good time before Raleigh's arrival. On his return he wrote a letter of apology to Cecil.

Raleigh anchored clear of Curiapan, which was only a dozen miles from the Orinoco delta, across the Serpent's Mouth through which the currents swept so alarmingly at the change of tide. The northern part of the island was protected by mountains, and sheltered the Puerto de los Hispanioles, or Port of Spain, and Berrío's San José de Oruña. Raleigh spent the next four or five days quietly exploring every cove and looking for watering places, 'the better to know the island' and keeping well away from the Spaniards.

One river was salty and here on the lower branches of mangroves at low tide he found oysters. His mention of 'oysters upon branches of trees' was ridiculed when he got back to England, but their existence was and is real enough: no great delicacy, it has to be admitted, although Raleigh said they were 'well tasted'. Near the point at Tierra de Brea he also came across the famous Pitch Lake, evidently rather more spectacular than it is today. Now it is much smaller, half a mile across, and sinking. The pitch came bubbling up in 'little springs of fountains' and would then harden. As now, it was possible to walk across, jumping over the fissures, and there are even warm sulphurous pools in which one can swim. Abraham Kendall had found the pitch 'good to patch vessels', and Raleigh made his men use it for caulking their ships, finding it 'excellent good and [it] melteth not with the sun as the pitch of Norway'. It is still in use for making asphalt.†

* This 'villainy' was probably connected with Kendall in 1591 having abandoned a man called John Segar, a tailor, on the island of St Helena. Segar was discovered two years later, naked and 'crazed in mind', and taken to Trinidad where, unable to sleep, he had died. His story, like that of the much later Alexander Selkirk, is thought possibly to have given some inspiration to Defoe, who placed Robinson Crusoe on a desert island visited by man-eating Caribs, near Trinidad. So Tobago has become known as Crusoe's island.[13]
† Sir Robert Schomburgk in the 1830s visited the Pitch Lake and thought the pitch 'well adapted for preserving the bottoms of boats against the destructive worm, the *teredo navalis*'. On the other hand he said that Admiral Lord Cochrane had made several experiments with it, and had found that too much oil was needed for mixing with the pitch, and this made it expensive to use.[14] In 1857 the world's first successful oil well was drilled near the Pitch Lake, and full commercial production began before the First World War.

Grains of gold, Raleigh later heard, were to be found. On the other hand the island 'hath store of deare, wyld porks, fruits, fish and fowle', with soil suitable for growing sugar cane and ginger. At last he sailed up to Puerto de los Hispanioles, where he found a landing place with a few Spaniards on guard. The Spaniards made a sign of peace, and Raleigh sent Whiddon to speak to them. They appeared anxious to trade, so some were invited on board. That evening two Indians turned up in a canoe; one of them was the local *cacique*, called Cantyman, and he remembered Whiddon. Thanks to him much information was gathered about the strength of the Spanish garrison and other matters, including the whereabouts of Berrío.

Raleigh was to write that there were several tribes on Trinidad, but generically they were Arawaks (Arwacas). Dudley described them as 'fine shaped and a gentle people, all naked and painted red, the commanders wearing crowns of feathers'. The redness would have been some sort of protection against mosquitoes and sand flies. Before the coming of the Spaniards these Arawak Indians lived in constant dread of the Caribs, who were cannibals.

The Spaniards wanted to buy linen, so they were invited on board again. Raleigh arranged for them to be 'entertained kindly and feasted after our own manner'. This included opening some of the barrels of wine, which delighted their guests, 'having been many years without wine'. 'A few draughts made them merry', so it was easy to get them to talk about the riches of Guiana. Raleigh all the time pretended only to be mildly interested. He told them he was really on his way to relieve the English at Virginia, and had been driven to Trinidad because of bad weather.

Raleigh admitted in his narrative that he had two reasons for spending time in Trinidad. He wanted revenge for the killing of Whiddon's eight men by Berrío in 1593, and he wanted to winkle out every detail possible about Guiana, 'its rivers and passages' and any difficulties or problems encountered by Berrío, and how they could be solved. He then went on to tell how another *cacique* told him that Berrío had given notice that any Indians who came to trade with the English would be hanged and quartered (Raleigh heard later on that two of them had already suffered this fate). 'Every night there came some with more lamentable complaints of the Spaniards' cruelty.' Indians were kept in chains and bizarrely tortured by having burning bacon dropped on them. Raleigh came across five chieftains all chained together, 'almost dead from famine and wasted with torments'.

Raleigh now reached the conclusion that if he plunged into the interior of Guiana, leaving behind ships at the mercy of the Spaniards, 'I should be savoured very much of the ass'. So, having got all the information he wanted out of his guests on board, he duly put the whole lot to the sword. (Let us hope that they were too drunk to know what was about to happen to them.) He then marched with 100 men to San José de Oruña, which was easily captured. The Spaniards were all 'dismissed', coldbloodedly slaughtered, except for Berrío himself and his Portuguese companion, Alvaro Jorge, both of whom he brought back to his ship. San José was burnt down.

We now turn to two Spanish accounts of Raleigh's doings in Trinidad, one written by Pedro de Salazar, the new Governor of Margarita, the other by the *licenciado* Pedro de Liano. In the first Raleigh is referred to as Monsieur Raeles, Earl of Cornwall, and in the second as Milor Guaterral. We learn that on arrival at Puerto de los Hispanioles Raleigh sent Berrío a friendly letter, with a gold ring as a token of friendship. He explained in it that he had only come to Trinidad to get wood for his settlement on the coast of Florida. So Berrío sent his nephew Rodriguez de la Hoz with eight soldiers and presents of food in order to get more information about Raleigh's plans. The nephew and some of the soldiers were invited on board 'to amuse themselves and drink each other's health'. More food and drink was sent to the Spanish soldiers on land.

This is Governor Salazar's account of what followed:[15]

A signal was made from the flagship to the four soldiers with Berrío's nephew and also to the fourteen [on the shore] who were busy eating. These were stabbed with poniards and halberds. Thus they were killed without being able to help or defend each other. Presently there landed from the fleet one hundred and twenty men, and that night, accompanied by native Indians and guided by those they had brought from England, they set out by the land road in the direction of the place where the Governor Berrío was, about three leagues distant; and without the slightest warning, they fell upon the place at daybreak and slaughtered all the Spaniards they could lay their hands on. They captured the said Governor Berrío and one of his captains, called Alvaro Jorge, and did not spare one Spaniard on whom they could lay hands. There escaped from this affray sixteen Spanish soldiers and some women who hid themselves in the forest, also a Franciscan friar, chaplain to the said Berrío.

Liano's version is that Raleigh had marched to San José with 200 men and some Indians. They entered the town crying out 'Peace! Peace!'. 'And saying these words they went on killing and wounding those whom they met.' Seventeen soldiers were killed in the town, and the rest fled into the marshes.*

---

* The scarlet ibis, a great attraction in Trinidad's marshes, are said by some to be the descendants of birds which were stained with the blood of Spaniards who had been mortally wounded by Raleigh's men.

The capture of Berrío at Trinidad. From de Bry's America VIII, *1599.*

He said that Guaterral (Raleigh) had spent two days in the town, carrying away anything of interest, including papers and documents, and then burning the churches and houses.

On that same day Raleigh reported in the *Discoverie* that the *Lion's Whelp* and Keymis's *gallego* arrived at Puerto de los Hispanioles, and in them 'divers gents and others, which to our little army was a great support and comfort'. He then called together all the chiefs of the island and through an interpreter gave a lecture about his being a servant of a queen, a great *cacique* of the north and a virgin, who had more *caciques* under her than trees on the island. He explained that she was an enemy of the *Castellanos* (Spaniards) and had sent Raleigh to defend Guiana from Spain. He showed them a picture of her which was much admired. They called her Ezrabeta Cassipuna Aquerewana, meaning Elizabeth the great princess or greatest commander.

Berrío and Jorge were now taken to the English encampment at Curiapan. Raleigh was impressed by Berrío's bearing, and found him 'very valiant and liberal'. 'I used him according to his state and worth in all things I could, according to the small measures I had.' At the same time, in long conversations he pumped him for all possible information about El Dorado, still pretending that he was really on his way to Virginia. He heard Juan Martín de Albujar's story.* He was also anxious to know the truth of those warlike women the *Amazones*, 'because of some it is believed, of others not'. The truth, for what it was worth, was that these ladies would summon the kings of bordering countries. The Queen would have first choice, but after that the rest would cast lots for their 'valentines'. For one whole month 'they feast, dance and drink of their wines in abundance, and the Moon being done, they all depart to their own provinces. If they conceive, and be delivered of a son, they return him to the father, if a daughter they nourish it, and retain it, and as many as have daughters send into the begetters a present, all being desirous to increase their own sex and kind.'

He added that it was not true that the women cut off their right breasts to make shooting with a bow easier. In wars they were very cruel and bloodthirsty. And, importantly, they had a 'great store of plates of gold'.

Having felt that he had gained all the information he could possibly want, Raleigh told Berrío the real truth, and how it was he who had sent Whiddon to gain intelligence. 'Berrío was stricken into a great melancholy and sadness, and used all the arguments he could to dissuade me, and also assured the gentlemen of my company that it would be labour lost; and that they should suffer many miseries if they proceeded.'

Berrío added that the channels leading into the Orinoco were very low and sandy, and that when he had travelled along them his canoes were always being grounded. Sometimes there was only twelve inches of water. Moreover, on their approach, the natives would all run away, having first burnt their houses. In the winter the water of the river would rise and there would be a very great current, 'impossible to stem'. And much else, which in fact turned out to be mostly true. Their chief had decreed that they should not trade with any Christians for gold, 'because the same would be their overthrow, and that for the love of gold the Christians meant to conquer and dispossess them of all together'. Which was also true.

Berrío also told Raleigh that the land of Morequito was 600 miles inland, but this piece of information Raleigh kept from the rest of the company. (In fact as the crow flies the mouth of the Caroní is about 125 miles from Trinidad.)

Some Spaniards had managed to escape by canoe to the island of Margarita, a journey of about twenty-four hours. The Governor Salazar sent back a canoe with spies in order to find out more about the enemy. He was told that the English were very busy felling trees and making defences and a fort,

* p. 220.

and that they had three pieces of artillery. Indians were helping them. It was confirmed that Berrío was being entertained and had been persuaded to give up letters he had written to King Philip. Then Salazar heard that the General (Raleigh), having obtained all the information he wanted, 'intended to deliver up the said General Berrío to the Indians to be slain by bowshot, and Captain Alvaro Jorge to be hanged, if they did not declare the way to Guiana'.[16]

Raleigh now sent out parties to reconnoitre the main channels of the delta.

Guiana
1595

Captain Gifford in the *Lion's Whelp* and Captain Calfield in his bark were sent to the mouth of the Capure caño, almost directly opposite Icaros Point and across the Serpent's Mouth. It was found that at high tide the water was only nine feet deep and at low tide five feet. What was more, there were dangerous sand bars – known now as the Barra de Cocuina, where fishermen build their huts on stilts.* So the master of the *Lion's Whelp*, King, was sent off further west in his ship's boat to the bay of Guanipa, into which flowed the *caño* Manamo, the largest of the entrances (there were said to be thirty-seven) into the Orinoco. Once again the water was found to be too shallow. What was more, King's Indian guide warned him that the local people were cannibals, and might also attack them with poisoned arrows. If 'he hastened not back', they would be lost.

Fearing the worst, Raleigh had his carpenters cut down the *gallego* so it would draw five feet, and fit it with banks for eight oars. There were to be no more reconnaissances and it was decided, cannibals notwithstanding, to head for the Bay of Guanipa where there were 'four goodly entrances', the least being as wide as the Thames at Woolwich, and all in effect tributaries of the Manamo. Raleigh himself went in the converted *gallego*, which now he called his galley, and into which were 'thrust' sixty men, including Captain Thynne, Raleigh's cousin John Grenville, his nephew John Gilbert, Jacob Whiddon, Lawrence Keymis, and Edward Hancock. Captain Calfield had Raleigh's cousin Butshead Gorges and six others in his wherry. Captain Gifford had nine more in the *Lion's Whelp* wherry, and there were ten more in the ship's boat. On one of these boats, perhaps in the galley, were Raleigh's sixteen-year-old cabin boy Hugh Godwin and young Francis Sparrey, both to be important in the story, especially Sparrey who was to write accounts of his experiences. Altogether there was a total strength of 100 men, with enough victuals for a month. The fleet was left anchored,

---

* Alarming for guests sleeping in hammocks at a time of high wind.

231

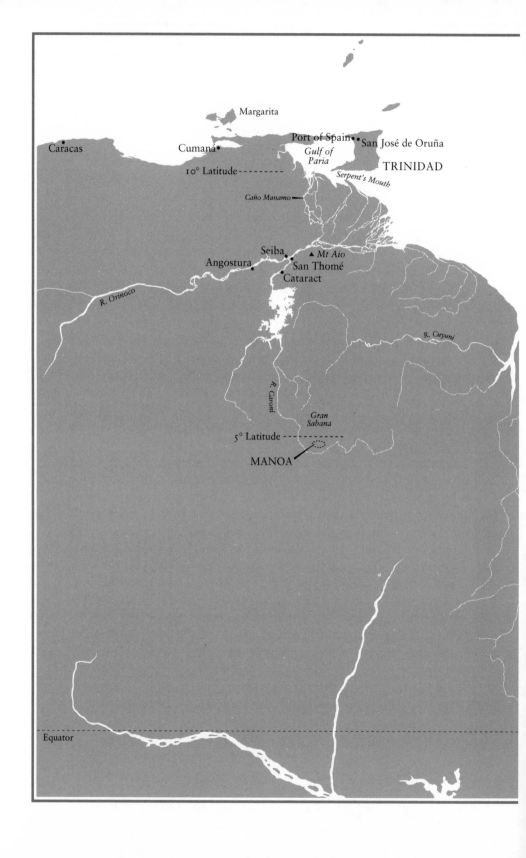

Margarita

Caracas

Cumaná

Port of Spain • San José de Oruña

Gulf of Paria

TRINIDAD

10° Latitude - - - - - - - - -

Serpent's Mouth

Caño Manamo

Seiba

▲ *Mt Aio*

Angostura

San Thomé

Cataract

R. Orinoco

R. Cuyuni

R. Caroni

Gran Sabana

5° Latitude - - - - - - - - - - -

MANOA

Equator -

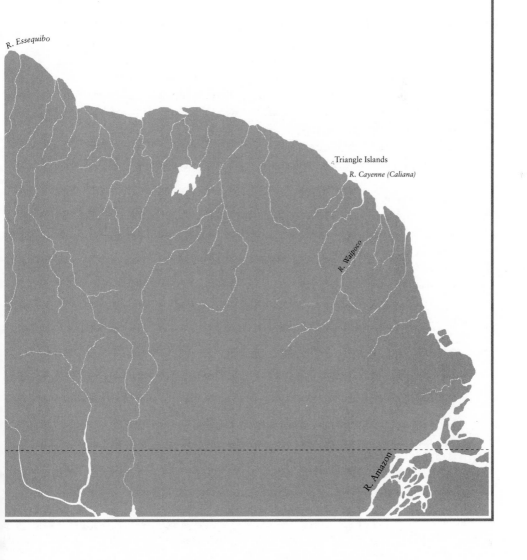

R. Essequibo

Triangle Islands

R. Cayenne (Caliana)

R. Waipoco

R. Amazon

protected from the winds, near the fort at Curiapan, where the disconsolate Berrío and Jorge were kept prisoner.

When the *Discoverie* was republished within Theodore de Bry's lavish and monumental work *America* in 1599, it was illustrated with pictures of Raleigh and his followers dressed immaculately in late 16th-century fashion, in padded jerkins and beplumed headgear. The reality would have been quite different in that relentless humid heat and sudden downpours. For some years Raleigh, as he admitted, had been used to living in comfort, but now they were 'being all driven to lie in the rain and weather, in the open air, in the burning sun, and upon the hard boards, and to dress our meat, and to carry all manner of furniture in them, wherewith they were so pestered and unsavoury, that what with the victuals being most fish, with the wet clothes of so many men thrust together and the heat of the sun, I will undertake that there was never any prison in England that could be found more unsavoury and loathsome, especially to myself, who had for many years before been dieted and cared for in a sort far differing.' He did not mention the mosquitoes, the vampire bats and jigger worms.

It was an ordeal crossing the Gulf of Paria in those small boats, some forty kilometres, 'in a great billow, the wind and current being both very strong'. They had brought with them an Arawak guide called Fernando,* who turned out to be entirely useless, admitting that he had not been to the Orinoco for twelve years, and that when he was very young.

If God had not sent us another help, we might have wandered a whole year in that labyrinth of rivers, ere we had found any way, either out or in, especially after we were past the ebbing and flowing, which was in four days: for I know all the earth doth not yield the like confluence of streams and branches, the one crossing the other so many times, and all so fair and large, and so like one another, as no man can tell which to take: and if we went by the sun or compass hoping thereby to go directly one way or other, yet that way we were also carried in a circle amongst multitudes of islands, and every island bordered with high trees, as no man could see any further than the breadth of the river.

They were in the peaty brown waters of the mangrove swamps, where great tentacles blocked the passages and had to be hacked away. This particular channel had no identifiable name, so they called it the Red Cross river, because they were the first Christians to enter it: the cross of St George of England; or even named after the knight in Spenser's *The Faerie Queene*.

* In the *Discoverie* Ferdinando.

Most likely it was the *caño* Pedernales, at the head of which now there is a decayed settlement built for workers in defunct oil wells on a nearby island, its wooden jetties watched over by vultures perched on poles, and known in Venezuela as 'the town that refused to die'.

On 22 May, rowing up the river, they espied a canoe with three Indians, which they overtook. There were more Indians watching from the bank, and when these people realized that no harm was meant they offered to do some trading. Fernando and his brother were sent ashore to buy fruit and to 'drink some of their artificial wines'. But they were at once seized by the local chief, who accused them of bringing strangers into their territory 'to spoil and destroy them'. They both escaped, Fernando's brother managing to get back to the barge, but Fernando ran into the forest and was hunted with 'deer dogs', and 'with so many a cry that all the woods echoed with the shout they made'. Raleigh then seized an old man as a hostage, threatening to behead him. Meanwhile Fernando at last reached the river's edge and climbed up a tree, from which he jumped and swam to the barge. Raleigh decided to keep the old man as an extra guide, even though he turned out to be often in 'doubt'. In fact he felt that but for him they would never have found their way to the Orinoco.

Raleigh called the people of the delta Tivitivas, which probably was near enough to the original word; Berrío's lieutenant Felipe de Santiago referred to them as Tivetives. In fact they are the equivalent of the present-day Waraos. As Raleigh's *Discoverie* was mainly designed as a propaganda document, he was at pains to praise their virtues. 'I never beheld a more goodly or better favoured people, or a more manly'. He continued with a passage that, like oysters on trees and Amazon women, was ridiculed by his enemies: 'In the summer they have houses on the ground as in other places. In the winter they dwell upon the trees, where they build very artificial towns and villages . . . as those people do near the gulf of Uraba. For between May and September the river of Orinoco riseth thirty feet upright, and then are those islands overflown twenty feet high above the level of the ground, saving those few raised grounds in the middle of them.'

He himself was to witness the alarming rise of the Orinoco, and today one can see Indian houses with floors flooded and hammocks and calabashes slung from rafters. Sometimes the Waraos do have to escape the flood waters and build temporary platforms in upper branches of trees. The mention of Uraba refers to the houses that are still built on stilts near Lake Maracaibo (as at the Barra de Cucuina); hence the origin of the word Venezuela, meaning little Venice.

The Waraos of today are indeed mostly good-looking, rather flat-faced, but not nearly so beautiful as some tribes on the Brazilian frontier, such as the Oyanas and especially the Yanomanis, now being persecuted by gold-miners and foresters. They are kindly people and tend to be hard drinkers. The Venezuelan government has given them subsidies and has built concrete-block houses. As a result there is less incentive to work, and there is a lot of lounging in hammocks.

As for their food, Raleigh pointed out that because of the floods no sowing was possible. The people used *palmitos* for bread (as today) and otherwise existed on wild fruits, fish and the meat of deer, 'porks' (*acures*, like guinea-pigs) and birds. *Palmitos* are the heart of the *moriche* palms, in which are also found large succulent grubs called *gusanos*, much sought after and a great delicacy, repellent-looking to Europeans, but when boiled tasting like sweetbreads, though the natives prefer them raw.* In Raleigh's day the Tivitivas ground the bones of their ancestors into powder and, as a special treat, sprinkled it into their wives' and friends' 'several sorts of drinks'.

Three days later the galley ran aground and Raleigh thought it would be stuck there for ever, and that he would have to leave some of the men behind, to live 'like rooks upon trees', like the Indians. But after throwing out some ballast, and after much tugging and hauling, they got her afloat again. On the fourth day, at last, they reached 'as goodly a river as ever I beheld'. This was the Manamo, 'which ran more directly without windings and turn-ings than the other'. They were no longer affected by the tide from the sea, but now they had to contend with a strong current. The gentlemen took turns with the rowing. After three days more they began to despair. The weather, already extremely hot, was getting worse, and the tall trees on either side of the river kept out any breeze. Also the current was increasing. The bread was finished and they were running out of drinking water. They were becoming weaker just when more strength was needed, living on such fruits as they could find, and on fish and birds which they shot with their fowling pieces. Raleigh kept on saying that there was only one more day's journey to go, and at the same time telling them that if they turned back they would certainly starve. And then 'the world would also laugh us to scorn'.

'We saw birds of all colours, some carnation, some crimson, orange tawny, purple, green, watchet [pale blue].' Apart from parakeets and scarlet ibis, these would have included macaws, toucans, orioles, and the fantastic

---

* The wood of the *moriche* palms is still central to the Waraos, and is turned into dugout canoes as well as bowls and platters. The fibres are prized. The 'artificial wines' also come from the fruit of the *moriches*, fairly potent and mixed with the women's saliva to make it ferment, and known as *cachire*.

hoatzins, not unlike female peacocks. In the great silence of the jungle he would have heard the eerie calls of the red howler monkeys. There were giant lilies with spade-shaped leaves, and among the flowering shrubs enormous cerulean blue butterflies.

The old Indian, now their guide, persuaded them to branch off down a creek where he said there was an Indian village that would let them have bread, hens, fish and palm wine. Raleigh set off with a small party, expecting to return that night. After rowing for three hours there was no sign of this village, and the Indian kept saying that it was just a little further on. Three more hours passed, and still no village. Again he said just a bit further. The sun was about to set, and the men were exhausted. The suspicion now was that he might be leading them to where there were Spaniards who had escaped from Trinidad. They reckoned that they had been rowing for forty miles.

They were even wondering whether to hang the old Indian, but then they realized that if they did this it would mean having to find their way back by night. It was 'dark as pitch' already, and the river was so narrow that they had to keep slashing at overhanging branches with their swords. They had eaten nothing since breakfast. 'It was now eight o'clock at night, and our stomachs began to gnaw apace.' Still the old man kept on saying they should continue. Then at about 1 a.m. they saw the light of a village and heard dogs barking, and a few people came to meet them.

The English, almost collapsing, were taken into the chief's house – he had left for the mouth of the Orinoco to buy women from the cannibals – and there they found all the food and drink they needed. The next day they did some trading and returned to their anxious colleagues with a good quantity of bread, fish and poultry.

On they went, and soon 'on both sides of the river were passed the most beautiful country that ever mine eyes beheld'. They had left the jungle which had seemed so oppressive, and now they were passing through grassy plains.

In divers parts [there were] groves of trees by themselves, as if they had been by all the art and labour in the world so made of purpose; and still we rowed, the deer came feeding by the water's side, as if they had been used to a keeper's call.

It was not all Arcadian idyll though.

Upon this river there were great store of fowl, and of many sorts; we saw in it divers sorts of strange fishes, and of marvellous bigness [fresh-water dolphin], but for *lagartos* [alligators] it exceeded, for there were thousands of these ugly serpents, and the people call it for the abundance of them the river of *lagartos*, in their language. I had a Negro, a very proper young fellow, that leaping out of the galley to swim in the mouth of this river, was in all our sights taken and devoured with one of those *lagartos*.

These days there are fewer alligators to be seen, at any rate by day. Electric eels appear to be the greater danger.

Once again the supply of food ran low. Captain Gifford had gone ahead to look for a landing place where he could build a fire, when to his delight he saw four canoes approaching. He gave chase but two escaped; the others were run ashore and found to be laden with bread, than which as Raleigh said nothing on earth could have been more welcome next to gold. Spirits rose at once, and the men cried out: 'Let us go on. We care not how far'.

Raleigh now landed, having sent a party to search for the fugitives. As he was creeping through the bushes he came across an Indian basket that had been hidden there. It was a refiner's basket, and in it he found not only quicksilver, saltpetre and 'divers things for the search of metal', but some gold dust. Eureka! Meanwhile the fugitive Indians had been rounded up. They were Arawaks and revealed that there had been three Spaniards with them, and that they had taken with them a quantity of gold. This was even more exciting, and Raleigh offered a reward of £500 to any soldier who would capture one of them.

The Spaniards were never found. One of them would certainly have been a great catch, as has been revealed in Spanish correspondence – though Raleigh was never to know it. He was Felipe de Santiago, protégé of Berrío, on his way to Margarita. All Raleigh knew was that he was a *caballero*, and that the other two were a soldier and a gold refiner.

The senior-seeming captured Indian, whom the Spaniards had called Martín, was now taken as a guide. He had been afraid that the English would eat him. The other Arawaks were set free and given back one of the canoes. The old man and Fernando, the first pilot, were given the other canoe and allowed to return. English standards of behaviour were clearly a revelation to Martín and later to other Indians when compared to the 'deceit and purpose' of the Spaniards who 'took from them their wives and daughters daily, and used them for the satisfying of their own lusts'. Not one of his company, Raleigh said, had ever molested any of the Indian women, 'and yet we saw many hundreds, and had many in our power, and of those very young and excellently favoured which came among us without deceit, stark naked'. Nor did he allow anyone to take so much as a pineapple or potato without paying for it, though he 'confirmed it was very impatient work to keep the meaner sort from spoil and stealing'. 'I caused my Indian interpreter at every place when we departed to know of the loss or wrong done, and if ought were stolen or taken by violence, either the same was restored, and the party punished in their sight, or else it was paid for to their uttermost demand.'

A day or so later the galley went aground yet again, and they almost despaired. At last they managed to pull her off. On the fifteenth day of their journey they saw far off the mountains of Guiana 'to our great joy', and towards evening they reached the great Orinoco itself. Very likely these mountains were the Sierra Imataca, still far from the mountain range that Berrío had seen and described, and which had been the escarpment of the Gran Sabana. They made friends with more Indians, who brought them fish and turtles' eggs.

Thousands more turtles' eggs were discovered on a beach where 'three goodly rivers' met. These eggs were found to be 'very wholesome meat and greatly restoring'. It is difficult from a map to pinpoint exactly where this place was: possibly where the Manamo meets the Capure and Tucupita rivers. Here they were visited by the local *cacique*, by name Toparimaca, with thirty or forty men, and with more presents of food. In return the Indians were given some Spanish wine, brought all the way from Trinidad and 'which above all things they love'.

Raleigh 'conferred' about the way to Guiana with Toparimaca, who conducted the galley and boats to his port, some way off, and then to his 'town' called Arowacai, which would seem to be near the present Barracas, a place with English associations, for quite different reasons.* Here some of Raleigh's captains 'garoused' the local wine until they were 'reasonable pleasant'. Also at this place they encountered two *caciques*, each lying in cotton hammocks and attended by two women who ladled wine into cups, which the *caciques* drank three at a time. One of them was a neighbour of Toparimaca, but the other was a stranger who had come up the river to trade. This last was accompanied by his wife.

In all my life I have seldom seen a better favoured woman. She was of good stature, with black eyes, fat of body, of an excellent countenance, her hair almost as long as herself, tied up again in pretty knots, and it seemed she stood not in that awe of her husband, as the rest, for she spake and discoursed, and drank among the gentlemen and captains, and was very pleasant, knowing her own comeliness, and taking great

---

* The original settlers are said to have been English and Irish during the war of liberation, in about 1818.

pride therein. I have seen a lady in England so like her, as but for the difference of colour I would have sworn might have been the same.

Presumably like the other Indian women she was naked. Who could this intriguing lady in England have been? Surely not Bess? Someone who had been swisser-swassered? A. L. Rowse's candidate of the Dark Lady of the Sonnets? At any rate a good piece of titillating propaganda. Against this Raleigh provided proof of the longevity of Guianans. He told how he saw many very aged people showing 'all their sinews and veins, without any flesh'.

The chief gave them a new pilot, an old man 'who was of great experience and travel, and knew the river most perfectly both by day and night'. This was very useful, because of the varying widths of the Orinoco, at times twenty or thirty miles wide, 'with wonderful eddies, and strong currents'; there were also many large islands to negotiate and dangerous rocks, and sometimes sudden gusts of wind that nearly overturned the boats.

One island, Raleigh judged, was as big as the Isle of Wight, and the river banks were mostly steep and stony. They passed rocks of a 'blue metalline colour, like unto the best steel ore', which Raleigh was sure it was. After a while the lands opened up, the banks 'very perfect red'. Raleigh sent ashore a party which reported that the country was all plain as far as you could see. The pilot confirmed that it went on for hundreds of miles, and told Raleigh about the various tribes which lived on it. One tribe was called the Aroras, black as Negroes, smooth-haired, 'very valiant, or rather desperate people, and have the most strong poison on their arrows, and most dangerous of all nations'.

Raleigh the alchemist wanted to know more about this poison, which the old man said caused the most insufferable torment, ending in a 'most ugly and lamentable death'. It drove victims 'stark mad, sometimes their bowels breaking out of their bellies, and are presently discoloured, as black as pitch, and so unsavoury, as no man can endure to cure, or to attend them'. The Spaniards used bribes and tortures to find out the secret of the antidote, but the Indians told it to Raleigh, and how certain juices and roots could 'quench' fever and heal internal haemorrhages. Such knowledge was to be invaluable to him in later years.

On the sixth day on the river they arrived at the port of Morequito, near the mouth of the Caroní river, and there Raleigh met the old chieftain, Topiawari, said to be aged 110, king of Aromaia, the uncle of Morequito who had been killed by Berrío's men.* Raleigh had already heard at Trinidad that Topiawari was now king. The centenarian had walked fourteen miles

* Candide's Cacambo was aged 172.

to meet him, and was accompanied by a great company, including women and children, bringing quantities of victuals, 'venison, pork, hens, chickens, fowl, fish, with divers sorts of excellent fruits, and roots, and great abundance of *piñas*, the princess of fruits'. They also brought bread, wine, and a kind of parakeet, 'no bigger than wrens', and several other birds, large and small.

One of them gave me a beast called by the Spaniards armadillo, which they call *cassacam*, which seemeth to be barred over with small plates somewhat like to a rhinosceros, with a white horn growing in his hinder parts, as big as a great hunting horn.

He was told that a little powder ground from the horn cured deafness. In return Raleigh gave presents. Raleigh had put up a tent for Topiawari to rest in, and there through an interpreter he explained the purpose of his visit, which was to offer the support of the Queen of England against the tyranny of the Spaniards; and he also expatiated on her beauty, virtues, sense of justice and concern for all oppressed nations. He then moved on to the delicate subject of Guiana, and was told about the people who lived beyond the mountains – where Raleigh believed was Manoa. With a great sigh Topiawari told him that his eldest son had been killed in a battle there. These people had 'come as far off as the sun slept', and wore 'large coats and hats of crimson colour'. They were called Oreiones and Epuremei, and had slain many of the original inhabitants, and had built a great town called Macureguarai; and their houses had many rooms, built one over the other, and their borders were defended by 3,000 men.

This story of an invasion by semi-civilized people was evidently well established, and is repeated in an account written by Domingo de Vera. Raleigh was also able to link it with what he had been told by Berrío, for later on he refers to the Epuremei as being 'subjects to Inga, emperor of Guiana and Manoa'.

Topiawari now wanted to leave, because he had far to go, saying that he was 'old and weak, and was every day called for by death'. He refused Raleigh's offer to stay the night, but said he would return another day. Raleigh 'marvelled to find a man of that gravity and judgement, and of so good discourse'.

It has to be said that Francis Sparrey,* in an account he was to write, gives another slant to Raleigh's arrival at Morequito.[1] As Raleigh's men

* p. 231.

Raleigh with the Indian Chief Topiawari, from de Bry's America, *1599.*

drew near they encountered some Indians in canoes who fled and were chased. Five or six were caught and brought before Raleigh who 'embraced' them and gave them gifts. In such a way their confidence was won and an appropriate message was sent to Topiawari. All this seems reasonably true, for why else would Topiawari have been prepared to meet Raleigh with such warmth and generosity? Unless of course advance recommendations had been sent to him by the chief Toparimaca at Arowacai.

The next day Raleigh's expedition left the port and sailed up the Caroní, which Raleigh had been told led to the land of the Epuremei. The current was too strong even for rowing. Another *cacique* appeared, called Wanuretona, and once again presents were exchanged, and there were more stories about the Epuremei and their great wealth. It was in this area that Alvaro Jorge had said that there was a silver mine.* Various reconnaissance parties were sent out; Raleigh, being 'a very ill footman', stayed behind. He climbed

---

* In 1989 the author of this book was taken to a recently discovered mine near the mouth of the Caroní, with an underground furnace, obviously constructed so that it was easy to cover up in an emergency and believed to have been used for smelting silver.

a bank and soon realized that it would be impossible even to sail up the Caroní because of a series of great cataracts, the second and most spectacular being known now as the Salto La Llovizna. Earlier he had heard the great roar and fall of the river, and now

When we ran to the tops of the first hills of the plains adjoining to the river, we beheld that wonderful breach of waters, which ran down Caroní; and might from that mountain see the river how it ran in three parts, above twenty miles off, and there appeared some ten or twelve overfalls in sight, every one as high over the other as a church tower, which fell with that fury, that the rebound of the waters made it seem as if it had been all covered over with a great shower of rain and in some places we took it at the first for a smoke that had risen over some great town.*

He was persuaded by his companions to get closer to this strange 'thunder of waters'. From the next valley

I never saw a more beautiful country, nor more lively prospects, hills so raised here and there over the valleys, the river winding into divers branches, the plains adjoining without bush or stubble, all fair green grass, the ground of hard sand easy to march on, either for horse or foot, for deer crossing in every path, the birds towards the evening singing on every tree with a thousand several tunes, cranes and herons of white, crimson and carnation perching on the river's side, the air fresh with a gentle easterly wind and every stone we stooped to take up promised either gold or silver by his complexion.

This is one of the best-known passages in the *Discoverie*. Raleigh's companions wanted to hack out some pieces of rock, but they had only their daggers and fingers 'to tear them out', and the rock was as hard as flint. When the others returned they brought with them several stones which were coloured but had no gold in them, though some looked like sapphires.

It was at this stage in his narrative that Raleigh recorded something that was to bring him much ridicule. Far inland, to the west of the Orinoco, he said, there was a great lake called Cassipa, perhaps forty miles across, and it was near here that grains of gold were found in the river beds. Further west still were people called the Ewaipanoma.

* The sight is still spectacular, though somewhat diminished as a result of the Guri hydroelectric dam up the river. There is now a great town nearby, Ciudad Guyana, a huge industrial complex, a truly modern city. The valley of the Caroní is also famous for its diamonds. San Félix is on the site of the port of Morequito; from here, among rotting hulks, the ferry crosses the Orinoco, past the island of Fajardo, which Raleigh called Caiana.

They are reported to have their eyes in their shoulders, and their mouths in the middle of their breasts, and that a long train of hair groweth backward between their shoulders.

He admitted that it could well be a fable, yet every child in the provinces of Aromaia and Caroní believed in it. Topiawari's son, whom Raleigh was to bring back with him to England, told him that the Ewaipanoma were the mightiest warriors of all, and used bows, arrows and clubs three times as big as any others in Guiana. They had killed many hundreds of his father's people. Raleigh heard about this only when he had left the district, but if he had known about it then he would have tried to bring back one of these creatures, 'to put the matter out of doubt'. 'For mine own part, I saw them not, but I am resolved that so many people did not all combine or forethink to make the report.'

Much further west, at San Augustín in Colombia, in country now notorious for guerrillas, are quantities of mysterious carved figures dating from pre-Incan times, probably from the 5th century. Nothing is known about the people who created them. Nearly all are grotesque, squat with jaguar fangs and big round eyes. Very many have shoulders on a level with their mouths. Could they be the origin of the legend of the Ewaipanoma?

Another possibility is the head-dresses used by certain tribes on ceremonial occasions, as for example, the Tayrona above Santa Marta on the Colombian coast.

The whole affair may have been treated as a joke by Raleigh's detractors, but it caught the imagination of his contemporaries. In *Othello* there are the lines:

> And of the Cannibals that each other eat
> The Anthropophagi, and men whose heads
> Do grow beneath their shoulders. This to hear
> Would Desdemona seriously incline.

And Gonzalo asks in *The Tempest*:

> When we were boys,
> Who would believe . . .
> . . . that there were such men
> Whose heads stood in their breasts?

Raleigh did not want to waste time at this place:

Especially for that the fury of Orinoco began daily to threaten us with dangers in our return, for no half day passed, but the river began to rage and overflow very fearfully, and the rains came down in terrible showers, and gusts in great abundance; and withal, our men began to cry out for want of shift [change of clothes], for no man had place to bestow any other apparel than that which he wore on his back, and that was thoroughly washed on his body for the most part ten times in one day; and we had now been well near a month.

They returned to the port of Morequito, and Raleigh sent for Topiawari, who duly arrived with a 'rabble of all sorts of people, and everyone laden with somewhat, as if it had been a great market or fair in England'. He took the aged Topiawari into his tent, and they remained there alone with an interpreter. They spoke about Manoa, and Topiawari strongly advised against any attempt to go there, not only because of the time of the year but because the 'Emperor' had such a strong army. It would only be possible to invade that part of Guiana with the help of friendly tribes. Topiawari suggested that Raleigh should leave behind fifty men, whom he would feed, until Raleigh returned the following year as promised. Calfield and Grenville would have liked to stay, but Raleigh would not permit this because of the danger of Spaniards arriving from New Granada and Caracas (possibly Berrío's son and Domingo de Vera).

Topiawari feared the arrival of the Spanish, remembering the time when they had led him by a chain like a dog until a ransom of a hundred gold plates was paid. When, he said, in the following year, Raleigh got ready to invade Macureguarai he would be helped by neighbouring tribes, whose wives and daughters had been snatched by the Epuremei. It was usual in these tribes for men to have ten or twelve wives, but now they had been reduced to a mere three or four. He said this very sadly, adding: 'In truth they were more for women than either for gold or dominion.' The Epuremei liked to have between fifty and a hundred wives each.

He then agreed that Raleigh should take his only remaining son to England. In return Raleigh said he would leave Francis Sparrey, who wanted to stay, and the cabin-boy Hugh Godwin, not as hostages but as a 'pledge'. Godwin was to learn the language. Sparrey was a bit of a writer and 'could describe a country with a pen'; he also was given the dangerous mission of taking 'merchandises' to Macureguarai and to try to get to Manoa.

Finally Raleigh asked how the Epuremei made their plates of gold. He was told that the gold was not 'severed from the stones', but collected as dust or in small heaps and then mixed with copper; 'otherwise they could not work it'. Then the mixture would be put into an earthen pot with holes in it. Canes were then fastened to the holes, into which men blew, increasing the fire until the metal ran. They then threw the liquid gold into moulds of clay or stone.*

So Raleigh and his men left Topiawari, having been given faithful promises that his people would become servants of Her Majesty of England, and if need be resist the Spaniards. Raleigh was then invited by a chief called Putijma to visit his country further down the river, with a promise to show him a mountain which had stones the colour of gold – evidently in the plains of the present-day Upata.

After spending a night at Putijma's 'port', Raleigh took most of the gentlemen in his company in the direction of that mountain, passing along a river called Mana (the present Supamo?). Once again he was impressed by the beauty of the country, and by the lakes and rivers full of fish and wildfowl. They rested at a clear lake, and one of the guides made a fire so that they could dry their shirts which had become heavy with sweat. They then looked for a ford to cross over in the direction of the mountain, which was called the Iconuri. They came across another lake, and here they caught a manatee, 'as big as a wine pipe' and 'very wholesome meat'.

Another half day's march lay ahead, and as 'I was not able myself to endure it' Raleigh sent off Captain Keymis and six others, with Putijma as guide to a promised mine. The plan was to meet again at the river Cumaca (the Tipurua?) further down the Orinoco. It was this expedition by Keymis on which Raleigh based his hopes in 1617.

Raleigh and the rest rowed down the Orinoco to another tributary river, and here he was told where there was a mountain of crystal. Because of the 'evil season' and the distance he could not make the journey there, but he was able to see it far away 'like a white church tower of exceeding height'. 'There falleth over it a mighty river which toucheth no part of the side of the mountain, but rusheth over the top of it, and falleth to the ground with a terrible noise and clamour, as if 1000 great bells were knocked one against another. I think there is not in the world so strange an overfall, nor so wonderful to behold.' This description would seem to be an embroidery to this story, for there is no such waterfall in that part of Venezuela. Perhaps he was repeating something told to him by Berrío, who very probably had

---

* This description has reinforced a theory among students of pre-Colombian metallurgy that the system of alloying gold with copper and silver, creating low grade gold objects, originated in the Orinoco highlands, and was brought to the Andean region by Carib invaders, perhaps in the 4th century or even earlier, and after that spreading north to Mexico and southern Florida. The alloy is commonly known as *tumbaga*, but in the Arawak language it was *guanin*, and in Carib *kavakoli*.

seen these extraordinary and beautiful phenomena, known as *tepuyes*, pouring down the table-top mountains. The most famous and greatest is the Angel Falls, far to the west on the Auyán *tepuy*.

There were several other encounters with tribesmen, not always happy ones. One group was found 'drunk as beggars'. All the same 'we that were weary, and hot with marching, were glad of the plenty, though a small quantity satisfied us, their drink being very strong and heady.' Some local *caciques* had told him that he must meet Carapana, 'one of the greatest of all the lords of Orenocqueponi'. But it turned out that Carapana had fled, having been forewarned by some Spaniards that Raleigh intended to destroy him.

Raleigh did his best to win everybody's confidence, assuring them that he was the enemy of the Spaniards. It was no use, and he never encountered Carapana, regarded as 'notable wise and subtle fellow', aged one hundred, and an 'old fox'. (Later he was to pretend that he had met him.) In any case the weather was becoming stormy, 'full of thunder and great showers', and they were afraid 'both of the billow and the great current' of the Orinoco. There must be no further delay in returning. It took some time to find Keymis, and nothing was said in the *Discoverie* about what he had found or seen. Putijma was very distressed at their urgent departure, and offered to let them take his son to England; 'but our hearts were cold to behold the great rage and increase of Orinoco'. It was at this stage that Topiawari's present, the poor captive armadillo, was killed, and they 'feasted' on it, evidently with much enjoyment, its meat being soft as a pig's.

They were not able to reach the Manamo, so they returned instead by the Capure. It was a tedious journey, and at the mouth of the river they encountered another huge and frightening storm. This was the 'bitterest moment' of all; 'for I protest before God that we were in a most desperate state'. The longer they stayed there, the worse it became. The only thing was to abandon the galley altogether, and to make the crossing huddled in the other boats. So at midnight 'we put ourselves into God's keeping, and thrust out into the sea'.

And so being all very sober, and melancholy, one faintly cheering another to show courage, it pleased God that the next day about nine of the clock we descried the island of Trinidad, and steering for the nearest part of it, we kept the shore till we came to Curiapan, where we found our ships at anchor, than which there was never to us a more joyful sight.

This part of the great journey was now over, and it was time to 'leave Guiana to the sun, whom they worship, and steer away towards the north'.

Raleigh had a few plates of gold, presents from Topiawari, and some mineral specimens, herbs and balsam. Sparrey was to say that Raleigh had no less than 808 calabashes full of treasures, but it must have been an exaggeration.[2] Even so; all this was not enough to reimburse the investors. Not surprisingly Raleigh decided that some privateering would have to be the answer, and he needed to plunder the towns along the Spanish Main.

None of the following appears in the *Discoverie*, presumably because the results were so disastrous. The details are mostly gleaned from Spanish reports.[3]

With Berrío and Jorge on board, he went first to the island of Margarita, famous for its pearls, arriving on 16 June at the well-fortified main port, Pampatar, then Manpatone. Its Governor, Salazar, at once despatched fifty mounted arquebusiers to be ready to defend the place. The English then threatened the Rancheria, where pearls were mainly fished, but were beaten back. Four English were captured. Raleigh's ships sailed on and anchored at Punta Mosquito, the corner of the island nearest to the mainland, a truly dreary place, a wasteland of scrub and cacti. Probably his men marched on to the nearest inhabited spot, La Isleta, near a lagoon. The Spaniards reappeared, and according to a Simón Bolivar, *contador* of Margarita, in a letter to Madrid of 8 July, the 'enemy' produced Alvaro Jorge and three others, demanding a ransom of 1,400 ducats. This sum was agreed, but the Governor intervened. The deal was off and the English sailed on to Cumaná on the mainland, about sixty miles from Punta Mosquito.

Cumaná, on a large bay and in a kind of ampitheatre with mountains behind, was possibly the first Spanish settlement in South America: it was to be cursed over the centuries with a sequence of war, revolution and earthquake. The Castillo de San Antonio is on a commanding site, and Raleigh found the place more difficult to attack than he expected. Its Governor, Francisco de Vidés, was of course Berrío's great rival and hate.

In one of the Spanish accounts we read:[4]

There arrived at the port of this City an English pirate with three great war-vessels and one pinnace or galliot with oars and four launches; and it is commonly believed that the commander of the fleet is an Englishman named Milo Guatterral, who embarked a large number of two hundred and ten fighting men, musketeers and pikemen, who landed to burn, pillage and devastate this city.

The battle was fierce, and the English captured some heights with 'devilish fury'. The Spaniards retaliated with concentrated musket-fire, and Captain Calfield was killed, as was soon afterwards John Grenville. They also claimed to have killed the 'captain of the little galliot, Thechen,' who may have been Thynne.

In his report Vidés wrote:[5]

Many more were wounded, they became so exhausted, that they were compelled to abandon the height, and began to flee . . . Then as they were retiring I rallied all the people who were with me in one of the forts, and all who were able followed up the victory to the seashore . . . On nearing the harbour the enemy was completely broken, and rushed into the sea in an endeavour to get to their boats, so that our men and the Indians shot them down at pleasure; and consequently they left us all the arms which they had brought, including muskets and the rest of their belongings. Our people took much spoil from them, and we found forty-eight Englishmen killed, besides the wounded who must be numerous. For I have been informed that twenty-seven have died aboard the ships.

Some of the English escaped by swimming. Vidés said that the final number killed was ninety-five, though another report said eighty. True or not, it was all a great disaster for Raleigh, and a deep sadness for the loss of his cousin Grenville and his trusted Calfield. In the *Discoverie* he said that Whiddon had been 'buried in the sands of Trinidad', but perhaps in reality he had been killed at Cumaná.

According to Vidés, Raleigh was so upset by the cries of the wounded that during the day he sought relief by calling on some Flemish merchantmen somewhere in the vicinity, returning later in the evening.

Another curious comment from a Spanish source is that on 'another day' Raleigh went to dine with Lucas Fajardo at a place a league from Cumaná, Fajardo 'being on good terms with English passers by'. 'For this reason proceedings are being taken against him . . . He [Raleigh] sent him certain gifts and presents, and the said Fajardo likewise to him'. This Fajardo was another of Berrío's enemies.*

Raleigh now decided to release Berrío, who had been his captive for eleven weeks. No ransom was asked; instead he was exchanged for a captured drummer boy who had been wounded in the leg. Perhaps Alvaro Jorge was handed over as well, unless he had been simply abandoned at Punta Mosquito. According to Vidés, not one Spaniard or Indian was

* p. 219.

wounded, but this certainly is questionable. No wonder when Berrío was handed over to Vidés, 'he was little favoured and badly received'.

Raleigh may originally have had plans to raid Rio de la Hacha and Santa Marta after Cumaná: two favourites for English privateers. But after the losses at Cumaná this seems hardly possible. On 30 June Vidés added to his report: 'Today the Englishman has sailed away in the direction of Macanao. It is said that he does not go away as pleased as he could wish.'

Raleigh must still have hoped to find some Spanish ship to capture. All we know is that two weeks later he ran into Preston and Somers off Cuba.* One of Preston's men, Robert Davie, wrote how they met Raleigh, 'returning from his painful and happy discovery of Guiana, and his surprise of the Isle of Trinidad'.[6] 'With glad hearts' they kept him and his fleet company for another week. Raleigh had indicated that he might visit Virginia, in the hope of finding clues about the fate of the Lost Colonists. Instead he headed home for England, arriving in Plymouth on about 5 September.

* p. 223.

Drake's Last Voyage
1595

Bess was at Sherborne when news reached her about Raleigh's return and the enthusiastic welcome he had received. In her excitement she could not resist writing at once to Cecil, her spelling tumbling over itself:[1]

Sur hit tes trew I thonke the leveng God Sur Walter is safly londed at Plumworthe with as gret honnor as ever man can, but with littell riches. I have not yet hard from him selfe. Kepe thies I besech you to your selfe yet: only to me lord ammerall. In haste this Sunday. Your poure frind E Raleg.

Then some less comforting information reached her, and she added a postscript.

Mani of his mene slane; him selfe will now. Pardon my rewed wryteng with the goodnes of the newes.

On the face of it Raleigh had little to show – much would depend on the assayers' verdict on the stones and earth that he had brought back. He had also to explain away the deaths of so many trusted companions.

Rowland Whyte, friend of Sir Robert Sidney,[2] wrote:

Sir Walter Rawley is returned with an assured loss of his bravest men . . . his wealth, in my Lord Treasurer's opinion 'tis made little; in Sir Robert Cecil's very great.

This was written on 25 September. Two days later he wrote again.

Sir Walter Rawley's friends do tell Her Majesty what great service he hath done unto her by his late voyage, in discovering the way to bring home the wealth of India, and in making known to that nation her virtues, her justice. He hath brought back a supposed prince, and left hostages in his place. The Queen gives good ear to them. I am promised, for you, his own discourse to the Queen of his journey.

From this we note that Robert Cecil's enthusiasm or hopes were not shared by his father Lord Burghley. Cecil must still have been counted as one of the friends at Court. The 'discourse' could have been the *Discoverie* which Raleigh was rushing out at speed, to counteract the malicious rumours by enemies such as Oxford and Henry Howard that he had never been to Guiana at all but had been skulking in Cornwall, and that all those pretty stones and bits of so-called gold had really come from the Barbary coast.

Undoubtedly the Queen would have been interested in the reports, but she was far from sharing any enthusiasm, and there was no sign of his returning to favour. She took no notice. More important things were worrying her. There had been another bad harvest, after three years of wet summers. In January English troops under Sir John Norris had withdrawn from Brittany, having prevented the Spaniards from capturing Brest by the successful storming of Crozon nearby. But that did mean that Spanish galleys were more free to sail round the Cornish coasts almost without check, and in May some of them had captured a fishing boat in Falmouth harbour. The fishermen were questioned about a major expedition it was known in Spain that Drake and Hawkins were planning, but disappointingly for the Spaniards they knew little or nothing.

Then, much more serious, on 23 July four galleys, having first attempted to raid Padstow on the north coast, rounded Land's End, and out of the sea-mist appeared opposite Mousehole. Men were landed and proceeded to burn down the little fishing port and the neighbouring village of Paul. More Spaniards came ashore, perhaps 400, and set fire to Newlyn and Penzance. A thanksgiving mass was held on the high ground above: it was regarded by the Cornish as the final insult.

All this while the Lord Lieutenant had been away in Guiana. His deputy, Sir Francis Godolphin, had sent an urgent message to Drake and Hawkins at Plymouth, who both had been almost ready to sail. They sent round several ships to try to intercept the invaders, but due to a sudden change in the direction of the wind they arrived too late.

Now, on his return, Raleigh was expected to assert himself. He was ordered to go down to Cornwall and make sure that levies were properly trained, and that his deputy lieutenants were arranging for the most vulnerable towns to be fortified. Owners of castles and large houses near the coast, from Cornwall to Dorset, were to be told to be ready to help in defence, 'upon pain of forfeiture of their livelihoods and further punishment'.

Raleigh also learnt that Drake and Hawkins had only recently left Plymouth: twenty-seven ships in all, with 2,500 men under the command of Sir Thomas Baskerville. This would have been a great worry for him, as he had known all about their plans before leaving for Guiana. It is clear that he had intended to bring Berrío to England, both for the ransom and to substantiate his stories about El Dorado – but when in Trinidad, in order to encourage Berrío to speak openly, as if for a *quid pro quo* he had recklessly given details of Drake's plan to capture Panama. Now that Berrío had been freed he would be able to relay all this important information to Madrid: which was exactly what happened.

Berrío wrote to Philip on 11 July. He told how, according to Raleigh, Drake and Hawkins were to have joint command of this large fleet (he exaggerated the size), and on some of the ships there would be flat bottomed boats. It was intended to land 2,000 men in these boats on the river Chayre, and then to head for Panama on the Pacific coast. The ships would dock at Nombre de Dios, in preparation for the sacking of Cartagena. 'This', Berrío wrote, 'is the account related to me by General Guatarral, who is captain of the Queen of England's guard.'

As it happened, the Queen at one stage had thought of diverting the whole expedition to Ulster, where the rebellion was becoming serious, but then well substantiated evidence had arrived to the effect that a Spanish invasion fleet, commanded by Bernardino de Avellaneda, was being planned for the summer of 1596. A strict order was therefore issued to Drake and Hawkins that they would have to return to England by May. It was also suggested that instead of sailing to the Caribbean it might even be better just to go to the Azores and catch the *flota* there.

Then came the dramatic report that a large Spanish galleon loaded with treasure had been badly damaged in a storm and had taken refuge in the harbour of San Juan at Puerto Rico, and was lying there unrigged and immobilized. So Elizabeth agreed that Drake and Hawkins should make straight for San Juan – which must have been a relief for Raleigh. (It did not seem to have occurred to anybody that the Spaniards would hardly leave such a valuable ship unprotected with its cargo still on board.)

In spite of this new order, Drake and Hawkins were determined to sail on to Panama in whatever time would be left available.

Raleigh wrote a long and obviously impressive paper for the Privy Council[3] on the defences of the west, pointing out the special vulnerability of Cornwall, its southern coastline being eighty miles long; it was virtually an island, easily invaded. To send relief troops there in the event of attack would, he said, be difficult, because of the barrier of the River Tamar. He also pointed out that Falmouth with its large and deep harbour 'could receive the greatest fleet that ever swam': an ideal base for the Spaniards. In this he was justified, as Falmouth was to have been the objective of Avellaneda's new armada.

He was still on tenterhooks about reactions to his reports on Guiana. By any standards it had been a stupendous effort, and it had been at stupendous expense. He had given a promise to his Indian friends that he would soon be back, but this time it would have to be with official and substantial support from the Government. Speed was in any case essential, because of the danger of Spanish reinforcements which could already be on their way.

In October he was in London, and Dr Dee noted in his diary that he dined with Raleigh on the 9th at Durham House.[4] This must have been out of courtesy, for old Dee was becoming a spent force, having somewhat reluctantly agreed to be warden of the Collegiate Chapter at Manchester, which meant having to leave London.

A little while later Rowland Whyte wrote with the amusing news that 'Raleigh goes daily to hear sermons, because he has seen the wonders of the Lord in the deep'.[5] But he also added: ' 'Tis much commended and spoken of'. If true, this was certainly a good riposte to all those accusations of atheism.

On 10 November Raleigh wrote gloomily to Cecil from 'this desolate place' (by which he meant his beloved Sherborne) with the excuse of telling him about a rumour that a fleet of sixty Spanish ships had been spotted, possibly preparing to sail for Ireland. His real concern, though, was Guiana, whether people were taking it as 'history or fable'. He had heard that 'Master Dudley and others' were planning to go out there again. If so, he said, all his good work in winning over the friendship of the chieftains would be cancelled out.

Then, suddenly, there was a wonderful boost: a vindication of so much that had been laughed at. Captain George Popham arrived, at long last, with a bundle of Spanish letters that he had captured the previous year. They were all to do with El Dorado and included official accounts of the mission of Domingo de Vera to Morequito, on behalf of Berrío, in 1593. The *Discoverie* had not yet been published, so the story of a tribe with men who had heads beneath their shoulders would have been passed around the Court only as a good joke, but here it all was, in one of the letters: men with 'points of their shoulders higher than the crowns of their heads'. Not only that, there were references to people who 'anointed their bodies with stamped herbs of glutinous substance and then covered themselves with gold dust'.

The documents, needless to say, had been written to impress officials in

Madrid, and they made out that Vera's mission had been a triumph, every *cacique* welcoming Spanish sovereignty. This was to be expected, but most thrilling of all was a communication from Jamaica that spoke of a giant golden idol, weighing 47 hundredweight, which had lately been discovered and was being sent to Spain.

Raleigh sent everything on to Cecil, presumably in translation, with a triumphant letter.[6] 'You will perceive by this relation [description] that it is no dream which I have reported of Guiana.' He reckoned that the idol would be worth £100,000. 'I know that in Manoa there are store of these.' He 'humbly beseeched' Cecil to 'move Her Majesty', so advantage could be taken of the good will of the chiefs, without interference from 'pilferers' (meaning Dudley). He was in any case, he said, sending out a bark 'to comfort and assure the people that they despair not'; in fact, though he did not say so at this stage, Lawrence Keymis was to be in charge of this little expedition.

He also urged Cecil to get hold of the map that Hariot had just completed, based on his own draft and perhaps after consulting Dr Dee, so that it could be shown to the Queen.

This map must be the great chart on vellum now rolled up in the British Library, in some ways stylized, but in other ways – where depicting the whole length of the Spanish Main, from Margarita to Nombre de Dios – surprisingly accurate.[7] Right in the centre is a grotesque object looking like a huge centipede. This represents the lake of Manoa, with tributaries all of equal length and at equal distances from one another, thirteen on each side, like legs. Above is shown the river Amazon, which he calls the Maranion, again with similar stylized tributaries at equal distances, making it look like some great wriggling eel that had grown feet. The city of Manoa is shown at the east end of the lake, a kind of Xanadu, all domes and spires; likewise the city of the Epuremei, equally exotic. Trinidad and the delta are also on the map, including Curiapan, the site of Raleigh's fort, and the caños Capure and Amana (Manamo).

In his letter Raleigh mentioned the gold samples and the diamonds he had brought back. It would seem that by then the assayers had agreed that the 'spar' did have some gold. Other stones were worthless, some being marcasite or 'fool's gold', as Raleigh had suspected. The diamonds were more promising. He was having a large one cut for Cecil, and was also sending him an amethyst 'with a strange blush of carnation'. 'I assure myself', he said, 'that there are not more diamonds in the East Indies than are to be found in Guiana'. The stones he had brought back 'bore witness of better'.

He was so delighted to have these documents from Popham that he

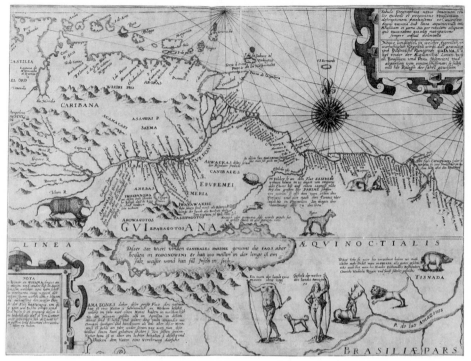

Guiana, from de Bry's America, *1599,*
showing a headless man and an Amazon.

decided to include some as an appendix to the *Discoverie*.* All the same, they failed to make an impression on the Privy Council, or on the Queen if she ever saw them. Two more weeks passed, and there was still silence. Winter was approaching, and unless a decision was made soon to send out an official expedition there would be no hope of victualling the ships for the summer, and that would mean farewell to Guiana, forever. He was now appealing to the Lord Admiral Howard, to whom he had also written to say that he had heard that ships were being sent out from Spain in pursuit of Drake and Hawkins. He urged that a couple of carvells or pinnaces should be sent to warn them. It would be disastrous, he said, if this Spanish fleet arrived at Nombre de Dios when the English soldiers were on the other side of the isthmus at Panama.

* In translation they are slightly abbreviated. The originals, in full, are in the British Library. Fortunately for the Spaniards, duplicate copies had been made, and they are now in Archivo General de Indias at Seville.[8]

Howard, of course, did not know what guilty motives lay behind this letter.

It was true that what had been intended as Avellaneda's invasion fleet, at present lying at Lisbon, was preparing to chase after Drake and Hawkins. A letter had reached him from the Canaries reporting an unsuccessful attempt by the English to land there.

But, unknown to both English and Spaniards, Hawkins had died on 11 November off San Juan, 'of grief' it was said. A little before leaving England he had learnt that his son Richard had been captured at sea, and he had been hoping that on this voyage he might somehow obtain his release.

He knew too that the whole venture was turning out a dismal failure. For one thing, there had been clashes of personality between him and Drake, almost from the start. The differences between them are well brought out in an account of a land captain, Thomas Maynarde, a protégé of Drake and therefore probably somewhat biased.[9] Drake, he said, had a lively spirit, and was resolute, quick, affable and easy of access, but with a stormy temper and was too pleased by open flattery. Hawkins was slow, jealous, and 'hardly brought to resolution'; he was also inclined to 'malice with dissimulation, rudeness in behaviour'. Both were 'faulty in ambition'. Although Hawkins was the less interested in self-promotion, Maynarde considered Drake the greater man.

The fleet had reached Guadaloupe on 29 October. Four days later disturbing news reached Drake and Hawkins that the *Francis*, which had become separated by strong winds, had been captured by five *gallizardos* or frigates that had sailed from the Canaries. They were not to know that the captain had failed to destroy his papers, in which it was revealed that San Juan was to be their next objective. As a result the Spanish commander, Pedro Tello, had immediately sailed to warn the garrison at San Juan.

The English wasted too much time at Guadaloupe, watering, trimming sails. Meanwhile defences were being frantically improved at San Juan. Silver and other treasures were being removed to the El Morro fortress guarding the harbour – the plan being, as a last resort, to throw everything into the sea. It was at this stage that Hawkins became ill. He died soon after the fleet had dropped anchor near El Morro.

There were furious bombardments from both sides, and on one occasion Drake's stool was said to have been shot away from under him. English ships were sunk, and Tello scuttled two Spanish cargo ships to block the harbour.

Greatly depressed at the failure Drake moved the fleet to the bay of San

Germán, taking on water, oranges and lemons. He then sailed on to Rio de la Hacha (now Riohacha). There were only fifty houses there, and most of the inhabitants had fled, taking with them, or hiding, anything of value. Nevertheless prisoners were taken and these were forced, either though threats or torture, to reveal some of the hiding places, so a little worthwhile booty was collected. The local pearl fishery was raided, and Drake took on board a hundred Negroes who had been working there. He stayed two weeks, again a dangerous waste of time, if he had known, given that Avellaneda was already in his way across the Atlantic. Then the town was burnt, except – unusually for Drake – the church, and some grand lady's house. Next he went to Santa Marta, supposed to have been one of Raleigh's targets, but it proved less productive. He burnt that too.*

He avoided Cartagena, realizing that it must have been prepared for his arrival, but possibly also because he was worried about the spread of sickness on his ships from a lethally infectious disease that been picked up at Rio de la Hacha. On he went to Nombre de Dios, which was easily overrun, yielding a small amount of profit. Baskerville disembarked six or seven hundred soldiers who set off along the muletrack to Panama on the Pacific coast. But they had chosen the wrong season for the long journey. Continual rain created mud into which men sank to their knees. A small Spanish force appeared, blocking the way. So after a few days the English had to turn back.

This was a terrible blow for Drake, and there was a great deal of bitterness among the men. Also the sickness, described as a 'bloody dysentery', was spreading alarmingly. On 5 January the fleet sailed for Nicaragua, and it was here that Drake himself caught the disease. He died on 28 January 1596. The body was put into a lead coffin and lowered into the sea off Porto Belo near the scene of his earlier triumphs, 'the trumpets in doleful manner echoing'.[10] Another who died on that same day was Abraham Kendall, the rough diamond who had accompanied him so often and had been to Trinidad with Robert Dudley.

Avellaneda had left Spain on 20 December, with a fleet of eight large galleons and some dozen other ships. He reached Cartagena on 17 February.

---

* Santa Marta was founded in 1520, and it was from here that the great Captain-General Gonzalo Jiménes de Quesada (p. 218) set out to conquer New Granada and found Santa Fé de Bogotá. Also near here, at San Pedro Alejandro, the liberator Simón Bolívar died on 17 December 1830. Riohacha, on the fringe of a mostly arid peninsula, is a free port and a great place for smugglers. The pearlers have mostly disappeared. The road between Riohacha and Santa Marta is these days not without risks for the unwary traveller, and the same could certainly be said about Santa Marta after nightfall.

Meanwhile Baskerville had taken over from Drake as commander. Discipline in the English fleet after Drake's death had been hard to enforce. The sickness was spreading and rations were short. Some vessels deserted and others were scattered by bad weather. The remaining fourteen ships encountered Avellaneda off Cuba. There was a fierce battle, though indecisive, and the English sailed homeward.

Early in January a small ship owned by Raleigh and Sir Robert Cross, the *Little Exchange*, had sailed from Plymouth, evidently to warn Drake of the Spaniards' approach. It was captured by Avellaneda about ten days after the battle off Cuba. And around the same time he also captured the *Hope*, one of the ships that had become separated from Baskerville. Some of the crews of both ships were put to the galleys and others were sent to Seville to be tried by the Inquisition.

No Forgiveness Yet
1596

Early in 1596 the *Discoverie* was published, with an impressive dedication to the two men whom Raleigh maintained had supported him most in the 'darkest shadow of my adversity':

To the Right Honorable my Singular good Lord and kinsman Charles Howard, knight of the Garter, Barron and Counceller, and of the Admiralls of England the most renowned: and the Right Honorable Sir Robert Cecyll Knight, Counceller in her Highnes privie Councels.

They had stood by him he said, when everyone else had abandoned him out of 'malice and revenge', and had shown him affection during his 'many miseries'. And he was ready to admit that his errors had been very great.

This new humility was mixed with self-pity. For he now considered himself past his prime: 'In the winter of my life [I did] undertake those travels, fitter for boys less blasted with misfortunes, for men of greater ability, and for minds of better encouragement'. (He was a good deal younger than Drake and Hawkins had been on their last voyage.) These travels had been accompanied 'with many sorrows, with labour, hunger, heat, sickness and peril'; they had been at his own expense, and he had returned a 'beggar and withered'.

In the dedication he also took the opportunity of publicly ridiculing his detractors who had made all those snide innuendoes against him, saying that he had led too easy a life to be able to attempt such a journey, that all the while he had been hiding in Cornwall; and, even more absurd, that he – of all people – would 'rather become a servant of the King of Spain'.

It would have been quite possible, he went on, to have held the Indian chieftains to ransom, and to have taken their gold in return. Instead he had made them his friends, and as a result they desired 'nothing more than her Majesty's protection' and the return of the English. He hoped that the Queen would view his labours in 'gracious part' and understand why he had chosen to bear the burden of poverty on her behalf. In other words he was hoping that she would now be inspired to send out an official expedition, with himself in command, in order to annex and govern Guiana. 'The shining glory of this conquest will eclipse all those so far extended beams of the Spanish nation . . . whatsoever prince shall possess it shall be the greatest'. In Guiana there were more rich and beautiful cities, more temples adorned with golden images, more sepulchres filled with treasure, than either Cortés found in Mexico, or Pizarro in Peru.

To conclude, Guiana is a country that hath yet her maidenhead, never sacked, turned nor wrought, the face of the earth hath not been torn, nor the virtue and salt of its soil spent by manurance [cultivation], the graves have not been opened for gold, the mines not broken with sledges, nor their images pulled down out of their temples. It has not been entered by any army of strength, and never conquered or possessed by any Christian prince.

He believed that only a small army would be needed to march on Manoa and subdue the Inca chief, who would thereupon be entirely happy to provide Her Majesty with a yearly tribute of the equivalent of £100,000, and would be prepared to subsidize an English garrison to help him to defend his country against the Spaniards.

His readers could have been excused for wondering how he reached such a conclusion. And what about that other great danger: those warlike Amazon women? He gave his answer at the end of the *Discoverie*:[1]

Where the south border of Guiana reacheth to the Dominion and Empire of the Amazons, those women shall hereby hear the name of a virgin, who is not only able to defend her own territory and her neighbours', but also able to invade and conquer so great empires and so far removed.

Even this eloquent peroration could not move the Virgin Queen. She showed no sign of being impressed by her new name, Ezrabeta Cassipuna Aquerewana. She knew her limitations; that was one of her strengths. Raleigh was to complain of this in his *History*: 'She did all things by halves, and by petty invasions taught the Spaniard how to defend himself'.[2]

In reality it had not been Raleigh who had 'discovered' Guiana, it had been Berrío. Yet it could not be denied that the whole expedition had been an immense and arduous adventure, a great achievement. He had been the first Englishman to penetrate South America. Because of the *Discoverie* Raleigh's name would forever be associated with El Dorado, and but for him Berrío's name would be forgotten, at any rate by non-Spaniards.

'To seek new worlds, for gold, for praise, for glory', he had written in the *Ocean to Cynthia*, and his expedition had been all of that. He had desperately wanted to win Elizabeth's forgiveness, but it was not forthcoming. Could his voyage also have been, as has been suggested, a kind of pilgrimage, a rebirth? Or was it just a great piece of theatre? 'For praise, for glory', and what about the gold? Did he visualize Manoa as a place to be ransacked? Would its sepulchres and temples be left intact? If not, how could its people be expected so joyfully to pay such a huge yearly tribute?

Throughout the *Discoverie* there is no mention of trying to convert these pagans to Christianity, or even of confronting the evils of Roman Catholicism, though in an unsigned propaganda piece, obviously not written by him but perhaps by Keymis, entitled *Of the Voyage to Guiana*, such matters are touched upon. Raleigh does, however, seem to have had a genuine feeling of humanity towards the Indians: treating them well was not just a pretence, a subtle way of breaking into Spain's ill-gotten gains.

The book sold widely, and was a greater success than the voyage. Written at speed, it had an immediacy and excitement stemming from the fact that, unlike his piece on the *Revenge*, Raleigh was a participator not just the narrator. It was immediately reprinted, and then again several times. There were four German editions between 1599 and 1602, and it was published in Dutch in 1598. There were Latin editions printed at Nuremberg and Frankfurt in 1599. The result was that there was no secret about Guiana any more, and Dutch and French expeditions were soon to be seen on the Orinoco.

It took a long time for the dream of El Dorado to fade. Raleigh's Arcadian descriptions have echoes in Milton's vision of Eden. In 1719, the year of *Robinson Crusoe*, Daniel Defoe wrote a pamphlet on Raleigh, 'humbly proposed' (dedicated) to the South Seas Company. In it he suggested in effect that the South Seas Company should follow in Raleigh's footsteps to Guiana, which had certainly been the 'greatest enterprise undertaken by any private person in the world'.

Probably by the time the *Discoverie* was published Raleigh had already begun to despair of regaining Elizabeth's 'princely and royal heart'. Apart from that, it was clear that the war with Spain was reaching a new crisis, and this was preoccupying her.

He had given his word to Topiawari and other *caciques* that he would return soon to help them against the Spaniards. But for the time being any further expeditions would have to be at his own initiative, and these could only be in the nature of maintaining friendship, liaison and obtaining new information, though naturally there was always hope that some gold would also be acquired. He had already arranged to send out Lawrence Keymis, primarily to locate the mountain mine that the *cacique* Putijma had spoken about, but also to find a channel into the Orinoco that would admit ships of a greater draft.

Keymis left on this new mission at the end of January 1596 in the *Darling of London*, with John Gilbert as pilot, and with a pinnace, that had been christened the *Discoverie*. On his return Keymis wrote a dutifully enthusiastic account of his adventures, such as they were, *A Relation of the Second Voyage to Guiana*.[3] He wrote how near the Cape Verde islands a storm arose, and he lost sight of the *Discoverie*. It was not until mid-March that he was able to reach the Orinoco delta. After cruising up and down for twenty-three days he at last found a suitable channel that would take his ship directly into the main river. Some *caciques* were delighted to see him, thinking at first that he was Raleigh come to defeat the Spaniards, and they spat into their right hands as a gesture of friendship. One important piece of news for Raleigh was that the golden city of Manoa was now said to be much further south, near the headwaters of the river Dessekebe (now Essequibo), from which it could be more conveniently reached.

Keymis also heard yet again about the headless men, whose 'mouths in their breast were exceedingly wide'. Francis Sparrey, he was told, had been captured but had ransomed his life with the gold he had collected, and was now in Cumaná. The cabin-boy Hugh Godwin, on the other hand, had been 'eaten by a tiger'. Topiawari was dead, after fleeing from Berrío's men who had returned to the mouth of the Caroní. His son, whom Raleigh had taken to England where he was known as Gualtero, would now be king on his return. Putijma had gone into hiding.

This time the wind was right for sailing up the Orinoco (which Keymis had renamed the Raleana), much easier than rowing. After eight days he reached the port of Morequito, only to find that near there Berrío had built a village of some twenty or thirty huts within a fort, which he called Santo Thomé. It was too risky to proceed further up the Caroní, so he was forced to return to the open sea. There he found the pinnace *Discoverie* waiting for him, but in such a bad state that he decided to burn her rather than leave her to be taken over by the Spanish. At first, as they set out for home, there was considerable danger from cannibals. They were not even able to pick up any tobacco, which at least would have helped to pay for the cost of the expedition. Thus Keymis on his return had to confess that he had emptied Raleigh's 'purse'.

In December Raleigh sent out the pinnace *Watte* under Captain Leonard Berry, with the object of exploring the rivers south of the Orinoco, and he was encouraged by the result. Berry reported among other things that the Dessekebe was so large that the Indians called it the brother of the Orinoco.[4] He said that 'after twenty days navigating they [the Indians] convey their canoes by porterage of one day from the river Dessekebe to a lake which the Jaos called Roponowini, and Charibes [Caribs] Parime. This lake is as large as a sea; it is covered with an infinite number of canoes; and I suppose that this lake is no other than that which contains the town of Manoa.'*

Francis Sparrey had indeed been captured by the Spaniards, and had eventually been taken to Madrid, where he remained in prison until 1603. He was interrogated by the *licenciado* Pedro de Liáno at Margarita, at the end of February 1596, and it is from this report that we learn that he and Hugh Godwin were treated very kindly by the Indians, who gave them presents and respected them.[5] But:

In the month of June in the year 1595, the younger of the two Englishmen [Godwin] going out into the country in English dress, was attacked by four tigers [jaguars] who tore him to pieces. The other Englishman, when sailing down the river, was seized by four Spaniards, who brought him to the Island of Margarita on the 25th of February this year.

Sparrey was interrogated again in Madrid. In the transcripts at the Archivo de Indias – where he features as Francisco Esparri, Raleigh as Guaterrale and Cecil as Conde Sicilia – it was claimed that the gifts Raleigh received from the Indian chiefs in the 808 calabashes included bars of gold, precious stones and balsam, and were worth a million ducats. In return the Indians were given small mirrors, knives and combs.

Sparrey had said that he became tired of living among savages, and that when he had been captured he was hoping to find English ships coasting along the delta. On his return to England he wrote a description of his time in Guiana which was eventually published by Purchas in 1625. From this it is clear that he travelled far inland in the direction of Peru.

---

* Reponowini would be the present Rupununi, a river which runs into the Essequibo. In the rainy season there is a good sized lake in the area, called the Amuku, but otherwise it is dry. In 1740 a German surgeon, Nicholas Hartsman, was sent to the upper Essequibo to search for El Dorado and found the Amuku in flood. The local Indians then directed him to Mount Ucucu-amo, which they called the 'mountain of gold', but when he got there he found nothing but rock crystals.

Camalaha is a place where they sell women at certain times, in the manner of a fair. And there you shall buy colours such as the savages paint themselves with. In this fair ... I bought eight young women, the eldest whereof I think never saw eighteen years, for one red-hafted knife which in England cost me one half penny. I gave these women to certain savages who were my friends at the request of Waritue, the king's daughter of Morequito.

He also reached a 'most sweet pleasant and temperate island' called Athul, perhaps on the river Apure. 'If I had company to my liking, I could have found in mine heart to have stayed there and spent my life.'

As for the fresh water pearls, they were 'nothing round, orient, not very great', and his Spanish captors later told him that they were topazes. He seemed to have been daunted by the wilderness ahead, and more especially no doubt by the alarming legends around the *tepuy* Auyán, 4000 feet, sacred to the Indians, that stood in his way like a sentinel in the rainforest.*

As for Berrío, it was unfortunate for him that Raleigh should have left him at Cumaná with his deadly enemy, Francisco de Vidés, and indeed he was 'little favoured and badly received' there. He managed to get across to Margarita and then to Trinidad and the ashes of his town, San José. Soon afterwards he proceeded up the Orinoco to the port of Morequito, where he built the fort of San Thomé. To his great relief his son and thirty soldiers joined him there from New Granada. This was the situation when Keymis arrived in March 1596.

In the following month Domingo de Vera arrived at last at Trinidad, with six flyboats carrying 1,500 would-be settlers, including women and children, also various monks and priests. His enthusiasm and persuasive tongue had resulted in his raising large sums of money in Spain. Nevertheless to dump all those people in such a remote part of the world, surrounded by cannibals, was a lunatic idea, one that was to turn into a tragedy.[7]

First Vera had to gain control of Trinidad, which had been occupied by supporters of Vidés. Next came the task of moving everybody to San Thomé, but attacks by cannibals followed by hurricanes meant that only three canoes survived. Several people were drowned. Foodstuffs and munitions were lost. So the journey had to be made on foot, and such baggage as was left was loaded into the canoes. It was a dreadful journey through this

* According to Spanish documents he married in Madrid and had a son. He also became a Catholic, having promised to guide an expedition to hidden treasure on the banks of the Orinoco – all of which came to naught. He was returned to England, with or without wife and child, in exchange for a Portuguese Jesuit.[6]

unknown and dangerous country, hacking their way through jungle and swamp, only to find that they were to be left in a place unsuitable for the 'rich and costly gala dresses' which they had brought with them. As soon as they were settled, Berrío despatched an expedition of 300 men under his old friend Alvaro Jorge, now in his sixties, up the Caroní to look for a gold mine. But after thirty miles or so Jorge died, and immediately all discipline collapsed. Until then local Indians had been welcoming and friendly, but now their villages were looted and women were raped. There was swift retaliation, and 230 Spaniards were massacred.

Vera arrived from Trinidad with more men, but quarrelled with Berrío and had to return. The complete lack of discipline meant that no more expeditions could be planned. To make matters worse there was a terrible plague of insects. Plots to murder Berrío were also discovered. So finally he gave permission for the surviving settlers to leave, and they hurried off in groups of twenty or thirty in boats, all except three being drowned in the dangerous currents.

Berrío remained at San Thomé, where he died in 1597, 'surrounded by the wreckage of his hopes' but just after the arrival of his son Fernando. Vera, who had been given the warrant to be Governor of Guiana, visited Fernando and was impressed by his 'great sagacity and quiet demeanour'. So he decided to hand over his warrant, and Fernando duly became Governor.

From now on there was a permanent Spanish presence on the Orinoco. When Keymis returned to England, with the news of a fort established at San Thomé, Bess – in the absence of Raleigh abroad – wrote to Cecil: 'You hear your poor friend's fortune, who, if he had been well credited in his reports and knowledge, as it seemeth the Spaniards were, they [Raleigh's men] had now been possessors of the place.'[8]

The irony of this saga of hope and disillusion is that great quantities of gold have been discovered in modern times beyond the Serranía Imatica. In 1853 some quartz (Raleigh's 'spar') from El Callao was assayed and found to contain the equivalent of fifty grams of gold per ton, and there was an immediate scramble by treasure-seekers to stake out claims; in 1857 a gold nugget was discovered weighing over fifteen pounds. The result was that until the opening of the Rand Mines in South Africa the area around El Callao was the most productive of gold in the world. The first mine was British, the second American. Two hundred kilometres north-east of El Callao is the mine of Bochiniche, which has been suggested as the site of the mine spoken of by the chief Putijma.

Further south the gold is panned from river beds (like the gold dust mentioned in the *Discoverie*) or separated by mercury from the orange-red earth or mud. The mercury-water sweeps over the landscape, killing all vegetation, so that the scenery around the chief shanty town, Las Claritas, is like pictures of the Somme in 1917: skeletal trees, craters, thick mud. It is a desperate and dangerous world, a morass of greed, squalor and degradation, but at least not comparable to the horrors of the Brazilian *garimpeiros*, who are ready to slaughter Indians who get in their way. Diamonds are found here too. A straggle of shacks on the main road is or was simply known as Kilometro 88, with one or two doss-houses available for travellers or one-night stands.

There is also now a town called El Dorado, between Las Claritas and El Callao. Down the river Cuyuni, a mile or two from El Dorado, is a mining co-operative called Payepal, where the use of mercury is more controlled. The coffee-coloured Cuyuni runs eventually into the Essequibo.*

The Essequibo is within the present country of Guyana, once British Guiana. The territory began as a Dutch colony and changed hands several times between Dutch, English and French. At the Treaty of Breda in 1667 it was ceded by the English to the Dutch in exchange for New Amsterdam, which became New York. In 1814 Guyana was finally ceded to the British.

---

* Across the river from El Dorado is a prison where once 'Papillon' was an inmate. At the time of the author's visit a boat from the prison capsized, carrying twenty-eight convicts who were all killed by *tembladores*, electric eels. A convict, returning from working in the fields, offered him a live anaconda for two dollars ('tastes like chicken'). One of the sights of Las Claritas is the prostitutes, picking their way through the muddy street in high heels, and, because of so much rain, holding umbrellas. They demand gold dust in payment, and at night carry torches which are shone in the faces of clients before acceptance.

Cadiz
1596

The burning of Penzance by the Spaniards had been a huge shock. Retaliation was now important; not only that, something must be done to boost the English coffers. The disastrously wet summers had continued, and the harvests had been the worst ever recorded. Resentment was growing against the government and the Queen. The bright light of the reign of Gloriana was losing its lustre.

An ambitious new plan was being hatched by Essex and the Lord High Admiral: a full-scale attack on the Spanish mainland, more ambitious than the ill-fated expedition into Portugal, from which lessons had been learnt. The place chosen was Cadiz and its great harbour from which the *flota* usually sailed for the West Indies. For a long while the destination was kept secret, but everyone became aware that some sort of major preparation was in hand. The City of London had been asked to have ships in readiness, and the inland counties were asked to make preparations for the victualling of 12,000 men. The Dutch were also asked to supply ships. Elizabeth had been forced to approve the idea of such an expedition, but stipulated that it had to be followed by an attack on the treasure fleet.

This time there was no Francis Drake to consult or assist. Hawkins was gone too, so was Frobisher. Since it was to be a combined naval and military assault, Raleigh was one of the few remaining with suitable experience. The trouble was that he was still not welcome at Court. Cecil's confidence in any expedition commanded by Essex had to be won. Rowland Whyte, being on the fringes of the Essex circle, wrote to his patron Sir Robert Sidney, who at that time was Governor of Flushing:[1]

Sir Walter Raleigh hath been very often very private with 1000 [code for Essex] and is mediator of a peace between him and 200 [Cecil], who likewise has been private with him. Sir Walter alleges how much good may grow by it. The Queen's unquietness will turn to contentments. Despatches for all matters of war and peace will go forward to the heart of common enemies.

The assumption has usually been, especially by Spanish historians, that Antonio Pérez had long been urging an attack on Cadiz as the surest way of damaging the war capability of Spain. He had certainly been giving the English information on undefended and weak points along the coast. Whether or not he received a pension from Elizabeth is debatable, but he did admit that he had been living on the liberality of Essex. Spanish children are brought up to regard Pérez as the prime example of an odious traitor; his treachery, it was even said in Spain during his lifetime, 'will weigh eternally on his memory'.

Sir Francis Vere, considered to be the most experienced commander on land, was ordered to withdraw troops from the Low Countries as reinforcements. This was very soon followed by a great new crisis: a Spanish advance into northern France and a threat to Calais. Henri IV had decided to become a Roman Catholic, but the Spaniards were unimpressed, since this was not accompanied by any serious effort against Protestants. Elizabeth had offered help to Henri, in return for her having Calais – at which he was reputed to have said that if his choice was to be eaten by a lion or by a lioness, he would rather be the victim of a lion.[2] In any case the prospect of Calais in Spanish hands meant that the whole enterprise against Cadiz would have to be postponed. Essex now begged to be allowed to go across and relieve the town. He claimed that it was possible to hear the sound of the siege guns at Greenwich. Elizabeth dithered, still trying to make a bargain with Henri. At last, on 14 April she gave permission for Essex to leave. It was too late. On that very day Calais fell.

In spite of panic in London, it was decided that the attack on Cadiz must be launched as rapidly as possible. For it came to be realized that the capture of Calais was not such an immediate threat to England; the harbour could be easily blockaded and was not suitable for a major fleet. Vere therefore advised Essex not to weaken the expedition he had planned for Cadiz.

One imagines that Elizabeth would only reluctantly have agreed to Raleigh's participation, and that it would have been at the insistence of Essex. A council of war was formed, consisting of Essex, Lord High Admiral Howard, Lord Thomas Howard, Sir Francis Vere, Sir George Carew, and Raleigh. The fleet would be divided into four squadrons, comprising nearly a hundred ships, and the Dutch were asked to provide a further squadron with twenty ships. Raleigh's particular task was to round up or pressgang sailors in the London area and to collect supplies. He also had to build up a fleet of victuallers. This was his great opportunity.

The task was not easy. 'As fast as we press men one day, they run away another and say they will not serve,' he wrote to Cecil early in May. When

Cecil sent him a letter by courier, he had to be followed to a country village a mile from Gravesend, 'hunting after runaway mariners and dragging in the mire from ale house to ale house'. The weather was terrible too, the wind so strong. He could only reply on a miserable scrap of paper: 'I cannot write to our general [Essex] at this time . . . Sir, by the living God there is no king nor queen nor general nor any else can take more care than I do to be gone.' He could not be expected to row up and down to London from Gravesend with every tide. He was 'more grieved than ever I was in anything of this world for this rough weather'.[3]

At least he felt he was once more back, or nearly back, at the centre of affairs. In one day he wrote four letters to Cecil, and not just about victualling and the rounding up of sailors. There were Irish problems. He wanted to get rid of the Bishop of Lismore and Waterford, Miles Magrath, who had 'of late dealt very badly with me', taking advantage of his fall from royal grace, with the help of course of Fitzwilliam. He was also worrying again about Widow Smith, to whom he still owed £500. He did not want her to start contesting the conveyance during his absence.

Essex (who had now grown a beard, which had turned out ginger) was at Plymouth and desperate to get away. The ships from the Low Countries had arrived and were waiting; supplies and ammunition had been without much supervision; Essex had been forced to try soldiers by martial law for desertion and an attempt at mutiny, and had directed they should be executed, so it was recorded, 'in a very fair pleasant green called the Ho'. He must have had a soothing letter from Cecil, for he wrote an unusually friendly and generous letter to Raleigh, evidently realizing that he was genuinely ready to move but held up by yet another strong wind.[4]

Your pains and travail in bringing all things to that forwardness they are in doth sufficiently assure me of your discontentment to be now stayed by the wind. Therefore I will not entreat you to make haste, though our stay here is very costly, for every soldier in the army has his weekly lending out of my purse. But I will wish and pray for a good wind for you. And when you are come, I will make you see I desire to do you as much honour, and give you as much contentment as I can. For this is the action and the time in which you and I shall be taught to know and love one another, and so I wish you all happiness and rest.

Your very assured friend Essex.

At last Raleigh was able to venture out from Gravesend, but at Dover there was such a storm that seven or eight of his ships let slip their cables and anchors. So there was yet another delay. Malicious tongues were at work again. Anthony Bacon wrote to his brother Francis that 'Sir Walter Raleigh's slackness and stay by the way is not thought to be upon sloth but upon pregnant design'.[5] He wrote this because of new difficulties with the Queen, whose changes of mind over the siege of Calais had already greatly irritated Essex. Now she had told him that she might recall both him and the Lord Admiral, suggesting that the command could be given to persons of lesser rank. The rumour going around was that Raleigh was trying to arrange to take over the command himself – complete nonsense, as Elizabeth would never have dreamt of such a thing.

There was an explosion of fury at Plymouth about the Queen's suggestion, and a joint protest was sent, signed by the chief land and sea officers. Essex wrote to Cecil asking to be rid of this 'hellish torment' of indecision. Relations between him and the Lord Admiral were in any case becoming very strained. Howard, recognized as the hero of the Armada, was now saying that he would rather withdraw than be a 'drudge' to Essex, and Essex told Cecil that it was 'purgatory' to govern such an unwieldy collection of men and to keep 'these sharp humours from distempering the whole body'.

Raleigh arrived at Plymouth on 21 May. Whether he was actually present at a dinner party where a violent argument took place is not clear from a letter from Anthony Standen to Anthony Bacon – who was always eager for news detrimental to Raleigh.[6] Sir Francis Vere had been 'in drink', and 'in the presence of my lord's generals and the Flemings of the Low Country fleet there passed some words against the marshal [Vere] by Arthur Throck-morton [Bess's brother?], a hot-headed youth, who deborded in such words as my lords ordered him from the table.' Standen added that Raleigh had been the subject of the quarrel, which evidently was an argument about precedence – whether Vere as marshal of the army should be entitled to issue orders to Raleigh when at sea. This was indeed a matter which required to be settled before sailing, so Essex decreed that Raleigh should have precedence on land, and Vere at sea; a fair compromise.

Arthur Throckmorton was over forty and hardly a hot-headed youth, so maybe this Arthur was some younger member of the family. Whatever he had said caused him to be cashiered from the Army and put under guard. Before long, however, he was reinstated; he was after all not a regular soldier or in any command, just a gentleman volunteer.

Through all this Raleigh was doing his best to keep on good terms with Essex, which caused a typical sneer from Standen: 'Sir Walter's carriage to my lord of Essex is with the cunningest respect and deepest humility that ever I saw or trowed.'

The expedition had attracted many fashionable young men on whom

Standen also commented. He also praised Essex's attitude towards ordinary people, behaving like a true aristocrat – and it was this which made him so generally popular:

We have 300 greenheaded youths covered with feathers, gold and silver lace, at the least ten thousand soldiers, as tall handsome men as ever I cast eyes on, who being conducted by a lion must work lion's effects: our navy in this port beautiful to behold, about 150 sail, whereof 18 of her Majesty's own, since her reign never so many before . . . My lord's demeanour as well with the meanest soldiers as mightiest colonel is such as all receive contentment, as willingly embrace his empire, equity and justice, shining indifferently on by which he wrought to himself a wonderful regard in the army.

This was a slight exaggeration, in that any contentment among the upper echelons was only on the surface; it had been discovered that Lord Admiral Howard had snipped off Essex's signature from a joint letter because he did not want it to be as high as his own.

The twenty-four-year-old poet John Donne was almost certainly one of the volunteers. Other literary men included Henry Wotton, Henry Cuffe and William Alabaster. William Trevelyan who 'went the voyage' with Francis Drake in 1586, as a penalty for sheep-stealing, was also a volunteer.*

Elizabeth had made it clear that she expected all plunder to be brought back to defray her expenses. If this was really thought to be true or enforceable, there would have been no gentlemen volunteers – they had joined the expedition not just out of bravado or patriotism, but because they were looking for loot. In any case Elizabeth had sent Anthony Ashley, Clerk to the Privy Council, to watch over her interests. It was also laid down that the second phase of the expedition must be to look for the treasure fleet in the Azores. She stipulated that on no account must Essex be exposed to danger.

On 3 June the great fleet finally sailed from Plymouth Sound. It was the largest ever assembled in England, well over a hundred ships, of which seventeen were the Queen's and twelve were London men o' war. There were up to 8,000 soldiers on board of whom 2,000 had been serving in the Low Countries, and 1,500 sailors. With pennants flying – 'bloody crimson' for the Lord Admiral, 'tawney-orange' for Essex, blue for Lord Thomas Howard, and white for Raleigh – and each ship bearing the flag of St George,

* p. 114.

the spectacle must have been thrilling for watchers on the shore. The Lord Admiral's flag-ship was his favourite *Ark Royal*, with the *Lion's Whelp* and the *Darling* included in his squadron. Essex was in the *Due [Dieu] Repulse*, accompanied by Sir William Monson in the *Rainbow*. Lord Thomas Howard was in the *Merhonour*, and had with him Robert Dudley in the *Nonpareil*, and Henry Moyle (Raleigh's friend whom he had rescued when stranded in a ford in Ireland) in the *Moon*. Raleigh was in the *Warspite*, belonging to the Queen, a new galleon with two decks and forty guns. He was accompanied by Sir George Carew in the *Mary Rose*, Sir Robert Cross in the *Swiftsure*, and fourteen victuallers and transports. The Dutch squadron consisted of twenty-four vessels, of which eighteen were fighting ships.

Almost from the start, according to the Lord Admiral's doctor, there were 'certain great strife and contentions', even at sea, between the two generals. Both were popular with their men, which resulted later in competing loyalties.[7] A few small ships were taken near the north-west Spanish coast; a captured Franciscan priest wrote that Essex, when he interrogated him, was dressed immaculately in white satin with a short brocaded cloak. By this time the Spaniards had been alerted, and the guess was that the English fleet was heading for Lisbon, causing much alarm in the city. But when the English sailed past it was realized that Cadiz must be the destination, and there was no time to send a warning.

A little before their arrival an Irish merchantman bound for Waterford was taken. She had just left Cadiz and her captain confirmed that the harbour was packed with ships, only a few of them warships, and that nobody had an inkling of what was in store. 'Good Lord,' wrote the Lord Admiral's doctor, 'what a sudden rejoicing there was! How every man skipped and leapt for joy, and how nimble was every man to see all things were neat, trim and ready for the fight'. Good booty lay ahead!

They reached Cadiz on 20 June. Even Spaniards in that doomed city were to admit later that it was a beautiful and awe-inspiring sight. To understand something of the English strategy and the resulting confusion and the course of the battle, it is important to say something about the geography. The town and its forts were like an island or the head of a snake at the end of a six-mile sandy isthmus, in some places hardly more than half a mile wide. To the east the mainland curved in towards the isthmus, forming an entrance, again only half a mile across or less, into a wide and deep harbour, beyond which was another but smaller harbour and the town of Puerto Real where the Spanish merchant fleet was anchored, laden with supplies for the Caribbean. At the south end of the harbour and the isthmus there

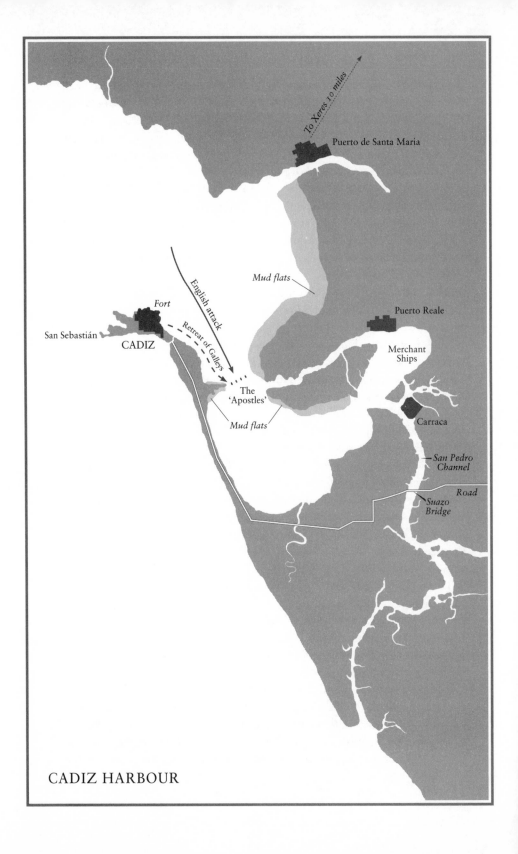

To Xeres 10 miles

Puerto de Santa Maria

Mud flats

English attack

Fort

Retreat of Galleys

San Sebastián

CADIZ

Puerto Reale

Merchant
Ships

The
'Apostles'

Mud flats

Carraca

*San Pedro
Channel*

Road

*Suazo
Bridge*

CADIZ HARBOUR

was the San Pedro channel, which could be used as an escape route into the Mediterranean by small vessels; a bridge over the channel was the link to the only road to Cadiz.

Raleigh's first assignment was to scour the coast for fugitive ships and to chase them back into the harbour. Once again there was a division between the generals. Essex had been all for entering the harbour at once, but it was decided that this would be too much of a risk for the Queen's ships. So it was agreed that he should make a landing directly below the steep walls of the San Sebastián fort (which was in the process of being repaired) while Howard gave him cover. But there was a heavy Atlantic swell. Two landing craft capsized and men were thrown into the water – some in heavy armour were drowned. It was all taking much longer than was expected.

Two long letters from Raleigh describing the Cadiz action have survived, one to Arthur Gorges, the other found among his papers after his death;[8] there is also an account by the old sea-dog Sir William Monson. Raleigh, on rejoining the fleet, realized that total disaster loomed, and that the whole enterprise was in danger. He had always supported the idea of entering the harbour, so he at once made for the *Due Repulse* and confronted Essex, convincing him of the mistake. Essex put the blame on Howard, whereupon Raleigh rowed over to the *Ark Royal* and persuaded the Lord Admiral to change his mind. 'When I brought back news of this agreement to the Earl, calling out of my boat to him *Entramos* [In we go], he cast his hat into the sea for joy, and prepared to weigh anchor.' This boyish gesture by Essex was grist to the legend that grew up round him.

The change of plan caused delays. Darkness was about to fall, and there were many 'seeming desperately valiant who were all for moving in at once' – which was what Drake would have done, so it was thought. It was decided to wait until first light, by which time a definite plan of action would be ready.

At ten o'clock that night Raleigh wrote a letter to the Lord Admiral. He knew that guarding the harbour were four of those great galleons known as the Apostles: the *San Felipe*, the *San Matéo*, the *San Andrés* and the *Santo Tomás*. His suggestion was that the Queen's ships should go straight in and batter them. Two flyboats should be allocated for each galleon for boarding. To his delight he was given the command of the vanguard. The ships appointed to him were the *Mary Rose* (Carew), the *Lion* (Southwell), the *Rainbow* (Vere), the *Swiftsure* (Cross), the *Dreadnought* (Sir Conyers and Alexander Clifford, brothers), the *Nonpareil* (Dudley), as well as some Dutch men-o'-war.

Lord Thomas Howard objected that his rank gave him the right of precedence over Raleigh and that he should be in command. It seems that the generals thereupon gave in. So Lord Thomas then handed over his flagship, the *Merhonour*, to Dudley and took over the *Nonpareil*, in order to head the attack. Raleigh, however, was not to be thwarted, 'holding mine own reputation dearest', and at the 'first peep of day' he was off in the *Warspite*, shouting '*Viva La Reina de Inglaterra*'.

At the sight of the English fleet approaching the four Apostles retreated to the neck of sea that led to the harbour, broadsides to seaward, with three frigates alongside. As Raleigh approached, the guns from a fort opened fire, as did seventeen galleys moored close to the shore beneath it. Raleigh ignored them, disdaining those 'wasps'. 'To show scorn to all which, I only answered the fort, and afterwards the galleys, to each a blur of a trumpet.' The ships following the *Warspite* 'beat' on the galleys, which took to their oars and made for the harbour. When they came near Raleigh he 'bestowed a benediction amongst them'.

He wanted to concentrate on the *San Felipe* and the *San Andrés*, because these two ships had boarded the *Revenge*; as he said, he had 'resolved to revenge the death of the *Revenge* or to second it with mine own'. Lord Thomas came alongside in the *Nonpareil*, and was joined by the other ships. Then Essex, hearing 'the thunder of the ordnance', could not bear being out of the battle any longer and anchored near Raleigh. This was against the rules, and the Lord Admiral decided to take part in the fight as well. But Raleigh, cock-a-hoop in this jostling for power, was to write: 'Always I must, without glory, say for myself, that I held single in the head of all'.

After three hours the *Warspite* might have been in danger of sinking from the broadsides of her foes, so Raleigh jumped into a skiff and rowed across to Essex's flagship to ask for the promised flyboats for boarding. 'The Earl, finding that it was not in his power to command fear, told me that whatsoever I did, he would second me in person upon his honour.' This was the greatest moment of their new-found comradeship.

The passage into the harbour was so packed with ships that the flyboats could not get close, and the same applied to the *Ark Royal*. The Lord Admiral thereupon transferred himself to the *Nonpareil* with Lord Thomas. Raleigh now found that in his absence Vere in the *Rainbow* had moved ahead of *Warspite*, still very much afloat, and so had the *Nonpareil*. He was not going to allow this, and pushed round the *Rainbow*, blocking its passage. He then found that Vere had secretly attached a rope to *Warspite*'s stern, and had been using it to pull himself closer. He had this rope cut. Another round in the battle of precedence.

Spanish shot tore through the *Warspite*'s rigging. 'The volleys of cannon and culverin came as thick and as fast as volleys of musketry', and still Raleigh 'urged on his men to exertions almost more than human'. The English cannons were replying with even more ferocity, battering and splintering the sides of the galleons, smashing into the ranks of Spanish soldiers. Blood could be seen pouring from the decks. Raleigh now made his great decision. With no hope of flyboats, he made as if to board the *San Felipe*. Suddenly the Spaniards panicked, morale was broken. The Apostles cut their cables and were swept by the tide onto the mainland sandbars.

Some [of the crews] saving themselves with boats, others leaping into the sea, the rest crying *Misericordia* [shades of Smerwick]. The noise and outcry was marvellous and the spectacle lamentable. The *Saint Philip* [*San Felipe*] and *Saint Thomas* [*Santo Tomás*] set themselves on fire, a most fearful and piteous sight to see so huge a flame.

The *San Andrés* and *San Matéo* were captured. 'The men tumbled out of the galleon like coal being poured from sacks. Some with their clothes alight, some falling into the mud and sticking there. Very many hanging by the ropes' ends by the ship's sides, under the water even to the lips; many swimming with grievous wounds, stricken under water, and put out of pain.' The gunpowder on the burning ships exploded. 'If any man had a desire to see Hell itself, it was there most lively figured.' The Flemings, with their ingrained hatred for the Spaniards after years of war, showed no mercy towards any survivors who came near their ships; this in spite of the fact that they had done little or nothing in the fight. They had to be beaten off by Raleigh and the Lord Admiral (a contrast this time to Smerwick).

Raleigh hoisted the arms of Spain as a trophy on his mizzenmast, and received 'many embracements and thanks' from Essex. It was only at this stage in his letters that he said that he had been wounded: 'a grievous blow in my leg, interlaced and deformed with splinters', which he had to pull out one by one over the next days. He was lucky that it did not turn gangrenous. For the rest of his life he walked with a limp and used a stick.

Essex now was in a hurry to land and storm the town, not bothering to consult the Lord Admiral. It did not occur to either of them that it would be more sensible to go forward and seize all the merchant ships huddled at the far corner of the harbour at Puerto Real. Three regiments were sent to the bridge over the San Pedro channel to block any possible reinforcements (there were none), but were too late to prevent twelve galleys escaping. Then Essex and Vere landed on the isthmus with the 2,000 soldiers brought from the Low Countries. There was a short skirmish with Spanish cavalry, and then with 'sudden fury' the walls were scaled. It was at this stage that an officer, Sir John Wingfield, was killed.

In four hours the town was taken, apart from the fort that fell some while afterwards. The citizens of Cadiz (known in Spain as *Gaditanos*) fled into the churches – there were 3,000 crowded in the cathedral. Orders had been expressly given by Essex that churches should be left untouched. And as Raleigh said: 'All mercy was used. Four thousand ladies, gentlewomen and merchants' wives [were] sent out in all their glorious apparel, with their jewels about them, without any touch, with the greatest honour used by any nation or any war.' This evacuation of ladies in their best clothes and with their jewels is confirmed by Spanish sources, and it caused some amazement. Monks and friars were also allowed to leave, and as reported back to Philip, not a single person was killed in cold blood. For this, great credit was given to Essex. As Philip had to admit: 'Such a nobleman was not be seen among heretics'.[9]

But the soldiers, seamen and gentlemen volunteers had come for the plunder, and they were not be held back any more. Chaos broke out, as houses and shops were ransacked. Raleigh had watched the capture of Cadiz from the *Warspite* and had himself carried on shore on the shoulders of his men. The Lord Admiral gave him a horse, but that did not help. 'I was not able to bide an hour in the town for the torment I suffered, and for fear that I had be shouldered in the press, and among the tumultuous disordered soldiers.' This would have been his great chance of getting some much-needed booty for himself, and after the part he had played in securing the victory he felt it was ironical that he was not able to take advantage of it.

Merchants were taken prisoner, and handed over to the land commanders, who then released them in return for ransoms of thousands of ducats. The streets were littered with broken furniture, ornaments tossed from windows, broken bottles, papers, almonds, raisins and spices, even dead horses. Some Spaniards had secretly taken advantage of Essex's decree against the sacking of churches by hiding their valuables inside tombs. All the same there was plenty more to be found, and according to Monson the 'lower class of Spaniard' joined in the fray.

Raleigh returned to his ship partly because 'I was unfit for ought but ease at that time', but chiefly because there was 'no Admiral left to order to the fleet, and indeed few or no people in the Navy, all running headlong to the sack.' He was worried about the great cluster of merchant ships, now defenceless at the far corner of the bay and loaded with the richest spoil of all. When morning came he sent John Gilbert and Arthur Throckmorton to Essex for instructions. 'But, the town now taken, and the confusion great, it was almost impossible for them to order many things at once, so I could not receive any answer to my desire.'

The two commanders realized this serious operational mistake too late, by which time the Duke of Medina Sidonia had arrived from his estates at Sanlúcar de Barrameda several miles further north. As Governor of the province and responsible for the defence of Cadiz, he sent a deputation to his old adversary Lord Admiral Howard, offering him and Essex two million ducats if the merchant ships, thirty-six in all, could leave unharmed. The English generals did not think this enough (Raleigh had estimated the cargoes' worth at twelve million), and wanted double the amount. Then Medina Sidonia made a dramatic gesture of defiance. He ordered the whole merchant fleet to be burned. Of all the ships that had been in Cadiz only the two galleons captured by the English remained, and twelve galleys that had fled down the San Pedro channel.

Medina Sidonia's decision to scuttle the merchant fleet was a gigantic loss for Spain, but also for the English – for them the result of sheer greed; and there were to be furious recriminations in London. Raleigh, watching the pillars of smoke, had been appalled.

The English stayed on at Cadiz for two weeks. Sir John Wingfield was buried with full military honours in the cathedral, and a grand banquet was held in the priory of San Francisco. Discussions were even held between English scholars and Spanish theologians, and indeed the poet Alabaster was converted to Catholicism. Essex dubbed no less than sixty-six knights; an amazing piece of arrogance, for he was debasing an honour traditionally the monarch's preserve. He had already been strongly reprimanded by Elizabeth when of his own accord he had created those knights at Rouen. There was a lot of joking later about the knighthoods. It was believed (and probably rightly) that they had not been a reward for merit but to create a following, an insurance for the future. The Queen threatened to cancel them all.

The Lord Admiral wrote to Medina Sidonia offering to exchange fifty-one prisoners for the same number of Englishmen serving as galley-slaves; this was accepted, as an agreement between gentlemen. Not quite so gentlemanly was the behaviour of the English towards certain Spanish prisoners who were taken back to London. These included the President of the *Contratación* of Seville and all the prebendaries of the cathedral. Not enough ransom had been paid, and Philip refused to help. So they were kept in prison until July 1603 – very unhappily too, complaining of cold and wet.

The question now for the English was whether to stay in the wrecked city or to move on. A march on Seville would have been possible, though in the long run disastrous. Exchange Cadiz for Calais? Move on to Gibraltar,

Ceuta, Tangier? Lisbon? Essex was all for keeping Cadiz as a permanent English base, with some collaboration from Morocco (thirty-eight Moorish slaves had been given a small vessel to return to Morocco, which had been much appreciated). But this, it was argued, would have been contrary to his instructions and would have to be approved by the Queen's Council. Raleigh was anxious to leave, resentful that so little had come his way after promises that he would not be forgotten when of necessity he had been marooned on board his ship *Warspite*. As he was to say: 'Either I spake too late or it was otherwise resolved . . . I have naught but poverty and pain.'[10] He had also had a violent disagreement with Vere, which was by no means healed.

Unburied bodies ashore had attracted a plague of flies, and this probably hastened the decision to leave. On 1 July preparations were begun; cannons, munitions and church bells were loaded onto the ships; walls and fortifications were demolished. Then the city was set alight. About a third of the houses were burnt, and some churches caught fire too. The English sailed away on 5 July.

Out to sea Raleigh gave a letter for Cecil to Anthony Ashley, one of the many knighted by Essex and who was returning with despatches for the Queen. It was full of tactful praise for Essex:[11] 'The Earl has behaved himself, I protest unto you by the living God, both valiantly and advisedly in the highest degree, without pride, without cruelty, and hath gotten great honour and much love of all.' Confident that Ashley would be loyal to him in his report, and that his letter would be shown to Elizabeth, he added:

I hope Her most excellent Majesty will take my labours and endeavours in good part. Other riches than the hope thereof I have none: only I have received a blow [his wound] which now, I thank God, is well mended. Only a little eyesore will remain. If my life ended withal, I had then paid some part of my great debts which I owe her, but it is but borrowed and I shall pay it, I hope, to Her Majesty's advantage if occasion be offered.

He was being modest about his wound, which was no mere eyesore. He also need not have worried so much about his reputation at Cadiz. Carew wrote to Cecil that 'those who were formerly his enemies do now hold him in great estimation'. And Sir Anthony Standen, once so prejudiced against Raleigh, now wrote to Burleigh.[12] 'Sir Walter Raleigh did, in my judgement, no man better; and his artillery most effect. I never knew the gentleman till this time, and I am sorry for it, for there are in him excellent things beside his valour; and the observation he hath in this voyage used with my Lord of Essex has made me love him.'

A landing was made at Faro in the Algarve. Its inhabitants had already been aware of a possible English attack, and had escaped into the mountains with their prized possessions. Essex, however, did appropriate the library of Bishop Jerónimo Osorio, and this formed part of the nucleus of the newly formed Bodleian Library at Oxford. Afterwards the town was set on fire.

Discussions continued about other towns that could be attacked. Lisbon was rejected, as it was decided that the fleet was not ready for another major action. Essex wanted to head for the Azores as the treasure *flota* would soon be due, and this of course had been the desire of the Queen. Both Howard and Raleigh were against this, taking into account the restlessness of the crews and soldiers wanting to get home with all their loot. Also Raleigh claimed that 'great and dangerous infection' had broken out on some of the ships. It was decided to call at La Coruña, but once again there had been advance warnings of their arrival, and they found the harbour empty. So they sailed on to Plymouth, the first ships arriving there on 6 August.

Only a week before the Spanish *flota* had reached Lisbon, with treasure aboard estimated as worth two million ducats. Its commanders were astounded to learn that the English ships had sailed past less than forty-eight hours before.

At first the return of the fleet was greeted with excitement. Elizabeth sent a message: 'Let the army know I care not so much for being Queen, as that I am sovereign of such servants'. And the Venetian ambassador wrote: 'What a woman! If only she were a Christian.'[13]

Her attitude soon changed. When Essex reached London on 12 August, he found himself received with anger and bitterness. She had heard about the looting at Cadiz. This had been a national enterprise, not a private one, and the proceeds were to have offset the nation's expenses. £50,000 had been invested, and now she found that she was not to get any dividends. Worse, her officials at Plymouth had reported on some blatant embezzling and looting. 'In this town', said William Killigrew, her Groom of the Chamber, 'for all the little stay the fleet make here, there is much landed, but in huxters' handling'.[14] And William Stallenge said: 'All or most part of the goods landed in this place was given by the Generals to men of desert, and is by them sold to others and the money received, which will hardly be gotten by them'.[15] The royal officials were helpless: a commentary on the inability of the state to enforce discipline in cases such as these.

Then there was the question of the knighthoods, which had enraged Elizabeth. Instead of being treated as a conquering hero Essex found himself in deep disgrace. He also discovered that in his absence Elizabeth had appointed Robert Cecil as her Principal Secretary. Thus Burghley had achieved his great ambition, for which he had worked so many years; his son would now have a full share in government, and would be in a stronger position to stand up to Essex.

Raleigh's enemies were becoming irritated by so much praise for his alleged bravery and fine judgement at Cadiz. As one of Anthony Bacon's friends typically said: 'A blind man may see where he aimeth. His friends in Court do as immoderately broach and publish his praise, as well as by letters as by speech.'[16] Thus, when news reached London of the appearance of the Spanish *flota* at Lisbon, with its hugely valuable cargo, the Bacons were only too delighted to pin the blame of losing it on Raleigh. Not that Essex was by any means exonerated by Elizabeth, who believed him to be ultimately responsible. She declared that she would confiscate all the ransom money that he had received. When Burghley tried to intervene on his behalf, she turned furiously on him: 'My Lord Treasurer, either for fear or favour you regard my Lord of Essex more than myself. You are a miscreant! You are a coward!'[17]

Anthony Ashley was in utter disgrace, for it had been revealed that chests from Cadiz had been carried into his house, and that he had sent a huge diamond to be broken up and sold to jewellers when it should have gone to the Queen. He was dismissed from her service, and sent to the Fleet prison, never to be forgiven. Vere owned up to receiving £3,628 worth of goods, Sir Conyers Clifford to £3,256. Raleigh's profit was given as £1,769, his spoils being made up of plate, pearls, gold ornaments, a Turkey carpet, tapestries, wines, hides and a chest of printed books.

Essex, in an attempt to soothe the Queen, volunteered to go to Calais and drive out the Spaniards, but she was not going to waste any more money just to benefit Henri IV. Her preoccupation was to recoup some of the plunder from Cadiz, and to get rid of sailors and soldiers without paying them – the fact that they had grabbed so much in Spain meant that they did not need to be paid. Orders were given to Raleigh and others to search their chests: an extremely unpopular operation. Pots, pans, kettles, some ivory, sugar, even bedsteads were revealed, but no signs of money or jewels, which had conveniently disappeared.

The scandal became even more explosive when reports from Spain claimed that the value of the merchant ships set on fire by Medina Sidonia was estimated at twenty million ducats. Essex found himself confronted by Cecil, secure now in his new position of authority. 'I was more braved by your little cousin', he wrote sardonically to Anthony Bacon, 'than ever I was by any man.'[18]

*

Philip II's life was coming to an end. He was suffering from dropsy and confined to a wheelchair. The sack of Cadiz was a terrible humiliation for him and the whole of Spain. Carew had written to Cecil from Cadiz that 'the wiser sort of Spaniards that are prisoners with us confess in one voice that a greater grievance could not have been done unto him, in so much as they are of the opinion that the people with one clamour will enforce him to seek for peace from her Majesty.' These last words were wishful thinking; but the affair did undermine confidence within Spain, and has been seen as a turning point in the country's prestige. Cervantes wrote a contemptuous sonnet on the shame felt by the whole country.

Only in May there had been general rejoicing in Madrid when news came of the death of Drake. Philip had said: 'This good news will help me to get well rapidly.'[19] Now all was changed. In a sense the relatively good behaviour of the invaders – no murders or rapes – did not help. The churches he was told had not been profaned,* though it was true that the common soldiers, mainly the Flemings, had dressed up in religious vestments and had paraded through the streets shouting 'Hang the Pope!'

On hearing about Cadiz the King was said to have seized the candelabra on his table and to have cried out that he would pawn even it to be revenged on the Queen of England. The time had come for retaliation, and a final attack on England. His honour was at stake, as was his financial credit. Loans had to be repudiated, and he was forced to dishonour the bills of his Governor in the Netherlands.

The *Adelantado* (Governor-General) of Castile, Don Martín de Padilla, was given the task of assembling the invasion fleet. Father Robert Parsons, that persistent scourge of Protestant England, advised an invasion of Ireland through Cork. However, with Calais still in Spanish hands, it was decided that a more direct attack from the Low Countries or Brittany was more feasible.

The season was late, but the King was determined that a new Armada should sail forthwith. At the end of October eighty-one warships and some smaller vessels sailed from Lisbon and La Coruña, ostensibly for Ireland though the real destination was Brittany and the capture of Brest. In the Bay of Biscay the fleet was struck by a tremendous south-westerly gale. Almost

---

* At Hampton Court there is a large canvas, *The Calling of St Matthew* by 'The Master of the Abbey of Dilighem'. This is captioned as having been taken from a church at Cadiz in 1596 and given anonymously to Charles I. In the chapel of the English College at Valladolid there is another relic from the Cathedral: a damaged Virgin known as the *Vulnerata*, arms and nose sliced off. Students and staff still perform an 'act of reparation' before her every Wednesday evening.

immediately a galleon with all the wages on board went down. The storm continued, forcing the whole fleet to disperse, some ships managing to reach the northern ports, but more than the half the ships, including seven galleons and some 3,000 men, were lost.

Warnings of the approach of this fleet had reached England in November. Essex, now back in favour with the Queen, was appointed head of a council of war. Alarm beacons were set up along the south coast and some 70,000 local militia put in arms; a scorched earth policy was one of the measures agreed if the enemy were to land. There was no time to collect and prepare ships for defence. It was not until after Christmas that the fate of the Spanish invasion fleet was learned.

The crisis had the effect in the public mind of enhancing Essex's reputation as a military leader. But neither Philip nor Padilla had given up hope of subduing England, and yet another Armada was being planned for 1597.

An Uneasy Triumvirate
1597

Raleigh wrote some remarkable letters during his life, and one which appears sometimes in anthologies was to Robert Cecil on the death of his wife, written on 24 January 1597. Born Elizabeth Brooke, the daughter of the 10th Lord Cobham, she had died in childbirth. Her epitaph describes her as 'silent, true and chaste', and although she was not considered intelligent and had little interest in politics, her husband loved her deeply; it was said that his hair literally turned grey after her death (though portraits do not confirm this). She appears to have been fond of Bess. Raleigh, for his part, had recently become close to her brother, Henry Brooke.*

The letter, all the more extraordinary as a letter of condolence for being so long, also marks yet another phase in Raleigh's life which has been described as 'Reflective Stoic'.[1] Its references to God appear sincere – the lofty sentiments make it read almost like a sermon. Once more, as in his poetry, he wrote about the inevitability of decay and death.

He began by saying that he was not going to call on Cecil until he knew it was Cecil's own pleasing, but 'I had rather be with you now than at any other time if I could thereby either take off from you the burden of your sorrows or lay the greatest part thereof on my own heart.' Cecil certainly would not have wanted to see Raleigh. When his cousin Sir Edward Hoby called on him, he was so horrified by his appearance that he left without saying a word.

Raleigh's letter continued:

... There is no man sorry for death itself, but only for the time of death; every one knowing that it is a bond never forfeited to God. If then we know the same to be certain and inevitable, we ought withal to take the time of his [death's] arrival in as good part as the knowledge, and not to lament at the instant of every seeming

---

* The Brookes of Cobham had been outraged by Shakespeare's caricature of their fat ancestor Sir John Oldcastle in *Henry IV* and had made him change the name, to Falstaff.

adversity, which we are assured have been on the way to us from the beginning. It appertaineth to every man of a wise and worthy spirit to draw together into sufferance the unknown future to the known present, looking no less with the eyes of the mind than those of the body – thereon beholding afar off, and the other at hand – that those things of this world in which we live be not strange unto us when they approach, as to feebleness, which is moved with novelties. But that, like true men, participating immortality and knowing our destinies to be of God, we do then make our estates and wishes, our fortunes and desires, all one.

It is true that you have lost a good and virtuous wife, and myself an honourable friend and kinswoman, but there was a time when she was unknown to you, for whom you then lamented not. She is now no more yours, nor of your acquaintance, but immortal, and not needing of your love or sorrow. Therefore you shall but grieve for that which now is as then when not yours, only bettered by the difference in this, that she hath passed the wearisome journey of this dark world, and hath possession of her inheritance.

He went on to say that he believed that sorrows were dangerous companions, converting bad into evil.

The mind that entertaineth them is as the earth and dust whereon sorrows and adversities of the world do as the beasts of the field tread, trample and defile. The mind of man is that part of God which is in us, which by how much it is subject to passion, by so much it is farther from him that gave it us. Sorrows draw not the dead to life, but the living to death . . .

Yours ever beyond the power of words to utter, W. Ralegh

'Of all which past the sorrow only stays', he had once written, and this to some extent summed up what he was now saying.

A few weeks later it began to be noticed among Court gossips that there seemed to be a growing friendship between Essex, Raleigh and Cecil. After Cadiz, Essex and Raleigh had their bond of comradeship in arms, but apart from this it was obvious that the three needed one another. Essex was still being lionized by the masses as the great hero and was eager for more military glory, but he knew now the value of Raleigh's experiences of battle and overall strategy. And Raleigh knew that friendship and collaboration with Essex would help towards his reinstatement. As for Cecil, he knew well enough that in the long run there could never be a true reconciliation with Essex, but for the present he was a useful link with the Queen. There were advantages for him when Essex was out of the country – that was how he had won his Secretaryship. Quite what his innermost feelings were about

Raleigh at this stage are by no means clear; Raleigh obviously felt that he had cultivated a genuine friendship, and looked to him as an ally at Court. Both Cecils also appeared to have faith in Raleigh's privateering ventures, and were thought to have invested in Lawrence Keymis's expedition; that was another reason for keeping on good terms with him.

So on the 4th of March we have Rowland Whyte writing to Robert Sidney, who at the time was Governor of Flushing, that '24 [his code number for Raleigh] hath been very private with 1000 [Essex] and is the mediator of a peace between him and 200 [Cecil] who likewise has been private with him.'[2]

On the very next day Lord Cobham died and the whole delicate edifice seemed about to crumble. He had been a Privy Councillor and Warden of the Cinque Ports, the latter being an important military post, the five ports being the most vulnerable in case of attack from across the Channel. Essex had been having one of his sulks because of yet another row with Elizabeth, but now he came tearing up to London in order to secure the post of Warden for Robert Sidney, whom he considered his protégé. The Queen retorted that Sidney was too young and inexperienced, and told him that Henry Brooke, the new Lord Cobham, was the most appropriate. It would be an insult to the Cobham family if the post went to someone of a lesser degree.

Essex made his violent objections at the Privy Council in the presence of Lord Treasurer Burghley. He said that he 'had just cause to hate Lord Cobham, for his villainous dealing and abusing of me; that he hath been my chief persecutor, and most unjustly; that in him there is no worth.'[3] Presumably Cecil, Cobham's brother-in-law, had listened to this tirade. It was awkward too for Raleigh, whose close friendship with Cobham was generally known.

When Essex had returned from Cadiz, Francis Bacon had advised him to play the courtier more, and to seek some major civil office which would bring him closer to the Queen again. His desire for military greatness would turn her against him, he said, remembering the struggles of her predecessors against over-mighty barons in the past centuries. But Essex longed to be Earl Marshal of England, or even Master of Ordnance, which would put him in charge of the country's artillery. Instead, Bacon advised him to ask for the office of Lord Chamberlain, which was then vacant – far too dull for this impetuous young man, and in the end it went to Lord Hunsdon, the Queen's cousin.

It was at this stage that Bacon decided that it was foolish if not dangerous to remain too involved with such an erratic creature, so now he secretly made overtures to Lord Burghley, even apologizing for having backed Essex in the past and thus impeding Burghley's designs. A wise decision, as it turned out.

On 9 March Elizabeth summoned Essex and told him that the new Lord Warden was to be Cobham. As she expected, he flounced out and rode from London in a fury. But she was ready for this, and sent a messenger ordering him to return. When he reappeared she told him that he was to be her Master of Ordnance. It had all been a great game, designed to show that she had and always would have the upper hand. Essex was of course delighted, especially as it gave him control over the royal munitions in the major new expedition that was now being planned. He again was to have the command, for him an additional relief in that it would give him the chance of keeping at a distance from the Queen, who it was obvious to many people was increasingly irritating him.

In years to come Sir Robert Naunton tried to analyse the reasons behind such tempestuous swings to extremes in their relationship:[4]

The first was a violent indulgence of the Queen which is incident to old age when it encounters with a pleasing and suitable object . . . The second was a fault in the object of her grace, my Lord himself, who drew in too fast like a child sucking on an over-uberous nurse; and had there been a more decent decorum observed in either of these, without doubt the unity of their affections had been more permanent, and not so in and out as they were, like an instrument ill tuned and lapsing to discord.

Essex's plan, supported by Raleigh, was to follow up the success of Cadiz with some great blow that would finally destroy the naval capacity of Spain, at any rate for the foreseeable future. It was known that the remnants of Philip's abortive invasion at the end of 1596 had taken refuge at Ferrol in north-west Spain, so this should be their target. The Queen and Burghley had at last given their consent, with a proviso that after the destruction of the ships at Ferrol the English fleet should sail on to the Azores and there intercept the Spanish *flota*, for the English coffers badly needed a replenishment. Raleigh should once again be in charge of the victualling of the land forces. And as usual he was to be responsible for the musters in the South-West.

Rowland Whyte's newsletter of 9 April not surprisingly relayed this bit of hot information:

Sir Walter Raleigh is daily in Court, and a hope is had he shall be admitted to the execution of his office, as Captain of the Guard, before his going to sea. His friends you know are of greatest authority and power here, and 1000 [code for Essex] gives it no opposition, his mind being full, and only carried away with the business he hath in his head of conquering and overcoming the enemy.

Who else were these powerful friends at Court besides Cobham and Cecil?

Soon Whyte was able to provide further fascinating developments. Cecil, Essex and Raleigh had dined together at Essex's house in the Strand. 'After dinner they were very private all three for two hours, when a treaty of peace was confirmed'. Raleigh had undertaken to provide victuals for 1,000 men for three months, and for this he would be allowed nine pence a man per day. 'He protests he may be the loser of it, but few are of that opinion besides himself.'

The destination was kept secret. Ireland? Calais? This new friendship *appeared* well cemented, and the social activity was kept going, but those who had experience of little Cecil's devious plotting and planning were suspicious about such cosiness. Essex's uncle, Sir William Knollys, sent his nephew a warning note: 'If we lived not in a cunning world, I would assure myself that the Secretary were wholly yours. I pray to God it have a good foundation, and then he is worthy to be embraced. I hope for the best, yet will I observe him as narrowly as I can. But your Lordship knows best the humour of the time and person.'

Then came a hiatus. The Queen was going through one of her changes of mind. She was horrified by the mounting costs and declared that she was not interested in making war, only in defence. The whole project must be cancelled. All preparations must cease. It took two days to get her to relent, and Cecil was able to write to Essex: 'The Queen is so disposed now to have us all love you, that she and I do every night talk like angels of you.'

Then at last, on 2 June 1597, for Raleigh the great longed-for moment:

Yesterday my Lord of Essex rode to Chatham. In his absence Sir Walter Raleigh was brought by 200 [Cecil] to the Queen, who used him very graciously, and gave him full authority to execute his place as Captain of the Guard, which immediately he undertook, and swore many men into the places void. In the evening he rode abroad with the Queen, and had private conference with her; and now he comes boldly to the Privy Chamber, as he was wont. This was done with the Earl of Essex's liking and furtherance.[5]

Even so the gossip was that Essex could not bear to be present at the reconciliation. Five years almost to the day had passed since Raleigh had fallen from grace. Time had stood still for the Queen, as always, but he was older, more discreet, a married man, one of the few leaders left from the heady Armada days. There were no more poems, at least none which have survived, but he no doubt gave her the flattery she expected. Essex, in contrast, was becoming increasingly bored with the charade of Gloriana.

She was nearly sixty-four, and Raleigh was forty-three. Essex was twenty-nine. Later that year the new French ambassador, Herault de Maisse, described an audience with Elizabeth and was amazed by her silver, white, and crimson dress covered with gauze, opened at the front so that the whole of her bosom, 'somewhat wrinkled', down to her stomacher was revealed.[6] She would, he said, open the front of her robe frequently as if she were too hot. She wore a reddish wig with a number of spangles and a garland of rubies and pearls, 'with two great curls' down to her shoulders. 'As for her face, it is and appears very aged. It is long and thin, and her teeth are very yellow and unequal . . . Many of them are missing so that one cannot understand her easily when she speaks quickly . . . When anyone speaks of her beauty, she says that she was never beautiful, although she had that reputation thirty years ago. Nevertheless she speaks of her beauty as often as she can.'

Unpredictable, maddeningly liable to changes of mind she might have been, but that same ambassador found her 'fine and vigorous in mind', and the old sharpness had hardly dimmed. Later that year a new Polish ambassador arrived, and was given a public reception. He was good looking, which she appreciated, and with due formality he kissed her hand. But to everybody's astonishment and horror he then, speaking in Latin, launched into violent abuse of the Queen herself, complaining about the interception of Polish ships trading with Spain. No foreigner had ever before dared to make a personal attack on her sacred Majesty on her home ground. But Elizabeth was ready. She waited, and in perfect and fluent Latin, she tore into him, insulting him in virulent language, and vindicating her policy. The ambassador apologized and retired in confusion. Elizabeth was delighted with herself, and the episode kept her in good spirits for a long while. 'God's death,' she said triumphantly to her councillors, 'I have been enforced this day to scour up my old Latin that hath lain long in rusting.'[7]

Raleigh was still a handsome man. He had his portrait painted, with a chart of Cadiz proudly shown in one corner. Now that he was safely back in favour, there is assurance rather than arrogance in his features, but his eyes have a wary look. It is the most powerful of his portraits, and the most magnificently dressed. (He perhaps would have been glad to know that it would end up in the National Gallery of Ireland.) Over his white silk or satin shirt, his black doublet is heavily decorated with gold filigree and hundreds of pearls, some no doubt false, and the buttons appear to be of rubies and turquoises. He holds a cane in one hand, because of his wounded leg, and in the other he holds a sword with a finely worked gold hilt. No earrings this time, but an expensive-looking lace ruff. His thinning hair is no longer dark, but seems touched up, perhaps artist's flattery. On his left arm he wears an enormous bow of gauze, evidently the latest Court fashion.

Essex was also painted at this time. His portrait shows him looking older than his years, absolutely sure of himself, beady dark eyes, dark curly hair, with a ginger spade-shaped beard, and dressed all in his favourite white, pearl buttons down the front, but with no other ornamentation except for a gold belt, dagger and sword hilt, the Garter on his leg and the blue ribbon of the Privy Council round his neck. 'A man with a nature not to be ruled,' as Francis Bacon said. From this picture it is easy to visualize the rage that would erupt whenever he was thwarted by the Queen. He was not always so splendidly dressed, it being said that he was 'more attentive of business and less curious of dress'.

A portrait at Hatfield House of Robert Cecil, the third member of the triumvirate (which everyone felt must surely be doomed), is a contrast to the others. He is dressed in deep black, a cloak concealing his crooked back. He also wears the blue ribbon. The face is distinguished, with arched eyebrows, a pointed beard and shrewd eyes. Bacon, in his essay on *Deformity*, written after Cecil's death but obviously with him in mind, said that people who are deformed, knowing that they are 'exposed to scorn', watch and observe weaknesses in others, so that they 'may have somewhat to repay'. All this one sees in the portrait. Cecil's motto is boldly shown, *Sero, sed serio*, which could be translated as 'I sow, but in earnest', but in fact means 'Late, but seriously'.*

The Queen now approved an ambitious plan for Essex's expedition. First and foremost, the fleet was to destroy all the Spanish ships refitting at Ferrol. If any of these ships were encountered on the high seas they must be engaged and destroyed. The fleet would then sail on to the Azores to intercept and capture treasure ships from the West Indies or any carracks arriving from the East Indies. This done, the island of Terceira should be taken and garrisoned, and if possible other islands would also be occupied.

Sir Francis Vere had been summoned from the Netherlands, bringing 1,200 musketeers to join the other largely inexperienced troops. Indeed Essex complained that many of the pressganged men had never been to sea in their lives, and did not know one rope from another. Now another old

---

* The portrait was painted when he was created Earl of Salisbury by James I. 'Late' in the motto is supposed to refer to his lateness in becoming a peer, but could it have a double meaning?

quarrel (from Cadiz) had to be patched up, and Raleigh and Vere were made to shake hands. Vere said that he did this the more willingly 'because there had nothing passed between us that might blemish reputations'. And in the *History of the World* Raleigh was to return the compliment by saying that Vere was one of the Queen's captains who had done 'as great honour to our nation as ever any did', adding that, like Sir John Norris, he had never been adequately rewarded by the Queen for his services.

The fleet numbered about a hundred ships, divided into four squadrons, one of them Dutch. Essex as Lord General was in the *Merhonour*, with five of the Queen's ships including the *Mary Rose* and the *Swiftsure*, and six armed merchantmen. Lord Thomas Howard was Vice-Admiral or second-in-command in the *Due Repulse*, with seven of the Queen's ships and one armed merchantman. Raleigh was Rear-Admiral or third-in-command in the *Warspite*, with Sir Arthur Gorges as his flag captain. In his squadron were the two captured Apostles, the *San Matéo*, now anglicized as *St Matthew*, with Sir George Carew captain, and the *San Andrés*, now *St Andrew*, with Marcellus Throckmorton, related to Bess, captain. Also in Raleigh's squadron were his nephew John Gilbert, who had been knighted at Cadiz, in the *Antelope*, two armed merchantmen, the *Guiana* and the *Consent*, ten transports and twenty 'voluntary barks of the west country'.

There were said to be 500 gentlemen volunteers, all eager for the adventure and, after the example of Cadiz, in hope of fabulous loot. Just as Raleigh gathered around him friends and kinsmen he could trust, so Essex had his own special group (most of them disliking Raleigh), including the Earls of Southampton and Rutland, married to Essex's stepdaughter, and Lord Mountjoy, lover of Essex's sister Penelope Rich; also Sir Gwyllym or 'Gelli' Meyricke, one of the Cadiz knights and Essex's steward. The poet John Donne was again to be in the company, sailing in Essex's flagship.

There was still time for Essex and Raleigh to go up to London for a final consultation with Cecil. Afterwards, on 6 July, Raleigh wrote a puzzlingly ambiguous letter from Weymouth, on returning from a last farewell to Bess and Wat at Sherborne. He began by apologizing for bothering Cecil at such a time of 'haste and confusion of businesses, among so many wants'. He went on: 'I acquainted the Lord General with your letter to me, and your kind acceptance of your entertainment. He was also wonderful merry at the conceit of Richard the Second. I hope it shall never alter, and whereof I shall be most glad of, as the true way to all our good, quiet and advancement, and most of all for her sake whose affairs shall therefore find better pro-gression.' The ending was suitably sycophantic: 'Sir, I will ever be yours. It is all I can say and I will perform it with my life and with my fortune.'

Did this mean that Cecil had taken them to a performance of Shake-speare's latest play at the Globe, *The Life and Death of King Richard the Second*? Cecil enjoyed the theatre, and at the end of the previous year had been invited to the play by Sir Edward Hoby. It was certainly not a play to be merry about, and there are not many jokes in it. But there were topical references, and these were to redound on Essex and help to cause his ruin four years hence. With the question of Elizabeth's succession still in the air, and complaints about her being too influenced by favourites, there were inevitable comparisons between him and Bolingbroke. The play was published in 1597, and went through three editions – with the deposition scene omitted. It was not reprinted until after Elizabeth's death. In 1601 Elizabeth, when being shown the archives of the Tower, 'fell upon' the reign of Richard II. 'I am Richard II,' she said, 'know ye not that?'

Raleigh's letter also included a request for Cecil to help in the hastening of supplies, which were evidently becoming short at Plymouth because of delays and the 'multitudes of bodies', who were ever more restless and discontented. Even so, by the time Cecil would have read this letter, the main fleet was about to sail.

Yet Cecil still had time to write a jaunty letter to Essex, it would seem enclosing a copy of Raleigh's of 6 July, referring to 'Good Mr Raleigh, who wanders at his own diligence, because diligence and he are not familiar'. He also said that he himself could not 'bear to be accused of dullness [being too slow], especially by your rear admiral [Raleigh] who making haste but once in a year to write a letter by post, has dated his latest despatch from Weymouth, which I know was written from Plymouth'.

There is no harm in friends making fun of one another behind his or her back. Cecil here was referring to the fact that Raleigh was a demon for hard work ('He can toil terribly'), and an indefatigable letter-writer. The reference to Weymouth is certainly strange, and some have thought that the whole letter was a piece of deliberate malice, as though Cecil was becoming uneasy about Raleigh and Essex being too close. It could have been just a harmless slip.

On the very day of departure, 10 July, Raleigh signed his will which had been drawn up two days before, the only will of his that has survived. Within six years it had been superseded; and after that it totally disappeared – to be discovered 300 years later in a bundle of deeds at Sherborne. It was witnessed by Adrian Gilbert, William Strode a landowner near Plymouth and a Member of Parliament, Christopher Harris with whom he would have been staying and a Vice-Admiral of Devon, and his steward John Meere still in favour.

Mentions of 'my reputed daughter' and Alice Goold have always been regarded as the most sensational items in the will. It is a long document and starts off portentously:[8]

In the name of God the father the sonne and the holye ghoste three persons and one god, the eighth Daye of Julye anno domini 1597.

I, Walter Raleghe of Colliton Raleghe in the County of Devon, acknowledging that all fleshe ys grasse and the day of our birthe ys the firste steppe to death, though the hower be uncertaine when the spiritt shall retorne to the Lord that gave it, do ordeyne, declare, and make this my laste will and testament in manner and effecte followinge . . .

Briefly, after provision had been made to Bess and bequests to friends and servants, the estate was to pass to the four-year-old Wat, and failing him to the next male heir (who would be Raleigh's brother Carew). The trustees were Arthur Throckmorton, Thomas Hariot, and Alexander Brett, a relative of the Throckmortons. Two main groups of land were affected: his 42,000 acres in Ireland and other purchases there, and the leases of Sherborne and properties in Dorset, Wiltshire and Somerset; possibly also a house at Colaton Raleigh, of which he was lord of the manor – hence its mention at the beginning of the will. Bess had been left the lease of a farm at Haselbury Plucknett, ten miles from Sherborne, evidently intended as a dower house, because all the woods around it were left to Wat. There was an interest in 'Spilmane, Her Majesties Juillers house neere Durham House, London', from whom had to be redeemed two large silver gilt flagons and pieces of obviously valuable silver which were to go to Wat. Durham House was not included in the will, since he was occupying it only at the Queen's pleasure.

He also listed as an asset Bess's marriage portion of £500 still owing from the Earl of Huntingdon, and another £500 owing from the Earl of Derby. He ordered that his ship the *Roebuck* should be sold, with all her anchors, tackle, artillery etc.; from the proceeds 500 marks were to go to the 'reputed daughter', and Hariot was to receive £200 and Lawrence Keymis £100. The rest of the money from the *Roebuck* was to be used for paying off his debts. Hariot was also to receive £100 a year from the wine patent, which evidently would continue after his death, and the rest of the income would go into the residuary estate.

Wat was specifically left two large silver gilt pots, a silver basin and a ewer; also a bedstead embellished with mother-of-pearl, a Chinese bedspread embroidered with silk and gold, and 'furniture thereto belonging', with eight pieces of 'my richest hangings having my arms on them'. A porcelain 'suite' set in silver and gilt was to go to Sir Robert Cecil, should Wat die before coming of age. All this presumably was at Durham House.

All the books and furniture in Hariot's own room and in Raleigh's room at Durham House were to go to Hariot. Arthur Throckmorton was to get his best horse and saddle, George Carew his next best horse and saddle. Alexander Brett would get his 'long black cloak now in my wardrobe at Durham House', and his 'loving kinsman' Arthur Gorges his best rapier and dagger. Meere was to have an annual income of £20. Particular instructions were given to Bess prohibiting her from ploughing up the park at Sherborne, or 'spoiling' any part of the castle and its outholdings, its gardens, orchards, walks, fish-ponds, trees; the same conditions were applied to the farm at Haselbury Plucknett.

The mention of Robert Cecil in the will shows that Raleigh must still have regarded him as a genuine friend. It is strange that the *Roebuck* appears to be the only one of his ships remaining. He often maintained that he had sacrificed all his worldly goods in the war against Spain; but much had also gone into the building works at Sherborne.

The Islands Voyage
1597

Scarcely had the English fleet left Plymouth when a storm arose, with thunder and lightning. Raleigh and his squadron became separated from the rest on the very first day. His own squadron became scattered too, and on the morning of the 11th he found that he was left with just the *Bonaventure*, the *St Matthew* and *St Andrew*, and some flyboats. The wind suddenly changed and blew both from the south and west, and as huge waves billowed up from the Bay of Biscay he began to fear for the two great lumbering Apostles. On the *Warspite* they had to lower the sails, or they would have been torn to pieces. As he was later to report, the ship lurched about so vehemently that all the beams and stanchions seemed about to be rent apart, insomuch as he and his crew 'made account to yield ourselves to God'; the tossing of the waves, had smashed open the bulkhead, and the bricks of the cookhouse were ground to powder.[1]

Raleigh decided that there was nothing else but to return to Plymouth, which he did on the 18th of July. This was a shameful thing to have to do, but on arrival he was worried to find that the rest of the fleet was still somewhere out to sea. So he dashed off a letter to Cecil explaining what had happened. He was alarmed about Essex, of whom there was no news, and worried that he might be blamed for abandoning him. The *Merhonour* had already been leaking before she left, and the Queen had begged Cecil not to let Essex go out in that 'crazed vessel'. However, on the next day Raleigh was able to report that the ship had struggled into Falmouth, 'in great extremity and in imminent peril of sinking into the sea'. The mizzen mast was broken, as were those of most of the other ships. Longboats and barges had been lost. 'I beseech you', Raleigh wrote, 'work from her Majesty some comfort to my Lord General, who I know is dismayed by these mischances, even to death, although there could not be more done by any man, God having turned the heavens with that fury against us, a matter beyond the power or valour or wit of man to resist.'[2]

Cecil showed part of this letter to Elizabeth, who nearly wept. She wrote to Essex, saying that she would send another ship, the *Golden Lion*, to replace the *Merhonour*. Others of the fleet arrived, sometimes one by one, including the *St Matthew* and the *St Andrew*, which Raleigh had feared were lost. But there was no sign of Howard.

Essex, we are told, rode overland 'all night post over the rugged mountains of Cornwall', in other words over Bodmin Moor. Raleigh asked him, with the Earl of Rutland and some others, to dine on board the *Warspite*. Essex spent the night there, Raleigh having said that he would have 'taken it unkindly if my Lord had taken up any other lodgings until the *Lion* comes'. There were desertions, and as Rowland Whyte said,[3] the storm had 'killed the hearts of many voluntary gentlemen' – literally in the case of Sir Richard Ruddale, who had died of seasickness. Some of these gentlemen even left without saying goodbye. Sir Ferdinando Gorges, who was to have been sergeant-major of the expedition, and was now Governor of Plymouth, also had to back out. Raleigh himself, always prone to sea sickness, had suffered a great deal. One trusts that the violence of the storm had not damaged the luxurious decorations of his cabin, which must have been made available to Essex – Stebbing tells us that he was accustomed to have pictures on its walls, and that after his death relatives 'treasured' a bedstead he used on board that had green silk upholstery and gilt dolphins for legs (much in keeping with those bequests in his will).

Morale at Plymouth was altogether very low. A despatch arrived from Lord Thomas Howard, announcing that he had got through the storm and was waiting outside La Coruña, hoping to lure out enemy ships so that they could do battle. This was embarrassing, and there was a frantic rush to repair some of the ships in order to join him. But still the winds were blowing too hard. Then on 31 July Howard turned up at Plymouth, blandly dismissing the great storm as a 'stiff gale'.

On the next day Essex and Raleigh rode to London, to discuss alternative plans: perhaps abandoning the Ferrol plan altogether and instead heading for some pillaging in the West Indies. This idea was rightly dismissed for it would mean the fleet being away for some months at a time of danger from another Spanish attempt at invasion. Sir Arthur Gorges observed the two men together while in London, and noted that although Essex had many doubts and jealousies 'buzzed into his ears' against Raleigh he still appeared to prefer Raleigh's counsel and company to others who thought themselves more in his favour.

An infection of some sort was spreading among the troops at Plymouth and Lord Thomas Howard reported that if the soldiers went to sea they would 'die in heaps'. So it was decided to disband all except the thousand brought over by Vere from the Low Countries. It was also now decided that it would be too dangerous to make a direct attack on Ferrol, given that it lay at the end of a narrow two-mile channel. Instead fire-ships would have to be sent in, and among those selected were the two unlucky Apostles, which Raleigh had decided were too unwieldy to stand up to really rough weather. The sending in of the fire-ships would be his responsibility. And once again the Queen gave orders that Essex should be kept well away from all danger.

A letter from Cecil to Essex at this stage contained another curious comment concerning Raleigh: that the next storm to be endured at sea by Essex was not to be appeased by 'praying until Jonah be thrown into the sea, which will be the captain of the *Warspite*'.[4] Was this a clumsy attempt at humour? It does not quite seem like it.

Essex's flagship was now the *Due Repulse*. The chief commanders in the expedition made up his council of war. These were Lord Thomas Howard, Lord Mountjoy, Sir Walter Raleigh, Sir Francis Vere, and Sir Anthony Sherley (a cousin of Essex who had succeeded Sir Ferdinando Gorges as sergeant major). Arthur Gorges was still Raleigh's captain in the *Warspite* and John Davis (of the expeditions to the North-West Passage) his master. Sir George Carew remained with the *St Matthew*, and Marcellus Throckmorton with the *St Andrew*. The wind blew day after day; then suddenly it dropped. On 17 August the much reduced fleet was towed out of Plymouth in search of a breeze. So began the drama of the celebrated Islands Voyage.

The ships drifted down the Channel, but on the seventh day in the Bay of Biscay back came a storm, and with a vengeance. The *St Matthew* broke her foremast, and Sir George Carew just managed to steer her into La Rochelle harbour, where her great size caused a sensation.*

Off Cape Ortegal on the Spanish coast the *Due Repulse* sprang a leak, and an attempt was made to plug her by 'ramming down pieces of beef and clothes wrung together'. Not surprisingly this was a failure, and the ship was made to lie to in order to raise the hull out of the water, a tricky exercise in such weather. On the same day, the 27th, the *Warspite* broke her main yard, and as a result Raleigh could only let her run before the wind, taking him to Cape Roca near Lisbon, which had been the pre-arranged second rendezvous, the first being Cape Finisterre.

In Galicia the rugged and stormy coast beyond Ortegal is locally known

---

* Carew said that the ship dwarfed all the others in the harbour. About 4,000 sightseers came aboard, including thirty ladies of rank who 'for three long hours talked of the Queen's beauty, wisdom and government'.[5] Eventually he managed to get the ship back to Portsmouth, and at once he set out again in the *Adventure*, hoping to join Essex.

as the Costa da Morte, because of the great number of wrecks, partly due in later years to the magnetic rocks. Raleigh would not have wanted to risk being left to drift in such a notoriously dangerous place. Meanwhile, the Spaniards had become alerted to the arrival of English ships, and beacons were being lit.

When Essex arrived off Finisterre he found that not only was the *Warspite* missing, but so were twenty other ships from the squadron. He had in fact known that the *Warspite* had sent up a distress signal, and that *St Matthew*'s foremast had been broken, but even so 'evil tongues' began to suggest that Raleigh had gone off 'for his own purpose'. Essex, however, was prepared to believe that the rest of Raleigh's squadron had obediently been following his stern light. In any case, without Raleigh, sending fire-ships to Ferrol was no longer possible, and the Spaniards were obviously fully prepared for attack. It all amounted to a good excuse for calling off an operation which neither he nor Raleigh had relished in the first place.

Rumours, mistaken as it turned out, reached both of them that the *Adelantado* Padilla* had already gone to the Azores to protect the *flota*. On 8 September Raleigh was off Terceira, where he wrote a kind of explanation to Cecil, saying that for ten days he had not dared go to bed or even to his cabin. Essex also hurried to Terceira, arriving after Raleigh had left but not knowing that he even had been there. Meanwhile, the *Adelantado*, who had never left Spain, took the opportunity of removing the ships from Ferrol to La Coruña. This meant that he now had a fleet of ninety-eight vessels, of which twenty-four were galleons, being prepared for a new invasion of England.

Essex was waiting at Flores when Raleigh arrived there on 15 September. What Raleigh had been up to during the intervening week is not known, but those evil tongues were at work again. Had he just been enjoying sailing in that deep blue sea, followed by dolphins and gulls, and watching the distant whale spouts? At any rate Essex was very friendly, saying that he 'never believed he would leave him, although divers persuaded him to the contrary'. Indeed, Gorges said, Essex seemed the 'joyfullest man living for our arrival'.[6] He even named those persons of 'scandalous and cankered dispositions' who had spoken against Raleigh. A council of war was called, and it was decided that the fleet was now to be separated into three commands.

Essex had also surveyed Terceira, and had realized the great problems of attacking it. As Raleigh was to say in the *History of the World*, 'there are

* p. 283.

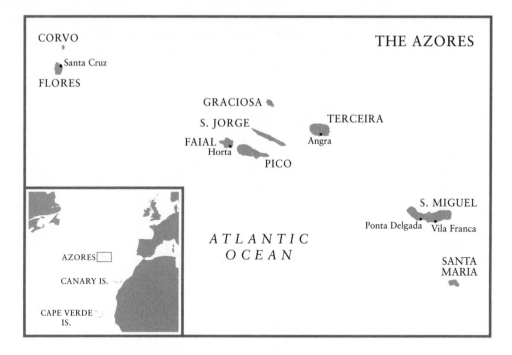

not many islands in the world better fenced by nature, and strengthened by art'.[7] The main harbour, Angra, was indeed virtually impregnable, probably once a volcanic crater, perfectly circular with a narrow entrance, and protected on one side by a rocky bluff known as Monte Brasil, and on the other by a fort. All treasure fleets and their convoys from the West Indies would call there for refitting and watering. Flores would always be the first port of call, again perhaps for watering, and afterwards the *flota*, with the great volcano on Pico, 2345 metres high, as a guide, would pass either Fayal or Graciosa, more usually Fayal, on the way to Terceira. So Essex and Raleigh were to attack and seize Fayal, and Lord Thomas Howard and Sir Francis Vere would capture Graciosa. The two cousins Lord Mountjoy and Sir Christopher Blount would tackle São Miguel, the largest and most easterly of the islands, where East Indian carracks usually called on their way to Terceira. The Dutch contingent would attack the sparsely inhabited Pico, only a couple of miles across the straits from Fayal.*

---

* Both Fayal and Pico were to become famous as whaling centres, especially in the 19th century. Pico and Graciosa started producing wine commercially in the 18th century, probably not at all at this time – contrary to what some writers have said.

Raleigh being 'distressed for water' asked if he could wait a while at Flores. With him were Sir Gelli Meyricke (a Cadiz knight) in the *Swiftsure*, Sir William Harvey in the *Bonaventure*, and Sir William Brooke in the *Dreadnought*. Loading casks of water was a long and arduous job and the work had hardly started when the next day at midnight a message came from Essex telling Raleigh to report at Fayal immediately with the other ships; he could continue getting water at Fayal. When he duly arrived there the next morning, to his surprise there was no sign of Essex, and he could see the Spanish flag flying from the fort at the island's capital, Horta. He waited, without a sign of Essex. Two Portuguese swam over to the *Warspite* with information about the strength of the military, and no doubt warning him that the Spaniards were beginning to remove their property into the hills above. In fact the indigenous population was only partly Portuguese and mostly Flemish, their ancestors brought there in the days of Henry the Navigator in the 1400s. Raleigh now called a meeting because his men were becoming restless and feeling that they were losing the chance of plunder. And there was still a great need for water.

Sir Gelli Meyricke insisted that no one should land until Essex's arrival. On the following day some cannon was fired from the fort, and it was seen that trenches were being dug on the beach. So on the fourth day, Essex having still not arrived, Raleigh sent boats ashore to a bay north of Horta to fetch in water. They were fired on. At this Raleigh lost patience and decided to land himself. He took 260 men and was accompanied by some of his gentlemen, all 'men assured', including Arthur Gorges, Henry Thynne, Marcellus Throckmorton, Lawrence Keymis, Leonard Berry and one or two others who had followed him on his previous adventures.

Horta has a long semi-circular beach, protected by two headlands. The fort was in the centre, but there was another on the south headland, Monte da Guia. Raleigh made for the one on the north, and found himself faced with perhaps 500 Spaniards. The fire was so heavy that the crews of his longboats began to hesitate, as if they meant to turn back. According to Gorges, Raleigh 'did not spare to call them openly and rebuke aloud with disgraceful words, seeing their baseness'. He shouted to them to row 'full on the rocks, and called to all who were not afraid to follow him'.

The rocks were of jagged black lava, and there was a considerable swell. Two of the boats were badly damaged and overturned.

And so, clambering over the rocks and wading through the water we passed pell mell with swords and pikes . . . Thereupon the Spaniards began to shrink, and seeing us to come faster upon them, suddenly retiring, cast away their weapons, turned their backs and fled.

Raleigh now sent back for 200 Low Countries soldiers, officially under the command of Vere but agitating to join in the fight.

Our Rear-Admiral accompanied with divers gentlemen of the best sort, to the number of forty, in the head of all the troops, with his leading staff, and no armour than his collar (a bravery in a commander not to be commended) led on the company with soft march, full in the face of the fort, descending down a little hill, whilst with their great ordnance and musketry we were very shrewdly pelted.

Raleigh, it must be remembered, was lame from his wound at Cadiz. Some of the men began to falter again. 'Our Rear-Admiral and we cried out on them for this shameful disorder.' He now asked for volunteers to find ways into the town, but as the country was so exposed nobody wanted to go. So he impatiently said he would go himself, and called for his helmet and breastplate. Berry, Gorges and a few others said that they would accompany him.

They worked their way up the hill and along the old walls, which were being battered by cannon balls, sending bits of stone flying. Two men had their heads cut clean off. Gorges was shot through the left leg with a musket bullet, but it was only a flesh wound, the bullet burning his silk stocking and buskin as if they had been 'singed with a hot iron'. Raleigh too was shot through his breeches and doublet sleeves in two or three places.

And still they plied us so fast with small shot as that (I well remember) he wished me to put off a large red scarf I then wore, being (as he said) a very fair mark for them. But I was not willing to do the Spaniards so much honour at that time, albeit I could have wished it had not been on me, and therefore I told the Rear-Admiral again that his white scarf was as eminent as my red, and therefore I would now follow his example.

When they at last reached the fort they found it deserted. They decided to attack the hill fort the following day, and to spend the night in the deserted houses.

It was on the next morning, 22 September, that Essex finally arrived. One theory about his absence is that he believed that the treasure fleet was on its way and had been searching for it, cruising round the islands. Another is that he had been chasing a carrack that got away. Whatever the reason, he

1. Katherine ('Kat') Astley, born Champernowne, Elizabeth's governess and Raleigh's great-aunt.

2. Hayes Barton, Raleigh's birthplace.

3. (*Above left*) The Duke of
Alba spearing the enemies of
Philip II: Queen Elizabeth, the
pro-French Pope Paul IV, and,
apparently, the Elector of
Saxony, though William the
Silent is more probable.
Polichrome statue in the
Palacio de Liria, Madrid,
artist unknown, *c.* 1575.

4. (*Above right*) Sir Humphrey
Gilbert, portrait at Compton
Castle, artist unknown.

5. (*Right*) Raleigh, miniature
by Nicholas Hilliard, the
Queen's 'dear minion'.

6. Queen Elizabeth, the 'Ermine Portrait', painted in 1585 by Sir William Segar;
at Hatfield House. The ermine was a symbol of chastity.

7. (*Above left*) Philip II, artist unknown.

8. (*Above right*) Sir Richard Grenville as a young man, artist unknown.

9. (*Right*) Sir Francis Drake, aged 43, with symbols of the great circumnavigation and his knighthood. Engraved by Jodocus Hondius.

10. Raleigh as Captain of the Guard. He wears the 'Green Greenwich Armour', which is to be seen in the Tower of London: typical armour used by fashionable young men at the tiltyard.

11. Elizabeth ('Bess') Raleigh, born Throckmorton, about the time of the marriage in 1591.

12. John White's portrait of the wife of the chief of Pomeioc with her daughter. Hariot said that Indians 'pounced' their skins, that is, tattooed as well as painted. The girl is obviously delighted with her doll, which is in Elizabethan dress.

13. (*Below*) The Indian village of Pomeioc by John White. Top right, a temple or charnel-house. A dog shown is top left.

14. The gateway at Sherborne Castle, looking across to the ruins of the old castle.

15. Sherborne Castle. The wings and turrets were added about 1625 by John Digby, Earl of Bristol.

16. (*Top*) An Indian house on the Orinoco delta. As the water rises so the family has to retreat upwards.

17. (*Above*) The *tepuy* Auyán seen from the Gran Sabana, on the border of Venezuela and Brazil.

18. (*Left*) At Payepal near the present town of El Dorado in Venezuela: hosing down the mud in preparation for panning for gold, using mercury.

19. The mysterious Lake Guatavita in Colombia where the legend of the Golden Man may have originated. The gap was made by prospectors in an attempt to drain the lake.

20. (*Above*) A 'headless man', detail from Theodor de Bry's *America*.

21. (*Right*) One of over 300 megalithic sculptures or idols, usually near funeral mounds, at San Augustín, Colombia.

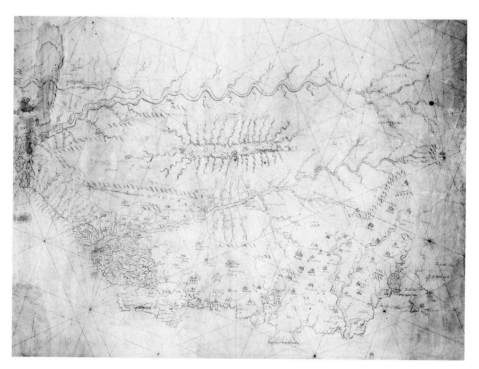

22. (*Above*) A detail from Hariot's map of Guiana showing the fabled lake and city of Manoa between the Orinoco and the Amazon. The stylized tributaries make the lake look like an enormous centipede. The northern coast of Guiana is at the bottom, as it is in the original.

23. Robert Devereux, 2nd Earl of Essex, a portrait now at Montacute House, painted after his return from the Cadiz expedition in 1596. After Marcus Gheeraerts the Younger.

24. Raleigh, back in favour after Cadiz and in full splendour. Because of his wound he carries a stick. Artist unknown.

25. (*Above left*) Robert Cecil, 1st Earl of Salisbury, painted by John de Critz the Elder. At Hatfield House.

26. (*Above right*) Lord Henry Howard, created Earl of Northampton by James I and Raleigh's bitter enemy. Portrait at Petworth House. Artist unknown.

27. (*Left*) James I, by John I. de Critz.

28. Bess Raleigh, her face showing the stresses and anxieties of living with such a husband. The portrait is mentioned by William Oldys as being in the possession of Captain William Elwes, related to the Raleighs, *c.* 1730.

29. (*Left*) Don Diego Sarmiento de Acuña Conde de Gondomar, aged 54. Engraved by Guillermo Passeo, 1622.

30. (*Below*) The coffin of the Conde de Gondomar in the crypt of San Benito el Viejo, Valladolid.

31. (*Right*) A posthumous miniature of Raleigh's son Wat with a battle scene below. At Belvoir Castle, artist unknown.

32. (*Below*) Robert Pigott, great-great-great grandson of Raleigh and his last authenticated descendant, who died aged 13 in 1751. A marble relief in St Leonard's Church, Grendon Underwood, Buckinghamshire.

33. (*Right*) From the cover of a pre-World War I cycle catalogue.

34. (*Bottom*) A popular brand of cigarettes in Mexico.

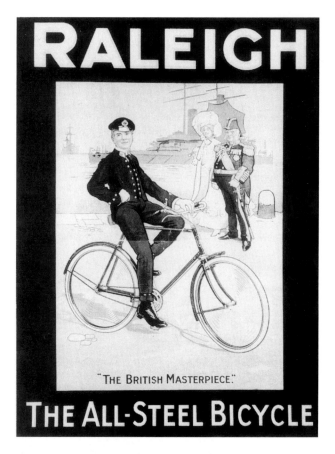

"THE BRITISH MASTERPIECE."

THE ALL-STEEL BICYCLE

should have informed Raleigh. As soon as he arrived Sir Gelli Meyricke came on board blazing with hostile talk about Raleigh having deliberately disobeyed orders, and how he had landed and engaged the enemy solely to steal the honour from Essex. Other haters of Raleigh – Sherley, Blount and Vere – now saw their chance. Raleigh's offence in landing could not be pardoned. It was a court-martial offence. He should be beheaded.

Essex sent for Raleigh's senior officers who had spent the night at Horta, and told them that all who had accompanied Raleigh were now cashiered. Then Raleigh was summoned. He arrived expecting congratulations but found 'all men's countenances estranged as he passed through them'. Essex gave him only a perfunctory welcome, and then accused him of a breach of order: it was an offence to land troops without the General's presence or order. Raleigh had to defend himself quickly against this volatile young man. The important point made against him was that no captain of a ship or company should land without direction. Raleigh said that he was not a captain but a principal commander, therefore not subject to court martial. In the absence of Essex or Lord Thomas Howard he was entitled to act. He had waited four days. Essex had told him to land on Fayal and take on water, and this was what he had attempted to do, and he had been attacked. It would have been dishonourable not to retaliate. It was true that Sir Gelli had asked him not to go, but it had come to a point where his own men were becoming restless and making out that he did not dare go into the attack.

After a long argument Essex relented and was ready to make friends again with Raleigh. But Christopher Blount was not going to let this pass and 'fanned discontent' all over again. By this time Lord Thomas Howard had arrived, ready to act as peacemaker. Raleigh had already made up his mind that if it was a question of his going to trial he would return to the *Warspite* and forcibly resist arrest; either that, or he would return to England. The whole day had been spent in argument. As a result, during that night the Spaniards in the upper fort, having seen such a large fleet assembled in front of Horta, had loaded up as much as they could and had taken refuge in the interior of the island.

The next morning Lord Thomas Howard, in the best aristocratic tradition, went to see Raleigh and guaranteed that, if he went to see Essex there would be no more trouble. This was done. Raleigh gave his apology and it was accepted. The cashiered officers were also pardoned.

When the time came to make a report on the Islands Voyage, all mention of the Fayal incident was omitted. It was signed by the whole council of war, including Raleigh; but not of course by Meyricke or Blount, who were not on the council. Some fifteen years later in the *History of the World*, Raleigh wrote of the episode with a commendable lack of bitterness: 'There was no purpose to defraud me of any honour, but rather an opinion; but the enterprise was such or so ill-managed, as that no honour was due unto it'.[8] He admitted that he had more regard of reputation in the affair than of safety. He had in mind, he said, the honour of Queen Elizabeth – meaning that if he had not counterattacked after being provoked it would have been a reflection on England itself. He also said that he had at first refused the assistance of the Low Countries men, and had taken men of his own squadron.

Essex now decided that the fort on Monte da Guia must be attacked. Escape routes were blocked and there were calls for instant surrender, to which of course there was no response. The fort was found to be empty, apart from six large cannons. There were also corpses of two prisoners, one English and one Dutch; their throats had been cut. In revenge, the town was set on fire.

There were new complaints from Essex supporters that Raleigh had not done anything to prevent the Spaniards from escaping. The reply was obvious: time had been wasted in 'disciplining and correcting our own pretended faults of landing' – otherwise there would have been a chance of capturing the Spaniards and ransoming them.

The fleet now sailed off to the tiny island of Graciosa, where they were joined by the Dutch from Pico, who according to Gorges had behaved with cruelty to the wretched inhabitants scraping a living from growing woad. The denizens of Graciosa were Portuguese, and only too glad to supply wine, fruit and fresh victuals. In return nobody was taken for ransom. Now Essex was persuaded to direct all the squadron on to São Miguel, way down to the south, about 150 miles away. He had been told, presumably by Mountjoy and Blount, that there was a good anchorage there and that the island would be easy to capture. It was a ridiculous and disastrous decision; if, as it was still hoped, the Spanish treasure fleet was about to arrive, there would be no question of it going all the way down to São Miguel. It would head straight for the safety of Terceira.

Due to some muddle, four ships had been left behind near Graciosa, one of which was Sir William Monson's *Rainbow*. Only three hours after Essex's departure, the *flota* was sighted. Monson desperately sent up flares and fired guns to attract Essex's attention, but it was far too late. There were forty-three vessels in the *flota*, afterwards said to be carrying ten million pesos' worth of silver.

It could well be wondered why Howard and Raleigh had not attempted to prevent Essex from making such a stupid mistake. Perhaps they felt it was best to avoid another confrontation, especially if his great confidants Mountjoy and Blount had been involved. At any rate one Spanish ship was captured, with a satisfactorily lucrative cargo of cochineal. The rest made their way unscathed to Angra harbour. Richard Hawkins, son of Sir John, was a prisoner on one of the galleons. Later, after his release, he was to say to Essex that if the English fleet had been there it would have been an easy victory.

Essex, not surprisingly, was seething when the news reached him. He was all for attacking Terceira immediately, his plan being to storm Angra from the rear, landing in the north of the island. Howard and Raleigh even offered 3,000 sailors to augment the landing party but this must have been bluff, for they well knew that the colonels of the military were not at all keen on such a project. So Essex gave up the idea: a bitter decision. At least, if São Miguel were captured, it would be a base for a forming a blockade between the Spanish mainland and the Azores. Also the lack of water for his fleet was again desperate.

On the way to São Miguel he managed to take three prizes, and Raleigh captured a small ship from Brazil, with a cargo which if sold would pay for the wages of the *Warspite*. They arrived on 4 October. The plan now was for Raleigh to sail up and down in front of the capital Ponta Delgado as if preparing for a frontal attack, blowing trumpets and beating drums, and with some bombarding, as a decoy to distract the garrison. Meanwhile Essex would make a landing further down the coast and attack from the rear.

It was almost a repetition of the Fayal fiasco. Essex landed at the town of Vila Franca, and found the countryside around so fertile and so full of delicious fruits, especially melons, and the abandoned houses so comfortable, that he decided to rest there for a time. Once again Raleigh was not informed, and he was kept waiting, not daring to land. The bemused inhabitants of Ponta Delgado simply gathered up his spent cannon balls from the beach.

And so Essex missed the appearance of a large carrack of 1,500 tons from the East Indies, heading all unconcerned for Ponta Delgado. There are conflicting stories about what happened next, but one version is that a Dutch ship moved up without orders and began firing on the carrack, just as she was about to enter the harbour where she would have been trapped. The Spanish captain immediately changed direction and made directly for the shore, running the ship aground and setting on fire the cargo of molasses and spices. Raleigh went in his barge to try to put out the fire, but he was too late, and the molten molasses poured into the surf turning it into blinding steam. The carrack burnt all the next day. So another rich prize had been lost. Essex could not blame Raleigh this time and ordered him to bring his squadron to Vila Franca. Raleigh's last sight of Ponta Delgado was of its inhabitants waving flags and firing guns in contempt.

The season of autumn gales had begun. Essex in his usual way created a few knights. On 10 October, amid an atmosphere of recrimination and disillusion, the ships put out to sea for the return journey. The Spaniards for their part, on reoccupying Vila Franca were surprised to find the churches and the pictures in them untouched. What was more, so it was reported back to Madrid, five women who had lagged behind during the flight from the town had been taken to Essex, and that he, finding them not bad looking, put them in a house under guard and out of temptation. The governor of the island was amazed at this. 'It may well be,' he wrote, 'that if we invaded England we might not have shared the same restraint'.[9]

In the worsening weather, with north-easterly gales, discipline deteriorated. Each ship now made its best way home. Raleigh did his utmost to follow the *Due Repulse*, but had to give up. The *Warspite* and the *Mary Rose* both sprang leaks. Water was short again, and on the *Warspite* 'we were fain to begin to set our great stills to work' (was this some kind of desalination?). Many of Essex's ships were swept as far as Ireland. Raleigh managed to reach St Ives. Essex made Plymouth on 26 October.

They arrived to find the country in a state of turmoil. News had just come that yet another Spanish armada was on its way under the *Adelantado* Padilla. One of his ships had been captured with information that the destination was to be Falmouth. The panic was greater than in 1588, because there was no fleet to oppose the Spaniards. The Privy Council had ordered troops to be brought back from France and the Low Countries. Essex on reaching Plymouth typically swore to beat the Spaniards even if 'we eat ropes' ends and drink nothing but rain water'.[10] He dashed up to London to arrange for supplies and financial help, while Raleigh set about organizing the coastal defences.

It was discovered shortly afterwards that the invading Spanish fleet had been broken up by the very same gales that had struck the English ships returning from the Azores. Padilla had left La Coruña on 18 October with over 17,000 men; he had pleaded to Philip that they were not sufficiently prepared, but the King had said if he did not sail at once he would hang him 'at his wife's neck'.[11] The plan had been to call first at Brittany where other ships were available, and then to capture Falmouth. This done, the fleet would station itself off the Scillies, waiting for the return of Essex, who would be destroyed. It would them return to Falmouth and move on to capture Plymouth.

But once more God blew and they were scattered, and Padilla returned to Spain with only three galleons and twenty-four transports, though other ships were able to reach Brittany and Ireland. A few more were picked up by the English, and it was reported that 560 Spanish prisoners had been taken to Plymouth.

Then the Furies took over. The Queen had already received good reports of Raleigh's exploits, but she now wanted to know why Essex had failed to follow up her instructions about Ferrol. Rowland Whyte wrote mildly that the Queen was not well pleased with Essex for his service and was saying that he could have done more than he did.[12] But Essex was raging, declaring that his long, dangerous and expensive ordeal had all been on his sovereign's behalf. As Whyte said: 'I hear his proceedings against Sir Walter Raleigh in calling his action to public question before a council of war, where, by a full court, he was found worthy of death, are greatly misliked here. Sir Walter is happy to have so good and constant friends, that are able by their wisdom and authority to protect him and comfort him.' He now feared that the peace between Essex and Cecil 'will burst out into terms of unkindness' – which was to prove no exaggeration.

Elizabeth had taken advantage of Essex's absence to grant Cecil the coveted post of Chancellor of the Duchy of Lancaster, which apart from the prestige provided useful profit and opportunities for patronage. More insulting to Essex was the conferring, on 23 October, of the Earldom of Nottingham on Lord Howard of Effingham, the Lord High Admiral. This was a very obvious snub. The wording of the patent commended the new earl not only for his services in 1588 but for the Cadiz expedition of 1596, indicating that he rather than Essex had been the principal victor there. Worse still was the fact that Howard would now be the Lord Steward of the Parliament that was about to assemble, thus giving him precedence over Essex, who would have to walk behind him in processions: a matter of great symbolic importance.

It was acknowledged by all at Court that this was a deliberate demotion, as the Earldom had been granted before the Queen even knew the outcome of the Islands Voyage. In tremendous dudgeon Essex rushed off to his house at Wanstead, where he shut himself into his room, wrapping himself in cloaks and blankets, pretending to be desperately ill. This was a crafty move, as a French delegation was about to arrive in London and would expect to be received by Essex who was on friendly terms with Henri IV. Inevitably the row would be seized on with glee and reported back to France.

He had behaved like a child, and the Queen treated him like a child. But she started to worry about his illness, and let him know that she was worried. So he consented to return to London, refusing to attend Parliament or Council meetings, and spending much of his time skulking at Essex House on the Strand.

Raleigh on the other hand was enjoying his return to eminence. As senior knight for Dorset he was entitled to sit in Parliament, but he had first to attend to defences and Stannary business, as well as some 'discontentment' among the Dutch about the Brazilian prize, which they felt was rightfully theirs. But he was exhausted, and not well, so after a while he and Bess went to Bath to take the waters. The Privy Council sent a message for his quick recovery, and the Speaker of the Commons authorized Adrian Gilbert, who was also a Member of Parliament, to go down to Sherborne to convey the best wishes of the House.

Raleigh had recovered enough to return to Parliament by December, for on the 21st he was on a committee to consider a bill against persons falsely pretending to be soldiers or sailors. He also reported to a shocked House of Commons that when he and other delegates went to the House of Lords to discuss this bill, they had to remain standing while their lordships did not even take off their hats. A kind of justification for such behaviour did arrive from the Lords, and the matter was dropped. But it had been a deliberate insult, and conceivably had been directed against Raleigh, who was still regarded by many in the Upper House as an ambitious upstart. In the Commons he also spoke on subjects to do with the Navy and the recruitment of men for the Services.

Essex had worked himself up into a tantrum again, and was demanding that the new Earl of Nottingham or one of his sons should fight a duel with him, to settle this question of precedence. 'Here is such a do about it', Rowland Whyte wrote, 'as it troubles this place [the Court] and all other proceedings. Sir Walter Raleigh is employed by the Queen to end the quarrel, and to make an atonement between them.'

Raleigh's suggestion, which was accepted, was that Essex should be given the vacant title of Earl Marshal of England, which in effect gave him all the precedence he wanted. Not only that, but the terms of his patent gave him due credit for his achievements at Cadiz. An overjoyed Essex received a further boost when Sir Francis Vere, who had been ill and away from Court, arrived with glowing accounts of his conduct in the Azores – most of them invented.

Now it was the turn of Nottingham to plead illness. He left the Court in umbrage before the Christmas festivities, and was never again on the same friendly terms with Raleigh, in spite of his 'kinship' and all those compliments in the dedication to the *Discoverie*.

So Essex consented to meet the French ambassador, who was impressed by his charm but alarmed by such delusions of grandeur.

Crisis in Ireland
1598

December 1597 could have been a dangerous month for Raleigh in his relations with Essex, but now all had changed. This also applied to Cecil. The Court gossips were all agog with the 'too too great familiarity that is grown between the Earl of Essex, Sir Robert Cecil and Sir Walter Raleigh'.[1]

Raleigh was now comfortably settled in his old role at Court, as confirmed by a vignette in one of Rowland Whyte's letters about yet another quarrel, this time between Southampton and Ambrose Willoughby.[2] These two, with Raleigh and a Mr Parker, had been playing a game of primero in the Presence Chamber one evening in January. The Queen had gone to bed, and Willoughby, as her Squire of the Body, asked them to leave:

Soon after, he spake to them again, that if they did not leave, he would call in the Guard to pull down the board, which Sir Walter Raleigh seeing, put up his money and went his ways. But my Lord Southampton took exceptions to him, and told him he would remember it; and so finding him between the tennis court wall and the garden, struck him, and Willoughby polled off [cut] some of his locks.

From his portrait, Southampton must have been proud of his exceptionally long girlish locks. And what was it about the tennis court that provoked such silly rows? At least the Queen did thank Willoughby, and said it would have been better to have Southampton shut up in the Porter's Lodge.

As always there were hidden reasons behind what was to be a very short-lived love affair within the Essex–Cecil–Raleigh threesome. As Whyte again said: 'I understand Sir Walter Raleigh desires to have a reward of service. Within these two days he has been with 1000 [code for Essex] and desired, by his means, some might be laid upon him.' It seemed, he said, that Raleigh hoped to be Vice-Chamberlain and to be admitted to the Privy Council. In the case of Cecil, he was about to leave the country on a mission of some months to Henri IV in order to try to prevent a peace treaty being signed between France and Spain; also he was to retrieve a loan that had been made by Elizabeth. He was going somewhat unwillingly, because of his aged father's failing health, and he did not want any adverse manoeuvring at Court while he was away.

Raleigh now offered Essex a share of his prizes, and Cecil persuaded the Queen to offer him all the cochineal and indigo captured in the Azores, at the bargain price of £50,000, nearly half its market value; what was more, all further importation of cochineal would be forbidden for two years. Cecil even managed to get the usually parsimonious Queen to grant Essex a further gift of £7,000 from the proceeds.

Even more amazingly it was agreed that Essex should act as Secretary of State during Cecil's absence. In return for this a promise was obtained from him that he would do nothing harmful to Cecil during that period. For all his grasping vanity and paranoia there was still at times a touching naivety in Essex's behaviour; he had given his word of honour and he would keep it. He had also promised to help Raleigh in some of his aspirations – not, as it turned out, with much success.

So now Cecil's friends, such as Raleigh, Bess and Lords Cobham and Southampton, gave him a series of farewell banquets and entertainments, including performances of plays. One of Shakespeare's latest plays, *Henry IV, Part Two*, might well have been thought suitable. *As You Like It* was also first performed in 1598.

Cecil left on 11 February. His stunted frame and splayed feet did not at first appeal to the King of France, who played a deliberately elusive game, inviting him to come out hunting wolves instead of talking business. Eventually the Englishman's courteous manner had some effect, although he soon discovered that Henri was bent on making a separate peace. He returned at the end of April, without having got the money, and in May France and Spain signed a treaty at Vervins recognizing Spanish rights in the Low Countries and returning Calais and other outposts to France. England and the Netherlands were left to fight alone.

Essex had indeed kept his word. For him his greatest achievement had been a personal matter, though it took a long time to get Elizabeth's agreement. This was to allow his mother Lettice, the former Lady Leicester and now married to Sir Christopher Blount, to return to Court. Even so her encounter with the Queen was brief and frigid, and Essex's insistence had only served to irritate Elizabeth. He himself renewed an affair with a Maid-of-Honour, and facilitated Southampton's liaison with another, Elizabeth Vernon, who eventually produced a child.

There was still no sign of Raleigh becoming a Privy Councillor. If he but knew, it was Cecil who was blocking it. There were other more suitable and less controversial candidates in that hothouse of jealous courtiers. But in March, Whyte reported the astounding news that Raleigh was in line to be the new Lord Deputy of Ireland; Sir Robert Sidney's name had also been canvassed. The other proposed candidate was Sir William Russell, who had held the post briefly before, but he absolutely refused to return to this poisoned chalice. For that matter, said Whyte, Raleigh also 'doth little like it'. The matter was indeed urgent, because the last Lord Deputy, Lord Burgh, had died after only a few months in office, rumoured to have been poisoned, though more likely it was from 'Irish ague'; and because meanwhile the Earl of Tyrone was ravaging Ulster.

As it happened, neither Sidney nor Raleigh were acceptable to the Queen, in spite of Raleigh being acknowledged as an expert on Irish affairs and frequently consulted on policy. He would have found it hard to refuse if he had been offered the job. All the same, from a personal point of view, he had long lost interest in his Irish estates and only two years before had tried to sell the whole lot for £2,000.

He was looking forward to spending a summer with his family at Sherborne. This time he was not expected to trail round after Elizabeth on her summer progresses from country house to country house, though on occasions he did put in an appearance. It must have been a relief to the long-suffering Bess to have him with her for a change. Adrian Gilbert was still helping them with the layout of the gardens and walks, and in the stocking of cattle; later he was to claim that he had spent £700 of his own money at Sherborne over seven years. The works continued until 1601.

Most importantly, thanks to the arrival of a new and more malleable Bishop of Salisbury, Raleigh had managed to acquire the property for his own absolutely – with, needless to say, a nice little *quid pro quo* for the bishop, namely arranging for him to keep a benefice in Hampshire. As a result Raleigh was able to draw up a conveyance to his son Wat, 'without power of revocation renewed', provided Wat would pay his mother £200 a year after Raleigh's death – otherwise much as along the lines of his will the previous year.[3] Once again it seems that Bess was kept in ignorance.

The Islands Voyage was to be the last of Raleigh's adventures overseas for a long while, though Guiana was still much in his mind, and he also continued to organize privateering expeditions. There were evidently some worries about expenses, for he complained that he was 'mad with intricate affairs and want of means'. There were also other anxieties in the South-West, what with disputes in the Stannaries and the overseeing of garrisons in the coastal towns. Simmering in the background were new tensions with

Essex, for reasons mostly unrecorded. There may have been some tactless remarks; and his enemies at Court had not forgotten those years of ruthless ambition.

He was not of course present at the Council meeting after Cecil's return from France, but the furious arguments that took place were to have an indirect effect on him. As a result of the new dangers following the French peace with Spain, Burghley was for a winding down of the expensive war, but Essex was all for fire and bombast. At a moment of high tension Burghley took out his prayer book and pointed to Psalm 55 verse 23: 'Bloodthirsty and deceitful men shall not live out half their days'. The prophecy of the Psalmist was to prove only too true, but any vestige of friendship with the Cecils was over, and Essex at once assumed that Raleigh was lined up with them against him.

Essex now wrote a letter to Anthony Bacon, which he called an *Apology*, 'against those which jealously and maliciously tax me to be the only hinderer of the peace and quiet of my country.'[4] One of his themes was that Catholic Spain was not to be trusted and was only biding its time to go into the attack again. He vaunted his own military achievements, complaining that while he was enduring dangers and hardships, he was merely leaving 'my own enemies elbow room to see their own and their friends' advancement'. Copies of the *Apology* were made and circulated round the Court. The Cecils were furious, but Essex pretended that it had been leaked without his permission and that some servant must have found loose pages under his bed and had copied them out.

Suspicions were growing that there were other motives behind this arrogance and beating of the war drums. In a time of national discontent Essex knew that he could rely on popular appeal, and was obviously doing all he could to encourage it. His looks and charm were an undeniable asset, and he took pains to acknowledge the salutes of passers-by in the street. This provoked satirical attacks, but also alarm, and once again comparisons were being made with Bolingbroke in *Richard II*, a play which Essex made no secret of enjoying:

> What reverence he did throw away on slaves,
> Wooing poor craftsmen with the craft of smiles
> And patient underbearing of his fortune,
> As 'twere to banish their affects with him.
> Off goes his bonnet to an oyster-wench;
> A brace of draymen bid God speed him well . . .

A dictator was in the making.

The crisis came in July at a private meeting between the Queen and Essex, with only Cecil, the new Earl of Nottingham and Thomas Windebank, Clerk of the Signet. It was an extraordinary scene. They were discussing the question of the new Lord Deputy of Ireland. Elizabeth proposed Sir William Knollys, who was Essex's uncle, but Essex said he wanted Sir George Carew, who as Raleigh's cousin was counted by him as belonging to the enemy camp – the plan, transparently, was to get Carew away from Court. What happened next is recorded by Birch in his *Memorials of Queen Elizabeth*.[5]

Finding that his advice on this point made no impression upon her Majesty, he turned his back upon her in such a contemptuous manner as exasperated her to so high a degree that she gave him a box on the ear, and bid him go and be hanged. Upon this he put his hand to his sword, and, when the admiral [Nottingham] interposed, swore that he neither could nor would bear such indignity, nor would have taken it even from Henry VIII, and so left the Court.

Back he went to his house at Wanstead. The Court waited for the next move. There had never been such an episode before; to draw a sword on the Queen was an act of treason. This was something that went beyond a relationship between monarch and subject. But she did nothing, and he had not even been banished from Court. She just let him brood and sulk, treating him like a recalcitrant child. He, on the other hand, behaved as if he were reacting against a tiresome old woman who was jealously frustrating his path to greatness. As Sir Henry Wotton was to say, he was not like his stepfather Leicester, who was able to 'put all his passions into his pocket'.

On 5 August Lord Burghley died, and Elizabeth was deeply affected, retiring to her room to weep alone. Fifty years before, when she was a princess aged fourteen, she had said that William Cecil was the one honest man whom she could trust. As he lay dying she had fed him with soup she had made herself. It was another turning point in her reign. This being so, as the Lord Keeper Egerton warned Essex, it would be foolish to be away from the seat of power, as he would be letting advantages slip away to his rivals.

Essex replied with a long and bitter letter, with dangerous phrases that were to be used against him.[6] He had been treated as a villein or slave, he had suffered the vilest of indignities. 'What, cannot princes err?' he wrote. 'Cannot subjects receive wrong? Is an earthly power or authority infinite? Pardon me, pardon me, my good lord, I can never subscribe to such principles.' In saying such things he was questioning the monarch's divine authority. It was not only treason but heresy.

As for Raleigh, the death of Burghley opened up new hopes for a place in the Privy Council. It might even bring him the chance of a peerage. Rumours of such machinations, and not only Raleigh's, were being relayed back to Essex. He fell ill, genuinely ill. Elizabeth's 'maternal' heart was touched and she sent him her own physicians. For a while, on the surface, all was forgiven on both sides.

The place in the Privy Council went to Lord Shrewsbury, husband of Bess of Hardwick and who for a long while had been Mary Queen of Scots' jailor. Lord Buckhurst, friend of Cecil, became Lord Treasurer. In October Whyte reported that Raleigh was 'discontented' and 'thrives no better', while Essex's supporters wrote 'with redoubled violence' about his blatant ambitions. Obviously the Queen herself was not in favour of having Raleigh on the Council. She knew his limitations too well from of old. He had great administrative abilities, but was overbearing, too impatient to be a committee man, too contemptuous of those who were intellectually inferior. And in any case Cecil did not want him.

On 13 September Philip II of Spain died, covered in sores and in terrible suffering, but borne with very great courage. After Vervins he had handed over the Netherlands to his eldest daughter, the Infanta Isabel Clara Eugenia, who was to marry his nephew the Archduke Albert of Hapsburg; they were to be joint sovereigns. Isabel, being descended from the first wife of John of Gaunt, was thus in line to claim the throne of England, and as such was the Catholics' prime candidate.

The death of Philip may have been a cue for Raleigh to try once more to urge the Privy Council to take an interest in the quest for El Dorado. He had already been negotiating for some sort of collaboration with the Swedish Duke of Sudermania, later Charles IX, who had been impressed by the *Discoverie*. As it happened, a message had already reached the Lord Treasurer Buckhurst that the Swedes were ready to provide twelve vessels fully victualled to go to Guiana. No information exists about subsequent negotiations, and obviously the English Government was not interested. However, in October there were strong rumours that Raleigh was preparing to go out independently to Guiana, with his nephew Sir John Gilbert. The news was relayed to Spain and caused some concern. It was said that the fleet would consist of thirteen ships, mostly pinnaces, carrying settlers – in addition, presumably, to the Swedish contingent.[7]

All this may have been a false alarm, for no such expedition went or could go out. Even so, in January 1599, orders were being given at Seville for the increase of fortifications at Trinidad. The fact that pinnaces were mentioned does appear to confirm Raleigh's acceptance of the opinions of Keymis and

Berry that the best way to find Manoa was up the river Essequibo, where large vessels would be useless. But it does not seem likely that Raleigh would have been interested in establishing settlers at this stage. Gold and silver were the priorities.

One very strong reason for the postponement of Raleigh's expedition was the fearful news from Ireland, and the fact that Raleigh's entire seignory had been overrun by the native Irish. Those who were able had fled to walled towns such as Youghal and Cork.

The crisis had begun on 14 August. Sir Henry Bagenal, Marshal of the English army, had marched from Armagh with some 4,000 infantry and 300 cavalry to relieve a small garrison on the Blackwater, the main entrance to the territory of the Earl of Tyrone, leader of the revolt in Ulster. On the way he was ambushed at the Yellow Ford on the river Callon, and there was an appalling slaughter. The English lost between 1,300 and 2,000 men, including Bagenal and thirty of his officers.

As news spread the whole of Ulster erupted, and one chieftain after another gave his allegiance to Tyrone. The rebellion spread with ferocious speed, to Connaught and then to Leinster. Bands marched into the English Pale, and up to the walls of Dublin. Then it was the turn of Munster, which rose up under the Sugan, nephew of the late Earl of Desmond. The massacre was merciless, with terrible atrocities. Tongues were cut out, noses slashed off, babies dashed against walls and wives made to wipe up their husbands' blood with their aprons. Among those who managed to escape from the hordes tearing down from the mountains were Edmund Spenser and his family – although a newborn child is said to have died when Kilcolman was set on fire. This was at a time when he had reached the pinnacle of his fame, and had been recommended as Sheriff of Cork.*

There is a strange letter from Raleigh to Cecil dated 26 October, which seems to suggest that Raleigh had found a 'knave' ready to assassinate Tyrone. He reassures Cecil that there is no 'disgrace' in giving head-money

---

* Spenser appeared to have had some premonition of disaster. *A View of the Present State of Ireland* was published in April 1598. Ireland had given him inspiration for *The Faerie Queene*, but just how much was this gentle poet in reality a ruthless administrator? That is a question still being argued. He arrived virtually destitute in London, and died in 1599 'for lack of bread' according to Ben Jonson. Essex, to his credit, paid for his burial in Westminster Abbey, near the tomb of Chaucer. In his *History of England* (1945 edn, p. 362) G. M. Trevelyan wrote: 'If Raleigh and Spenser were stone-blind to the realities of the Irish religious and racial problem under their eyes, it was not likely that the ordinary Englishman at home would comprehend it for several centuries to come.'

for the killing of rebels, which had been usual in Munster in the 1580s. This was a much cheaper way of dealing with the Irish problem . . .

Raleigh's settlement at Tallow was totally destroyed, and Mogeely castle was besieged for four months. We are told that on Barry's land fifty-four 'towns' were burnt, and that the rebels took 10,000 cows, 5,000 horses and nearly 60,000 sheep and hogs. For many Undertakers it was ruin, though for Raleigh the situation was not quite so devastating. He had invested about £1,000 and had recouped most of it through selling leases. Spenser on his return to England had called for vengeance, but Raleigh accepted the inevitable and began once more to attempt to sell his lands.

In the Calendar of State Papers there is this brief comment:[8]

The misery of the English was great. The wealthier sort, leaving their castles and dwelling houses, and their victual and furniture, made haste into walled towns, where there was no enemy within ten miles. The meaner sort (the rebellion having overtaken them) were slain, man, woman and child; and such as escaped came naked to the towns.

Essex had boldly suggested that he should be Lord Treasurer in place of Burghley. Elizabeth had of course ignored this, and she also refused his bid to take on the lucrative office of Master of the Wards, which would have given him some hold over sections of the gentry. Arguments continued about the Council's policy on Ireland, and he then grandly announced that as the greatest man in the kingdom only he was fit to save that country for England. The Queen wavered, realizing that his popularity would be a great asset, and eventually decided that she had no choice. Musters were already in hand, and once again Vere had been ordered to send over 2,000 seasoned troops. It would be the greatest army ever sent to Ireland during her reign.

Nevertheless, there was general astonishment in the Court about the appointment. The risks were immense, but for Essex there were the glittering prospects of fame and martial glory. Given that he was becoming ever more resentful of others who seemed close to the Queen, it was also surprising that he was prepared to remove himself for so long from Court.

He was planning to take with him many of those on whom he had conferred knighthoods in his various campaigns. One he had in mind was Lord Grey of Wilton, son of the Lord Deputy in Raleigh's time, but Essex was suspicious that he was being 'too kindly received' by the Queen. He accosted him 'roughly' and asked him bluntly whether he was becoming a friend of Cecil. To which Grey replied that he would not alter his friendship just to please Essex, and he had certainly received favours from Cecil. At which Essex told him that in future if he wanted rewards he would have to get them from Cecil, because none would be forthcoming from him. From then onwards they were declared enemies.[9]

Essex was now determined that Raleigh was poisoning the Queen's mind against him. The very mention of Raleigh's name was enough to make him lose his temper. When a celebration of the Queen's accession day on 17 November was planned in the tiltyard, he saw the chance of insulting Raleigh publicly in what was to be described as a 'glorious feather triumph'.[10] He had heard that Raleigh was to lead a retinue wearing orange-tawny plumes (this was a colour that Essex considered his own; how dared he?). When Raleigh had his men settled round the Queen, Essex entered the tiltyard with a much more splendid and larger troop, displaying *two thousand* orange-tawny feathers. It was all very childish, and evidently Elizabeth thought so too, for she called off the ceremonies before the finish.

Essex did not set off for Ireland until 27 March 1599. He rode down the Strand with a crowd following, shouting 'God save your Lordship' and 'God preserve your Honour'. They followed him to Islington, where there was a sudden downpour of rain and hail, drenching everybody. It was not considered to be a good omen.

Age Like Winter Weather
1599

In 1599 Hakluyt published the second volume of his *Principall Navigations*, and in it he urged Cecil to sponsor the revival of the Virginia enterprise. He advised him 'not to meddle with the state of Ireland, nor that of Guiana' when 'there is under our noses the great and ample country of Virginia'. He recommended sending out one or two thousand settlers, and in this way not only would the Queen's dominions be vastly increased, but her 'coffers will be enriched in a short space' and pagans would be converted to the faith of Christ.

Raleigh would have had mixed feelings about Hakluyt's reference to Guiana, but he was certainly beginning to turn his attention again to North America. Between 1591 and 1598 knowledge of the mainland northwards from Virginia had been increasing as a result of merchants sending out fishing vessels and making contact with the Indians. There had even been a proposal to form a colony on the island of Ramea off Newfoundland.

Ireland was a different matter. It was not just a question of 'meddling'. Ireland was in turmoil, militarily and strategically, with the ever-present danger of Spanish troops being landed to join Tyrone. To the public at large in most of England, especially London, the Earl of Essex was the obvious choice to defend the country's honour. He was young, still only thirty-one, and had the surface glamour, the ambition and self-confidence. After all, it had been his father who had been in charge of the colonization of Ulster. Also, it was the turn of the century, a time for change, for new excitements, new adventures, new victories. The Queen was ageing, with no designated successor. There was a general feeling of unease and disillusion.

'Hot blooded youths' and well-born contemporaries looking for adventure flocked to join Essex. They were impatient with the remnants of the old brigade, stuck with the memories of the glories of the Armada days, and who still dominated the Court, the Council and the Queen; Raleigh specifically was the great enemy, untrustworthy, intriguing, dripping poison into the Queen's ear. Cecil was only a little older than Essex, but he also was not to be trusted – and hardly a figure of glamour. The truth was that Elizabeth's inner circle was becoming alarmed by the degree of mob support for Essex.

The size of the army and the supplies was unprecedented. Southampton, still in disgrace with Elizabeth because of his marriage to Elizabeth Vernon, had gone with him. Essex wanted him as his Master of Horse, but she had forbidden it. As Southampton was Shakespeare's patron, topical compliments to Essex were woven into *Henry V*, just being completed, and these appear towards the end of the play, in the prologue to Act V. The first refers to the crowd of admirers who had accompanied Essex out of London, needless to say exaggerated.

> How London doth pour out her citizens!
> The Mayor and all his brethren, in best sort,
> Like to the senators of th'antique Rome,
> With the plebeians swarming at their heels,
> Go forth and fetch their conqu'ring Caesar in –

The next lines are even more explicit:

> As, by a lower but high-loving likelihood,
> Were now the General of our gracious Empress
> (As in good times he may) – from Ireland coming,
> Bringing rebellion broachèd on his sword,
> How many would the peaceful city quit,
> To welcome him!

In fact the whole campaign was a catastrophe, far worse than the Islands Voyage, and Essex behaved with outrageous and unaccountable disregard of the orders given him. Instead of advancing north against Tyrone, he turned south, wasting his resources in futile encounters and sieges. There was a slight victory at the Pass of Plumes, but this was followed by a humiliating defeat in the Wicklow Hills, almost as bad as at the Yellow Ford. He disobeyed the Queen by making Southampton his Master of Horse, and created no less than eighty-one knights, many of them undeserving but patently in an attempt to make sure that they would remain his faithful and grateful followers.

The Queen sent him stinging and angry letters, and in reply he wrote passionate protests: 'Why do I talk of victory or success? Is it not known that from England I receive nothing but discomforts and soul's wounds?'[1]

He was infuriated to learn that Cecil had been created Master of the Wards, which meant a handsome income that he badly needed and had hoped for. His sense of persecution was egged on by cronies such as Sir Gelli Meyricke, who wrote blaming Raleigh, Cobham and Sir George Carew, 'infamous here for their service'.[2] So he wrote to the Queen in June:

Is it not lamented of your Majesty's faithfullest subjects, both there and here, that Cobham and Raleigh – I will forbear others, for their places' sakes – should have such credit and favour with your Majesty when they wish the ill success of your Majesty's most important action, the decay of your greatest strength, and the destruction of your faithfullest servants?[3]

It was absurd to suggest that Raleigh of all people, the greatest of the English landowners there, should wish defeat in Ireland.

As so often in Ireland, the army began to be reduced not just by casualties but by illness and desertion. By July Essex found himself able to muster only 4,000 men, about a third of the army's establishment and too few to attack the north. He wrote complaining of his 'banishment and proscription in this most cursedest of islands'. He had failed, and it was his fault, and he did not want to believe it. His followers also began to think that they too were the victims of malignant conspirators at home.

By August there was alarm in London that the *Adelantado* was planning yet another massive invasion and was heading for the Isle of Wight. In the general panic chains were put across the streets, and barricades went up. Raleigh 'took leave at Court of all the ladies'[4] and went to join the fleet as Vice-Admiral under Lord Thomas Howard. He was at sea for nearly a month, patrolling along the Downs. On 25 August he wrote that he had received intelligence from the French Governor of Brest that seven Spanish galleons were in the harbour of Le Conquet, and that 200 sail of ships had been spotted.

When it was discovered that it had all been a false alarm, rumours began to circulate that the mobilization of the fleet had been for a quite different reason, that Essex was known to be plotting an invasion from Ireland and this display of strength was designed as a warning that he had not left the country defenceless. Indeed two years later Sir Christopher Blount (under threat of torture?) confessed that Essex had thought of landing his army at Milford Haven and marching on London. It could therefore have been significant that at this point the Queen sent Essex an order that on no account was he to leave Ireland.

The final débâcle came when Essex met Tyrone for a parley, in direct contravention of the Queen's orders. The two men spoke privately, without witnesses, and when she heard about it the Queen became exceedingly suspicious. Again the rumour was that Essex had agreed to most of Tyrone's demands, in return for help if Essex decided to invade Wales or England. Another unauthorized conference was held, at which a truce was agreed, renewable every six weeks.

In September word came that Cecil and Raleigh 'do infinitely desire to be barons, and they have a purpose to be called unto it, though there be no Parliament.'[5] Although the Queen took no notice of their desire, it was enraging news for Essex. Soon afterwards he received a letter from Elizabeth. She had not heard about the truce, and ordered that none should be signed. She would not in any circumstance agree to a pardon for Tyrone, and demanded to be told what had been said at that private meeting. Essex, realizing that disaster was impending when she came to hear the truth, decided that he must hurry to London, leave the army to care for itself, and rely on his charm to soften the Queen and wipe out the stigma of his errors.

He reached the Court at Nonsuch Palace in Surrey on 28 September, at about ten in the morning. He burst into her bedroom to find her newly up and dressing with 'her hair about her face', therefore without her wig and cosmetics, and probably showing scrawny arms and legs. He himself was 'so full of dirt and mire that his face was full of it'.[6] He threw himself at her feet and kissed her hands, while she kept her composure and appeared to receive him with kindness.

His carelessness in dress in recent years was well known. It had already been said that he 'scarcely knew what he had on when he went to see the Queen'.* But she had certainly never allowed him to see her in this state. Nor had anyone ever dared to burst in on her in this way. What about that guard, one might well ask, of which Raleigh was the captain? She gently told Essex to return when they both had time to prepare themselves; she said that his boots stank.† She needed that time to find out reasons for his intrusion. Could it be a prelude to some rebellion or a coup in the streets outside?

They met again an hour later, and she questioned him closely for an hour. She still appeared friendly, leading him on to pour out his heart and give his explanations. He emerged smiling. Dinner, the midday meal, followed and it was observed that two groups had formed. The one presided over by Cecil consisted of the Earls of Shrewsbury and Nottingham, the Lords Thomas

---

* The great man's bedroom would be filled with people when he rose in the morning, and he allowed his servants to dress him as they thought fit. Meanwhile he would be discussing business matters. 'Only in his baths he was somewhat delicate'.[7]

† Elizabeth was outspoken about courtiers having smelly feet.

Howard, Cobham and Grey of Wilton, Sir Walter Raleigh and Sir George Carew. Essex's group consisted of the Earls of Worcester and Rutland, the Lords Mountjoy, Rich and Lumley, Lord Henry Howard and some of the newly created knights. The account was given by Rowland Whyte to Sir Robert Sidney, and it is interesting to note that he warned against Henry Howard as a 'ranter';[8] Sidney should 'take heed of him, and not trust him'. Howard was to be revealed in the next years as by far the most dangerous of Raleigh's opponents: a 'subtle serpent', the mother of Francis and Anthony Bacon once described him.[9]

Essex's third audience with the Queen, in the afternoon, was very different. She tore into him, reduced him to stuttering and mumbling. He was unable to excuse himself. She dismissed him with contempt, ordering him to keep to his room. She was never to see him again, and she was in a fury. 'By God's Son,' she screamed at Sir John Harington, who had been with Essex in Ireland, 'I am not Queen. That man is above me.'[10]

The next day Essex was summoned to meet the Lords in Council and was with them for five hours. He was charged with 'contemptuous disobedience' of Her Majesty's letters and will in returning to England, with writing presumptuous letters, with ignoring instructions he had been given before leaving England, with making an 'inordinate and unjustifiable number of idle knights', and with being overbold in breaking into Her Majesty's bedchamber.

On receiving the reports the Queen ordered that Essex should be put into the custody of Sir Thomas Egerton and be held at York House on the Strand. Nobody, not even his wife, would be allowed to visit him, and he would not be allowed into the garden. She said she would give her reasons publicly at a later date.

A poem attributed, though wrongly, to Shakespeare, had appeared that year in William Jaggard's little book, *The Passionate Pilgrim*, and now seemed alarmingly prophetic:

> Crabbed age and youth cannot live together,
> Youth is full of pleasance, age is full of care;
> Youth like summer morn, age like winter weather;
> Youth like summer brave, age like winter bare.

Essex descended into a deep melancholia and turned his thoughts to religion. Elizabeth now decided that Lord Mountjoy should take his place in Ireland. This could seem odd, given that Mountjoy was one of Essex's closest supporters and the acknowledged lover of his sister. There were

The ageing Queen, engraved by F. Delaram after a miniature by Nicholas Hilliard.

indeed potential dangers, but it was to be an inspired choice. When Mountjoy tried to refuse, pleading ill-health, she took no notice. As a counterbalance Raleigh's cousin and confidant, Sir George Carew, was to be Lord President of Munster: to prove another excellent choice.

Francis Bacon met the Queen soon after Mountjoy's nomination, and found her still raging. When he made the mistake of mentioning Essex's name, she turned on him in a great passion: 'Essex! Whensoever I send Essex back into Ireland, I will marry you. Claim it of me!'[11]

Essex fell ill, troubled with 'Irish looseness'. Scandalous graffiti against Cecil appeared on walls, including those of his own house, such as 'Here lies the Toad'. There were reports of bawdy tavern songs about Elizabeth and Cecil. Then 'swordsmen and captains tired of Irish service' began appearing in London, proclaiming their support for Essex.

When Elizabeth sent not only a doctor to visit him, but also her personal representative Sir John Fortescue, it was thought that she was beginning to relent. As Whyte said, these marks of favour 'gave his enemy Sir Walter Raleigh so much chagrin that he fell sick about it'. But Elizabeth sent her doctor to see Raleigh too.

Raleigh, however, was well enough to attend the Lords of Council on 29 November, when a public declaration was made about Essex's imprisonment. In December Essex became so much worse that it was rumoured he was dying. The Queen did not believe it, and was annoyed when church bells tolled, as though he was already dead. Nevertheless, she sent eight of her best physicians to York House, and they brought back some truly alarming reports. His liver had 'perished', his 'entrails and guts were exulcerated', and there was a 'grinding of the kidneys'.

There was a suggestion that Elizabeth might even have visited York House, but without actually seeing him. Meanwhile his chief supporters, notably Mountjoy and Southampton, had been having secret meetings. Mountjoy was not to leave for Ireland until February, and he now began a coded correspondence with James VI of Scotland, making clear that Essex and his allies strongly supported the king's claim to the throne of England, and assuring him that it was all false that Essex had designs on the Crown for himself. But at this stage little interest was shown by James. The possibility of arranging for Essex to escape to France was also discussed.

Essex recovered enough to send Elizabeth an expensive New Year's gift. She would not accept it. On Twelfth Night she was observed dancing several galliards.

Rage and Rebellion
1600

Early in the New Year Raleigh was called to the Council to discuss Irish affairs. Surprisingly, he recommended a defensive war, but this was not found acceptable. On 2 February he was writing to Cecil with first-hand news sent from Lisbon. Two thousand men, he had heard, were to be embarked on thirty ships, said to be bound for Flanders. But, he darkly suggested, their destination could well be Ireland.

There was to be a Star Chamber indictment of Essex on 7 February, with Essex himself present, but at the last minute it was cancelled. Cecil had visited Essex at York House and had persuaded him to write an apologetic letter to the Queen, which he did in a suitably humble fashion: '. . . God is witness how faithfully I vow to dedicate the rest of my life to your Majesty, without admitting my worldly care'.[1] For the time being this was considered acceptable, though nobody really believed him.

Raleigh may have felt that Cecil was softening, and this could have been the reason for a letter which on the face of it seems quite shocking.[2]

Sir, I was not wise enough to give you advice, but if you take it for a good council to relent towards this tyrant you will repent it when it shall be too late. His malice is fixed, and will not evaporate by any of your mild courses, for he will ascribe the alteration to Her Majesty's pusillanimity, and not to your good nature; knowing that you work but upon her humour and not out of any love towards him. The less you make him, the less he shall be able to harm you and yours, and if Her Majesty's favour fail him, he will again decline to a common person.

Raleigh had plenty of experience of being reduced to a common person. He went on to cite various great figures in the past who had been eliminated but whose heirs had not taken revenge against those who had been responsible. If Essex were to be 'kept down' there need be no fear of a blood-feud between his son and Cecil's son Will. 'If the father continue, he will be able to break the branches, and pull up the tree, root and all.

Lose not your advantage. If you do, I read your destiny. Yours to the end, W. R.'

He added a postscript:

Let the Queen hold Bothwell [in other words Essex] while she hath him. He will ever be the canker of her estate and safety. Princes are lost by security; and preserved by prevention. I have seen [foreseen] the last of her good days, and all of ours, after his liberty.*

A Machiavellian and cold-blooded letter perhaps, as some have said, but events were to prove him right. He never went as far as saying that Essex ought to be executed, or even murdered, but he was obviously looking beyond Essex having been reduced to a common person. In any case he should never have put all this in writing.

Cecil ignored Raleigh's advice: Essex had not yet committed a treason.

Once again there were alarms about Spanish attacks, probably on account of the arrival of the 2,000 men in Flanders. Raleigh was therefore kept busy on coastal defences in the south-west, as was Cobham in his Cinque Ports. Friends of Essex claimed that all this was merely an excuse to build up an army in case of an insurrection.

Gelli Meyricke and Christopher Blount continued to whip up suspicions against Raleigh. But John Chamberlain, purveyor of Court gossip, wrote on 29 February that the Earl 'hath been somewhat crazy this week', and that on 9 March he appeared 'quite out of his mind'.[3] And Whyte said that 'Her Majesty's displeasure had nothing lessened':[4] encouraged by Raleigh, it was generally thought.

For all that, at the end of March, Essex was allowed to return to his house on the Strand, under a new keeper. But he was still in solitary confinement, though allowed two servants. His wife was now permitted to visit him occasionally by day. Outside in the streets the populace was restless and dangerous. He was still their hero.

Raleigh was desperate to get onto the Privy Council and had hoped at least to be a commissioner in the important negotiations that were taking place in the Netherlands. As Whyte said: 'But her Majesty, as it is thought, begins to perceive that if he were one, he would stand to be made a Councillor, which she has no fancy thereto.' Raleigh was patently discontented, but

---

* In Scotland there had been various outbreaks against James, particularly by the Earl of Bothwell, who by this time was an exile in Spain. The inference was that if Essex were to be set free and then allowed to continue with his schemes he would be as great a menace as Bothwell had been to James.

now he had an eye on another chance. The Governor of Jersey, Sir Anthony Paulet, was dying, and he at once put in an application to be his successor. If he did not get that post, he told Cobham, he would have to resort to keeping sheep. He badly needed the money – or so he maintained. Meanwhile he decided to retire for a while to the country, and he took with him Cecil's nine-year-old boy Will, who had not been well. On the way they stopped at Syon House just west of London and had dinner with the Earl of Northumberland. Thanks to the clean air of Sherborne Raleigh was able to reassure Cecil that Will had lost his 'looseness', and that the 'beloved creature' was in good health and able to get on with his books.[5]

Evidently Will was to spend much of the summer at Sherborne with Raleigh's Wat. But he was also having to have some tutorial work at Bath under a Dr Sherwood. It would seem that in temperament he took more after his mother. We are told that he was an affectionate child, but slow and lazy, not very good-looking and growing up to be rather dull, wasting his time at Cambridge and only interested in horses.

Raleigh that spring also had to visit Dartmouth, from where his nephew John Gilbert was operating a lively privateering business, often of doubtful legality. There had been trouble over a Venetian prize, laden with sugar, said to be 'to Sir Walter Raleigh's use'. The matter, embarrassingly, had to be referred to the Privy Council.[6]

Elizabeth was greatly annoyed to learn of the slanderous talk in the taverns and elsewhere that Essex had been condemned unheard. She therefore ordered a special commission of eighteen high-ranking persons to sit at York House where he was being held, with an audience of two hundred, from varying backgrounds. It was led by the Attorney-General Sir Edward Coke, whose characteristically scathing invectives merely had the effect of creating a certain sympathy for Essex. It was also a shock when Francis Bacon completed the case for the Crown against his former patron, quoting the damning passages from the *Apology* of two years back: 'Cannot Princes err? Cannot subjects suffer wrong?'

The hearing began on 5 June at eight in the morning and continued until nearly nine at night. Essex at last submitted 'with tears in his heart' that he had 'quenched all the sparkles of pride that were in him'. Nevertheless, the court decided to dismiss him from the Council and suspended him from the offices of Earl Marshal and Master of Ordnance, and ordered that he should remain in confinement until the Queen in her mercy chose to remit his punishment. It had all been a great performance, and a 'most pitiful and lamentable sight to see him, that was once a minion of fortune, now unworthy of least honour'.[7] Some spectators wept.

Two months were to pass before the Queen granted him his liberty. He was, however, still to be banned from Court.

Those sparkles of pride had, needless to say, not really been quenched. Mountjoy had arrived in Ireland on 26 February, and in April Essex sent him a letter by Southampton, asking him to leave Ireland sufficiently guarded and to land 4–5,000 men in Wales. He must then march on London and seize the Court by force. It was all crazy. But Mountjoy, now safely out of reach of his mistress Penelope Rich, Essex's sister, and his cousin Christopher Blount, Essex's stepfather, decided that his duties in Ireland were more important, and refused. At the end of July Essex, egged on by his secretary Henry Cuffe, a brilliant but sinister character,* and the inevitable Meyricke, made yet another appeal to Mountjoy, pointing out that James of Scotland had, whether by design or accident, a strong force poised north of the border. Mountjoy annoyingly responded by merely asking him to be patient.

All this time Essex was sending loving epistles to his 'most dear and most admired Sovereign', and signing himself 'your Majesty's humblest vassal, pining, languishing, despairing'.[8] Elizabeth was not to be fooled. As she told Bacon, she had been moved by such dutiful letters, but knew only too well that what was behind them was his hope that his 'farm of sweet wines' would be renewed at Michaelmas, when it was due to expire. This was of vital financial importance to him, as he had lost the income from so many other offices, leaving in effect only his position as Master of the Horse. His debts were enormous, and in particular a sum of £5,000 was due for instant repayment. If the 'farm of sweet wines' was not renewed he would be bankrupt.

In June Raleigh was making another unsuccessful bid for the Vice-Chamberlainship. In July he and Cobham 'stole away' to Ostend, which was being besieged by the Spaniards under Archduke Albert. The Essex faction thought this very suspicious, and with some reason, because the journey seems to have been unofficial, although they did bring a message from Cecil to Lord Grey of Wilton, Southampton's enemy, who was in charge of an English contingent over there. It was reported back that the 'two gallants' had been 'entertained with much honour and extraordinary respect, but have seen little.'[9] If this was sightseeing, they just missed an Anglo-Dutch victory at Nieuport.

---

* Cuffe had been Essex's professor of Greek. Sir Henry Wotton described him as 'a man of secret ambitions of his own, smothered under the habit of a scholar, and slubbered over with a certain rude and clownish fashion' – clownish here meaning provincial.

Then in August Raleigh at last had the official sanction that he was to be Governor of Jersey. He invited both Cecil and Cobham to Sherborne, but Cecil, greatly overworked, could not possibly accept. There is an attractive little letter from Will Cecil at this time, proudly passed on to his father, and reflecting well on Raleigh, who obviously enjoyed the company of the boys:[10]

Sir Walter, we must all exclaim and cry out because you will not come down. You being absent we are like soldiers when their captains are absent, they know not what to do: you are so busy about idle matters. Sir Walter, I will be plain with you. I pray you leave all idle matters and come down to us.

Bess and little Wat accompanied Raleigh to Weymouth to see him off to Jersey, and went aboard his ship. He left in fine weather, but strong winds kept him at sea for two days and nights. He had, as he put it, a royal reception on arrival, and took the oath of office on 20 September. He wrote to Bess that he had never seen a pleasanter island, but did not think its value was as he had expected.

With all his usual energy he set about the completion of the Isabella Bellissima fort (Elizabeth Castle) on the islet off St Helier, paying for some of it himself. He also halted the demolition of the Mont Orgueil castle, until recently the seat of government – it had been decided that it would be too exposed in case of an attack by artillery. This was a popular move, the castle being a 'stately fort of great capacity and both a countenance and comfort to all that part of the island next to Normandy'.

While he was away there was a fire at Durham House, affecting only the stables along the Strand, but serious nevertheless. Bess told Cecil that she was relieved that the 'feeiar' went 'noo fardar, other wies, hit had rid ous of all our poour substans of plat and other thinges'.[11] The fault was not due to any negligence by her servants, she said, but to her cousin Sir Edward Darcy's servant, 'a woman that delleth just under our logging, and anoyeth ous infenitly'. She hoped that Darcy would now 'remouve heer'.

By 14 October Raleigh was writing to Cobham that he was back from Jersey, which he described as his 'little commonwealth', and was off on his 'miserable journey into Cornwall' – miserable presumably because of all the tinners' grievances that had been mounting up, keeping him away once more from London at this time of impending drama. On 27 October he attended a Stannary Parliament on the windswept heights of Crockern Tor on Dartmoor. An important problem that had to be solved was a complaint from Plymouth that tinners were drawing off too much water. He then moved on to Cornwall, to the more commodious Stannary Hall at

Lostwithiel. Here he had to deal with complaints from dealers that the Queen was buying tin at a specially low price – the monarch had the right of pre-emption on tin. Raleigh as Lord Warden was of course acting on the Queen's behalf, and this led to attacks in Parliament in the following year that he was using the right of pre-emption for his benefit. His answers, as will be seen, were not all that convincing.

He was not able to return to Sherborne until about 12 November. By that time Elizabeth had come to her final decision about the 'farm of sweet wines': Essex's licence would not be renewed. She would keep the revenues for herself.

This threw Essex into a panic, which soon developed into a maniacal fury with wild paranoid accusations about his woes being all due to the evil machinations of his enemies. In all this he was encouraged as usual, not only by Meyricke and the dreadful Cuffe, but by Southampton, Christopher Blount, and now by Sir Charles Danvers; not to mention his sister Penelope who urged him not to be a coward. Much as they all doted on Essex, and longed for their own profit and advancement, they must surely have realized that he was becoming mentally unbalanced. Sir John Harington, who once had admired Essex, but who also was the Queen's godson, became so alarmed by his tirades that he escaped to the country. 'He [Essex] shifted from sorrow and repentance,' he wrote, 'to rage and rebellion so suddenly, as well proveth him devoid of good reason as of a right mind. His speeches of the Queen became no man who hath *mens sana in corpore sano*. He hath ill advisors, and much evil has sprung from the source . . . The man's soul seems tossed to and fro, like the waves of a troubled sea.'[12] Mad and insulting words spoken by Essex were reported back to Elizabeth: that 'she was cankered, and her mind as crooked as her carcass'.[13] As Raleigh was later to say they alone were enough to cost him his head. Certainly they made it impossible for him ever to be forgiven.

Essex wrote to James in Scotland, with the claim that Cecil was plotting to put the Spanish Infanta on the throne.* The fact that Raleigh had been made Governor of Jersey was all the more suspect; the island would be the jumping-off point for a Spanish invasion. Raleigh also controlled the ports of Cornwall, while Cobham had the vital Cinque Ports. The Treasury and the Navy were controlled by Buckhurst and the Lord Admiral Nottingham, Cecil's allies. The Lord President of the North was Cecil's elder brother

* It was indeed true that in 1599 Cecil had secretly set about procuring portraits of the Infanta and her husband the Archduke Albert, no doubt as a kind of insurance. Whether they were actually delivered to him is not known.

Lord Burghley. Sir George Carew, Raleigh's cousin, now in Munster, was likely to succeed Mountjoy as Lord Lieutenant of Ireland. And there were others in this great evil conspiracy, like Lord Grey of Wilton and Lord Thomas Howard. All would have to be eliminated. The exception was Sir Ferdinando Gorges, a relative of Raleigh and Governor of Plymouth Fort, but nevertheless a loyal follower of Essex.

James was also by now receiving secret correspondence from the 'subtle serpent' Lord Henry Howard, warning him against not only Cobham and Raleigh, but also the Earl of Northumberland. These men, he said, were without principles of religion or morality, a triplicity who denied the Trinity. Northumberland in particular was a 'very contemptible person'.[14] James became so alarmed by all these accusations that he sent a delegation under the Earl of Mar, with the official task of discussing the succession with Elizabeth. By the time Mar reached London in February the following year it was too late to broach any such inflammatory subject.

Essex House at the end of 1600 was now open to virtually anyone who was disgruntled or had grievances against the Queen and her government, including both Puritans and Catholics; the place was packed with a rabble of adventurers and unemployed soldiers. It was said that Puritan divines preached there daily. But there was an informer in their midst, possibly one Gabriel Montgomery, and reports were relayed back to Cecil and the Council. Events were leading confusedly to a tragic and terrible climax.

Machiavelli and Parliament
1601

On 9 January 1601 the Earl of Southampton met Lord Grey of Wilton riding down the Strand near Durham House. Perhaps a look of scorn on Southampton's face or an insulting remark was enough for Grey to set about the young man with a sword. Soon a fight broke out between rival retainers, during which Southampton's page lost a hand. Elizabeth promptly dispatched Grey to the Fleet prison. Nevertheless, for Essex this was a signal for rebellion.

A summons was sent out to all his supporters in every part of the country to join him at Essex House. Meyricke set about organizing a contingent from Wales. Disaffected army officers came over from Ireland. Among Essex's followers were earls, barons, knights and gentlemen, to the number of about 120, the majority of them resentful at lack of promotion at Court, but some also in financial trouble which they blamed on the government. One main supporter who did not come into either category was Sir Ferdinando Gorges.

Gorges was part of a committee that met at Drury House, where Southampton was living, near the present Drury Lane Theatre. The other members besides Southampton were Sir Charles Danvers, and two followers from Wales, Sir John Davies and John Lyttleton. Essex kept away, but sent ideas in writing for discussion. It was decided that Meyricke should assemble an armed force in the courtyard of Essex House. But what next? Should they march on the City, where a mysterious character called Sheriff Smyth had said he could mobilize a thousand men? Or should they capture the Tower of London, or seize the Court? This last suggestion was most favoured, but Gorges was unhappy about it, and such a vital decision had to be left unresolved.

That was on 3 February. Grey had been released from the Fleet, regarded as another ominous sign. In their euphoric state friends of Essex hit on the idea of arranging a special performance of *Richard II* at the Globe Theatre. The actors, possibly Shakespeare included, were reluctant – it was an old play, some of them had forgotten the lines, etc. – but finally they agreed after a subsidy of forty shillings was promised. So on Saturday, 7 February, the play was duly performed, enthusiastically applauded by Essex and his colleagues, delighted to 'feast their eyes' on the deposition of a sovereign.

That same evening the Lords of the Privy Council sent Essex an order to appear before them immediately. He refused, pretending to be ill. Soon afterwards he received an anonymous note, warning him to provide for his safety without delay, and to beware of Raleigh and Cobham. He briefly considered flight to France. But he knew that his great moment had arrived; he could wait no longer. There now were 300 men armed and ready to accompany him. So it was decided that the next morning, Sunday, he would ride with them to the City in time to catch the congregation coming out of St Paul's, who would surely join him, and afterwards they would all join up with Sheriff Smyth's thousand men. They would then return to Whitehall and seize the Court. Essex would force his way to the Queen, and Cecil, Raleigh, the Howards, Grey and any others in their gang would be rounded up and dealt with.

Very early in the morning of the 8th Raleigh sent a message to Ferdinando Gorges, asking him to come by water to Durham House. Essex gave permission to Gorges to go, but told him that he must meet Raleigh in mid-river opposite Essex House, and that Gorges must take two guards who would act as witnesses and would make sure of his safe return. Raleigh agreed to these conditions and rowed out alone. Gorges said later that Christopher Blount had urged him to kill Raleigh, but that he had refused.[1]

Raleigh advised Gorges to return at once to Plymouth, because there was a warrant out for his arrest. 'Tush, Sir Walter,' Gorges is reputed to have said, 'this is not the time to talk of my going to the Fleet. Get you back to Court, and that with speed, for my Lord of Essex hath put himself into a strong guard at Essex House, and you are likely to have a bloody day of it.' Raleigh tried to reason with Gorges, but he refused to leave Essex. As they were speaking, someone – possibly Blount – fired four shots at Raleigh from the bank. They all missed. Then armed men were seen coming down the steps of Essex House and climbing into a boat. At this Gorges pushed his cousin's boat away with his own hands, and told him to hurry home.

Raleigh instead went to raise the alarm at Court, and set about getting the Guard ready to defend his Sovereign. At once Cecil sent a warning message to the Lord Mayor and Aldermen who were gathering for the service at St Paul's. The Council decided on one more attempt at a peaceful settlement, and a deputation of four distinguished councillors were sent to Essex House: Lord Keeper Sir Thomas Egerton, Lord Chief Justice Sir John

Popham, Sir William Knollys, who was Essex's uncle, and the Earl of Worcester, who was a friend of Essex. Egerton took with him the Great Seal of England.

They arrived to find a jostling and jeering crowd. It was all becoming very ugly, with shouts of 'They will betray you! Kill them! Cast the Great Seal out of the window!'[2] Essex gave orders for all four to be locked in a room. The mob now rushed out towards the City, while Essex with his troop of young noblemen rode up Fleet Street and up Ludgate Hill, crying out 'For the Queen! For the Queen! A plot is laid for my life!' By the time they reached St Paul's the service had been long over and there was no crowd to greet them. Indeed the few onlookers appeared to be merely curious. Some of them cheered, but most just watched in pity. When the dreaded word traitor got around, they all melted away, as did some of Essex's followers.

The Sheriff proved useless. His thousand men were nowhere to be seen. Now at last Essex began to realize that he had overestimated his popularity. He began to sweat and called for a new shirt; he saw that there was nothing for it but to return to Essex House. But when he reached the Lud Gate, he found it barred with chains and soldiers. There was a scuffle, during which Blount was wounded in the face by a pike, but Essex managed to escape by boat.

He arrived back to find that Gorges had slipped away before him and had released those four distinguished prisoners. The house was surrounded by royal troops who were soon reinforced by artillery under the command of the Lord Admiral. Essex set about burning papers, including a special letter from James VI and a mysterious key that he always kept in a black taffeta bag round his neck.

The Lord Admiral threatened to blow up the house, so in the evening Essex surrendered, and he was taken to the Tower of London. A week later he and Southampton were brought to trial at Westminster Hall. Dressed dramatically all in black, he behaved calmly, arrogantly – impudently, some thought. It was a contrast to those days of hysteria and fake illnesses. Raleigh was called as a witness. 'What boots it to swear the fox?' he said with contempt, perhaps alluding to the foxes as supporters on Raleigh's coat of arms.[3] He attempted to discredit every witness, but when it came to Cecil he had to admit defeat over the story of his support for the Infanta's claim to the English throne – it had been quoted out of context, and Cecil had never once spoken in her favour. Both Essex and Southampton were sentenced to be hanged, drawn and quartered, but in the case of Essex it was changed to the more merciful beheading, in deference to his high rank; and Elizabeth changed Southampton's sentence to imprisonment in the

Tower, because of his youth, and because of his successful pleading that he had been led on by his love for Essex.

Meyricke and Cuffe however did meet that full dreadful fate. Blount and Danvers were beheaded. Gorges had a short spell in prison, but was let out on account of his rescue of the four councillors, though his kinship with Raleigh may have played a part. Mountjoy's role was overlooked because of his successes in Ireland. Other aristocratic conspirators were heavily fined; the Earl of Rutland bought his freedom for £20,000.

Blount at his trial admitted that neither he nor Essex really believed that Raleigh and Cobham intended to harm Essex; the report had merely been a 'word cast out to colour other matters'.[4] On the scaffold there had been an attempt to cut short his prayers and confessions (he was a Catholic), but Raleigh who was there as Captain of the Guard insisted that he should finish in peace. Blount asked for him, and called out: 'Sir Walter Raleigh, I thank God that you are present. I had an infinite desire to speak to you, and for my particular intent towards you. I beseech you forgive me.' He had indeed done a good deal of harm to Raleigh, especially at Fayal, and had perhaps even attempted to murder him, but nevertheless Raleigh gravely replied: 'I most willingly forgive you, and I beseech God to forgive you and to give you His divine comfort.'

Raleigh had also to be present at Essex's execution on 25 February, Ash Wednesday. He stood close to the scaffold and began listening to Essex's long and sometimes emotional speech of confession, but there were murmurs in the crowd around him, that – in Camden's words – 'he came to feed his eyes on a sight of the Earl's sufferings, and to satiate his hatred with his blood.' He therefore withdrew to the Armoury where he could watch unseen. So he missed Essex saying that he bore no malice towards himself and Cobham, and knew them to be 'true servants of the Queen'. He had hoped that Essex might wish to speak to him, and for the rest of his life regretted that he had not been there when Essex did indeed ask for reconciliation.

The story went around afterwards that Raleigh 'gloated' over the execution from his window and blew out puffs of tobacco smoke.[5] This was patently a malicious fable, like that other fable concocted in 1596, that he never really had gone to Guiana.

Essex's head was severed in three blows, one hopes the first sufficient to knock him senseless. A crowd attacked the headsman as he came out of the Tower, and he had to be rescued or he would have been killed.

There is also a famous legend, almost as well known as the one about Raleigh throwing down his cloak in the mud, about Essex sending back a ring Elizabeth had given him years before and which could have saved his life; how it reached the wrong person, Lady Nottingham, and how she was forbidden by her husband to give it to the Queen; and how Lady Nottingham confessed this on her deathbed to Elizabeth; at which the Queen cried out: 'God forgive you, for I never can!' and rushed from the room. The first reference to it was in 1620, and it has been almost universally regarded as made up. But it is a harmless story and the existence of such a ring is undeniably in character, and certainly some of Elizabeth's more sentimental biographers wish it to be true.

For a long while after Essex's execution Elizabeth was in a state of depression, and would shut herself weeping in her room. Sir John Harington wrote how 'The Queen walks much in her privy chamber and stamps her feet at all ill news, and thrusts her rusty sword at times into the arras in a great rage'.[6] But then when she smiled, 'it was pure sunshine, that everyone did choose to bask in, if they could.'

Raleigh when returning to Durham House was observed to be deep in gloom. It was ironical that he should come to be regarded as the man most responsible for Essex's death. But at first Cecil was just as unpopular. People shouted at him in the street: 'Robin with the bloody breast'. Essex had become a symbol of all the glories of the past age. Ballads were printed: 'Our jewel is gone, the valiant knight of chivalry . . .' and 'Sweet England's pride is gone . . .'

A song was written about Cecil, his elder brother (now Lord Burghley), and Raleigh.[7]

> Little Cecil trips up and down;
> He rules both Court and Crown,
> With his brother Burghley clown,
> In his great fox-furrèd gown.
> With the long proclamation
> He swore he saved the town
> Is it not likely?
>
> Raleigh does time bestride
> He sits twixt wind and tide,
> Yet uphill he cannot ride,
> For all his bloody pride.
> He seeks taxes in the tin,
> He polls the poor to the skin,
> Yet he vows 'tis no sin–
>   Lord, for thy pity!

But far more vicious was another rhyme about Raleigh.[8]

> Essex for vengeance cries
> His blood upon thee lies,
> Mounting above the skies,
> Damnable fiend of hell,
> Mischievous Machiavell!

It was Cecil who deserved more the name of Machiavelli, as Raleigh was to discover. He had now reached his peak of power, but like everyone else at Court was concerned about the delicate matter of the succession, a subject that was absolutely forbidden in the Queen's presence. She had an obsessional horror of death, fearing also that to proclaim an heir would create a centre of unrest, and that discontented persons would gather round him or her with an eye for their future advancement. 'The name of my successor is like the tolling of my own death bell,' she once said. 'I can by no means endure a shroud to be held before my eyes while I am living.'

In fact it was clear that James, brought up a Protestant, would be the most obvious candidate as the nearest in consanguinity, although there were other descendants of Henry VII like Arabella Stuart. The Infanta Isabel could claim to be the senior descendant of John of Gaunt, but Cecil still had to quash once and for all the claim by Essex that he with Raleigh and Cobham supported her candidacy (which in the case of Raleigh was certainly ludicrous). He also needed to dissociate himself from the others. It was of course essential that the succession should be tranquil and orderly, but above all James had to be convinced that *he*, Cecil, should continue to hold the reins of government. And so in March he began a secret correspondence with the Scottish Court.

Raleigh behaved as if he were indifferent to his unpopularity, almost obtusely so, still treating Cecil as if he were his dearest friend, and his letters still kept up the tone of implicit faith. In some ways he had reached the zenith of his career; the Queen trusted and confided in him. He was aware that he had enemies at Court, but (as far as he knew) they were of no immediate threat. What he was now confidently expecting was that place on the Privy Council.

The building work at Sherborne was virtually complete. If domestic bliss and happiness are a feature of many of Raleigh's letters, there was also a nagging irritation that continued until 1602. This concerned John Meere whom Raleigh had replaced as bailiff with a John Dolberry. Adrian Gilbert had also been appointed 'constable of Sherborne Castle', a somewhat nebulous title, one might think, but another sore point for Meere, who referred to Adrian as a 'gorbellied rascal'. Meere brought a Star Chamber case against Raleigh, claiming that he had been appointed bailiff for fifty years – should he live that long.

It became clear that he had been caught forging Raleigh's signature. Meere at one stage actually had Dolberry arrested, but Raleigh's supporters released him and instead Raleigh put Meere in the stocks in Sherborne market-place, walking off with the keys and leaving him there for six hours. Meere complained that Raleigh's servants sang ribald songs outside his house when he was in bed; this would seem to have been because Mrs Meere had put her head out of the window shouting indecent things about Lady Raleigh – or it could have been the other way round. All was made more complicated, even dangerous, when Meere's elder brother Henry enlisted the support of Lord Thomas Howard. Then yet another Howard, Lord Howard of Binden, Raleigh's neighbour, began intriguing on behalf of Meere when Raleigh was abroad in Jersey.

As a result comments about Meere's villainy were often woven into Raleigh's letters of greater importance, whether dealing with the latest intelligence from Spain or on Court matters: 'Yet more notorious cowardly knave never lived'; 'The rogue Meere continues his knavery as violently as ever', and so on. In a letter to the Western Assize Judges, Raleigh described how he had rescued this 'wretch' whom he had taken 'eaten with lice out of prison, because it was told me that he had all the ancient records of Sherborne, his father having been the Bishop's officer.'[9] He told them that besides being a forger, Meere had also been a coin clipper, and had twice been imprisoned. This seems to have had the effect of suppressing the nuisance, though only temporarily. The wonder is that Raleigh had employed him at all.

Raleigh was also having trouble with Henry Pyne in Ireland, who somehow – because of successes by Mountjoy and Carew – had been reviving the pipe-staves industry.* Raleigh and his partners are recorded as having petitioned the Privy Council against Pyne on the grounds that he was swindling them.

More profitable was his share in his nephew John Gilbert's privateering activities. Gilbert had captured a Brazilian prize, with a cargo of porcelain and silk, probably from the East Indies. Bess was to have some of the porcelain, and Raleigh wanted a specially fine saddle and what he called

* p. 153.

pied silk for some curtains.[10] There was a reference in a letter to Spanish books which had to be reserved for Lord Cobham: an odd request since these books had been filched from Jesuit priests, and had subsequently been described as 'very scandalous and not fit to be suffered'. There was also avuncular advice: 'Use your fortune wisely in this hard world. I hear you spend vainly and use carousing. It is time to be wise and look to your estate ... harken not to begging companions but make the best of your fortune.' But these words were not taken to heart, as Raleigh found in the following year.

Bess was often affectionately quoted in Raleigh's letters to Cobham and Cecil, both of whom were invited to stay at Sherborne during the summer. Sometimes she added cryptic postscripts. To Cobham for instance he wrote: 'I hope your lordship will be here tomorrow or else my wife says her oysters will be all spoilt and her partridge stale ... Bess remembers herself to your lordship and says your breach of promise shall make you fare accordingly'. And when she sent Cecil a present of gloves, he wrote: 'Bess says that she must envy any fingers whosoever shall wear her gloves but your own'.[11]

Meere, Pyne – just how good was Raleigh in judging character? But Hakluyt, Hariot, Keymis and the Durham House 'set', they were men of intellect and loyalty, whom we can admire. His great attachment to Cobham remains a mystery. Cobham was Cecil's brother-in-law, a wealthy land-owner, Warden of the Cinque Ports, these were advantages, and it would seem that he was bookish; but ultimately he was a weak character, referred to as loquacious, a good conversationalist, full of schemes, unstable, and to Sir Anthony Weldon 'a silly lord'.* His marriage in 1602 to Frances Howard, the widowed Countess of Kildare, was an odd twist for Raleigh, in that she was the daughter of the Lord Admiral, no longer friendly. Even more complicated was her animosity towards Bess, who longed to be allowed back at Court but complained that Lady Kildare took every chance of criticizing her before the Queen. 'For the honour I bear her name', Bess said to Cecil, 'and the ancient acquaintance of her, I wish she would be as ambitious to do good as she is apt to the contrary.'[12]

In contrast to the hothouse of Court intrigue, and in spite of the lampoons in London, in his native South-West Raleigh could still command support and admiration. Soon to be published was *A Survey of Cornwall* by Richard Carew of Antony, a minor classic of the language, a work of much more than regional interest. Admittedly Carew, one of the least egotistical of men, was Raleigh's cousin and a deputy-lieutenant, but there is genuine warmth

* In *The Court and Character of King James.*

in his dedication to Raleigh, praising his kindness to the Cornish people, and how 'your ears and mouth have ever been open to hear and deliver our grievances, and your feet and hands ready to go and work their redress'.

Raleigh being a fluent linguist, it was now expected that he would be available for welcoming foreign dignitaries. In March he escorted the Spanish envoy around the sights of London. In the summer the mighty Duc de Sully arrived, unheralded, at Dover. Raleigh had however been warned, and Sully tells in his memoirs how Raleigh came tiptoeing into his room when his back was turned, and jokingly called out: 'I arrest you as my prisoner, in the Queen's name'. Sully turned and recognizing Raleigh burst into laughter. 'It was the Captain of her Guard. I returned his embrace, telling him I should consider such an imprisonment as a great honour.'[13] All of which shows that they must already have been on quite friendly terms; also that Raleigh had more of a sense of humour than has sometimes been credited.

It was awkward for the Queen and the government when on 5 September the Duc de Biron, Constable of France, arrived in London with a huge retinue, his purpose being to inform Elizabeth that Henri IV was to marry Marie de Medici. Something had gone wrong, and there was no one to greet him. The Queen was on a progress at Lord Sandys's house, The Vyne at Basing, and Cecil was with her. Raleigh luckily was in London. As he wrote: 'I am glad I came hither for I never saw so great a person so neglected.' He took the Duke round the monuments of Westminster and entertained him and other French nobles at the Bear Garden at Southwark, which was much enjoyed. There were difficulties about finding enough horses to take them to Basing, and accommodation had to be arranged for the night at Bagshot en route. 'I have laboured like a mule,' said Raleigh.[14]

Meanwhile, tapestries and plate had been brought from Hampton Court, and local gentry were made to provide 140 beds for the French visitors. Raleigh noted that the French wore 'all black and no kind of bravery [decoration] at all', evidently the latest fashion, very different from the colourful dress of the Elizabethan Court,[15] and as a compliment to the Queen's guests rode all night back to London to get himself a plain black taffeta suit and a black saddle. The Queen was so pleased with him that she knighted his brother Carew.

Another grand visitor was the Duke of Lennox, who had been asked by James VI to sound out Cobham and Raleigh. According to Henry Howard, Cobham gave 'abundant assurances of his earnest attachment to the King', but Raleigh turned down the suggestion of a secret meeting, merely saying that he was 'over-deeply engaged and obliged to his own mistress to seek favour anywhere else, that should divert his eye or diminish his sole respect to his sovereign'.[16] Afterwards Raleigh, again according to Howard, 'full of brave flourishes of confidence and love' went to see Cecil and proudly told him how he had 'denied any kind of proffer of devotion or kind affection to have been made to King James from the Duke'. Howard could well have added a little twist detrimental to Raleigh in his account of this saga, but the sly reply of Cecil, who was already in lengthy correspondence with James, rings absolutely true: 'You did well; and as I myself would have made the answer, if the like offer had been made to me.' Raleigh wanted Cecil to tell the Queen about such a great gesture of loyalty. This alarmed Cecil, and he firmly counselled Raleigh that it was quite the wrong thing to do. Even at this stage, he said, Elizabeth might think that Raleigh was trying too hard to ingratiate himself with her. So Elizabeth knew nothing, and James remained convinced that he was a potential enemy. Raleigh had behaved loyally, but also unwisely.

On 19 September Raleigh told Cecil that he had received reports that a Spanish fleet, including twenty-five warships and with up to 7,000 soldiers, was about to sail from Lisbon, bound either for Ireland or the Low Countries. Then on 26 September, he had definite news that the Spaniards were on their way to Ireland, aiming for Cork or Limerick, with an even greater force and 'well furnished with victuals, munitions and money'. They had also apparently brought many women.

It was true that the Spanish armada, under the command of Don Juan de Aguila, had left Lisbon on 24 August. The destination was to be Cork harbour, and at this stage they were already approaching the Irish coast. The women could possibly have mostly been Irish refugees wanting to return, though the commanders were said to have brought their wives and children, so confident were they of victory. Aguila was accompanied by several priests, including Matéo de Oviedo, the titular archbishop of Dublin. The Spaniards landed eventually on 23 September, not at Cork, because of an unfavourable wind, but at Kinsale further west and not so early defendable. Unaware of the recent successes of Mountjoy and Carew, they immediately set about adding to its fortifications. Messages were sent to Tyrone, asking him to hasten south, bringing horses which Aguila desperately needed. Perhaps 4,000 men had been landed. But within a fortnight Mountjoy had arrived with a larger force and immediately took over strategic positions, blocking off the harbour. So now the Spaniards found themselves in a state of siege. And it was a long time before Tyrone could manage to reach them; he did not leave Ulster until early November. As

Raleigh put it, this was the last of all his hopes – if the Spaniards had come at the beginning of the rebellion, all Ireland would have been lost.[17]

Raleigh had also guessed, correctly, that Kinsale had been chosen as an alternative landing place by the Spaniards because it adjoined territories controlled by the chieftain Florence MacCarthy. But as the Spaniards were soon to discover, he had already been arrested by Carew and was safely locked up in the Tower of London.

Raleigh was not well that September and was not even able to make the journey to take the waters at Bath. However, he had recovered sufficiently to attend the opening of the new Parliament, the tenth and last of Elizabeth's reign, on 27 October. Indeed he was in confident and abrasive form there, almost the dominant figure, and gave some great performances. His hope of becoming a Privy Councillor had once again been dashed, and there was a definite if temporary coolness now in his relations with Cecil, both in correspondence and in the House.

But for the Essex rebellion Parliament would have met earlier. Money was badly needed because of the situation in Ireland. Essex had spent wildly, and now there was this substantial Spanish army to be dealt with at Kinsale. Thus the main item of business was the subsidy, and as everyone knew tax assessments were too low. The Queen, in view of the crisis, had asked for the session to be kept brief.[18]

Raleigh was sitting as senior knight for the county of Cornwall. The House was in a restless and aggressive mood, and with so much shouting, hawking and coughs of disapproval there were many calls to order from the Speaker. Members agreed to take off their spurs, but would not be parted from their boots and rapiers. On one occasion Cecil complained that they were behaving as if they were in a grammar school instead of in Parliament.

The Queen had granted freedom of speech, but on arrival for the opening she seemed depressed and aloof. Then, when she left, few greeted her. Cecil had said that £30,000 was needed by Easter, and when the time came to discuss the subsidy there was at first silence, as if waiting for someone from the Council to take a lead – as Lord Burghley would have done in the old days. It was Raleigh who spoke first, from his seat. The situation was so urgent, he said, that in order to raise money the Queen had been forced to sell her own jewels and land, 'sparing even out of her own purse and apparel for our sakes'. Large loans made by her to her subjects were still unpaid. During his speech there was an interruption from Sir Edward Hoby, who had arrived late and, unable to find a seat, had to stand near the door. He was evidently in a sulk, and was irritated by Raleigh's low voice. 'Speak out!' he shouted. 'You should speak standing, that the House might hear you.' Raleigh merely stared at him 'with a countenance full of disdain'. It was Cecil who had to smooth matters, and Hoby in due course apologized.[19]

There was discussion about tax on lands valued below £3. Raleigh was in favour of their not being exempted; Cecil agreed and in his speech made the remark that 'neither pots nor pans, nor dish nor spoon should be spared when danger is at our elbows'.[20] On the face of it this might seem a joke, but it was evidently spoken with such an air of smugness that Raleigh was annoyed. 'I like it not', he said, 'that the Spaniards our enemies should know of our selling our pots and pans to pay subsidies; well may *you* call it policy, but I am sure it argues policy in the state.' His gratuitously offensive tone to his friend was noted. The subsidies were voted on and agreed. But afterwards Francis Bacon made a surprisingly priggish and pedantic speech, commending the decision to tax the poor as well as the rich; it was *dulcis tractus pari jugo*, he said, right to draw in equal yoke. 'Call you *par jugum?*', Raleigh asked scornfully, 'when a poor man pays as much as the rich? Peradventure his estate is no better, or little better than he is assessed at, while our estates are £30 or £40 in the Queen's books – not the hundredth part of our wealth. It is neither *dulcis* nor *par*.' He had spoken fairly but it only added to his reputation for inconstancy. On the other hand it was hardly prudent to attack two such potentially powerful allies on trivialities.

He spoke well on other matters. He attacked the government's proposal to compel all farmers to plough up a third of their land. Some land was suitable for cultivation, some not, some farmers might not be able to afford to buy seed corn.[21] 'I think the best course is to set it [the land] at liberty, and every man free, which is the desire of a true Englishman'; and again: 'For my part, I do not like this constraining of men to manure [cultivate] or use their grounds at our wills; but rather, let every man use his ground to that which it is most fit for, and therein use his discretion.' He swayed the House decisively, and the bill was 'absolutely rejected'.

Then on the question of exporting iron ordnance, he spoke with the authority of the old warrior-patriot. He said that too many cannons made in England had found their way to the Spaniards. 'I am sure heretofore one ship of her Majesty's was able to beat a hundred Spaniards; but now, by reason of our own ordnance, we are hardly matched one to one.' His practical approach showed up again when debating a bill on the enforcement of church attendance. He was against putting so much power into the hands of churchwardens. 'Say, then, there be 120 parishes in a shire; there must now come extraordinarily 240 churchwardens. And say but two in a parish offend in a quarter of a year; that makes 480 persons, with the offenders, to appear. What multitudes this will bring together; what quarrelling and danger may happen, besides giving authority to a mean churchwarden!' The bill was lost by one vote only. Then Raleigh caused an upset. A member complained that he had wanted to vote but had been pulled back by another. Cecil said that the member should be named, at which Raleigh said: 'Why! If it please you, it is a small matter to pull one by a sleeve, for so have I done myself oftentimes.' Such flippancy caused 'a great loud speech and stir', followed by a shocked silence. There was a suggestion that he should be made to apologize. Cecil's implicit censure on Raleigh was much applauded; he said that any man whose vote could be drawn backwards and forwards like a dog on a string would never be returned to the Commons again.

Besides the subsidies, the main issue discussed in the Parliament was the Crown's long practice of granting monopolies to private individuals, and there were those who regarded it as a major injustice. In this Raleigh had been for long a figure of particular hate and envy, with his monopolies on the export of broadcloths, on the control of certain sorts of wine, and the right to license innkeepers. Then of course he was also Lord Warden of the Stannaries. When the list of monopolies, including soap and salt, was read out and reached packs of playing-cards, Raleigh was actually seen to blush (unaccountably, since this monopoly was Sir Edward Darcy's). A sarcastic voice was heard saying, 'Is not bread there?' Nevertheless Raleigh was prepared to defend himself on tin, as there was a strong reason for the Crown regulating the industry, and he was acting as the Crown's representative. (The suspicion had always been of course that some of the Crown's benefits found their way into his own pocket.) He said:

I am urged to speak in two respects. The one because I find myself touched in particular; the other, in that I take some imputation of slander offered to her Majesty, I mean by the gentleman that first mentioned tin; for that being one of the principal commodities of this kingdom, and being in Cornwall, it hath ever, so long as there were any, belonged to the Dukes of Cornwall, and they had special patents of privilege. It pleased her Majesty freely to bestow upon me that privilege; and that patent being word for word the very same as the Duke's is, and because by reason of mine office of Lord Warden of the Stannaries I can sufficiently inform this House of the state thereof, I will make bold to deliver it unto you.

For benefit of the uninitiated he then gave some details of the working of the tin industry, proudly revealing that he had been able to have the miners' wages doubled.[22]

When the tin is taken out of the mine, and melted and refined, then is every piece containing one hundred weight sealed with the Duke's seal. Now I will tell you, that before the granting of my patent, whether tin were but of seventeen shillings and so upward to fifty shillings a hundred, yet the poor workman never had above two shillings a week, finding themselves. But since my patent whosoever will work may; and buy tin at what price soever, they have four shillings a week truly paid. There is no poor that will work there but may, and have that wages.

Notwithstanding, if all others be repealed, I will give my consent freely to the cancelling of this as any member of the House.

He had spoken sharply, and for a while there was silence. This peroration had stunned the House. Then Sir Francis Hastings congratulated Members on giving Raleigh a fair hearing, but wondered if everyone's memories of the facts and figures were the same. No other holder of a monopoly spoke or offered to give up his privileges. It was the whole system of patronage that was under attack, and everyone knew that the royal prerogative over monopolies had to be reviewed.

The Queen realized that she must react at once. She sent word through the Speaker that she would indeed review the entire system of monopolies. A few were to be abolished and others were to be subject to trial at common law.

The Members were summoned to the Council Chamber at Whitehall to present their humble and heartfelt thanks. It was then Elizabeth made one of her greatest speeches, afterwards always known as the Golden Speech – patently a kind of farewell, the end of an era. It was a long speech but contained these much remembered words:[23]

For myself, I was never so much enticed with the glorious name of a king, or royal authority of a queen, as delighted that God hath made me his instrument to maintain his truth and glory, and to defend his kingdom . . . from peril, dishonour, tyranny and oppression. There will never queen sit in my seat with more zeal to my country, care to my subjects, and that will sooner with willingness yield and venture her life – for your good and safety than myself. And though you have had and may have princes more mighty and wise sitting in this seat, yet you never had or shall have any that will be more careful and loving.

After her speech all present came forward to kiss her hand.

Parliament was dissolved on 19 December. It has since been said that if nothing else contributed to Raleigh's renown he would have been remembered as one of the most active parliament men of his time. Many pretensions had been ruffled, but he had spoken with conviction and in some degree in the manner of parliamentarians of the next century.

Tyrone reached the outskirts of Kinsale on 9 December, with a force of about 6,000. The English army had been reduced by about the same amount, what with sickness and desertion. It was also very short of food, not helped by the deliberate devastation of the country around. The final battle, on Christmas Eve, was brief and decisive. Tyrone was routed, leaving perhaps 1,200 dead. It was a battle that changed the course of Irish history, and it was Mountjoy's greatest moment as a soldier. On 2 January the Spaniards surrendered, on honourable terms; their forces were to be shipped back to Spain, taking with them their colours, artillery, money and private possessions.

It has been suggested that the victory at Kinsale marked the end of the old Celtic culture.[24] For Elizabeth and England a deadly peril had been removed.

Malice and Betrayal
1602

Early in 1602 Raleigh began once more to plan expeditions to America, north and south. He was to say later that he had already twice sent out vessels to search for the lost colonists, each time under Captain Samuel Mace, a Weymouth man. In March Mace was again despatched with two ships to look for suitable trading places in and around Virginia. Before leaving he had taken the trouble to get ideas from Hariot about such things as suitable gifts for Indians, and had tried to learn a few words of their language. He landed at Cape Fear, about 200 miles south of Roanoke, spending a month there and bringing back sassafras wood, china root (a kind of sarsaparilla), and other plants of medicinal value. He excused himself for not searching the islands for the colonists because of the 'extremity of weather'.

At about the same time, unknown to Raleigh, Bartholomew Gilbert,* Bartholomew Gosnold and the Revd John Brereton left for Norumbega, with twenty intended settlers. They traded around what is now Portland, Maine, then went further south collecting sassafras and cutting down young cedar trees. Some sort of row ensued, so they returned with the settlers, but still apparently intending to found a new colony which was to be called North Virginia.

Raleigh encountered Bartholomew Gilbert at Weymouth and was at first furious with him, complaining that the voyage had been in breach of his Virginia patent; he was also afraid that the price of his investment in sassafras wood would be affected. Some of the cargo was apparently confiscated. It was on this occasion, on 12 August, in a letter to Cecil, that he wrote the famous and often quoted words about Virginia: 'I shall yet live to see it an English nation'.†

---

* Bartholomew Gilbert, a goldsmith from London, was no relation of the Gilberts of Compton Castle.

† Early in 1603, before the world suddenly crashed around him, Raleigh had been thinking of sending out Mace on trading missions to both Virginia and Guiana. In the event Mace seems to have made for Chesapeake, with potentially diastrous results (p. 159). In May Raleigh sent

Amyas Preston, one of those knighted by Essex at Cadiz, challenged Raleigh to a duel in 1602. The cause of the quarrel is unknown, but perhaps Raleigh had made some slighting remark about Preston having gone privateering in 1595 instead of joining him off Guiana. Raleigh declined the challenge without, as Thomas Fuller was to say in the next century, 'any abatement of valour'. Differences in age, and especially in rank, were good enough reasons, and as Raleigh was later to write, after a duel the hangman was the one who bestowed the garland on the victor.[2] At any rate he and Preston were later reconciled.

Raleigh now decided to divest himself of his Irish seignories, which had been a burden on his resources with many appalling anxieties. They were sold on 7 December for £1,500 to Richard Boyle, the future Earl of Cork whom Sir George Carew had rescued from the 'verge of ruin' and had made a clerk in the provisional government of Munster. Castles, lands and fisheries, with the extra bonus of the ship *Pilgrim*, were included, though Raleigh held back the castle of Inchiquin which had been let for life to the ancient Dowager Countess of Desmond. Boyle could raise only £500, and the balance was still outstanding when Raleigh was attaindered. James tried to confiscate the lands, but Boyle managed to have his title confirmed by paying him the balance of £1,000 in 1604.

Boyle was to maintain that the price was perfectly fair, because the property was 'woefully dilapidated' and he had been faced with an expenditure of £3,700. All the same, it turned out to be a spectacular bargain, one great advantage being that he was not an absentee landlord, as had been the case with Raleigh.

There was another quarrel, this time between Raleigh and his nephew John Gilbert (who had also been knighted at Cadiz), and connected with the distribution of profits in a privateering venture. It would seem that Gilbert had written to Cecil, who had been a substantial investor, asking that Raleigh should be excluded in the shareout. The Lord Admiral was also a investor, though on a smaller scale, and Raleigh was said to be entitled to part of the Lord Admiral's proceeds. The actual details are obscure, but Raleigh wrote bitterly to the young man about his ingratitude and disloyalty.[3] It took a long time for this family rift to heal.

Bartholomew Gilbert in the *Elizabeth* to search for the lost colonists around Chesapeake. Gilbert inadvertently landed north of Chesapeake, and there was a fight with Indians, during which he and several others were killed. The *Elizabeth* with its diminished crew was able to return only with great difficulty – by which time Raleigh was a prisoner in the Tower of London.[1]

Another worry was a robbery at Durham House. From the Middlesex County Records we learn that two men, one a yeoman, the other a tailor, 'broke burglariously into the dwelling-house of Sir Walter Raleigh'.[4] They stole two linen pillowslips fitted with silk and gold worth £10, a linen cushion cover adorned with silk and gold, and a 'diaper tablecloth' worth 40 shillings. Bess asked Cecil for a more secure leasehold because of the great cost of repairs; but he turned it down, inferring so it would seem that the fire and general dilapidations had made them unsatisfactory tenants: all of which was a bit hard, seeing that Raleigh had taken over the supervision of Cecil's newly acquired and run down estate of Rushworth, and was also giving him advice about selling timber.

But the Raleighs were not to know that behind Cecil's refusal were secret negotiations with the Bishop of Durham, Tobie Matthew, for his repossession of Durham House.

The great issue of the day was still of course the succession. Cecil was only too aware of his unpopularity after the death of Essex, who James of Scotland now referred to as 'my martyr'. If he were to remain in power after the death of Elizabeth it was essential to win over James's trust, and this would mean unloading the chief odium on Raleigh and Cobham. Raleigh in his closeness to the Queen appeared totally confident about his future whoever might succeed (most probably he assumed it would be James), and was aloof from politicking. Cobham was making some efforts to ingratiate himself with James, and in this way his brother-in-law saw him as a rival.

There were at least a dozen possible candidates for the throne of England besides James, the most spoken of being the Spanish Infanta – in reality an impossibility* – and Lady Arabella, or Arbell, Stuart, who was James's first cousin. Others included Edward Seymour Lord Beauchamp, who represented the ill-fated Lady Jane Grey's family, and the Earl of Huntingdon who was descended from the Duke of Clarence. When Elizabeth died the line of Henry VII would of course come to an end. Both James and Arabella/Arbell were descended from daughters of Henry VII, James's grandmother being the elder, which made him the obvious choice. Not much was thought of Arbell: too lightweight and too young, and not very religiously inclined; in any case it was felt that another long female reign was to be avoided.

Cecil continued to write to Raleigh as his 'faithful friend' and to Cobham as his 'loving relative'. All the same, he managed to block Raleigh from a peerage which Elizabeth had suggested, and told him that if he wanted to

---

* The Infanta was soon to abandon her claim. Word was sent that Spain would support any candidate who would grant religious toleration and peace.

be a Privy Councillor he would have to give up being Captain of the Guard, a condition he knew Raleigh could not possibly accept as it would mean becoming detached from Elizabeth. Cecil meanwhile continued to flatter her in the way she loved, calling her a nymph and complimenting her on the 'crystalline beams' of her eyes.

Soon after the execution of Essex, Cecil had a secret meeting with the Earl of Mar, James's envoy, and pledged his support for James. He made it clear that if James left everything in his hands he would make certain that the succession would run smoothly. A secret correspondence was arranged, using code numbers for names and arranging special routes for letters between Scotland and England on some occasions apparently via Dublin.

The correspondence began at the end of May. James, 'a great lover of subtle conceits', fancied himself as a scholar and theologian, and was impressed by Cecil's long-winded letters, sprinkled with Latin tags and allusions to the Bible. But Cecil needed to explain away his once publicized friendship with Raleigh, as well as – rather more difficult – his keeping up with Cobham. The result was this stunningly disloyal letter.[5]

I do profess . . . that if I did not sometimes cast a stone unto the mouth of those gaping crabs . . . they would not stick to confess daily how contrary it is to their nature to resolve to be under your sovereignty; though they confess (Raleigh especially) that natural policy forceth them to keep on foot such a trade against the great day of mart. In all which light and sudden humours of his, though I do in no way check him, because he shall not think I reject his freedom or his affection, but always (under seal of confession) use contestation with him . . . yet, under pretext of extraordinary care of his well being, I have seemed to dissuade him from engaging himself too far, even for himself . . . Would God I were . . . from offence to God in seeking, for private affection, to support a person [Raleigh] whom most religious men do hold anathema.

He was of course alluding to Raleigh's so-called atheism, which still clung to him. It was a clever shaft, shrewd and damaging, that hit its mark. For James had a Calvinist upbringing, and to him there was nothing more dangerous than an atheist, both to religion and the monarchy.

Cecil also sought to isolate Raleigh from influential friends. One such was Raleigh's relative and close ally, Sir George Carew, now President of Munster. Carew was recognized as a man of exceptional probity and had won renown for his victories in Ireland, so it was obvious that he would continue to be highly regarded in the next reign. Cecil sent him a present of tobacco and referred to Raleigh's desire to be a Privy Councillor, and how

Cecil would not allow it unless he handed over the Captaincy of the Guard to Carew; if this were to happen he would easily be able to add 'some matter of profit' (a nice bribe). He complained that for some reason Raleigh and Cobham had been unfriendly to him, which was a lie, 'but I have covenanted in my heart not to know it'. And plaintively he added how much he resented 'the mutinies of those whom I have loved'. He asked Carew to be careful what he wrote in his letters, as Raleigh and Cobham were very indiscreet and 'show all men's letters to every person'.[6]

Not surprisingly he did not succeed in turning Carew against Raleigh.

Keeping this correspondence secret was always Cecil's nightmare. Once when driving with the Queen in a coach, a post messenger came riding up, blowing his horn. He had with him an urgent packet of letters from Scotland. Cecil offered to cut the string and was horrified to find in it a letter to himself. Knowing that the Queen hated bad smells, he said: 'Faugh! It smells vilely', at which she shrank back in disgust and hid her face. He then slipped the letter into his pocket.[7]

Cecil hit on another way of destroying Raleigh's reputation with James, one which would also avoid his having to commit himself too much on paper. 'But why', he craftily wrote, 'do I thus presume to trouble your ears with my poor private griefs at his ingratitude to me, when I resolved to record my private joys? I will therefore leave the best and worst of him, and other things, to 3's relation, in whose discretion and affection you may *dormire securus*.'

He was referring to the dread Lord Henry Howard, whose code number in the secret correspondence was 3. For the last twenty years Howard had been Raleigh's avowed enemy, ever since those early days at Court when they both consorted with the Earl of Oxford. In the secret correspondence Cobham was 7, Cecil 10, Raleigh 2, the Queen 24 and James himself 30. Howard needless to say was already writing derogatory letters against Raleigh and others he disliked to the King, all mixed with the sort of extravagant flattery in which he excelled.

Tall, saturnine, gloomy-looking, Howard was now over sixty. In recent years he had been readmitted to the presence of the Queen, to whom he was related, and had become a great friend of Essex, though he had not taken part in the rebellion. Born a Catholic, he had for years been lurking in the background of the Court, and was regarded by many as a suspicious character. When in 1595 Lady Bacon had written to her son Anthony warning him that Howard was a dangerous man, a 'subtle serpent', she had added: 'He will betray you. He, pretending courtesy, worketh mischievous perilously'. And in poisoning the King's mind he was a main instrument in Raleigh's eventual downfall.

It has to be admitted that Howard had a disastrous family history. His grandfather, the Duke of Norfolk, had been sent to the Tower. His father, the soldier-poet Earl of Surrey, had been executed by Henry VIII, and his brother the fourth Duke of Norfolk, the country's premier Duke, had been executed for plotting on behalf of Mary Queen of Scots, whom he had actually hoped to marry. His nephew, the Earl of Arundel, was sent to the Tower, where he died. Proud and embittered, Howard resented being excluded from the power and position at Court to which he considered his birth entitled him. For years he had been living on a meagre income, having to rely on the generosity of a sister, Lady Berkeley. In the early 1580s he had been friendly with the Spanish ambassador Bernardino Mendoza, who had persuaded Philip II to give him a welcome pension of 1,000 crowns a year in return for information, but this ended when Mendoza was expelled from England.

Once he had been Reader in Rhetoric at Cambridge University, at a time when it was unusual for a nobleman to take up teaching. He was interested in theology and had translated the Psalms into verse. Thus his academic background and his sympathy for Mary Queen of Scots, coupled with his dislike of militarism and wish for peace with Spain, were all important recommendations to James. Another link was that they shared the same sexual preferences.

For so many years Howard had regarded the Cecils, father and son, as implacable enemies. Now Robert Cecil had to unravel all this, with the bait of recommending him to high office when James succeeded to the throne. What Cecil described to James and his two close advisers, the Earl of Mar and Edward Bruce, as Howard's 'wisdom and sincerity' was in reality a stream of furious slander and innuendo against Raleigh and Cobham, sometimes almost incoherent in its rabid hate. References to 'that accused duality', 'that damned crew', and 'those wicked villains' developed into even more explicit gems such as 'Hell did never spew up such a couple, when it cast up Cerberus and Phlegethon [one of the rivers in Hell]', and 'Cobham and Raleigh, who hover in the air for an advantage, as kites do for carrion'. If, he said, Cobham had the 'rough hand of Esau', then Raleigh had the 'soft voice of Jacob in courtly hypocrisy'. And of course Raleigh had a 'pride above the greatest Lucifer that ever lived in our age'. In one letter he described the two of them as *duo erinacii* (two hedgehogs), which in contrast to all the above is surprisingly mild.[8]

Bess was not spared either – 'The league is very strong between Sir Walter Raleigh and my Lady Shrewsbury [Bess of Hardwick] and Sir Walter Raleigh's wife. Much hath been offered on all sides to bring her into the

Privy Chamber to her old place, because she is a most dangerous woman, and full of her father's inventions.* *Sed canunt surdae* [But the two women sing tone-deaf].' Lady Shrewsbury was mentioned because of her being Arbell Stuart's grandmother, which made the connection seem even more sinister. In a letter to Cecil, Howard described Bess as being 'as furious as Proserpina with failing of that restitution in Court which flattery had moved her to expect.' 'All my revenge', he concluded, 'shall be to heap coals on their heads.'[9]

The subject of Raleigh's atheism was not of course to be resisted, and here he involved Northumberland, whom he now described as a 'fool'. That 'diabolical triplicity' who denied the Trinity – Raleigh, Cobham and Northumberland – were meeting daily at Durham House for consultation, 'which awaked all the best wits of the town out of suspicion of every kinds, to watch the chickens they could catch out of those cockatrice eggs that were daily and nightly sitten on.' Raleigh and Cobham were simply playing up to Northumberland, putting 'their heads under the girdle of him they envy most'. He also said that Northumberland had told his wife, Essex's sister, that he would rather the King of Scots were buried than crowned.

Northumberland, unaware of the slanders against him, but suspecting a campaign against Raleigh and Cobham, wrote a long letter to the King, and in it he defended both of them.[10] He admitted that he did not know Cobham well, but he gave a very neat assessment of Raleigh, especially of his faults.

... I must affirm Raleigh's ever allowance of your right. And although I know him insolent, extremely heated, a man that desires to seem to be able to sway all men's fancies, all men's courses, and a man that out of himself, when your time shall come, will never be able to do you much good nor harm, yet must I needs confess what I know, that there is excellent good parts of nature in him, a man who is disadvantageous to me in some sort, which I cherish rather out of constancy than policy, and one whom I wish your Majesty not to lose, because I would wish that not one hair of a man's head should be against you that might be for you.

It was no use. The damage had been done. James was now irretrievably 'exceeding far inamorat of Raleigh and Cobham'. Cecil was safe. Howard was safe. Letters from James to Howard would be addressed to 'My dear and trusty 3' or 'My dear and worthy 3', and in ending one of them he wrote of his 'infinite thanks which my heart doth yield to my dearest 10',

---

* Sir Nicholas Throckmorton had been prosecuted for high treason in the reign of Mary but had managed to be acquitted on a legal technicality.

adding 'I bid you heartily farewell, ever praying to rest more and more assured of the constant affection of your most loving friend, 30.'

Unaware of the crevasse that was opening before him, Raleigh in July went again to Jersey and stayed there, somewhat impatiently, for several weeks. Yet again there had been anxieties about the Spaniards. Raleigh ostensibly had been sent to see to the island's defences and to try to obtain some intelligence about Spanish fleets, but Cecil was obviously glad to keep him out of the country. Raleigh's letter to him of 20 July has therefore an unconscious poignancy.

You will I hope give my leave to salute my Lord Cobham and you both in a letter. I can send no news from hence. I hear not from any part of the world just yet. I cannot send a bark for Spain, the wind blowing continually at west and north east. From France I have heard nothing ... I beseech you bestow a line on me that live in desolation, and if you find no cause to stay me here I would willingly return ... I shall ever rest to do you both service with all I have, and all my life to boot. W. Ralegh. Bess will convey letters if you send any.

But he was not one to waste his time, even in exile. Among other things he promoted a profitable trade between Jersey and the fishing grounds of Newfoundland. He created a register of Jersey lands and abolished compulsory service for those living in the district of Mont Orgueil castle. He also acted as judge in the island courts. Probably on this visit he arranged the marriage between his illegitimate daughter and Daniel Dumaresq, son of the seigneur of Saumarez.

By 12 August he was back in England, writing to Cobham in the hope that they might meet at Bath. He was expecting Northumberland at Sherborne. It seemed that the Queen had been more than a little annoyed by his long absence from Court (just as Cecil had intended?). But he was not feeling well, and from Bath he told Cecil that he was in pain and could not write much. Possibly his wounded leg had became arthritic.

The ageing Queen tried to keep up her spirits. She played her virginals and still danced, though rarely in public. In August she went on a ride lasting 10 hours (which did tire her). All the same, Sir John Harington was soon to write: 'Our dear Queen, my royal godmother and the state's most natural mother, doth now bear show of human infirmity.'

The Main and the Bye
1603

Cecil was still behaving towards Raleigh as a trusted friend and partner in business. In January he commissioned him to send out a privateering vessel and said that he would pay for half the victualling. The other half, he told Raleigh, 'may be borne between my Lord Cobham and you, or for such part as any of you will not receive let it remain upon my head.'[1] All this had to be kept secret, for James was known to detest privateering and it would be disastrous for Cecil if he discovered that the Queen's Secretary was acting as partner in such an enterprise, and with the very man he was expected to hate.

Dr Dee had cast Elizabeth's horoscope and had sensibly advised her to leave Whitehall and the London fogs. So she went to Richmond, her 'warm box'. She was now in her seventieth year. The death of Lady Nottingham affected her deeply – which rather gives the lie to the legend of Essex's ring. She fell into deep depression, and it became obvious to everyone around her that the end was close. Her throat was ulcerated, like a 'chain of iron', she said. She would barely speak or barely eat. Her own coronation ring, which had become embedded into the flesh of her finger, had to be sawn off. She would not change her clothes or go to bed, believing that if she did she would never get up again. Instead she sat on the floor propped up by cushions. Once she asked to be lifted to her feet, and to her attendants' horror remained standing for fifteen hours.

William Weston, a Catholic priest then in the Tower, wrote how during this time 'a strange silence descended on the city . . . not a bell rang out, not a bugle sounded.'[2] After three weeks, 'what by fair mean, what by force', she was taken to her bed. Archbishop Whitgift knelt by her, and she would not let him leave. At last, at 3 a.m on 24 March, she died, having just been able to signify with her hand that she agreed that James of Scotland should be her successor. She went 'mildly like a lamb, easily as a ripe apple from a tree.'[3]

Horses had been kept in readiness along the Great North Road, and her young relation Sir Robert Carey went galloping off at once, the first to reach Holyrood House in Edinburgh with the news, after only three days. Meanwhile Cecil called the Privy Council to announce James's accession, and then went on to Whitehall and to Cheapside to proclaim the new king to the expectant crowds.

There was a great rush to greet James on his progress south. Howard was waiting for him at Berwick-on-Tweed, as was the Bishop of Durham. At York he received the Lords of the Council. He created over a hundred knights, pardoned some criminals but had one or two others hanged without trial (not a good precedent?). As he was known to love the chase, special hunts were arranged for him en route, including hares which were released from baskets along the roadside. A proclamation had to be issued by Cecil 'against the too free resort to the King on his journey'. The excuse was to prevent overcrowding but the rumour went around that it was to keep away Raleigh, who had been in the West Country at the time of Elizabeth's death, and was known to be on his way, accompanied by a large retinue. But Raleigh was too grand to be deflected like this, and he duly appeared at Burghley House in Northamptonshire where James had arrived on 3 May.

Perhaps it had been feared that after all James would have been impressed by this tall haughty figure, confident that his long experience near the seat of power would be accepted as invaluable to the new sovereign. If so, Raleigh was to be proved quite wrong, James being already deeply prejudiced against him. The impression one gets is that Raleigh was distrusted and feared more than ever before – he was out of date, irrelevant, a relic of the past, a menace to the stability of the realm.

It is hard for anyone writing about Raleigh to be sympathetic towards James. The remark about him by Henri IV of France, 'the wisest fool in Christendom', has stuck to him forever. Then we have that classic summing up in Sellar and Yeatman's *1066 and All That*: 'James I slobbered at the mouth and had favourites; he was thus a Bad King. He had however a very logical and tidy mind, and one of the first things he did was to have Sir Walter Raleigh executed for being left over from the last reign.'

From the evidence of a contemporary, the admittedly hostile Sir Anthony Weldon, we learn that although James was peaceable and merciful, witty and 'ready with jests', delivered with a poker face, he was 'crafty in petty things' and 'of timorous disposition'. He did indeed have a tongue too large for his mouth, which made watching him eat an unpleasant sight; and he was crippled, which meant that he had to walk leaning on somebody's shoulder. He was terrified of assassination, with some good reasons from the past, and wore a padded doublet, proof against stilettos, and stuffed breeches, which apparently he only changed when they wore out. Now aged thirty-seven, he had once been considered good-looking, and a portrait of the period shows an intelligent but sombre face with a downturned mouth and a thin square beard, blue eyes and light brown hair. He never washed his hands, only wiping his finger ends with a wet napkin, and was said to be constantly fiddling with his codpiece (fleas?). His language was sometimes coarse and blasphemous, and he drank heavily though never to excess. He must have smelt.

His admiration for handsome youths was notorious. As Weldon tactfully said; 'He was not very uxorious, though he had a brave Queen that never crossed his designs and was of a mild spirit in his change of favourites'. This lady, Anne of Denmark, has gone down in history as a very different character, frivolous and party-loving, but the poor woman must have suffered on several counts, and a good mark was her support and admiration for Raleigh in later years. For all that, James's better qualities have recently been emphasized, notably his distaste for extremism and his desire to find a middle way in reform and politics. G. M. Trevelyan summed him up as 'easy to love or despise, impossible to hate'.[4]

There had been a rumour that Raleigh had once said, when Elizabeth was likely soon to die, that it would be better for the English to keep the government in their own hands, and set up a commonwealth, 'and not to be subject to a needy beggarly nation'. It is not very likely that he would have said such a thing, and it could well have been yet another choice piece of malice spread around by Henry Howard and passed on to James. Thus, when at last the King and Raleigh came face to face at Burghley, James produced one of his famous puns: 'Raleigh, Raleigh, O my soul, mon, I have heard rawly of thee'.[5]

The reason given by Raleigh for disobeying Cecil's proclamation was that it was essential for him to have letters with the royal signature in order to be able to continue with certain legal processes in Cornwall, in particular over 'waste of woods and parks' within the Duchy. The King could hardly at this stage have been expected to concern himself with such far-off matters, but he did want to get rid of Raleigh as soon as possible. He therefore instructed Sir Thomas Lake, who was acting as his Secretary, to prepare the necessary letters, adding: 'Let them be delivered speedily, that Raleigh may be gone again'. As Lake reported to Cecil: 'Raleigh hath taken no great root here.'[6]

Cobham was not able to meet the King on this occasion. When Cecil mentioned the possibility, James merely 'made good sport on the matter, and passed it over'. But Raleigh was not to be dismissed so easily from

Burghley. 'It was a most stately sight,' so Aubrey was to write in his *Brief Lives*, 'the glory of that reception of his Majesty, where the nobility and gentry were in exceedingly great equipage, having enjoyed a long peace under the most excellent of Queens.' Aubrey then went on to describe a conversation between Raleigh and the King, one which caused great offence.

The company was so exceedingly numerous that their obedience caused a secret dread with it. King James did not inwardly like it, and with an inward envy, said that he doubted not but that he should have been able on his own strength (should the English have kept him out) to have dealt with them, and get his right. Said Sir Walter Raleigh to him: 'Would to God that had been put to the trial'. 'Why do you wish that?' said the King. 'Because', said Sir Walter, 'that then you would have known your friends from your foes'. But that reason of Sir Walter was never forgotten nor forgiven.

Whatever Raleigh said was bound to be misconstrued. But such a conversation seems hardly credible. If true, however, was Raleigh hinting that behind all the magnificence some danger was really lurking? It was at this stage that Aubrey also made an often quoted comment on Raleigh: 'He was such a person (every way) that (as King Charles I says of Lord Strafford) a Prince would rather be afraid of than ashamed of. He had that awfulness and ascendancy in his aspect over other mortals.'

Three days later Raleigh was back in London for the funeral of Elizabeth. As Captain of the Guard, in a long black cloak down to the ankles and wearing a tall black hat, he led his ten Guards in the cortège, each man carrying a halberd, reversed to signify mourning.

Not long afterwards Raleigh was summoned before the Council and abruptly told that Sir Thomas Erskine was now to be Captain of the Guard, as he had held that post in Edinburgh. This was to be expected, and it was written in the Council book that Sir Walter Raleigh 'in a very humble way did submit himself'. He received recompense however: a remission of £300 a year that he had been paying to the Crown out of his revenue as Governor of Jersey.

On 3 May James was a guest at Theobalds, Cecil's house in Hertfordshire. Here he gave the order for Southampton to be released from the Tower, along with others imprisoned after the Essex rebellion. He also raised Cecil to the peerage, as Lord Cecil of Essendon. Thomas Howard became Lord Chamberlain and was given the title of Earl of Suffolk. Henry Howard's advancement was yet to come; he was given a place on the Privy Council and was to be made Earl of Northampton. There was a certain amount of agitation at Court about the advancement of so many Scots, particularly in the lesser posts such as Gentlemen of the Bedchamber and Master of the Harriers, which kept them on close familiar terms with the King.

Now Raleigh received yet another blow. James recalled all the monopolies granted by Elizabeth 'for scrutiny'. Wine licensing was not strictly a monopoly but the Council forbade the levy of all dues; this meant the removal of the major part of Raleigh's income.

On his first round of visits James went to Beddington in Surrey, the house of Sir Nicholas Carew. Raleigh's hopes must have risen because Sir Nicholas was Bess's uncle, and Raleigh knew the place well. So there was yet another confrontation. One cannot but wonder at his ignorance of James's character and the present mood of the government, which was for peace with Spain. Most people knew that James had an absolute horror of war, but Raleigh seemed to think that in the great Elizabethan tradition he longed for military glory. So he presented him with a pamphlet he had written with the title of *A Discourse touching a War with Spain, and of the Protecting of the Netherlands*. It was a well-composed and lucid document about the strategic reason for England's long involvement in the Low Countries, with a warning of how disgraceful it would be to abandon the Dutch, who if antagonized could turn out to be rivals both in trade and warfare. He even offered to take across 2,000 men at his own expense. James's response has not been recorded.

Yet another, worse, blow was in store. When James had met Tobie Matthew, the Bishop of Durham, at Berwick-on-Tweed, the worthy cleric had lost no time in putting in a request for the return of Durham House. But it was not until 31 May that James issued an order to the Councillors to 'give warning and commandment' to both Raleigh and his co-tenant Sir Edward Darcy to 'deliver quiet possession' of the house to the Bishop. On hearing this good news Bishop Tobie at once wrote to Sir Thomas Egerton, as Lord Keeper of the Seal, and soon to be raised to the peerage as Lord Ellesmere, asking for the return of the house as soon as possible, for he had heard that 'those wranglers' were plotting to stay on until Michaelmas at the end of September. He was afraid that if given time Raleigh might remove fixtures such as the wainscoting, and in any case he needed to use the summer months for repairing the 'dilapidations and decays which he [Raleigh] by so many years hath made or suffered'.[7] The King's Commissioners thereupon ordered Raleigh to quit Durham House at once.

This was plain malice, and the Bishop was behaving as deviously as the rest. Raleigh was rightly outraged and wrote angrily pointing out that he had occupied the house for nearly twenty years and had spent £2,000 on the place. The order was 'contrary to honour, to custom and civility'; the 'meanest gentleman' would have been given six months' notice, and the 'poorest artificer in London' at least a quarter's warning. What was more, he had already made provisions for forty people and had brought in hay and oats for twenty horses. He wanted to appeal to the King, but the Commissioners were adamant, only agreeing to extend the notice until midsummer.*[8]

Sometime between the 12th and 16th of July Raleigh, still apparently hoping for a return of royal favour, went to Windsor to join the King in a hunting party. On a fine summer's day he was waiting on the terrace when Cecil came up to him 'as from the King' and told him he was to stay behind, as the Councillors needed to put some questions to him. By the 20th he was in the Tower on suspicion of high treason.

There is such a 'thick cloud of words' about what came to be known as the Bye and Main Plots that it is hard to unravel the sequence of events, with all the recriminations, charges and countercharges. Raleigh's eventual trial is among the most notorious in English legal history, even though no official transcript exists. We have to rely chiefly on reporters' notes hurriedly jotted down and later written-up. Neither have we transcripts of Raleigh's examinations. Most writers on the events leading up to the trial have relied on the two 19th-century biographers, Edwards and (especially) Stebbing, though these are sometimes contradictory and are not now considered to be entirely reliable. But in 1995 a major discovery in a 'random trawl' at the Bodleian was published by Mark Nicholls: a document prepared for the prosecution against Cobham and Raleigh, constituting the so-called Main Plot.[11] It would seem to have been written about five weeks before the trials

* Bess might have had mixed feelings about leaving Durham House which she had always considered to be 'a rotten house'. And if James but knew, the Bishop had once formed a very unfavourable impression of his own character. In 1594 he had written to Lord Burghley that King James of Scotland was 'a deeper dissembler than is thought possible for his years . . . I pray God that the King's protestations be not too well believed.'[9] It is also worth noting that after three years Tobie was advanced to the Archbishopric of York, and this entitled him to another grand mansion in London. So he took the opportunity of doing just what he had complained that Queen Elizabeth had done; he alienated the house from the See of Durham to the Duke of Buckingham. He also transferred the outbuildings and stables – those that had been damaged by fire in 1600 – to his eldest son, who in turn sold them for £1,200 to Robert Cecil, by then further ennobled as Earl of Salisbury. It was Cecil/Salisbury and his son who converted these buildings into the huge and very profitable New Exchange, or 'Britain's Bourse'.[10]

and commissioned by Sir Thomas Egerton. In spite of further evidence that emerged, the document settles several important points.

The Bye (or 'Surprising') Plot was also known as the Treason of the Priests, since it was in essence a Catholic plot, at the centre of which were two priests named Watson and Clarke. They had been to see James in Scotland, and had been under the impression that he would ease the heavy penalties on Catholics when he succeeded to the throne of England. They were to find themselves quite mistaken. 'Na, na, we'll no need the Papists noo' was the much quoted response of James when approached about more toleration for the Catholics. So a conspiracy was hatched, revolving mostly round the area of the Sherwood Forest and including two men whom the priests had recruited and usually referred to as 'impecunious swordsmen', Sir Griffin Markham and Anthony Copley. Their crazy plan was to seize or 'surprise' the King, imprison the members of the Council in the Tower, and force through assurances that Catholics would be placed in positions of power.

Meanwhile, there was a curious alliance with Protestant plotters, led by George Brooke, brother of Cobham, and Lord Grey of Wilton, both of whom had their grudges against Cecil. Grey was a Puritan and wanted more latitude in religious worship and freedom of expression. He was infuriated by the release of Southampton and had thereby conceived a deep dislike for the King. Each group knew of the other, but Grey never met the priests. In fact his plan was very different. With his military background he was wanting to raise a regiment that would be used to surround the King and force him to agree to his demands.

This is a simplification of a tortuous and muddled double-headed affair. Both Cobham and Raleigh had known about the arrest of the priests at the beginning of July, and on 12 July we have Copley's first recorded examination, which led to the arrests of Markham and Grey. Then on the 14th George Brooke was also arrested. Two days later Cobham was therefore examined, but he denied any knowledge of the Treason of the Priests.

As Raleigh, in the words of the prosecution document, was as 'dear to Cobham as his hand and heart', it was not surprising that he too should be questioned. Hence his encounter with Cecil on the terrace of Windsor Castle. But this may have been in consequence of further blabbing by George Brooke on the 17th, that had led to Cobham being cross-questioned about his dealings with Arbell Stuart. The prosecution document says that on that day Cobham admitted that he had corresponded with her, but he had burnt the letters. But on the 19th Brooke went very much further, claiming that

Cobham had sent him to Arbell, to ask her to write letters to the King of Spain, the Infanta and the Duke of Savoy (their brother-in-law) asking them 'to favour and assist her title to the Crown, with a promise of three things if it succeeded: first a firm peace with Spain, second toleration in religion, and lastly to be ruled by them in the choice of her marriage.'[12]

Brooke seemed to have got it into his head that by incriminating his brother he might be able to save his own life. It also seems that Cobham denied anything so treasonable. But now Raleigh's name surfaced. On the 17th Brooke had said that his co-conspirators had decided that Raleigh was a 'fit man' to join them, being already discontented and humiliated by the new regime. What was more, they felt that he would surely be able to win over the King's fleet. It was wild talk, but enough to put Raleigh under suspicion.

This then was the real start of the more important Main Plot. Raleigh denied absolutely any complicity with the Bye. Nevertheless, he was put under arrest in the house of Sir Thomas Bodley. Somehow he managed to send secret messages to Cobham, also under house arrest, using Lawrence Keymis as go-between. This was only discovered a week or so later, and Keymis was promptly put under arrest. The excuse was that it was all in connection with a large pearl and a diamond that had been given by Cobham to Raleigh in payment towards the £4,000 with which Cobham was going to buy a fee farm from the Crown. But other more serious reasons were suspected, and revealed, and Keymis was even threatened with torture.

Both Raleigh and Cobham were also asked about dealings with Charles de Ligne, Count of Aremberg, who had been sent by Archduke Albert to congratulate James on his accession. Aremberg was known to be a friend of Cobham, and indeed Cobham had earlier informed Cecil of an approach to him by Aremberg about the possibility of a peace with Spain; this was a perfectly proper thing for Cobham to have done, though the King was not pleased, it being considered that such a matter was not within Cobham's sphere.

Raleigh and Cobham would of course have continued to deny anything underhand. But the prosecution document shows that there was a dramatic turn on 19 July when Brooke admitted that the plan had been to obtain the large sum of five to six thousand crowns from Spain, 'as far as he knew to supply a second action for the surprise of the King'. By 'second action' he meant something different from the one planned by the Bye clique. Presumably the finger was directly pointed at Cobham, whose name might even have been mentioned.

Things now moved swiftly. On that same day an Antwerp merchant,

Matthew La Renzi, or Laurency, was interviewed. He was working in some way for Aremberg, who could not be questioned because of his diplomatic immunity. La Renzi confirmed that several letters had passed between Cobham and Aremberg. The document also adds that La Renzi said that 'Cobham in the night time went secretly only with him to the Count's lodgings and was brought up a back way'. Much more damning was the assertion that 'at another time' he delivered a letter to Cobham from Aremberg promising the money, when Raleigh was present, and that Cobham and Raleigh had gone upstairs 'into a chamber privately', leaving La Renzi alone below. 'At another time' may refer to a further examination of La Renzi after 19 July.

Raleigh was again probed about Cobham and Aremberg, but once more was not to be drawn. Perhaps all he was told was that it was now known that La Renzi had brought letters to Cobham. At any rate soon afterwards he had qualms – he had not been entirely truthful, and this could turn out to be a fatal mistake, so he wrote a letter to the Lords in Council, with, according to the prosecution document, this somewhat cryptic message:

If your honours apprehend the merchant of St Helen's, the stranger will know that all is discovered of him, which perchance you desire to conceal for some time. All the danger will be lest the merchant fly away. If any man know any more of the Lord Cobham, I think he trusted George Wiet of Kent.

The 'merchant' was meant to be La Renzi, and the 'stranger' Aremberg. Nicholls has identified George Wiet as George Wyatt, son of the Marian rebel Sir Thomas Wyatt. It is possible of course that La Renzi was interviewed only *after* the Lords had received Raleigh's letter.

This was to be reckoned a crucial letter – up to now Raleigh's biographers have assumed that it said something quite different: that he had noticed that Cobham, after leaving Durham House one evening, had not gone straight home to his house at Blackfriars but had rowed across the river to where La Renzi was living. Either version might be considered fairly innocuous. On the next day, however, 20 July, Cobham was again examined by the Council, in the course of which he was shown Raleigh's letter. He at once 'broke out into passion', accusing Raleigh of 'ruining his own honour, life, and estate, crying out three or four times: "O villain! O traitor! I will now tell you all the truth".'[13] He then poured out an admission that he had indeed asked Aremberg for this large sum of money, but it had all been at Raleigh's suggestion. He would never have got himself involved in these 'courses' but for Raleigh's instigation. He was to have gone to Spain to collect the money and then return home via Jersey, where he would meet Raleigh and discuss how it could be distributed among English malcontents.

Having recorded all this, the writer of the prosecution document was justified in remarking:

What colour of cause should move Cobham jointly to accuse himself and Rawleigh [as he wrote the name throughout] of high treason, ruinating thereby his own honour, life, and estate, except they thereof were guilty, against whom before that his confession nothing was proved? . . . Cobham by accusing Rawleigh seeketh not to excuse himself, but by the same his accusation condemneth himself guilty of the selfsame treason.

This was 'not the accusation of an enemy but of a vowed and dearly beloved friend'. But then, some days later, even more surprising, Cobham retracted all his accusations, every word.

Stebbing has added another twist, namely that Cobham also said that he had been afraid that when Raleigh had got him to Jersey he might arrest him and send him to the King. Those who were convinced of Raleigh's duplicitous nature, Stebbing wrote, would find confirmation in Aubrey's *Brief Lives*, where Aubrey claimed that he had been told this very story by an intimate friend of the Earl of Southampton: that 'really and indeed Sir Walter's purpose was, where he had them [the conspirators] there, to have betrayed them and the plot, and to have them delivered up to the King and made his peace.'

It has of course to be remembered that Southampton was one of Raleigh's particular enemies. For all that, the theory has its supporters, including A. L. Rowse, who believed that Raleigh in his parlous state had to do something that was desperate and striking if ever he were to recover himself. 'We have seen that, at the top, almost anyone would betray almost anyone else.'[14]

That is one theory. The confession of Cobham on 20 July, in spite of the retractions, remained the high point of the attempts to construct a case against Raleigh. So Raleigh was at once transferred to the Tower. The unfortunate Arbell also was put under house arrest.

Raleigh was sent to the Bloody Tower, which had two rooms and was reasonably comfortable, and was allowed two servants of his own. Nevertheless, he was in a state of abject depression, knowing that in State trials for treason the end was nearly always a foregone conclusion, and that against such a phalanx of enemies there was little hope. When he had been cast down by Elizabeth there had always been a chance of forgiveness. James had made it clear that he was in no mood for that.

Sir John Peyton, the Lieutenant of the Tower, wrote to Cecil on 23 July: 'I never saw so strange a dejected mind as in Sir Walter Raleigh. I am extremely cumbered with him; five or six times a day he sendeth for me in such passions as I see his fortitude is impotent to support his grief.'[15] Raleigh asked one of his servants to buy him a long narrow knife, he said to stir wine, but the man refused.

On 27 July while at dinner with Peyton he suddenly tore open his vest, grabbed a table knife and plunged it into his chest, crying out, 'There an end!' The knife hit a rib, but he bled a lot. As it happened, Cecil and some Councillors were in the Tower at the time, examining the other prisoners, and they were hastily summoned. To Cecil it was not a serious attempt, and he considered it to have been merely a ruse designed for public sympathy. However, as he was also to write, Raleigh did appear to be 'in some agony' and 'seeming to be unable to endure misfortunes and protesting innocency, with carelessness of life'. And he added: 'In that humour he had wounded himself under the right pap, by no means mortally; being in truth rather a cut than a stab.'

One conclusion at the time was that at the last moment he lost his nerve about killing himself. There have also been doubts about whether he even really meant to commit suicide. Always the great actor, he could have been whipping up a drama, knowing that Cecil and the others were in the Tower. Five days later Peyton was writing to Cecil that 'Sir Walter Raleigh's hurt is nearly well', and on the 4th of August we have Cecil writing to Sir Thomas Parry, ambassador in Paris: 'He is very well cured, both in body and mind.'[16]

That he had intended to kill himself is shown in a farewell letter to his wife, which in the end she probably never saw and which has found its way to All Souls at Oxford.[17] He may have given it for safe keeping to one of his servants, or to Peyton. For a while it was wrongly considered by biographers to be a forgery, partly because of some mawkish passages quite untypical of his usual style, and partly because of a mention of an illegitimate daughter – who of course has since turned out to have existed, as a result of the discovery of his will of 1597. The letter is not nearly so moving as yet another farewell letter, a superb piece of writing, that he wrote to Bess a few months later. All the same it is important and revealing, and much of it needs to be quoted.

Receive from thy unfortunate husband these his last lines, these the last words that ever thou shalt receive from him. That I can live to think never to see thee and my child more I cannot. I have desired God and disputed with my reason, but nature and compassion hath the victory. That I can live to think how you are both left a spoil to my enemies and that my name shall be a dishonour to my child I cannot; I cannot endure the memory thereof. Unfortunate woman, unfortunate child, comfort yourselves, trust God and be contented with your poor estate. I would have bettered it if I had enjoyed a few years.

Thou art a young woman, and forbear not to marry again. It is now nothing to me; thou no more mine, nor I thine. To witness that thou didst love me once take care that thou marry not to please sense but to avoid poverty and so preserve thy child. That thou didst also love me living, witness it to others, to my poor daughter to whom I have given nothing, for his sake who will be cruel to himself to preserve thee. Be charitable to her, and teach thy son to love her for his father's sake.

For myself, I am left of all men, that have done good to many, all my good turns forgotten, all my errors revived and expounded to all extremity of ill. All my services, hazards, and expenses for my country – plantings, discoveries, fights, councils, and whatsoever else – malice hath now covered over. I am now made an enemy and a traitor by the word of an unworthy man. He hath proclaimed me to be a partaker of his vain imaginations, notwithstanding the whole of course of my life hath approved the contrary, as my death shall approve it.

Then comes one of the passages that made one writer dismiss the letter as a 'palpable concoction inflicted on posterity'.[18]

Woe, woe, woe be unto him by whose falsehood we are lost. He hath separated us asunder, he hath slain my honour; my fortune, he hath robbed thee of thy husband, thy child of his father, and me of you both. Oh God thou dost know my wrongs, know then thou my wife and child, know then thou my Lord and King that I ever thought them too honest to betray, and too good to conspire against.

He asked Bess to forgive his enemies, even Lord Harry (Howard), 'for he was my heavy enemy'; also Cecil – 'I thought he would never forsake me in extremity; I would not have done it him, God knows'. He reminded her that Cecil as Master of the Wards would have charge of their boy and might therefore have compassion on him.

The central and important passage, in any attempt to try to understand Raleigh, follows next. To commit suicide was a Christian sin, and he gave his explanation.[19]

Be not dismayed that I died in despair of God's mercies, strive not to dispute it but assure thyself that God hath not left me nor Satan tempted me. Hope and despair live not together. I know it is forbidden to destroy ourselves but I trust it is forbidden in this sort, that we destroy not ourselves despairing of God's mercy. The mercy of

God is immeasurable, the cogitations of men comprehend it not. In the Lord I have ever trusted and I know that my redeemer liveth. Far is it from me to be tempted with Satan; I am only tempted with sorrow, whose sharp teeth devour my heart. Oh God thou art goodness itself, thou must not be but good to me. Oh God that art mercy itself thou canst not be but merciful to me.

This is not the cry of an atheist. Raleigh is often portrayed as the paragon of the Elizabethan age, but the passage here emphasizes the unconventionality of his religious views.

Turning to mundane matters, he listed his debts, which were considerable, at least £1,500. The largest was £600 to Peter Vanlore, the royal jeweller. He also mentioned money due to a baker and a brewer at Weymouth in connection with the privateering ship that he had shared with Cecil and Cobham. He did not yet know the fate of Bartholomew Gilbert in Virginia, so he asked Bess to make sure that the men's wages would be paid out of the sale of their cargo (which probably turned out to be virtually non-existent).

He referred to the conveyance of the Sherborne estates to Wat – a vital matter, because if he was convicted as a traitor they would otherwise be forfeited to the Crown. And this makes one wonder whether, when he made the conveyance in 1602, he did in some way fear disaster after the death of the Queen. He also told Bess that his silver plate was 'at gage' (held as security) in Lombard Street.

Then once more he descended into a quasi-hysterical outpouring.

Oh what will my poor servants think at their return when they hear I am accused to be Spanish, who sent them, to my great charge, to plant and discover upon his [the Spaniard's] territory. Oh intolerable infamy. Oh God I cannot resist these thoughts. I cannot live to think how I am derided, to think of the expectation of my enemies, the scorns I shall receive, the cruel words of lawyers, the infamous taunts and despites, to be made a wonder and a spectacle. Oh death hasten thee unto me that thou mayest destroy the memory of these and lay me up in dark forgetfulness. O death destroy my memory which is my tormentor; my thoughts and my life cannot dwell in one body.

He asked Bess to rely on the help of Adrian Gilbert, and to be good to Keymis, 'for he is a perfect honest man and has suffered much wrong for my sake'.

There is no doubt about the sincerity of the ending.

I bless my poor child. And let him know his father was no traitor. Be bold of my innocence, for God – to whom I offer life and soul – knows it. And whatsoever thou choose again after me, let him be but thy politic [expedient] husband, but let my son be thy beloved for he is part of me and I live in him; and the difference is but in the number and not in the kind. And the Lord for ever keep thee and them and give thee comfort in both worlds.

The writer of the prosecution document was certain that it had been Raleigh's intention to commit suicide: 'Rawleigh's purpose and attempt to murder himself strongly presumeth the guiltiness of his own conscience, for so the civil law construeth the same'. Yet Cecil had obviously been at pains to prevent the episode from being publicly known.*

As for King James, his comment on hearing of the suicide attempt was that Raleigh should be 'well probed' by a good preacher.

* A curious footnote to this episode appears in Lefranc's *Sir Walter Ralegh Ecrivain*, p. 669. Lefranc discovered in John Hutchins's *History of Dorset IV* (1870 reissue) a reference to Raleigh's secretary Edward Hancock having committed suicide on the same day. No other reference to this has been discovered, and it is true that Hancock's name never reappears in correspondence.

The Trial
1603

The report of the French ambassador, Comte de Beaumont, to Henri IV would seem to give the most likely reason for Raleigh's attempted (or pretended) suicide: 'Sir Walter Raleigh is said to have declared that his design to kill himself arose from no feeling of fear, but was formed in order that his fate might not seem as a triumph to his enemies, whose power to put him to death, despite his innocence, be well known.'[1] It was certainly strange that no mention of the incident was made in the treason trial that was to follow. Even if the whole thing had been a charade, the mere fact of an attempted suicide would be shaming enough to his accusers, the assumption being that he had been driven to it through ill treatment.

Raleigh's guilt was generally taken for granted. He was doomed from the start, and he knew it; the jurors would also know what was expected of them. As Stebbing said, Raleigh was always an enigma, feared for his brilliance and unorthodox ideas. 'Who is Sir Walter Raleigh?' wrote the author of the prosecution document. 'A man of extraordinary wit, and thereby the better furnished to shadow his misdoing. Secondly, a man too much more than ordinary policy, and therefore the better provided to prevent the discovery of his secret unlawful purposes.'

Those clinging on to their newfound power simply wanted him out of the way. They knew that his reputation as a man of adventure, courage and vision could also be used in the event of national unrest. And if Cecil did not feel any remorse, he had at least to put on the semblance of believing in Raleigh's guilt. As he wrote to Sir Thomas Parry: 'Few men can conceive that Sir Walter Raleigh's denial comes from a clear heart'.[2] But Sir John Harington, one of the few who still had some sympathy for him, said: 'I doubt the dice not fairly thrown, if Raleigh's life be the losing stake'. And there were vultures waiting for what morsels that they could still pick for themselves out of his ruin. Beaumont was convinced that Cecil acted 'more for interest and passion than for the good of the kingdom'.

The tradition in English law that a person is innocent until proved guilty did not yet apply. And Raleigh knew well enough that a person accused of treason was not allowed legal assistance and was usually not even informed of specific charges until the trial began. After the government's investigations had been completed and all the evidence gathered in, he would be assumed to be guilty, and it was up to him to prove his innocence. He had not studied law when he was at the Inns of Court, and was ignorant of changes in the treason laws. It was ironical that he was secretly relying on the example of his own father-in-law, Sir Nicholas Throckmorton, who had been acquitted of treason through a trick of law at the time of Queen Mary.*

Throckmorton had been in trouble because he had been one of those who had signed the Letters Patent favouring Lady Jane Grey on the death of Edward VI. He had also been a friend of Sir Peter Courtenay, one of the plotters in the Wyatt rebellion and the man whom Raleigh's father had helped to escape to France. At his trial statutes from the reign of Edward III had been invoked, whereby execution for treason was only for those who had actually plotted the death of the sovereign or had been engaged in an overt act to depose him. The accused was also entitled – and this was the important point – to call two witnesses.

Such was the gist of the message that Keymis had really taken to Cobham, so it was later claimed, although Raleigh was to deny it. Cobham had certainly been forewarned about Raleigh's intentions to bring it up at the trial. It is possible that Raleigh had simply *discussed* it with Keymis, who on his own initiative had told Cobham, in order to give him some encouragement.

Soon after the presumed suicide attempt Cecil questioned Cobham and reported that on 'being newly examined, he seemeth now to clear Sir Walter in most things, and to take the burden on himself.'[3] Yet, according to the prosecution document, on 2 August Raleigh admitted that there had been a plan for Cobham to meet him in Jersey on his return from Spain.

There was a suspicion that Raleigh was using Peyton's young son for carrying messages, but although probably true it was dismissed. On being questioned again on 10 August Cobham merely said that he had seen Raleigh talking to the boy out of a window, and that when the boy had come to visit him three hours later he had said: 'I saw you with Sir Walter Raleigh – God forgive him! He hath accused me, but I cannot accuse him.' To which the boy had answered: 'He doth say the like of you – that you have accused him, but he cannot accuse you.'[4]

It was decided that Peyton's family was becoming too friendly with

* pp. 173, 354.

Raleigh, so a tactful way had to be found of removing Peyton himself. Promotion was the answer. James now declared that Raleigh's governorship of Jersey had been 'forfeited to us' because of the 'grievous treason intended against us' (though not yet proved), so the post was given to Peyton. And Peyton was replaced as Governor of the Tower by a much tougher character, Sir George Harvey. But Harvey had a son who also fell under the spell of this legendary man; so he too began taking messages to Cobham.

At Whitehall there was excitement and speculation about the fate of Raleigh's properties at Sherborne. Cecil told Sir John Elphinstone that he was the twelfth person to have applied for them. In due course the farm of wines, which had been Raleigh's main income, passed to the Lord Admiral, Lord Nottingham, and in the general partition of spoils Henry Howard managed to acquire for himself Cobham's Wardenship of the Cinque Ports. At least it was a friend of Raleigh, Sir Francis Godolphin, well away from Court intrigues, and acting as High Sheriff of Cornwall, who was authorized to take the county's musters – 'the Commission of Lieutenancy granted to Sir Walter Raleigh becoming void and determined.'

At intervals Raleigh was cross-questioned by Sir William Waad, or Wade, a bully and known as an adept at obtaining confessions in the torture-chamber; but always Raleigh remained obdurate. On 13 August, however, he was examined by three Commissioners, namely the Attorney-General Sir Edward Coke, Lord Wotton, and the snakeish Henry Howard, and he then admitted that, when Cobham told him of his scheme of getting money through Aremberg, he had said that he was to be offered 10,000 crowns for 'the furthering of peace between England and Spain'. 'I told him,' said Raleigh, ' "When I see the money, I will make you an answer". For I thought it one of his ordinary idle conceits; and therefore made no account thereof. But this I think was before Count Aremberg's coming over.' Which seemed to bear out that Cobham's plot had been fomenting as early as May.[5]

Coke and of course Howard would have been hostile, but not necessarily Wotton, a distinguished diplomat and a friend of the Throckmortons* (also of Cecil). Raleigh in any case was unhappy about the outcome, and wrote a special appeal jointly to Cecil and three Councillors, the Lord Admiral Nottingham, Lord Thomas Howard now Earl of Suffolk, and Lord Mountjoy now Earl of Devonshire. He begged them to study his replies to the Councillors 'seriously before there be any further proceedings', and not 'to leave me to the cruelty of the law of England . . . before your understandings and consciences be thoroughly informed.' He reminded them of his constant

* His son, the second Lord Wotton, was to marry Bess's niece.

enmity towards Spain, and repeated how he had spent vast sums of his own money in his various enterprises, including the plantations in Virginia. He absolutely denied any conspiracy against the King, and insisted that he had never accepted any money from Spain. The letter was evidently designed to be shown to James, who was appropriately described in Latin as a *rex pius et miserecors et non leo coronatus* (a pious and merciful king and not a crowned lion).[6]

On 23 August Brooke said that he had been given a book by his brother that questioned the right of James to the throne of England. Cobham on being asked about this said he had got it from Raleigh. On the next day Raleigh admitted that he did once have a book 'written against the title of the Queen of Scots', but did not know what had become of it. This was regarded as especially sinister and was to be brought up at the trial.

Also on 23 August the priest Watson from the Bye plot, backed up by Markham, claimed that he had heard Brooke making the altogether shocking statement that Cobham meant to destroy the King 'with all his cubs' and replace him with Lady Arabella Stuart. Brooke then confirmed this, but Cobham denied that he had ever said such a thing, though he did admit that he had spoken 'discontentedly and inadvisedly'.[7] Raleigh's name seems to have cropped up somehow, but there was no direct accusation about involvement over the 'cubs'.

Brooke had been visited by the Bishop of London, Richard Bancroft, who had told him that 'the only way to procure favour is to open all that you possibly can'. So he let his imagination fly. He had already implicated Sir Arthur Gorges, who had been arrested and released. Now he accused Sir George Carew and Sir Henry Brouncher, custodian of Arbell, but in both cases this was quickly recognized as spurious. Then Copley said that Brooke had told him that Raleigh had suggested stirring up rebellion first in Scotland. And Watson claimed that Brooke had told him that he had been present at an assembly at Cobham's house when Raleigh and Grey had been there; everyone had been showing great discontent, especially the two lords, Grey 'uttering treason with every word'.

Even the Commissioners must at times have been bemused by such a mishmash of accusations and betrayals. While all this was going on Raleigh was secretly using one of the Tower servants, Edward Cottrell, for carrying yet more messages to Cobham. Some of their subterfuges might have been worthy of *The Faerie Queene*. On one occasion a letter for Cobham was hidden inside an apple which was thrown into his window while Sir George Harvey was at supper. The answer Raleigh received was not, however, to his 'contenting', so he asked for another. This time the reply, slipped under

Raleigh's door, was considered 'a very good letter', and Raleigh hid it in his pocket. Cobham had written:

To clear my conscience, satisfy the world and free myself from the cry of your blood, I protest upon my soul and before God and his angels, I never had any conference with you in any treason; nor was ever moved by you to the things I heretofore accused you of. And, for anything I know, you are as innocent and as clear from any treasons against the King as is any subject living . . . and so God deal with me and have mercy on my soul, as this is true.

In one of his letters Raleigh warned Cobham to beware of clergymen or preachers trying to wheedle out a confession: 'Do not as my lord of Essex did, take heed a preacher. For by his persuasion he confessed and made himself guilty.'[8] It was typical of Cobham that before Raleigh's trial not only did he tell the Commissioners about this, but that he had written that 'very good letter', which he then proceeded to retract just before the trial began.

Less than a month before the trial, Cobham had written another important letter in Raleigh's favour, this time to Sir George Harvey, asking him to arrange for him to address the Privy Council: 'God is my witness, it doth touch my conscience . . . I would fain have the words that the Lords used of my barbarousness in accusing him falsely.' But Harvey kept back the letter and did not show it to Cecil until after Raleigh's conviction. He gave it to him then because his son had been imprisoned for helping Raleigh (once more revealed by Cobham).

Plague had struck London again, at its peak causing 3,000 deaths in a week. The Court moved first to Hampton Court and then to Woodstock, Winchester, and Wilton. Bells tolled ceaselessly, and the streets were cluttered with infected bedding and straw. The carts of 'carcase-carriers' roamed the streets, to the terrible cry of 'Cast out your dead'.* There were deaths in the Tower. It was decided that the trials should be held at Winchester.

The date for Raleigh's trial was to be 17 November. Before leaving the Tower he wrote a desperate and painful last letter to Cecil.[9]

Sir: To speak of former times it were needless. Your lordship knows what I have been towards yourself and how long I have loved you and have been favoured by you, but change of time and mine own errors have worn out these remembrances (I

---

* Some 30,500 were consigned to the plague-pits.

374

fear) and if aught did remain, yet in the state wherein I stand there can be not friendship. Compassion there may be, for it is never separate from honour and virtue . . . I cannot despair but some warmth remaineth in cinders . . . A heavy burden of God to be in danger of perishing for a prince [the King of Spain] which I have so long hated and to suffer these miseries under a prince [King James] whom I have so long loved. Sir, what malice may do against me I know not. My cause has been handled by strong enemies.

Again he asked for mercy from James, as a 'true gentleman and a just man beside being a King'.

For yourself (my Lord Cecil) and for me sometime your true friend and now a miserable forsaken man, I know that affections are neither taught nor persuaded, but if aught remain of good, of love or compassion towards me, your lordship will now show it when I am most unworthy of your love and most unable to deserve it . . .

At the trial and especially afterwards there were certainly signs that Cecil did have pangs of conscience.

Raleigh was indicted at Staines on 21 September 1603:

that he did conspire, and go about to deprive the King of his Government; to raise up Sedition within the realm; to alter religion, to bring in the Roman Superstition, and to procure foreign enemies to invade the kingdom. That the Lord Cobham, the 9th of June last, did meet the said Sir Walter Raleigh in Durham House, in the parish of St Martin in the Fields, and then and there had conference with him, how to advance Arabella Stuart to the Crown and royal throne of this kingdom.

It had been intended to hold the trial earlier, but it was postponed either because of the plague or perhaps because of yet more disclosures pouring out from the accused in the Bye. The prosecution document found at the Bodleian was probably drawn up in October. It dealt separately with Cobham and Raleigh, and opened along the same lines as the indictment.

Cobham, it warned, regarded Raleigh as his 'second self, of whose love, fidelity, wit and policy he had so great opinion and belief.' In the matter of his relations with Arbell, it appears that Brooke had first told her that Cobham was anxious to 'have intelligence with her'. Her lady-in-waiting, Frances Kirton, who was related to the Brookes, had written to Cobham asking why this should be so. Nevertheless, Arbell wanted to meet him and 'be advised by him', which was how the correspondence had begun.

Apparently Cobham had 'specially bid her beware how she dealt with any Scots' – a confession, as the writer of the document said, from which 'many strong inferences may be gathered'.

There was another warning about Raleigh's hold on his 'unhappy disciple'.

The nature of the treason is violent and bloody, and not to be executed but by the sword and arms. Cobham of himself is neither of the sword nor ever professed arms, and therefore it is probable (as he affirmeth) that Raleigh being a man of both was the inciter of him thereunto.

In the case of Raleigh, reasons – hardly convincing ones – were given for not calling witnesses in trials for treason: in effect his offence was of such 'vile and horrible nature' that no witness could be trusted. This was of course something Raleigh was confident he would be able to refute.

All those accused of the Bye and Main plots, with the exception of Raleigh, had already been sent down to Winchester with an escort of fifty light horse. Raleigh left on 10 November in his own coach, accompanied by Sir William Waad and Sir Robert Mansel. Waad told Cecil that Raleigh was now much altered – he had not been well in the Tower. A group of well-wishers, friends and relatives had gathered at Wimbledon to cheer him as he passed, but generally the crowds on the way showed nothing but hatred. Waad wrote that it was 'hob or nob' whether or not Raleigh 'should have been brought out alive through such multitudes of unruly people as did exclaim at him'. Tobacco pipes, sticks, stones and mud were thrown by the mob, and not only in London. 'If one hare-brained fellow amongst so great a multitude had begun to set upon him, as they were near to do it, no entreaty or means would have prevailed; the fury and the tumult of the people was so great.'[10]

It took them five days to reach Winchester. Raleigh was said to have ignored the insults of the crowds, and to have sat calmly in his coach puffing at his pipe. From Bagshot he wrote a last, confident, but patronizing letter to Cobham: 'You know in your soul that you never acquainted me in your Spanish imaginings . . . I trust in God that you never spoke those words to the King, and if you be clear of it your peers will never condemn you.'

The trials were to be held in Winchester Castle's Great Hall, built by Henry III and in many ways still unchanged, with its polished Purbeck marble columns and flint and stone exterior walls. The famous Round Table of King Arthur was then at the east end, and the plastered walls would have been covered with patterns and coats of arms. There is a hole in a wall traditionally supposed to have been used by James to eavesdrop on the proceedings – in fact very unlikely, for he and the Court were at Wilton near Salisbury.

The trials of the priests, Brooke, Markham and others in the Bye Plot took place on 15 November and all were found guilty, apart from the less important Sir Edward Parham, who was lucky to be a friend both of the foreman of the jury and of Cecil. He was the first person to be acquitted for treason since Sir Nicholas Throckmorton. The two noblemen, Cobham and Grey, were to be tried on 18 November, the day after Raleigh.

Raleigh's chief prosecutor was the Attorney-General, Sir Edward Coke, tall and handsome, red faced, abrasive, a master of invective as had been shown when he had prosecuted Essex. But his vicious attacks on Raleigh were outrageous even by contemporary standards.* He was assisted by a very different character, Sergeant Hele, prone to making bad jokes – he had actually acted for Raleigh in his case against his bailiff John Meere.

The Lord Chief Justice, Sir John Popham, presided, seated at the west end of the Hall on a raised platform and under a brocaded canopy. His portrait confirms Aubrey's description of him as a huge, heavy, ugly man. There was gossip about his background – stolen as a child by gypsies, behaving like a highwayman when a young man, and amassing a huge fortune in peculiar ways. The other judges were Chief Justice Anderson and the Justices Gawdy and Warburton.

The seven Commissioners sat on either side of Popham, and were people hardly likely to be well disposed to Raleigh, all anxious to prove their loyalty to the new king. Four of them were familiar faces, now at the heart of the government of England: Cecil, Suffolk, Devonshire and, needless to say, Henry Howard. The others were Raleigh's jailor Waad, Lord Wotton and Sir John Stanhope the Vice-Chamberlain, both Cecil's men. Raleigh was provided with a stool. He knew people in the crowd at the back of the Hall and cheerfully saluted them.

The trial began at eight o'clock in the morning and was to last until seven in the evening.[11] The indictment was read out by Hele, who gratuitously elaborated on each charge. When he came to the mention of Arbell Stuart, he did manage to make Raleigh smile: 'As for the Lady Arabella, she, upon my conscience, hath no more title to the crown than I have; which, before God, I utterly renounce.' Raleigh then pleaded not guilty. He was asked if

---

* It has to be said that in later years, and in posterity, Coke was to achieve a quite different fame as a champion of the independence of English law against the royal master he was now serving.

he wished to challenge any of the jury, said to be all from Middlesex,[12] and replied: 'I know none of them; but think them all honest and Christian men. I know my own innocency and therefore will challenge none. All are indifferent to me.' Sir Thomas Fowler was chosen as foreman. There was a rumour that three of the jurymen had been replaced the night before, in case they were known to Raleigh. Could this have been because of objections to the release of Sir Edward Parham?

Raleigh made a request. His health was not good and his memory failing. There would be many points to answer, and he asked if he could reply to each one as it came out, and not have to carry them all in his head when the Crown had completed its case. Coke, the chief prosecutor, did not like this. 'The King's evidence', he said, 'ought not to be broken or dismembered; whereby it might lose much of its grace and vigour.' There was not much grace in the way he was to present the evidence. In any case in this instance he was overruled.

Coke then launched his attack with a lengthy discourse on the Bye plot, rambling on without interruption from the judges until Raleigh was forced to protest: 'I pray you, gentlemen of the jury, remember I am not charged with the Bye, which was the treason of the priests'. 'You are not,' retorted Coke, 'but your lordships will see that all these treasons, though they consisted of several points, closed in together, like Samson's foxes, which were joined in the tails, though their heads were severed.' On he went, citing the murder of Edward II, the treason of Perkin Warbeck, and of Edmund de la Pole in the reign of Henry VII, finally returning to the damning words attributed to Cobham by his brother Brooke that 'it will never be well in England until the king and his cubs were taken away'. Now he turned on Raleigh: 'To whom, Sir Walter, did you bear malice? To the royal children?'

Thus began the great battle.

RALEIGH: Mr Attorney, I pray you to whom, or to what end, speak you all this? I protest I do not understand what a word of this means, except it be to tell me news. What is the treason of Markham and the priests to me?

COKE: I will then come close to you. I will prove you to be the most notorious traitor that ever came to the bar. You are indeed upon the Main, but you have followed them of the Bye, in imitation; I will charge you with the words.

RALEIGH: Your words cannot condemn me; my innocency is my defence. I pray you go to your proofs. Prove against me any one thing of the many wherewith you have charged me, and I will confess all the indictment, and that I am the most horrible traitor that ever lived, and worthy to be crucified with a thousand torments.

COKE: Nay I will prove all; thou art a monster; thou hast an English face, but a Spanish heart. You would have stirred England and Scotland both; you incited the Lord Cobham, as soon as Count Aremberg came into England, to go to him; the night he went, you supped with the Lord Cobham, and he brought you after supper to Durham House, and then the same night by a back way with La Renzi to Count Aremberg, and got from him a promise of money; after this it was arranged that the Lord Cobham should go to Spain and return by Jersey, where you were to meet him to consult about the distribution of money, because Cobham had not so much policy or wickedness as you. Your intent was to set up the Lady Arabella as a titular queen, and to depose our present rightful king, the lineal descendant of Edward IV. You pretend that this money was to forward peace with Spain. Your jargon was peace, which meant Spanish invasion and Scottish subversion.

RALEIGH: All this while you tell me news, Mr Attorney.

COKE: Sir Walter, I cannot blame you, though you be moved.

RALEIGH: Nay, you fall out with yourself; I have said nothing to you; I am in no case to be angry.

Coke warned Raleigh not to provoke him, or 'I will not spare you'. On he went about Raleigh having corrupted Cobham, who was just a simple man from an ancient and noble house, 'never a politician nor swordsman'; about how Raleigh had sent Keymis with the message that a man could not be convicted of treason with only one witness and had warned him against confessing to a preacher. 'Now you shall see the most horrible practices that ever came out of the bottomless pit of the lowest hell ... came this contrivance, think you, out of Cobham's quiver? No, but out of Raleigh's devilish and Machiavellian policy.'

RALEIGH: What is that to me? I do not hear yet that you have spoken one word against me. Here is no treason of mine done; if my Lord Cobham be a traitor, what is that to me?

COKE: All that he did was by thy instigation, thou viper, for I *thou* thee, thou traitor. I will prove thee the rankest traitor in all England.

RALEIGH: No, no, Mr Attorney. I am no traitor. Whether I live or die, I stand as true a subject as any the King hath; you may call me traitor at your pleasure; yet it becomes not a man of quality and virtue to do so, but I take comfort in it, it is all that you can do, for I do not hear you charge me with any treason.

SIR JOHN POPHAM: Sir Walter Raleigh, Mr Attorney speaks out of zeal of his duty for the service of the King; and you for your life; be patient, on both sides.

COKE: I charge Sir Walter Raleigh with contriving and conspiring all this that I have recited; and now I will read my proofs for it.

To use 'thou' instead of 'you' was insulting, as though Coke was speaking to an underling or servant. Raleigh had hit back, insinuating that Coke was no gentleman.

Coke next read out Cobham's confession of 20 July, to which was added the 'O traitor!, O villain!' outburst. Raleigh coolly demanded to see it, and it was shown to him.

RALEIGH: Now, gentlemen of the jury, I beseech you hear me. This is absolutely all the evidence that can be brought against me. This is that which must either condemn me or give the life, which must set me free or send my wife and child to beg their bread about the streets. This is that must prove whether I am a notorious traitor, or a true subject to the King . . .

He absolutely denied ever having heard plots about Arbell. If it were to be proved otherwise, he would be ready to be found guilty of ten thousand treasons. He pointed out that Cobham had repented of what he had said against him and had acknowledged that he had done him wrong.

RALEIGH: Whether to favour or disable my Lord Cobham, you may speak as you will of him, yet he is not such a babe as you make him, but hath dispositions of his own, and passions of such violence that his best friends could never temper them. But 'tis very strange that I, at this time, should be thought to plot with the Lord Cobham, knowing him a man that had neither love nor following in England, and myself at this time having just resigned a place of very best command, the Wardenship of the Stannaries in Cornwall.

Moreover, I was not so bare of sense but I saw, that if ever this state was strong and able to defend itself, it was now. The kingdom of Scotland united, whence we were wont to fear all our troubles; Ireland quieted, where our forces were wont to be divided; Denmark assured, whom before we were want to have in jealousy; the Low Countries, our nearest neighbours, at peace with us; and instead of a lady whom time had surprised, we had now an active king, a lawful successor to the crown, who was able to attend to his own business. I was not such a madman as to make myself in this time a Robin Hood, a Wat Tyler, or a Jack Cade. I knew also that state of Spain well; his weakness, and poorness, and humbleness, at this time. I knew that he was discouraged and dishonoured. I knew that seven times we had repulsed his forces, thrice in Ireland, thrice at sea, and once at Cadiz on his own coast. Thrice had I served against him myself at sea, wherein for my country's sake I had expended of my own properties £40,000 . . .

'A lady whom time had surprised' was to become one of his most quoted phrases, and must have struck home to everyone in that hall. It had been a long speech, delivered with extraordinary ease and restraint.

Cobham's second examination was read out, and the jury was confused. Cecil this time decided to explain. He began:

CECIL: I am divided in myself, and in great dispute what to say of this gentleman at the bar; for it is impossible, be the obligations never so great, but the affections of nature and love show themselves. A former dearness betwixt me and him, tied upon the knots of his virtues, though slacked since by his actions, I cannot but acknowledge, and the most of you know it . . .

There were clear hints here that he believed Raleigh guilty. Raleigh now demanded that Cobham should be brought to the bar, so that he could confront him face to face. It was at this stage that he triumphantly referred to the statutes that had saved Throckmorton. But the court was prepared for this, having of course been forewarned. That loophole had long ago been closed, and the treason laws had been amended. Raleigh argued that it was still unfair that a man should be condemned for treason without two witnesses. He was again overruled. But he still persisted that the common law of England was by trial and witnesses. No, said Popham, it was by examination. 'If three conspire a treason, and they all confess it, here is never a witness, and yet they may all be condemned of treason.' 'I know not, my lord', Raleigh said, 'how you conceive the law; but if you affirm it, it must be a law to all posterity.' 'We do not conceive the law,' Popham answered grandly. 'We *know* the law'.

So Raleigh was to be convicted on hearsay. The trial continued, dragging in declarations by Watson and Brooke, and quoting Raleigh on 13 August when he confirmed that Cobham had offered him 10,000 crowns for 'furthering the peace' between England and Spain. This was mere jargon, Coke said. It was clear that the money was to be used for discontented persons, and Raleigh was to have part of it; he was a discontented person and therefore a traitor.

RALEIGH: It is true my lord Cobham had speech with me about the money and made me an offer; but how and when? Voluntarily one day at dinner, some time before Count Aremberg's coming over. For he and I being at his own board arguing and speaking violently, he for the peace, I against the peace, the Lord Cobham told me that when Count Aremberg came, he would yield such strong arguments for the peace as would satisfy any man; and withal told (as his fashion is to utter things easily) what great sums of money would be given to some councillors for making the peace; and named my Lord Cecil and the Earl of Mar. I answering bade him make no such offer unto them, for by God they would hate him if he did offer it. Now, if after this, my Lord Cobham changed his mind as to the use to be made of the money and, joining with the Lord Grey and the others, had any such treasurable interest as is alleged, what is that to me? They must answer it, not I. The offer of the money to me is nothing, for it was made me before Count Aremberg's coming; the offer made to the others was afterwards. Let me be pinched to death with hot irons if ever I knew the money was to be bestowed on discontented persons.

So Raleigh was admitting that he had been offered money and had not informed the authorities. Here was the great enemy of Spain even considering a Spanish bribe. Henry Howard could not resist weighing in.

HOWARD: Allege me any ground or cause wherefore you gave ear to my Lord Cobham for receiving pensions or money in matters you had no business to deal with.
RALEIGH: Consider, my good lord, I pray you, how could I stop my Lord Cobham's mouth?

This was a weak reply, and again he asked that Cobham should be brought to the court. 'I am here for my life.' The Lord Chief Justice's reply to this might have been concocted by the 20th-century writer Franz Kafka.

POPHAM: There must not such a gap be opened for the destruction of the King as would be if we should grant this. You plead hard for yourself, but the laws plead as hard for the King. Where no circumstances do concur to make a matter probable, then an accuser may be heard; but so many circumstances agreeing and confirming the accusation in this case, the accuser is not to be produced; for having first confessed himself voluntarily, and so charged another person, if we shall now hear him again in person, he may for favour or fear retract about formerly he hath said, and the jury may, by that means, be inveigled.

Coke went back to the examinations of the Bye Plot priest Watson and how he had referred to Jesuits plotting to murder the sovereign and his children, and what Brooke had told him about a conversation that had taken place between Raleigh and Cobham.

COKE: . . . to this effect saying 'There is no way of redress save only one, and that is to take away the king and his cubs', for these were his words as they were to me delivered, 'not leaving one alive'.

RALEIGH: O barbarous! Do you bring the words of these hellish spiders against me? If they, like unnatural villains, used those words, shall I be charged with them?

COKE: Thou art thyself a spider of hell, for thou dost confess the King to be a most sweet and gracious prince, and yet thou hast conspired against him.

And so it went on. Next was brought up the matter of the book which Cobham said had been given to him by Raleigh. This turned out to be by a certain Robert Snagge, and was about the right of Mary Queen of Scots, and therefore James, to the English throne. Raleigh denied giving it to Cobham, but admitted that he had found it in Lord Burghley's study after his death and had borrowed it without permission. Cobham likewise had borrowed it without Raleigh's permission. Cecil at once came to his father's defence. It was his duty, and had been his father's duty, to have such books in his library. He had allowed Raleigh in there to look for some maps and books about Indian discoveries, and Raleigh had abused his trust. 'You did me wrong, Sir Walter Raleigh, to take it thence.' Raleigh said he had brought it away by mistake, mixed up with other papers. There were probably other similar books in his own library containing libels against the late queen.

COKE: You were no councillor of state, Sir Walter, nor I hope never shall be.

CECIL: Sir Walter Raleigh was truly no sworn councillor of state, yet he hath often been called to consultations.

Things were not going well for Raleigh. This was definitely a bad mark. Now the name of Keymis came up, as having carried messages from Raleigh to Cobham in the Tower. Raleigh maintained there had never been such messages, and that such a confession from Keymis had been extracted through torture. This caused a sensation, and Howard denied that the rack had been used: 'The King gave charge that no rigour should be used'.

THE OTHER COMMISSIONERS: We protest before God there was no such matter intended to our knowledge.

RALEIGH: Was not the keeper of the rack sent for, and he threatened with it?

WAAD: When Mr Solicitor and myself examined Keymis, we told him he deserved the rack, but did not threaten him with it.

COMMISSIONERS: That was more than we knew.

Keymis had of course taken messages, but Raleigh had managed to twist the story round in his own favour.

Arbell was mentioned. This was the cue for a dramatic intervention. The elderly Lord Admiral, Lord Nottingham, appeared from the back of the court with Arbell herself on his arm. 'The lady', he announced, 'doth here protest, upon her salvation, that she never dealt in any of these things, and so she willed me to tell the court.' These words could not have been altogether welcome to the prosecution, as they removed the one person for whom the plotters had been ready to risk their lives. Arbell, remembering no doubt the fate of her cousin Lady Jane Grey, had her own head to save. But it made a mockery of Raleigh not being allowed to call in his accuser, and he demanded his presence once more.

HOWARD: Sir Walter, you have heard that it cannot be granted; pray importune us no longer.
RALEIGH: Nay, my lord, it toucheth my life, which I value at as high a rate as your lordship does yours.

Undaunted, Coke produced a witness of his own: one of the most ludicrous episodes in the whole trial. A ship's pilot called Dyer said that he was just back from Lisbon and had been asked some time in July if the new King of England had been crowned yet. Dyer had replied that he did not know. 'Nay,' said the Portuguese, 'your king should never be crowned, for Don Cobham and Don Raleigh will cut his throat before he come to be crowned.'

Raleigh was rightly outraged. 'This is the saying of some wild Jesuit or beggarly priest, but what proof is it against me?' 'It shows that your treason had wings,' said Coke.

Sergeant Phillips wound up for the prosecution, and it seemed as if the trial was coming to an end. Raleigh still maintained that nothing had been proved against him directly, only on circumstantial evidence. He turned to Coke:

RALEIGH: Mr Attorney, have you done?
COKE: Yes, if you have no more to say.
RALEIGH: If you have done, then I have somewhat more to say.
COKE: Nay, I will have the last word for the King.
RALEIGH: Nay, I will have the last word for my life.
COKE: Go to, I will lay thee upon thy back for the confidentest traitor that ever came to the bar.
CECIL: Be not so impatient, good Mr Attorney, give him leave to speak.
COKE: I am the King's sworn servant, and must speak; if I may not be patiently heard, you discourage the King's counsel, and encourage traitors.

Coke now sat down in 'chafe' or huff, and refused to speak again until the Commissioners urged him to continue. After more fuss he got up and went over all the evidence again. Raleigh, fed up with the repetitions, interrupted him and protested that he was doing him wrong. Coke turned on him in a rage.

COKE: Thou art the most vile and execrable traitor that ever lived.

RALEIGH: You speak indiscreetly, uncivilly, and barbarously.

COKE: Thou art an odious fellow; thy name is hateful to all the realm of England for thy pride.

RALEIGH: It will go near to prove a measuring cast between you and me, Mr Attorney.

COKE: Well, I will now lay you open for the greatest traitor that ever was. This, my lords, is he that hath set forth so gloriously his services against the Spaniard, and hath ever so detested him! This is he who hath written a book against the peace! I will make it appear to the world that there never lived a viler viper on the face of the earth than thou. I will show you wholly Spanish, and that you offered yourself a pensioner to Spain for intelligence . . .

The mood of the spectators had changed. There were even groans when Coke got up to speak, and there were hisses. They had come to enjoy the spectacle of a great and famous man being destroyed, but instead Raleigh had behaved with courage and dignity, and they now pitied him.

Coke was about to produce his trump. He brought out a letter from Cobham that he had actually written *since* his arrival at Winchester, probably only the day before. In this he told of the apple being thrown through his window and what he had written in response. He said that soon after Aremberg's arrival in England, Raleigh had asked him to procure an annual pension of £1,500 from Spain in exchange for intelligence. He also said that but for Raleigh he would never have dealt with Aremberg. Raleigh was the original cause of his ruin.

Raleigh was clearly taken aback by this letter, but after a while seemed to pull himself together. 'You have heard a strange tale of a strange man,' he said. 'You shall see how many souls this Cobham hath, and the King shall judge by our deaths which of us is the perfidious man.' From his pocket he drew the 'very good' letter from Cobham which he had kept for such an emergency. In spite of Coke's objection, he passed it to Cecil to read out loud, as he was familiar with Cobham's handwriting. Cecil did so, but it obviously made no difference to the case.

Addressing the jury for the last time, Raleigh admitted that he had been offered £1,500 a year pension for intelligence, but insisted that he had never attempted to accept it. He also admitted that it was his fault to have concealed it. 'But for attempting or conspiring any treason against the King or the State, I still deny it to the death, and it can never be proved against me.'

The admission of the pension offer merely reinforced the rest of Cobham's accusations. By this time Raleigh knew he was lost. One wonders what went on in the mind of Lord Henry Howard, as a crypto-Catholic who long ago had received a regular Spanish pension. Only a few months after the trial when peace was made with Spain, Cecil accepted a pension from Spain of £1,000 a year, which was subsequently raised to £1,500. The Earls of Nottingham, Dorset and Devonshire also accepted pensions, though the Earl of Suffolk refused (the Spaniards paid it to his avaricious wife instead). Howard, when he became Earl of Northampton, also received £1,000 a year, as well as gifts of jewels.

The jury took less than fifteen minutes to reach the verdict of guilty, which Raleigh received with his usual calm and dignity. Before pronouncing the sentence, Popham made a long speech, regretting that a man of Raleigh's intelligence had been entangled with so many treasons. 'I grieve to find that a man of your quality would have sold yourself for a spy to the enemy of your country for £1,500 a year.' Raleigh's two great vices, he said, had been 'eager ambitions' and 'corrupt covetousness'. Not only that:

You have been taxed by the world, Sir Walter Raleigh, with holding heathenish, blasphemous, atheistical, and profane opinions, which I do not like to repeat, because Christian ears cannot endure to hear them; but the authors and maintainers of such opinions cannot be suffered to live in any Christian commonwealth. If these opinions be not yours, you shall do well, before you leave the world, to protest against them, and not to die with these imputations upon you. But if you do hold such opinions, then I beseech you renounce them, and ask God forgiveness for them as you hope for another life.

He asked him not to let Hariot, nor any such 'doctor', persuade him that there was no eternal life in heaven – 'lest you find an eternity of hell-torments'. The fact that he had dared to advise Cobham not to confess to a preacher had been most irreligious and wicked.

Poor Hariot, everyone's bogeyman. Popham continued: 'It now only remaineth to pronounce the judgement, which I would to God you had not to receive this day of me; for if the fear of God in you had corresponded to your other great parts, you might have lived to be a singular good subject to His Majesty.'

He put on his black cap. And then came the terrible sentence.

That you shall be led from hence to the place whence you came, there to remain until the day of execution; and from thence you shall be drawn upon a hurdle through the open streets to the place of execution, there to be hanged and cut down alive, and your body shall be opened, your heart and bowels plucked out, and your privy members cut off, and thrown into the fire before your eyes; then your head to be stricken off from your body, and your body shall be divided into four quarters, to be disposed of at the King's pleasure. And God have mercy upon your soul.

Raleigh obtained leave to speak to the Commissioners, to ask them to intercede with the King, that his death might be honourable and not ignominious. Given his rank, he could expect to be spared those grisly tortures – tortures which he had watched many times when he was Captain of the Queen's Guard.

Waiting for the End
1603

It was said that after the trial some members of the jury came up to Raleigh and begged forgiveness on their knees.[1] Cecil was even supposed to have had tears in his eyes. The reaction throughout the country was extraordinary, as news spread of Raleigh's heroic demeanour against Coke's rantings and of the obvious flimsiness of the prosecution. As the magisterial 19th-century historian Samuel Gardiner was to say: 'With unerring judgement posterity has reversed the verdict of the Winchester jury.'[2] In 1650 Anthony Weldon was writing: 'To this day it could never be known that ever there was any such treason, but mere trick of State to remove such blocks out of the way.' In 1904 G. M. Trevelyan, speaking of the Jacobean legal system, said: 'The prejudice of the court against the prisoner led to results like the condemnation of Raleigh for a crime he would have abhorred to commit, and of hundreds of witches for crimes no one can commit at all.'[3] Rumours of all sorts circulated against the verdict. Weldon repeated one of them, that the 'villain Wade' had got Cobham to sign a blank sheet of paper and had then himself written the supposed charges above. One of the judges, Gawdy, was supposed to have said on his deathbed: 'Sir Walter Raleigh's trial injured and degraded the justice of England.'[4]

Sir Dudley Carleton wrote to his friend John Chamberlain that 'never was a man so hated and so popular in so short a time', and that Sir Walter Raleigh had 'answered with that temper, wit, learning, courage and judgement, that, save it went with the hazard of his life, it was the happiest day he had ever spent.'[5] Sir Thomas Overbury, who wrote a report on the trial, said of Raleigh that he had behaved in a manner 'humble but not prostrate ... affable but not fawning ... persuading with reason, not distemperedly importuning with conjuration.' Faced with Coke's crude tirades and insults he had never once been 'overtaken with passion'.[6]

Two courtiers scurried off to the King at Wilton, with what would have been received as bad news. One declared that 'never any man spake so well in times past, nor would do in the world to come'.[7] The other, a Scot, told him that 'whereas, when he saw him first, he was so led to the common hatred, that he would have gone a hundred miles to have him seen him hanged, he would, ere he parted, have gone a thousand to have saved his life.'[8]

It was significant that because of the unease and unanswered questions that had emerged, the trials of Cobham and Grey were postponed. It must have been obvious that Raleigh knew more and that he was anxious to avoid telling the whole truth. He had obviously lied about Lawrence Keymis. But it was hardly conceivable that a man with his reputation should dream of supporting a Spanish invasion, or even of putting the unremarkable Arbell on the throne. All the same Cobham's last letter contained dramatic new accusations: about the pension of £1,500 and secret information to be given to Aremberg on Raleigh's 'coming from Greenwich one night'. And why should Cobham be prepared to incriminate himself at the same time as Raleigh? And could it have been really possible, as Cobham insisted, that Raleigh had been the original instigator or stirrer up of Cobham's discontent?

Cobham was interviewed again on 22 November and gave more sensational information about that return from Greenwich. He claimed that Raleigh had suggested that the King of Spain should be urged to send an army to Milford Haven. For years the English government had realized that the best point of invasion for the Spaniards would be Milford Haven, and its very name in time of war stoked up fears. This was where Essex had wanted Mountjoy to land the army from Ireland. How Coke would have loved to set off such a firework! At least it was now decided that the plot about Arabella had been all in George Brooke's imagination.

The Commissioners made a brief visit to Raleigh's cell, to confront him with this latest development. He was evidently shocked, and suddenly he seemed to lose his composure. He wrote a joint letter to the Commissioners:[9] 'It was so late ere your Lordships came, as I could not, in good manners, beseech you of longer time. It was your pleasure to tell me of a new accusation – of the landing of Spaniards at Milford Haven.' This, he said, was just another ploy of Cobham's, in his 'cruel desire to destroy me, hoping thereby to exterminate his own offences.'* Raleigh had already blamed Frances Howard, Lady Kildare, Cobham's wife, for urging Cobham to speak out against him as a way of mitigating his own guilt, perhaps saving him from the block. That old despair, which had made him contemplate

* Milford Haven is never mentioned in Spanish papers in this connection. It was here that Henry Tudor landed in 1485.

suicide, had now returned. He asked for at least a year's stay of execution. 'And if I may not beg a pardon or a life, yet let me beg a time at the King's merciful hands. Let me have one year to give to God in a prison and to serve him. I trust his pitiful nature will have compassion on my soul, and it is my soul that beggeth a time of the King.'

He wrote abject letters, of which he was soon to be ashamed, to individual nobles, to Cecil and very likely to the King, who must have been glad to read the grovelling of this once powerful and haughty servant of Queen Elizabeth. The Bishop of Winchester, Thomas Bilson, visited both Cobham and Raleigh, ostensibly for spiritual reasons but in reality to obtain further information (just as Raleigh would have suspected). Cobham insisted on the Milford Haven story; Raleigh said that he did not deny 'lending a patient ear' to Cobham's unwise and lavish projects but otherwise his stance was adamant. At any rate the Bishop decided that Raleigh was at least nominally a Christian.

That Greenwich night could well have been the flashpoint of the whole affair. It is easy to imagine Raleigh boiling with frustration, furious at the favours given to his rivals, realizing that he was faced with financial ruin, appalled that Cecil, the man who had been his friend, should not stand up for him. He could have just received the peremptory and insulting order to clear out of Durham House. He might well have burst out with indiscretions that put ideas into Cobham's foolish head, including those secret details, which evidently had been about James's wish for peace with Spain. If there were to be peace with Spain, he could also as Gardiner suggested have decided in his bitterness that he might as well apply for a Spanish pension. Under the circumstances the idea that he suggested an invasion seems wild. Yet he never denied the proposed meeting at Jersey.

The evidence of La Renzi about being present when a letter from Aremberg arrived, and Cobham going upstairs with Raleigh, does, however, ring suspiciously true. As Mark Nicholls has said, Raleigh's eclipse appears to have owed a great deal to ill fortune, and to the fact that he was regarded as politically expendable.

The importance of Raleigh's trial is that it was a first flicker in the change of attitude towards rights of individuals against the power of the mighty State. Here was an individual fighting for his life and brilliantly defending himself against ruthless and implacable bias, and condemned to a hideous death on presumption and conjecture. In this way the fact that he had lied and that he had not admitted to all that he knew is beside the point.

*

Queen Anne was supposed to have asked her husband to save Raleigh's life. The Spanish ambassador also was said to have interceded; if true, this again could have been thought suspicious. Lady Pembroke, Sir Philip Sidney's sister, perhaps urged on by Adrian Gilbert who sometimes worked for her, sent her handsome son to James to plead for Raleigh.

Bess wrote a confused and pleading letter to 'the most honourable my Lord Cisseil' (Cecil), which in translation began:[10]

If the grievèd tears of an unfortunate woman may receive any favour, or the unspeakable sorrows of my dead heart may receive any comfort, then let my sorrows come before you – which, if you truly knew, I assure myself you would pity me, but most especially your poor unfortunate friend which relieth wholly on your honourable and wonted favour.

She implored him, in the name of their young sons, and in memory of past friendships, to speak to the King about her Walter:

For Christ's sake, which rewardeth all mercies, pity his just cause; and God for his infinite mercy bless you for ever, and work in the King's mercy. I am not able, I protest before God, to stand on my trembling legs, otherwise I would have waited now on you; or be directed wholly by you.

She that will truly honour you in all misfortune, E Ralegh

Cobham's behaviour at his trial was very different from Raleigh's. 'Never', wrote Carleton, 'was seen so poor and abject a spirit.'[11] He heard his indictment with much 'fear and trembling'. He still blamed Raleigh for everything, and when asked to explain the contradiction between his two letters, one excusing Raleigh and the other condemning him, he insisted that the last was the truth, and that the other had been 'drawn from him by device in the Tower by young Harvey, the Lieutenant's son, who Raleigh had corrupted and carried intelligence between them'.

Cobham was tried by a court of thirty of his fellow peers, who did not take long to find him guilty. After receiving his sentence, Cobham 'begged a great while for life and favour, alleging his confession a meritorious act.'

Raleigh now decided to write to the King himself, a grovelling letter.

... I do therefore on the knees of my heart, beseech your Majesty to take council from your own sweet and merciful disposition, and to remember that I have loved your Majesty now twenty years, for which your Majesty hath yet given me no reward

... Save me, therefore, most merciful Prince, that I may owe your Majesty my life itself; than which there can be no greater debt. Lend it me at least, my Sovereign Lord, that I may pay it again for your service when your Majesty shall please. If the law destroy me, your Majesty shall put me out of your power; and I shall have then none to fear, none to reverence but the King of Kings.

The two priests, Watson and Clarke, were executed on 29 November, 'very bloodily handled'. Clarke had to be pinioned as he struggled and screamed while being disembowelled and castrated. Their four quarters were displayed at the gates into Winchester, and their heads were stuck on a turret of the castle. Brooke was treated more mercifully in that he was merely beheaded, on 6 December. Before putting his head on the block he made a cryptic remark that there was 'somewhat yet hidden, which one day will appear for my justification'.

Cobham, Grey and Markham were to be executed on the morning of Friday 10 December, Raleigh on the Monday following. As the day of his death approached Raleigh recovered his nerve and, incredibly, wrote one of his finest and most famous poems, 'The Passionate Man's Pilgrimage':

> Give me my scallop-shell of quiet,
> My staff of faith to walk upon,
> My scrip of joy, immortal diet,
> My bottle of salvation,
> My gown of glory, hope's true gage,
> And thus I'll take my pilgrimage.
>
> Blood must be my body's balmer,
> No other balm will there be given
> Whilst my soul, like a quiet palmer,
> Travels to the land of heaven,
> Over the silver mountains,
> Where spring the nectar fountains;
> And there I'll kiss
> The bowl of bliss,
> And drink my eternal fill
> On every milken hill.
> My soul will be a-dry before,
> But after it will ne'er thirst more.
>
> And by the happy blissful way
> More peaceful pilgrims I shall see,

That have shook off their gowns of clay,
And go apparelled fresh like me.
I'll bring them first
To slake their thirst,
And then to taste those nectar suckets
At the clear wells
Where sweetness dwells,
Drawn up by saints in crystal buckets.

And when our bottles and all we
Are filled with immortality,
Then the holy paths we'll travel
Strewed with rubies thick as gravel,
Ceilings of diamonds, sapphire floors,
High walls of coral, and pearl bowers . . .

And this is my eternal plea
To him that made heaven, earth, and sea:
Seeing my flesh must die so soon,
And want a head to dine next noon,
Just at the stroke, when my veins start and spread,
Set on my soul an everlasting head.
Then am I ready, like a palmer fit,
To tread those blest paths which before I writ.

James, with a warped sense of humour, had decided on a cruel game. He had signed the death warrants on 8 December and had sent them to the Sheriff, Sir Benjamin Tichbourne, but on the day before he had written a stay of execution for Cobham, Grey and Markham and this he secretly gave to a young Scottish Groom of the Bedchamber, John Gibb, with instructions to hand it to Tichbourne on the day of their execution, preferably when on the scaffold.

It was a cold and drizzly December day. Raleigh was watching from a tower above the castle yard. 'A fouler day could scarcely be picked out, or fitter for such a tragedy,' said Carleton.[12] Markham was to be the first to have his head chopped off. Apparently he had thought that he was going to be reprieved, and when confronted with the headman on the scaffold he recoiled in horror. Someone offered him a napkin to put round his eyes, but he threw it away, saying that he could look upon death without a blush. He knelt to say his prayers, and just as the axe was about to be raised there was shouting from the crowd. It was young Gibb who had been unable to get to the front because he had been made to stand among the boy apprentices. Frantically he called out that he had a message from the King and managed to attract the attention of one of the magistrates, Sir John Hayes, who was standing on the scaffold. Hayes climbed down and received the message. He conferred with Tichbourne, and Markham was told that as he was evidently unprepared for death he had been granted two hours' respite. He was thereupon sent to the Great Hall and locked inside.

Grey was next. He emerged, accompanied by a group of courtier friends. His appearance was quite different. 'Such gaiety and cheer was in his countenance that he seemed a dapper young bridgegroom.' He made a speech saying that his ancestors had spent many lives in their Princes' service, and he could not therefore beg his. 'God send the King', he cried, 'a long and prosperous reign, and your lordships all honour.' Then he knelt down and prayed for half an hour. Tichbourne seemed to have entered the mood of James's harlequinade. He now gave Grey the same message, and had him locked inside the Great Hall.

Then it was Cobham. He came looking sprightly and unconcerned, very different from his behaviour at his trial. Perhaps he was relieved not to see blood on the straw of the scaffold. In his speech he swore 'upon the hope of his soul's resurrection' that all he had said about Raleigh was true. He knelt to pray, staying on his knees for so long that the crowd began shouting catcalls. When at last he had finished he was told by the sheriff that his execution had been stayed. The two others were summoned, and all three men were made to stand together like actors on a stage at the end of a play. Tichbourne, evidently enjoying the sadistic game, asked them whether their crimes were not heinous, and whether they had been justly tried and convicted. When they had all agreed, Tichbourne cried in a loud voice for all to hear: 'Then see the mercy of your Prince, who of himself hath sent hither a countermand and given you your lives.' So they were not to die. The crowd clapped and cheered, duly applauding the King's 'mercy'.

Raleigh, looking down from his tower, so Carleton wrote, must have had hammers working in his head, wondering what was the meaning of it all. According to the Comte de Beaumont, someone said that he was seen to smile. If so, it could have been a smile of relief, and for himself hope.

Markham was sentenced to be exiled, as had been Copley in an earlier trial. Cobham and Grey were to be imprisoned.

Raleigh was still kept in suspense. Typically he at once dashed off a letter to the Commissioners.

We have today beheld a work of so great mercy and for so great offences the like have been seldom, if ever, known . . . And although myself have not been brought so near the very brink of the grave, yet I trust that so great compassion will extend itself towards me also, every way being hopeless as the rest, and who shall as truly pay that most great debt of borrowed life on any that ever hath or ever shall be therefore bound . . .

By Sunday, the day before he was due to be executed, he still had not received any response about his fate. As he prepared himself for death, he wrote a farewell letter to Bess, a beautiful and agonized piece of writing, one of the great love letters from any husband to wife:[13]

You shall now receive, my dear wife, my last words in these my last lines. My love I send you, that you may keep it when I am dead, and my counsel, that you may remember it when I am no more. I would not with my last will present you with sorrows, dear Bess. Let them go into the grave with me and be buried in the dust. And, seeing it is not the will of God that ever I shall see you in this life, bear my destruction gently, and with a heart like thyself.

First, I send you all the thanks which my heart can conceive, or my pen express, for your many travails and cares taken for me, which, though they have not taken effect as you wished, yet my debt is to you not the less; but pay it I never shall in this world.

Secondly, I beseech you, for the love you bare me living, that you do not hide yourself many days, but by your travail seek to help your miserable fortunes and the right of your poor child. Thy mourning cannot avail me: I am but dust.

He told her that he had made a conveyance for Wat the year before.

And I trust that my blood will quench their malice that desire my slaughter, and that they will not also seek to kill you and yours with extreme poverty. To what friend to direct thee I know not, for all mine have left me in the true time of trial; and I plainly perceive that my death was determined from the first day. Most sorry I am, as God knows, that being thus surprised with death, I can leave you no better estate; I meant you all my office of wines, or all I could have purchased by selling it, half my stuff and jewels – but some few for the boy. But God hath prevented all my determinations, and even that great God that ruleth all in all. If you can live free from want, care for no more, for the rest is but vanity. Love God, and begin betimes to repose yourself on Him. Therein you shall find true and lasting riches, and endless comfort. For the rest, when you have travailed and wearied your thoughts over all sorts of wordly cogitations, you shall but sit down by sorrow in the end. Teach your son also to serve and fear God while he is young, that the fear of God may grow up in him. Then will God be a husband unto you, and a father to him; a husband and a father which cannot be taken from you.

He listed some money owed to him, including arrears in the 'farm of wines' which had accrued before the patent had been transferred to Nottingham. Those he hoped would pay his debts.

When I am gone, no doubt you shall be sought unto by many, for the world thinks that I was very rich. But take heed of the pretences of men, and of their affections, for they last not, but in honest and worthy men. And no greater misery can befall you in this life than to become a prey, and afterwards to be despised. I speak it, God knows, not to dissuade you from marriage – for that will be best for you, both in respect of God and the world. As for me, I am no more yours, nor you mine. Death hath cut us asunder; and God hath divided me from the world, and you from me.

Remember your poor child for his father's sake, who chose you and loved you in his happiest times.

He now regretted those shameful letters that he had written to the Commissioners and others.

Get those letters, if it be possible, which I writ to the Lords, wherein I sued for my life; but God knoweth that it was for you and yours that I desired it. But it is true that I disdain myself for begging it. And know it, dear wife, that your son is the child of a true man. And one, who in his own respect, despiseth Death, and all his misshapen and ugly forms.

I cannot write much. God knows how hardly I steal this time when all sleep, and it is also high time that I should separate my thoughts from the world. Beg my dead body, which living was denied thee, and either lay it Sherborne, if the land continue, or in Exeter church, by my father and mother.* I can write no more. Time and Death call me away.

The everlasting, infinite, powerful, and omnipotent God, that Almighty God, that is goodness itself, mercy itself, the true life and true light, keep thee and thine, and have mercy on me, and teach me to forgive my persecutors and accusers; and send us to meet in His glorious kingdom. My dear wife, farewell. Bless my poor boy. Pray

---

* Bess had not been allowed to visit him in the Tower, nor presumably at Winchester. For a long while historians assumed that by 'Exeter church' Raleigh meant Exeter Cathedral. But in the register of St Mary Major at Exeter the burial of 'Walter Rawlye gentleman' on 23 February 1581 is recorded. Raleigh's mother died in 1594, and her will shows that she had been living in the parish of St Mary Major, where a number of Gilberts were also living (p. 212).

for me. My true God hold you both in his arms. Written with the dying hand of sometime thy husband, not now, alas, overthrown.

Yours that was; but now not my own, W: R:

The next morning he was told that he had been reprieved. 'And therefore', James triumphantly told his courtiers, 'I have saved the life of them all.' By 16 December Raleigh was back in the Bloody Tower; he was to remain there for the next thirteen years.

Life in the Bloody Tower
1604

Raleigh, Cobham and Grey were delivered to the Tower on 16 December 1603. Raleigh returned to the Bloody Tower, on the south side by the river, once part of Henry III's watergate and next to the massive Wakefield Tower where Henry III had sometimes stayed. The legend was that both the Duke of Clarence and the two Princes, Edward V and his brother, had been murdered in the Bloody Tower. Until a few years before it had been known as the Garden Tower, since it adjoined the garden of the Lieutenant's lodgings.

Life for those who were not close prisoners was much easier than in Tudor times. There was almost a village atmosphere. A certain freedom of movement was now permitted, and long-term prisoners were allowed servants and visitors. Raleigh could have his wife and ten-year-old son living with him, and they had three servants: a serving man called Dean, a maid for Bess, and Raleigh's secretary John Talbot, who also acted as tutor for Wat. A waterman called Owen brought ale and beer.

Raleigh was about fifty, not in good health, and work was needed to make the Bloody Tower more habitable. It was also too small to accommodate his family, so an upper floor was to be added. Thus for the first months he was allocated the Brick Tower, used by the Master of Ordnance but with accommodation for persons of rank. It would seem that Wat was in lodgings nearby.

Cobham was kept a safe distance away, in the Beauchamp Tower on the west side, with the use of an adjoining garden. This had been built for Edward I, and was kept for important political prisoners. Evidently some work had to be done there too, as an existing window dates from 1604. He was allowed two servants, in addition to a visiting cook and an apothecary. His wife was also permitted to visit, had either she or he wished it, which was exceedingly unlikely. Grey was on the east side of the Inner Ward with the liberty of the King's gardens. He too was allowed two servants, as well as a barber who came daily. As he was not married, his mother and sister were regular visitors.

Another prisoner but with less freedom, was Florence MacCarthy,

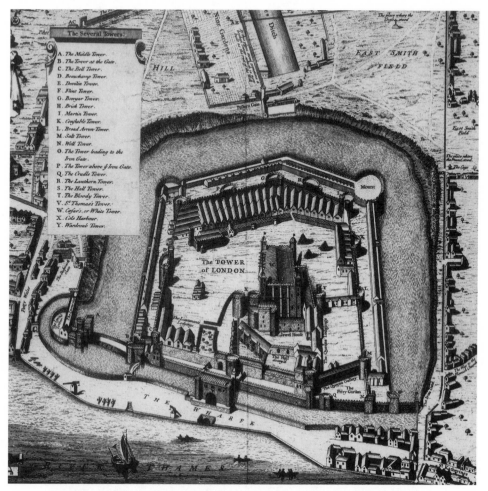

The Tower of London from A True and Exact Draught of the Tower Liberties, *1596, by Gulielmus Haiward and J. Gascoyne. In front is Traitor's Gate. The Bloody Tower has the small archway behind; on Raleigh's arrival two storeys were added. To its left are the Lieutenant's lodgings and garden.*

Raleigh's old foe from his Irish days. Very likely they made contact through messengers, as MacCarthy was writing the mythic history of Ireland, a subject which interested Raleigh.

Cobham and Grey were allowed £416 a year for food, coal and candles, but Raleigh being a knight got only £208. He complained about this, and as a result all three were given an extra £100 a year. There were also special allowances for clothing and medicines. The Lieutenant of the Tower was responsible for making the payments and was reimbursed by the Exchequer, which in turn recouped from the sale of prisoners' assets. Traitors' lands were automatically confiscated, but in Raleigh's case he had already arranged for his Sherborne estate to be conveyed to his son, but giving himself a life interest, and it was this that would now be forfeited to the Crown. In Cobham's case, the majority of his property was entailed, and a young cousin was the heir; again income from his life interest would go to the Crown. Grey lost everything.

Legally Raleigh, Cobham and Grey were considered dead, but all three – Raleigh especially – felt that they had hopes of an eventual reprieve. Raleigh never admitted guilt, protesting his innocence, and such was his unquenchable vanity remained convinced that the country needed and deserved his talents. The government for its part was well aware of his new-found popularity and intellectual reputation, and was prepared to be reasonably lenient.

As soon as he arrived at the Tower he wrote another letter to the King, one that has also been much copied. Cecil had asked Sir George Harvey to wish Raleigh well, which must be why a draft of the letter in Raleigh's hand was found among Harvey's papers.[1]

The life which I had, most mighty Prince, the law hath taken from me, and I am now the same earth and dust out of which I was made . . . Name, blood, gentility or estate I have none; no not so much as a being, no not so much as *vita plantae*. I have only a penitent soul in a body of iron, which moveth towards the lodestone of Death, and cannot be withheld from touching it, unless your Majesty's mercy turn the point towards it which repelleth . . . This being the first letter which ever your Majesty received from a dead man, I humbly submit myself to the will of my supreme lord and shall willingly and patiently suffer what his great and generous heart shall determine.

It was a long letter and as ever he insisted that he had always honoured, loved and admired James.

Cecil was now on easier terms with Raleigh (in theory at least), and he did make some important efforts to protect his interests. Guilt inevitably must have played a part. Soon Raleigh was sending him an anguished plea on behalf of Bess, reminding him that the King had promised that she would be allowed to keep her personal chattels.[2] But now tenants at Sherborne were refusing to pay rents, and coppices were being cut down. People were even breaking into the house. Later he was to say that his debts were over £3,000, and the value of his goods would not nearly cover them. To his utmost dismay Meere had reared up again, 'that so infamous and detested a wretch', and was busy cutting down trees to pay his own debts.

In fact the King did keep his word, and this may well have been because of a letter to him from a Thomas Morgan, who had acted as Mary Stuart's agent in Paris, written before the Winchester trial. In this Morgan had said that Lady Raleigh's father 'was a Protestant, but yet in his time did very grateful service in England to you and your mother; which should lead you to have compassion upon her in case he [Raleigh] suffers death.'[3]

Bess, as a proud Throckmorton, was certainly not to be humbled. She swept grandly in and out of the Tower in her coach. She also lashed at Henry Howard, accusing him of malice towards her husband. In return, Howard wrote to remind her that Raleigh had never lost the opportunity of 'shooting me through and through so long as he had any powder left', and that Raleigh himself had shown malice towards Essex, still considered a national hero.

Very likely Howard's letter was intended to be shown first to the King, who by now had already granted him the precedence of a duke's son. In it he wrote:[4]

I could thank your Ladyship for putting me in mind of the griefs and sorrows of my own honourable family (because nothing more contenteth and pleaseth the dispositions of men than to look back to the rocks and billows of the sea after they are arrived in safe harbour) if I did not find this warning powered with many grains of . . . bitterness . . . none of these committed thither nor convicted after they came thither upon so just grounds as we committed Sir Walter.

Bess, being a mere commoner, and the wife of a commoner convicted of treason, had been suitably snubbed, or so he must have thought.

The handing over of the seal of the Duchy of Cornwall, which Raleigh had taken with him into the Tower, was a symbolic act that caused him almost the greatest pain. On 14 January the Earl of Pembroke had received the Stewardship of the Duchy and the Wardenship of the Stannaries, and Raleigh was outraged when he sent a servant to collect the seal which, he pointed out, had been ceremoniously received from the very hands of Queen Elizabeth. He therefore sent it direct to Cecil asking him to present it personally to the King.

Cecil put a stop to the depredations at Sherborne, and also arranged for a trust to be drawn up, with John Shelbury and Robert Smythe as trustees, in order to supervise the payment of Raleigh's debts and the maintenance of Bess and Wat. This was very satisfactory, as both men were good friends of Raleigh. Shelbury had been managing the wine licences since the break with Sanderson, and as Raleigh put it was a 'man I can better entreat than I known how to reward'.[5]

The Lord Admiral Howard, Earl of Nottingham, was trying to claim for himself arrears of payments in the wine licences before they had even been granted to him. Bess was determined to see Cecil about this iniquity. In a letter she pointed out that the Lord Admiral had already received the sum of £6,000 and was to get £3,000 a year 'by my husband's fall' – 'And since it pleaseth God that his Lordship shall build upon our ruins, which we never suspected, yet the portion is great and I trust sufficient out of one poor gentleman's fortune to take from us the debts past, which your Lordship knows were stayed from us, by a proclamation before my husband was suspected of any offence.'[6] Attached to the letter was a list of eighteen distinguished ladies who backed her.

At the same time Raleigh told the Privy Council that he had been forced to sell the 'rich hangings' at Durham House for £500 to the Lord Admiral, who also seems to have had his eye on a very grand bed – but this had already been sold for £300 to Cobham when Durham House was being emptied.[7] As for his plate, 'which was very fair', and valued at £800, this had been pawned to the goldsmith Cheyney of Lombard Street, and it was impossible to redeem it.* He pointed out that his income from Jersey, the Stannaries, and the half share with his brother in the Rangership of Gillingham Forest and the Lieutenancy of Portland Castle had been at least £3,000 a year.

Thus we understand that Raleigh's income before the arrival of James, and taking into account the wine licences, had been at least £6,000 a year, apart from any rents from other properties besides Sherborne, privateering and suchlike. It was at this stage that he succeeded in being granted another £100 a year as his pension allowance in the Tower. And Cecil did block the arrears in the wine payments to the greedy Lord Admiral.

The three prisoners had to be moved out of the Tower to the Fleet prison in readiness for the Sovereign's annual visit at Easter. This was also a time when amnesties were granted, and there were some releases, but none for the newcomers. In normal times James would have expected to stay in the Tower, but this was not to be the case because of the danger from plague, now re-erupting. For that same reason there were to be no processions to and from Westminster. The journeys had to be by royal barge. Nevertheless there was plenty of pomp, and James entered under a gorgeous canopy and carried by six members of the Privy Council (such were the duties of

* p. 368.

402

Ministers of the Crown in those days). The entertainments included bull-baiting and lions being set upon by mastiffs.[8]

Raleigh was in the Fleet for two and a half weeks. He was relieved on his return to find the Bloody Tower ready for occupation, but against that he also discovered that the citizens who had been let in from the streets to cheer the King had left behind the plague. He at once complained to Cecil, telling him that all the time he had been in the Fleet Wat had been sleeping in a room next to a woman with a running plague sore, and whose child had recently died from the disease – there had only been a 'paper wall' between them.[9] Bess had therefore snatched Wat away, and had found lodgings on Tower Hill, near All Hallows Church.

Raleigh's rooms on the first floor in the Bloody Tower have in modern times been restored with contemporary furnishings, and give a very good idea of what they must have looked like. One room was partitioned off as a bedchamber. Mullioned windows that still exist date from 1604, and the patterned tiles are original. The portcullis and its machinery for the water-gate below were (and still are) left intact. It was all a far cry from the grandeur of Durham House and Sherborne Castle, but the great open fireplaces must have given a certain comfort. It was an ideal atmosphere for the creative flowing from his pen which was soon to develop.

Bess sometimes stayed with him, and it was here in the Bloody Tower that another child was conceived. It was to be a boy, called Carew, like Raleigh's brother, and with the ever loyal Richard Carew of Antony, author of the *Survey of Cornwall*, as godfather. The boy was probably born in the lodging house on Tower Hill, but in the register for 1605 at the chapel of St Peter ad Vincula on the green within the Tower we read: 'Carew Rawley was baptized ye 15th of February the sonne of S. Walter Rawley'.

Raleigh took his exercise along the top of an inner wall. Striding up and down in a long black cloak and wearing a velvet and lace cap, jewelled buttons no doubt flashing, he became one of the sights of London, and crowds gathered to watch him from the wharf below, or from ships, and he most certainly would have acknowledged them. He seemed to have had plenty of visitors, including Keymis who had been released on New Year's Day, Hariot, George Carew, Shelbury, Alexander Brett, his physician Dr Peter Turner, the jeweller Peter Vanlore, even Indians who had been brought on various expeditions from Guiana and Virginia – indeed some of these Indians are supposed to have been lodged within the Tower precincts and to have gone to him 'for instruction'. After a while Raleigh also asked for a preacher, Dr Hawthorne, and 'three boys in ordinary' for help in serving.

There was hardly any need for Harvey to be asked to wish Raleigh well.

His whole attitude had changed, and he was obviously fascinated by his famous prisoner, frequently asking him to dine. He allowed the door from the Bloody Tower into his garden to be kept perpetually open, so that Raleigh could plant out his special herbs and shrubs, including tobacco. At the end of the garden there was a lath and plaster hut, which had been latterly used as a hen-house but had once been Bishop Latimer's prison before Queen Mary had him burnt. Harvey gave Raleigh permission to have the hut repaired and to use it for his chemical and medicinal experiments.

Raleigh would rise at dawn. It was said that his servant Dean would take an hour dressing his hair and curling his moustache and beard; his vanity had not left him, or perhaps he wanted to be sure that he looked his best for unexpected important visitors. He would spend the morning writing, and afterwards work in the garden, then play bowls and quaff a horn of beer with Harvey, and no doubt the preacher.

As for Cobham, he appears to have led a more subdued life. Books we are told were his great consolation. When he died there were a thousand books in his room, mostly in foreign languages – the treatises of Seneca were especially mentioned. This love of books does at least give one reason why Raleigh and he had become friends.

Cobham's wife, who had kept her grander title Countess of Kildare, had been for a while governess to the King's daughter Princess Elizabeth. Like her father, the Lord Admiral, she had no scruples about grabbing as much money as she could, whatever miseries might thereby be imposed on other people. So she succeeded in persuading James to let her keep the income from Cobham's entailed estate, and even entertained him at Cobham Hall on one of his progresses. She also looked for further evidence incriminating her husband – just in case there was ever talk of his getting a reprieve. As Cobham said: 'Jezebel was never like her . . . she will never suffer me to come out of prison if it be in her power.'[10]

Cobham died a pauper, covered with lice, after a stroke in 1619; he had been allowed the year before to go to Bath for treatment. His body lay un-buried for a long time, apparently because his wife refused to bear the cost.

Grey was the last in the family's main line, and he died in the Tower in 1614. In that year he had been made a close prisoner (which meant windows boarded up) for supposedly sending a message to Arbell Stuart, who by then was also a prisoner. He said he had only been flirting.

In the Tower Raleigh was to achieve a new renown, as a 'chymist'. He fitted up his little hen-house with copper tubing and retorts, and here he brewed essences and medicines which one assumes must in the first instance have been based on herbs and roots that he and others had brought back from Guiana and Virginia. The fame of his 'Great Cordial', otherwise known as the 'Balsam of Guiana', a kind of cure-all, lasted for the rest of the century and beyond. It was administered to William III on his death-bed in 1702; Sarah Duchess of Marlborough regarded it as a remedy for everything, especially smallpox.[11]

Raleigh had long been interested in medicine. As far back as the early 1580s John Hester had dedicated his 114 *Experiments and Cures* to him. The book was denounced as the work of Paracelsus, the German occultist healer, but there was nothing occultist about Raleigh's work. He was not looking for the philosopher's stone or the elixir of eternal youth. Chemistry as practised by him was distinct from alchemy, which Ben Jonson satirized and which to some people was a quasi-religion, and to others an opportunity for exploitation and fraud. By the end of the 17th century it was said to be debatable whether Raleigh was more famous as a statesman, explorer, seaman, historian or scientist. Aubrey wrote:

Sir Walter Raleigh was a great chemist, and amongst some receipts I have seen some secrets from him. He studied most in his sea voyages, where he carried always a trunk of books along with him, and had nothing to divert him. He made an excellent cordial, good in fever etc. Mr Robert Boyle has the recipe.

It is likely that Raleigh used some of the antidote to poison that he mentioned in the *Discoverie*, 'that quencheth marvelously the heat of burning fevers'. Keymis in his account listed four 'herbs good against poison'. Conceivably this antidote could have been quinine, or something similar.[12]

The ingredients of the Cordial were for a long while a mystery, but at an early meeting of the Royal Society Charles II asked his French physician Lefebvre (or Le Fèvre) to publish them. They were quite a concoction, including crushed pearls, hart's horn, bezoar stone (found in the intestines of certain ruminants), musk, ground ambergris, and quantities of herbs from angelica to cardamon, all boiled up in 'spirit of wine', the equivalent of *aquavita* or the Spanish *aguardiente*, fire-water; but nothing apparently from Guiana.[13]

Sir Kenelm Digby insisted that viper's heart should be included. Sassafras was another ingredient, but the one that mystified Lefebvre was 'serpentary of Virginia', which does in fact exist, once used as a cure for the bite of a rattlesnake or a rabid dog.

One of Raleigh's medical notebooks is in the British Library. Some of the remedies are certainly curious, particularly the stone that you must clench in your hand to enable you to 'piss blood'.[14] Tobacco is also recommended for headaches.*

Visitors to the Tower who came to see the lions usually hoped to glimpse old Raleigh working away among his retorts. One of these was the Comtesse de Beaumont, wife of the French ambassador, who managed to get him into conversation. She asked him for some of his famous Cordial which he duly sent her by means of a Captain Whitelocke (an unfortunate choice of messenger, as he was to discover).[15]

He also built a small furnace for smelting metals. He worked on ways of distilling sea water for drinking, and for preserving meat on long voyages, using cloves and ginger. And he cured his own tobacco. This last did not please James when he got to hear of it, so he published a treatise *A Counterblaste against Tobacco*. Smoking, the King wrote, was 'a custom loathsome to the eye, hateful to the nose, harmful to the brain, dangerous to the lungs, and, in the black stinking fume thereof, nearest resembling the horrible Stygian smoke of the pit that is bottomless.' There was also an attack on Raleigh himself, 'a father generally hated' who had obtained the habit from 'beastly Indian slaves to the Spaniards, refuse to the world, and as yet aliens to the holy covenant of God.'

Becoming desperate about his finances, Raleigh decided that he must sell a magnificent jewel composed of diamonds that Queen Elizabeth had given him and which he had passed on to Bess. The jeweller Peter Van Lore had offered £1,000. Not surprisingly, Bess was extremely reluctant to part with it, the more so because they had already had some unhappy dealings with Van Lore in the past.[16]

And indeed the result was disastrous. No sooner had Van Lore got the jewel in his hands than he reminded Raleigh that he owed him £600, which Raleigh in his distraught state of mind had quite forgotten.† So Van Lore would pay him only £400. Bess was furious, so furious that she refused to have dinner with Raleigh that night.

Van Lore was of course delighted, and told Shelbury that Sir Walter had 'dealt with him the most nobly of any gentleman that ever he had to do withal . . . and was the best payer of debts he ever known'.

---

* Tobacco also appears in Hilary Spurling's *Elinor Fettiplace's Receipt Book* (1986): 'Serop of Tobaccho' and 'Tobacca Water'. The former involved adding whites of egg and sugar to three ounces of tobacco; it was said to be good for old coughs and loosening phlegm. The other was more potent: two gallons of muscatel, crushed aniseeds and raisins were added to a pound of leaf tobacco, distilled with a 'soft fire'. This Lady Fettiplace was the sister-in-law of Raleigh's brother Carew.   † p. 368.

There were bright spots, however. In August Bess went to see Cecil, and returned with exciting news. Sherborne Castle and its manors were to be granted by Letters Patent to her cousin Sir Alexander Brett and George Hall, second husband of Raleigh's sister Margaret, in trust for herself and Wat for sixty years, 'should Sir Walter live so long'. Raleigh therefore at once shot off a letter to Cecil, rather pathetically and prematurely assuming that a pardon might also soon be arranged.[17] First he dutifully thanked Cecil for having helped to save his life and his estate, and for *having 'kept me* and mine from utter ruin'. If freed, he said, he would willingly serve Cecil as his 'true and only creature', though he did of course realize that he might still have to be 'constrained or confined'. In that case he would be quite happy to be 'confined within the hundred of Sherborne', and if that was not possible he would be content to live in Holland, or 'to get some employment upon the Indies'. Or perhaps he could be appointed to 'any bishop, or other gentleman or nobleman . . .'.

Thus spoke the once mighty Sir Walter Raleigh. He also said that if he could not get to Bath that autumn 'I am undone for my health and shall be dead or disabled forever'. But he had no response.

Cecil had more important things on his mind, for on 28 August, at long last, a peace treaty was signed with Spain: regarded as one of Cecil's masterstrokes in statesmanship. The Spanish commission had arrived in May, and the conference, lasting nearly three months, took place at Somerset House, under the aegis of the new Spanish ambassador, the Conde de Villamediana. Aremberg also took part, which must have been awkward. The English delegation, headed by Cecil, consisted almost entirely of those Privy Councillors who had presided at the Winchester trial. The Spaniards were not impressed by the English weather, let alone the heavy drinking, the bad food and the fleas. Several of them were pickpocketed, and one commissioner lost his jewelled cap badge when he stuck his head out of the window of his coach and had his hat snatched away. Queen Anne took a lead in their entertaining, but they hardly understood English and were bored by the plays she arranged.

Philip III sent over the Constable of Castile, Don Juan Fernández de Velasco, to sign the treaty when all details had been settled. Velasco arrived at Dover with a retinue of 234 and a large supply of ice to cool his wine. James arranged for him to stay at Somerset House, and for his apartments to be hung with costly tapestries. Twelve Grooms of the Chamber were allocated to serve him.

By the treaty the Spaniards had at last put an end to English privateering.

The English had also scored several important points, one being that they were permitted to continue trading with South America, and it was agreed that they should be allowed to carry goods for the Dutch. They also refused to prevent the Dutch from paying English mercenaries. After the signing James gave a banquet, bringing out all his gold plate. There was a display of horseback riding and tumbling. Velasco was proudly presented with a melon and six rather green oranges that had actually been grown in England.

The 'Spanish Peace' was not popular with Londoners. Maybe Raleigh was cheered by a wicked little anecdote (which could have been an invention). Velasco gave Anne a necklace which he said he had brought as a personal present from the Queen of Spain. But it was soon revealed that this necklace had been bought in London. What was more, it had been given by Anne to Cecil, who had sold it. (Why should Anne want to give Cecil a necklace?)[18]

After the departure of the Spaniards Cecil went to Bath for a rest and a cure. So Raleigh had to wait.

There being no inkling about a pardon, Raleigh began to suspect that Cecil had felt that he had not been showing enough gratitude over the Sherborne trust. What was more, the number of visitors he was allowed was suddenly reduced. Even his brother Carew was struck off the list. By this time Cecil had been raised to the rank of Viscount Cranborne. So Raleigh wrote to him, in about November.

Since the time that my wife was last with your lordship I have withered in body and mind, by whom [Bess] I perceived a sad change in your lordship's favour towards me, on which my hopes have ever lived and made me live . . .

For the times past, whatsoever your lordship hath conceived, I cannot think myself to have been an enemy or such a viper [Coke's terrible insult], but that this great downfall of mine, this shame, loss and sorrow, may seem to your lordship's heart and soul a sufficient punishment and revenge. And if there be nothing of so many years' love and familiarity to lay on the other scale, O my God, how my thoughts have betrayed me in your lordship's nature, compassion and pity. For to die in perpetual prison I do not think that your lordship could have wished to your strongest and most malicious enemies.

What Raleigh had still to comprehend was that Cecil (as time would show) had absolutely no intention of ever letting him out of the Tower. Cecil was prepared to help Bess and Wat as much as was feasible, but he believed that if Raleigh was again on the loose he would be a danger not only to him but to the stability of the country.

In his letter Raleigh also said he was ill, 'daily in danger of death by the palsy, mightly by suffocation by wasted and obstructed lungs'. This may have been an exaggeration, but the mists and damp rising from the Thames were affecting him, as his physician Dr Turner confirmed. Plague was spreading again, and Bess and Wat had once more fled the Tower, he knew not where.

Evidently he had not perfected his Balsam of Guiana, or else he might have tried it on himself. But with the coming of spring his health did gradually improve.

Friendship with the Prince
1605–7

Suddenly there was a shock. During the winter of 1604–5 someone, some-how, threw doubts on the validity of Raleigh's deed of transfer of the Sherborne properties to Wat. Raleigh dashed off a long, despairing and confused letter to Cecil, as though unable to grasp this new disaster. The conveyance, he pointed out, had been drawn up by an eminent lawyer, Sir John Doddridge. An opinion from the highest authority would now have to be sought, and this would have to be none other than the Chief Justice Sir John Popham and the Attorney-General Sir Edward Coke. There was no option. 'If they shall judge fraud herein, God judge them with more grace than they have judged of it and me.'

The result was not necessarily a foregone conclusion, but it turned out to be a catastrophe. There was a genuine flaw in the deed of transfer. The clerk who had drawn it up had missed out some vital words. Sherborne was thus legally still Raleigh's property, and as he had been found guilty of treason it was to be forfeited to the Crown.

Bess had fought hard for him, appealing to the King and Cecil, keeping creditors at bay, selling off jewels and mortgaging plate, and at the same time determined to keep up her dignity and style. Now she could bear it no longer, and came raging in to see him, carrying her new-born child and bringing Wat as well.[1] She accused him of 'unnatural negligence', letting them starve while all the while he was happily brewing his potions and planting his herbs. This meant another urgent letter beseeching help from Raleigh to Cecil, who was just about to accompany the King on a progress: 'I shall be made more than weary of my life by her crying and bewailing who will return in post [haste, from Dorset] when she hears of your lordship's departure and nothing done . . . These torments, added to my desolate life . . . are sufficient either utterly to distract me or to make me curse the time that ever I was born into the world.'

What was more, Raleigh claimed that he was ill. Speaking as he put it in 'the presence and fear of God', he wrote: 'I am every second or third night

410

in danger either of sudden death, or the loss of my limbs and sense, being sometime two hours without feeling or motion of my hand and whole arm . . .'. Cecil very probably dismissed this outburst as yet another piece of self-dramatization, but there could have been some truth in it, as several months later in the following year Raleigh's physician Dr Turner reported that he was complaining that all his left side was cold and numb, and that the fingers of his left hand were contracted; there was also something wrong with his tongue that made him speak weakly, 'and it is to be feared that he may utterly lose the use of it'.

This sounds very like a stroke. Dr Turner recommended that he should be moved to warmer quarters, even to the 'little room which he hath built in the garden adjoining to his still-house' and away from the river mists.[2] The better weather helped him, and Raleigh did not seem altogether keen about living in the hen-house – which makes one wonder whether it might all have been a ruse to have him removed from the Tower on 'compassionate' grounds.

Cecil ignored his appeal for help over the conveyance, so Bess wrote to the King, who was either moved by her plight or fed up with her letters. He therefore instructed Cecil to cause a grant to be drawn up in her and her children's favour, 'that we may be no more troubled with their pitiful cries and complaints'. Cecil ignored this too – ultimately with disastrous consequences for the Raleigh family. It might have been because Raleigh, instead of quickly and gratefully accepting such a gesture of royal mercy, at once began agitating for the freehold. If he could have the freehold, he suggested a bargain: Cecil himself could use it (rent it?) as his country seat. But Sherborne was too far from London for Cecil even to contemplate such a suggestion, and in any case in 1607 he was to hand over his home Theobalds to the King in exchange for Hatfield House, which he proceeded to rebuild and enlarge on a magnificent scale.

In 1605 Sir George Harvey was suddenly removed from the Lieutenancy of the Tower, and in his place came that unpleasant character who had been Raleigh's gaoler, Sir William Waad. It is not at all surprising to learn that on the day before Waad was sworn into office he told Cecil (now advanced to the Earldom of Salisbury)[3] 'Sir Walter Raleigh used some speeches of his dislike of me . . . yet sithence he doth acknowledge his error, and seemeth to be very well satisfied'. Cobham was not so tactful, and he had less to lose by being outspoken, especially with a social inferior known for his 'brutality of language'. Waad told Cecil:

My Lord Cobham did forget himself toward me yesterday in the afternoon in such sort as I could do no less than shut him up with his lodging . . . and if I should say to your Lordship privately what I think, his passions when the fit takes him goeth beyond choler and I wish that which he said had been private, and not so loud, as it was heard into the court.

Waad was not pleased by all the comforts that were being allowed to his prisoners. There certainly were to be no more dinners for Raleigh. Cobham had one more servant than he was supposed to have, and the door of his rooms were left open so that people came and went as they chose. All this was dealt with. Raleigh too had the 'access of divers', and then there was that hen-house, 'where he doth spend his time all day in his distillations'. He did not want to remove him, but he did want the use of his garden. The fence was very broken down and low, which did not give Waad enough privacy, so he was given permission to build a broad brick wall to hem him in. Raleigh promptly used it by walking along the top on his daily walk, visible both inside and outside the Tower. Visitors who came to see the Tower's great new novelty, the whelping lioness, would stare up at him and he would stare back: typical of what Waad claimed was his 'cunning humour'.

Waad was also irritated by the way Bess would come driving into the Tower in her coach, so he ordered her to leave it outside the gates. For a while she took no notice, but eventually had to give in. There were plenty of other examples of his petty tyranny, the most drastic being a curfew at 5 p.m. When the bell rang, all visitors including wives and unauthorized servants had to leave, and prisoners had to retire within their lodgings and lock their doors.

On 5 November 1605 church bells rang in the City on the discovery of the famous Gunpowder Plot, which was to set back Catholic emancipation into the far future. All James's fears of assassination had been revived and it also seemed to put an end to hopes of release for Raleigh.

The plot seemed to have been hatched in 1603 by Sir Robert Catesby and Thomas Percy, both bitter at James's wavering policy towards Catholics. In a cellar beneath the House of Lords Guy Fawkes stacked twenty barrels of gunpowder, on which he loaded faggots and iron bars. At the opening of Parliament it was hoped to blow up the King, Queen, Prince of Wales, and all the Government, and that this would lead to a nation-wide Catholic uprising.

The Raleighs at once fell under suspicion. For one thing Bess was a cousin of Lady Catesby, born a Throckmorton. And why had she been seen scouring the rusty armour at Sherborne?[4] As for Raleigh, his reputation made him a natural target. But what seemed especially to compromise him was his choice of Captain Whitelocke for sending the bottle of his Cordial to the Comtesse de Beaumont. This Whitelock had not long before been seen with Archduke Albert in Flanders. He was a dependant of the Earl of Northumberland and had actually dined with him on 4 November. Also present at the dinner had been Thomas Percy, who was related to the Earl, and Thomas Hariot. During the meal Percy had been called outside to speak to a messenger from London, and this messenger had been Guy Fawkes.

Raleigh was thus called before the Privy Council. He wrote a 'declaration' about Whitelock, denying any formal acquaintance. He said that he had sometimes asked him to find out Northumberland's disposition towards him, and had only received back a 'dry and friendless answer'.[5] He had not communicated directly with Northumberland. Evidently he acquitted himself well, and he was soon returned to the Tower.

Thomas Percy was Northumberland's steward, and had planned to use £4,000 of the Earl's money towards the Catholic rising. This was without Northumberland's knowledge, but the fact that he had dined at Syon House was enough for Northumberland to be tried before the Star Chamber, and to be found guilty of misprision (concealing knowledge) of treason and of criminal negligence. He was also fined the giant sum of £30,000, the largest recorded.

The ninth Earl of Northumberland was the grandest and richest peer in the kingdom. There were other reasons for suspicion about him. He had long been a friend of Raleigh and had possible leanings towards Catholicism; as the 'Wizard Earl' he was interested in all new philosophical and scientific ideas, as well as in the occult. Then of course, James was already prejudiced against him, thanks to Henry Howard's malicious libels when Elizabeth was still alive. Since James's accession Northumberland had made very few appearances at Court, which had also seemed significant.

He was not able to pay all his fine, so some of his leases were appropriated, though later he was able to recover them after paying £10,000. Grey was turned out of his lodgings to make way for him and sent to the Constable Tower. But Northumberland was not satisfied, and was well able to stand up to Waad's bombastic pretensions. He told him he wanted to move: 'As the summer growth on, I find this little garden, that lieth all the day in the sun, to be very close; these galleries very noisome with the savours of the ditches'; and when it rained the air was not 'wholesome'.[6] So he was transferred to the Martin Tower on the north-east corner, and here he set himself up in great splendour. He had his rooms enlarged, with new windows, displayed his coat of arms, laid out a gravel path, and created a bowling alley under a canvas roof. Like Raleigh he built a still and a furnace.

He gave Waad £100 a year, so that he would not have to eat Tower food, and lavishly tipped wardens who in effect became his servants. He gave Waad's daughter two ruby pendants. He created a large library, especially of Italian books, many of them abstruse or on scientific subjects. A strong believer in the inferiority of women, he had his son removed from his wife and took a lease on the Brick Tower nearby to accommodate him. In one year his housekeeping charges reached £1,400. Like Raleigh he was addicted to tobacco.

Hariot was also arrested and sent to the Gatehouse prison. One must imagine that he had been greatly upset by the Lord Chief Justice in his final speech at Raleigh's trial, branding him as an evil influence and an atheist. A letter of deep distress from him to the Lords in Council is dated 16 December. In this he points out that he was never a 'busy meddler in matters of state' and had never sought preferments.[7] All he wanted was to lead a private life 'for the love of learning that I might study freely'. Like Raleigh he also pleaded ill-health: 'Great windiness in my stomach and fumings in my head rising from my spleen, besides other infirmities'. He must have been let out of prison very soon after, for his notes show that he was resuming his study of the refraction of light and corresponding with the great astronomer and worker on optics, Johannes Kepler.

It is sometimes said that Hariot took voluntary lodgings in the Tower, so that he could be near both Northumberland and Raleigh, with whose financial affairs he was still concerned, and to whom he was allowed access, but there is no firm evidence of this. Northumberland may have insisted that he should spend the occasional night there. Hariot's biographer John Shirley believes that he commuted to the Tower at intervals from Syon, where Northumberland had let him have a house; he also had a pension of £80 a year from Northumberland. Anthony à Wood says that he and his fellow 'magi', Hues and Warner,* had a table in the Tower at the Earl's charge, and that Northumberland 'did constantly converse with them, either singly or all together, as Sir Walter Raleigh, then in the Tower, did'.

The arrival of Northumberland must have given Raleigh a new dimension in his life. It is unlikely that he would have been allowed to visit the Martin Tower, but Waad could hardly have prevented Northumberland's occasional excursions to him before the five o'clock curfew. Northumberland seems to have been especially interested in making alcoholic drinks, and created a so-called whisky made out of stale beer, ambergris and musk, which hardly sounds appetizing. He also distilled a liqueur which he called

* p. 119.

Spiritus dulcis: this was created from eighteen gallons of sack (white wine from Southern Europe), four pounds of sugar candy and 'spirit of roses'.[8]

Raleigh suddenly found that he had a new important patron: Queen Anne. She had been struck down by a 'violent malady', and on the advice of the French ambassador had asked for some of Raleigh's Cordial, which she believed had cured her. She therefore called on Raleigh in the Tower and was enchanted by him, so much so that she even put in a plea to James for a pardon. Not surprisingly James took no notice, but she continued to see Raleigh which must have been unsettling for Waad. The fact that George Carew, Raleigh's cousin and close friend, was her Vice-Chamberlain would certainly have been an advantage. (Carew was given a peerage in June 1605.)

This royal interest must in some degree have counteracted Raleigh's worries over an enquiry by the Council about Sir George Harvey's conduct as gaoler at the Tower. There were continual efforts to find further incriminating evidence, and it was at this stage that the Tower servant Cottrell confessed to having taken messages between Cobham and Raleigh in the autumn of 1603.

Later in 1606 Anne's brother King Christian IV of Denmark paid a state visit to England. James was suspicious that she would try to get him interested in Raleigh, and maybe she had even told Raleigh that she would try to get him to ask for a pardon. So on the King's arrival James at once said: 'Promise me that you will be no man's solicitor.' The King had the reputation of a Viking's thirst and this was certainly shown to be the case at banquets arranged in his honour. Even court ladies were unable to keep up with his drinking, spewing on the floor.*[9] There were deer hunts in the royal parks, tournaments, bear-baiting, excursions up and down the Thames, even a visit to the Tower to look at the crown jewels and the ordnance. In the end King Christian broke his promise and did ask for Raleigh's pardon – he wanted him as his admiral of the fleet.†

James's refusal was a terrible blow to the Raleighs. Once again Bess decided that she must act, and she drove to Hampton Court to confront James. Simply seeing her must have appalled him, for he brushed past her without saying a word.

* At one such banquet the 'Queen of Sheba', very drunk, was to have presented the King with food and wine on a platter. She tripped and spilt everything over him. After he had been cleaned up a little, he insisted on dancing with her. They both fell down and were sent to bed, and the festivities continued.

† A similar request, turned down by James, was evidently made by the Prince de Rohan, the Huguenot leader.

It has usually been assumed that it was some time in 1607 or early in 1608 that Anne brought her son Henry, the Prince of Wales, to see Raleigh. Henry had been born in 1594, so he would have been only about thirteen. He was an outstanding, brilliant boy, taciturn and withdrawn, very different in character to his father, and everyone predicted great things for him. The Venetian ambassador described him as 'little of body, and quick of spirit – ceremonious beyond his years, and with great gravity'.[10] He was fond of sports, except hunting, which was his father's passion. Even in 1604 he was being considered by men of learning as a proper patron of their works, and books were dedicated to him.

He soon fell under the spell of Raleigh, as the great survivor from England's past, a warrior and intellectual who had known Drake, Sidney and Spenser and could talk of the Armada, Virginia and El Dorado. Raleigh was flattered and delighted. Not only did this raise new hopes of his eventual release, but he felt that the boy's gifts and enthusiasms could restore the prestige of England after what he considered to have been a shameful peace with Spain. Henry even at this age showed a precocious interest in politics and foreign relations, as well as military matters. Waad's curfew in a way now proved a blessing for Raleigh, because it gave him time in those long evenings to write treatises on a variety of subjects which he felt would entertain and interest the young Prince.

Henry soon showed a rejection of his father's way of life, and he especially hated his young favourites. 'No one', he said, referring to Raleigh, 'but my father would keep such a bird in a cage.'[11] He disapproved of his father's drinking and bad language. The atmosphere in his house was monastic; he kept a 'swear-box' into which you had to put a fine if you misbehaved, and there were worse penalties for drunkenness.

In 1604 the Lord High Admiral Nottingham had presented the boy with a small ship, which had thrilled him. She had been designed by the master shipwright, Phineas Pett, at the Chatham shipyard, was only twenty-eight feet long and was elaborately painted and decorated with carvings. The Prince christened her the *Disdain* and Pett was sworn in as his servant. Possibly Henry had been impressed by his Danish uncle's warships, and this had inspired him to build a great new man of war on similar lines. Raleigh wrote him a long letter of advice based on his own experiences of building the *Ark Royal*, in particular emphasizing that the ship should not be over-loaded and made top heavy with too much ordnance.[12]

Much of the advice in this letter was repeated in a treatise, *Observations and Notes concerning the Royal Navy and Sea Service*, which Raleigh wrote with Arthur Gorges. In November 1607 Phineas Pett produced his ambitious design for a three-decker, beautifully presented in a model 'fairly garnished with carving' and even 'curtained with crimson taffety'. The ship was to be called the *Prince Royal*, and the keel was laid in October 1608.

Henry was also an enthusiastic supporter of the revival of plans to recolonize Virginia, which had been an immediate consequence of the peace with Spain. After Raleigh's conviction all rights in his patent had reverted to the Crown, so he must have watched developments with mounting frustration and envy – though also with a certain amount of pride. There were four companies: London merchants from the City companies, headed by Sir Thomas Smythe, who had been one of Raleigh's grantees in 1589; a Plymouth group, headed by old Sir John Popham, but also including Sir Ferdinando Gorges and Humphrey Gilbert's two sons, Sir John Gilbert and Raleigh Gilbert, more concerned with fisheries and trade in what was known as North Virginia, the equivalent of New England; a Bristol group of wealthy merchants, headed by Richard Hakluyt, also interested in North Virginia and which had sponsored a successful reconnaissance in 1603 by Martin Pring; various individuals under the Earl of Southampton who had aimed to form a Catholic colony but had been forced to abandon it after the Gunpowder Plot.[13]

Hakluyt was the link between the London and Bristol merchants, and it was decided that together they would exploit South Virginia. The charter for all three companies was finally signed on 10 April 1606. The Plymouth group soon afterwards sent out separately two reconnaissance ships, one captained by Henry Challons, the other by Martin Pring. The former had the misfortune to run into the Spanish treasure fleet which at once assumed that he must be a pirate, and sank his ship, having taken him and his crew prisoner. Not a good omen. Pring arrived back in 1607, and soon afterwards a colonizing expedition was despatched under the command of Captain George Popham, a nephew of the Chief Justice (who died that year) and the same man who had captured the Spanish documents which Raleigh had included as an appendix to his *Discoverie*.* Raleigh Gilbert was his second-in-command or Admiral.

They landed in August at the mouth of the Sagadohoc (now Kennebec) river, in the present-day state of Maine, and at what must at first have seemed a paradise. Immediately they set about building a fort, designed more as a trading post and called Fort St George. But supplies were insufficient, winter was fearsome, and relations with the Indians were deteriorat-

* p. 256.

ing. With the death of George Popham and other settlers, and with the news of the death of Sir John Gilbert, Raleigh Gilbert decided to return with the rest of the group in September 1608.* It was to be twelve years before the enterprise was revived, under Sir Ferdinando Gorges, the first Governor of New England.

The three small ships of the London Company, with the Bristol Company participating, left for Chesapeake Bay, under Captain Christopher Newport and Bartholomew Gosnold, with 105 settlers. They landed at the mouth of the James River on 13 May 1607.† And so, after incredible hardships and much danger, the first permanent English colony was established, in the region to which Raleigh and Hakluyt had wanted White's colonists to be directed in 1587. There were many deaths that first winter, including Gosnold's. The famous Captain John Smith was president, Newport having returned to England.[14]

Smith was captured by the Algonquin chief Powhatan's men, and according to legend was saved from execution by the chief's daughter Pocohontas. For a while he managed to keep the Indians happy, and grappled with indiscipline, quarrels and laziness within the fort, which had been named Jamestown. (The complaint was that the gentlemen among the settlers were not used to labour.) More supplies and reinforcements arrived, including women. But this colony was no Mexico or Peru, and it was realized that diversification was needed if the colony were to survive, and with more money from City investors. Thomas Hariot was consulted about his experiences in the time of Governor Lane. The Spanish ambassador Don Pedro de Zúñiga got to hear of this, and from his letter of 5 July 1609 to Philip III it appears that Raleigh also gave advice in writing – and that Zúñiga obtained

---

* The Spanish ambassador somehow obtained a copy of the plan of Fort St George and sent it to Madrid. It is now in the Archivo General at Simancas. Excavations of the fort are in progress, at what is mostly a summer resort, Popham Beach, and have revealed the site of Raleigh Gilbert's house, as well as artefacts such as glass buttons, pieces of German stoneware and pistol balls. Raleigh Gilbert, probably born in 1583, posthumously after his father's death, seems to have shared some of his uncle's characteristics, having been described as proud, arrogant and headstrong. But Sir Walter would not have approved of his treatment of the Indians, which was to be regarded as disgraceful – dogs were set upon them. Having discovered at first hand the tremendous resources of the mid-Maine coast, he decided that his father's patent had been unfairly passed on to Sir Walter and that it had rightfully belonged to his brother John and himself. He began writing to associates in England about his claim, which was firmly quashed by Ferdinando Gorges after intercepting the correspondence. From his brother he inherited Compton Castle, where his descendants still live.

As for Sir John Popham, on his deathbed he had asked for some of Sir Walter Raleigh's Cordial, but died an hour after taking it.   † p. 158.

a copy of it: 'I have a paper which Walter Raleigh wrote, who is a prisoner in the Tower, and it is he who discovered that land and whom they consider a very great personage. The members of the Council of Virginia follow this paper . . .'[15]

We hear no more of Raleigh connections with Virginia. By now he was entirely obsessed by Guiana. He had been encouraged by accounts of recent journeys organized by two brothers, Charles and Oliph Leigh, to the Waipoco river, which in spite of disasters, massacres and the murder of Charles Leigh had revived hopes of good trading, and especially gold. A ship's captain, John Wilson, had written about the riches and commodities of the region, and had also told how many of the local people had spoken of Sir Walter Raleigh, and how a man had arrived from the Orinoco to ask about him, complaining that he had promised to return.[16]

Raleigh told Cecil that a piece of stone he had picked up in Guiana and put to one side, believing it to be marcasite, had at (long) last been assayed and traces of gold had been found in it. This had inspired him to make yet another desperate bid for his liberty. He swore he could go to where that very stone was found – but he would travel as a private individual, in a ship with a master and officers appointed by Cecil, so that there would be no possibility of his turning renegade. The cost would be £5,000, and he suggested that one third might be borne by Queen Anne, 'to whom I am bound by her compassion', and another third by Cecil; he had some friends who would provide the rest. If the Queen and Cecil did not want to put up the money, he would find means to bear the entire cost, and he would present the Queen and Cecil with half the proceeds. He would also bring bellows and bricks for a furnace so that they would be able to melt down the gold on the spot, and bring it back in ingots. For secrecy's sake the journey could be made under the pretence of going to Virginia. 'We will break no peace, invade none of the Spanish towns. We will only trade with the Indians.'

He also tried to interest John Ramsay, one of James's young favourites, recently made Viscount Haddington, in leading an expedition. This time the bait was 'a mountain near a navigable river covered with gold and silver ore'.

On the face of it the idea was wild, hopeless, and the assayer's report does sound suspicious. But amazingly the Council seriously considered the proposal. It had been suggested that Keymis should be sent out, and if he returned with a sample of ore Raleigh would be freed and a regular working of the mine begun. One wonders who made the suggestion – surely not Cecil. At any rate it was put to Raleigh, who insisted that he would have to accompany Keymis on the first voyage. But this did not appeal to the Council, and the whole project was abandoned.

An event in 1607 which was to have a grave effect on Raleigh and his family was the sudden rise to eminence of Robert Carr or Kerr, then aged about twenty-one. He was a Scot and had been employed as a Groom of the Bedchamber: somewhat androgynous in appearance, pert, blue-eyed, fair-haired and virtually beardless. At the annual tournament held on the King's accession day, 24 March, he had been thrown from his horse and had broken his leg. James was distraught and visited him constantly, finally falling in love. Within months Carr had been given property sequestered from a Catholic, with a pension of £600 a year (soon increased to £800). On 23 December he was knighted and promoted to Gentleman of the Bedchamber. There was no doubt any more at Court about James's sexual inclinations. This was only a preliminary.

The Great *History*
1608–9

In January 1608 the Court of Exchequer ordered Raleigh to produce a proper title whereby Sherborne should revert to his heirs. All he could show was the conveyance with its fatal missing words. It soon became clear that the King was meaning to give Sherborne to Carr.

The terrible truth, which Raleigh was not to know, though he may have suspected it, was that it had been Cecil who had made the recommendation, taking advantage of having disobeyed James's order to have the grant drawn up in favour of Bess and her children. James had wanted to give Carr land but it was difficult because he had just been forced to agree to entail the Crown estates. He was immensely relieved: 'The more I think of your kind remembrance of Robert Carr for yon manor of Sherborne, the more cause I have to conclude that your mind ever watcheth to seek out all the advantages for my honour and contentment'.[1]

On the death of the Earl of Dorset, Cecil became Lord Treasurer as well as Chief Secretary. In a time of mounting financial crisis he was by no means inclined to subsidize the greedy and worthless Carr, on whom the infatuated James had already lavished so much in money, jewels and fine clothes. Rents from the Sherborne estate would therefore have seemed an excellent solution. On the other hand Henry Howard was also attracted by Carr, at the same time realizing that it would be much in his interest to keep on intimate terms with the King's current favourite. So there is every reason to suspect that in reality it was as much Howard's idea that Sherborne should be bestowed on him.

As it happened, James had already become aware of deficiencies in Howard's character. Some incident involving Howard must have upset Cecil, which impelled James to write him a long letter of reassurance: '. . . What large and eternal proof of 3 [Howard] his fidelity ye best know, and yet I would no more trust him than one of the corruptest lawyers in the trial of a mean error upon one of his dearest friend's.' He also added, by way of a joke: 'Set another leg beside mine, I warrant 3 will swear the King's sweet leg is for the finest.' He had no illusions about his own spindly shanks.

The situation dragged on throughout the year, and on 27 October judgement was given in the King's favour. Bess was once more ready for war. She requested an audience, and when this was ignored marched off to Hampton Court and placed herself at a strategic corner where James must pass. He was embarrassed, and all he could do was to mutter as he shambled on: 'Na, na. I mun hae the land, I mun hae the land for Carr.'[2]

Years later, at the time of the Commonwealth, her younger son Carew was to write this in a petition to the Commons:[3]

She being a woman of very high spirit, and noble birth and breeding, fell down upon her knees, with her hands heaved up to heaven, and in the bitterness of spirit beseeched God Almighty to look upon the justice of her cause, and punish those who had so wrongfully exposed her, and her poor children, to ruin and beggary.

It was just as well that the King was out of earshot and did not hear her curses. But as Carew darkly added: 'What hath happened since to that royal family is too sad and disastrous for me to repeat.'

Raleigh and his wife did at least have the good news that Wat had graduated at Corpus Christi, Oxford, on 30 October 1607. He was aged then fourteen. His tutor was the brilliant young Dr Daniel Featley, who however had to report that the boy was addicted to violent exercise and apt to mix with 'strange company.'[4] With reason, so it would seem. According to Aubrey, whose cousin had been with Wat at Oxford, he was a 'lusty stout fellow, very bold, and apt to affront, but – for good measure – could speak Latin fluently.' He was also a 'notable disputant and courser, and would never be out of countenance or baffled; fight lustily and, one time of coursing, put a turd in the box and besmeared it about his antagonist's face.'

Some years back Wat had been betrothed to Elizabeth Bassett, a ward of Cobham with an income of £3,000 a year. This had been cancelled, and just as well for Elizabeth (who ended up as Duchess of Newcastle). Raleigh, obviously a little alarmed about Wat's behaviour, wrote a warning poem:*

> Three things there be that prosper up apace
> And flourish, whilst they grow asunder far,
> But on a day they meet all in one place,

---

* Much admired by the late Peter Levi who told the present author that the lines 'still taste like fresh honey and have a sting like bees'.

And when they meet they one another mar;
And they be these – the wood, the weed, the wag.
The wood is that which makes the gallow tree,
The weed is that which strings the hangman's bag,
The wag, my pretty knave, betokeneth thee.
Mark well, dear boy: whilst these assemble not.
Green springs the tree, hemp grows, the wag is wild;
But when they meet, it makes the timber rot,
It frets the halter, and it chokes the child.
　　Then bless thee, and beware, and let us pray
　　We part not with these at this meeting day.

In the long evenings imposed by Waad's 5 p.m. curfew Raleigh was pouring out essays, letters, treatises, many of them intended to help and instruct Prince Henry, whom he saw as a potential saviour. He was flattered by the boy's attention and took it upon himself to attempt to mould and shape him towards an enlightened sovereignty, and to inspire him with the glories of the past regime. He immediately set about writing an essay with the imposing title of *The Present State of Things as they now stand between the three great Kingdoms, France, England and Spain*. This was followed by *A Discourse of the Invention of Ships, Anchors, Compasses etc.*, and the *Observations concerning the Royal Navy and Sea-Service*, which in fact was mainly a reworking of an address to Elizabeth of about 1598. He especially encouraged the Prince's interest in the revival of England's maritime power, always with an eye to reopening the struggle with Spain. There were also warnings against the perils of corruption and incompetence.

Quite a lot of this is daunting stuff for the present-day reader, especially when references are made to special occasions which are no longer of interest. Even so there are plenty of vivid flashes reminiscent of the style of the *Discoverie* and the famous essay on Grenville and the *Revenge*. Raleigh also wrote on ethical and metaphysical subjects, and on political philosophy – with titles such as *The Sceptic, A Treatise of the Soul, Maxims of State* – some of them extremely hard going today, and not necessarily aimed at Henry. Where Raleigh could not compete was in the visual arts, which were of passionate interest to Henry and whose luminaries included Inigo Jones, Salomon de Caus and Isaac Oliver.

Raleigh's most uncharacteristic piece is *Instructions to His Son*: pompous, and – to use an anachronism – Blimpish. When exactly it was composed is not known. It could have been at this stage, or four years later after hearing stories of Wat's escapades with Ben Jonson in Paris. Or it could have been written for the child Carew, who was growing into a rather more stable personality.

Raleigh in his mind must have contrasted the behaviour of Wat with the godlike Prince of Wales. Stebbing says that Wat fought a duel with Robert Tyrwhitt, a retainer of Suffolk's, and it thus became necessary for him to leave the country, so that Raleigh had sent him off to the Netherlands, with a letter of introduction to Prince Maurice. This may well fit in with the suggestion made by Camden that he should go to Europe with Ben Jonson as guardian, supposedly in order to control his 'planetary and irregular motions'. But on reaching Paris, Wat was as 'knavishly inclined as ever' and distinguished himself by pinning girls' favours (love tokens) on his codpiece.[5] He also took advantage of Ben Jonson's fondness for the bottle:

He caused him to be drunken, and dead drunk, so that he knew not where he was; thereafter laid him on a car, which he made to be drawn by two pioneers [labourers] through the street, at every corner showing them his governor straitened out, and telling them, that was a more lively image of the crucifix than any they had.

Such behaviour could have been dangerous in a country so recently recovered from religious wars. But when news of these pranks reached Bess, she merely laughed, saying that 'his father young was so inclined'. Raleigh on the other hand was exasperated and 'abhorred it'. (A classic case of an impetuous and possibly unhappy young man without, for practical purposes, a father?)

The pair stayed on in France for nearly a year, no doubt creating other scandals, and then went on to Brussels. By the time they reached Antwerp they were in financial trouble and had to be bailed out by someone said to have been Raleigh's agent. According to Isaak Walton, 'they parted (I think in cold blood), with a love suitable to what they had in their travels (not to be recommended)'.[6]

Bess was of course right about Wat's behaviour having been somewhat like his father's – 'riotous, lascivious and incontinent Raleigh' – which makes the stuffiness of the *Instructions to His Son* all the more peculiar, dealing with subjects such as friendship, marriage and servants, without a drop of charity or generosity, or for that matter humour. The message appears to be that self-interest is all. Raleigh advises his son to choose his friends wisely, 'for by them thou shalt be judged what thou art', but he needed to avoid making friends with those of poorer or inferior rank, because they 'will only pursue it for necessary ends'. Marrying a woman just for her beauty should also be avoided, because beauty does not last and he would be stuck with her for the rest of his life. She must not be ugly either; 'for comeliness in children is riches' (assuming that good-looking women automatically produce good-looking children.) The preservation of the estate was all-important. Provision for a wife must be made in case of her widowhood, but she must forfeit all her benefits if she remarried, and these would have to be passed on to the children.

Most surprisingly, for one who had notoriously dressed like a peacock, Raleigh warned against overspending on clothes and 'bravery' (jewels etc.): 'Money in thy purse will ever be in fashion, and no man is esteemed for gay garments but by fools and women'.

Very different is *A Discourse of the Original and Fundamental Cause of Natural, Arbitrary, Necessary and Unnatural War*, some of it with an obvious debt to Machiavelli, some of it relevant even today. His attitude to war had changed since he wrote about Cadiz; now it was never a glorious thing. He had a special horror of civil war.

The terribleness of civil war and dissensions will be sufficiently made out, by observing the methods of divine Providence; for never was any place threatened with terrible judgements and desolations as Jerusalem, the capital city of the Holy Land, and the seat of religion for above eleven hundred years.

And he wrote with feeling for those who die in battle in ignorance of the selfish and base motives, and the mistakes, of their leaders:

What deluded wretches, then, have a great part of mankind been, who have either yielded themselves to be slain in causes which, if truly known, their heart would abhor, or been the bloody executioners of other men's ambitions! 'Tis a hard fate to be slain for what a man should never willingly fight, yet few soldiers have laid themselves down in the bed of honour under better circumstances.

He was also producing occasional poetry. Perhaps the sonnet to Wat had been the spur. This poem, with a well-known first line, and of which there have been other versions, appeared in 1612 in Orlando Gibbons' *The First Set of Madrigals and Mottets*.

> What is our life? A play of passion;
> Our mirth, the music of division;
> Our mothers' wombs the tiring houses be,
> Where we are dressed for this short comedy.
> Heaven the judicious sharp spectator is,

That sits and marks still who doth act amiss;
Our graves that hide us from the scorching sun
Are like drawn curtains when the play is done.
Thus march we playing to our latest rest –
Only we die in earnest, that's no jest.

Thus wrote the great performer. The metaphor of life as a comedy, with death as the only reality, appears again and again in his writings. With this poem he had almost written his own epitaph.

Another poem could have been composed at this period. Written in Raleigh's hand, it was first published only in 1952, having been found at the back of a recently discovered notebook, containing among other things part of his library list in the Tower. Conceivably it could have been written at the time of Elizabeth's death, or even earlier, for a masque in her honour.*

These are the first stanzas:

Now we have present made
To Cynthia, Phoebe, Flora,
Diana and Aurora,
Beauty that cannot fade.

A flower of love's own planting,
A pattern kept by nature
For beauty, form and stature,
When she would frame a darling.

She is as the valley of Peru,
Whose summer ever lasteth,
Time conquering all she mastereth
By being always new,

As elemental fire,
Whose food and flame consumes not,
Or as the passion ends not
Of virtue's true desire . . .

Presumably Raleigh had kept other lists, but there are no books of poetry in the notebook, apart from the works of Petrarch; not even *The Faerie*

---

* The notebook, large quarto and vellum-bound, still with the remnants of its original green silk ties, is now in the British Library. Its discovery is told in Walter Oakeshott's *The Queen and the Poet* (1960).

Queene. Many are in French or Italian. Hakluyt is there, and there are books by Machiavelli, Copernicus and Pico della Mirandola. There are books about travel, America and medicine. One book mentioned is *Lacademie francois*, which must be Primaudaye's *French Academy*, a dense tome that begins with the creation of an academy not dissimilar to the opening scene in *Love's Labour's Lost.*

The greatest interest of the notebook is its bearing on Raleigh's masterpiece *The History of the World*, which could even have been started in 1607, though he may have been thinking about it for several decades, judging from all those trunks of books he carried on his sea voyages. Some lines he wrote in the *Ocean to Cynthia* might also have been significant:

> We should begin by such a parting light
> To write the story of all ages past,
> And end the same before th'approaching night.
> Such is again the labour of my mind . . .

The inspiration for this colossal work of a million words – when published, a folio leather-bound volume weighing eight pounds – had been his friendship with Henry, for whom it was intended: 'It was in the service of that inestimable Prince Henry, the successive hope, and one of the greatest in the Christian world, that I undertook this work. It pleased him to peruse some part thereof, and to pardon what was amiss.' Nearly seven hundred sources were quoted. In the century that followed it was vastly influential, but later it became the fashion to treat it as some sort of collaborative effort, following Isaac D'Israeli who wrote in his *Curiosities of Literature*: 'The truth is that the collection of the materials of this history was the work of several persons', among whom were said to be Ben Jonson, Hariot and especially Dr Robert Burhill, Rector of Northwold in Norfolk, once Raleigh's chaplain.

It is true that Jonson (when drunk) said that Raleigh had the assistance of some of the 'best wits in England', and that he himself had drafted the section on the Punic Wars, which Raleigh had amended. Raleigh also admitted that he had 'borrowed the interpretation of my learned friends', and that he had no Hebrew and preferred reading Greek authors in English or Latin translation. D'Israeli's reference to Burhill is based on Aubrey, who was told by Burhill's widow that her husband had dealt with 'all the greatest part of his book, for criticisms, chronology and reading of Greek and Hebrew texts'.

It is hardly a surprise that Raleigh should have sought the advice of specialists. His own research was immense, and the conception, interpretation and narrative style of the *History* was absolutely his own; indeed he has been regarded as one of the founders of modern historical writing. His eye for human interest, his gift for characterization and his own personal observations, from a long and varied experience, make the book far easier to read than most of the prose works of his contemporaries. He certainly would have relied, as always, on Hariot's advice, and probably consulted the other two 'Magi'. He may have borrowed some of Northumberland's books. He asked Sir Robert Cotton, the great figure at the Society of Antiquaries, which had been founded in 1580, for the loan of books. Aubrey said that the wit and lawyer Sir John Hoskyns when he was in the Tower (for speaking too freely against Scottish favourites), was supposed to have been 'Sir Walter's Aristarchus'* and that it was his function 'to review and polish Sir Walter's style' – quite likely he did help, but it would have been long before, as Hoskyns only arrived in the Tower in 1614, the year of the book's publication. Arthur Gorges would also have been ready to assist him with advice or seeking out books of reference. Then there was Raleigh's secretary John Talbot, who remained with him in the Tower for eleven years: 'my honest friend, an excellent scholar, and as faithful and true man as ever liveth'.[7] He must have taken down dictation or made the fair copy.†

The book went through eleven editions in the 17th century, outselling even Shakespeare's collected works. Oliver Cromwell recommended it to his son, and John Locke regarded it as ideal reading for 'gentlemen desirous of improving their education'. It was the favourite reading of Sir John Eliot and John Hampden, and for Puritans sacred literature, with Foxe's *Book of Martyrs*. Milton owed him a great debt, and was delighted to discover one of Raleigh's essays, *The Cabinet Council*, which he arranged to have published.

The plan had been to divide the book into three parts, but in the end, as will be explained later, only the first was published, taking the history of the world from the Creation to the Roman conquest of Macedonia in 146 BC. The intention appears to have been to continue with the history of Great Britain, presumably after the Roman invasion, and bringing it up to date, but stopping short of very recent times – for, as he said: 'Whosoever, in writing a modern history, shall follow truth too near the heels, it may happily strike out his teeth'.‡ He had lost too many teeth already. It did

* Aristarchus of Samothrace, grammarian and philologist, director of the library at Alexandria.
† Let us hope with better spelling than his master's – 'Cronikell of Teuxbery' was one of the books asked for from Sir Robert Cotton.[8]
‡ This phrase was borrowed by many 17th-century writers, including Clarendon and Pepys.

not however prevent him alluding indirectly to Elizabeth, and to his own experiences, especially war.

The main framework, as he was to explain in his preface, was the idea of Providential history – the traditional medieval view, that history is a record of God's will: 'God, who is the author of all our tragedies, hath written out for us and appointed us all the parts we are to play'. Throughout history God has intervened to punish or reward the actions of rulers, either directly or on their descendants. Thus Raleigh stresses the vanity of human pomp and, especially, the principle that no monarch is above the law of God, or can expect to evade His justice. Power had the terrible effect of creating ambition for more power, which led to tyranny and corruption.

So it was not surprising that James found the book 'too saucy in the censuring of princes',[9] especially after reading the preface – which will be referred to again later, it being the last part of the book to have been written.

The Biblical section is in huge detail, and is probably that which most inspired Milton. Classical history, including myths, is interwoven, bringing in the siege of Troy, Perseus and Andromeda, the rape of Proserpina, the punishment of Tantalus, along with translations from Ovid and Virgil, the aim being to show that figures such as these could be considered contemporaneous with Moses or Gideon. Raleigh's concern was with chronology, proving God's dominance over human affairs at all times in the past. It is from the study of history that we see how the world has been governed throughout the millennia, and how lessons can be learned; how the world 'was covered with waters and again repeopled, how kings and kingdoms have flourished and fallen, and for what virtue and piety God made prosperous, and for what vice and deformity, he made wretched, both the one and the other.' Having established the argument that there was no contradiction between classical history and that set out in the Bible, Raleigh then came to his main theme: the rise and fall of kingdoms, through the achievements and failures of their rulers, all being illustrations of the judgement of God.

It is with some amusement that we note Raleigh's problem at having to explain away the animals in the Ark. His solution is almost Darwinian, in that he points out the dogs turned into wolves, that the dogfish of England are in effect the same creatures as the sharks of the southern ocean, and that English blackbirds and thrushes have their equivalents in Virginia, only their colours are different.

Raleigh has few heroes in his book. On the whole he approves of Hannibal, but then Hannibal never had complete power. It is Epaminondas who gets his fullest sympathy.[10]

So died Epaminondas, the worthiest man that was ever bred in that nation of Greece, and hardly to be matched in any age or country: for he equalled all others in the several virtues, which in each of them were singular. His justice, and sincerity, his temperance, wisdom and high magnanimity, were no way inferior to his military virtue; in every part whereof he so excelled . . . a perfect composition of an heroic general. Neither was his private conversation unanswerable to those high parts, which gave him praise abroad. For he was grave, yet very affable and courteous, resolute in public business, but in his own particular way easy, and of much mildness; a lover of his people, bearing with men's infirmities, witty and pleasant in speech, far from insolence. To these graces were added great ability of body, much eloquence, and very deep knowledge in all parts of philosophy and learning.

So here was the model for Prince Henry to follow, or what Raleigh hoped he might become.

In contrast Raleigh shows his contempt for those rulers whom God has justly punished: Jezebel thrown to the dogs, Nebuchadnezzar eating grass. Then there was Rehoboam, who was 'transported by familiars and favourites' and whose counsellors were all 'witless parasites'.[11] This was regarded by his readers as a subtle warning to James, and it did not escape him: in 1614 he told Parliament that he was no Rehoboam 'that took young and new counsellors and rejected the old'.

A more direct reference to James was seen in Ninias, 'esteemed no man of war at all, but altogether feminine, and subjected to ease and delicacy', in contrast to his powerful predecessor Queen Semiramis.[12] As for Darius, with his corrupt pacifist court, he was a 'Maygame king', more of a 'masker than a man of war', dressing his courtiers as women and 'honouring them with the title of King's Kinsmen'.[13] Alexander too 'fell into the Persian's luxury', surrounding himself with a 'shameless rabble', including sodomitical eunuchs.[14]

In the section about Alexander, Raleigh writes about the march on Bessus, and how Alexander smoked out his enemies from an otherwise invincible place. It is then that we have the often quoted digression* about Raleigh's own experience in Languedoc during the Huguenot wars, when bundles of burning straw were let down into the caves where the enemy was hidden. 'There were also, some three years before my arrival in Guiana, three hundred Spaniards, well mounted, smothered to death, together with their horses by the country people who did get long dry grass on fire to the eastward of them (the wind in those parts being always east) so as notwith-

* p. 14.

standing their flying from the smoke there was not anyone who escaped.*
Sir John Borough also, with a hundred English, was in great danger of being
lost at Margarita, in the West Indies, by having the grass fired behind him.'[15]

Elsewhere he sarcastically writes about omens and miracles – how an
eagle hovered over Alexander's head at the battle of Issus, and a flight of
crows guided him through the desert to a temple of Jupiter. On the other
hand:

The strangest things I have read of in this kind being certainly true was that the night
before the battle of Navarra, all the dogs which followed the French Army ran from
them to the Switzers, leaping and fawning upon them as if they had been bred and
fed by them all their lives, and in the morning following, Tremulzi and Tremouille,
Generals for Lewis the twelfth, were by these Imperial Switzers utterly broken and
put to ruin.[16]

Raleigh's distrust of Switzers – Swiss mercenaries – much used on the
Continent, inspired a section on its own, *The Dangers of the Use of Mercen-
ary Soldiers and Foreign Auxilaries*,[17] which also includes a reference to
Machiavelli:

The extreme danger, growing from the employment of such soldiers, is well observed
by Machiavell, who showeth that they are more terrible to those whom they serve,
than to those against whom they serve. They are seditious, unfaithful, disobedient,
devourers and destroyers of all places and countries wherein they are drawn, as
being held by no other bond than their own commodity. Yea, that which is most
fearful among such hirelings is that they have often, and in times of great extremity,
not only refused to fight, in their defence [of] those who have entertained them, but
revolted unto the contrary part, to the utter ruin of those Princes and States who
have trusted them.

Raleigh may have been attacked as a 'mischievous Machiavell', but he was
not ashamed to show how closely he had studied Machiavelli's works. At
least readers of the *History* could not now accuse him of being a 'damned
atheist'. But given the continual emphasis on the judgement of God on the
behaviour of individuals, we cannot but notice that nowhere is there any
sense of the Incarnation, Redemption, or the coming of Christ. This may of
course be because the book ends in 146 BC, but it could also be a reflection
on Raleigh's religious beliefs. He was fiercely Protestant, but from the

* This story was told him by the Indian chief Topiawari, and appears in the *Discoverie*.

History it could easily be assumed that he was more of a deist than a true Christian.

As the time drew near for Sherborne to be handed over, Raleigh with obvious distaste decided to write on 2 January 1609 directly to Carr. He did not demean himself by begging for mercy, but appealed to Carr as a gentleman. Carr was still young, in his dawn of life, and could be assured of many favours from the King, but Raleigh was in his 'evening' and asked him not to 'begin your first buildings on the ruins of the innocent' [meaning his heirs].

It was too late. A week later, on 9 January, Sherborne passed to Carr, and as John Chamberlain put it, Raleigh was like Job: 'Naked came I into the world and naked will I also go out'.[18] Chamberlain also added a sly little remark about the original assignment, which seemed to show that there were still people at Court who had little love for Raleigh: 'The error or oversight be so gross that men do merely ascribe it to God's own hand that blinded him and his counsel'. This in fact was to be the very theme of the *History of the World*: God intervenes to punish the wicked.

The whole affair of the gift of Sherborne to Carr was however generally regarded as a very great scandal. John Webster was writing *The White Devil* in 1609, and in it there is a clear reference to Raleigh's plight. Gossipers could not help noticing the irony, and Raleigh must surely have been conscious of it: Robert Carr had been a penniless young man from Roxburghshire, and his good looks were bringing him wealth and possibly fame from a doting monarch. Raleigh had been a penniless young man from Devon, slightly older admittedly when he came to Court, and his good looks had attracted Elizabeth, as a result of which he was to receive wealth and great fame. The difference was that Carr had *only* his looks to recommend him.

Raleigh wrote a poem, among his best, known as *Petition to Queen Anne*, a cry for help, and usually regarded as having been written in 1618 when he was in far more desperate straits. But there is another poem which, because of some similarities, including an identical stanza, is thought to be a draft for the *Petition*, and which does fit his mood in 1609. The dating of the second poem is one of the many minor mysteries in Raleigh's life. Some believe that both could even have been written for Queen Elizabeth in about 1592 when he was disgraced over Bess, since the first lines in the 'draft' are the same as those of the unfinished *22nd Book of the Ocean to Cynthia*:*

* p. 183.

> My day's delight, my springtime joys foredone,
> Which in the dawn and rising sun of youth . . .

The lines that followed were to be much quoted:

> For as no fortune stands, so no man's love
> Stays by the wretched and disconsolate;
> All old affections from new sorrows move.
>
> Moss to unburied bones, ivy to walls,
> Whom life and people have abandoned
> Till th'one be rotten, stays, till th'other falls . . .

There are several more stanzas. Whether it was because of the combined pleas of Anne and Henry, or, more likely, simply out of bad conscience, James finally agreed that Bess should be given £8,000 in compensation for the loss of Sherborne and that there should be a pension of £400 a year to her and her elder son during their lifetimes. This was generous, though it did not take into account the declining value of money. The first part of the trustees' assignment was signed on 24 July 1609, the signatories on Raleigh's side, besides himself, being his most loyal supporters: George Carew, George Hall, Thomas Hariot, John Shelbury, Robert Smythe, and Lawrence Keymis. On the other side were Salisbury (Cecil), Northampton (Henry Howard), Nottingham, Carr, and Sir Julius Caesar the Chancellor of the Exchequer. Bess lent £3,000 from the compensation to the Countess of Bedford, presumably with good interest.

The dream of Guiana never left Raleigh, and it also inspired Prince Henry. In March 1609 an expedition led by Robert Harcourt, and sponsored by the Prince, sailed for the 'Wild Coast' of Guiana, between the Amazon and the Orinoco. It was because of Henry's support that Harcourt was able to obtain the King's consent to establish a colony there.[19] He was also a friend of Raleigh, but James might not have known this.

Harcourt left with three ships and ninety-seven men, arriving at the mouth of the Waipoco on 17 May. He was welcomed by the local chieftain who turned out actually to have been in England with Raleigh, 'to whom he beareth great affection', and had been christened with the good English name of Leonard. 'He loveth our nation with all his heart', Harcourt wrote in his eventual report.

Harcourt was tactful when local people asked him why Raleigh had not come back to Guiana: 'I excused his not returning according to his promise, by reason of other employments'. He also explained about the accession of a new sovereign, King James. It was unfortunate that Leonard's offer to guide him to diamond mines only yielded topazes (though diamonds are now found in the area), but Harcourt's descriptions of fruitful meadows, valleys and woods echo the enthusiasm of the *Discoverie*. Although he had no authority to annex territory, he in his own words 'took possession of the land by turf and twig on behalf of our Sovereign Lord King James'. Inevitably, gold was what his followers really wanted; even so, he was sceptical about the possibility of gold mines, although he thought some white spar seemed promising. He left behind his brother Michael with sixty men, with the task of finding a route to the elusive city of Manoa.

By the end of 1609 another group of adventurers was preparing an expedition to Guiana, under Sir Thomas Roe, famous later as ambassador at the court of the Great Mogul in India and to the Sublime Porte at Constantinople.[20] This time Raleigh was one of the sponsors, amazingly putting up the sum of £600 (from Bess's £8,000?). Roe and partners had collected together £1,100, and the Earl of Southampton, evidently now on friendly terms with Raleigh, £800. Raleigh's old bedfellow from the Inns of Court days, Sir Stephen Powle, had subscribed a modest £20. The purpose of the expedition was, as usual, primarily to look for gold and the city of Manoa. Cecil seems to have put up money, and possibly Henry had done so also.

Harcourt's report was not published, but he kept a detailed notebook which Roe must have studied. The expedition was a badly kept secret, for the Spanish ambassador wrote to Philip III that two ships were preparing to leave for Guiana, he claimed under the command of the 'pirate' Sir Walter Raleigh. How Raleigh would have yearned to go . . .

Headpiece from a chapter opening in the History of the World.

O Eloquent, Just and Mighty Death!
1610–12

For some unexplained reason, in 1610 Raleigh was put under restraint for a while, and his wife and family were banished from the Tower. It could have been due to the arrival, as a prisoner, of the wretched Arbell Stuart.

For the past years she had been well treated at Court, as a princess of the royal blood, and had been promised a subsidy and a household when she married. No effort was made to find her a suitable husband, but suddenly at the age of thirty-five she fell violently in love with her cousin, William Seymour, aged twenty-three, and he with her. This was forbidden fruit because Seymour could have been in line for the throne, as a descendant of Henry VIII's sister Mary and nephew of Lady Jane Grey. When James heard that they had been secretly married, Seymour was despatched to the Tower and she was sent up to Durham. Both escaped and Seymour reached the Continent safely, but Arbell was recaptured and put into the Lieutenant's house in the Tower, where Raleigh could easily have seen her and spoken to her from the top of Waad's wall.

She was moved to the Bell Tower nearby (where Sir Thomas More had spent four months until his execution) and allowed to live in relative comfort. After the collapse of a plot to rescue her she became depressed and had delusions, complaining that she was being made a spectacle.

The *Prince Royal*, the ambitious three-deck warship modelled by Phineas Pett of Chatham three years earlier, was launched on 24 September 1610. There had been complaints about her design and expense, fostered by the Earl of Northampton, Henry Howard. She was certainly an unusual ship, rather ungainly, high above the water line, and in response presumably to Raleigh's suggestion the number of guns had been reduced from eighty to fifty. There were problems about getting the ship through the dockhead, at first thought to be too narrow. Prince Henry, after whom she was named, obsessed with building up the maritime power of the country, which had been entirely neglected by his father, commissioned Pett to build him a pinnace for the ship. There were rumours that he had an ambition to be Lord High Admiral. In all this Raleigh kept in touch as closely as possible.

In February 1611 a series of lawsuits began between Raleigh, represented by John Shelbury and Robert Smythe, and William Sanderson in connection with the memorandum drawn up before Raleigh set off for Guiana in 1595, with the charge that Sanderson was accountable for £60,000 debts.*[1] Sanderson had brought a countersuit, claiming forgery. The whole matter is obscure and the final judgements have not been discovered, but there are suspicions of sharp practice on both sides. The name of John Meere reappears, accused of forging Raleigh's handwriting, and it was claimed by Sanderson that Shelbury had paid him for it (Raleigh had of course maintained long ago that Meere had been an accomplished forger).† It was Hariot who had kept back the memorandum on the reverse of which this presumed forgery had been written. He had taken suspiciously long to produce it and denied absolutely that he had forged anything, though he was unable to swear that anyone else could have done so. A bracelet of seed pearls was somehow involved as a bond, and Raleigh claimed that Sanderson had acquired £36,000 worth of goods from the *Madre de Dios* in 1592. There was also an unexplained reference to Sanderson getting hold of a further £46,000.

It also appears that a judgement of £500 against Raleigh had been expected. This decidedly murky family squabble is all the more distasteful given the close relationship (Sanderson seems to have had a son called Raleigh Sanderson) and the fact that Sanderson had backed so many of Raleigh's enterprises. Evidently disappointed investors in the Guiana venture had decided to take advantage of Raleigh, having heard that his effects were being sold to pay his debts. Very likely in the end the enormously rich Sanderson found himself landed with having to pay the investors, and Raleigh had to contribute his £500.‡

The affair could have had a bearing on Raleigh being put under further restraint for at least three months in July 1611. Or there might have been other difficulties over his neighbour Arbell. Grey was to be in trouble because he had tried to communicate with her,§ but now he was complaining that other prisoners enjoyed more privileges than himself. Arbell was notoriously extravagant and even in prison spent wildly on clothes, including £1,500 for a dress to wear at Princess Elizabeth's wedding to which she never was asked or would be allowed to attend. She died, her mind com-

---

* p. 222.   † p. 339.

‡ In November 1612 Adrian Gilbert bought a Chancery suit against Raleigh, claiming £3,303 debts from his half brother.   § p. 404.

pletely broken by the strain, in 1615, aged forty. There was at once an inquiry from the Privy Council about her jewels and other finery, including a dress 'powdered with pearls'. Raleigh was ordered to hand over any goods of hers that he might have in his possession – which does sound suspicious.*²

Raleigh's troubles were even more likely due to James's concern over his influence on Prince Henry, who made no secret of his intense dislike of Carr, promoted in March to Viscount Rochester, and to the Garter in April. Some time in 1611 Henry told his father that he wanted Sherborne for himself, the obvious reason being that he meant in due course to hand it back to Raleigh. James had to agree, and gave £20,000 to Carr in compensation.

Henry now had Arthur Gorges in his household, obviously very useful for Raleigh. The *History*, again through Henry's influence, was entered in the Stationers' Register in April 1611. This would normally mean that publication was imminent, but something happened to delay it – it has been suggested that Henry asked for more about the Romans. There does appear to be a slight sense of hurry towards the end of the last section of the book, and fewer digressions.

Apparently, at Raleigh's examination by the Privy Council in 1611 there had been some 'sharp words' from Cecil, including as Raleigh said 'terms . . . which might utterly despair anybody else'. Realizing that it was hopeless to correspond with Cecil any further, Raleigh wrote instead to Sir Walter Cope, now Chamberlain of the Exchequer, asking him to mediate in allowing Bess back in the Tower to live with him. By now he must have come to the conclusion that Cecil would never allow him to be released, and this is clear in a sarcastic passage in the letter to Cope: 'The blessings of God cannot make him cruel and that was never so, nor prosperity teach any man of so great worth to delight in the endless adversity of an enemy.'³

Henry Howard had also been at that Privy Council encounter, and wrote to Carr: 'We had a bout with Sir Walter Raleigh in whom we find no change, but the same boldness, pride and passion, that heretofore hath wrought more violently, but never expended itself in stronger passion . . . The lawless liberty of the Tower, so long cockered and fostered with hopes exorbitant, hath bred suitable desires and affections, and yet your lordship may assure His Majesty that by this publication he hath won little ground.'⁴

---

* Arbell's body was taken at midnight from the Tower to Westminster Abbey and laid, it was said without any solemnity, on top of the coffin of Mary Stuart, recently brought from Peterborough. Arbell's coffin was made of such cheap wood that when the crypt was opened in the 1860s it was found to have crumbled away, and her skull and bones were clearly visible.

'This publication' may have been the leaking of an essay that Raleigh had written on the suggested marriage of Henry to a daughter of the Duke of Savoy, which had been proposed towards the end of March 1611.[5] There had been a previous suggestion that Princess Elizabeth should marry Don Filiberto, second son of the Duke. Raleigh had already expressed in an essay addressed to the King his views on this Don Filiberto; he was careful to say that he had been asked to do so by Henry, but such presumption could hardly have been welcome. The Savoy royal family was of Spanish descent and Catholic, and Raleigh had made clear that his hatred of Spain was as unrelenting as ever. The Prince was strongly anti-Spanish – as now was Cecil, in spite of receiving such a large Spanish pension, and who in fact was in the throes of negotiating an entente with France.

In any case there was a rival claimant for the Princess's hand, a Protestant, Frederick, Elector Palatine, and by 1611 it had been decided in his favour. As James loved to imagine himself in the role of peacemaker in Europe, he was now wavering towards a Catholic alliance by Henry's marriage into the heart of the Counter Reformation. There would be a double marriage: to a Protestant and a Catholic.

But Henry was utterly against marrying a Catholic, and for this reason had asked Raleigh to write another essay for his father. As he put it, he was resolved that 'two religions should not lie in one bed'. Henry Howard was pressing a Spanish wedding, but the only available Infanta was still a child, and James had already scornfully dismissed her saying: 'They offer their Infanta to everybody.' The financial side was, however, an important aspect – the Savoys were not rich, but as Howard pointed out the Spaniards would be guaranteed to provide a large dowry. Cecil proposed a match with the wealthy Medicis of Florence.

Both essays were lucidly written, the one concerning Princess Elizabeth showing especially an impressive grasp of European history. Raleigh also pointed out the obvious fact that Savoy was a long way off, and it would be disastrous if England became entangled in its political problems. An alliance with Savoy might force England to remain neutral in any future war between Spain and the Netherlands. 'It is the *Spaniard* who is to be feared,' he wrote, 'the Spaniard who layeth his pretences and practices with a long hand'. He said that Spain was not as strong as people thought, and he quoted one of their own proverbs, that the lion is not so fierce as he is painted. If the late Queen Elizabeth had listened to her men of war (such as himself) instead of scribes (such as Cecil) 'we had in her time beaten that great empire to pieces and made their kings kings of figs and oranges'.

One passage was prophetic, with Europe in only a few years' time about to erupt into the slaughter of the Thirty Years War (due to the reckless folly of Frederick):*

Seeing that we have nothing in hand; seeing there is nothing moves; seeing the world is yet in a slumber, and that this long calm will shortly break out in some terrible tempest; I would advise the prince to keep his own ground for a while, and in no way to engage or entangle himself. While he is yet free, all have hope.

Henry was still young, a Prince Charming, full of his own ideals and dreams. He certainly did not feel ready to marry, and showed very little interest in women – though some thought there was a liaison with Lady Essex, the ruthless Court beauty, married to the third Earl of Essex, son of the great hero. But the decision was not to be his, and he was in a state of helpless resignation. James did seem eventually to come round to thinking that there was a political advantage in keeping him free. It is something of a surprise to find Raleigh actually coming round to recommending the possibility of a French bride, but this was for strategic reasons, a safeguard against any further Spanish aggression in the Netherlands: 'By holding France, we hold the Low Countries, which will make us invincible'.

Sir Thomas Roe did not return from South America until July 1611. In his ship the *Lion's Claw* he had journeyed 300 miles up the Amazon, and left a colony of twenty men near its mouth.[6] Afterwards he spent many months on the 'Wild Coast' and in attempting to penetrate the Guianan highlands by canoe, hoping to find the way to the elusive Manoa. He is said to have negotiated thirty-two rapids, and to have eventually reached a plateau (the Gran Sabana?), but had to return because of the inability to find food. In February he arrived at Trinidad where he wrote a letter to Cecil which Raleigh must have seen or heard about. Not only had he to admit that he had failed to find Manoa, which had been a main object of the expedition, but more importantly he had come to the conclusion that it did not exist at all, confirming opinions of Dutch explorers. Raleigh had to accept this, and from then in all his schemes the word Manoa was not mentioned.

At Port of Spain in Trinidad Roe said he had found fifteen ships, English, French and Dutch, loading up tobacco, which from the Spanish government's point of view was illegal. He then went on to tell of Spanish treachery and insolence, and how in spite of the Anglo-Spanish truce the Spaniards

---

* England, because of the marriage, was also to be put in danger of being drawn into the war.

behaved towards the English as if they were Moors. Recompense was being demanded by 'all seamen here'. He did not describe the particular outrage (which could be an exaggeration) that later came to the notice of Raleigh: thirty-six men had been tied back to back and had their throats cut. Roe also said that the king of Spain was now determined to colonize the Orinoco area, 'for the river runs into the heart of the Main', and was already sending out cattle and horses. The Spaniards planned to enlarge and fortify San Thomé, which was still being governed by Fernando de Berrío, who was 'lazy, and inapt for labour, and hath more skilful in planting and selling tobacco than in erecting colonies or marching of armies'. Then came, on the face of it, an odd remark: 'But the town is infinite rich and weak, and may easily be taken away, and as easily held'. Next there was a reference to a renegade Spaniard, Don Juan de Gamboa, a former Governor of Caracas, whom he was trying to trace and who knew all the secrets of the land, including the whereabouts of mines.

The clear indication of all this was that Cecil was sincerely interested in the possibility of acquiring San Thomé, or at least of continuing explorations along the Orinoco. He had already been protesting about the ill-treatment of merchants, and not long after receiving Roe's letter threatened to withdraw the English envoy from Madrid. Although in some ways Roe's expedition had been a failure, he had acquired information which was to prove extremely valuable to Raleigh. 'I have seen', he wrote, 'more of the coast, rivers and inland from the Great River of the Amazons under the line to Orenoque in 8 degrees than any Englishman now alive'.

James had dissolved Parliament in February 1611, having reached a complete deadlock over finances and the so-called Great Contract, which had been devised as a compromise by Cecil – in effect a permanent settlement of £200,000 a year for the King, and bringing to an end his prerogative power to raise money without Parliament. Apart from two months in 1614 Parliament was not to meet again until 1620. The financial situation was extremely grave, and not helped by the King's extravagance. Raleigh saw that this was his cue: gold from the Orinoco would solve all problems.

He had in 1610 already written a desperate letter to Queen Anne, offering his service in Virginia, and asking her 'to engage your word for me with the Earl of Salisbury'. 'I may rather die in serving the King and my country', he had written, 'than to perish here'.[7] In fact by Virginia he must have really meant Guiana, for when the Guiana expedition had been proposed in 1607 the plan had been that it should be under the pretence of going to Virginia, and she must have been aware of that. Even letters to the Queen could get into the wrong hands.

His letter also contained a dramatic and scarcely believable sentence, after saying that in the event of failure he would leave his wife and sons as pledges for his good faith: 'My wife shall yield herself to death if I perform not my duty to the King'. As his 19th-century biographer Stebbing said, one can almost see Bess stooping over him and forcing him to write these words. But he went further; he said he would even be prepared to tell his officers and mariners 'to sail elsewhere that they may cast me into the sea'.

It must have been because of Roe's letter to Cecil that Raleigh wrote both to Cecil and the Lords in Council, in effect reiterating the propaganda of 1607.[8] He even sent them copies of that original letter. He also said that he was writing because he had been persuaded to do so by 'some honourable friends of mine', one of whom was to be revealed later as George (Lord) Carew. But this time there was a difference. He was prepared for Keymis to go out alone to the Orinoco on a preliminary expedition, and if he brought back a sample of ore (half a ton!) he – Raleigh – would ask for his liberty in order to be free to make a regular working of the mine. If Keymis was unsuccessful then Raleigh would pay for the whole cost of the expedition. Once again his wife and sons would be his surety. Evidently he now considered that Roe's reference to the renegade de Gamboa was a sufficient guarantee of gold deposits.

One of the incentives mentioned in his letter to Cecil was that the gold he had in mind was not deep down but 'found at the root of the grass, in a broad and flat state.' Reference to the *Discoverie* would have shown that there was nothing to prove that this was true.

It does seem however that serious consideration was being given to this proposal, at least as far as sending out Keymis was concerned. Cecil would never have allowed his old rival to be released. Nor would be have been prepared to risk a war with Spain unless there was proof of abundant deposits.

All was put on hold when Raleigh was placed under restraint in July. Carr, by now the leader of the pro-Spanish party, must certainly have had a hand in blocking the plan. The months went by, and Raleigh decided to write yet again to the Queen.[9] She was sent a copy of his earlier letter to Cecil. 'That there is nothing done therein I could not but wonder with the world, did not the malice of the world exceed the wisdom thereof.' He complained that he was locked up 'as straightly as I was the first day', and that he was being punished for 'other men's extreme negligence' – which must refer to the leaking of a document. Now he was also asking for pity because of his extreme 'shortness of breath', and this made him despair 'of obtaining so much grace to walk with my keeper up the hill within the

Tower', implying that he had not been entirely confined within the Bloody Tower, but accustomed to move around outside.

Then he decided to write to the King himself, also enclosing a copy of the 1607 letter, denying that it was just a trick to set him free, and claiming that the discomforts of a voyage to Guiana were far more 'grievous' than being shut up in the Tower of London.[10] He 'lamented' that James had refused 'a most easy way of being enriched, both in despite of your malicious enemies abroad and of your grunting subjects at home' – the 'grunting subjects' being a shrewd dig at James's troubles with Parliament.

Did James ever bother to read the letter? The events of 1612 were to make any thought of Raleigh being sent to Guiana totally impossible.

Cecil's health was visibly failing. He suffered from dropsy and complained of stomach pains. The failure to push through the Great Contract had distressed him, and it had angered the King. His unpopularity had also increased, the populace still blaming him for the death of their hero Essex and the gentry despising him for hanging on to power and jealous of the scale and grandeur of Hatfield House, completed in 1611 – it had cost over £38,000 (no doubt paid for in part by the Spanish pension). Carr and most of the Scottish faction, as he well knew, were working on the King to have him ousted.

In February 1612 he was taken very ill, probably suffering from cancer. He rallied a little, went to Bath and came back to find that Carr, scenting power, had been admitted to the Privy Council. He returned to Bath, his condition made worse by the rattling of the coach on a five days' journey, and he realized that he had not long to live. He felt he must return to London to face his 'underminers', but on reaching an inn at Marlborough he collapsed, and was carried to the parsonage where he died on 24 May, aged forty-eight.

He had already approved the design for his tomb at Hatfield, in High Renaissance style. And there he still lies in his Lord Treasurer's gown, on a black slab of marble supported by white marble allegorical figures of Justice, Prudence, Temperance and Fortitude. Below, at ground level, is a marble skeleton lying on a pallet.

Chamberlain wrote of him:[11] 'His friends had fallen from him apace. I never knew so great a man so soon and generally censured.' There were rumours of syphilis, probably unjustified, though in recent years he had a reputation as a womanizer. A bitter epitaph circulated, and some said it was written by Raleigh, though it is not at all in his style, even if he had plenty of reasons to hate his once trusted friend:

Here lies Hobinol, our pastor while ere
That once in a quarter our fleeces did shear . . .
For oblation to Pan his custom was thus,
He first gave a trifle, then offered up us;
And through his false worship such power he did gain
As kept him o' the mountain and us on the plain.
Where many a hornpipe he turned to his Phyllis
And sweetly sung Walsingham to's Amaryllis.
Till Atropos clapped him, a pox on the drab,
For (spite of the tarbox) he died of the scab.*

James was disgusted by this jingle, and said he hoped that whoever wrote it would die before him. For Raleigh Cecil's death meant that a major obstacle to his release had gone. Henry realized that too, and he made his father agree that Raleigh should be freed by Christmas.

At the beginning of October Henry fell ill, after swimming in the filthy water of the Thames at Richmond, though he had already complained of giddiness and nosebleeds. He recovered enough to play tennis, but it did him no good, and his 'putrid fever' became worse. 'Looseness' affected him fifteen times a day. Doctors were called, and their diagnosis has been recognized as typhoid.

The remedies prescribed were bizarre.[12] The Prince's head was shaved and newly killed pigeons spread all over it. A live cock was cut in two and pressed against the soles of his feet. His nose was bled. Then the revered Parisian physician Dr Theodore de Mayerne was summoned. His favourite remedy, which no doubt was administered, was a syrup made of snails, frogs and crawfish boiled up in water of coltsfoot.

The desperate Queen sent for Raleigh's Cordial, but there were prevarications. For one thing Raleigh had been condemned as a traitor. Then there was gossip about the pills he had sent to the Countess of Rutland, Sir Philip Sidney's sister, who had subsequently died. It was decided to try out the Cordial on dogs, and then on some members of the Privy Council. All survived. Raleigh had said that it would cure the fever, but was not proof against poison, and had to be administered immediately. Valuable days had been lost. At last some of the elixir was poured into Henry's mouth. Miraculously he opened his eyes and even sat up and spoke. But it was only a last rally, and he died on 6 November.[13]

---

* Hobinol was a country lout in Spenser's *Shepheard's Calender*. Atropos was one of the three Moirae or Fates: the Fate that cannot be avoided. A drab = a slut or whore. 'Walsingham' refers to the popular ballads on which Raleigh's was based (p. 122).

The grief everywhere was tremendous. This brilliant, active and athletic young man, only eighteen, had been the great hope of England's revival.[14] 'Our Rising Sun is set ere scarce he had been there,' wrote the Earl of Dorset to Sir Thomas Edwards. For months the Queen could not hear his name without weeping. She was convinced that he had been poisoned, and said so in public.

As for Raleigh, the death of his patron and pupil meant utter disaster. There was no hope now of release. Sherborne reverted to the King, and he immediately gave it back to Carr, who however was made to pay £25,000 for it. In compensation Carr was to be given the title of Earl of Somerset.

Raleigh lost all will to continue with the *History*. There were to have been two more books, but they were abandoned. Some of the first volume might already have been in proof, but it is clear that his preface – which so infuriated James – was written after Henry's death, as he may also have written his magnificent peroration on the inevitability of death: how the great monarchies of the past had considered themselves imperishable, but had been brought down by 'storms of ambition'; powerful princes and mighty men might have blamed Infidelity, Time, Destiny, or the Instability of Fortune, but 'to those undertakings the greatest Lords of the World have been stirred up, rather by the desire of *Fame*, which plougheth up the Air, and soweth in the Wind'.[15]

I have considered, saith Solomon, *all the works that are under the Sun, and behold all is vanity and vexation of spirit*; but who believes it until Death tells it us?. . . It is therefore Death alone that can suddenly make man to know himself. He tells the proud and insolent, that they are but *Abjects*, and humbles them at the instant; makes them cry, complain, and repent, yea, even to hate their forepassed happiness. He takes account of the rich, and proves him a beggar; a naked beggar, which hath interest in nothing, but in the gravel that fills his mouth. He holds a Glass before the eyes of the most beautiful and makes them see therein, their deformity and rottenness; and they acknowledge it.

O eloquent, just and mighty Death! whom none could advise thou hast persuaded; that none hath dared, thou hast done; and whom all the world has flattered, thou only hath cast out of the world and despised; thou hast drawn together all the far stretched greatness, all the pride, cruelty, and ambitions of man* and covered it all over with these two narrow words, *Hic jacet*.

* p. xv, the quotation by Anthony Powell.

Then comes the final sad paragraph, his dirge for Henry, again with his italics.

Lastly, whereas this Book, but the title it hath, calls itself *The first part of the General History of the World*, implying a *Second*, and *Third* Volume; which I also intended, and have hewn out; besides many other discouragements, persuading my silence; it hath pleased God to take that glorious *Prince* out of the world, to whom they were directed, whose unspeakable and never enough lamented loss, hath taught me to say with Job, *Versa est in Luctum. Cithara mea, et Organum meum in vocem fluentium* [My lyre is changed into mourning and my organ into the voices of those who weep].

Headpiece from a chapter opening in the History of the World.

The Overbury Affair
1613–15

The marriage between Princess Elizabeth and the Elector Palatine Frederick had been delayed because of Henry's death. It took place on 14 February 1613, with all due extravagance. Nine thousand pounds were spent on fireworks and river spectacles, some of which Raleigh must have been able to watch from his prison. Elizabeth was to become famous as the Winter Queen of Bohemia, the romantic Queen of Hearts, mother of Rupert of the Rhine.

James was becoming even more dependent on Carr, who was acting as Secretary of State. The complaint was that the country was being run from the Bedchamber; if for instance James was out hunting, Carr would open important documents and reply to them. Henry had been the main focus of opposition to him, and regroupings were forming. Henry Howard, now Earl of Northampton, in particular took the opportunity of drawing closer to Carr; as Lord Privy Seal he was one of James's main advisers, and had hopes of becoming Lord Treasurer. He certainly showed talent as an administrator and put forward useful ideas about reforms; in the process he had become vastly rich, building a stately London mansion, Northampton House, near Charing Cross. The rumour was that he was using his position as Warden of the Cinque Ports for smuggling in Catholic priests.

His nephew, the Earl of Suffolk, was Lord Chamberlain, and his cousin, the ancient Earl of Nottingham, was still Lord High Admiral. The Howards were not quite a homogenous group, but they were sympathetic to Catholics and represented the pro-Spanish party. Their opponents were headed by William Herbert, Earl of Pembroke, and George Abbot, the Puritan Archbishop of Canterbury. All of them detested Sir Thomas Overbury, who was Carr's closest friend, secretary and mentor, and therefore at the heart of government decisions. The Queen also could not stand either Carr or Overbury, and had once even threatened to go back to Denmark because of their rudeness to her.

In some ways Overbury's unpopularity was like Raleigh's when he was at the height of Elizabeth's favour. There is no record of their having met, but Overbury was present at the trial and had reported on it. Aubrey said: 'It was a great question who was the proudest, Sir Walter or Sir Thomas Overbury, but the difference that was, was on Sir Thomas's side.' Overbury, as Weldon said, was prone to 'over-valuing himself and under-valuing others', whereas Raleigh, as Northumberland had written,* had the 'desire to seem to sway all men's fancies.' A poet, Overbury had once been a friend of Ben Jonson, but they had quarrelled, it was thought because he had tried to seduce the Countess of Rutland. When Carr fell in love with Lady Essex, Overbury helped him with poems and letters.

The beautiful Countess of Essex, born Frances Howard, was the daughter of Suffolk and great-niece of Henry Howard. If Prince Henry had ever fancied her, it was only a phase. Perhaps he realized that she was a completely unscrupulous and immoral character, for he was said to have described her as a 'stretched glove'. She had married the third Earl of Essex when they were both children. They had lived apart at first, and Essex had afterwards gone on a grand tour of Europe. On his return they had found themselves temperamentally and sexually incompatible.

Overbury thought that Carr – at the time still Viscount Rochester – only wanted to bed Frances, but when he discovered that they were both seriously in love he was furious, calling her a 'filthy base woman', something that was never to be forgotten or forgiven, to his very great cost.[1] She was now deter-mined to divorce Essex for non-consummation, and in this she was encour-aged by her great-uncle, who wanted to break Overbury's hold on Carr. Unfortunately, Carr was not at all liked by her father. She had even resorted to the well-known 'cunning man' Simon Forman for love philtres to keep Carr sexually interested in her, and for various devices to make Essex impotent, such as sticking needles through the genitals of a wax image.

The affair was in the long run to have an effect on Raleigh. James had first to be won over in this matter of exchange of husbands. Oddly, he never seemed to mind when his favourites married, and he liked Frances. Soon he was persuaded to favour an annulment, and this meant that Suffolk had to swallow his prejudices. But Overbury continued to work against her with his beloved master, hating the way Carr just to please her had his hair 'frizzled' and wore ludicrously flamboyant clothes. Then Henry Howard came up with an idea. Overbury could be got rid of by sending him abroad on some diplomatic post. By April, James, who was getting tired of Overbury, agreed to this, but Overbury refused, and his insulting reply was relayed

* p. 354.

back to the King. This resulted in his being sent to the Tower and put in close confinement. Meanwhile a commission under the extremely reluctant Archbishop of Canterbury was set up to investigate the Essex marriage.

At the hearings Frances dragged out all the sordid details of the bed, and bishops found themselves having to parry questions about ejaculations and penetrations, while servants were called to report on the state of bedclothes. Then it was demanded that Frances should be proved *virgo intacta* – a decidedly awkward matter. She was examined by a panel of 'grave matrons' and experienced midwives, but for modesty's sake insisted that her head and upper body should be kept covered. The matrons vindicated her, though it was generally believed that there had been a substitute.[2]

Frances was convinced that Overbury would continue to denigrate her and prejudice Carr against her, even from the Tower. It would seem likely that Henry Howard knew what was in her mind, and that he had decided that Sir William Waad would prove an obstacle, which would mean that he would have to be removed from the Lieutenancy of the Tower. Waad had mellowed and was behaving rather more leniently towards his prisoners, though he was still known to have strong principles. Nevertheless he was swiftly replaced by the more compliant Sir Gervase Elwes, who had to pay £1,700 for the honour – of which Howard kept £1,400 for himself.[3]

During the next months Frances and her great friend Mrs Anne Turner would send tarts, jellies, and venison pasties laced with arsenic to Elwes, who at first was innocent of the ingredients, for passing on to Overbury's gaoler, Richard Weston, once an employee of Mrs Turner's late husband. Overbury began to suffer agonies and vomits, and to burst out in boils. Dr Mayerne was called in, knowing nothing about the real cause of his suffering. The recipe he prescribed for Overbury was as bizarre as that inflicted on poor Henry. A deep cut was made between the shoulder blades and kept open with several peas. Then a 'balsam of bats' was administered, consisting of putrefied bats, snakes, puppies and earthworms, boiled up with oil, sage and wine, along with other ingredients. Afterwards there would be a 'glister' or enema, mostly made from the 'honey of dog nettles'.[4]

Overbury died on 15 September, according to Weldon after a poisoned enema, with Weston and another providing the *coup de grâce* by suffocating him with bedclothes. Variations on the cause of death were to be raked over later in the trials of everyone concerned, including Frances, Carr, Mrs Turner and Weston. The enema had not been Mayerne's, and the apothecary's boy who had applied it was known to have fled the country. An enormous suppurating ulcer was found on the miserable man's back – which also suggests that he could as easily have died of gangrene.

Howard at once sent this gleeful news to Carr, at the same time telling him that the corpse 'stank intolerably'. He also told Elwes to have it buried as quickly as possible: 'If the knave's body be foul, bury it presently [immediately]. I'll stand between you and harm.' He asked him to burn the letter.[5] Foul play was not suggested for the time being, though rumours began to circulate. The divorce was pronounced just after Overbury's death, with the Archbishop abstaining. It had been a messy, distasteful affair and had done little for the reputation of the Court, or indeed of James, who was still obviously besotted by Carr.

It was at this time that Carr was created Earl of Somerset, the object being that he would be of equal rank to Frances. They were married in the Chapel Royal on 26 December, in the usual extravagant manner. James gave the bride £10,000 worth of jewels, which he could not afford. There was an elaborate masque devised by Thomas Campion, but as some of the stage mechanics failed to work it was not a great success.

The History of the World was published on 29 March 1614. There was no title page or author's name – these had been forbidden – but everyone knew the author was Sir Walter Raleigh. There was an elaborate allegorical frontispiece, obviously designed by Raleigh but executed by Renold Elstracke. An athletic female figure denoting History, her gown inscribed *Magistra Vitae*, Mistress of Life, bore aloft a globe of the world, on which were shown a sea-battle, the course of the Orinoco, the Garden of Eden and Noah's Ark. She was trampling on Death and Oblivion, and on each side were figures of Experience and Virtue, the former old and gaunt and the latter young and Rubenesque. Above them all was the huge eye of Providence. A dedicatory poem, again anonymous but written by Ben Jonson, explained the symbols.* The publisher was Walter Burre, and the printer William Jaggard, the same who later printed the First Folio of Shakespeare's plays. The price is said to have been between twenty and thirty shillings, quite expensive but then it was very large tome. The sale went well, and it was not until 5 January 1615 that a letter from Archbishop Abbot reached 'My very loving friends the Master and Wardens of the Stationers Company', telling them that he had express orders from His Majesty that the book should be suppressed and withdrawn from shops.[6]

By this time the book had nearly sold out, and it does appear from the letter that the Archbishop may once have praised it. John Chamberlain told Carleton that he had heard that Raleigh took the withdrawal of his book

* p. 471.

very much to heart, 'for he thought he had won his spurs, and pleased the King extraordinarily.' It certainly would have been a very great blow, but after writing his preface Raleigh could scarcely have thought that James would have been pleased with him.

The preface was immensely long, in some places defensive and in others self-pitying. He began with a kind of apology, saying that it might perhaps have been better if in the 'very evening' of his tempestuous life he had written about recent English history, on account of the 'inmost and soul-piercing wounds' he had received, that were as 'ever aching while uncured', and because he would have liked to satisfy those few friends 'which I have tired by the fire of adversity'.

Prosperity and Adversity have evermore tied and untied vulgar affections. And as we see in experience, that dogs do always bark at those they know not; and that it is their nature to accompany one another in these clamours; so it is with the inconsiderate multitude ... who condemn, without hearing; and wound, without offence given ... For myself, if I have in anything served my country, and prized it before my private; the general acceptation can yield me no profit at this time, than doth a fair sunshine day to a seaman after shipwreck; and the contrary no other harm than an outrageous tempest after the port attained. I know that I lost the love of many, for my fidelity to Her, when I must still honour in the dust; though further than the defence of Her excellent person I never persecuted any man.

Nevertheless it is from the study of history that we may gather 'a policy no less wise than eternal, by the comparison and application of other men's forepassed miseries, with our own like errors and ill deservings'.

He then proceeded to his 'saucy' catalogue of the sins of most of the previous kings of England one by one from William I to Henry VIII, with their inevitable punishments. Retribution had come to them all. 'They were lovers of men's misery, and misery found them out.' He was careful to be tactful about Henry VII and to praise his wisdom and justice, as being the direct ancestor of James, and in so doing (which must have amused some readers) he also praised James's 'temperate, revengeless and liberal disposition'. James, asked why he had objected to the book, had seemed surprised, and had said that Raleigh had written irreverently about Henry VIII – whom he himself had so often railed against.

It was also said that James forbade the book not just because of the faults of princes but because some passages were offensive to Spaniards. And it was true that Raleigh mercilessly dismissed Spanish kings from Pedro the Cruel to Philip II.

Oh by what plots, by what forswearings, betrayings, oppressions, imprisonments, tortures, poisonings, and under what reason of state, and politic subtlety, have those forewarned kings, both strangers and of our own Nation, pulled the vengeance of God upon themselves, upon theirs, and upon their prudent ministers!

Raleigh ended the preface with a tribute to the 'inestimable Prince Henry, the successive hope, and one of the greatest of the Christian World', for whom he said he had undertaken the work.

It may have been after learning about the suppression of the book that, as Aubrey said, he was 'put in a passion', and that before the very eyes of his publisher Burre he had thrown all the material he had gathered for the second volume into the fire, saying 'If I am not worthy of the world, the world is not worthy of my works'. The book in fact was reissued in 1617, and another theory about this episode (if it was true) is that he was enraged in the following year when Burre told him that the new edition was selling slowly. A further possibility is that his notes were burnt with his other papers after the death of Hariot, in accordance with the instructions in Hariot's will.

Whatever James may have thought of the book, his daughter Elizabeth obviously liked it, for she is known to have possessed a copy of the first edition. After the outbreak of the Thirty Years War the copy was captured in Prague by the Austrians. It was recovered by the Swedes in 1648.

The appointment of Sir Ralph Winwood as Secretary of State on 29 March 1614 was good news for Raleigh, who regarded him as an ally. Winwood, just returned from acting as agent to the States General in Holland, was a strong Protestant and although opposed to any gesture of friendship towards Spain had been Carr's nominee, though Carr was soon to regret it. Shortly afterwards, Parliament was called. After the bad feelings of 1610 James had hoped that this would be a 'Parliament of Love', which would provide the solution to his overwhelming debts. He was to be badly mistaken. The Addled Parliament – so called because nothing was achieved – lasted only two months, and in considerable acrimony. As Chamberlain said: 'There never was known a more disorderly house, many more times like a cockpit than a grave assembly, and many that sat there were more fit to have been among roaring boys than in that assembly.'[7] Six years were to pass before another Parliament was called.

Raleigh could have felt little remorse when Henry Howard died on 15 June – he had been suffering from a gangrenous leg, and just before he died was received back into the Catholic church. Relations with Carr had cooled, but no doubt his great-niece missed him. If he had lived a year or so longer, the *Fata Mala*, one of the symbols depicted in the *History*'s frontispiece, could well have claimed him, and he might have ended his life in the Tower of London. The effigy of the old humbug can still be seen at the Trinity Hospital, Greenwich, piously kneeling with his hands in prayer.

At the end of 1613 Sir John Digby, the ambassador to Spain, had returned to England and had revealed that Howard, Cecil, the Countess of Suffolk, Sir William Monson, Admiral of the Narrow Seas, and Mrs Drummond, First Lady of the Bedchamber to the Queen, had all been receiving Spanish pensions. After James had recovered from the shock he decided not to take any action. Carr took the document and filed it among his own papers (which, when discovered, was thought to be suspicious).

On 10 July 1614, Suffolk was appointed Lord Treasurer and Carr took his place as Lord Chamberlain. A few weeks later James, while staying at Apethorpe, seat of Sir Anthony Mildmay in Northamptonshire, espied a figure of dazzling male beauty, with remarkably long legs, a young man of twenty-three called George Villiers. Opponents of Carr at once noticed that James was attracted, and efforts were made to tidy up this newcomer and present him at Court. He was intelligent and had good manners. Carr soon became suspicious and strongly objected to his being made a Groom of the Bedchamber, so instead Villiers became the King's Cupbearer, his Ganymede.

Carr's objections now developed into 'furious assaults', causing James insomnia, and there were many angry exchanges. Meanwhile, Carr's enemies enlisted the support of the Queen, who was delighted with the prospect of having him replaced by such a charming person, and it was at her insistence, in April 1615, that Villiers was dubbed a knight.

During the spring of 1615 Raleigh settled down to write a long essay dedicated to the King entitled *A Dialogue Between a Counsellor of State and a Justice of the Peace*, no doubt and as always unwelcome but nevertheless a readable and lively piece of political theory. It circulated in manuscript copies, but in 1628 was published in a pirated edition, slightly changed, as *The Prerogative of Parliaments*.

With the failure of the Addled Parliament in mind, Raleigh in the *Dialogue* touched on such matters as freedom of speech and the need of the monarch to cultivate the love of his people – the writing being tempered of course with large doses of flattery. Cooperation with Parliament and the removal of evil counsellors, 'moved by the love of their own future and glory', were main themes, and historical examples were given. This time there was no reference to the judgements of God; it was the will of the people that counted. He also turned to James's desperate need for money. In the past kings had been compelled to make reforms, but having got their money had broken their promises, 'for all binding of a king by law upon the advantage of his necessity makes the breach itself lawful in a king . . . The bonds unto subjects to their kings should always be wrought out of iron, the bonds of king unto subjects but with cobwebs.' This apparently pro-monarchist comment worried some of Raleigh's later Puritan admirers, but it could have been ironical. In any case he insisted that it was essential to recall Parliament, and to listen to the members' grievances.

At the same time he could not forbear the opportunity of complaining about the unjustness of his own imprisonment, and in his preface he compared himself to a dog, snapping back at those persecutors who had wrongly advised James to have him imprisoned. In any case, he pointed out, five out of the six people who had signed the warrant were dead, 'rotting' in their graves. The political climate having changed, Raleigh was hoping that James would at last recognize the value of his experience, and that this would result in his early release.

Raleigh also saw that opportunity had come to revive his plans for Guiana. In July he wrote to Winwood, sending copies of the letters he had written to Cecil (spelt 'Secill', no need any more to refer to him by his title Salisbury), the Queen and the King. As he put it, there had been many 'inventions to enrich His Majesty', but most of these would be in the long term. His proposal would cost the King nothing, and would not cause any 'offence to a Christian King'. He would take with him none but 'such as His Majesty shall acknowledge as his faithful servants', and he would give the King whatever proportion he wanted out of the riches that he brought back. He was old (sixty-one) and unfit, near the end of his life, and if he did not survive he would be 'exceedingly happy' to have to died 'in the way of His Majesty's service'.

Soon he wrote again, pointing out that the late Prince, the Queen and James's brother-in-law, the King of Denmark (who had visited England again in 1614), had all been pressing for his release. 'To die for the King and not by the King is all the ambition I have in the world.'[8] As it happened, he did soon become seriously ill, some said because he had been overcome by fumes in his laboratory. It could have been another stroke.

The new Spanish ambassador, Don Diego Sarmiento de Acuña, better known to posterity by his eventual title Conde de Gondomar, would not have been happy if he had learnt of those letters. To him and to most Spaniards, the name of Raleigh as an abhorred pirate was only second to the dreaded *corsario* Drake, the terror of the high seas in the time of the Jezebel of England, and he would have hoped that he would be shut away in the Tower for ever. Moreover he was a Galician and as a young man had been at the family home of Gondomar near Bayona at the time of Drake's raid in 1585. According to family tradition he had helped to 'chase' Drake's men to Vigo and had actually rescued a drowning Englishman from the sea.

Now aged forty-eight, he had arrived in England in August 1613, and he had set the scene at Portsmouth by refusing to dip his flags before the royal standard.[9] Although below medium height, he had a formidable presence, with a high forehead, pointed beard, brown hair and penetrating light blue eyes that enchanted English ladies but were regarded by their husbands as Machiavellian. Nevertheless he soon formed an unlikely and close friendship with James. In spite of alarming flares of temper, which frightened James, he had a fund of comic stories and would even burst into Spanish gypsy songs, and he knew that James loved to be flattered. Ben Jonson called him the Spanish Aeneas. He spoke French, but he and James usually spoke to one another in Latin, and when James corrected a mispronunciation (or thought he had) Gondomar tactfully apologized and told the King that he spoke the language like a 'master of arts'.

Gondomar's first task was to guide James away from a French marriage for his son Charles, which James had hoped would solve some of his financial troubles. It was natural that on his arrival he should at once have gone to see Henry Howard, whom he described to Philip III as the 'first gentleman of the kingdom,' praising him for his 'courage, virtue, prudence and refinement', a 'true celibate'.[10] Howard had apparently urged Gondomar to consider the possibility of a Spanish Infanta for Charles, and his sudden death was undoubtedly a shock to the Spaniard.*

Tempted by the prospect of a large dowry, James became interested in the possibility of a Spanish match for Charles. The proposal was referred by Philip III to the Pope, who – according to the Spanish ambassador in Rome – was full of doubts, particularly about the Infanta losing her faith if she married a heretic, but also because it was 'well known that the kings of England always consider it permissible to repudiate their wives when they have no children'.[11]

Gondomar was friendly with Sir John Digby, and advised James to leave the matter in his hands. But Carr had become aware of this, and had decided that a way of regaining favour with James would be to take over the

---

* Gondomar said in his letter to Philip that it was he who had encouraged Howard to return to the Catholic faith, which he did on his death bed.

negotiations from Digby. When it became known that Carr was communicating with Gondomar, the hatred of his enemies, including Winwood, became obsessive. They decided that once and for all he must be crushed.

By July whispers about Overbury's death had been gathering momentum. The apothecary's boy who had administered the fatal enema had been discovered in the Netherlands, and a story he had told had been relayed to Winwood. This must have been why Elwes, Lieutenant of the Tower, was so suddenly called in for examination. At the end of August Elwes decided that he must make a full declaration. Arrests followed swiftly, and the formidable and much feared Sir Edward Coke, who was now Lord Chief Justice, was put in charge of the trials. The first to be tried and found guilty was the gaoler Weston. Two days later, on 25 October, he was hanged at Tyburn. On that same day Elwes was removed from the Lieutenancy. On 2 November Carr was sent to the Tower and stripped of his seals of office. Frances was heavily pregnant, and thus for the time being only under house arrest. Mrs Turner was the next to be hanged, on 14 November.* Then it was the turn of Elwes, and he was hanged six days later. The apothecary was hanged on 8 December.

Carr had pleaded with the king to have the investigation quashed, but James would not allow 'such a crime to be suppressed and plastered over'. At the farewell scene James embraced him frequently, 'slabbering his cheeks', and had sent his love to Frances. But when Carr left his manner changed, and he said with a smile: 'I shall never see his face again'.

---

* Mrs Turner held the patent for making yellow starch for ladies' ruffs. After her execution yellow starch went out of fashion.

Release
1616

By early 1616 the release of Raleigh from the Tower was seeming inevitable. James was under pressure from Winwood and other enthusiasts in the anti-Spanish faction, and whether he liked it or not Raleigh's popularity as a symbol (or relic) of a lost golden age had been steadily increasing. Apart from this, if all that Raleigh had been claiming about Guiana gold were true, an addition to the Exchequer would be exceedingly welcome.

Raleigh had also had the idea of involving young Villiers. The rumour went about, which was probably correct, that he had given bribes of £750 each to Sir Edward Villiers, the favourite's half-brother, and Sir William St John, a cousin of Sir Edward's wife. On 17 March he was writing to Villiers: 'You have by your mediation put me again into the world . . . If it [the Guiana expedition] succeed well a great part of the honour shall be yours, and if I do not make it profitable unto you I shall show myself exceeding ungrateful.'

But he had been kept in suspense until the last moments, as is shown in a letter written by Edward Dyer on 7 March:[1]

For the news about town, no talk but of Sir Walter Raleigh and as I understand it is his own election to come out upon some conditions proposed, that he will presently be shipboard, and to remain in the Tower till ships be provided, and so to go the voyage to Guiana, but he doth not accept of those conditions, but entreats that he may have some time to walk about the town to show himself, for the comfort of being free is not so much as that others should take notice of it. And that he might propose so to furnish himself for the voyage, and because most of his substance will be expended towards the voyage he entreats likewise that something might be allotted by the State towards the maintenance of his wife and children if he should chance to suffer shipwreck or be robbed by pirates, and this he doth propound which is thought will be granted.

We can appreciate Raleigh's desire to show himself to the world at large, but there was also a great deal of preparation to be done for the voyage, which he had personally to supervise. He would indeed have been lucky if James agreed to make provision for his family, and it was not surprising that no notice was taken of such a suggestion. He was released by royal warrant on 19 March: 'For the business for which upon your humble request His Majesty has been pleased to grant you freedom'. He was not entirely a free man however, and had to be accompanied everywhere by a keeper. Moreover, he was not 'to presume to resort' to the Courts of the King, Queen or Prince, nor to go to 'any public assemblies wheresoever without especial licence obtained from his Majesty'.[2] As Carew told Roe in India, he 'remains unpardoned until his return'.[3] Carew also said that there were many kinsmen and friends who were eager to join the expedition, but 'only if they might be commanded by none but himself'.

According to Chamberlain,[4] Raleigh's release had been principally due not only to his ally Sir Ralph Winwood but to the Countess of Shrewsbury, who was now confined to the Tower, her crime being that she was Arbell's aunt, and had helped her to escape. The Countess, as Bess of Hardwick's daughter, was still a power, besides being immensely wealthy, and was given privileges which would have included being allowed to call on Raleigh.

Among those still in the Tower were Florence McCarthy and the Earl of Northumberland, who also had kept his privileges, and of whom it was joked that he had turned the place into a university. No doubt Raleigh went straight to his wife's house in Broad Street. Chamberlain wrote how soon afterwards he went 'up and down seeing sights and places built or bettered since his imprisonment'. Because of his bad leg much of this sightseeing would have been on horseback, and one can imagine the salutes – even cheers – of onlookers, curious to glimpse the still handsome face of this grey-haired legend. Durham House would have been a first objective, and there he would have seen Cecil's two-storeyed New Exchange on the site of his old stables. Ivy Bridge Lane, on the east side of Durham House, had been moved some yards to its present position to make way for the building of Little Salisbury House, adjoining Great Salisbury House. On the west side was Northampton House, Henry Howard's mansion.* He would have noticed a new chancel that had been added to St Martin-in-the-Fields by Prince Henry. The Banqueting Hall in Whitehall, where he had dined so often with Queen Elizabeth, had been demolished and rebuilt, 'very strong

---

* According to Gondomar 'when furnished it was one of the finest in Europe'. Howard in his will had left it to his nephew, the Earl of Suffolk. The New Exchange was still popular fifty years later. Pepys recorded going there to buy books and ribbons for his wife.

and stately,' in the new Palladian style (it was to be burnt down in 1619 and rebuilt once more by Inigo Jones).

It was ironical that only eight days after his leaving the Tower, his rooms should receive new and famous, or infamous, occupants, the Earl and Countess of Somerset, Frances Howard and Robert Carr.[5] Frances, after being separated from her baby, had been assigned to the lodgings of her victim Overbury, which threw her into such hysterics that the Lieutenant had to move her to the now vacant Bloody Tower. According to Carew, in his letter to Roe, it was her husband who actually lived in the Bloody Tower and she was put in Raleigh's 'new building'. Elsewhere it has been said that she was sent to Raleigh's garden house – the old hen-house, which must therefore have been enlarged and rebuilt. At any rate she made the place suitable for someone of her station. Her bedroom was decorated with crimson velvet and gold fringes, and her chairs were covered in satin. She was also allowed three maids, and there was a communicating door with her husband's rooms. Carr insisted on wearing his Garter and was permitted to wander around the Tower and to pay visits on Northumberland.

Bacon, who was now Attorney-General, conducted Frances's trial on 24 May. She pleaded guilty and soon afterwards Carr was also found guilty. Both were sentenced to be hanged, but were later pardoned. They remained in the Tower until 1622. At his trial Carr had furiously denied ever having received payments from Spain; but in fact Gondomar's letters reveal that he had asked for a pension of £1,500, as being the equivalent of that paid to Cecil, but at the time of the trial the first instalment had not arrived.[6] Many believed that there was also a 'foul stain of suspicion' upon Henry Howard, and if he had lived there is no doubt that he would have been brought to trial. Elwes on the scaffold denounced him, and Bacon was sure of his guilt. Gondomar's reactions have not been recorded.

Within a few days of his release Raleigh went to see Phineas Pett at Deptford, and advanced him £500 to build a great new ship of 440 tons. She was to be called the *Destiny*, and she was to be his flagship.[7] In due course he assembled six other ships on the Thames. Then there was the question of finance. Without Sanderson it was hard to get the City companies involved. At this time there tended to be more interest in the Muscovy Company, which had produced some good dividends from whaling, and in the development of the East India Company, which by then had established its first warehouse, at Surat north of Bombay.

Raleigh enlisted the help of Peter Van Lore and asked him to write to his brother-in-law in Amsterdam for assistance, in return for a share of the profits from Guiana.[8] Quite what this assistance was to be is unclear –

either a loan or for some Dutch ships, or perhaps even to round up English mercenaries who were serving under the Prince of Orange.* Bess was made to call in the £3,000 that she had loaned to the Countess of Bedford, and she sold her property at Mitcham† for £2,500. In all he himself spent £10,000, some of which he had to borrow on bills. As he was to say later, when he sailed for Guiana he had only £100 left, of which £48 was given to Bess.

The Crown contributed 700 crowns in tonnage money, in accordance with an Act of Parliament for the encouragement of shipbuilding. Bess's relatives the Earls of Huntingdon, Pembroke and Arundel between them provided £15,000 as sureties, and Huntingdon also provided two cannon for the *Destiny*. Raleigh asked for each gentleman volunteer to contribute up to £50. A total of £30,000 was said to have been invested in the expedition.[9]

He was still the same plausible Raleigh – gambler, energetic, obstinate, and as ever the actor. Did Bess really believe that he would succeed? He was a bird set free from a cage, ready to take any risks, any hardships, even in his sixties and weakened by strokes. She really had no option but to support him.

Unfortunately, some of the gentlemen volunteers were a rough lot, and as Raleigh put it drunkards, blasphemers, and such as their fathers, brothers, and friends would consider it 'an exceedingly good gain to be discharged of, with a mere hazard of fifty pounds, or even forty or thirty'.[10] Some were so obstreperous that he was obliged to discharge them before sailing.

Against this, and as so often in the past, were several loyal friends. Among them, inevitably, was Lawrence Keymis, while others included his nephew George Raleigh, who had been serving under Prince Maurice in the Netherlands, his cousin William Herbert who was also related to Pembroke, Roger North a friend of Hariot and Lord North's brother, and whom Aubrey described as an algebrist, Charles Parker a brother of Lord Monteagle, and Edward Hastings the brother-in-law of Huntingdon but who turned out to be a liability[11] for he was to die on the voyage because as Raleigh said 'both his liver, spleen and brains were rotten'. Then there was his son Wat, coming up to twenty-two, who was to be the captain of the *Destiny*.

Raleigh was being dined by Winwood and many influential friends. Aubrey tells a story that was told to him by Sir Benjamin Rudyerd, a poet and politician. Both Raleigh and Wat had been invited by 'some great personage'. On the way there Raleigh said to his son: 'Thou art such a

---

* Raleigh's letter to Van Lore was produced at the Court of Chancery in June 1622, when Bess sued Van Lore for the £600 that he had deducted in 1605 from the sale of the jewel which she said was her property (p. 406).   † p. 173.

quarrelsome, affronting creature that I am ashamed to have such a bear in my company.' At this Wat 'humbled himself' and promised to behave himself. He was placed next to his father at the dinner, and was 'very demure' for at least half the meal. Then suddenly he burst out with:

I, this morning, not having fear of God before my eyes, but by the instigation of the Devil, went to a whore. I was very eager of her, I kissed her and embraced her, and went to enjoy her, but she thrust me from her and vowed I should not: 'For your father lay with me but an hour ago.'

Raleigh, as might well be imagined, was 'strangely surprised' and 'put out of countenance at so great a table'. He gave his son

a damned blow over the face. His son, as rude as he was, would not strike his father, but strikes over the face of the gentleman that sat next to him, and said: 'Box about. 'Twill come to my father anon.'

The story became well known and another great joke. 'Box about' for a while was a favourite catchword.

Inevitably Raleigh would have been eager to meet members of the Virginia Company, and to receive first-hand news from colonists who had returned, among them Captain John Smith. Some of their experiences at Jamestown had been terrible, especially during the 'Starving Time' of 1609–10 which had included both pestilence and fever, and attacks by Indians. But by 1616, thanks to the rigid discipline of the Governor, Sir Thomas Dale, the situation was more stable, although there were only 381 settlers left. John Rolfe had begun growing tobacco in 1614, and this had been a success. Soon tobacco-growing was to become the life-blood of the colony.

Raleigh would also have wanted to meet the Indian princess Pocahontas, daughter of the chief Powhatan, who had married Rolfe.[12] They had arrived at Plymouth with their child Thomas early in June 1616. Everybody who was anybody wanted to see this exotic creature, now aged twenty-one. She quickly adapted herself to English ways and 'wore a hat and ruff and wielded a fan like a civilized fine lady'. James was sceptical about her royal status, and was so annoyed about Rolfe launching into tobacco-growing that he thought of sending him to the Tower. Queen Anne on the other hand (described by Gondomar in that year as more than ever *curiosa, jovial y vehemente*') gave parties for her. Pocahontas was also invited to the Banqueting Hall for Twelfth Night, when Ben Jonson's masque *The Vision of Delight* was performed with George Villiers as '*primer bailarin.*' Her husband however was excluded, being neither royal nor an aristocrat; so Pocahontas was accompanied by her relative Tomucomo.*[13]

For Gondomar the greatest worry at this *fiesta* was whether he should have precedence over the French ambassador. The Spanish and French ambassadors were always treated as the two senior diplomats and were entitled to sit on stools covered with brocade, whereas lesser fry had to have stools only covered with velvet. Gondomar was not well and had to have a chair with a back, but the back had to be removed when he sat down for the spectacle. James honoured him by making him sit beside the throne so that they could speak, whereas the French ambassador had to sit in front of Gondomar on a lower level (*Triunfo!*).[14]

Gondomar had been enraged by the release of Raleigh, whom he regarded as the deadly enemy of Spain, and by the news of his preparations for Guiana. What he found even more alarming was the general enthusiasm in the country, and more particularly the blatant anti-Spanish attitude of Winwood. It was ridiculous of James, he said, even to contemplate a Spanish marriage for Prince Charles and at the same time give this man his liberty. And why were preparations being made for arming his ships on such a scale? Raleigh, he told James, was merely making a pretence of looking for a mine; in reality he was going out as a pirate, intending to plunder the towns on the Spain Main and seize the treasure fleet at Mexico.[15]

Raleigh denied that he had any intention of turning pirate. One of his arguments was that Guiana was English because of its cession by the native chieftains on his journey there in 1595. The days had long past since the Spaniards could assert that they had rightful dominion over the whole of America from the Magellan Straits to the Arctic, and James himself had acknowledged this by permitting the founding of the Virginia colony, and by sponsoring the voyages of Harcourt and Roe. The French and the Dutch had also established forts on the American continent. He was of course aware of the creation of San Thomé, just a few huts, apparently, on the

---

* The famous story of Pocahontas saving the life of Captain John Smith was only revealed in 1624 by Smith himself in his *Grand History*. When he went to see her in 1616 she had difficulty in recognizing him. The excitements and entertainments of London were too much for the poor woman, and she died at Gravesend on 21 March 1617, just before she was due to return to Virginia. In 1957, on the 350th anniversary of the founding of the first permanent colony, the author of this book, who was representing Sir Walter Raleigh, went to Virginia as part of the UK Goodwill Mission. Others in the group included representatives of the City Companies which had subsidized the original expedition. Canon Selwyn Gummer, whose parish included Gravesend, represented Pocahontas, in place of Countess Mountbatten, her descendant.

Orinoco, but the mine to which he was aiming was a long way from that settlement.

Angry letters were sent by Gondomar to Philip III, telling how Raleigh 'with relatives and friends has created an Armada, and goes to Guiana along the river Orinoco, where he says there is a gold mine that so far has not been excavated by anybody and does not belong to your Majesty, and is far from your territories.' He now put up to James the cunning suggestion that Spain should provide an escort for Raleigh's fleet, and allow him to return with as much gold and silver as he had been able to find. Raleigh was certainly not going to be fooled by such a suggestion, and cited the report of the thirty-six men who had their throats cut.* [16]

Another point made by Gondomar was that if gold were to be found in any quantity in Guiana, it would immediately unleash a flood of English speculators, ready to sell up their properties in search of a vast reward, and they would be followed in a similar fashion by Dutch and French. Which would certainly have been true, as has been demonstrated with virtually every gold-rush and diamond-rush in history – ending inevitably in degradation and misery.†

James at first appeared to be accepting Raleigh's assurances that he had no intention of attacking Spanish property or Spanish people. The prospect of profits from gold seemed to override every objection. In any case all responsibility for avoiding a conflict would be on Raleigh, who after all still had the sentence of death hanging over him. As Professor Gardiner was to say: 'For James there was everything to gain. For Raleigh there was everything to lose.' [17]

Inescapably Don Diego Sarmiento de Acuña, Conde de Gondomar, will be remembered as Raleigh's most determined and deadly enemy, the ultimate cause of his ruin and death. He was born on 1 November 1567 at the family's *pazo*, Gondomar, the manor house he loved so much on the slopes of the little river La Ramallosa, surrounded by chestnuts, oaks, vineyards and orange groves, and which still has the columns and a fountain that he added – though there are now many houses in the valley below. [18] The Sarmientos were powerful in the south of Galicia, along the river Miño which forms the frontier with Portugal, both in relations with the Portuguese and as guardians of the coast from the river's estuary to Vigo. There were various branches of the family,

---

* p. 440.

† As observed by the author when visiting the gold-mines of Las Claritas in southern Venezuela, where the only beneficiaries were the prostitutes and the dealers, striding around with parrots on their shoulders and guns at their hips.

and the Conde must certainly have been related to Don Pedro Sarmiento de Gamboa, the Governor of Patagonia who was captured by the English in 1586. His grandfather had been *Corregidor*, equivalent to High Sheriff, of Granada and Governor of the Canaries, and his father had advised Philip II and the Bishop of Tuy, Diego de Torquemada, on Portuguese matters but had died young. His mother Doña Juana de Acuña came from a slightly grander family with distant royal links. He was married to Doña Constanza de Acuña, related to his mother but half Flemish (in fact illegitimate but this was glossed over); her father had been in the Army, and had been *Corregidor* of Alessandria in Lombardy. They had seven children.

Gondomar was educated at the Episcopal college at Tuy and at Toro, and probably studied law at Salamanca. He was *Corregidor* of Toro, then of Valladolid, where he bought the palace known as the Casa del Sol, and had created a famous library. When the capital was moved to Madrid, he continued to hold important offices, such as Councillor for Portugal and Notary in Chief for Toledo. He had been offered the Governorship of the Philippines but declined. He was also reluctant to go as ambassador to England, mainly because of the expense involved, but before he left he added a crypt to San Benito el Viejo, the church adjoining his palace in Valladolid, because as he disdainfully said he did not wish to be buried in an English *corral* (farmyard).

Doña Constanza and a son accompanied him to London. She proved a highly competent and well organized ambassadress – as she needed to be, because the house they rented in the Barbican had a household of seventy-two people. They had a large garden and a riding school for exercising the horses.[19] Also attached was a chapel which could accommodate 400, often the number present on Sundays. Their evenings were quiet because most courtiers were afraid of compromising themselves by visiting them. They played cards and dutifully read the life of each day's saint. The second volume of *Don Quixote* had just been published and was much enjoyed. Gondomar admired English literature (did he acquire a copy of Raleigh's *History?*), and when he left London he took with him forty chests of books. He also appreciated English tapestry-makers, goldsmiths and silversmiths. He was musical.

He found London water 'horrible', saying it gave him headaches and stomach aches, so he had casks of water sent from Mondariz in Galicia. He also sent for casks of Gondomar and Ribadavia wine, as well as fruit and Galician ham. On the other hand he appreciated English beef and fish, especially salmon and sole. He complained of snow in March, but said he was glad of the cool summers.

He was shocked by so many ruined monasteries and tombs, which he said had once been as fine as any in Europe after the Escorial. Then there was the sight of heads of Catholic traitors, so-called, at each end of London Bridge, and soon after his arrival there was a public burning of Catholic books outside St Paul's. He was indeed surprised by the size of the anti-Catholic and anti-Spanish faction close to the King, but his policy towards such people was to be generous with presents, usually wine. James was always ready for a barrel of Galician wine, especially Ribadavia, as was Francis Bacon. With ladies he had less of a problem; 'amber gloves' were a popular present. It was said that his female admirers waved handkerchiefs to him as he rode down the Strand. The Queen was very taken by his blue eyes, and was supposed to have confided her secrets in him; she was in any case a crypto-Catholic, though she attended Protestant services. She would also ask him to be her squire at parties, and to lead her in hand-in-hand *without* wearing gloves. It was the custom in England for men to greet ladies by kissing them on the lips, but Doña Constanza (understandably) would never allow James to do this.

Astute, bold, learned, strong-willed, crafty, intensely patriotic, witty: these are some of the epithets used when describing Gondomar. His 'barbed jocularity' and facetious jokes appealed to James, and he knew how to play up to the royal vanity, saying that Spain's King Philip looked upon him as the British Solomon and longed to put aside old quarrels. He went hunting with James and according to the Venetian ambassador 'vied with him in putting his hands in the blood of bucks and stags, doing cheerfully everything that his Majesty does and in this way chiefly he has acquired his favours.'[20] Such was his apparent ascendancy over the King that a popular nickname for James behind his back was Don Jacques or Don Jaime, and their relationship was frequently caricatured in pamphlets and plays. As the Venetian ambassador wrote to the Doge, you won James's favour 'by praising and admiring him and by making him believe that all those who have the honour to treat with him learn a great deal from his extraordinary wisdom'. In return James would open his heart, but as Gondomar said in the end you never quite knew what he was saying was really the truth.

Gondomar had expected a term of about three years in London, but James's reliance on him and his friendship were reckoned too valuable by the Council of State in Madrid. He continued to dangle the advantages of a Spanish marriage for Charles, by stressing the strength of Spain and the security that would come through Spanish friendship; then of course there was the possibility of a large dowry. The degree to which he managed to win James's confidence is shown by a letter (probably slightly exaggerated) which he wrote from Madrid some years after the end of his ambassadorial term: 'That a Spaniard should have been and still be a Councillor *not merely in your Majesty's Privy Council*, but in your private closet itself, does not exceed all possible merit of mine, but also exceeds all the services I can possibly have been able to render to your Majesty.'[21]

On 26 August Raleigh received the commission giving him authority to command the expedition to Guiana, but with the customary words 'trusty and well-beloved' erased, and sealed with the Privy Seal not the Great Seal. He was empowered to visit territories not under the dominion of any Christian prince, and was still 'under peril of the law'. The King reserved for himself a fifth part of all gold, silver, pearls and precious stones, but Raleigh was to be 'sole commander, to punish, pardon and rule according to such orders as he shall establish in cases capital, criminal and civil, and to exercise martial law in as ample a manner as our lieutenant-general by sea or land.'

And so we have the paradox of a man convicted as a traitor being nominated as the King's lieutenant-general, and although unpardoned allowed to pardon others.

There was at once a furious outcry from Gondomar, and as a result a promise was extracted from Raleigh that he should cause no injury upon the subjects of the Spanish King. The Doge of Venice had the translation of a letter from Winwood forwarded to him saying that if these orders were contravened 'Ser Vat Ralle' would pay with his head. Did Raleigh know that Winwood had actually written this letter?[22] If he did, then it dispels the theory that he sailed without knowing that he faced such a penalty.

Gondomar bombarded Winwood with requests for interviews, and in desperation Winwood suggested that he should meet the dreaded 'Gualteral' face to face. Such a suggestion, needless to say, was contemptuously refused. As for Raleigh, he certainly had no desire to fight the Spaniards, but he must have realized that it could hardly be avoided. He could scarcely have contemplated digging up a mine only a few miles from a Spanish settlement without some sort of confrontation.

There is a story, somewhat suspect, of a discussion between Bacon and Raleigh as they walked together in the gardens of Gray's Inn.[23] Raleigh was supposed to have boasted that he was prepared to seize the Spanish Plate Fleet if he failed to find the gold on the Orinoco. 'But that would be piracy,' said Bacon. 'Oh no,' was Raleigh's reputed reply. 'Did you ever hear of men who are pirates for millions? They who aim at small things are pirates.' It does seem rather unlikely that Raleigh would ever have made such a remark to the Attorney-General, a political opponent of Winwood, but the anecdote does make a point. Gold was everything. Raleigh believed that if he brought back enough all past sins would be put aside, as had happened in the days of Elizabeth; in theory she disapproved of piracy, but was perfectly prepared to reward Francis Drake and to demand a share of his profits. Raleigh misunderstood James if he thought he would do the equivalent.

As it happened, in 1618, the year of his return from Guiana, the value of the treasure brought from Mexico to Spain was reckoned at £2,545,454.

Raleigh's release had caused a sensation of a different sort abroad. The Doge wondered if in some way he could be of service to Venice. The Duke of Savoy, his ally, was now in a state of war with Spain, and was looking to France and England for help. The French were reluctant, so the Duke despatched an emissary, Count Scarnafissi, to James. In spite of the state of the English exchequer James had sent Savoy £15,000 the previous year. Now the suggestion was that he should form a league with Savoy, Venice, Holland, and the German princes. It was all very ambitious, but James was interested, or pretended to be interested, partly because he was annoyed at not having had word from Madrid about the proposed Spanish match.[24]

The city of Genoa had long been a worry for Savoy. It had a great harbour where Spanish ships were accustomed to land with reinforcements for their garrison at Milan. It was also exceedingly rich, a city of money lenders, and that winter they had advanced Spain a loan of the equivalent of £250,000. Whether Scarnafissi approached Raleigh first, or vice versa, is not clear. The suggestion is that Raleigh saw a lucrative and potentially safer alternative to Guiana, with a real chance of doing damage to Spain, and with the approval of Winwood and others who were urging for war. The plan that evolved was that he should make his ships available for the capture of Genoa, if James could be persuaded to add four more vessels. Further help might be obtained from Holland and France. As Lionello, the Venetian ambassador, wrote: 'This *cavaliere* is excellently informed upon the situation and the conditions of the place, and considers that he can take it by surprise'.

Delighted and full of hope, Scarnafissi went to James who again said he was interested. James asked him to continue the discussion with Winwood and Sir Thomas Edmondes, who had been ambassador in Paris. Playing his usual double game, he also said he wanted to be sure of a share of the booty.

Winwood and Edmondes were enthusiastic, and proposed a fleet of sixteen royal ships. But only a few days afterwards James announced that he did not wish to divert Raleigh from the Guianan expedition, which meant that the whole – admittedly risky – scheme had to be abandoned. Raleigh was very disappointed; it had been flattering to discover that he was held in such universal esteem. The real reason for James's decision would seem to have been that he had heard that a peace treaty was about to be made between Spain and Savoy.

The *Destiny* was launched on 16 December, as Phineas Pett said 'in float and good order', though there was much ado to get her into the water. Pett later was to complain that he had lost £700 on her and never received compensation.[25] As with the *Prince Royal* she had been one of the sights of London, and all the grandees had been to have a look, except for the Queen whose visit had been forbidden by the King. Even Gondomar had gone for a surreptitious check. Carew wrote to Roe that he 'prayed Heaven that she might be no less fortunate than is wished by me.'[26] He added that he had no doubts about Raleigh's sincerity and his confidence in the gold mine.

On 30 January Raleigh was told that he was to be freed from the necessity of being accompanied by a keeper. This still did not mean, however, that he had his pardon.

Earlier, Raleigh had learnt with the utmost bitterness that Sherborne had gone to Sir John Digby, who had proved a successful ambassador in Madrid and was later to be advanced to the earldom of Bristol. James had thought of giving it to Villiers, by now a Viscount, but to the young man's credit he had said: 'Do not build my fortune on another man's ruin.'[27] So instead Villiers had been given eleven manors. On 17 November by Privy Seal the discharge was awarded to Digby 'of the sum of £10,000 paid by him for the lordship, castle and manor of Sherborne heretofore belonging to Sir Walter Raleigh, attainted, and forfeited by the attainder of Robert, Earl of Somerset.'

As Chamberlain said: 'Besides the goodly house and other commodities [it] is worth £800 a year, and in a reasonable time worth double.' The Sherborne estate was in fact already worth double.

Aboard the *Destiny*
1617

Alarming rumours had reached the new French ambassador to London, Comte Des Marêts, suggesting that Raleigh had been approached by Huguenot leaders about making a raid on the port of St Valéry.[1] This at first does sound incredible, but there could have been something in it, Raleigh having already secretly decided to turn to the French for some form of assistance, as a safety net if things went seriously wrong in Guiana.

In case of bloodshed he wanted to be able to take refuge in a French port; from there he would be able to gain time and start negotiations with James. His other plan was to procure French ships that would accompany him to the Orinoco; they would act as a protection while he searched for the mine and dug out ore – and, more important, they would take the blame if fighting with the Spaniards were to be involved. He had already sent a messenger, a Frenchman called Captain Faige, to the Duc de Montmorency, Admiral of France, asking him to intercede with Louis XIII. Des Marêts might also have had an inkling of this, a complication being that he and his patron Richelieu were in the party opposed to Montmorency.

So Des Marêts went to visit Raleigh on board the *Destiny*. Having been duly reassured that Raleigh had no such raid in mind, he proceeded to flatter him and express regrets for 'all the sufferings inflicted on him by his long and unjust imprisonment, and by the confiscation of his property'. He appreciated, he said, how much Raleigh would have resented the grant of Sherborne to Sir John Digby.

Raleigh, duly encouraged, asked if they could meet again. This may have been because Gondomar was known to be making one last effort to prevent his ships leaving the Thames for Plymouth. Chamberlain reported that the Spanish ambassador's insistence had been such that 'Sir Walter Raleigh's voyage was within these few days in question and in great hazard to be overthrown here at home, when he is now *in procinctu* [prepared for battle] and in a manner ready to be gone.'[2] Carew told Roe that Raleigh was acting 'nothing appalled' by the prospect that Spanish forces were being sent to intercept him, and was as confident of finding the Guianan gold as he was 'of not missing his way from his dining-room to his bedchamber'.[3]

Gondomar had now been in London for nearly four years. Although his domination over James was as strong as ever, it was always on the surface; James had his own games, and Gondomar knew it. Gondomar could deliberately switch on a show of anger, even rage, but he knew that patience was important. He warned James that the dangers from Raleigh's intentions were so real that they could easily break the friendship between the two crowns. He was utterly convinced that Raleigh had designs on the treasure fleet. Why otherwise should his ships be so heavily armed? He also pointed out that among the crews were well-known pirates (true), and they certainly would not want to come back empty-handed if they failed to find gold – which he did not in any case believe existed. There were also rumours that instead of going to Guiana Raleigh might be planning to head for the East Indies.

Most of these arguments had been relayed to the *Junta de Guerra*, Council of War, in Madrid, and they had been passed on to the royal favourite and chief of staff, the Duque de Lerma, and then to the King. But so far there had been little action, apart from sending warning letters to the Governors of Trinidad, Margarita and Cumaná; replies were still awaited. Then came reports that six 'ships of adventurers' were being prepared in Holland in order to assist Raleigh. Either Gondomar's informants had been muddled, or 'Guaterale' really had been sounding out the possibility of help from Holland through Van Lore's contacts.[4]

Much more worrying at this stage for the *Junta* was the new suggestion from another source that these large and well armed ships of Raleigh's were not going to Guiana at all, or to the East Indies, but preparing to leave for Virginia. From there it was believed that he was intending to move on to Jamaica, and this was far more serious, because Jamaica was on the main route for the treasure fleet from Mexico to the Bahamas channel before crossing the Atlantic.

But Gondomar had said nothing about Jamaica. He had to be patient with the Spanish government, as it creaked towards action.

Meanwhile James told Gondomar that, if he attempted to prevent Raleigh from leaving, the whole country would 'cry out'. He had put the matter up to the Privy Council, and the verdict had been that on no account should Raleigh be stopped. He did however provide Gondomar with a consolation: he had ordered the Lord Admiral to make a survey of Raleigh's fleet, and the result would be passed on to him. He would also get Raleigh to write a letter confirming that he was indeed going to Guiana and would not harm

Spanish subjects or encroach on Spanish territory. And not only that, Raleigh would have to produce a map showing precisely where he was going, and where he believed the gold mine to be.[5]

On 15 March the Lord Admiral's officers went to Gravesend, and it was confirmed that the 440-ton *Destiny* had 36 guns; her master was Robert Burwick. On board would be 100 sailors, 20 watermen, 80 gentlemen, and various servants and labourers, some of whom may have been intended as miners.

The *Star*, otherwise known as the *Jason*, was 240 tons, with 25 guns, 80 men, and commanded by Captain John Pennington. The *John and Francis* (or *Thunder*) was 150 tons, with 20 guns, 60 soldiers, 10 land-men, 6 gentlemen and commanded by Sir William St Leger. The *Flying Joan* was 120 tons, with 14 guns, 25 men, commanded by Captain John Chudleigh. The *Husband* (or *Southampton*) was 80 tons, with 6 guns, 25 mariners, 2 gentlemen, and commanded by Captain John Bailey. The 25-ton pinnace, the *Page*, with 3 brass robinets (cannons), was commanded by Captain James Barker. So the total so far came to 1,215 tons, 431 men, 121 guns or pieces of ordnance. Then there was the *Encounter*, 160 tons, with 17 guns, one gentleman, commanded by Edward Hastings; to date her crew had not been picked.

The list, along with Raleigh's letter and the map, was given by Winwood to Gondomar. Raleigh was to complain afterwards that this had been a betrayal of confidence. But the letter contained virtually nothing that was not already known. It would have been easy for anybody to obtain a full list of the seven ships, with all the details of their armaments and commanders. The information given was exactly what Raleigh had been saying for months, but for him the inclusion of the map was potentially dangerous.

All this reached the *Junta* at the end of May. There were still objections, particularly about the cost of mounting a fleet to intercept Raleigh; it was also pointed out that apart from the *Destiny* the ships on the list were mostly small, hardly in the category of warships.[6] At least it was now possible to decide that Jamaica no longer appeared to be in danger, though as a precaution an engineer should be sent out to supervise the island's defences. It was also agreed that the Governor of Brazil should be alerted; he might have ships available for an emergency.

Such a cool reaction to Gondomar's warning was an advantage to Raleigh – if he but knew of it – rather than a betrayal. In any case, by the time the report reached Madrid he was just about to sail.

Arundel came aboard the *Destiny* before she left Gravesend. He took Raleigh by the hand and asked him to promise that come what may he

Frontispiece to the first edition of the History of the World.

would return to England.[7] Raleigh, who only a few days before had been conferring with Des Marêts, solemnly gave his word.

On 29 March Chamberlain wrote:[8]

Sir Walter Raleigh took his leave yesternight of Master Secretary [Winwood] and goes this morning toward Dover where he hopes to find his ship, though his followers are yet in the river and make no haste after him. He makes away with all the speed

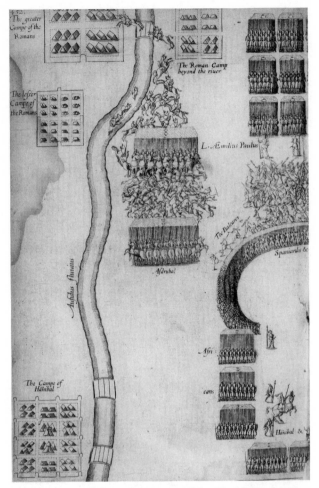

The Battle of Cannae, from the History of the World, *Book IV, p. 452.*

he can for fear of a countermand, by reason of some message brought by the Lord Roos . . . and it is observed that the Prince is no friend to the journey, but hindered the Queen from going to see his ship as she had appointed on Wednesday last. God knows there needs no such working to overthrow the voyage.

Lord Roos, as ambassador,* had arrived from Spain with a message from Philip III, namely that the theologians had at last agreed that the possibility of a Spanish marriage for Prince Charles could be investigated.[9] As a result

---

* This disreputable character was to be accused of incest with his stepgrandmother Lady Exeter.

James had decided to make a public declaration on the subject. This was bad news for Raleigh, but Carew spoke for all those who loved and admired him. 'God grant he may return loaded with Guianan gold!' The blue waters of the open seas were getting tantalizingly close.

Des Marêts had said to Richelieu that he had been too busy to see Raleigh before he left. Nevertheless on 14 April he told him that Raleigh had said that 'seeing himself so easily and tyrannically treated by his own King, he had made up his mind, if God sent him good success, to leave his country, and to make the King of France first offer of whatever might fall under his power.'[10] That Raleigh should ever have said such a thing must again surely be unlikely; if he did, and if he really meant it, his wife and family would have to face ruin and disaster, and he would also be betraying loyal friends. Perhaps Des Marêts had misunderstood him, or his memory was at fault – or he wanted to give Richelieu the impression that his influence was greater than it really was.

In any case, Richelieu's curt comment was that Raleigh was a '*grand marinier et mauvais capitaine*', a great sailor and a bad captain; even so, he was by no means discouraging about a possible collaboration.[11]

Troubles began long before Raleigh reached Plymouth. While still on the Thames the *Southampton*'s anchor cable had fouled the *Destiny*'s and John Bayley was infuriated when Raleigh ordered his cable to be cut. At the Isle of Wight Bayley decided to marry a local girl, and announced that he would continue on the expedition only if he could be the first to bring news home. The way things turned out, it would have been far better if Raleigh had refused, and had let this arch trouble-maker stay behind.

Off the Downs Warham St Leger had trouble with his ship, and repairs were needed. More worrying was when Raleigh's vice-admiral, John Pennington, again at the Isle of Wight, had been forced to stop there because he had run out of money. Even the bakers were refusing to supply bread for his ships, and he had to ride off in haste to London to ask for help from Bess. All the unfortunate woman could do was to give him some letters of credit, to be cashed at Portsmouth. Almost worse, Raleigh was forced to sell some of his remaining plate to pay for feeding Thomas Whitney's sailors on the *Encounter*.

Four more ships were waiting for him at Plymouth. They were commanded by Sir John Ferne, Richard Wollaston, Samuel King, and Lawrence Keymis (in command of the *Convertine*). More money had to be raised for Ferne, a rapscallion who had once been an embarrassment to the East India Company and had been forced to take refuge in France. Samuel King was a trusted friend, but Wollaston was a slippery character, more than half a pirate. Altogether Raleigh counted on a strength of 1,000 men.

The delays in departure, as in the days of Essex, resulted in much ill-temper and unrest. There had already been a riot at Gravesend, when the towns-people had driven some of Raleigh's men into the 'mud of the river', while James Hancock, a ship's officer, reported from Plymouth that there were 'continual quarrels and fighting' and 'many dangerous hurts'.[12]

Faige arrived at Plymouth with a letter from Montmorency with a some-what guarded promise that he would do his best to allow Raleigh into a port on his return journey, bringing with him any goods he might have acquired by trade '*ou conquis*', or conquest.[13] The great news from France at this time, and appreciated all over Europe, was the assassination of the Queen Mother's hated favourite, the Italian Concini. Raleigh expressed his own joy in a letter to De Bisseaux, previously ambassador in London and now a member of the French Council of State. He rejoiced, he said, at 'this happy change in affairs', which 'gives me hope and courage, assuring me that the Spanish party will not now be so powerful.'

This letter was given to Faige with a copy of Montmorency's letter and a request for confirmation about entry into French ports. Faige was to be accompanied by one Antoine Belle, one of the many worthless characters in whom Raleigh was fated to put his trust; they had been in communication when Belle was in prison in London. Faige and Belle were afterwards to take charge of four vessels which were being fitted out at Le Havre and Dieppe, and with the aid of a map would join Raleigh's main expedition off the Guianan coast. If all this had worked out according to plan, the outcome of the venture might have been very different.

The two emissaries had their own ideas, however. Instead of making their way to De Bisseaux they went straight to collect at least one of the ships and then set off to the Mediterranean for some trading on their own account, which they imagined would be less perilous and more profitable than sailing up the Orinoco to fight Spaniards. They had made a bad mistake, for they were soon captured by Algerian pirates.

Faige eventually ended up ill in a debtors' prison at Genoa. Belle reached Rome, where he confessed to have worked for the infamous *corsario* Sir Walter Raleigh, and at his own request was sent to Madrid, taking with him all the papers that had been entrusted to him and Faige, and which had been miraculously saved from the pirates. Under interrogation he insisted that it had been Raleigh's intention to attack and plunder Margarita and Trinidad after working on the mine, and that afterwards he meant to return to Europe for reinforcements. Thus De Bisseaux never received his letter, and no French ships joined Raleigh at the Orinoco.* Belle was sent back to England with a *propina*, tip, of 100 ducats. Whatever Raleigh had originally thought of him, he would hardly have been likely to confide plans such as these, even if they were genuine.

On 3 May Raleigh issued his *Orders to be Observed by the Commanders of the Fleet*, a lengthy document described by a member of the expedition as a 'model of godly, severe and martial government'. They certainly do not read as if they were compiled by someone bent on turning renegade, and it is hard to believe that this motley collection of rogues would be ready to live up to such lofty precepts.[15]

There was to be divine service twice a day, with a psalm sung every night before the setting of the watch. There was to be no blaspheming, stealing, gambling by dice or cards, smoking between decks, or eating or drinking between meals. Only meat that had been salted for several hours should be eaten, and certainly not 'over-fat hogs or turkeys'; and no fruit should be eaten that birds or animals refused to touch. He would only allow swimming in places which Indians considered safe (remembering that experience in 1595 when a Negro was eaten by an alligator). No man should strike an officer or rape a woman, 'Christian or Heathen', under pain of death. And there was to be no sleeping on the ground. There were explicit instructions about firefighting, signalling emergencies or the sighting of a strange ship, and cleaning firearms.

There may have been discontent among his crews at Plymouth, but on his arrival he had a great welcome, as the last of an heroic generation which had brought the south-west such great profit from privateering. The mayor, Robert Trelawny, was awarded £9 for 'entertaining Sir Walter Raleigh and his followers at his house', and this was 'done by general consent'. A drummer was given twelve pence for beating the tattoo as Raleigh mounted the gangplank to his flagship.[16]

The fleet sailed on 19 June, and out to sea were joined by 'loiterers', which brought up the total of vessels to thirteen. Almost immediately there was a storm and they were driven back to Plymouth. They re-emerged, but there was yet another storm, and they were blown into Falmouth harbour where as James Hancock said, 'We attend the pleasure of Almighty God for a fair wind'. The wait for His pleasure turned out to be 'very tedious and without comfort', and there were yet more quarrels and fights: 'But I thank God we have not lost a man yet ... we still feed with hope'. Raleigh took the

* The correspondence and papers are now at Simancas, where they were discovered by Gardiner in the 1860s.[14]

opportunity of dumping the worst offenders on land, the excuse being that he expected to be away a year and needed to save victuals.

Out to sea there was once more another gale, even worse, and a pinnace was lost off the Scillies. One ship managed to reach Bristol. 'Himself and some others', wrote Chamberlain, 'are in several ports in Ireland', chiefly Kinsale and Cork. 'God speed him and send him a better voyage than I can hope for'.[17]

Raleigh stayed at Cork where he was well entertained by old friends and old enemies, including Lords Barry and Roche, but especially by Richard Boyle, now Lord Boyle and soon to be remembered as 'the great Earl of Cork', and to whom Raleigh had sold his estate in 1602. The gales continued and they could not leave for three weeks, thus losing the best part of the season for crossing the Atlantic. Raleigh was to be criticized for the delay, and he certainly enjoyed being in Ireland again, going out hawking with a FitzGerald at Cloyne and riding up for a last look at beautiful Lismore Castle, once his and which he had begun to repair, and the silvery Blackwater river winding below. It seems that he could not bear to visit the house he had loved so much at Youghal.

Boyle was still having trouble with that 'grasping and litigious spirit' Henry Pyne,* and Raleigh gave him help in a legal case, and this meant going to Mogeely, where he had started the timber business.[18] Boyle was said to have kept open house to Raleigh and his followers, and through his generosity the stay in Ireland proved a considerable advantage. He lent Raleigh £350, and provided the ships with 100 oxen and many stores, including beer, biscuits and iron ballast to the value of 600 marks. He also gave Raleigh a 32-gallon cask of whisky. In return Raleigh told him that he would abandon certain claims which were outstanding on the estate.

At long last, on 19 August, the fleet managed to sail, 'in a frank gust of wind': southwards to trouble.[19]

* p. 339.

Chronicle of Death
1617

'The 19th of August at 6 o'clock in the morning, having the wind at NE, we set sail in the river of Cork where we attended a fair wind seven weeks.'[1] So ran the first entry in Raleigh's *Journal* for the voyage to Guiana. Now this *Journal* is in the British Library: twenty-three pages of close script, very faded, the narrative continuing until 13 February when it comes to an abrupt stop. It is a moving document to hold, not just because of the tragedies ahead and the horrors it describes, but because of its glimpses of wonders such as rainbows, moonlight reflections and shoals of fish, written by a man who for so many years had been shut away from the natural world.

Eleven days after their departure, off Cape St Vincent four suspicious-looking ships were sighted and given chase. They turned out to be French. Captain Bailey boarded them and seized a net, a pinnace and some pipes of oil, claiming that the men were pirates and had plundered Spaniards in the West Indies. He was enraged when Raleigh insisted on paying the market value of 61 crowns for these things, maintaining that it was lawful for the French to capture Spanish ships 'beyond the line', west of the Canaries and the Azores. 'I did not suffer my company', Raleigh wrote, 'to take from them any pennyworth of their goods, greatly to the discontentment of my company who cried out that they were men of war and thieves, and so indeed they were, for I met with a Spaniard afterward of the Gran Canaria whom they had robbed.'[2]

With a favourable wind behind them they reached the island of Lanzarote in the Canaries late on 5 September. They anchored in the bay of Arrecife, where there were a few dwellings and a castle on a spit of land, the Castillo de San Gabriel. Raleigh badly wanted water and provisions for his ships. In the morning he landed some 400 men 'to stretch their legs' on the beach, greatly alarming the locals who thought they must be those same Barbary pirates who had recently raided Porto Santo off Madeira. The Governor, by name Captain Hernán Peroya, emerged from the castle with an armed band and a flag of truce. It was arranged that he would meet Raleigh face to face, provided that each would be accompanied by a single companion only, equipped with a rapier and no other weapon. Raleigh brought with him Captain Bradshaw, who was partly Portuguese and could speak Spanish. 'The Governor's first desire was to know whether we were Christians or Turks, whereof being satisfied, he demanded what I sought of him from that miserable and barren island peopled in effect by Moriscos.' Raleigh assured him of his peaceful intentions and said he only wanted to buy fresh food and collect water. The local people, however, after seeing Bradshaw's swarthy complexion, were still convinced that the intruders must be Turks.

There happened to be an English merchant ship in the harbour, bringing wine from Tenerife and loading up with grain. The Governor asked Raleigh to put his request in writing, and promised to send him 'some few muttons and goats' for himself and his captains. The next morning therefore Raleigh sent him a note by means of the captain of the merchant ship asking for 'wheat, goats, sheep, hens and wine', for which he would pay, and giving his word that his men would not go inland further than a mile or two.

Lanzarote was indeed a very poor island, volcanic with a weird desert-like landscape of extinct cones, so it would have been difficult to supply Raleigh's 1,000 men with all the food they needed. The only town was Teguire, seven miles inland, well away from pirates and other marauders – at least, so the inhabitants hoped. Raleigh waited, spending the day 'training and mustering our companies on the sea-shore', which could not have been an encouraging sight for the '*conejeros*', rabbit-keepers, as the local people were known to the Spaniards. On the next morning Peroya sent his reply, assuring Raleigh that 'on the faith of a *caballero*', gentleman, he would send the provisions the following day.

Raleigh suspected that Peroya was merely playing for time, to enable him to move goods and women and children up to Teguire, and he was right. The men became restless and demanded to march on the town, but Raleigh refused because he said it might put the English merchant in danger, and in any case the way up there was mountainous and stony. Also the Spaniards had a force of 300 men, ninety of them being musketeers, and had the advantage of superior ground. Two days passed and there was still silence from Peroya, so Raleigh sent him a fierce letter, saying that if he did not know that it would 'offend the King my sovereign' he would have pulled the Moriscos from their town 'by the ears'. At the same time he gave the English merchant twenty shillings to 'buy some hens and other trifles'.

Peroya beat the merchant for daring to attempt to buy things without his leave, and sent him with a note to Raleigh saying that now he knew he really was a Turk, and that even if he were English he – Peroya – would be hanged for helping him.* Back was sent the unfortunate merchant, with a scathing letter from Raleigh, in effect saying that judging from the shabbiness of his clothes Peroya must be in need of cash and Raleigh would have been glad to send him 40 *rials* to buy a doublet. And with that he sailed away.

Only later in the *Journal* did Raleigh reveal that two of his men had been killed on Lanzarote. He blamed it on the 'madness and vanity' of a sergeant who with two other men had wandered off without permission. They had met a group of thirteen islanders, who pretended to be friendly and had then attacked them. The sergeant and another were killed, but the third escaped with twenty-four wounds from which he was to die several days later.

Raleigh had refused to take reprisals. He does not mention in the *Journal* that it was at this stage Bailey deserted, claiming to be upset by such supine behaviour. But there was much more to it than that, for according to a Spanish report Bailey was pursued by Raleigh's ships in vain for three hours.

The fleet sailed on to Gran Canaria, and moored off the southern end of the island. Raleigh sent copies of his correspondence with Peroya to the Governor, who happened to be the Conde de Salvatierra, a Galician and – which of course Raleigh was not to know – related to Gondomar. He said that he had come in peace, and was only looking for water and fresh meat; he also asked whether, as the Spanish king's Lieutenant of the Canaries, Salvatierra had given instructions to Peroya not to deal with him. (If so, Raleigh would know that warnings about his possible arrival had already been sent from Madrid.)

The weather was extremely hot, and some of the men were sick, so Raleigh decided that he would wait only a day longer for an answer. Meanwhile he landed a force of sixty men, some to fish and some to fill casks with water. The *Journal* records that a few islanders crept up by 'favour of the trees' and attacked the sentinels, wounding one,

but he behaved himself so well as he slew one of them and recovered his pike. Captain Thornehurst being a valiant and active man hastened to their rescue and with a horseman's piece shot another of them. Mr Hawton with his pick wounded the third, so as all three died in the place, the rest took to their heels.

As at Lanzarote the southern coast of Gran Canaria had and has little rainfall, and the springs had virtually dried up. So once more Raleigh sailed on, this time for the island of Gomera.

* As it happened, in May 1618 a fleet of sixty Turkish and Algerian ships arrived at Lanzarote and sacked Teguire, carrying off 900 people into captivity, no doubt including Peroya.

It was maintained later in Spain that he had robbed a caravel of salt and wine. He did admit that a fishing vessel from Cape Blanc (in Morocco) with fourteen men aboard had been taken by a pinnace, and that one of the men had 'asked' (*sic?*) to accompany him – presumably the man was a Spaniard and the rest were Moors.

As for the request for fresh meat, what – it could be asked – had become of Lord Boyle's gift of 100 oxen?

Bailey's return caused a sensation in London. As Carew wrote to Sir Thomas Roe: 'The cause of his abandoning the fleet he allegeth to be the fear that Sir Walter would turn pirate . . . which for my part, I will never believe.'[3]

The news came just when Winwood had died, so Sir Thomas Lake, acting as Secretary of State, brought the news to Gondomar, and as expected there was an immediate explosion of fury. This was exactly what Gondomar had predicted. And now there were stories going around that Raleigh had really meant to capture Lanzarote and lie in wait there for the treasure fleet from the Caribbean; it was monstrous, an act of war . . .

Gondomar was not at all well, and said to be in a state of 'nervous irritability'. He had been dangerously ill in January, and in July had been unable to accept James's invitation to accompany him to Scotland. He had often asked Madrid that he should be relieved, but had always been over-ruled because of the importance of his personal influence over the King, who now to all intents treated him as his most intimate friend. Gondomar was also upset because he had heard that valuable books from his library at Valladolid had been stolen.

On 22 October he wrote at length to Philip, enclosing a letter from Lake, which expressed the great grief of King James:[4]

The King promises that he will do whatever we like to remedy and redress this outrage. Although I judge Lake to be a very honest man, and sincere in what he says, I look upon it as absurd to expect that a fitting redress will be afforded here for so atrocious a wickedness as this, as I clearly foresaw and foretold . . . The captain [Bailey] says he had sailed with him [Raleigh] under the belief that his intention was to discover unknown countries, but when he saw his evil object he returned hither to the Isle of Wight, where he now is . . . Raleigh's friends are greatly perturbed, and are trying to find excuses for him . . .

He recommended that an embargo on English shipping should at once be put into effect by the authorities in Seville, as if of their own volition. A fleet *must* be sent out to punish this pirate – it should be easy, as Raleigh's force was small. Every man captured should be put to death, at once, except for Raleigh himself and his officers who should be publicly executed in the plaza at Seville. 'This is the only way to treat such pirates and disturbers, and a necessary step for preservation of peace with England, France and Holland.'

He also said that Raleigh had written to Lord Southampton from the Canaries, saying that he had decided to wait there for the arrival of the Plate Fleet, and that some French ships had joined him. This was nonsense and must have been based on gossip, as such a claim was never repeated elsewhere. Very likely Gondomar was confused by the fact that Bailey's ship had been the *Southampton*.

Next day Gondomar wrote again to Spain, urging that the authorities in Seville and the Canaries should act quickly and decisively, to show the English that they would tolerate these outrages no longer. James, clearly upset and worried, was publicly saying that if what Bailey had said was true Raleigh and his backers must pay with their heads. Meanwhile, he said, friends of '*el Ralle*' had made his wife demand that Bailey should be brought to justice for traducing her husband.

Members of the crew of the *Southampton* were indeed questioned, some agreeing that Raleigh was a pirate, others saying that they had not wanted to desert him. Then in December the captain of the merchant ship who had been at Lanzarote with Raleigh, referred to as Master Reeks, arrived in London and was examined. His story gave Raleigh a complete clearance – and in fact what he said coincides with the *Journal*, which of course nobody had seen.[5] He said that Raleigh had throughout been careful not to transgress his commission, contrary to the desire of his captains who had wanted revenge. He also spoke about the clash on Gran Canaria, but in his version it had been the governor who had attacked, not the 'islanders', and one English sailor had been killed.

Bailey was now brought before the Privy Council and his demeanour was considered very unsatisfactory: 'He blancheth and deals not ingenuously with his answer,' so it was reported.[6] As a result he was committed as a close prisoner to the Gatehouse prison, for having 'behaved himself undutifully and contemptuously' and making 'foul and base imputations' as well as 'threatening speeches' against Raleigh. There he remained for seven weeks, until released on 27 February, having made 'humble acknowledgement under his hand of his offence and hearty sorrow for same'.[7]

Gondomar being again ill, his secretary Antonio Sánchez de Ulloa wrote to Madrid reporting all this, but saying that the ambassador considered that it made no difference and that *medicina segura*, preventive medicine, must still be taken. The Spanish government remained indecisive; but quite independently information had reached Seville about Raleigh's exploits at Lanzarote; there the story went that Raleigh's men had actually robbed people of wine and food. As a result English ships at Seville were impounded and demands made for compensation for the islanders.

Raleigh had been told that Gomera was the 'best of all the Canaries', with a good supply of water. Columbus had stayed there on his second journey, and although it was forbidding-looking from out at sea, the interior had fertile valleys with plenty of fruit. He found on arrival that the little town of San Sebastián and its castle stood on the 'very breach of the sea', but that the 'billows do so tumble and overfall as it is impossible to land upon any part of the strand except by swimming, saving in a cove under steep rocks.' And, sure enough, even before they could anchor, they were fired upon from those rocks. So 'we to let them know that we had good ordnance gave them some 20 demiculverin through their houses and then forbore.'

The 'friendly' Spaniard picked up from the fishing boat at Gran Canaria was sent to reassure the Governor of Raleigh's peaceful intentions. This Governor turned out to be the Conde de Guzmán, from another grand Spanish family, and he had already been alerted about a foreign fleet lurking around the Canaries, possibly those Turks who had raided Porto Santo. The situation was duly sorted out, and Raleigh was allowed to send unarmed men to fill casks from Columbus's well.

Raleigh had heard that the Governor's wife, although Flemish, had English forebears,* and he sent her six 'exceeding fine' handkerchiefs and six pairs of gloves (strange luggage for the tropics). She was enchanted and 'sent me answer that she was sorry her barren island had nothing worthy of me, and with her letter sent me 4 very great loaves of sugar, a basket of lemons which I much desired to comfort and refresh our many sick men, a basket of oranges, a basket of most delicate grapes, another of pomegranates and figs, which items were better welcome to me than 1000 crowns could have been'. More exchanges followed. He sent her twelve ounces of ambergris perfume, an ounce of extract of amber, 'a great glass of rosewater in high estimation here', a cutwork ruff and, oddly for such a staunch anti-Catholic, a 'very excellent picture of Mary Magdalene' (loot from the French ships off Cape St Vincent, perhaps). She sent back more fruit, two dozen fat hens and a 'basket of delicate white machete [bread].'

---

* According to Raleigh, from the Stafford family. It is said in Gomera that she had been born Maria Van Dalle y Vandeverde. The island, incidentally, is famous because of the adventures of another great lady of legend, the beautiful Beatríz de Bobadilla.

This was one of the last happy episodes in Raleigh's life. He managed to fill 240 pipes of water, and before his sailing away, on the evening of Sunday 21 September, the Conde sent a friar aboard the *Destiny* with a letter addressed to Gondomar which told him 'how noble we had behaved ourselves, and how justly we had dealt with the inhabitants of the island'. Raleigh also left behind the Spanish fisherman, to whom he gave eight ducats.

The wind had dropped, which meant a delay, but later picked up strongly. Two men died on the *Destiny* and there were fifty men sick. They reached the Cape Verde Islands but decided to avoid the most westerly island São Antão, having heard – erroneously – that it was 'desolate', and headed for Brava further south, which was known to be inhabited. Meanwhile, there were more deaths, including the master-surgeon Mr Nubal, a great loss, also one of the quartermasters and the sailmaker. A pinnace was sunk during the night, having been driven under the *Destiny*'s bowsprit, but its crew was saved 'though better worthy to have been hanged than saved' – a curious remark, but presumably because of their lubberly shiphandling.

Brava was the most south-easterly of the islands, very small, with plenty of water and some maize and cattle, but there was 'very inconvenient anchorage' and a hurricane suddenly swept up 'with the most violent rains, and broke our cables at the instant, greatly to the damage of the ship, and all our lives . . . I was myself so wet as the water ran in at my neck, and out at my knees, as if it had been poured on with pails.' All the ships lost their cables and anchors, and another pinnace sank. One of his trumpeters and a man from the cookroom died.* So Raleigh was forced to sail on, without even having been able to land on the island, or bring in some fish, which were known to be abundant in those waters.

After being buffeted by the weather, the ships now being virtually half manned, and swept south by a strong current, they suddenly found themselves in a great calm and unable to move; as in the *Ancient Mariner* upon a painted ocean. And so the journey which could have taken a fortnight lasted nearly forty days. In the stifling heat the sickness turned into an epidemic.

In his *Journal* Raleigh recorded the terrible chronicle of death. On 6 October there 'died to our great grief our principal refiner Mr Fowler', who had been vital to the enterprise. This was followed by a loyal supporter, Richard Moore, who had been Governor of the Bermudas. Then 'Crab died, so I had not any one left to attend me but my pages.' Crab had been with

---

* Trumpeters were always at the captain's command and stayed on the poop, ready for orders, alarms, hailing ships, boarding etc.

him in the Tower, as had John Talbot, who died on 13 October, 'my honest friend'. Also on 13 October he lost Captain John Pigott who was to have been his second-in-command of the land forces, his personal cook Francis, and 'Mr Gardner and Mr Mordent two very fair conditioned gentlemen.'

'By reason of the tornado at Brava, failed of our watering we were at this time in miserable estate not having in our ship above 7 days of water, 60 sick men, and nearly 400 leagues off the shore, and becalmed.' Then the sky became so dark 'we steered our ship by candlelight.'

Violent rain and wind followed, and they just missed a waterspout. Double and even triple rainbows heralded yet more foul weather, but on 22 October there was a clear night and 'we saw Magellan's Cloud round and white which riseth and setteth with the stars'.* On 29 October 'the circle about the moon on Tuesday night and the double rainbow on Wednesday morning paid us towards the evening with rain and wind, in which gust we made shift to save some 3 hogsheads of water, besides the company having been many days scanted and pressed with drought drank up whole quarter cans of the bitter rainwater.'

Then Raleigh himself was struck down. He had slipped on deck and had been badly bruised. Then:

The last of October at night rising out of bed, being in a great sweat by reason of a sudden gust and much clamour in the ships before they could get down the sails, I took a violent cold which cast me into a burning fever than which never man endured any more violent nor never man suffered a more furious heat and an unquenchable drought. For the first 20 days I never received any sustenance, but now and then a stewed prune but drank every hour day and night, and sweat so strongly as I changed my shirts thrice every day and thrice every night.

Here must be interpolated some comments by the Revd Samuel Jones, made at the inquest on the voyage later in London. He said that there were complaints from the sick and dying about Raleigh's 'hard usage' of them, and that he had even denied 'large adventurers things upon necessity'.[8] Pigott had complained of this on his death-bed. On the other hand, when Raleigh himself fell ill with his 'dangerous fever', Jones did say that he 'grieved for the gentlemen more than for himself.'

On 11 November, at long last, land was sighted. They had reached the river Waipoco, but Raleigh was not able to leave his bunk. He sent a skiff

* The Magellanic Clouds are two galaxies visible in the southern hemisphere, similar to the Milky Way.

to look for his old friend Leonard;* but was told he had gone thirty miles up country. So he decided to move on to the Caliana, now Cayenne, where the *cacique* was another old friend, a man who had lived with him as a servant in the Tower for two years. They anchored near an island where there were so many birds that you could kill them with staves. There were also 'great codds of hereculla silk' – capsules of the silk-cotton tree.

His old servant was called Harry, and had almost forgotten his English. He brought presents of cassava bread, roast mullets, pineapples, plantains and pistachios. At last Raleigh was able to leave his 'unsavoury ship, pestered with many sick men which being unable to move poisoned us with a most filthy stench.' He recovered enough to be able to eat some armadillo meat, but still had to be carried in a chair.

The body of Edward Hastings† had been kept on board, evidently for ten days, in spite of the heat, and was now buried on land, along with those of two others, Raleigh's sergeant-major Hart and Captain Henry Snedall (who could have been a kinsman, Raleigh's sister having married a Snedall). It took a good three weeks for the men to recover from their fevers, and there were more deaths. The ships were cleaned, torn sails mended and casks filled with fresh water. A forge was built for repairing damaged ironwork and tackle.

One of the captains, Peter Alley, was suffering from an 'infirmity of the head', that is, vertigo, which had been brought on by the rolling of the ship. It was decided to send him home with a friendly Flemish merchant called Janson whom they had found at the Caliana. He took a number of letters with him, including one from Raleigh headed 'For my dearest wife, the Lady Raleigh' which was later copied and much circulated. Bess must have found it alarming reading:[9]

Sweetheart: I can yet write unto you but with a weak hand for I have suffered the most violent calenture [fever] for fifteen days that ever man did and lived. But God, that gave me a strong heart in all my adversities, hath also now strengthened it in the hellfire of heat.

We have had the most grievous sickness in our ship of which forty-two have died and there are yet many sick. But having recovered the land of Guiana this twelfth of November I hope we shall recover them. We have yet two hundred men [on the *Destiny*] and the rest of my fleet are reasonably strong, strong enough I hope to perform what we have undertaken – if the diligent care at London to make our strength known to the Spanish king by his ambassador have not taught the Spaniards to fortify all the entrances against us. Howsoever we must make the adventure, and

* p. 433.   † p. 459.

if we perish it shall be no honour for England nor gain for His Majesty to lose among many other an hundred as valiant as England hath in it.

He was able to reassure her that Wat was well, and in 'never so good health, having no distemper in all the heat under the line [the Equator].' He told her that at the Caliana he had received such a welcome that 'to tell you that I might be here the king of the Indians now were a vanity, but my name hath still lived among them . . . All offer to obey me.' He also told her about Gomera and the Countess, how her presents of fruit had saved his life. He still had some fruit left, 'preserved in fresh sands'. He asked that she should give 'my most devoted and humble service' to Queen Anne.

'As for Captain Bailey's base running away from me at the Canaries see a letter of Master Keymis to Master Scury, and of the unnatural weather, storms, rains and winds'. This was old Silvanus Scory, an associate of the Earl of Northumberland and son of an ex-Bishop of Hereford – who in his dotage had been against the whole expedition, ludicrously urging Raleigh to give a 'moral example' rather than attempt a feat of valour.

At the Caliana nobody of course knew of the furore that Bailey had created in England, though they might have guessed it. Keymis in his letter suggested that Bailey could just have been anxious to get back to his 'young gentlewoman' on the Isle of Wight. 'He left without leave-taking beyond all expectation; to the wonder of most of the fleet he set sail homewards and we never heard of him since that time.' Another suggestion he made was that Bailey could have realized that his ship was not adequately victualled for the voyage ahead. These were charitable excuses. After Bailey's release from prison more of his misdeeds were to be revealed. It was said that when in Ireland he had robbed a Scottish ship and had stolen a shallop. He had also quarrelled with Wat and 'fled his challenge'.

According to Keymis in that same letter there appeared to be some unease about the behaviour of Captain Wollaston in Ireland, for which Keymis insisted they were not responsible. Apparently Wollaston had taken on board some adventurers, but had abandoned them 'without means or money to return to their friends'. His ship had now been 'cast off', as unfit for service, and his men had been dispersed amongst the rest of the fleet. Wollaston was soon to cause Raleigh much worse trouble.

The vertigo-stricken Peter Alley also brought with him a peculiar document headed *Newes of Sr Walter Rauleigh*,* dated 17 November 1617 and signed

* see p. 559.

R. M., 'a gentleman of the fleet', possibly Molyneux. It did not contain much news, but was in reality a great piece of propaganda both for Guiana and Raleigh, beginning with a swipe at all those 'envious and evil-disposed people' who sought to 'poison the worthy labours of the most noble attempters'. It also included a complete transcript of Raleigh's *Orders* to his commanders before he left England, the aim being to emphasize his expert knowledge of seamanship, his wisdom and godliness.

What was more, if Manoa no longer existed, there was still the prospect of its equivalents, apparently just waiting to be pillaged: 'In this place the soldier may fight for gold and pay himself with plates of gold a foot broad: that the commanders which shoot at honour and abundance may find there more beautiful cities, more temples adorned with golden images, more sepulchres filled with treasure, then either was found in Mexico or Peru, and that the shining glory of this conquest would eclipse all the beams of the Spanish nation.'

In addition to such fabulous wealth, there were the delights of an abundant and fertile land, full of exotic products and packed with every sort of wild game and animals to be hunted. Much of this had been said many years before, and laughed at. The document would have been circulated among friends, but it was published only at the end of 1618 – too late to help Raleigh.

But Peter Alley also returned to England full of horror stories about the voyage. As Sir Edward Conway told Carleton, the letters from the Caliana 'come charged with misfortunes and tears, and his [Raleigh's] wife is in great affliction.'[10]

For Gondomar such stories were good news. Enemies of Raleigh relayed other disasters to him, which he unhesitatingly accepted. He wrote to Spain:[11]

A ship has arrived recently at Posemuna [Portsmouth] from where Gualtero Ralle now is, and it is said that many of his best men have died, including the master of his flagship; and that he has mistaken the way into the river Arenoco, where he is going to look for the mine, but instead he has gone to a port full of currents, which makes it hard to get out, and there is a great lack of provisions, so that most of his people are desperate, some of the letters to be sent on the ship were taken away by Ralle. He [Raleigh] opened one letter from a gentleman, saying what misery they were in, and that if things did not improve it was decided to throw him into the sea and return to England. Gualtero Ralle wanted to arrest this gentleman, and showed him his own letter, but the others would not allow it … they think that if the enterprise fails, those who remain with him will either be lost, or if they are able to get out, will turn pirates.

It was true that there had been problems getting into the harbour at the Caliana, and Raleigh had to wait for the right tide. The rest of the ships had mostly anchored outside, where the currents were probably strong. Raleigh eventually managed to catch the spring tide, and on 4 December he had with some difficulty emerged. By 10 December, the fleet had reassembled at the Triangle Islands, now known as the Isles de Salut (one being the notorious Devil's Island), about forty miles from the Caliana and still some 500 from the Orinoco delta. It was from here that the expedition to the gold-mine was to be launched.

Mutiny was certainly a strong possibility. Raleigh's age had caught up with him; he was still weak from his illness, being carried around in a chair, so there was no question of his leading the expedition. Pigott having died, the most obvious choice as commander would have been Warham St Leger, but he had been taken 'extreme sick' at the Caliana. So the choice fell on Lawrence Keymis.

'My Brains Are Broken'
1618

There were only five ships with draught shallow enough for navigating the Orinoco delta. At the Caliana it had been rumoured that Spanish reinforcements were already on their way, and the alarm had been such that officers and men insisted that they would not leave unless Raleigh promised that whatever might happen he would be waiting for their return; he was the only one whom they trusted to guarantee their defence. Even Professor Gardiner, usually one of Raleigh's sternest critics, was able to concede admiration for such a tribute: 'His followers were ready enough to grumble at him; but when the time of trial came they knew well enough what his value was.'[1] Raleigh gave his promise: 'You shall find me at Punta Gallo [Icacos Point at Trinidad], dead or alive. And if you find not the ships there, yet you shall find their ashes, for I will fire with the galleons, and if it comes to extremity, run away I will never.'

Keymis (usually spelt Kemish by Raleigh) was hardly the ideal leader for such a riff-raff, in spite of his past experiences at the Orinoco. Raleigh had given him instructions in writing, and had told him to sail past the mountain Aio, which they had seen in 1595, 'from whence you have less than three miles to the mine, and to lodge and encamp between the Spanish town and you, if there be any town near it.' His first duty was to create a protective screen in case of attacks by the Spaniards.

There were two possible mines to exploit, and it is not clear which one Raleigh meant. Monte Aio was some twenty-three miles from the mouth of the Caroní, and it was inland from here that the chief Putijma had indicated there was the fabulous mountain 'covered with gold and silver ore' – but that was a good fifteen miles further on. The other mine was connected with the possibly gold-bearing stones of quartz that Raleigh had picked up some three miles from the site of Morequito's port, up the Caroní. As far as he knew, the so-called town of San Thomé, which Keymis had seen in 1596, was on the site of Morequito's port. Perhaps he was hoping that further enquiries from Indians would reveal a mine near the Caroní.

489

In any case Keymis was to 'make trial what depth and breadth the mine holds, and whether or no it answereth our hopes'.[2] If the mine was found to be 'royal' and the Spaniards attacked, then the sergeant-major, Raleigh's nephew George, was authorized to repel them; but 'if you find the mine be not so rich . . . then you shall bring but a basket or two, to satisfy his Majesty that my design was not imaginary, but true; though not answerable to his Majesty's expectations'. He also said that if the Spanish reinforcements were indeed waiting on the Orinoco, 'so that, without manifest peril of my son, yourself, and other captains, you cannot pass towards the Mine, then be well advised how you land, for I know (a few gentlemen excepted) what a scum of men you have. And I would not, for all the world, receive a blow from the Spaniards to the dishonour of our nation.'

George Raleigh was a courageous and dashing young man in the true family mould, and had seen some action in the Netherlands, while Wat, as his father knew, was apt to be reckless and impulsive. Raleigh was under no illusions about the dangers with these two young men wanting to prove themselves. Even if there was no clash of arms on the Orinoco, there were plenty of perils on the journey out, as he himself had experienced twenty-two years before. 'The crisis of his fortunes had come,' Gardiner wrote, and he was having to stand aside 'while the stake upon which his life and honour were set was being played for by rough sailors and beardless boys.'[3] The donnish Keymis was hardly in the category of a rough sea-dog, but he was devotedly loyal to Raleigh, who nevertheless must have been aware that he could be dangerously indecisive.

The five ships destined for the voyage to the Orinoco were commanded by Captains Wollaston, Whitney, King, Smith and Hall (all certainly in the category of sea-dogs), and with them were 150 mariners and 250 soldiers. There were five company commanders besides Wat: Captains Parker, North, Thornehurst, Bradshaw and Prideaux. Some small launches were also taken for the landings, and provisions were provided for a month 'or somewhat more'. Raleigh told Keymis to call first at the river Surinam, to find out if there was more news about those Spanish reinforcements, and then to go on to the Essequibo, which with its tributaries was the nearest main river to the Orinoco, and where he could pick up Indian pilots.

After Raleigh's death, when James issued *A Declaration of the Demeanour and Carriage of Sir Walter Ralegh, Knight*, it was claimed that Raleigh at his so-called Council of War on board the *Destiny* had said that San Thomé must be captured before looking for the mine. One of his officers was supposed to have said that this would mean a breach of the peace, at which Raleigh had retorted that he had orders by word of mouth 'to take the town if it is any hindrance to the digging of the mine'. Which does sound like an afterthought invented by his enemies.

On 15 December Raleigh and his mostly sick and convalescent men landed at Punta Anegada near the mouth of the Orinoco, probably the present Punta Araguapiche which is in swampy country – *anegada* meaning inundated in Spanish. From there he continued to Punta Gallo, where they obtained fish, armadillos, guavas and other fruit; also a kind of pheasant, which had 'exceeding fat and delicate meat'. Then he went to see the amazing Pitch Lake, which he had visited in 1595.

Because of the strong currents at the Serpent's Mouth he had to keep on the move. Somewhat rashly he sent a boat belonging to Sir John Ferne up to Port of Spain to try to trade for tobacco. The Governor of Trinidad and Guiana, Don Diego Palomeque de Acuña,* had already been warned from Madrid about the possibility of Raleigh's arrival. He was in fact at San Thomé, but his men were at the ready, so the boat was met with a volley of musketry at close range. No one was hurt, and as the boat pulled away the Spaniards shouted out insults and all sorts of 'opprobious speeches'.

By now the Spaniards were fully alerted. One of Ferne's men was sniped while 'boiling of the country pitch'; another escaped by swimming, though a cabin boy was captured.

If an avenging Spanish fleet had appeared, there would have not have been much hope. Raleigh was to write to Winwood (still not knowing that he was already dead): 'Had they set upon us, our force divided – the one half at the Orinoco, 150 miles from us – we had not only been torn to pieces, but all those in the river had also perished, being of no defence at all for a sea-fight; for we had resolved to have burnt by their sides, and to have died there, had the armada arrived.'[4]

As it happened, no armada was due. And no action, apart from those warning letters to Governors, had been taken by Madrid after receiving Gondomar's letter, partly for bureaucratic reasons, partly because the Council was still unconvinced of the urgency. All that happened was that the various Governors had been told to have troops ready if required.

Raleigh continued patrolling the southern end of the island and made contacts with Indian villages on the mainland. He also collected herbs. On 31 January he was at Punta Gallo, hoping to meet men back from the Orinoco. Instead seven Indians were discovered, pretending as it turned out

---

* Very likely Palomeque was related to Gondomar, whose mother and wife were of the Acuña family.

not to be able to speak Spanish and probably sent as spies. Raleigh kept three of them on board, and had twelve of his men escort the rest to their village. It was there that one of his men, who had been in Guiana only two years before, recognized an Indian and knew he could speak Spanish. He took him by the arm and using threats got him to confess that the three on board the *Destiny* could indeed speak Spanish. Raleigh was told this, and after more threats received some exceedingly worrying information from their chief, that 'certain Indians of the drowned lands inhabited by a nation called Titivitas, arriving in a canoe at his port', had told him that the English in 'Orenoke' had taken San Thomé and that they had killed the Governor and two others. Two English captains had also been killed. The rest of the Spaniards had 'fled into the mountains'.

The story was confirmed soon afterwards by another Indian. In the anxious days that followed Raleigh sent forays to various villages, sometimes taking hostages. One of his prisoners was made to show him where he could find some balsam trees which produced aromatic seeds, said to smell like angelica, 'very rare and precious'. He was annoyed when his sailors stupidly untied this man who promptly bolted off into the woods.

On 14 February 1618 he received a letter from Keymis, written on 8 January, with the devastating news. There had indeed been a clash with Spaniards; San Thomé had been taken, and Wat had been killed.

Some months later, when Raleigh was compelled to explain his expedition's 'ill success', he wrote an *Apologie*, and in this he included not only his own instructions to Keymis but part of that letter of 8 January, leaving out what must have been the terrible first sentences announcing Wat's death. He did, however, add Keymis's praise for the boy's 'extraordinary valour and forwardness', and Wat's supposed last words: 'Lord have mercy on me and prosper your enterprise'.

Keymis knew very well what the effect of his letter would be on Raleigh, and he was to say that he feared that in Raleigh's weakened state it could even have killed him. The shock did completely undermine Raleigh mentally and for the rest of his life he never fully recovered, except perhaps when he spoke from the scaffold. This bungling by Keymis and the apparently flagrant disregard of his orders were, he knew, his own death warrant.

The letter had been brought to him by someone who had been his servant, Peter Andrews, and from him Raleigh learnt more details about casualties and something about the circumstances of the attack on San Thomé. Keymis had attempted to add a kind of encouragement, saying that he had found some refiners' houses in the town, and that there was a gold mine eight miles away.[5] He admitted that there had been 'murmurings, disorders and vexations' which had 'tormented' the sergeant-major George Raleigh, but things were easier now. As soon as he had tried out this mine, he would return by the *caño* Manamo. Meanwhile he was sending Raleigh a parcel of papers, a roll of tobacco, a turtle, and some oranges and lemons.

It was claimed long afterwards by Raleigh's younger son Carew that among these papers were not only a copy of Gondomar's warning letter to the King of Spain but the list of his ships and their itinerary in Raleigh's own handwriting.

It had taken Keymis three weeks to negotiate the 'unspeakable misery' of the delta and the shifting currents of the Orinoco. At an early stage the ships of Captains Whitney and Wollaston had run aground on mudbanks and were not able to rejoin the others until after the fall of San Thomé. Keymis had found the Titivitas at the delta and the Chaguanas on the Orinoco reasonably friendly, but an Indian fisherman near where there is the present town of Barrancas had spotted the English fleet and had gone ahead to warn the Spanish Governor.

A Chaguana man was taken on as a pilot. On 2 January Monte Aio was duly passed, but instead of halting nearby they sailed on to the creek Aruco only a short distance from the Caroní and San Thomé, arriving at about 11 o clock in the morning. Six boatloads of men were unloaded on the shore, and afterwards – provocatively, one might think – the ships anchored opposite the town. And indeed they were fired on by two cannons.

This was Keymis's first mistake. When he had last seen San Thomé it had been a makeshift place, 'a town of stakes, covered with leaves of trees'. Now it was walled, and on a much larger scale, with a church and substantial houses round a plaza. It was square with buttresses at each corner and surrounded by a moat.

The Governor Palomeque had been appointed in 1615 in place of Fernando de Berrío and had a reputation for harshness and a strong temper. According to residents later a rebellion was even simmering. Under the easy-going Berrío there had been much illegal trading in tobacco with visiting Dutch and English merchants, but now Palomeque had slapped all this down. It was also claimed later that there were English spies within the town, working with the rebels, and that Keymis had known about them. After the fisherman's warning Palomeque had hurriedly called in tobacco growers from outside and had distributed arms. He also had loopholes made in the larger houses. Altogether he was able to muster fifty-seven men, though at least a dozen of them were said to be invalids.

Spanish and English versions of the story now differ. The Spaniards said that as darkness was falling the English began to advance, so one of the tobacco growers, Gerónimo de Grados, was sent with ten men to lie in ambush on a hillock 'three musket shots' from the town.[6] The English version was more probable. They said that they were settling down for the night when a Spanish patrol suddenly attacked with a shower of bullets and shouts of 'perros ingleses' (English dogs). It seems that nobody was hurt, but panic followed and the English were only rallied by the determination of the officers, among whom Wat Raleigh was outstanding.

The English now marched up to the town which was easily entered, apparently at one o'clock in the morning (by moonlight?). Wat was in charge of the pikemen, but now 'more desirous of honour than of safety' he rushed ahead shouting 'Come on my hearts! This is the mine you must expect! They that look for any other are fools!'[7] – words which when repeated later were held against his father, as proof that he never expected to find a mine. He slashed at one of the Spaniards, some said it was Palomeque himself, and killed him, and in the struggle was hit by a musket ball. Bleeding and probably mortally hurt, he pressed on and struck at a Spaniard named Arias Nieto who defended himself with the butt of his musket, knocking Wat to the ground, which was when he uttered those brave last words.

Captain Parker was to write of Wat's 'unadvised daringness', cynically adding that he was given no time 'to call for mercy to our heavenly father for the sinful life he had led'.

The chief Spanish account is that of Fray Pedro Simón, and he wrote of an Englishman at the head of the rest who came shouting 'Victory! Victory!' and was killed by Grados with a sword stroke 'at the left side of his gullet which sent the heretic to re-echo his song in Hell'. The Englishman could have been Captain Cosmor, who led the 'forlorn hope' or storming party. Three other English officers were killed, and the Spanish deaths numbered four. The English set fire to the houses where there had been loopholes, but in so doing, as they were to discover, they destroyed a precious hoard of tobacco.

The invaders' superiority in numbers forced the Spaniards to retreat. It was said by one of Simón's witnesses that Palomeque was left alone with his two trusted lieutenants, Arias Nieto and Juan Luís Monje, and that they fought with great valour. Their dead bodies were stripped naked and bound together with horse halters. The rest of the Spanish garrison withdrew to the fortified island of Seiba (now Fajardo), near the mouth of the Caroní, bringing with them the invalids and women and children.

It is conceivable that Keymis was taken by surprise at the sight of a walled San Thomé, and that he had underestimated the determination of its defenders. By landing a substantial force he may have thought it sufficient to intimidate them while he pondered his next move. After all, Raleigh had wanted a screen between San Thomé and Monte Aio. If he had chosen a spot for his encampment further away from San Thomé that still might have been feasible. As for the 'spies' within the town, given that one of the men left with Raleigh had been on the Orinoco only two years before, he probably knew that there was hostility against Palomeque and might have told Keymis before he left that this would be an advantage. If indeed he had said so, he was wrong, for Grados had been one of Palomeque's chief opponents, and that did not mean that he was ready to surrender to the English.

In his letter to Raleigh breaking the news of Wat's death Keymis had said that Wat's daring had 'led them all on, when some began to panic and recoil shamefully', though adding that but for Wat 'this action had neither been attempted as it was, nor performed as it is, with his surviving honour'. This curious phrase could mean that Keymis was going as far as he dared in blaming Wat for the attack.

When the Revd Samuel Jones, who had been on board the *Chudleigh*, back at Trinidad, was called to make a deposition before the Privy Council he appeared to confirm that Keymis had not intended to attack San Thomé that night.[8] He said that the men had been all for rushing straight for the mine, but Keymis kept worrying about the strength of the enemy and the likelihood of revealing to them the whereabouts of the mine. 'During the night of this consultation, our men, ready to repose themselves for that night, were assaulted by the Spaniards from the skirt of the wood, in pursuit of whom they were brought to the town almost before themselves knew of it. In which conflict some four or thereabouts of either side were slain, the rest of the Spaniards quit the town and fled.'

Now everyone was expecting to move on to the mine, but still Keymis held back. He seemed to care more about 'the tobacco, apparel, household stuff, and other pillage; often saying that these would help if all failed'. Then one night he secretly crept out with some men 'and brought in some mineral ore which he cheerfully showed to Captain Thornehurst; but being tried by a refiner, it proved worth nothing, and was not more spoken of'. Naturally the suspicion grew that both Keymis and Raleigh had been 'deluded in the ore and the place' – and that was not far from the truth.

It seems fairly clear that Keymis either did not know or had forgotten exactly where Raleigh had collected those gold-bearing pieces of quartz – only that it was somewhere near the Great Cataract, with its 'strange thunder of waters'. Raleigh had spoken of the stones as coming from a

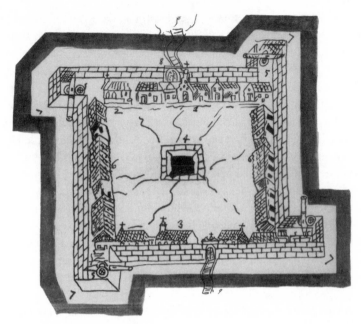

San Thomé. 1 Church. 2 Governor's house. 3 Gunpowder and munitions store.
4 Water cistern. 5 Bastion. 6 Houses. 7 Moat. 8 Gateway to land with portcullis.
9 Gate to river. 10 Walls.

mine, but he had never *seen* the mine. It was true that he had said that a
Spaniard from Caracas had assured him that the stones were *madre del oro*,
mother of gold, which would mean that there was probably solid gold deep
down. But at that time, as he had said, the ground was as hard as flint, and
they had only their fingers and knives to dig with.

So why had Raleigh waited all those years between 1597 and 1603
without sponsoring expeditions to the Orinoco? How reliable had his
assayer been? Could it have been another case of Burchard Cranach and
Frobisher's black ore from Newfoundland, mixing real gold with the rock
so that he could be sure of having the job of assaying and smelting should
gold be eventually found in real quantities?* Only after Raleigh had been
in the Tower some while had gold from Guiana loomed so importantly in
his mind – it had suddenly become the road to liberty. He had convinced
himself that he had really seen a mine; imagination had turned into reality.

When the time came for Keymis to make his excuses to Raleigh for not
broaching either mine, he lied, saying that San Thomé had been moved

---

* p. 22.

downstream twenty miles. Raleigh believed him and repeated this in England. It was in fact true that San Thomé was in a different position from where it had been in 1596, but only a question of a mile or so.*

Only one Spaniard had been left behind at San Thomé, and this was a priest, Padre Francisco de Leuro, who was so crippled in his hands and feet that he was unable to leave his bed. He was discovered by the English who, it was acknowledged by the Spanish sources, took great care of him. Two Indian women were captured and put in charge of the old man; they also had to grind maize and make *arepas*, cakes, day and night it was said, until they were exhausted and finally managed to escape.

One of the women broke down when asked to identify Palomeque's body, and it must have been a ghastly sight – the whole of the left side of his face had been sliced away to his teeth. The five English bodies were covered over and laid in front of the church. The next day they were put on planks and carried in procession around the plaza, with muffled drums, reversed muskets and dipped banners. Wat and Captain Cosmor were buried in front of the high altar, and the other three in the nave. Palomeque and his two lieutenants were put in a shallow pit and lightly covered over.†

It was during the funeral that Whitney's and Wollaston's ships arrived. A Portuguese boy had also been left behind. His hands were bound and he

---

* In its history San Thomé, or Santo Tomé de Guayana as it is now known to Venezuelans, was moved six times. The first, which was the stockaded village seen by Keymis in 1596, was almost certainly on the site of Morequito's port, the equivalent of the present San Félix. Berrío moved it in 1598 and built the fortifications. In 1629 it was sacked by the Dutch, and had to be moved inland. Even then it was not proof against Dutch attacks, so it was transferred to further inland, up higher ground. In 1642 an entirely new and strategic situation was chosen, about twenty-three miles downstream from the Caroní, nearly opposite to where the delta *caños* meet the Orinoco, and in fact near Monte Aio. Partly because of what Keymis had said, it was for many years believed that this was the San Thomé of 1618, and indeed today there are Venezuelans who are convinced that this is the site.

The French were the next to cause trouble, and they actually occupied San Thomé in 1684. In 1764 for the sixth and last time it was transferred to near the famous narrows of the Orinoco, several miles upstream from the Caroní and known as Angostura. On this site there is now the town of Ciudad Bolívar.

The 1642–1764 site is now popularly known as Los Castillos, consisting of two forts, the Fuerte Villapol and the Fuerte Campo Elias, both extensively restored; even if they are not associated with 1618 they are regarded as being symbolic of that year and of Sir Walter Raleigh's quest for El Dorado. Important excavations are in progress. For a long while after the removal to Angostura the buildings were used by Capuchin missionaries.

† After the English departed they were apparently left unburied four months. This because of Palomeque's unpopularity.

was led from house to house in the hope of his being able to show where gold was hidden. When nothing transpired he was beaten, but afterwards he was set free and allowed to wander round the town. A Negro, a half-caste and two Indians, all slaves, were found and later taken to England. The half-caste, known as Pedro the Creole, was especially popular with the English and ate with them; he was also given smart clothes, a sombrero and new shoes. One of the Indians was called Christoval; he had been Palomeque's personal slave and was to witness Raleigh's execution before being returned to Guiana.

Chaguana Indians arrived with presents of food and in return were given some of the plunder. The local Indians however kept well away and appeared hostile, contrary to Raleigh's promises. A messenger arrived from the Spaniards waving a white handkerchief, with the naive demand for the return of the Governor and a request that the English should 'go away'. He was taken to see Keymis, whom he was to describe as a tall slender man, aged about sixty, with a cast in one eye, clearly of gentle birth and of grave demeanour. Palomeque was dead, he was told, and there was no question of the English leaving. This was the signal for Gerónimo de Grados, who was now in charge, to send off a small group assisted by some friendly Arawak Indians, to ask for help from the Governor of Margarita.

The English went out foraging, burning down barns and farms. They seemed to think that they were in their rights, because whenever they were attacked they would cry 'Fair play Spaniards!'.[9] In comparison the Spaniards were very few, but had the advantage of being on horseback.

Keymis now appeared to be in a state of paralysis. The whole object of the expedition to been to bring back gold. It might have been thought that he would have turned his attention to Putijma's mountain, but there was still the fear of meeting Spanish reinforcements coming up the river. The painful truth of course was that neither he nor Raleigh had ever seen that mine. The mountain had merely been pointed out to them. Now without a guide it would be almost impossible to hack a way through the jungle undergrowth.

It was probably the Indian Christoval who told him about another mine only a few miles up the Orinoco. This must have seemed a heaven-sent solution, and the dangers of possible Spanish reinforcements were forgotten. Two launches therefore set off, manned with 'gentlemen, soldiers and sailors', but Keymis must have forgotten about the island of Seiba, which he had noted in 1596 as being a fortified place of refuge. Grados had already been warned of their approach and had mobilized his invalid Spaniards and some Indians for an ambush overlooking the channel between the island and the mainland. The English were met with pelting arrows and a fusillade of musket fire. Two were killed, and six or seven more were wounded by the arrows, including Captain Thornehurst who was shot in the head and became 'crazy and distempered in his body'.

The English retreated to San Thomé and reassembled. It was decided that the Spaniards must have been guarding the entrance to the mine. George Raleigh was especially eager to get going, so on 13 January he and Keymis set off once more in a shallop with two barges, and managed to circumvent Seiba without any hostilities. They were, however, observed by the Spaniards, who saw them making frequent soundings as they disappeared towards the Angostura narrows.

As Keymis put it, they passed 'great sands and rocks', 'in a large river of very great swiftness'. There was no sign of a mine, and by now the discomforts and the baking heat were too much for the men in the barges and they decided to turn back. What was more, according to the Revd Jones, they had only taken provisions for four days. Nevertheless Keymis and George Raleigh continued alone with fourteen men. They were away three weeks, and if Spanish sources are to be believed they travelled three hundred miles, desperately looking for some new mine, as far as the river Guarico, near the present town of Caicara. Not an ounce of gold was discovered, but they called frequently on local tribesmen, who were Caribs and cannibals, giving them presents of knives and in return urging them to rise up and kill and presumably eat the Spaniards.

On 24 January they found themselves 'embayed amongst the sands' and could not go further – which, if they really did get as far as the Guarico, was indeed very likely. Keymis made six of his officers sign an affidavit, that the intention had been to take them 'to a certain place in Guiana where he had in former times taken ore out of the ground' (not true, of course), and that Keymis had used all his 'endeavour and willingness ... to perform this design'.

Afterwards there were different opinions about the journey. The Revd Jones acidly noted that 'whereas the mine was described to be three miles short of the town, they went not only three miles, but three score leagues beyond it, till at last they were forced to return; and had they found a mine they must have come back for spades, pickaxes and refiners, for none of these carried any with them.' Captain Parker was to be even more scornful:[10] 'When we were possessed of the town Captain Keymis took divers gentlemen to find the mine, and trifled up and down some 20 days keeping us in hope still of finding it, but at last we found his delays mere illusions and himself a mere machiavell, for he was false to all men and most odious to himself.'

Keymis's party returned to find San Thomé a rubble of burnt ruins, and the English ships waiting a league from the town, the crews despairing and mutinous after twenty-nine fruitless days in the place. There had been many deaths from illness and disease, and according to Simón there had been much harassment by both Spaniards and Indians, who had one night tried to fire the rest of the town but had been thwarted by heavy rain which had soaked the thatched roofs. This had been followed the next night by a second attack when, wrote Simón, 'much havoc was wrought among the heretics', who as usual when in trouble began to call out for fair play. In daytime stragglers outside the town were caught and killed, and there were daily and nightly alarms of guerrilla attacks. Then a number of English were ambushed when trying to steal stacks of maize, and it was claimed that fourteen or fifteen were killed. So finally the English left, having set fire to the remains of the town, but forgetting about poor old Padre de Leuro who was burnt in his bed. They did however carry off as much loot as they could, including arms, gunpowder, cannons, six hundred *reales* in coins, two gold ingots, some gold ornaments, church bells, tobacco, maize and the rest of the archives.

Out in the river, while waiting for Keymis, the English hoisted a flag of truce, but no notice was taken. The humiliating reality was that they had been defeated by a handful of exceedingly brave Spaniards, aided by local Indians who Raleigh had said should have been friends. Only 150 English were supposed to have survived out of the original 400 (perhaps an exaggeration). So, Keymis having arrived, on they sailed, handing out knives and hatchets to Indians in villages lower down the Orinoco in the hope that they would be used against the Spaniards. On reaching the area of Monte Aio the question arose as to whether or not an excursion should be risked to the mountain, but everyone was anxious to get away before the threatened Spanish reinforcements arrived. Also there was always the possibility that Raleigh might not still be alive. And they were running out of food.

On 9 February Keymis sent another letter to Raleigh as he prepared to return up the delta. He gave a further reason for not attempting Putijma's mountain: the original entrance bay had become choked up with sand, and the water there was only two to three feet deep. He seemed to suggest that Raleigh might consider returning after March when the level of the Orinoco began to rise. 'The disgrace of not bringing our men to this mine will, I know, whilst I live rest heavy upon me in the judgements and opinions of most men, and it will be argued and enforced that I have wittingly deluded many noble and worthy gentlemen with vain hope.' Too true, alas. But he insisted that he had done 'the utmost endeavour . . . that any man can do'. It was a very long letter, attempting to explain away that long mad journey upstream, which he claimed had only been forty leagues.

Raleigh in his *Apologie* said that a friendly *cacique* called Carapana had actually volunteered to guide Keymis to yet another mine, and as proof of its existence had offered to leave behind hostages. If this Carapana was the same 'old fox' of the *Discoverie*, he was already supposed to be aged 100 in 1595.

Apart from the hardships of weaving through the jungle and mangrove swamps of the delta, and the sudden tropical downpours, it must have been a hideous journey back for Keymis, dreading the encounter with Raleigh and surrounded by loathing and contempt. The party reached Punta Gallo on 2 March.

The Revd Jones had said that after receiving Keymis's first letter Raleigh maintained that he would call Keymis to public account before he spoke to him privately. It was not to be quite like this. Raleigh first behaved towards Keymis with a certain magnanimity, which was wilfully exaggerated in the King's *Declaration*: 'He had him to dinner and supper, and used him as familiarly and kindly as before.' The same was said to have applied to George Raleigh. But the more Raleigh heard the more he was appalled, and it did nothing to lessen the depths of his grief at Wat's death. Any consideration of past loyalties and affection had turned into icy fury. Some few days passed, then in Raleigh's words:[11]

He came to me in my cabin, and showed me a letter which he had written to the Earl of Arundel; to whom he excused himself for the not discovering the mine, using the same arguments, and many other which he had used before, and prayed me for to allow of his apology. But I told him that he had undone me by his obstinacy, and that I would not favour or colour in any sort his former folly. He then asked me whether that were my resolution; I told him it was; he then replied in these words, 'I know then, Sir, what course to take', and went out of my cabin up into his own, into which he was no sooner entered that I heard a pistol go off. I sent up (not suspecting any such thing as the killing of himself) to know who shot the pistol; Keymis himself made answer, lying on his bed, that he had shot it off, because it had been long charged, with which I was satisfied. Some half an hour after this, his boy going into his cabin, found him dead, having a long knife thrust under his left pap through his heart, and the pistol lying by him, with which it appeared he had shot himself; but the bullet, lighting upon a rib, had but broken the rib, and went no further.

This all makes extremely painful reading. In his accounts, Raleigh showed absolutely no remorse, only scorn, as if Keymis's suicide was a confession of guilt. He had lost his beloved son, the expedition had been a total failure, his instructions had been disobeyed, and now he faced ruin and the scaffold. Almost it seemed as if he was losing his mind.

The irony was that Keymis would have been the chief witness, if not the only witness, for the defence in the inevitable examinations ahead. He had lied, but his lies had been meant to help Raleigh, the man whom he admired and loved most in the world. This was of course not the first time that his good intentions had placed Raleigh in serious trouble – but those damaging remarks that he had relayed to Cobham in 1603 had resulted in his own imprisonment and the threat of torture.

Raleigh now became convinced that they must return to the Orinoco, and this time he would be in charge. The captured Spanish documents that Keymis had brought back gave proof of the existence of mines near San Thomé, and now Christoval was confirming that there was ore only two hours away from the town – he had deliberately not said where it was at the time, because his master and his friends had been killed, and 'they [the English] had made a drudge of him, setting him to grind corn, and took away his apparel and did not respect him'.[12] There were still enough men and ships available to deal with any further opposition from Spaniards. If he were to die, Raleigh said he would happy for his body to lie next to his son's.

Not surprisingly, nobody else was ready to die for this phantom gold, let alone set out again on that fearful journey. As the Revd Jones put it: 'Our men were weary, our boats split, our ships foul, and our victuals well-nigh spent.' One of the cabin boys spread the malicious rumour that Raleigh had 24,000 guineas hidden under his bed. There were those who wanted to leave him marooned at Trinidad, grab the money, and abandon him to the mercy of the Spaniards.

It was in any case vital to get away from Trinidad before those Spanish reinforcements appeared. At the Grenadines there were angry discussions with Whitney and Wollaston who then deserted him, intending to recoup their losses through piracy, or as Captain Parker put it, 'to look for homeward bound men', meaning the Spanish treasure fleet. Wollaston was an old lag, but Raleigh was especially bitter about Whitney, as he regarded him as a special friend and it was for him that he had sold his plate at Plymouth. At Nevis on 12 March more ships melted away, so by the time he reached St Kitts he had only five ships left.

He arrived at the bay now known as Old Road or Stonefort on the north-west slopes of the island. The danger this time was from the local

Caribs who were notoriously warlike.* Here he stayed for two weeks. There were more arguments and much wild talk, with Raleigh uncertain about what to do next, though apparently determined first to move up to New-foundland where he would revictual. Sir Warham St Leger said afterwards he had told him that he was determined not to return to England, or he would be hanged. Others said that he had been thinking of returning to Guiana, or going to the Azores to catch homeward-bound Spaniards. There was also talk of a 'French commission'. Whatever he said they were desperate fantasies. He was doomed, and he had lost control.

A flyboat was sent home, with his cousin William Herbert in command, taking back some sick men and a 'rabble of idle rascals'. At last, in the words once more of the Revd Jones, he 'freely gave leave to any of the Captains to leave him if they pleased, or thought they could better themselves in their own interests'. One of these was Charles Parker who said that 'about the latter end of August I hope we shall have feathered our nest'. Roger North decided to return to England, and Raleigh gave him some letters, including one to Winwood with a précis of all the miserable events that had beset the expedition since leaving Ireland.

He could not resist in this letter complaining that the King had thought so little of him that he had given all the details of his voyage to the Spaniards through 'that braggadocio the Spanish ambassador'. He hinted that he had found many things of importance that could be exploited in the West Indies, and these he would explain later. 'What shall become of me now, I know not. I am unpardoned in England and my poor estate consumed, and whether any other Prince or State will give me bread I know not. I desire your Honour to hold me in your good opinion, and to remember my service to my Lords of Arundel and Pembroke, to take some pity on my poor wife, to whom I dare not write for renewing of her sorrow for her son.' He asked Winwood not to take notice of what was said by 'divers persons, good for nothing', who had already set off home. As for the men returning with Herbert, 'I beseech your Honour that this scum of men may not be believed of me, who have taken more pain, and suffered more than the meanest rascal in the ship.'

The letter came into the hands of the dead Winwood's successor, Sir Robert Naunton, who was not so well disposed towards Raleigh. It was

---

* The Caribs of St Kitts painted their bodies crimson, pierced their noses and wore necklaces of their enemies' teeth. In 1623 Sir Thomas Warner, the first English settler, arrived at this place. Nearby is Bloody Point, where 2,000 Caribs were massacred by French and English in 1626.

dated 21 March, but on the next day he decided he must write to Bess after all:

I was loth to write because I know not how to comfort you. And God knows, I never knew what sorrow meant till now. All that I can say to you is, that you must obey the will and providence of God; and remember that the Queen's Majesty bare the loss of Prince Henry with a magnanimous heart, and the Lady Harrington of her only son. Comfort your heart, dear Bess, I shall sorrow for us both. I shall sorrow the less because I have not long to sorrow, because not long to live. I refer you to Mr Secretary Winwood's letter, who will give you a copy of it, if you send for it. Therein you shall know what hath passed which I have written by that letter, for my brains are broken, and 'tis a torment for me to write, and especially of misery . . . I have desired Mr Secretary to give my Lord Carew a copy of his letter. I have cleansed my ship of sick men, and sent them home. I hope God will send us somewhat ere we return. Commend me to all at Lothbury.* You shall hear from me, if I live, from Newfoundland, where I mean to make clean my ship and to revictual; for I have tobacco enough to pay for it. The Lord bless and comfort you, that you may bear patiently the death of your valiant son.

   22nd of March, from the Isle of Christophers,

     Yours, W. Ralegh

His great and consuming grief made him add a long postscript, pouring out his heart about Wat, Keymis's betrayal, the disaster on the Orinoco, his bitterness about having to divulge his plans for transmission to Madrid.

I protest before the majesty of God, that as Sir Francis Drake and Sir John Hawkins died heartbroken when they failed of their enterprise, I could willingly do the like, did I not contend against sorrow for your sake, in hope to provide somewhat for you, and to comfort and relieve you. If I live to return, resolve yourself that it is the care for you that hath strengthened my heart. It is true that Keymis might have gone directly to the mine, and meant it. But after my son's death, he made them to believe he knew not the way, and excused himself upon the want of water in the river, and, counterfeiting many impediments, left it unfound. When he came back, I told him that he had undone me, and that my credit was lost for ever.

He answered, that when my son was lost and that he left me so weak that he resolved not to find me alive, he had no reason to enrich a company of rascals, who, after my son's death, made no account of him. He further told me that the English sent up into Guiana could hardly defend the Spanish town of St Thomas which they

---

* Broad Street, where Bess was living in London, was in the ward of Lothbury.

had taken, and therefore for them to pass through thick woods it was impossible; and more impossible to have victuals brought them into the mountains. And it is true that the governor Diego Palomeque, and four other captains being slain, of which my son Wat slew one ... There was never poor man so exposed to the slaughter as I was; for being commanded upon my allegiance to set down, not only the country, but the very river by which I was to enter it, to name my ships, number my men, and my artillery – this was sent by the Spanish ambassador to his master, the King of Spain. The King wrote his letters to all parts of the Indies, especially to the governor Palomeque of Guiana, El Dorado, and Trinidad; of which the first letter bare date the 19th of March, 1617, at Madrid, when I had not yet left the Thames, which letter I have sent the Secretary ...

My brains are broken, and I cannot write much. I live yet, and I have told you why. Whitney, for whom I sold my plate at Plymouth, and to whom I gave more credit and countenance than all the captains of my fleet, ran from me at the Granadas, and Wollaston with him; so as I am now but five ships, and one of those I have sent home – my fly-boat – and in her a rabble of idle rascals, which I know will not spare to wound me, but I care not. I am sure there is never a base slave in the fleet hath taken the pains and care that I have done; hath slept so little and travailled so much. My friends will not believe them; and for the rest I care not. God in heaven bless you and strengthen your heart.

Your W. Ralegh

'Piratas! Piratas!'
1618

In his agony of grief Raleigh had lost the confidence of his men. As the *Destiny* set off northwards, they became restless, alarmed about their fate if they dared to return to England. One thing was certain: they had no intention of returning to the Orinoco.

On nearing Newfoundland Raleigh discovered that there was a plot among the crew to follow the example of Wollaston and Whitney and turn to piracy. As he afterwards told Carew, a hundred of them were determined to break away as soon as the ship was hauled up on the beach for cleaning. On arrival at St John's some fishing vessels, English and Portuguese, were found to be anchored in the harbour. The mutineers decided to seize and plunder them by night, and then board the best ship of the English flotilla and sail off, leaving him stranded. He therefore called the whole company together and told them what he had learnt, saying that he had decided to make directly for England without taking in water or provisions. 'The conspirators revealed themselves, resisting and shouting they would rather die than return to England. They were the greater number, and some of the best men I had, some of them being gentlemen. All the arquebuses and swords were in the magazine with the armour for cleaning, and the mutineers had taken possession of them, refusing me admission into the magazine.'[1]

He was helpless and in great danger, though he may have tried to smuggle a message to the Governor of St John's. 'Finding myself in this peril, I gave way to the mutiny for a time . . . treating with some of the leaders to abandon the mutiny. With great difficulty, I persuaded them to do so, on condition that I would not return to England until they had obtained pardon for past piracies; and they demanded my oath.'

The Revd Samuel Jones was to confirm that Raleigh wished 'very confidently' to return to England.[2] According to James's *Declaration*, Raleigh had offered to give the *Destiny* to his officers if they would transfer him to a French bark, 'as being loath to put his head under the King's girdle'. But this of course could have been mere malicious tattle. The *Declaration* was mostly compiled by Bacon, who would not have been interested in favourable testimonials such as that of Jones.

Finally it was agreed to head for Ireland. Killybegs in Donegal was chosen, described by Raleigh as a 'miserable place frequented by corsairs', tucked away in a landlocked harbour. If he had not agreed to this, he would have been killed. Had he decided to turn to piracy, he was to say to Carew, within three months he could have easily have amassed £100,000. Instead he preferred to throw himself on the King's mercy.

They went, however, to Kinsale, to find that the three ships commanded by Captains Ferne, Pennington and King had already taken refuge there. This time there were no welcoming parties by local chieftains, and Lord Boyle kept his distance – rumours of troubles had already reached him, and Pennington seems to have already had a rough reception from the Lord Deputy. Of the three captains only King remained loyal.

Raleigh began his letter to Lord Carew while in Ireland. Since his arrival, he wrote, he had been 'not a little alarmed to be told that I have fallen into the grave displeasure of his Majesty for having taken a town in Guiana which was in the possession of the Spaniards.' When his men had heard of this report they became terrified that they would be hanged, and tried to force him to sail away again. On his refusal the majority of them had abandoned ship and disappeared into the countryside.

In his letter Raleigh restated some of the arguments given to Winwood from St Kitts: how he had never given authority for the storming of San Thomé; the Spaniards had attacked first, as he put it 'killing several and wounding many' (which of course was an exaggeration); his son had been cut down at the entrance to the town, and this had so enraged the men that 'if the King of Spain himself had been there in person they would have shown him little respect.' Then came what was his main argument, that he had taken possession of Guiana in the name of Elizabeth, 'by virtue of a cession by all the native chiefs of the country'. (In the *Discoverie* he had merely indicated that he had told Topiawari and others that there was this mighty English Queen who was ready and able to protect them against Spanish oppressors.) He said that James had accepted this, by virtue of his giving a grant to Harcourt in 1609 to found a colony, 'under the seal of England' (though that had not been on the Orinoco but further south, in territories where the Spaniards had never ventured).

I heard in Ireland that my enemies have declared that it was my intention to turn corsair and flee, but, at the manifest peril of my life, I have brought myself and my ship to England. I have suffered as many miseries as it was possible for me to suffer, which I could not have endured if God had not given me strength. If his Majesty wishes that I should have suffered even more, let God's will and His Majesty's be done; for even death itself shall not make me turn thief or vagabond, nor will I ever betray the noble courtesy of the several gentlemen who gave sureties for me.

These last words were important, since as everyone knew Arundel was one of those who had given a surety and he was on the Privy Council.

Raleigh added a postscript:

I beg you will excuse me to my lords [of the Council] for not writing to them. Want of sleep for fear of being surprised in my cabin at night has almost deprived me of my sight, and some return of the palsy which I had in the Tower has so weakened my hand that I cannot hold the pen.

Could he have suffered yet another stroke? Or was it arthritis?

With his depleted crew he then made his way to Plymouth, arriving it has been generally assumed on 21 June, but a Spanish source shows that it was well before 14 June.[3]

Both Wollaston and Whitney arrived at Newfoundland some time after the *Destiny* had left for England, and here they did show themselves true corsairs. Wollaston seized the entire cargo of dried fish from four French ships and took his booty all the way to Leghorn, selling it for £3,000. He had also appropriated one of the French ships and sold that as well at Leghorn for £2,400.

Whitney, even more surprisingly, turned up eventually at Malaga, also loaded with fish from Newfoundland. How much he managed to rake in is not recorded.

Gondomar was not convinced by Raleigh's confession about Lanzarote, which he believed had been manipulated by Raleigh's friends – and this, it must be said, is still the view of some present-day Spanish historians, who refer to Raleigh as *el pirata* or *el atroz* (the atrocious). Gondomar was frequently in agony from piles, and he was exhausted. He was hating the English weather and longed to be back among his Galician vineyards. Realizing that James was also suspicious about Bailey's confession, he nagged him constantly and at last extracted a renewed promise 'on faith, hand and word' that Raleigh would be handed over to Spain in the event of the least hostility.

This was a victory, and Gondomar wrote jubilantly to Madrid, receiving back congratulations, written on 19 April, from Juan de Ciriza, the Secretary of State:[4] 'Your Excellency's account of the conference you had with the King about the Raleigh affair pleased our people here so much that they found it almost too good . . . They say that there never was such an Ambassador before!'

On 3 May Madrid heard about San Thomé, but the news only reached London ten days later, after the arrival of William Herbert with his shipload of dissidents and sick men. The stories differed in some ways, but in the main confirmed the disaster. The Spanish version was that the Governor Palomeque had learnt about the English landing only at 10 o'clock at night and had made ready to attack, only to discover that the English were too numerous.[5] His patrol had therefore withdrawn, followed by the English. A messenger had been sent, warning the English that the town was Spanish, but no notice had been taken. San Thomé was stormed and pillaged, and houses were burnt. Afterwards another messenger was sent asking for the return of Palomeque, believed to have been captured, and with a plea: 'Be content with what you have already done to us, and leave us.' But no notice was taken, and more depredations by the English followed.

The date for Gondomar's departure from London had already been arranged, but now, such was the fury in Madrid, it was postponed, and he was ordered to stay for at least three more months. The story goes that before Herbert arrived, Gondomar – having already received the report from Madrid – stormed off to Whitehall, demanding to see the King, only to be told that he was engaged. He was not to be deflected, saying that he had but one word to say, and on that condition was allowed into the royal presence. He burst in, waving his arms and shouting *'Piratas! Piratas! Piratas!'*, and then made his theatrical exit, leaving a bewildered and (according to one version) terrified monarch.[6]

All this coincided with the return of Sir John Digby from Madrid with details of new prevarications over the proposed royal marriage. There followed much 'high language' at further meetings between Gondomar and James, mixed with a certain amount of bluff and manoeuvring. It was obvious that it was becoming increasingly difficult for Spain to control its vast American empire, and that there were too many weak areas virtually unguarded. Spain needed the friendship of Britain, but at the same time had to appear to be tough and unbending. Gondomar also played on James's innate timidity and hatred of war and violence, and – most importantly – his desperate need of finance (he had told Digby to bargain for a dowry of £500,000, 'besides the jewels').

It is hardly surprising that Gondomar should be remembered by historians in Spain as an example of *el perfecto diplomático*, the perfect diplomat.

On 23 May Captain Roger North arrived bringing with him Raleigh's letter to Winwood, and this resulted in his being summoned to an audience with the King. Whatever he said then was probably repeated in a jumbled way when after Raleigh's arrest he was called to make a statement to the Lords in Council. The main gist was that he did not think that Raleigh had ever believed in the existence of a mine, and that other captains also had their doubts. This was certainly pretty damning, and he was obviously full of rage against both Raleigh and Keymis; why, he asked, after castigating Keymis in public, 'in a sharp and round fashion', should Raleigh thereafter have had him in his cabin privately for several days 'without any words of expostulation'?[7] North said that Raleigh had indeed spoken of the possibility of going to France – North himself had also been friendly with the Frenchman Faige at Plymouth, who had told him that he was going to Normandy to fetch two ships which were ready to join Sir Walter Raleigh 'upon the seas'. He also said that Raleigh had been hoping to seize a very large quantity of tobacco, something that would have had disgusted James with his well-known hatred of the weed.

North had told enough to ignite the flames. On 9 June James issued a brief and dramatically worded *Proclamation*, that might almost have been at the dictation of Gondomar. It concerned not only 'Sir Walter Rawleigh' but 'those who had adventured with him'. Weaving in two references to 'our dear Brother the King of Spain', he denounced 'by common fame' the 'hostile invasion of the town of San Thomé' and the 'killing of divers of the inhabitants thereof', which had his 'utter mislike and detestation'. Raleigh and others unnamed were to be condemned for having 'maliciously broken and infringed the Peace and Amity which hath been so happily and so long inviolably continued between Us and the subject of both Our Crowns'. He asked all those who had knowledge of these 'scandalous and enormous outrages' to repair immediately to a member of the Privy Council.

Thus was Raleigh prejudged, although the words 'by common fame' were a possible loophole for escape. James's rage can be understood. If after all there had never been a mine he had been cheated. But he was in a dilemma. Were he to punish Raleigh he would be admitting his own error in allowing him to sail in the first place. If he did not punish Raleigh it would mean the end of his friendship with Spain and the final collapse of the Spanish marriage fandango.

Orders for Raleigh's arrest were given by the Lord Admiral on 12 June to Sir Lewis Stukeley of Afferton Castle, Vice-Admiral of Devon but at that time still in London. This seems to confirm that by then Raleigh had already reached Plymouth.

Stukeley was related to Raleigh, being a nephew of Sir Richard Grenville, and seemed in no hurry to leave. It may have been decided that Raleigh needed time to recover his strength and have some time with his wife, who also had to travel down from London. Raleigh was staying as so often in the past, at Radford outside Plymouth with Sir Christopher Harris, one of his staunchest allies, and who was acting as a deputy Vice-Admiral. In a sense therefore he was under house arrest. If he had wanted to escape he had at least a fortnight to do so.

On arrival he had been handed a statement by some of his captains, no doubt including North, and this made him add another page to his letter to Carew before despatching the letter to London. 'They are bound to plead their cause,' he wrote. 'The truth is that all of them, except Warham St Leger, wanted to turn thieves if they had a chance, but they were obliged to return . . . I hope to live to answer them to their faces, and to prove them all cowards, liars, and in spirit, thieves.' He asked for a copy of his whole letter to be sent to his wife, 'who with the loss of her son and these rumours, I fear will go mad.'

Excitement was buzzing around London. James Howell wrote to his benefactor Sir James Croft.[8]

The news that keeps greatest noise here now is the return of Sir Walter Raleigh . . . but it seems that Golden Mine is proved a mere chimera, an imaginary airy Mine; and indeed his Majesty had never any other concept of it. But what will not one in captivity (as Sir Walter was) promise to regain his freedom? Who would not promise not only Mines but mountains of gold for liberty? . . . The *Destiny* is like to prove a fatal destiny to him, and to some of the rest of those gallant adventures . . . many of those are like to make shipwreck of their estates by their voyage . . . I fear it will go very ill with Sir Walter, and that Gondomar will never give him over until he hath his head off his shoulders.

Raleigh had expected a hostile reception but never one quite so devastating as this. On 16 June he exploded in a letter to the King, writing more strongly that he had ever dared before. The beginning was important, setting out the credo to which he adhered until his death – though the effect was weakened by the pleading and confused tone of some of the rest.

It was copied out and given to Gondomar, who sent it on to Spain. A Spanish biographer of Gondomar has admitted its *admirable tenacidad*, but has also dismissed it as a *notable ejemplo del tono melodramatico y* *declamatorio*, which tended towards *autocompasión o al histrionismo*, self-pity or histrionics.*[9]

The letter began:

May it please your most Excellent Majesty. If in my journey outwards bound I had of my men murdered at the Islands [the Canaries], and yet spared to take revenge; if I did discharge some Spanish barks taken, without any spoil; if I forbare all parts of the Spanish Indies, wherein I might have taken twenty of their towns on the sea-coast, and did only follow the enterprise which I undertook upon Guiana – where, without any direction from me, a Spanish village was burnt, which was newly set up within three miles of the mine – by your Majesty's favour I find no reason why the Spanish ambassador should complain of me. If it were lawful to murder 36 Englishmen – tying them back to back, and then cutting their throats, when they had traded with them a whole month, and came to them on the land without so much as one sword amongst them all, and that it may not be lawful for your Majesty's subjects, being charged first by them, to repel force by force – we may then justly say, O miserable English!

He then when on to refer to the behaviour of two Englishmen, Parker and Moutam, who had burnt towns and killed Spaniards in the Honduras and had 'nothing said unto them at their return'. He on the other hand had not committed any offence in the West Indies; 'O miserable Sir Walter Raleigh!'

If I have spent my poor estate, lost my son, suffered by sickness and otherwise a world of miseries; if I have resisted with the manifest hazard of my life the robberies and spoils which my companies would have made; if when I was poor I could have made myself rich; if when I had gotten my liberty, which all men and Nature itself doth so much prize, I voluntarily lost it; if when I was master of my life I have rendered it again; if I might elsewhere have sold my ships and goods, and have put five or six thousand pounds in my purse, I have brought her [the *Destiny*] into England – I beseech your Majesty to believe that all this I have done because it should not be said to your Majesty that your Majesty had given liberty and trust to a man whose end was but the recovery of his liberty, and who had betrayed your Majesty's trust.

* The letter has hitherto been regarded as written from the Tower on 24 September. Only transcripts were found, one with that date because a copy had been made then for Sir Thomas Wilson, who had been put in charge of Raleigh at the Tower. The original letter was discovered by Latham and Youings at the Centre for Kentish Studies at Maidstone, with the date 16 June. Joyce Youings records that it was evidently written for Raleigh by a clerk but signed by him with a very shaky hand.

My mutineers told me that if I returned for England I should be undone, but I believed more in your Majesty's goodness than in their arguments . . . Your Majesty's wisdom and goodness I have made my judges, who have ever been and shall ever remain, your Majesty's most humble vassal, W Ralegh.

Gondomar, meanwhile, as James Howell predicted, was indeed bombarding James with demands that he should take prompt and severe public action, 'in order', he said at one of their meetings, 'that my master [Philip] may see by your Majesty's acts that you are really desirous of his friendship.' Now there were wild claims from Spain that Raleigh had been attacking towns all over Guiana and burning their churches. On 20 June Gondomar was saying that Raleigh had on board the *Destiny* enough stolen goods 'to make him and his supporters rich', and that simple justice demanded to have him and his crew hanged at once if James did not intend to keep his promise to have them all sent to Madrid. 'Raleigh's acts of war and damage were foretold to you in writing and speech a thousand times by me.'[10]

On the 21st James called his Councillors and lectured them on Raleigh's crimes. Raleigh's friends could not presume to contradict their sovereign, but they did object to Gondomar's presumption in demanding that Raleigh should be hanged in Madrid, as if England was a mere vassal of Spain. For a while James was taken aback. 'Though I am a peaceful man', he at last said, 'I need to defend my honour.' Buckingham (Villiers, who was now Marquess of Buckingham) and Sir Robert Naunton came to his rescue. Did that mean that his Majesty should now be prepared to go to war with Spain in order to defend his honour? Should he not punish those traitors who had advised him to let Raleigh go on his voyage? This last was a shrewd point, because some of the 'traitors' were sitting in front of the King. It was therefore agreed by all that Raleigh deserved some sort of punishment.[11]

On the next day James and Gondomar had a confrontation. James had spent the morning interviewing new witnesses, and most seemed to have laid the blame on Keymis rather than Raleigh for the attack on San Thomé. This was not what Gondomar wanted to hear, and he now put on his grandest and most condescending manner, telling James that he was not capable of judging Raleigh's conduct because of his being surrounded by Raleigh's friends; what was more, James himself had given Raleigh permission to leave. If he, Gondomar, had been Governor of the Canaries or Seville he would have exacted reparations at once, but the plain fact was that Raleigh still had not been hanged, and his friends in the Council were still at liberty.

Elizabeth would never have stood for this – her crushing of that impudent

Polish envoy in 1597 was famous.* Even James was put in a rage, but he reacted differently. He threw his hat on the floor and clutched at his hair, shouting that what might be justice in Spain was not justice in England. Until God forsook him, he would not condemn any man until he had been legally tried. Even if the Prince of Wales had been murdered, there would have to be a trial. Gondomar scornfully replied that yes, there was a difference between Spain and England: if a Spaniard had done to Englishmen what Raleigh had done to Spaniards his King would immediately have ordered his execution. He went through the catalogue of all the horrors of Raleigh's behaviour, and made James admit that such things were indeed terrible and needed to be dealt with swiftly. James, having been duly calmed and subdued, finally agreed that he would entrust Raleigh's case to 'noble gentlemen and not to the judges', and that on his conviction Raleigh with ten or twelve of his captains would be sent to Madrid to be hanged in the main square. He would have this confirmed by the Council.

On the 24th the Council met and once again there was strong opposition, with Buckingham supporting the King. James angrily broke up the meeting saying that he was King and would keep his promise to Gondomar 'without following the advice of fools and designing persons'.[12]

On the same day Gondomar sent to Spain a translation of Raleigh's letter to Carew that had been begun in Ireland.† Also sent to Spain was a document headed *Alegaciones de Walter Raleigh en su descargo*, Allegations by Walter Raleigh for his defence.

It must be said that those Allegations were faithfully and objectively recorded: how, for instance, Raleigh was claiming to be the first discoverer of Guiana; that the local chieftains were supposed to have recognized Elizabeth's sovereignty, in the light of which James had sent out Harcourt, etc. etc. But they did also include Raleigh's new claim, that every day the French were seizing goods and properties from Spanish subjects and then openly selling them.

On the 26th Buckingham on behalf of James wrote to Gondomar saying that one way or another justice would be done. Carew went personally to the King and, so it was said, knelt before him, pleading passionately for his cousin. The King's reply was: 'I may as well hang him as deliver him to the King of Spain; and one of these I must do, if the case be as Gondomar

---

* p. 290.

† The translation is now in the Archivo General de Indias at Seville where it was discovered by Martin A. S. Hume who retranslated it into English. The original and any other copies have been lost.

represented it.' When pressed for a more favourable answer he merely said: 'The most thou canst expect is that I should give him a hearing.'[13]

Gondomar had been expecting to leave shortly and had already said his farewells. Now he was ordered from Spain to stay on some days longer. To keep up the pressure he had been deliberately spreading rumours that embargoes on British shipping were already in force at the Canaries and in Seville. Then he heard that James had received an alarmist letter from his ambassador in Madrid, Sir Francis Cottington, about cries for vengeance and threats of reprisals. This meant that it should be easier to push James into a final decision, and at last he would be able to get away from England.

So he asked for an immediate audience. But James was on progress at Hatfield and not in the mood for yet another stormy encounter. He sent word that he would meet Gondomar at Greenwich on 2 July. This was not good enough for Gondomar, and he told Buckingham, who was holding the reins of government in James's absence, that he wished to see the whole of the Privy Council, *in person*. So an order was given to all members of the Council to wait upon His Excellency at whatever time and date he named. His Excellency decided on 5 o'clock on 29 June. He said that the matter was of such importance that he could not be kept waiting even one more hour.

On his arrival he was received by all members of the Council standing at the entrance to the chamber. The Archbishop of Canterbury told him that they had put aside business in his honour. What followed was described by Gondomar with considerable relish in a very long letter to King Philip.[14] He began by saying that he had heard from Spain that Raleigh had intended to commit far greater hostilities throughout the West Indies if his fleet had been strong enough. Even so, there had been night attacks, terrible acts of cruelty, deaths, burnings, looting, as in time of war. Such behaviour was a discredit to the whole English nation.

In Spain, he continued, and elsewhere there had been outrage that all this should have occurred in spite of Raleigh's promises. His Majesty the King had sworn that if those promises were broken he would be prepared to surrender Raleigh and his accomplices to be hanged in the *plaza* of Madrid, and that they would be made to bring with them everything that they had stolen. An armada had been kept ready at Seville for intercepting Raleigh, but it did not leave because of those promises and the fact that he had left under royal authority. Instead he had chased after every ship he had met, expecting it to be Spanish. Gondomar had been shown Raleigh's letter to Winwood in which he had proudly listed the names of the captains who had sacked San Thomé and slaughtered its inhabitants, as if they ought to be admired for their bravery and considered for further service by the Crown

. . . It was important that Raleigh should be punished as swiftly as possible if the friendship of the Spanish King was to be maintained.

'Having said that,' Gondomar said, 'I took off my hat, and calmly and with dignity told them that I had said all that I wanted to say, and put it on again.'

The Chancellor, Francis Bacon, whom Gondomar liked, now conferred in a low voice with the Archbishop and the Treasurer. Then he got up and spoke 'with the utmost cordiality', sympathizing with Gondomar's feelings, assuring him of full satisfaction – which of course would have to depend on the will of the King – and hoping that the incident would not affect the friendship between the two Majesties and their subjects.

The Archbishop's attitude was very different. With what seemed like '*suma malicia*', extreme malice, he took off his '*birreta*' and without looking at Gondomar in the face said that he was sure that the excesses of Sir Walter Raleigh as described by His Excellency were worthy of exemplary punishment but he would want to know what Raleigh would say in response. Gondomar cut him short and said that he was not acting as Raleigh's prosecutor, and the matter was not a case for tribunals – he had no more to say than that. At this point the Chancellor and the Treasurer intervened and were so courteous and flattering that Gondomar was obliged to reply to their compliments in a similar fashion, and that had to be that.

James needed to call the Council before the meeting at Greenwich. He was greeted with complaints about Gondomar's high-handed behaviour; no English monarch had ever been treated in such a way by a foreign ambassador. Again Buckingham defended James, who was working himself up into a passion, hobbling up and down the Council Chamber, asking questions and giving his own answers: how it was absurd to go to war just because of Raleigh; what would the world say; he was renowned as a man who kept his word, and he had given his pledge to Gondomar. All he wanted to know was whether Raleigh should be punished or not. Most of the Councillors agreed that this must be done, but Raleigh's friends abstained. James then announced that the vote was unanimous, and that if ever he heard anyone speaking favourably of Raleigh, in public or in private, he would treat him as a traitor.

So the next day Gondomar was rowed to Greenwich to hear the verdict. He and James met behind closed doors. Despite some harsh words, with Gondomar behaving like a headmaster lecturing a pupil, it was a fairly jocular meeting, and Gondomar was assured that the Council would now be made to decide on how Raleigh was to be punished. But this was still not what Gondomar had wanted.

As he gloomily walked in the garden with the Earl of Lennox, a messenger arrived from James with a basket of cherries, which Gondomar began to eat as he went along. Suddenly there were shouts of laughter from the window of a summer house under which they was passing. He looked up and there was His Majesty, who had been lying in wait. 'Where's your gravity now?' James shouted. 'An Ambassador, eating cherries out of a basket!' Gondomar had to pretend to be amused and waved to him.[15]

On 4 July James summoned the Council again, this time to be met with almost complete opposition to the sending of Raleigh and his captains to Spain. James said he had given his promise and would not break it. Bacon, no friend of Raleigh, was the most vocal. He said that however important it was to be on good terms with Spain, even to suggest sending an Englishman there to be executed would have been 'mere talk' and not something to be taken literally. At this James threw a tantrum, shouting that 'mere talk' was nonsense, and he would listen no more to such ignorant chatter.

The next day was to be the farewell meeting between the two friends. James hugged Gondomar again and again, swearing friendship forever. They played the sort of game that James loved, with Gondomar acting as 'Secretary', to whom James dictated a letter. But the letter once again turned out not to be what Gondomar wanted: James must be more explicit about the fate of Raleigh's captains – surely it was not too much ask for ten or a dozen of the worst of them to be executed in Spain? Raleigh's ship the *Destiny* must be sent as well, along with all its plunder.

The more James hesitated, the more Gondomar urged him. Digby and Buckingham were called in, and a deal was made in their presence. Raleigh would be sent for execution in Spain, unless King Philip decided otherwise, in which case the execution would be in London. Gondomar said that he must have this in writing. James said that Buckingham would write the letter. Afterwards the King and the ambassador were left alone, so that 'some familiar and domestic things could be discussed'.

James had once told Gondomar that Buckingham was a 'greater Spaniard than the Ambassador himself'. It was said that the letter Buckingham wrote would have been enough to make the dead Elizabeth rise from her grave. Buckingham did add in it, however, that there had to be a legal process, 'which cannot be altogether avoided', and said the King would be as severe in punishment as if the attack on San Thomé had been on an English city.[16]

To give Buckingham his due he had (unlike Digby) refused a Spanish pension until – as he put it – he did something to deserve it.

Gondomar expected to leave London on 15 July. It was usually the practice to allow departing Catholic ambassadors to take with them a few priests who had been liberated from prison, on condition that they would not return to England. Gondomar was allowed to take all the priests who had been imprisoned or sentenced to death, seventy-three in total. James had at first attempted to be adamant about one of them, Father William Baldwin, a Jesuit, who was believed to have been implicated in the Gunpowder Plot and had been extradited back to London by the Count Palatine – he had been eight years in captivity, more or less incommunicado. As usual Gondomar had his way, and Baldwin was sent to him in the company of Buckingham, who had also brought a diamond in the shape of a heart. James in a letter said that by sending Baldwin he was giving Gondomar a 'jewel that was an even finer present'.*

Just before Gondomar's departure one of his retainers knocked down a small boy in the Strand. Although the child was not badly hurt, an angry crowd formed and rushed to the Spanish embassy in the Barbican throwing stones at windows and hacking at doors. Gondomar himself was out, having supper with the Earl of Worcester. The Chief Justice was summoned, along with the Mayor and some Aldermen, and the crowd was only pacified when a trial was promised and the culprit led away (in fact he was sent back very soon afterwards). Buckingham wrote to express his regret to Gondomar, who asked that the rioters should not be dealt with harshly.

Gondomar left with a train of fifty carriages, and with his trunks of books. He was going first to Brussels and then to Paris. James told him that no ambassador had been so much loved and respected in England.

Gondomar's confessor, Fray Diego de la Fuente, wrote on the next day, 16 July, to another priest in Spain, Fray Antonio de Sotomayor, to say that before he left the ambassador had two meetings with King James, 'one more than an hour and a half in Latin (which he spoke *elegantemente* on matters of religion) . . . But I cannot avoid adding that the King gave the Conde two presents such as have never been accorded to any other ambassador in this kingdom. The first was all the artillery that Drake took from the city of Cadiz, and all that was taken at sea in the Indies and from Santo Domingo, said to be of the value of 200,000 ducats and not wanted in this country

---

* Writing to Cardinal Robert Bellarmine on 4 July Gondomar said:[17] 'I have Father Baldwin in his own Jesuit robe here now in my residence, even saying mass publicly. Catholic people flock to see him and many to make their confessions to him. This is the reward for all the other anxieties and difficulties that I have borne and still bear here.' At least Gondomar had promised a concession. He wrote to Pope Paul V asking him to release John Moll, who was being held by the Inquisition in Rome and had been tutor to Lord Roos.

On 24 September 1618 Sánchez de Ulloa, Chargé D'affaires at the embassy, wrote to Madrid saying that most of the priests who had left with Gondomar had returned and were to be seen openly in the streets – such was the relaxation of restrictions on Catholics.

Raleigh's portrait as frontispiece to the third edition of the History of the World.
The second edition, published when he was still living, had the motto Amore et
Virtute *below, adopted originally in honour of Elizabeth. This new motto can be
loosely translated as 'He followed the destiny appointed him'.*

because the metal used here is of better quality. The *Conde* is arranging for
all those things to be sent to Flanders.' The other present was somewhat
bizarre: a parchment signed by James and with the Great Seal authorizing
Gondomar and his successors to 'take every year from England six horses,
six dogs and six hawks'.[18]

*

We can only imagine the agony of the reunion between Raleigh and Bess. At least she would have been able to bring Raleigh a copy of the new edition of the *History of the World*, published at the end of 1617 and soon to be reprinted. This time it had his name on the title page with his portrait in armour, authoritative, holding a baton, and underneath showing his coat of arms and the famous motto, *Amore et Virtute*. Undoubtedly she and his faithful captain Samuel King would have urged him to escape, which he would have refused. In the *Declaration* it was said that he did try to escape immediately on arriving at Plymouth: another deliberate lie by Bacon.

In the second week of July Raleigh and Bess decided to ride to London. It was a brave decision. But just outside Ashburton, some twenty miles from Plymouth, they were met by Stukeley, who told him that he had orders to apprehend both him and his ship. Raleigh tried to make a joke, saying that he had saved Stukeley the trouble by arresting himself.

So they returned to Plymouth, and waited for the written order for Raleigh's official arrest. Another strange lull followed. Stukeley busied himself with disposing of the *Destiny*'s cargo of tobacco, hardly paying any attention to his charge, almost as if the government was still hoping that he would escape – which would certainly have saved everyone a lot of trouble.

By now Raleigh knew that there was very little hope for the future, and once more he wrote to Carew, in a style different from his last, rambling and repetitive though with some additional points.[19] He did his best to exonerate the King, perhaps regretting his outburst, by saying that he now admitted that he had never made it known to him that the Spaniards had a 'footing' on the Orinoco (which in effect he had) and that James had nothing to do with the attack on San Thomé. From the letters captured at San Thomé he had discovered a copy of one dated 9 March 1617 from the Spanish King to Palomeque, referring to *los anglos enemigos* (the English enemy), and saying that all Spaniards and Indians who traded with them were to be put to death. He also referred yet again to the thirty-six men who had their throats cut, this time identifying them as 'Hall's men', Hall perhaps being his own brother-in-law. How therefore, he asked, could *enemigos* also be peacemakers?*

With Stukeley, for whatever reason, taking so little notice of Raleigh, Bess did seize the opportunity of urging her husband to flee. Samuel King

---

* The original letter from Madrid appointing Palomeque Governor of Trinidad and Guiana in 1615 still exists in the archives at Seville.[20] It specifically mentions that 'the enemy' had established colonies in Guiana for growing tobacco. These colonies, it says, had to be destroyed. There were plans for a garrison of 500 men at Trinidad, and there was to be a 'complete extirpation of the enemy, from every point on the island where they have secured a footing.'

was in contact with a French captain called Flory and had persuaded him to take Raleigh in his bark aross the Channel to France. So one night King rowed Raleigh out to the ship. They had scarcely gone a few hundred yards when Raleigh had a change of mind and demanded to be taken back, saying that he found the idea of flight intolerable and humiliating. (The version given in the *Declaration* was that they could not find the ship in the dark.) Once more, on the following night, he was persuaded to be rowed out, and once more he asked to return.

On 13 July, with Gondomar about to depart, the Privy Council decided it was time to send a peremptory order to Stukeley to bring Raleigh to London: 'We command you, upon your allegiance, that, all delays set apart, you do safely and speedily bring hither the person of Sir Walter Raleigh to answer before us such matters as shall be objected against him on his Majesty's behalf.'[21]

Stukeley closed the tobacco sales and whatever else he had been up to (he was said later to have kept some of the profits for himself), and on 15 July the party set off, accompanied by an enigmatic character called Manourie, a French doctor, generally described by subsequent biographers as a quack.

Cold Walls Again
1618

Raleigh did need to be accompanied by a doctor, and he probably looked forward to chatting with Manourie about the 'many chymical receipts' he took with him. Manourie was to be revealed as a sly rogue, on the make: just another case of Raleigh's misplaced friendships. He could well have been recommended for the job by Stukeley.

They were staying at a Mr Drake's* house when the order came from London. Manourie said afterwards that he noticed the shock on Raleigh's face. Watching from the top of the stairs he saw him in his room, which had the door open, and he was stamping his feet and tearing at his hair, muttering and swearing. 'God's wounds,' he heard him say, 'is it possible that my fortune should thus return upon me again?'[1]

This piece of so-called evidence was not particularly damning but was one of the various scraps of talk that Manourie stored in his mind, to be repeated later. The cavalcade moved on to the house of Mr Horsey, probably a connection of the Sir Ralph Horsey of the Cerne Abbas inquiry back in 1594. Here Manourie had a conversation with Samuel King, unkindly described in Bacon's *Declaration* as 'an old domestic', who spoke to him of the 'infortunity' of his master. 'I would we were all in Paris,' King had remarked. When asked why, he answered: 'Because as soon as we come to London they will commit Sir Walter Raleigh to the Tower and behead him.' This was to be taken as proof that Raleigh was again thinking of escaping to France. Manourie expressed appropriate sorrow for Raleigh's troubles and meekly said that he was ready to do all he could to help him.

They reached Sherborne, and there was the view of the gabled house that Raleigh and Bess had created and loved so much, with its park and plantations in their July splendour, and with the castle across the river. Raleigh turned to Manourie and sighed, saying that once all this had been his and that it had been unjustly taken from him. He, Bess and Stukeley

---

* No doubt one of the family of Raleigh's father's first wife.

stayed with 'old Master Parham', Sir Edward Parham, but Manourie, Samuel King and the servants were put up at the George Inn, which must have caused some local excitement. Raleigh was to say that whilst he was at Sherborne Sir John Digby actually came to see him, and informed him that he would not be caught under common law but would be prosecuted under both civil and admiralty law (for suspected piracy).[2]

The next day they continued to Salisbury, a long and tiring journey of thirty-five miles. They passed Wilton, which Raleigh had known so well, and here he dismounted, asking Manourie to join him as he walked down the hill. He had heard that James was coming here on his summer progress, and he wanted time to prepare for his defence in the form of a document which could be presented on arrival. 'Give me a vomit,' he said to Manourie.[3] 'It is good for me to evacuate many bad humours. By this means I shall gain time to work my friends, give orders for my affairs, and, it may be, pacify his Majesty before my coming to London.'

On arrival at Salisbury he went to bed, complaining of dizziness and loss of sight. Then he got up, and leaning on Stukeley's arm stumbled and hit his head violently against a post in the gallery outside.

The next day he sent Bess, Samuel King and most of the servants on to London. Digby's warning had made him decide that after all he must be ready to escape to France. It seems that on various occasions during the journey King had said to Raleigh how much he had regretted that decision to row back to land, and that once Raleigh had replied: 'I can blame nobody but myself.' King told him that he knew of a former boatswain called Hart, who kept a ketch at Tilbury which would take him to France. He would enlist the help of Edward Cottrell, the Tower servant who had been helpful to Raleigh, and ask him to contact Hart and arrange for a boat to take them to Tilbury. Bess had been told of this plan, also about the pretended illness.

Afterwards Samuel King said:[4] 'I was ready to do anything that might procure his safety; being well assured, in my conscience, that though he ought to absent himself till the Spanish fury was over, yet . . . that the misery would never make him disloyal to his King or his country.' He also added that in spite of what Manourie was to say, he had never heard Raleigh 'name his Majesty but with reverence'. (Bacon in the *Declaration* wrote that Raleigh had complained that Sherborne had been taken from him *by the King*, which was a deliberate untruth.)

The next morning Raleigh's servant came rushing in to Stukeley's room in a state of excitement, saying that his master was out of his wits, on all fours in his nightshirt scratching and gnawing the rushes on the floorboards. Stukeley arrived just as Raleigh was vomiting, after which he went into convulsions, drawing up his legs and arms which Stukeley and others wrestled to straighten out. When they had gone Raleigh laughed and said to Manourie that all this had given Sir Lewis Stukeley good exercise and had taught him how to be a physician.

He showed absolutely no remorse about such antics. He was determined to finish his defence, which he called his *Apologie for the Voyage to Guiana*. As he put it: 'In spite of King and Council, in spite of courtiers and of scaffolds, Englishmen shall know all about Guiana.' He also had a Biblical reference to hand, how David had deliberately pretended to be mad in order to gain time, allowing spittle to fall on his beard, and how he had scrabbled at the gate.

Now he asked Manourie to get him an ointment that he could rub over himself making him look 'horrible and loathsome, without offending the principal parts'. Manourie duly obliged, and purple pustules and blotches appeared all over his face, arms and chest, greatly alarming Stukeley who thought he must have leprosy. The Bishop of Ely was in Salisbury, being the new Bishop of Winchester designate, so Stukeley went to him for help. The Bishop sent round two physicians, who were so baffled that they called in a third, Dr Heydock, 'a bachelor in physic'. Heydock took his pulse, which was normal – all the more surprising. All they could do was to sign a certificate saying that Raleigh's condition was extremely serious, and that he could not be moved for several days.

Raleigh decided that they might ask to see his water, so he got Manourie to rub round the inside of his piss-pot with a substance that turned his urine 'all earthy humour, of a blackish colour'. This had a great effect on the physicians, who then decided that his end must be near. To keep up the pretence of sickness, Raleigh gave out that he had eaten nothing for three days. In fact he had sent Manourie round to the White Hart Inn to smuggle in a 'leg of mutton and three loaves', which he ate in secret.

Meanwhile, he was writing frantically, day and night. The very first paragraph of the *Apologie* reveals the mental strain and his passionate determination to clear himself. He cited not only the 'greatest Princes of Europe', such as Charles V, but Francis Drake, Hawkins and Sir John Norris as having made great mistakes that had been condoned. Then he went on to repeat the familiar themes: Guiana was English because of its cession by native chiefs and his 'conquest' of 1595; Guiana was a rich country, not just because of its gold. He also repeated Keymis's assertion that San Thomé had been moved, and once more insisted that the Spaniards had been the first to attack. He emphasized that no French ships had been involved, that he did not attempt to ambush the Plate Fleet. Some of his enemies had claimed that he had invented the myth of a mine, but this was completely untrue. And so on.

It is ironic that, nearly three centuries after his death, Raleigh should have been vindicated by the British Government. This was to happen at the time of the boundary dispute between Venezuela and British Guiana when the United States was arbitrator. By then it was also recognized, in the words of Cecil's descendant, the Prime Minister Lord Salisbury, that there were large tracts of land south of the Orinoco 'which from their auriferous nature are known to be of almost untold value'.

The results of the dispute were published in the Blue Books of the British Foreign Office between 1896 and 1899. Raleigh's claim that Guiana was an uninhabited region (by Europeans) was proved to be literally true, except for the area around San Thomé.* There had been frequent trading by Dutch and English ships up and down the lower Orinoco before 1618 and some time afterwards. In the report of the American commission it was stated: 'There is no perfect evidence of the existence before 1648 of any other Spanish settlement than San Thomé in the region between the Orinoco and the Essequibo, or any other than a temporary occupation of any position in that area.'†

Raleigh's defence of himself in the *Apologie* reached its climax with an attack on his great opponent Gondomar:

But in truth the Spanish Ambassador hath complained against me to no other end than to prevent my complaint against the Spaniards . . . My men . . . were invaded and slain before any violence was offered to any of the Spaniards; and I hope the Ambassador doth not esteem us for so wretched and miserable a people as to offer our throats to their swords without any manner of resistance. Howsoever, I have said it already, and I will say it again, that if Guiana be not our Sovereign's, the working of a mine there and the taking of a town there had been equally perilous to me; for by doing the one I had robbed the King of Spain and been a thief and by the other a disturber and breaker of the peace.

James arrived at Salisbury on 1 August, and was not pleased to learn of the

* By the 1890s an important quicksilver mine had been discovered near the mouth of the Caroní.
† The resulting settlement is still not accepted by Venezuela, and a military road has ominously been built along the frontier, with a large portion of what is now Guyana marked on maps as 'Disputed Territory'.

presence of Sir Walter Raleigh. The *Apologie* had been completed, and, to the doctors' amazement, Raleigh's blotches had suddenly cleared up. So he had not contracted leprosy after all. Whether or not the *Apologie* was handed to James at that time is not known; in any case he did not bother to read it. Stukeley was ordered to remove Raleigh immediately and to continue to London.

On the journey Raleigh confided in Manourie about his plan to escape to France, and said if he would help him, he would pay him £50 a year. He had been told that Hart's ketch 'would go with all the winds'. Manourie asked him why he needed to escape if he had written his *Apologie*. To which Raleigh curtly replied 'Never tell me more; a man that fears is never secure.'[5]

According to the *Declaration* Manourie also said that Raleigh used 'unchivalrous words' against the royal person, some of them 'hateful and traitorous', which Raleigh was vehemently to deny. When Manourie worried about his own fate, in case it might become known that he had been in on the secret, Raleigh suggested that as a Frenchman he could join him in France.

They went to Andover and on to Staines. Manourie now divulged Raleigh's plans for escaping to Stukeley, and Raleigh soon became aware that Stukeley had suddenly become much more watchful. Not knowing why this should be so, he decided that Stukeley must be drawn into the plot, another reason being that Manourie would soon be leaving them. The bribe this time was a diamond and ruby jewel worth £150, and £50 in cash, plus another £1,000 when he had arrived safely in France. Stukeley was happy to accept.

But Raleigh's plan to escape soon reached Stukeley from a quite different source, and he became involved in a plot which would trap and destroy Raleigh for good and all. The boatswain Hart and the Tower servant Cottrell had realized that there was good money in the story, and had passed on the information to William Herbert and Sir William St John (this William Herbert was a cousin of Stukeley and not the Herbert who went with Raleigh to Guiana). Sir William St John was a kinsman of Buckingham and it was he whose pocket had been filled to enable Raleigh to get out of the Tower in 1616. The Council had therefore been informed – except perhaps for Raleigh's allies, Carew, Arundel and Pembroke – and although the Lieutenant of the Tower had already been warned to expect Raleigh as soon as he reached London, it was decided that he must not be prevented from going to his home in Broad Street; this was so that developments could be secretly watched, and an arrest made at the right moment. Herbert and St John had gone galloping off to Salisbury to inform the King about this decision, and had run into Stukeley and Raleigh at Bagshot on their way to Staines. Herbert and Stukeley went into private conference, which Raleigh assumed was simply an exchange of news between two relatives.

The next stop was Brentford, and here Raleigh was surprised to be met by a Frenchman, David de Novion, who had the title of Sieur de La Chesnée. This man brought a message from the French agent or acting ambassador, Le Clerc, who said he was eager to meet him in London. No doubt Stukeley was told about it. How La Chesnée knew that Raleigh would be at Brentford has not been revealed,

Two days later Le Clerc, accompanied by La Chesnée as his interpreter (which for Raleigh as a fluent French speaker was not necessary), came to Broad Street. It seems that at the time the house was full of Raleigh's friends, but Raleigh maintained later that Le Clerc only passed through the crowded parlour and nobody knew who he was. He also said that he was surprised by the visit and had asked who the man was with the white feather in his hat, and that he was told that it was the French agent.[6]

Le Clerc wanted to tell him that he would help him to get to France, where he would have a good welcome on arrival. Raleigh thanked him, but said that he had already arranged to escape in an English boat. After Le Clerc had left, Raleigh told Stukeley about it, and Stukeley congratulated him and even volunteered to flee with him. Stukeley then asked for a loan of £10 so that he could pay off his servants, to avoid suspicion – so he said.

The next evening Raleigh went down to the Tower dock, where Samuel King was waiting.[7] He was accompanied by Stukeley, Stukeley's son and a page who carried his cloak-bag. Even more farcical, Raleigh was wearing a false beard. We are also told that he wore a hat with a green band and that he carried four pistols. He gave two of the pistols to Stukeley. As they were about to leave, Stukeley surprised King by asking him 'whether thus far he had not distinguished himself an honest man'. King merely replied 'that he hoped he would continue so'. Raleigh and the Stukeleys were in one wherry, King and Hart in the other. They had hardly gone twenty strokes when it was apparent that a larger boat, well manned, was following them. Raleigh was at once alarmed, but Stukeley calmed him and told the watermen to keep rowing. But Raleigh was still worried and after a while asked the men what they would do if told to stop in the King's name. This was a foolish thing to have done, and he went further, making up a story about a 'brabbling matter' with the Spanish ambassador. As a result the 'great boobies' became frightened and refused to go on.[8]

Stukeley started cursing Raleigh and saying that he regretted ever getting involved with a man so full of doubts and fears. All the while the shadowing boat was waiting in the darkness. Raleigh threatened to kill the watermen if they did not go on. They had got as far as Galleon's Reach when the watermen said that they had lost the tide. Stukeley insisted that if they could get as far as Gravesend he was certain that they could cross to Tilbury. The watermen said that they could not make Gravesend before morning. There was some discussion about landing and looking for horses. Then three ketches were seen, and Hart said that he wondered if one of them could be his. Raleigh was now convinced that he had been betrayed and ordered the men to row back to Greenwich.

At this stage their pursuers were hailing them in the name of the King. Raleigh and Stukeley began whispering together, Raleigh handing over some valuables to Stukeley and Stukeley embracing him. They landed, to be followed by the men from the other boat who were wearing the livery of Sir William St John. Now 'Sir Judas' Stukeley, as he was soon to be known, arrested both Raleigh and Samuel King. They went into a tavern, and Raleigh begged Samuel King to say that he was an accomplice of Stukeley, but he refused. Raleigh's reproach to Stukeley was surprisingly mild: 'Sir Lewis, these actions will not turn out to your credit.'[9]

At dawn, on 10 August 1618, Raleigh entered the Tower for his third and last imprisonment. He and Samuel King had been kept separate, but now King in great distress was allowed to say goodbye. Raleigh comforted him and told him he need not fear; 'It is I only that am the mark shot at.' As King was later to say: 'I was forced to take my leave of him. I left him to His tuition, with whom, I doubt not, his soul resteth.'[10] He was taken to another, less exalted, prison.

Nothing of this sordid last episode appeared in the *Declaration*.

The Lieutenant of the Tower was Sir Allen Apsley, who was genuinely friendly towards Raleigh. He had been in Ireland, had fought at Cadiz, and was a supporter of the Virginia colony; his late wife had been a niece of Lord Carew, almost an adopted daughter. The new Lady Apsley admired Raleigh and was also an enthusiast about the new chemistry. These two were the parents of Mrs Lucy Hutchinson, whose Civil War memoirs of her husband were to be famous.

So at first Raleigh lodged with them. An official called Robert Meering said that on that first morning Raleigh paced up and down the dining chamber, cursing his trust in Manourie. The Somersets were still occupying the Bloody Tower, and the two other most commodious apartments were occupied by Northumberland and the Countess of Shrewsbury, Arbell's aunt, who was soon to buy herself out with the huge sum of £20,000.

Cobham, in the Beauchamp Tower, was very ill after his stroke and in due course Raleigh was given one of his rooms.

James, and Raleigh's enemies, were of course delighted that the old dodger had at last been caught and shamed. According to Aubrey, James was apt to say that Raleigh 'was a coward to be taken and conveyed, for else he might easily have made his escape from so slight a guard.' This would have been impossible, but could mean that James would actually have preferred him to escape. Chamberlain could not resist the puns: 'It was a foul *pas de clerc* [blunder] for an old cozener to be so cozened and overtaken.'[11]

Needless to say nobody was more excited than Gondomar when the news reached him. He was still in Paris on his way home. Full of joy, he at once wrote to Philip III:[12]

From England they write all marvellous things, how the King is at once putting in hand what he promised me about matters of religion and about Walter Ralé, who has been declared a traitor and a pirate and as such has been sent to the Tower, waiting for our master, Your Majesty, to order what should be done.

Gondomar had already suggested that it would advisable to have Raleigh executed in his native country; to send him to Madrid would greatly increase the already substantial antipathy towards Spain among the English. And in fact on 11 August his recommendation had already been accepted by the Spanish Council of State, which of course he did not yet know. But it was to be some weeks before the royal assent reached London.

On his arrival at the Tower Raleigh's valuables were removed from his cloak-bag and handed over to Stukeley. They included £50 in gold; a Guiana idol of gold and copper; a jacinth seal set in gold, with a Neptune cut in it and a piece of Guiana ore tied to it; a lodestone in a scarlet purse; a silver (sapphire?) seal with his own arms; a 'Symson' stone, set in gold; a wedge of 22-carat gold, and a 'stobb' (stub?) of coarser gold; a chain of gold with diamond sparks; a diamond ring of nine sparks; a naval officer's gold whistle set with small diamonds; sixty-three gold buttons; an ounce of ambergris; a diamond ring given him (which he later denied) by the late Queen; a sprig jewel, set with soft stones and a 'made' ruby in the midst (perhaps the jewel that had been offered to Stukeley at Staines); a gold-cased miniature set with diamonds; charts of Guiana and Nova Regnia, and of the river Orinoco and Panama; a sample of Guiana ore, with a description of it; four silver mine samples.

All of which shows that Raleigh had not lost his love of jewellery; but some of the things could also have been available for selling. The charts and

Guiana ore were evidently to be shown to French investors. He was allowed to keep the ambergris and the seal, but insisted on leaving the miniature, presumably of Bess, with Sir Allen Apsley, refusing to give it to Stukeley, who was even insisting that he still 'loved him as well as any friend he had in the world'.[13] Raleigh was later to wonder how many of these objects stayed in 'Sir Judas's' clutches.

He at once wrote a fawning letter to Buckingham, asking for pardon 'in presuming to address so great and worthy a person'.[14] It was of course to ask him to intercede with the King, and to explain that he had attempted to escape to France only to give time for the full truth about his innocence to be understood. He afterwards told Sir Thomas Wilson, who was to be appointed his guardian, that he had hoped that Queen Anne and other friends would intercede for his pardon. The poor woman, however, was very ill; she had dropsy, with grossly swollen legs, and was soon to sink into senility. Buckingham was backing the Spanish marriage, but she most certainly was not, and told Lady Carew that she would rather have a match with 'Madam Christienne,' presumably Henrietta Maria, still a child, daughter of 'His Most Christian Majesty' (Henri IV), than 'the Spanish lady with all her gold'.[15]

Not knowing the dreadful state Anne was in, Raleigh – as he had done some years before* – wrote her a *Petition* in verse:

> Oh had truth power the guiltless could not fall
>   Malice win glory, or revenge triumph;
> But truth alone cannot encounter all!

> Mercy is fled to God, which mercy made;
>   Compassion dead: Faith turned to Policy
> Friends know not those who sit in Sorrow's shade . . .

> Cold walls to you I speak, but you are senseless;
>   Celestial powers you hear, but have determined
> And shall determine to my greatest happiness.

> Then unto whom shall I unfold my wrong . . .

The King had long since ceased to take any notice of her appeals, as she knew. So Anne did her best by writing to Buckingham:[16]

My kind dogge, if I have any power or creditt with yow, I pray you let me have a trial of it at this time in dealing sincerely and ernestly with the king that Sir Vater

---

* p. 432.

Raleigh's life may not be called in question. If you do it so that the success answer my expectation, assure yourself that I will take it extraordinarily kindly at your hands and rest one that wisheth you well, and desires you to continue still, as you have been, a true servant to your master.

There was never any hope that he would take the least bother. Nevertheless rumours were rife; that Raleigh was to be executed at once, that he was to be sent to Spain, even that he was to be pardoned if he would divulge some information about the suspected misappropriation of royal property during the administration of Cecil and Suffolk. Recently James Montagu, Bishop of Winchester had died. As translator of the King's Latin works it was thought that he might have had some influence. James had visited him on his deathbed while staying at Wilton, but had been unmoved when the old man begged that Raleigh should not come to an 'untimely end'.

James was now searching for an acceptable pretext for eliminating Raleigh. There were three possibilities: treason, in complicity with the French; he had never meant to look for a mine, and had intended to use his ships for piracy; he had acted as trespasser, ignoring the authority he had been given by attacking a friendly people. James now appointed (shades of 1603) a Committee of six, and these were George Abbot the Archbishop of Canterbury, Francis Bacon now Lord Verulam and the Lord Chancellor, the Earl of Worcester who was Lord Privy Seal and a great friend of Gondomar, Sir Robert Naunton the Chief Secretary, Sir Julius Caesar Master of the Rolls, and Raleigh's old opponent Sir Edward Coke who was no longer Lord Chief Justice but still a leading jurist, and as formidable as ever.

They interviewed Raleigh on 17 August, and then on at least two other occasions. Other witnesses were called, but not George Raleigh, Charles Parker or Sir John Holenden, who had been on the expedition and had been regarded as especially close to Raleigh – the Revd Samuel Jones had already said enough in Raleigh's favour.* Sir Julius Caesar took notes but not many details have survived. Did Raleigh dare to remind Coke of his famous words in 1603: 'Thou art a monster; thou hast an English face but a Spanish heart'?

They tried hard to compromise him. A possible plot with the French seemed the most fruitful line of attack. The allegations about the non-existence of the mine had to be discarded; disgruntled colleagues may have said that it was myth, but Raleigh made it fairly clear that it was never a myth in his mind. There had been a rumour that he had never brought any

* p. 484.

mining equipment, but this was countered by his proving that he had paid £2,000 for the appropriate material, and by his having brought qualified refiners (one of whom had died on the voyage). It was hard to make him personally responsible for the burning of San Thomé, when he had not even been there; and if he was not responsible, then ought not those who took part in the attack also to be prosecuted? Raleigh continued to persist that Guiana was English, just as he denied that he had ever used 'contemptuous speeches' against the King. Whatever had been claimed by the Spaniards about his behaviour in the Canaries, nothing could be proved against him at Lanzarote and Gomera (what had happened to that letter from its Governor to Gondomar?), and it had been confirmed that the killing of the Spaniards at Gran Canaria had been in self-defence. He may have talked recklessly about taking the Spanish Plate Fleet, but he had wanted to prevent his captains going off on marauding expeditions. And he certainly did have crews who were well experienced in piracy and rough justice.

All these arguments he had put many times in writing. The Commissioners were not interested in his dreams of an English empire to rival Spain's. They looked upon his expedition in terms of self-enrichment – as indeed, it had to be said, had the King by giving him the authority to leave.

The matter of a conspiracy with France could have had sinister implications, or so they hoped. The French ambassador Des Marêts had visited the *Destiny* in 1617, and various witnesses had spoken about Faige, a French commission, and the possibility of French ships joining them in the West Indies. A main task for Sir Thomas Wilson when appointed as Raleigh's guardian would be to wheedle out confidences about all this, holding out hopes of a pardon in return for a confession.

Wilson was thought to be well experienced in subterfuge. He had been used as a spy by Cecil, and had been awarded a pension by the government for his work in the Bye and Main Plots. His official position at present was quite unconnected: Keeper of the State Papers. Hardly an inspiring character, dull and rather pious, he was no match for Raleigh, in whose company he was expected to be virtually all day long. They ate together, and he was even sometimes present at Raleigh's devotions. Raleigh knew exactly what he was up to. It was hardly surprising that Wilson had to put on an act of being just a plain humble simple-minded creature, overawed by the fame of this once mighty individual.

Bess was kept a prisoner in her own house. She too had a guardian: a wealthy London business man called Wollaston (unconnected one assumes with Raleigh's errant captain), who was made to live in her house. After about two weeks he was relieved by another City magnate, Richard Champion. She was not allowed any visitors, and all her furniture was removed, which does seem unnecessarily vicious – she even had to appeal to the Privy Council for the return of some household chattels and linen. Eventually she too was sent to the Tower under the care of Wilson, but not allowed to see her husband. She and Raleigh were encouraged to write to one another, and all their letters were opened and read in the hope of picking up something incriminating.

Bess also sent letters to the King, but he could not be bothered to read them. As Naunton wrote to Wilson, who tended to write overlong epistles: 'I forbear to send your long letter to the King, who would not read over the Lady's, being glutted and cloyed with business.'[17]

The Council called in La Chesnée the interpreter, but in spite of battering away at him they could get no information of any importance, so they sent him off to prison. Then the acting French ambassador Le Clerc was summoned. When he refused to answer any questions, claiming diplomatic immunity, he was suspended from his duties, ostensibly for having 'held secret intelligence and conference, to the notable disservice of His Majesty and the Estate, with one of His Majesty's subjects attainted of High Treason and since detected of other heinous crimes.' Lady Carew was sent to see Le Clerc, but met with no success. When she asked him what Raleigh would have done if he had managed to get to France, he merely replied: '*Il mangera, il boyera, il fera bien*', he would have eaten, he would have drunk, he would have been all right (had a good time). This became a great joke in London and James did not like it.

Raleigh could hardly be prosecuted for approaches which he had turned down. The French government was both annoyed and amused by these reports. There had of course to be reprisals, and the English ambassador Sir William Beecher was suspended from diplomatic functions. He wrote that he did not know whether he was a prisoner or a free man.

Wilson was grumbling about his quarters in the Tower, and he did not get on with Sir Allen Apsley. He wanted to have Raleigh moved to the Brick Tower, which officially was Lord Carew's lodgings as Master of the Ordnance but occupied on rare occasions by Northumberland's son. Raleigh was very 'discontented' about this and said he would not move except by force. Wilson made the point that there were two windows in Raleigh's room which meant that he could easily throw messages from them. He himself was in a 'poor walled prison chamber' immediately above Raleigh and had to share it with his men.

Raleigh was not at all well. A man came to dress his sores; he was 'sick

533

of the rupture' and his left side was swollen. He had not had the 'benefit of nature' for twenty-two days, except by medicine. An apothecary and a surgeon were allowed to attend to him, but otherwise he was not allowed any visitors.

A scrap of a letter from Raleigh to Bess survives, copied for Sir Thomas Wilson:[18]

I am sick and weak. This honest gent, Master Ed Wilson [his personal servant], is my keeper and takes much pain with me. My swollen side keeps me in perpetual pain and unrest. God comfort us. Yours W. R.

Written on the same letter is a note by Sir Thomas Wilson:

Memorandum that I asked Master Secretary's Counsel if I might send Edward with the box of spirits and cordials. He told me that there was no danger to send to her but to observe what came from her. Yet I kept the box till I talked with the apothecary.

Evidently Raleigh's chemical apparatus had been put in store when he left the Tower, and he now had access to some of it, possibly thanks to Lady Apsley.

Bess's reply was also copied for Wilson:

I am sorry to hear amongst other discomforts that your health is so ill. 'Tis merely sorrow and grief that with wind hath gathered into your side. I hope your health and comforts will mend and mend us for God. I am glad to hear you have the company and comfort of so good a keeper. I was somewhat dismayed, at the first, that you had no servant of your own left you, but I hear this knight's [Apsley's] servants are very necessary. God requite his courtesies and God, in mercy, look on us. Yours E. Ralegh.

It took some while before Wilson was able to report anything remotely useful to the Council. He had to listen to long complaints from Raleigh, about how Northampton (Henry Howard) and Suffolk (Lord Thomas Howard) tried to get rid of him. This 'arch hypocrite,' he said, was 'forever pulsing, pining, groaning, but when talking of his late voyage and former actions he will talk immediately with as great heartiness and signs of cheerfulness as the strongest and soundest man.'

Wilson kept telling Raleigh of the King's 'merciful disposition' and how if only he would open his heart and reveal all he would 'taste of the

King's graciousness'. But Raleigh was not to be fooled, and would turn the conversation back to Northampton and Suffolk. When Wilson tried to compare James to King David who showed mercy to those who had offended him, Raleigh was ready with answer: 'David left commission for his son to put them to death'.

Lady Wilson was now allowed to try her luck, with even less success. It was a game on both sides. Wilson continued to plead ignorance 'as the surest armour', he told Naunton, 'of proof for those that are to converse with cunning.' At last came a snippet: Raleigh denied that he had offered Stukeley £10,000 to help him to escape. He admitted that he had asked Manourie to sprinkle 'Aqua Fortis' on him, in order to gain time – but the Council knew all that.

Wilson kept numerous notes. Sometimes he made heavy handed jokes which he thought would appeal to James.

Since my last letter of yesterday morning I have been wholly busied in removing this man to a safer and higher lodging, which though it seems nearer heaven, yet is there no means of escape from thence for him to any place but Hell ... The things he seems to make most recking of are his chemical stuffs, amongst which there are so many spirits of things, that I think there is none wanting that ever I heard of, unless it be the spirit of God.

Wilson wanted to remove all drugs, but Raleigh said that if he wanted to kill himself he had only to bang his head against a post. Raleigh must have deliberately set out to alarm Wilson by telling of the bravery of Romans ending their lives. He told him that he would rather die in the light than in darkness.

There were times, Wilson said, when he felt that the only way to get information out of this 'arch impostor was by the rack or halter'. He suggested that Raleigh should write a letter to the King, opening the 'secret closets of his heart'. Raleigh did write, but the letter has not survived and probably was not considered of much interest.

He denied any plotting with Des Marêts, agreed that he had come to the *Destiny*, but so had the Venetian and Savoyard ambassadors. The Spanish ambassador had rowed round the ship but had not come aboard.

He did, however, say that Winwood and he had met Des Marêts, but this was because Sir John Ferne was one of Raleigh's captains. Sir John had been regarded as a nuisance by the French, but witnesses called by the Commission claimed that he had boasted about having an assignment from France, which would have permitted privateering 'beyond the Canaries'.

Raleigh also suggested that if the Spanish match went ahead, then surely there would be no need for him to be put to death. Wilson found this remark 'repugnant', as no doubt would have James if ever it had been relayed back to him. Raleigh also reminded Wilson of the last words of Judge Gawdy about his trial in 1603.*

Early in October Bess was back at Broad Street, and on the 4th Raleigh wrote to her about some business concerning the *Destiny*, in which William Herbert had a quarter share: 'As I remember the ship and her furniture, to wit her cables, anchors, sails, ordnance, bullets, powder, joiner's work, carving, painting and all else, doth amount unto £7,000 or near it, as you may perceive by the inventory'. He signed himself 'Your desolate husband W. R'. But he added a postscript:

There is in the bottom of the cedar chest some paper books of mine. I pray make them up altogether and send them me. The title of one of them is 'The Art of War by Sea'. The rest are notes belonging unto it. There is amongst the little glasses the powder of steel and pumex for to stay the flux. If you can find it now [send it], for I have a grievous looseness and fear it will turn into a bloody flux [dysentery]. Send me some betony [supposed to ease hernia].

This could have been his last letter to Bess – at any rate it is the last to have survived. A note added by Wilson indicates that all his papers and the chest had already been confiscated.

On that same day, 4 October, Wilson asked to be relieved of his duties, which were 'no longer useful or profitable'.

I perceive now that this man with whom I have to do, finding his subtlety encountered by my simplicity, thought me a fit subject to be wrought upon, and therefore assailed me with fair promises and some small presents, both from himself and his wife to me and mine, to try if I would be brought to nibble at a bait, but finding me one of those *qui timent daneos et dona ferentes* [who fear harm from bearers of gifts] he sets upon me with the other ordinary hook that catcheth fools, flattery and fair words ... that he would make me his ghostly father and tell me whatsoever any matter that I should require ...

All he could get were 'old matters' and 'delusory answers'. Raleigh had certainly set the hook and caught a fool, and all credit to him. On 15 October Wilson was allowed to return to his own house.[19]

* p. 388.

Perhaps Raleigh knew that his 'guardian' had applied for his relief, for on 4 October he wrote a letter to the King with the kind of information that Wilson would have liked to have extracted from him. He told James that he had now decided to give him the 'truth' about the French commission and promises of aid from France. But there was very little that was really new. He did, he said, have a commission from the Duc de Montmorency, and it had been relayed to him by Faige, who had told him that Des Marêts had letters confirming it. This commission was never taken up.

He also admitted that it was true that he had seen La Chesnée three times, once at Brentford and twice at his house in Broad Street, and that he had been told that the French agent Le Clerc would 'assist and favour my escape to France' and that 'certain gentlemen in France might receive me well and recommend me to the Most Christian King [Louis XIII].' Le Clerc himself had come to confirm this on the third occasion. But Raleigh had decided to save himself by his own means.

The cringing end to the letter would have given his sovereign some wry pleasure. As usual a copy was sent to the Spanish embassy.*

I pray you humbly, therefore, to pardon and have compassion on me, and if it may please your Majesty to grant my life even in imprisonment, I will reveal things which will be very useful to the State, and from which there will result great wealth and advantages, while my death could occasion nothing but gratification to those who seek it with so much vindictiveness and anxiety, contrary to the natural disposition of Your Majesty, who has always been inclined to goodness and clemency . . . I am, Sir, your Majesty's most humble and most unhappy subject, W Ralegh.

There were even new rumours that Raleigh might be spared execution. On 12 October Sir Edward Harwood wrote to Carleton that 'the King is much inclined to hang Raleigh; but it cannot handsomely be done; and he is likely to live out his days.'

Three days later, on 15 October, Sánchez de Ulloa, the Chargé D'affaires, went to the King at Royston to tell him that the King of Spain had decided that James should have responsibility for putting Raleigh to death.[20] James assured him that this would be done immediately and gave him two of the pieces of the Guiana gold that had been found in Raleigh's possession.

* The translation is now at Simancas, and the original has been lost.

Even Such is Time
1618

Raleigh must die. The King had decided on it, once and for all. Now there could be no excuses or quibbling. The problem was how to provide a veneer of legality, so the Commissioners were asked to work out some suitable procedure. As John Chamberlain wrote to Carleton: 'It is generally thought that Sir Walter Raleigh shall pay this new reckoning upon the old score – his treason conviction of fifteen years earlier'.

On 18 October Bacon delivered the Commissioners' report to the King. It was pointed out that as Raleigh was already attainted of high treason he could not be called in question for any crimes since committed. It would therefore be legal, as Chamberlain and many others expected, for a warrant to be issued to the Lieutenant of the Tower for his execution upon the conviction of 1603. A printed narrative would also have to be issued, as his 'late crimes and offences were not publicly known'.

The Commissioners made it clear however that they did not favour such a course. Their second suggestion was that Raleigh should be brought before the 'whole body of State', with the principal judges present, and witnessed by a selection of nobles and 'gentlemen of quality'. It would have to be explained that this procedure was necessary because Raleigh was already civilly dead. Afterwards he would be charged by Counsel with his 'acts of hostility, depredation and abuse as well of your Majesty's Commission as of your subjects under his charge, importunes, attempt to escape, and other his misdemeanours.' The King was advised to drop 'that which concerns the French, wherein he was rather passive than active.'[1]

This last was not what James had expected. On 12 October Padre Fuentes had reported that the King had told him that he was daily being told 'most extraordinary things' about Raleigh's collusion with the French.[2] Sánchez de Ulloa was also complaining that the delay in executing Raleigh was 'longer than needful'. So James replied to the Commissioners that he did not like either of their suggestions and had chosen a middle course. He agreed that there had to be some sort of trial – he had always insisted on this to Gondomar

– but to allow a repeat performance of the trial of 1603 would be disastrous: 'It would make him too popular, as was found by the experiment of the arraignment at Winchester, where by his wit he turned the hatred of men into compassion. To allow an audience of the nobility would be too great an honour for such a man – this procedure was only used in the case of persons of great quality, as had been the case of the Countess of Shrewsbury.'[3] The hearing should not be in the presence of the Council either, but of the Commission only, and behind closed doors. There were too many people on the Council who were well disposed to Raleigh. After this Raleigh would be told he must die, and a warrant for his execution would be 'sent to us to sign'.

Qué fárrago! It never crossed James's mind that the outside world would realize that Raleigh had been condemned in secret, and that feelings against the Spanish marriage would only be exasperated. And in fact the eventual *Declaration* that he was forced to have drawn up after Raleigh's execution did greatly increase the general disgust.

On 22 October Raleigh was brought before the Commissioners. The only record of the hearing, which lasted from 3 p.m. to 7 p.m., is based on some rough notes made by Sir Julius Caesar, Master of the Rolls, and briefly from a letter to Philip III by Sánchez de Ulloa. No doubt James had insisted on secrecy. The prosecution was led by the Attorney-General, Sir Henry Yelverton, who from his name was probably a Devonian and at heart well disposed towards the prisoner.

Raleigh was charged under three headings: 'Faults before his going this last voyage; Faults committed in his voyage; Faults committed since'. But first of all Yelverton was obliged to excuse the King for authorizing the voyage, which had been shown up to have been based on imposture; the King, he said, had given his permission because he believed it to be for the 'country's good'. The Solicitor-General, Sir Thomas Coventry, also added an account of those 'vile' words that had been spoken about the King to Stukeley and Manourie. Never, he said, had any subject been so 'obliged' to his sovereign as had Raleigh.

Raleigh was careful to agree that he had received extraordinary marks of royal leniency, but claimed that his release from the Tower had meant that 'His Majesty doth in his conscience clear him of all guiltiness.' He knew that the King had been heard to say, when speaking of the proceedings in 1603, that he would not wish to be tried by a Middlesex jury. Once again he repeated a Judge Gawdy's deathbed remark.* Also as previously he denied that he had ever spoken offensively against the King to Stukeley and

* p. 388.

Manourie. His only critical response then had been: 'My confidence in the King is deceived.'

Nearly everything he appears to have said was to be found in the *Apologie*: he denied that he had piratical intentions, he insisted that San Thomé was not within Spanish territory. He admitted that he had pretended to be mad, and 'to that purpose looked vomative', citing again the example of King David letting spittle run on his beard – 'I find not that recorded as a fault in David, and I hope God will never lay it to my charge as a sin.'

Then, in contrast to 1603, the prosecution produced two witnesses: Captains Pennington and Warham St Leger. It must have been especially painful for St Leger to have to confront his old friend and relative. Both testified that Raleigh had told them he was intending to lie in wait for the Spanish plate fleet. Raleigh countered this by saying that the remark had only been made after the failure to find the mine, and it had been merely to keep the 'turbulent and mutinous' fleet together. If he had earlier said anything to the same effect, it had merely been 'discourse at large'.

We can assume that the Commissioners paid little attention to any of Raleigh's arguments. According to Sánchez de Ulloa, Bacon as Lord Chancellor closed the hearing with a severe rebuke to Raleigh for the injuries that he had committed against the subjects of the King of Spain, and for abusing the confidence of his own sovereign.[*][4]

Bacon then told him that he would die, at which, said Sánchez de Ulloa, 'Raleigh lost consciousness for a time, and on coming to himself, I am told he spoke most wildly.'[6] He was taken back to the Tower and put in a different room. 'They changed his clothes and his servant, and appointed guards, who were relieved every hour, never leaving him alone day or night in order that everything he said might be known. This care was also necessary so that he might not put an end to his life by poison, the knife or otherwise.'

On the following day the law officers met to decide on the next formalities. On the 24th Raleigh was called before the King's Bench (or the 'Hinsbens', as quaintly transmuted by one of Gondomar's correspondents), and was told that he was to be executed on the old sentence of 1603. It was at least confirmed that he would be beheaded, and not hanged, drawn and quartered, which had been his original sentence.

So he was to die on the presumption that fifteen years before he had been

---

* Carew Raleigh was to say, much later, that on the occasion when Raleigh had walked with Bacon in the gardens of Gray's Inn, Bacon had actually assured him that 'You have sufficient pardon for all that is past already, the King having under his Great Seal made you Admiral, and given you power of martial law.' But if Bacon had really said such a thing, Raleigh surely would have tried to raise it at the hearing.[5]

ready to accept a pension of £1,500 a year for acting as a spy on behalf of the enemy, namely Spain; and now for having attacked a friendly nation, namely Spain. In reality he was being sacrificed for the hope of a dowry of £500,000, 'besides the jewels'.

The Queen, very ill and at Hampton Court, was said to have sent one more plea to save his life. This may have been in response to his letter to her – not in fact a direct appeal for help, but more in gratitude for past favours:[7] 'In the little time which I am to live [I must] acknowledge and admire your goodness and in all my thoughts, and even with my last breath, confess that you have beheld my affliction with compassion . . .'

Raleigh's son Carew, now aged thirteen, also wrote to the King, begging for the life 'of my poor father, sometime honoured with many great places of command by the most worthy Queen Elizabeth, the possessor whereof she left him at her death, as a token of her good will to his loyalty' – an argument hardly likely to appeal to James. Lord Carew wrote to the King, and a newly arrived Dominican priest is also supposed to have advised against Raleigh's execution, for fear of a popular reaction against Spain.[8]

There was to be yet another formality. Raleigh was woken early on 28 October and taken again to the King's Bench in Westminster Hall. He had contracted a fever, and had not bothered to comb his now overlong white hair. Once he had been so meticulous about his looks, and even Sir Thomas Wilson, surprised by his appearance, had suggested that he should call in a hairdresser – to which Raleigh's typically macabre reply had been that he would want to know who was to have his locks, and that if it was to be the hangman he was certainly not going to bother.

On the way to Westminster Hall he passed his old servant Peter, who had been on the Guiana voyage, and was now distressed by the sight of his old master looking so unkempt and ill and by his tousled head. 'Let them kem [comb] it that are to have it', Raleigh told him smiling, then added: 'Peter, dost thou know of any plaster to set a man's head on again when it is off?'[9]

He was accompanied by Sir Allen Apsley, as Lieutenant of the Tower. The Justices in their red robes were waiting. After the writ of habeas corpus had been read, the Attorney-General drew attention to how Raleigh had been sentenced to death fifteen years before for high treason, and His Majesty 'by his abundant grace' had been 'pleased to show mercy upon him till now':

Sir Walter Raleigh hath been a statesman, and a man who in regard to his parts and quality is to be pitied. He hath been a star at which the world has gazed; but stars may fall, nay they must fall when they trouble the sphere wherein they abide. It is, therefore, His Majesty's pleasure to call for execution of the former judgement, and I now require order for the same.[10]

The Clerk of the Crown read the record of the conviction and judgement, and asked Raleigh to raise his hand, which he did. Raleigh was asked if he had anything to say as to why execution should not be awarded against him. He was known for his low voice, but now he apologized for it on account of his fever. The Lord Chief Justice, Sir Henry Montague, replied that it was audible enough. Raleigh then reiterated his argument that the fact that in 1617 the King had given him power of life and death over others surely meant that he had been discharged of the judgement of 1603. It was to be his last attempt to plead his cause:

For by that commission I departed the land and undertook a journey, to honour my sovereign and enrich his kingdom with gold, if the ore whereof this hand hath found and taken in Guiana; but the voyage, notwithstanding my endeavour, had no other success but what was fatal to me, the loss of my son and wasting of my whole estate.

The Lord Chief Justice interrupted him, saying that none of this was to the point. The fact that he went to Guiana did not mean an implicit pardon. He must say something else to the purpose, 'otherwise he must proceed to the execution'.

Raleigh had to accept defeat. All he could do was to put himself at the mercy of the King. 'As concerning that judgement which is so long past . . . I think His Majesty, as well as others who are here present, have been of the opinion that in my former trial I received but hard measure.'

This was getting uneasily close to the truth. The Lord Chief Justice had to be firm: 'Sir Walter Raleigh, you must remember yourself; you had an honourable trial, and so were justly convicted; and it were wisdom in you now to submit yourself.' He then told him that all that happened in Guiana had a bearing on his sentence of execution. This was absurd, and he knew it – it had already been agreed on 18 October that as Raleigh was civilly dead he could not be convicted for further offences, though of course Raleigh was not aware of that decision. What Montague had now to say, however, was a good deal kindlier than those fearful words of old Sir 'Pompous' Popham in 1603:[11]

I pray you attend what I shall say unto you. I am here called to grant execution upon the judgement given you fifteen years since; all which time you have been as a dead man in the law, and might at any minute have been cut off, but the King in mercy spared you. You might think it heavy if this were done in cold blood, to call you to execution; but it is not so; for new offences have stirred up His Majesty's justice, to remember to revive what the law hath formerly cast upon you. I know you have been valiant and wise, and I doubt not but you retain both these virtues, for now you shall have occasion to use them. Your Faith hath heretofore been questioned, but I am resolved you are a good Christian, for your book which is an admirable work, doth testify as much. I would give you counsel, but I know you can apply unto yourself far better than I am able to give you . . . Fear not death too much, nor fear death too little; not too much, lest you fail in your hopes; not too little, lest you die presumptuously. And here I must conclude with my prayers to God for it, and that he would have mercy on your soul.

He ended with these words, 'Execution is granted.'

Montague's praise for the *History of the World* was significant. James had disliked the book for being 'too saucy in censuring princes', but he now had to beware of meddling with the judiciary. As G. M. Trevelyan was to say, the revolt of the judges against both James I and Charles I was only one example of how 'the ghost of Raleigh pursued the house of Stuart to the scaffold'.[12]

Raleigh asked for a few days' respite so that he could finish some work he had to do; he maintained that he had something of importance to impart to the King. He also asked for permission to speak from the scaffold.

But James had no intention of delaying the execution or of giving any time for yet more tiresome pleas for a pardon. Raleigh must be beheaded the next morning, and as early as possible. The 29th of October, the feast of Saints Simon and Jude, was to be the day of the Lord Mayor's Show, and he mistakenly hoped that the crowds would be assembling in the City for the processions and entertainments. He directed that the scaffold should be erected 'at or within our palace at Westminster'. He was also to regret not preventing Raleigh from making his speech. The execution was to produce a welter of satires and vicious poems against James. When the Spanish marriage negotiations finally collapsed, bonfires were lit in celebration all over the country, and there was dancing around them.

The warrant drawn up by Bacon, *De Warranto Speciali pro Decollatione Walteri Raleigh, Militis, A. D. 1618*, was signed immediately. James then left for some hunting at Theobalds and thereabouts. He was also working on his *Meditations on the Lord's Prayer*, which he intended to dedicate to Buckingham.

Raleigh was to spend the last night of his life in the Gatehouse prison, part of the old monastery of St Peter and dating from Edward III, near the west end of Westminster Abbey and close to the present Tothill Street. As he crossed the palace yard, where his scaffold was about to be erected, he spied an old friend from Cheshire, Sir Hugh Beeston.[13] He called out to him, asking if he would be present at the great show the next day. Sir Hugh said he hoped so, if he could find a place in the crowd. Raleigh gave a sardonic smile; 'I do not know', he said, 'what you may do for a place. You must make what shift you can. But for my part, I am sure of one.'*

'Stone walls do not a prison make; nor iron bars a cage', wrote Richard Lovelace, who in 1642 was also to be incarcerated in the Gatehouse. Raleigh was extraordinarily lively and cheerful, almost in a state of euphoria. Friends and relations were allowed to make their last farewells. He was reported as saying to one of them: 'The world itself is but a larger prison, out of which some are daily selected for execution.' One of the Thynnes, perhaps Francis and presumably a stepson of Raleigh's brother, was alarmed by the way he actually seemed to rejoice in his approaching death. 'Do not carry it with too much bravery,' he said. 'Your enemies will take exception if you do.'[14] He was thinking of that notorious pride or 'swank'. Raleigh replied: 'It is my last mirth in the world. Do not grudge it to me. When it comes to the sad parting, you will see me grave enough.'

Among those who apparently visited him was the son of William Sanderson, his great-nephew – to make amends, a fine gesture. Hariot must surely have come, also Raleigh's brother Carew, perhaps Adrian Gilbert, and Raleigh Gilbert. There were also business matters to be settled. In a testamentary note he referred to his meeting with Lord Boyle the last time he was in Ireland; he now retracted the support he had given against Henry Pyne and wished to remain neutral. He had never let land at Sherborne to a Captain Caulfield as claimed by John Meere. Stukeley must be made to give an account of the tobacco from the *Destiny* that he sold at Plymouth, and must return the £10 that he had been lent 'the Sunday we took boat'. Raleigh also asked his wife, 'if she should enjoy her goods', to take care of his servant Christopher Hamon's wife and especially the widow of John Talbot, his faithful secretary who had died on the Guiana voyage – 'I fear me, her son being dead, she will otherwise perish.'

In case, after all, he was not allowed to speak from the scaffold, in a second note he wrote down some further important points. These exonerated Carew and Lord Doncaster from urging him to escape, refuted the French commission and the £10,000 promised to Stukeley, insisted that it was his

* Beeston did manage to obtain a permit guaranteeing him a good place. It was handed to the Sheriff, who had left his spectacles at home and so ignored it.

'true intent' to find gold in Guiana and that a mine certainly did exist near San Thomé, denied that he had ever thought of capturing Trinidad or abandoning his fleet as Ferne had said, denied that he 'did carry with me 100 pieces' (presumably the money said to have been hidden in the cabin), denied that he had ever spoken disloyally or dishonourably about the King to Manourie. 'These things are true, as there is a God, and as I am now to appear before His tribunal seat, where I renounce all mercy and salvation if this be not a truth. At my death, W. Ralegh.'

That evening he was also supposed to have written a sprightly little couplet, 'On the snuff of a Candle', which certainly reflected his state of mind:

> Cowards fear to die, but Courage stout,
> Rather than live in Snuff, will be put out.

He was sent a priest to attend him in his last hours. This was Dr Robert Tounson, Dean of Westminster, a royal chaplain and a future Bishop of Salisbury. Like many others Tounson was bemused by Raleigh's jauntiness, and by the fact that the consolation he was proposing to give seemed entirely superfluous. About ten days later he wrote a vivid account of the evening to his friend Sir John Isham:[15]

He was the most fearless of death that ever was known; and the most resolute and confident, yet with reverence and conscience. When I began to encourage him against the fear of death, he seemed to make so light of it that I wondered at him ... He gave God thanks, he never feared death; and the manner of death, though to others it might seem grievous, yet he had rather die so than of a burning fever. I wished him not to flatter himself, for this extra-ordinary boldness I was afraid came from some false ground. If it were out of a humour of vain glory, or carelessness of death, or senselessness of his own state, he were much to be lamented. He answered that he was persuaded that no man that knew God and feared Him could die with cheerfulness and courage, except he were assured of the love and favour of God unto him; that other men might make shows outwardly, but they felt no joy within; with much more to that effect, very Christianly so that he satisfied me then, as I think he did all his spectators at this death.

Bess was the last to arrive. She had been again to the Commission, and the only concessions had been that she could 'sup' with Raleigh that night and have the possession of his corpse. She was brought to the prison in the coach belonging to Lord and Lady Carew, in whose house she was staying. As they made their last farewells she told him in a 'burst of anguish' that she had leave to bury him, thus avoiding the terrible tradition of exposing a traitor's body. Raleigh attempted a joke: 'It is well, dear Bess, that thou mayst dispose of it dead that hadst not always the disposing of it when it was alive.'[16]

The clock struck midnight, and soon after she left him.

It must have been then that he remembered the poem that he had written before they were married, and when she was his Serena.* The last verse beginning 'O cruel time, which takes in trust' had been meant as an exhortation to enjoy love before it was too late. Now he made a slight change, adding two more lines, turning it into an epitaph and a declaration of faith. The result is the most remembered and moving of all his poems.

> Even such is time, that takes in trust
> Our youth, our joys, our all we have,
> And pays us but with earth and dust;
> Who, in the dark and silent grave,
> When we have wandered all our ways,
> Shuts up the story of our days;
> But from this earth, this grave, this dust,
> My God shall raise me up, I trust.

The poem was said to have been found on a sheet of paper inside his Bible, which was given to Tounson the next morning.

Afterwards he slept for two or three hours.

During the night Bess wrote to her brother, Sir Nicholas Carew at Beddington in Surrey:†

I desire, good brother, that you will be pleased to let me bury the worthy body of my noble husband, Sir Walter Ralegh, in your church at Beddington, where I desire to be buried. The Lords have given me his dead body, though they denied me his life. This night he shall be brought you with two or three of my men. Let me hear presently. God hold me in my wits. E. R.[17]

Around 5 a.m. Tounson returned, and was obviously disturbed that his culprit should still view his fate with such composure. 'After he received Communion', he wrote, 'he was very cheerful and merry, and hoped to

* p. 174.
† Nicholas Throckmorton had changed his name to Carew after inheriting the Beddington estate from his uncle Sir Francis Carew in 1611.

546

persuade the world that he died an innocent man.' The good Dean then said that it was not right to speak against the justice of the realm. Raleigh agreed that justice had been done, and that therefore he must die, but insisted that he must still be allowed to protest his innocence.

Tounson reminded him that there might be earlier sins to which he ought to confess. For instance, there was the case of Lord Essex, 'how it was generally reported that he [Raleigh] was a great instrument of his death, which if his heart charge him with, he should repent and ask God forgiveness.' No doubt Tounson thought this was a shrewd and worthwhile move, and it must have put Raleigh in mind of saying something about Essex in his speech on the scaffold. All we get from Tounson's letter is that Raleigh replied that 'My Lord of Essex was fetched off by a trick, which he privately told me of.' Unfortunately nothing is explained about this trick. Could it possibly be to do with that romantic story about Elizabeth's ring which was never returned?

According to Tounson Raleigh ate a hearty breakfast and enjoyed a pipe of tobacco (which seems to have upset some people when they heard of it). 'He made no more of his death, than if it had been to take a journey.' He dressed carefully, putting on a black velvet gown over a 'hair-coloured' doublet, a black embroidered waistcoat, black taffeta breeches, a ruff band and ash-coloured silk stockings. We must assume that he also had his hair properly combed. Because of his recent fever he kept his lace nightcap under his hat. Before leaving the Gatehouse someone offered him a cup of particularly fine sack wine, which he drank. Asked how he liked it, he replied: 'I will answer you as did the fellow who drank of St Giles's bowl as he went to Tyburn, "It is a good drink, if a man might tarry by it".'[18]

By about 8 a.m. he said he was ready. According to Gondomar's correspondent he was escorted by sixty armed guards, which could have been an exaggeration.* A very large crowd had gathered, and another source says that he even had to push his way through, and that this made him breathless and a little faint. On the way he noticed an old man with a bald head and asked him why he had come out on such a raw morning. The old man said that he had come 'but to see you, and to pray God to have mercy on your soul'. Raleigh thanked him and threw him his nightcap 'which you need more of it now than I' (shades of Sir Philip Sidney).

A fire had been lit, and after he had mounted the scaffold he was asked if

---

* An engraving of the execution scene does admittedly show the scaffold platform entirely surrounded by pikemen, possibly more than sixty, but this was made many years later by an artist who thought it had happened on Tower Hill.

he would like to come down and warm himself. He declined, because he said his fever had temporarily left him and he was afraid that with the heat it might return; he did not want people to think he was trembling with fear. He looked around and saluted those he knew. Lords Arundel and Doncaster were on a balcony of Sir Randolph Carew's house, along with William Compton, the recently created Earl of Northampton (the title having become vacant after Henry Howard's death), and the the Earl of Oxford, son of Raleigh's old enemy. Some, like Lords Sheffield and Percy, Northumberland's brother, were still on horseback. Other grandees recorded were Sir Edward Sackville, Colonel Cecil and Sir Henry Rich. There were a few 'ladies of rank'.

Hariot was somewhere there, and took notes on Raleigh's speech. Also present were two West Countrymen: John Pym, the great future Parliamentarian, and Sir John Eliot whose life was to be totally changed after witnessing Raleigh's execution – having been a monarchist he turned into an opponent of the Stuarts.

Eliot wrote this account of Raleigh on the scaffold:[19]

All preparations that are terrible were presented to his eye. Guards and officers were about him, the scaffold and the executioner, the axe and the more cruel expectation of his enemies. And what did all this work on the resolution of our Raleigh? Made it an impression of weak fear to distract his reason?

Nothing so little did that great soul suffer. His mind became the clearer, as if already it had been freed from the cloud and oppression of the body. Such was his unmoved courage and placid temper that, while it changed the affection the enemies who had come to witness it, and turned their joy to sorrow, it filled all men else with emotion and admiration, leaving them only with this doubt – whether death was more acceptable to him or he more welcome unto death.*

Silence was called for, and Raleigh made ready to speak. No exact transcript survives, and he spoke – amazingly – for up to three quarters of an hour. There are many contemporary accounts (one by Archbishop Sancroft), all of which cover the same subjects, though not necessarily in the same order. All also catch what appears to have been the authentic voice, and include the subtle points so brilliantly and devastatingly woven into the speech.[21]

Taking off his hat, Raleigh asked for the indulgence of his audience. He

---

* John Trevelyan of Nettlecombe in Somerset was accustomed to receive regular 'Newes from London' from a relative, John Gyll or Giles. Early in November he was told: 'Sir W. Rawleigh was executed in the old Pallace at Westminster Thursday last, whose manner of dying won him more love than I can express.'[20]

had been ill with fever, which might return, and any weakness in his voice or appearance would be due to that. He then paused and sat down for a few moments. Standing again, he said he was worried that some of his friends might not hear what he had to say. 'I will strain myself,' he said, 'for I would willingly have your Honours hear me.' Lord Arundel called out: 'We will come upon the scaffold'. At which the four lords from the balcony jostled their way through the crowd and ascended the steps. One by one they shook hands with this man so soon to die.

Raleigh began once more: 'I thank God of his infinite goodness that he hath vouchsafed me to die in the sight of so noble an assembly, and not in darkness, neither in the Tower, where I have suffered so much adversity, and a long sickness.' He ignored the supposed reason for his execution being the conviction of 1603, but concentrated on demolishing 'two main points of suspicion, that his Majesty cannot be satisfied, which I desire to clear and resolve you of.' The first was his 'practices' with the French, before he sailed and after his return.

But this I say, for a man to call God to witness to a falsehood at any time is a grievous sin, and what shall he hope for at the Tribunal Day of Judgement? But to call God to witness to a falsehood at the time of death is far more grievous and impious, and there is no hope for such a one. And what should I expect that am now going to render an account of my faith? I do therefore call Him to witness, as I hope to see Him in in His Kingdom, which I hope shall be within this quarter of an hour. I never had any commission from the French King; neither knew I that there was an Agent, or what he was, till I met him in my gallery at my lodging unlooked for. If I speak not true, O Lord, let me never come into Thy Kingdom.

The second suspicion was that he had spoken disloyally of the King.

But my accuser was a base Frenchman, a runagate fellow, and who had no dwelling, a kind of chemical impostor, whom I afterwards knew to be perfidious. This fellow, because he had a merry wit and some small skill in chemical medicines, I entertained rather for his taste than his judgement. For being drawn by him into an attempt of escaping, in which I confess my hand was touched, he being sworn to secrecy overnight revealed it the next morning.

But in this I speak now, what have I to do with kings? It is not for me to fear or flatter kings. I have nothing to do with them. I have now to do with God, I am the subject of Death, and the great God of Heaven is my sovereign before whose tribunal seat I am shortly to appear. Therefore to tell a lie now to gain the favour of the King were vain. Therefore, as I hope to be saved at the last day, I never spake dishonourably, disloyally, or dishonestly of the King; neither to this Frenchman, nor to any other; neither had I, ever in my life, a thought ill of his Majesty. Therefore I can not but think it strange that this Frenchman being so base, so mean a fellow, should be so far credited. So much for this point. I have dealt truly, and I hope I shall be believed.

It is hardly conceivable that he had never 'a thought ill' of James. What would the great God of Heaven make of that at the tribunal seat?

He went on to admit that he did try to escape, but this was to save his life, and that he did pretend to be sick at Salisbury, and here again he invoked the precedent of David. He admitted that 'I did it to prolong the time until his Majesty came, hoping for some commiseration from him', but did not say that he also wanted to write his *Apologie*.

He said he forgave Manourie (not mentioned by name) as he forgave Sir Lewis Stukeley (specifically mentioned), his kinsman. For all that, he immediately launched into refuting the various lies made against him by Stukeley, including the suggestions that he, Raleigh, had warned Arundel and Doncaster that he was preparing to escape, and that he had been given a 'dram of poison' at Sir Edward Parham's house at Sherborne, presumably to help him to commit suicide if he had so wished.

And so, having demolished Stukeley as the arch-betrayer, he proceeded to invite God's mercy on him, 'as I hope to be forgiven.'

Now he glanced down at his 'notes of remembrance'. 'Well, faith be,' he said, 'This far have I gone, now a little more, and I will have done by and by.' He touched on slanders about the Guiana voyage, how it had been claimed that he had only gone there because he wanted to get his liberty, that there had never been a mine, and that he had never intended to come home after the failure to find the mine. He spoke of how he had been 'crossed and undone' by Keymis, who realizing the consequences of his mistake had killed himself, and then of the treachery of the mutineers – no forgiveness demanded for people such as these.

He turned to Arundel, standing by him on the scaffold: 'Being in the gallery in my ship at my departure, your Honour took me by the hand, and said you would request me one thing, that was, that whether I made a good voyage or bad, yet I should return again into England.' 'So you did,' said Arundel in a loud voice. 'It is true. They were the last words I spoke to you'.

'Another slander was raised,' Raleigh said, 'that I would have gone away from them and left them at Guiana, but there were a great many worthy men that accompanied me always, as my Sergeant Major George Raleigh and divers others [he named them] that knew my interest was nothing so.'

He then glanced towards the Chief Sheriff: 'I will speak but a word or two more, because I will not trouble Mr Sheriff too long.' He needed to deal with yet another slander, and that was his behaviour towards the Earl of Essex. He had never sat in a window in full view of Essex watching him being executed and puffing out tobacco smoke in disdain.

God I take to witness, my eyes shed tears for him when he died, and as I hope to look in the face of God hereafter, my Lord of Essex did not see my face when he suffered. I was afar off in the Armoury, where I saw him, but he saw not me.

I confess I was of a contrary faction, but I knew my Lord of Essex was a noble gentleman, and that it would be worse for me when he was gone; for those that set me against him, afterwards set themselves against me, and were my greatest enemies, and my soul hath many times grieved that I was not nearer to him when he died, because I understood that he asked for me at his death, to be reconciled unto me.

He had now reached his peroration.

And now I entreat you all to join with me in prayer, that the great God in Heaven, whom I have grievously offended, being a great sinner of a long time and in many kinds, my whole course a course of vanity, a seafaring man, a soldier and a courtier – the temptations of the least of these were able to overthrow a good mind and a good man; that God, I say, will forgive me, and that he will receive me into an everlasting life. So I take my leave of you all, making my peace with God.

He was dying a believer. He was no atheist. As one observer wrote:[22]

In all the time he was on the scaffold, nor before, there appeared not the least alteration in him, either in his voice or countenance; but he seemed as free from all manner of apprehension, as if he had come hither rather to be a spectator than a sufferer; nay the beholders seemed much more sensible than he.

He knelt down to pray, then stood up and gave away his hat and whatever money he had on him. He shook hands with the nobles, knights and gentlemen on the scaffold, including Tounson and the two Sheriffs. He took special leave of Arundel, thanking him for his company, and asked him to desire the King not to publish any scandalous writing that would defame him after his death (a fond hope). He embraced him and said: 'I have a long journey to go and therefore I will take my leave.'

After the scaffold had been cleared he took off his gown and doublet, and asked the headman to show him the axe. The man hesitated, but Raleigh insisted: 'I pray thee, let me see it.' He then ran his thumb along the blade, saying: 'This is a sharp medicine but it is a physician for all diseases.'

It was a superb piece of theatre. Next he went to each corner of the scaffold, kneeling down and asking the people below to pray for him. He was asked if he would like to be blindfolded, but refused. The executioner threw down his own cloak for him to kneel on, and then knelt himself asking for forgiveness. Raleigh placed both hands on his shoulders and said: 'When I stretch forth my hands, despatch me.'

He put his head on the block, but somebody called out that he was facing the wrong direction – he should face 'the east of our Lord's arising.' Raleigh said: 'So the heart be right, it is no great matter which way the head lieth.' But to satisfy the onlookers he stood up and rearranged himself.

He told the axeman to give him a little time for prayer. He put up his hands; and then again. Still the axeman faltered. 'Strike man, strike!' he called. The head was severed with two strokes, and it was noticed that as it tumbled to the ground the lips were still moving. The body did not shrink. The head was lifted by the hair, and shown at each side of the scaffold, but the familiar words, 'Behold the head of a traitor', were not spoken. A great groan went though the crowd, and someone cried out: 'We have never had such a head cut off.' There was such an effusion of blood that people said there must still have been plenty of vigour in his body.

His head was put in a red leather bag, and his body wrapped in his cloak.[23] One of Gondomar's closest friends, Juan Bautista Van Male, wrote a detailed and faithful description of this whole episode.[24] 'I promise Your Excellency', he added, 'that he died with such high spirits as if he was going to a wedding. I do not think that there was ever such a spectacle in the time of the Romans.' And Sánchez de Ulloa told Philip III: 'Raleigh's spirit never faltered, nor did his countenance change. On the contrary he was extremely brave throughout.'

Van Male described how the body was conveyed to a black mourning coach, drawn by two white horses. He then added a curious note: 'I forget to say that he asked for some broth which was brought to him in a silver bowl, but then refused it.' He also said that Raleigh had made no mention of the atrocities that he had committed in Guiana. He thought King James would now make it clear that Raleigh had died 'to satisfy the King of Spain'. He also said that the delay in the execution had been an advantage because in the meantime the intrigues of the French had been exposed.

Bess had the head embalmed and kept it in a special case. The body was not buried at Beddington after all, but in front of the main altar at St Margaret's, Westminster: the nearest place possible to where Raleigh had been executed. This was apparently done within twenty-four hours and maybe in deliberate defiance of the King. It was marked only with his coat of arms, but afterwards there was a wooden tablet, later replaced by one in brass, with these words:

Within the Chancel of this Church was interred the body of the great Sir WALTER RALEIGH, on the day he was beheaded, in Old Palace Yard, Westminster, October 29, 1618. Reader, should you reflect on his errors, remember his many virtues; and that he was a Mortal.

Afterwards

'Every word he spoke, as far as we can judge, was literally true; it was not the whole truth, and it was calculated in many points to produce a false impression on his hearers.' So wrote Professor Gardiner in 1883.[1] He was mainly referring to the French commission, and he was well qualified to make that comment – for it was he who discovered the letter at Simancas that Raleigh had given to Faige for De Bisseaux, and which contained the decidedly compromising request to '*obtenir le brevet qui m'est promis*', 'to obtain the warrant that was promised me'.

And what about those tears supposed to have been shed at the decapitation of Essex? Some of Raleigh's audience may not have felt all that convinced, and would have been even less so if they had been able to read Raleigh's alarmist letter to Cecil in 1600, in which he warned him not 'to relent towards the tyrant before it was too late'.

For all that, Raleigh's courage and the manner in which again and again he called God to witness, confounding those old accusations of atheism, and his admission that he had been a sinner, won the hearts of the people. As one observer, John Pory, said, it had been 'impossible to show more decorum, courage and piety'.[2] Weeks later Chamberlain was reporting that the town was still talking of nothing else. The execution had come to be regarded as a national dishonour; however misjudged Raleigh's enterprises, whatever mistakes he had made, his vision had always been the greatness of England. The appearance of a comet blazing across the November skies seemed a portent, and dire predictions followed from the leading astrologer of the day William Lilley.

There was an explosion of lampoons, ballads and pamphlets against Spain, but for the present Sir Lewis Stukeley and Manourie were the main objects of hatred, insomuch that Stukeley felt obliged to write his own *Apology*. Meanwhile, in a vain attempt to justify himself, James produced the *Declaration* – almost entirely based on hearsay. He probably wrote the pedantic first paragraph himself. In any case such a document was decidedly unusual for a reigning monarch to have sanctioned. Once again it was asserted that the mine had been purely imaginary, a hoax. After a trail through the disasters at San Thomé, and an account of the journey from Plymouth to London, with much emphasis on the faked illness, the *Declaration* made it clear that these 'just and honourable' proceedings had been to satisfy James's 'dearest brother the King of Spain': hardly likely to inspire much sympathy among his good people.

The Sheriffs were also in trouble for allowing Raleigh to speak so long. A wealthy goldsmith called Wiemark was reported as saying that Sir Walter Raleigh's head 'would do very well on the shoulders of Sir Robert Naunton', for which he was hauled before the Council and only escaped censure when he said that he had meant that two heads were better than one. Naunton, however, was able to exact his revenge. When Wiemark subscribed £100 to a fund for the repair of St Paul's, he was told that two £100s were better than one; the hint was duly taken.[3]

Gondomar was in Madrid when the news reached him. He urged Sir Francis Cottington not to wait for the formalities but to take the good news at once to the Escorial. 'I told the King of Spain', Cottington afterwards wrote to Buckingham, 'of the justice which the King my master had commanded to be done, and expressed, in the best terms I could, the great demonstration his Majesty therein made.'[4] Philip obliged with a handwritten letter of thanks.

Diego de la Fuente also echoed Gondomar's delight in a sarcastic letter to Boisschot, the Spanish ambassador from Flanders in Paris: 'So farewell to Raleigh and his dreams ... of becoming the *Señor* of the Indies. They have cut off his head in the *plaza* of Westminster, in spite of the efforts of his patrons and guarantors. Let us hope that his punishment will deter others known to be intriguing with certain ministers in France.'[5]

The pro-Spanish party in London was appalled by the violence of public feeling. The hugely popular booklet *Vox Populi or Newes from Spain*, purporting to be written by Gondomar before the execution, was published in 1620. It was written by Thomas Scott, a preacher exiled in Utrecht, and ran into nine editions within the year, in spite of attempts by Naunton and Buckingham to suppress it. In the booklet Gondomar was made to boast how he had worked to bring about the 'ignominious death of the old pirate, who is one of the last now living to have been bred under that deceased English virago, and by her fleshed in our blood and ruin.'

Gondomar returned, reluctantly, to England in March 1620, on his second embassy, staying for two years. 'There goes the devil in his dungcart,'

THE SECOND PART OF VOX POPVLI,
or
Gondomar appearing in the likenes. of
Matchiauell in a Spanifh Parliament,
wherein are difcouered his treacherous & subtile Practifes
To the ruine as well of England,as the Netherlandes .
Faithfully Tranflated out of theSpanifh Coppie by a well-willer
to England and Holland

Simul Complectar omnia.

G nhs Hifpanæ decus

Printed at Goricom by Afhuerus Janfs
1624 / Stilo nouo

*One of many cartoons of Count Gondomar, this one showing the chair designed
for his well-known affliction. His litter in the background is carried by mules.*

bystanders shouted as he was carried in his litter down the Strand. Arrests
for insults such as these were made, but had little effect. A second part to
Vox Populi featured Gondomar as a 'Machiavell' addressing an imaginary
Spanish parliament and explaining how he had spied out all the suitable
spots for invasion along the English Coast, made lists of naval ships and
armaments, and set about destroying Raleigh. Given the outrage in England
over the invasion of the kingdom of Bohemia by the Catholic League it was

particularly provocative that the dedication should be to Frederick and Elizabeth of Bohemia, and to Maurice of Nassau.

Even more scathing was the caricature of Gondomar in Thomas Middleton's play *A Game of Chess*. Another booklet, *Sir Walter Raleigh's Ghost, or England's Forewarner*, again by Scott and a big seller, appeared in 1626. In it the ghost of Raleigh appears in silver armour, holding a golden cup full of blood which he sprinkles on Gondomar, who confesses and asks for absolution but is told that Raleigh will watch over him as he plots further evils.

Although some Spanish historians appear to be slightly shocked by this spate of venomous literature, others have regarded it as a compliment to Gondomar's strength of character and the brilliance of his diplomacy. His biographer Luís Tobío has seen the careers of Raleigh and Gondomar in some way tangential: Raleigh as a symbol of the birth of the British empire, Gondomar as a symbol of the Spanish empire's decline.*

Manourie was paid £20 for his services in escorting Raleigh to London, much to the general disgust. Sir Lewis Stukeley, aghast at the reaction against him, according to Chamberlain 'makes suit to the King that his reputation might be repaired, and offers to take the Sacrament solemnly, in St Paul's or any other public place, that all he related of him [Raleigh] is true.' He had written his own *Apology* in August which had been merely jeered at. Sir Thomas Badger had unkindly told him, said Chamberlain, that swearing the Sacrament would not 'serve his turn unless he should presently be hanged and so seal it with his death.' The King had been glad to shift the blame, and had sent him off, roughly saying: 'I have done amiss. Raleigh's blood be upon thy head.'[6]

As Vice-Admiral of Devon Stukeley made a duty call on Lord Admiral Nottingham, to be greeted with a tirade from the old man: 'What thou base fellow! *Thou*, who art reputed the scorn and contempt of men, how darest thou offer thyself into my presence? Were it not in my own house, I would cudgel thee with my staff, for presuming to be so saucy.'[7] (Nottingham himself had done pretty well out of Raleigh's fall in 1603.)

---

* Tobío makes the point that the Spanish domains in America were conquered and held by people from Central Spain, from Castile and Extremadura, and to some extent from Andalucía: people of pastoral stock with no maritime experience, whereas the English, especially those from the south-west, were accustomed to make their living from the sea. Gondomar as a *Gallego* from Galicia, which did have a seafaring tradition, felt himself entitled to hammer away at the *Junta* on the theme that Spain could only hold on to its empire through creating more efficient maritime communications.

Stukeley now enlisted the help of a Devonshire parson, a Dr Sharpe, to concoct a *Humble Petition*, with some new 'revelations', such as Raleigh having asked the Keeper of the Gatehouse if there were any Romish priests in the prison – the insinuation being that he would have liked to be reconciled to the Church of Rome. The tone of the *Petition* was certainly not humble, and there were some telling points. 'This man's life was a mere sophistication', it ran, 'and as such was his death.' Raleigh had borrowed a 'tincture of holiness' in order to make it seem that he was dying a saint. It had all been play-acting, and he had invited friends on to the scaffold in order to 'spread the contagion of his seditious humour'. If he had managed to escape to France he would have been as dangerous to the Crown as Antonio Peréz had been to the King of Spain.[8]

Stukeley went again to see the King, who is supposed to have said: 'On my soul, were I disposed to hang every one that speaks ill of thee, there would not be trees enough in all my kingdom to hang them on'. Nevertheless on 29 December he was paid the very large sum of £965 6s 3d for 'performance of his service and expenses in bringing up out of Devonshire the person of Sir Walter Raleigh'. Within days, however, there was a sensation. Manourie was arrested at Plymouth for clipping gold coins, and he accused Stukeley of having been his accomplice.

It turned out that both Stukeley and his son had been clipping coins for years.[9] There was jubilation at this news – divine providence! The rumour went around that Stukeley had even been tampering with the coins that Raleigh had given him – blood money! He was sent to the Gatehouse, then to Raleigh's old cell in the Tower, and in due course sentenced to death. James however 'flung him a pardon', it was believed in consideration of a very large sum or money, nearly £1,000. Stukeley returned to Devon, where his job as Vice-Admiral had been given to Sir John Eliot. Still ostracized, 'Sir Judas' took refuge on the island of Lundy in the Bristol Channel, and there he died 'a raving madman amidst the howling of the Atlantic storms', on 24 August 1620, less than two years after Raleigh's execution.[10]

Sir Thomas Wilson considered that he needed some recompense for his six weeks trying to coax indiscretions out of Raleigh, admittedly without any success. James decided that it was less expensive to have him installed as Master of Caius College, Cambridge, and was so enthused by the idea that he said he would 'take no denial'. Instead, for some reason, the official letter was never sent.

As Keeper of the Rolls, Wilson felt justified in confiscating all Raleigh's books, maps, papers, globes and mathematical instruments, and for this he

NEVVES

Of Sʳ. Walter Rauleigh.

WITH

The true Description of GVIANA:

As also a Relation of the excellent Gouernment,
and much hope of the prosperity of the Voyage.

Sent from a Gentleman of his Fleet,

to a most especial Friend of his in London.

From the Riuer of Caliana, on the Coast of Guiana, Nouemb. 17. 1617.

LONDON,

Printed for *H. G.* and are to be sold by *I. Wright,* at the signe of the
Bible without New-gate. 1618.

*The text of this leaflet was sent from Caliana in November 1617 (pp. 486–7)
but not published until after Raleigh's execution. The portrait is probably
more of a true likeness than that used as a frontispiece to the third edition of
the* History of the World *(p. 519).*

received a royal warrant. His theory was that they would be 'of small use
to Lady Raleigh'. But Lady Raleigh thought differently, and as always was
ready for a fight. These things were her legitimate property she insisted,
with considerable passion, and were intended for the education of her son
Carew. Although the books were as yet still in the Tower, the mathematical
instruments had already been removed by Wilson, and one of them had cost
her husband £100. She wrote to Lady Carew begging her to intervene. She
admitted that it was right for His Majesty to have any of the books that

were rare or 'not to be had elsewhere', but she had been told that one Byll, a book-binder or stationer, had copies. She had been afflicted with 'so many unspeakable troubles and losses' that she needed comfort and help, not this kind of petty 'molestation'.[11]

Wilson also wanted to get his hands on Raleigh's manuscript *Treatise on the Art of War* and his list and assessment of the world's sea ports. What became of all this is unknown – they have disappeared. The affair of the books and other papers dragged on for at least a year, and it seems that James did allow Bess to keep most of them, judging from the books and manuscripts that were later being sold, evidently by the family.[12]

The government also requisitioned the *Destiny* and her contents, but Bess fought to prove her investment and was awarded £2,250.[13] Out of this sum £700 was held back, to meet a claim by Herbert. Then in 1621 a Spaniard claimed £700 for damages done to his property at San Thomé – this almost certainly must have been Francisco de Avila from Seville, a main trader at San Thomé and a kinsman of its Governor, Diego Palomeque, and therefore of Gondomar.*[14]

In 1622 Bess was ordered to pay £750 for claims against Raleigh out of her £2,250. The Earl of Huntingdon demanded back the two pieces of brass ordnance which he said had only been on loan. On the other hand she still had not had back her dowry of £500 from Huntingdon, a debt which evidently had been transferred to Lord Boyle in Ireland.

However hard Bess campaigned for her rights, she was no pauper. It seems clear that she lived partly at West Horsley, presumably the present West Horsley Place in Surrey, and if so it would have been in relative grandeur, as it was, and is, a very large house; possibly it was leased from Viscount Montague, who was lord of the manor. She also appears to have been a shrewd businesswoman, for somehow by 1628 she had accumulated enough capital to *lend* the government £4,000 towards Buckingham's ridiculous expedition to La Rochelle, though a bargain was involved. In theory she was still receiving a pension of £400 a year as part compensation for the transfer of Sherborne to Robert Carr, but there were arrears of £1,000; the pension was now to be surrendered and the £1,000 paid to her, and in due course she would receive £2,400, with interest of 8 per cent until the money was paid.[15]

In 1623 her house in the City was burnt down, and afterwards, when in London, she lived in the parish of St Martin-in-the-Fields, her name appear-

---

* The Herrick family papers, sold at Sotheby's on 15 December 1988, included a receipt from Avila, who must therefore had some satisfaction. Interestingly, Avila's papers include accounts of low morale at San Thomé before the arrival of Raleigh's men.

ing in a list of important people headed by Buckingham who were refusing to contribute to the mending of highways.[16]

Carew Raleigh entered Wadham College, then a new West Country foundation at Oxford, in the spring of 1621 when he was sixteen.* In that same year the House of Lords passed a Bill restoring him in blood, which meant renouncing his father's attainder – but James would not allow it. Carew wrote sonnets and a poem that was set to music, and after two years was introduced at Court by his mother's relative Lord Pembroke, only to be banished because James found him too much 'like the ghost of his father'. Pembroke therefore advised him to travel abroad, which he did until James's death the following year.

Charles I, the new King, had been opposed to Sir Walter Raleigh, so did not take kindly to a renewed application by Carew to be restored in blood, especially as Carew was also campaigning for the return of Sherborne. At last in 1628 the King sent for him and explained that, when he was Prince of Wales, Lord Bristol (Digby) had given him £10,000 in order to keep him safe in the estate,† and he therefore would not agree to restoration in blood unless Carew renounced his claim to Sherborne. At first Carew was determined to fight on, but friends advised him to succumb, and so he did.[17]

Thus at last the stigma was removed from the family name, and from 1635–39 Carew was a Gentleman of the Privy Chamber. Also in compensation for Sherborne he was allowed the £400 a year that his mother had renounced – the original pension was to have been paid to her and then to Wat for their lifetimes, so now Carew was receiving what would have been his dead brother's inheritance.[18]

In 1628 he bought the manor of East Horsley, which had been a Throckmorton (or Carew) property. About the same time he married Philippa Weston, the wealthy widow of Sir Anthony Ashley, who had been with his father at Cadiz, and by her he had two sons, Walter and Philip, and three daughters. This enabled him to petition the government for £2,765 in arrears of pension due to his wife. In 1639 he spent a while in the Fleet prison after a squabble when the King was out hunting, and was discharged on a bond of £1,000.[19]

---

* In his biography of Walter Oakeshott (1995) John Dancy describes how Oakeshott discovered a 1617 edition of Spenser's *Collected Poems* that had been owned by Carew Raleigh, obviously a present from his mother. Written in ink against Raleigh's two commendatory poems for *The Faerie Queene* was written, 'Bothe thes of your father's making', and against a shepherd in *Colin Clout* 'WR: Sheppard of the Ocion'. Later she identified herself by her maiden name, 'E Throckemorton his mistris'.

† p. 467.

Carew seems even to have made some sort of bid for recovering his father's Irish estates, possibly claiming that the price paid by Boyle had been inadequate. There had also been a query, on behalf of the Church, on the soundness of Boyle's title to Lismore Castle. For his part Boyle pointed out that between 1602 and 1617 he had given Sir Walter considerable pecuniary support. This put an end to the matter, and probably also affected Bess's effort to reclaim her dowry.

In 1643 Sir Nicholas Carew died, and Carew Raleigh was left the manor of West Horsley, which Sir Nicholas had bought only the year before. Carew certainly lived in West Horsley Place and is said to have spent £2,000 on it, and to have put in the staircase. Probably it was he who was also responsible for facing the timber-framed exterior of the house with brick.

His behaviour during the Civil War was equivocal. He had been a personal servant of the King but with estates in Surrey could not offend Parliament. What was more, his father's reputation as a martyr, historian and political writer was rapidly increasing among Parliamentarians. But when Charles left Hampton Court for the last time, he gave Carew 'a kind of token'.

In the flood of literature about Raleigh in the Commonwealth period he was often represented as the diehard republican hero and an advocate for an aggressive foreign policy. There had been various editions of *Instructions to his Son*, as well as other essays that are regarded now as 'attributed', including *Maxims of State* which is equally untypical of Raleigh's style. Milton published *The Cabinet Council* in 1658, which he said he had found among some other papers, but it has been suggested that his reason for doing this was 'ironic', as a warning to Cromwell. In 1646 came an inflammatory work entitled *Vox Plebis or The People's Outcry against Oppression, Injustice and Tyranny*, a manifesto of the Levellers using various themes from the *History of the World* such as Magna Carta and false imprisonment. In 1650 a condensed version of the *History* was produced by Alexander Ross in the *Manner of History*, but not entirely to Raleigh's credit.*

An attack on Raleigh's credibility by William Sanderson's son appeared in 1656, in some ways comparable to Stukeley's *Humble Petition*: and this

* An earlier example of the prestige of the *History of the World* is in St Mary's Church, Totnes, Devon, where there is a notice recording that a Christopher Blackhall in 1620 presented a library to the church, specifically including Sir Walter Raleigh's *History of the World*. C. V. Wedgwood in her *Montrose* (1952) writes that Montrose bought a copy of the *History of the World* when still a schoolboy at Glasgow. It was one of his especial favourites, and he was unwilling to be separated from it on going to St Andrew's University before he was seventeen – so much so that he himself personally carried the 'precious, ponderous volume' all the way.

provoked Carew to respond in an article as 'Lover of Truth', in which Sanderson is called a 'contemptible beggar'. A reaction was beginning to set in. Carew was furious with James Howell for referring to the Guiana mine as a 'mere chimera', and forced him to apologize.

Bess died in 1647, aged eighty-two. Less than two years later Charles I was to die on the scaffold, outside his Banqueting House, a few hundred yards from where her husband's scaffold had been. It is not known where she was buried. Carew was MP for Haslemere from 1648–53. Cromwell put him in the Tower for a few days in 1650 for having spoken 'passionate words'. He was one of the Rump of the Long Parliament, and thanks to General Monk a member of the Council of State from January to April 1660. In February Monk rewarded him with the Governorship of Jersey, his father's last official posting: a handsome and welcome gesture.[20]

In the summer of 1658 John Evelyn dined twice with Carew at West Horsley, evidently to arrange a mortgage. At the Restoration Charles II offered Carew a knighthood, but he declined and asked that instead it should be given to his eldest son Walter. This second Sir Walter Raleigh died from plague very soon afterwards, as did his only son and a baby daughter: all three were buried in St Mary's Church, West Horsley. Five years later Carew sold West Horsley to Sir Edward Nicholas, Secretary of State, and East Horsley to Henry Hildyard. He died in 1666, the year of the Great Fire, at his London home in St Martin's Lane, where his mother must have lived.

Carew was buried with his father at St Margaret's, Westminster. In the parish register he is described as 'killed', but for whatever reason is a mystery.[21] Evidently he did not die at once, for there was an nuncuperative (oral) will in which he left all his estate to his wife Philippa, who was also his executrix. The tradition is that he was buried with his father's severed head, which had been passed to him on his mother's death.*

Aubrey said that Elias Ashmole, the antiquary and astrologer, had been told by Carew that he had his father's skull, adding: 'Some years since, upon digging up the grave, his skull and neck bone being viewed, they found the bone of his neck lapped over' – which confirmed that it was not that of someone who had been hanged. The parish register of West Horsley says that Carew was buried there in September 1680, so there must have been a reburial,

---

* Bishop Goodman of Gloucester, once Queen Anne's chaplain, is quoted by the Devon historian Brushfield in his *Raleghana* as having written: 'No man doth honour the memory of Sir Walter Raleigh and his excellent parts more than myself; and in token thereof I know where the skull is kept to this day and I have kissed it often.' What irony, if this is true, that the head of the supposed atheist should be regarded as some kind of relic.[22]

which seems to be confirmed by Aubrey's story. It has always been assumed at West Horsley that the skull is buried with Carew in the Chantry Chapel.*

Thomas Hariot died on 23 June 1621. For some time he had suffered from cancer in his nose, probably from smoking, and this had spread horribly to his mouth. Three days before his death he made a will, which contained this clause:

Whereas I have diverse waste papers (of which some are in a Canvas bagge) of my Accompts of Sir Walter Rawley for all which I have discharges or acquitances lying in some boxes or other – my desire is that they may bee all burnte. Also there is an other Canvas bagge of papers concerning Irish accompts . . . which I desire also may be burnte as likewise many Idle papers and Cancelled deedes which are good for no use.

His wishes were fulfilled, and farewell 'to a very dark corner of Raleigh's and Hariot's association'.[23]

Negotiations over the 'Spanish match' finally collapsed in 1623 in humiliating circumstances after the well-documented farce of the visit of Prince Charles and Buckingham to Madrid, through no fault of Gondomar, but because of a clash between Buckingham and Olivares, the Secretary of State.

When Gondomar had returned to Madrid after his first London embassy, he was asked to give his opinion on the political life in Spain. He had been horrified by the inefficiency, corruption and immorality in the government. He wrote a scathing letter to Philip III, and it was probably because of this that Olivares took such a dislike to him.†[24]

On his return from his second embassy in 1622, after the death of Philip III the year before, he continued with his outspoken complaints and the need for a radical reform of the Catholic Monarchy. He was appointed State

* Now, alas, almost entirely filled with a second-hand church organ put there in 1945 – though presided over by a magnificent monument to Sir Edward Nicholas, believed to be the work of Grinling Gibbons.

† The letter, written on 28 March 1619, was certainly extraordinary, unusually direct. After giving his ideas about what he considered to be good government, he said: 'I confess that in a few years that I have been away from Spain I can hardly recognise it, judging from what I have seen in other parts of the country and the plague of unjust demands [for money, titles etc.). Because of the confusion and the lack of will either to remedy or to cure it, this Monarchy is sliding into danger [se va acavando por la posta]; its two greatest enemies are all the princes in the world [a reference to the start of the Thirty Years War] and all the Ministers and servants of the Crown.'

Councillor in 1623, and later Governor and Captain-General of Galicia. On the accession of the Prince of Wales as Charles I in 1625 it was proposed by Olivares that he should return to England for a third time, but he resisted this very strongly. For one thing his health was not good, and he was looking forward to spending more time at his great library at Valladolid. Being an ambassador in England had brought him no financial benefit; he was not well off, and indeed on his second embassy Digby had to lend him money. He was aware that Olivares wanted to get rid of him. On top of all this he was profoundly disillusioned. He regarded Charles, who was now about to marry the French princess Henrietta Maria, as double-faced, and there were rumours that Buckingham was preparing ships for an attack on Spain.* There was no doubt that England was growing into a strong military power. And the intransigence of the Puritans was growing.

Philip IV was obviously bored with Gondomar. He regarded him as a relic of the past regime, almost as though he were senile, a perpetual grumbler and responsible for bringing the Prince of Wales to Madrid. For a while Gondomar and Olivares where not on speaking terms. Eventually Gondomar went to Paris, where he conducted dealings with Richelieu that were satisfactory to Olivares and the Council of State. He was also frequently summoned to Brussels for advice by the Infanta Isabel Clara Eugenia.

His health became worse and early in 1626 he was allowed to return to Spain. It seems that he knew he was dying. He was mostly in Galicia but paid frequent visits to Madrid where he found himself virtually ignored by the Court. On 2 October 1626 he died, aged fifty-nine. Tobío has said: 'He had prepared for his death like a Christian and a gentleman, renouncing the pomp and vanity of the world'. He is now regarded in Spain as an ambassador *uno de los más eximios del siglo XVII*, one of the most eminent of the 17th century, and a great patriot.[25]

So was Raleigh a liar? The answer has to be yes, sometimes. But then most of his enemies were liars and cheats. Early in his career he was universally regarded as a liar, ruthless and untrustworthy. This conceivably could at first have been due to some unrecorded incident, which set the scene. He also seems to have believed in some of his lies – or were they fantasies? Not surprisingly he was desperate to get out of the Tower, but he does seem to have been genuinely convinced that there was gold out there in Guiana – as has turned out to be true. He appears also to have sincerely believed that

---

* True enough, resulting in the expedition to Cadiz in October 1625, a humiliating flop for the English.

Putijma's 'mine' really did exist, but its exact location had never been established, or it had been forgotten by Keymis, who proved a muddler and realized he had been a muddler – thus destroying the man he admired most in the world.

Raleigh was indeed a patriot, just as Gondomar was a patriot. That he had in 1603 plotted on behalf of a Spanish invasion must surely be nonsensical. At times of great anger and stress he blabbed out things that should never have been said: about the Aremberg affair; and about catching the Mexican treasure fleet in 1618. It is clear that there was more to be said about his dealings with Cobham, and he may have behaved deviously towards him. The fact that Cobham condemned him from the scaffold could be significant; you were expected to tell the truth before meeting your Maker.

It is impossible to give an outright verdict on Raleigh. He cannot be either wholeheartedly condemned or admired, as nearly everyone who has written about him has agreed. Ben Jonson said that Raleigh esteemed more of fame than conscience. This was not quite true. Raleigh was ambitious, but not just for fame and riches. His career has been aptly compared to a tumbling stream that rushes over boulders. An early biographer, Hume, said that his moral nature was inferior to his gifts. He was at times extremely brave, but could beg for his life like a coward, and some such episodes are truly despicable. He probably did respond emotionally to Elizabeth's attractions to him, but she was also his path to power and wealth. The desperation behind *The Ocean to Cynthia* can be understood for this latter reason, though the poem is still a mystery.

It has often been pointed out that his life was a series of failures. He failed to keep the trust and love of the Queen, he failed to establish colonies in Virginia and Guiana, he failed to finish the *History of the World*. He went to the scaffold a ruined man. Yet the memory of Raleigh endured in men's imagination and in the minds of those who succeeded to his work in North America. He himself wrote: 'True it is that as many things succeeded both against reason and against our best endeavours, so it is most true that men are the causes of their own miseries, as I was of mine.'[26]

The Tower, Rowse had said, was the 'best place for him'. It is hard to imagine how he would have behaved if let loose in the Jacobean world. He was regarded by his contemporaries as greedy and rapacious, but he had been ready to sink his great wealth into huge projects – his dreams. He also wanted to live in style, live in a great house, wear extravagant clothes and jewels, to impress people and be admired. This was understandable in a man of such alarming ambition and who had started from humble beginnings.

His love for his wife, and – especially – her love and support for him, are very much to his credit. He could be susceptible to hoaxers and a bad judge of character, but his behaviour towards Sanderson is worrying and not fully explained. The loyalty he inspired from Hakluyt, Hariot, Keymis, Samuel King, Grenville, Richard Carew, and George Carew, and his friendship with Prince Henry, Queen Anne, Spenser, Northumberland, Arundel and many others are also to his credit and impressive. All these people knew his weaknesses but supported him. No man is an island. The flaws in his personality and the mistakes he made were not enough, on their own, to destroy him. He was also brought down by other people's malevolence – and yet at times he seemed to encourage such enmities.

He is not among the greatest poets, but he did write some superb lyrics and justly famous lines, and his poetry was central to his fame. The *History of the World* is not read today, except for its preface and some extracts, but its influence as literature and in politics is acknowledged. Passages from the *Revenge* and the *Discoverie*, and from his letters, will always be admired. That the Durham House group of intellectuals formed a 'School of Night' must be far-fetched. Raleigh was ahead of his time in his interest in comparative religions and scientific experiments. Again and again in the *History of the World* we are shown that he was certainly not an atheist.

There is much to be argued over. Did he epitomize the whole spirit of an epoch? Was he the true Renaissance man? His life was so full of paradoxes that we cannot end with a neat little summary. We cannot fail to be awed by the vastness of his aspirations. Fashions change, especially in relation to the building of empires, its rights and wrongs, but his name is as secure as Drake's among the heroes of English history and for what Spaniards still regard as the wrong reasons.*

---

* On a recent visit to Mexico City the author of this book was surprised to see RALEIGH blazed in huge red neon lights. He was told that this was an advertisement for a popular brand of cigarettes.

Appendix:
Family Background

Many attempts have been made to disentangle the Raleigh family tree, but it is generally agreed that they originated at Pilton near Barnstaple. One source mentions a William de Raleigh having been killed at the Battle of Hastings, and that his widow Beatrix gave lands in his memory to the abbey at Battle. If true, this must mean that he had fought on the side of the Normans. The story could derive from the fact that in Domesday Book the manor of Pilton was known as Radelie or Radeleia and held by the Bishop of Coutances; previously it had belonged to one Britic (female?) with thirty-seven acres.[1]

Raleighs were recorded as owning the manor in the 12th century, and between then and the 14th century seven Raleighs were sheriffs of Devon, by which time the family had split into at least five branches, a main one being at Nettlecombe in Somerset. Another branch migrated to Mitchell or Michell in Cornwall (where in 1239 Walter de Raleigh and his wife Isabel obtained a charter for a yearly fair on St Francis's day), which could conceivably be why three centuries later Sir Walter Raleigh opted to be Member of Parliament for Mitchell (a house there is still known as Raleigh's House). By the 14th century Raleighs also appear in various roles as far away as in Warwickshire and Northamptonshire.

At the Devon Record office there are several Raleigh documents from 1253 onwards. In 1384 the manor at Pilton passed to the Chichester family, because of a marriage to a Raleigh heiress. It seems clear that Sir Walter Raleigh's descent came from a Nettlecombe younger son. The Nettlecombe property, set in its beautiful Quantocks valley, was granted to Sir Hugh de Raleigh around 1160; he was Sheriff between 1160 and 1167. One of his sons supported the barons at Runnymede and got into trouble as a result.

St Mary's Church, Nettlecombe, dating from the 13th century, stands next to the great rambling house, part Tudor, part 18th century, built on the foundations of the original mansion. In the south aisle are two large recesses in which two knights' effigies lie beside their wives. The earlier, on the left, is presumed to be Sir Warin de Raleigh, who had been a crusader and died in 1280. From Jerusalem he had brought back a fragment of the True Cross given to him by Queen Berengaria, wife of King Richard I, and until recently this was kept in a silver vessel at Nettlecombe. Sir Walter Raleigh's ancestor, Wymond de Raleigh, was Warin's uncle. This Wymond did well for himself by marrying an heiress who brought him the manor of Smallridge on the Devon–Dorset border, and it would seem that it was he who acquired the manor of Colaton, later to be known as Colaton Raleigh, and Bolham in South Devon.

The other effigy is of Sir John de Raleigh, with a massive coned helmet resting on his shoulder. He fought at Crécy and died in 1372. There used to be a tradition that Sir Walter Raleigh's ancestor had been at Crécy, but this is a confusion with the giant-like Sir John. Another was that he was related to Chaucer, but this again is garbled – it was Sir John's wife who had that connection. Nettlecombe in the next century passed through a marriage to the Whalesboroughs of Cornwall, and then by another marriage to the Trevelyans, also Cornish.

One of the sons of Wymond, William, who died in 1250, was treasurer of Exeter Cathedral and a counsellor to Henry III. The King objected to his appointment as Bishop of Winchester because he had reserved it for the Queen's uncle, William of Valence. Undaunted, Bishop William spent huge amounts of Winchester's money in securing his confirmation from the Pope. Evidently he was a man much to be wary of, for when the monks of Winchester objected to Valence, because he had 'slain many men', the king retorted that the Bishop had slain many more with his tongue. So William excommunicated the King and went to France where he made friends with Louis IX. This naturally alarmed Henry, who had to relent, and William was allowed to return to Winchester.

Two generations on and we come to another John de Raleigh who in 1303 married Hanna Newton, whose dowry was Fardel Manor in the parish of Cornwood on the edge of Dartmoor, an important property on a Saxon site. So Fardel rather than Smallridge became the main seat of Sir Walter's ancestors, who rebuilt it. Much of the medieval mansion is still to be seen, including a vaulted ceiling in the library, mullioned windows and a porch. Next to the house is a large chapel, built in the 15th century. An 'ogham' stone, with a Celtic or Druidic inscription, used to be a feature here and was regarded as a clue to buried treasure – 'Between this stone and Fardel Hall lies as much money as the Devil can haul'. It has now been removed to the British Museum.

Five generations more and we reach Sir Walter Raleigh's great-grandfather, married to the daughter of a great Cornishman, Sir Richard Edgcumbe, who had fought for Henry VII at Bosworth and had been appointed Controller of the Royal Household – he was also the owner of the now famous house Cotehele, on the wooded slopes above the Tamar river. Their son Wymond (some say he was called Walter) married the daughter of another Cornishman, Thomas Grenville. There were also family connections with the Courtneys, Tremaynes and Champernownes.

It was this Wymond who squandered his advantages and was fined 700 marks in 1502 for his apparent involvement with the Cornish uprising.* Worse, he may even have been supposed to have had sympathy for the pretender Perkin Warbeck. As a result he had to sell his Smallridge estate.

Wymond's son, Sir Walter Raleigh's father, also called Walter, was born in 1505 and inherited Fardel and three other remaining manors (Colaton Raleigh, Withycombe Raleigh and Bolham) while still a minor at his father's death in 1512. He was made the ward of Nicholas Vaux until 1526, when the lands were released to Walter and Sir Piers Edgcumbe, evidently acting as his adviser. Sir Piers created the magnificent great hall at Cotehele that still bears the arms of Raleigh.

Fardel having been let, Sir Piers must have been glad to have had Walter married off that year to Joan Drake, as the daughter of a prosperous merchant and shipowner.

The two sons of Walter and Joan Drake were George and John. George inherited Fardel Manor on his father's death in 1581.† He died in 1597, leaving it to his brother John. Evidently there had been a trust whereby Colaton Raleigh had been left to his youngest half-brother, the future Sir Walter. There is a house there still known as having been his and where he is supposed to have grown potatoes.

Both George and John were involved in shady privateering affairs, as in 1557 when they captured a Portuguese ship off the Scillies and threatened to throw the crew overboard. They were arrested, and their father agreed to bail them, which they promptly jumped, moving from place to place, with his connivance.[2] Otherwise virtually all we know about George Raleigh is that he was agitating for compensation because of the confiscation of a ship in 1588 for arming against the Spaniards, and that in 1591 there had been trouble about the ownership of two mills. It is said that he only left

* p. 1.   † pp. 1, 13.

illegitimate children. According to Vivian's *Visitations* he married Margaret Drake 'alias Blake' of Withycombe Raleigh on 15 April 1597, which would have been on his deathbed – the assumption therefore is that she was the mother of his children. In the church at Withycombe Raleigh there are various Drake and Raleigh memorials, but no sign of George's stone. From the church register it is recorded that his burial was delayed three weeks: another mystery.

As for John, information is also scanty. He rented part of Woodbury Common and owned an ale-house at Woodbury itself. He may or may not be the John Raleigh who was buried in the church there in 1629; if he so he would have been aged about a hundred. He was certainly alive in 1613, because in that year he sold Fardel to Walter Hele of Cornwood, thus ending 310 years of family ownership.

LATER RALEIGHS

Carew Raleigh, Sir Walter Raleigh's son who died in 1666, had two sons. The elder died of plague, as did two children.* The second, Philip, had four sons and three daughters. Walter, the eldest, died young. Brudenell, the second, was killed while on an expedition to the West Indies, and Carew also died at sea; both unmarried. That left Grenville who joined the Green Howards, formed at the time of the Monmouth rebellion in 1685. He died in 1717, and is recorded as leaving two sons and a daughter, but here there is a hiatus in the records, though direct male descent is still claimed by some, one having been the eminent historian and literary figure Sir Walter (Alexander) Raleigh, who died in 1922.[3]

It is not clear whether two of the daughters of Carew married or had children. The other daughter, Anne, married Sir Peter Tyrrell, a baronet, of Henslape and Castlethorpe in Buckinghamshire. They had a son and six daughters, two of whom were certainly married. The son, Sir Thomas Tyrrell, had a son, who died in infancy, and two daughters, Christobella and Harriot.

Christobella is still a legend in north Buckinghamshire. It cannot be said that she had many of her illustrious ancestor's characteristics, but she was a remarkable personality, and since so few people seem to have known about her descent from Sir Walter Raleigh she surely deserves a niche in this book. Born in 1695, she married three times and, as she put it when she reached the age of eighty-seven, she married first for love, second for riches, and third for honour. Her first husband was John Knapp, and the second

* p. 563.

John Pigott of Doddershall and Grendon Underwood, by whom she had a son, Robert Pigott, who died aged thirteen 'at school' on 27 November 1747. John Pigott died in 1751. Two years later Christobella married Richard 6th Viscount Saye and Sele. He was aged thirty-six, and it had been hoped that he would marry someone who would produce an heir, but she was on the way to sixty. He died aged sixty-four, and she outlived him.

In *The Gentleman's Magazine* there is a reference to Christobella's death on 23 July 1789, aged ninety-four: 'She tasted the good things of this world and enjoyed them long . . . She dressed even at the close of her life more like a girl of 18 than a woman of 90. She was supposed to be the Viscountess in Hogarth's print of the *Five orders of Periwigs, Coronets, etc.* Her favourite amusement was dancing, and she indulged in it almost to the last week of her life.' It was said that she would send haunches of venison to the men she wanted to dance with, and that as she grew older the haunches grew larger. She always hid her age, and would go to any book or church register where it was mentioned and cut it out.

Christobella's monument at St Leonard's Church, Grendon Underwood, reads: 'In her youth the beauty and elegance of her person were the admiration of all who beheld her. For her cheerfulness and pleasant manner she was beloved by all her friends and neighbours. Her charitable institutions are the strongest and most conspicuous proofs of her munificence, and her justice was so correct, that when she paid the last debt of nature she had no other debts to pay.'

She left £50 to the poor of Grendon, £2,000 in trust for six poor boys of Grendon and six of Quainton, yearly apprentices, 'such boys being legitimate'. In addition she left £4,000, of which half was to be for the workhouses of Grendon and Quainton, for 'poor industrious widows and others, to be employed in spinning, knitting and other useful industry'; the other £2,000 was to be at interest, proceeds of which were for the above. It took a long time for the provisions of the will to be put into effect. Sixteen years later the money was still in the hands of executors. According to Lipscomb's *History and Antiquities of the County of Buckinghamshire*, in 1847 the £4,000 had still not been made available, 'from causes or circumstances not hitherto satisfactorily explained'. The Trust, however, does still exist, as does a smaller 'Christobella Trust' at North Newington in Oxfordshire.

Christobella's sister Harriot died possibly without children. It could be said therefore that the monument of Christobella's son Robert at Grendon Underwood represents the likeness of the last definitely known descendant of Sir Walter Raleigh: his great-great-great grandson.

The other Carew Raleigh, Sir Walter's brother, had three sons. Gilbert married into the Wroughton family, relations on his mother's side. Walter was Dean of Wells from 1641 to 1646: he was taken prisoner at the surrender of Bridgwater in the Civil War, confined to Ilchester jail and ultimately to the Deanery of Wells, where he was murdered by his gaoler. George was Deputy Governor of Jersey in 1623 and married into the Jermyn family of Suffolk, and was thus related to the future Earl of St Albans. Whether any of these have descendants still living is not known.

Sir Walter's sister Margaret Hall does appear to have living descendants in the male line. Some are now in America. For several generations the Halls had plantations in Jamaica.

Notes

Family and Childhood

1. *Fragmenta Regalia* (1641).
2. Champernowne papers, Exeter.
3. Henry Manisty, *Sunday Times*, 4 March 1973.
4. Champernowne papers, Exeter.
5. Hooker/Holinshed, III, 1016. Caraman, 93.
6. Eamon Duffy, *The Stripping of the Altars*, 1992.
7. SP Dom, 5 February 1553. Rowse, *Tudor Cornwall*, 267.
8. Williamson, 50.
9. H. G. J. Clements, Vicar of Sidmouth, *Trans. Devon Assoc.*, VI, 1873.

With the Huguenots

1. *History of the World*, V, 2, 3.
2. Champernowne papers, Exeter.
3. *ibid.*
4. *History of the World, ibid.*
5. *History of the World*, V, 2, 8.
6. Champernowne, *ibid.*
7. *History of the World*, IV, 2, 16.
8. *History of the World*, IV, 2, 11.
9. Preface to Laudonnière's history of French voyages to Florida.
10. *Discourse of War in General.*

Desirous of Honour

1. Register of Privy Council, Elizabeth, IV, 726. Edwards, I, 24.
2. Powle, Commonplace Book, Bod Tanner ms 168 f2.
3. Brushfield, *Raleghana*, Part V, 1903 from Middlesex County Records.
4. Oldys, 178. For descriptions and illustration see *Gentleman's Magazine*, 1791.
5. *Conversations* (Ben Jonson) *with Drummond of Hawthornden*, III, 416.
6. Aubrey.
7. David Lloyd, *State Worthies*, 1676.
8. Quinn, Hakluyt Soc., LXXXIII, Vol. 1, 1938.
9. Holinshed.
10. SP Ireland 1574–85, 289.

11. See Simmons, *Meta Incognita*, for full documentation.
12. Quinn, Hakluyt, *ibid*. SP Dom 12/18, 1.
13. Carew papers, Antony C2/EE/32. Halliday, *A Cornish Chronicle*. Especially Andrew Foot's article

prepared for Royal Institution of Cornwall, *Journal*, 2002.
14. DIHE, XCI 229–30.
15. SP 1568–70, 4956.
16. De Thou, *Thouani Historia*, III, 608.
17. Williams, 20. Edwards, I, 79.

Foothold at Court

1. Lefranc, 341.
2. Aubrey.
3. *Prose Works*, 38–9.
4. APC, XI, 421.
5. E. K. Chambers, *Sir Henry Lee*, Oxford, 1936.

6. Camden, 227.
7. Dec. 1596.
8. Stebbing, 32.

Ireland

1. Spenser, *A View of the Present State of Ireland*, 1596?.
2. Philip Woodruff, *The Men Who Ruled India*, I, 1953.
3. Oldys, I, 30.
4. Quinn, *Gilbert*, I. Thomas Churchyard, *Generall Rehearsal of Warres*.
5. SP Ireland 1509–73, 425.
6. *History of the World*, V, 3, 21.
7. *History of the World*, IV, 2, 18.
8. Elton, 303.
9. Holinshed/Hooker, supp. vol. II, 1596, and for most anecdotes in this chapter.

10. *ibid*.
11. *Present State . . ., op. cit.*
12. Holinshed, *ibid*.
13. BL Cotton Titus, 13, XIII, ff. 313–17. See also Mendoza to Philip II, 11 December 1580. SP Spanish III.
14. *Present State . . ., ibid*.
15. Rowse, *Throckmortons*, 135.
16. Holinshed, *op. cit.*
17. 25 Feb. 1581.
18. Holinshed, *op. cit.*
19. *ibid*.
20. *Present State . . ., op. cit.*

A Kind of Oracle

1. SP Ireland, 88, 12.
2. Naunton.
3. Camden, *Annales*.
4. Francis Peck, *Desiderata Curiosa*.
5. Edwards, I, 61.

6. Drexelius, in *Trismegistus Christianus* etc.
7. Personal to author.
8. Oldys, VI, 'On the Fortunate Memory'.

9. Bacon, *Apophthegms*, no. 31.
10. Jenkins, 218.

11. SP Ireland, 358, 13.

Grandeur at Durham House

1. Brushfield, *Raleghana*, 1909.
Edwards, II, 19.
2. Camden Soc., 1842, ed. J. O.
Halliwell.
3. John Strype, *Annals*, Vol. II, 1854,
part I, 533.
4. Timbs.
5. Thynne papers, Vol. V, Longleat.
Transcribed in Quinn, *Parmenius*.
6. Brushfield, *Raleghana*, 1903.
7. Birch, 6 May 1583.
8. BL, Add 4231, fol. 85. Edwards II.
9. 17 March 1583.

10. Jones, *Sir Walter's Surname*, 270.
11. Quinn, *Gilbert*, also 10 September
1580.
12. DIHE, XCI, 535, 9 January 1581;
SP Spanish, 1580–86, no. 61.
13. SP Dom 12/153/14.
14. Close Rolls Eliz. Part 6 C54/1126,
also Part 7 54/1154.
15. Edward Hayes, *Narrative*, covering
subsequent events, in Hakluyt, 1589,
679–97, IV (1600), all transcribed in
Quinn, *Gilbert*. See also Brushfield,
Raleghana, 1909.

The First Virginia Voyage

1. Hakluyt, III, 1600, 165.
2. SP Dom 15/28. Add 54, 55.
3. 26 March 1583.
4. 10 February 1585.
5. 20 Febuary 1585.
6. Chapel Hill Control Folder 4577.
7. Cotton Roll XIII 48.
8. Dava Sobel, *Longitude*, New York,
1995.
9. Patent Roll 26 Eliz. pt. 1 38–40.
PRO C66 11251.

10. Hakluyt, 1589, 728–33; 1600, III,
246–51.
11. 26 July 1584.
12. Klarwill, 323.
13. Kamen, 270. Winton, 51.
14. Klarwill, *op. cit.*
15. Winton, 52.
16. *History of the World*, I, 8.

The Roanoke Fort

1. BL, Add 15891, fol. 147.
2. SP Foreign France 78/14 120.
3. Holinshed, III, 1587.
4. *Colección Navarrete*, XXV, no. 53,
Museo Naval, Madrid.
5. SP Colonial 1/14 *et seq.*

6. Birch, II, 434.
7. Carnsew diary in Cornwall Record
Office.
8. SP Dom, XXIX, 126.
9. Fuller.

NOTES

El Draque

1. *Character of Queen Elizabeth*, 1693.
2. BL, Lansdowne, 41, fols. 9–10.
3. Accounts and documents in M. F.
Keeler, *Sir Francis Drake's West Indian Voyage*, Hakluyt Soc., 1981, 46–7.
4. Keeler, *ibid*.
5. Quinn, *Roanoke Voyages*, I, 250.

More Riches

1. McCarthy Morrogh, 52.
2. *History of the World*, IV, 23, 4.
3. SP Spanish 8.1.87; SP Venetian 13.2.87.
4. BL, Add 6697 fols. 227–35.
5. Hatfield, III, 96.
6. John Bruce, *Correspondence of . . . Leycester*, Camden Soc., XXVII, 1844, 239.
7. *ibid.*, 190–94.
8. Hakluyt, 1589, 737–47.

A Competition of Love

1. College of Arms Vincent Old Grants ms 157 397–80.
2. *Trevelyan Papers*, I, Star Chamber Proceedings, 128, III, 24.
3. BL, Add mss V, 756.
4. Bagot to Dyer, May 1587, Thompson, 58.
5. Hardwick Hall HMC Third Report, 42.
6. BL, Tanner, 76, fols. 846–85a. SP Dom, 4, 20.
7. John Shirley, *Life of the Valiant and Learned Sir Walter Raleigh*, 1677.
8. Lloyd, *State Worthies*.
9. BL, Add 44963, fol. 37V, Rudick, 38.
10. Hakluyt 1589/764–70.

Armada

1. SP Dom, CC, VII, 87.
2. *History of the World*, V, 16.
3. Letter to Burghley, 21 December 1587.
4. Plymouth Municipal Records, Widey Court Book, 126.
5. SP 12/209 43.
6. Lefranc, 207.
7. *Report of the Truth of the Fight about the Isles of the Azores*, 1591, reprinted Hakluyt 39.
8. *ibid.*

Two Shepherds Meet

1. APC, XVI, 293, 378–9.
2. Birch, I, 156.
3. Oakeshott, 91.
4. Nicholas Canny, *Raleigh's Ireland*, in H. G. Jones.

5. Howell.
6. Pope Hennessy, 1–3.
7. Latham and Youings, 378–80, Appendix I, spelling modernized.

The Lost Colonists

1. APC, XXIV, 6–7. Raleigh to Burghley, 15 January 1593.
2. Andrews, 1964, 104.
3. Quinn, *Set Fair for Roanoke*, Chapel Hill, 1985, 316–17.
4. Hakluyt, III, 1600, 288–95.

5. 16 October 1590.
6. See Quinn, *The Lost Colonists*, 1984, for main substance of this section. *Roanoke*, by Lee Miller, London, 2000, has ideas and insights.

Grenville of the *Revenge*

1. J. H. van Linschoten, *The Last Flight of the Revenge*, Arber's Reprints, 1871.
2. Edwards, I, 130.
3. Colección Sanz de Barntell, Madrid, quoted Rowse, *Grenville*, 300ff.
4. *op. cit.*
5. *op. cit.*
6. Cobbett, *Complete Collection of State Trials*, 1809, 1 col., 1308. Strype,

Life and Times of John Whitgift, Oxford, 1821, 43, II, 98–100.
7. Edwards, I, 152.
8. Cobbett, *op. cit.*; Philip Caraman, *Other Face*from ms Stonyhurst Anglia, VI, 117, 258–62.
9. Rowse, *Court and Country*, 1987, 181ff.

Scandal and the Tower

1. *Nugae Antiquae*, I, 105.
2. John Hutchins, *History and Antiquities of Dorset*, 3rd edn, 1861–71.
3. 30 December 1591.
4. 10 February 1592.
5. Algernon Cecil, *Life*, 9.
6. Described in Rowse, *Throckmortons*, 158 et seq.
7. *op. cit.*, 61.

8. Latham and Youings estimate 26 July 1592.
9. Late July 1592.
10. HMC Ashmole 1729 vol. 171.
11. Birch, I, 79.
12. Birch, I, 80.
13. End July 1592.
14. HMC Hatfield vol. 140.
15. HMC Finch 133–4.
16. Andrews, 115.

17. *c.* 13 September 1592.
18. SP Dom, CCXLIII.

19. End January 1593.

The School of Night

1. Oakeshott, 52.
2. Published 1592 in Antwerp.
3. Shirley, *Renaissance Scientist*, 24; Lefranc, 356–93.
4. D'Ewes, *Journals*, 1682, 478, 490, 493, 508–9, 317; Edwards, I, 271.
5. *Elizabeth*, 310, *et seq.*
6. Latham and Youings note 9, 10 May 1593.
7. 10 May 1593.
8. 15 June 1593.
9. 27 August 1593.
10. HMC Hatfield IV, 364.
11. 25 August 1599.

12. Hutchins, quoting 'Mr Coker', 275.
13. *Acta Cancellariae*, ed. Monroe, London, 1847.
14. *Nugae Antiquae, op. cit.*
15. BL Harleian 6 348 185–6 190.
16. P. Edwards, 64.
17. Nicholl, *Reckoning*, 293.
18. *Reckoning*, passim.
19. BL Harleian 6848 190.
20. Nicholl, *Reckoning*, 57.
21. *The Assassination of Christopher Marlowe.*
22. Yates, passim.
23. Yates, *Florio*, 65–75.

The Mind in Searching

1. Birch, I, 150.
2. Birch, I, 151.
3. Edwards, II, 397.
4. Hakluyt (I) II 08–10; Andrews, 287–91.
5. Harrison, *Willobie*, passim.
6. 14 April 1594.
7. *Records of the English Province of*

the Society of Jesus, 1878, III, 492, Henry Foley SJ.
8. Harrison for transcript.
9. Enys Papers, Cornwall Record Office.
10. Brushfield, Trans. Devon Assoc., 1896. Halliday, *A Cornish Chronicle*, 24 *et seq.*
11. 4 March 1594.

Arrival at Trinidad

1. Dedication in his edition of Peter Martyr's *De Orbe Novo*, Paris 1587.
2. To Cecil, 20 September 1594.
3. Hakluyt Soc., 1899, ed. G. F. Warner, Naipaul, *El Dorado*, 44.
4. Harlow, *Discoverie*, p. L. Hakluyt Soc., 1861, introduction by Sir Clements Markham.
5. Letters from Berrió to the King, 24

May 1585, 26 October 1591, 1 January 1593, all transcribed in BL Add 36315 16, 245, 186.
6. AGI Patronato 54 4–6.
7. Harlow, *Discoverie*, lxxxvi.
8. PRO SP 12/250 no 46.
9. Written second week December 1594.
10. John Shirley, 'Sir Walter Ralegh's

Guiana Finances', Huntingdon Library Quarterly, 13, 1949. PRO *c.* 24/372 Bundles 125–6, STAC 8/260 Bundle 4.
11. Nicholl, *Creature*, 73.
12. Edwards, II, 398.
13. Hakluyt Soc. 1940, ed. Sir William Foster; Naipaul, *El Dorado*, 380.

14. *The Discovery of Guiana*, ed. Schomburgk, 1848.
15. AGS Patronato estante 54. BL add mss 3616. ff151 *et seq.*
16. *ibid.*

Guiana

1. AGI Indif Gen 747.
2. *ibid.*
3. AGI Patronato 5442. BL add 36316. ff151 *et seq.*
4. Francisco Lopez Urquilla, Scrivener of the Government leg 1011, 6 July 1595. HMC Hatfield, xxxi.

5. AGI Indif Gen 140 7 37, 28 June 1595.
6. Andrews, *Privateering*, 170. Hakluyt, 1600 edn III, 582.

Drake's Last Voyage

1. HMC Hatfield 5 396.
2. HMC Sidney 2 163–4 166.
3. 25 November 1595.
4. J. O. Halliwell, Camden Soc., 1842, 54.
5. HMC Sidney 2 173.
6. Dated 13 November 1595, but probably 12 (Latham and Youings).

7. BL Add Mss 17/940A.
8. BL Add Mss 3 6316 f30. AGI 1 1 1/ 26 33.
9. BL Add Mss 5209.
10. *A Summarie and True Discourse*, by Walter Bigges, 1652.

No Forgiveness Yet

1. Raleigh returns to the subject in *History of the World*, IV, 2, 15.
2. Hakluyt, x, 452.
3. Hakluyt, xi, 8f.
4. Purchas, 2, 6, II.

5. Nicholl, *Creature*, 340.
6. Simón, XII, 605.
7. Harlow, *Discoverie*, xcii.
8. Edwards, II, 402.

Cadiz

1. HMC Sidney II 173.
2. Oppenheim, Monson, I, 69.

3. 4 May 1596.
4. Devereux, I, 493.

5. Devereux, I, 342.
6. Birch, II, 15ff.
7. Dr Roger Marbecke, HMC Stowe 159 353.
8. 21 June 1596 to Gorges. In Oldys VIII, *A Relation of Cadiz Action*, 667–74.
9. Edwards, I, 223.
10. *Relation, op. cit.*
11. 7 July 1596.

12. BL Harleian 6845 fol. 101.
13. Williams, 144.
14. BL Cott Mss Otho, E IX, f337.
15. Oppenheim, Monson, II, 13.
16. Birch, II, 58.
17. Lambeth Palace Library, Bacon Paper Ms. Tenison 136.
18. Birch, II, 115.
19. SP Venice 1 x 201.

An Uneasy Triumvirate

1. Katherine Duncan-Jones, *TLS*, 22 October 1999.
2. Collins II (Sidney Papers) 18.
3. Collins, *op. cit.*, 52.
4. *Fragmenta Regalia*.
5. Collins, *op. cit.*, 54.

6. G. B. Harrison, *Journal of De Maisse*, 1931.
7. SP Dom 473.
8. Will printed in Latham and Youings, 381–6.

The Islands Voyage

1. Letter to Cecil, 18 July 1597.
2. 20 July 1597.
3. Collins, II, 50.
4. SP Dom 469.
5. Oppenheim, Monson, II, 57.
6. *Relation of the Islands Voyage*, Purchas, iv, 1938.

7. V 1 9.
8. *ibid.*
9. Vaz Continho, *Hist do Successo*, Lisbon, 1630. Oppenheim, II, 71.
10. SP Dom cclxiv 153.
11. Oppenheim, II, 77.
12. Collins, II, 54.

Crisis in Ireland

1. Collins, II, 79.
2. *ibid.*
3. 25 August 1598.
4. Birch, II, 384.
5. Birch, II, *ibid.*
6. Birch, II, *ibid.*, 15 October 1598.

7. McLure Chamberlain, I, 49.
8. SP Ireland 1598–9 326.
9. Collins, II, 98.
10. 17 November 1598; Stebbing, 145.

Age Like Winter Weather

1. Devereux, II, 40–41.
2. HMC Hatfield 1 x 343.
3. 25 June 1599; Stebbing, 147.
4. Collins, II, 117.
5. *ibid.*, 119.
6. Birch, II, 433; Collins, II, 128.
7. Sir Henry Wotton, *Reliquiae Wottonianae*, 1685.
8. Collins, II, 121.
9. Birch, I, 227; 14 April 1595. Lady Bacon to Anthony, 'For he pretending courtesy worketh mischief perilously. A dangerous intelligencing man.'
10. *Nugae Antiquae.*
11. Birch, II, 440; 31 October 1601.

Rage and Rebellion

1. 18 October 1600 SP Dom 479.
2. Undated, probably February 1600.
3. McLure, 90.
4. Collins II, 127.
5. 27 March 1600.
6. Raleigh's letter to Gilbert, 26 May 1600. McLure, I, 89.
7. R. Winwood, *Memorials of Affairs of State*, I, 300–301, Birch, II, 477.
8. 17 November; Birch, II, 473.
9. Edwards, I, 317.
10. HMC Hatfield x 459.
11. Edwards, II, 404.
12. *Nugae Antiquae.*
13. In his *Prerogative of Parliaments.*
14. Devereux II.

Machiavelli and Parliament

1. Birch, II, 465. Maclean, *Cecil*, 68.
2. Harrison, 286. Lacey, *Essex.*
3. Neale, 374; Stebbing, 150; Edwards, I, 258.
4. *Complete State Trials*, Cobbett, I, col. 1414. Thompson, 148. Lacey, *Raleigh*, 266.
5. Maclean, *Carew*, 72. Hume, 225. Edwards, I, 260.
6. *Nugae Antiquae.*
7. J. O. Halliwell, ed., *Poetical Miscellanies*, 1845. SP Dom cclxxviii 23.
8. G. B. Harrison, *Elizabethan Journal*, III, 174, 1938.
9. *Gentleman's Magazine*, 1853, pt II, 434–43, and 1854, pt I, 17–23.
10. 3 March 1602.
11. 31 October 1601.
12. 27 August, 25 September 1601.
13. Edwards, II, 405–6.
14. Sully, *Mémoires*, III, 29, 1814.
15. 7 September 1601.
16. Raleigh to Cobham, 12 September 1601.
17. Bruce, *Correspondence.*
18. D'Ewes, *Journals.* 19 Early October 1601.
19. *ibid.*, 7 November.
20. *ibid.*, 9 November.
21. *ibid.*, 9 December.
22. *ibid.*, 20 November.
23. *ibid.*, 659.
24. Falls, 317.

Malice and Betrayal

1. Quinn, *Lost Colonists*, 32.
2. Fuller, *Worthies*; Raleigh's *Instructions to his Son*.
3. Late April 1602.
4. Brushfield, Trans. Devon Assoc., V, 1603.
5. Bruce, 4ff.
6. Maclean, *Cecil*, 85–6.
7. Rowse, *Throckmortons*, 229.
8. Hailes, *Secret Correspondence*, Edwards, II, 436–44. Gardiner, I, 93–4.
9. Bruce, 66. HMC Hatfield XIV, 265.
10. Edwards, II, 439.

The Main and the Bye

1. HMC Hatfield xi 528; xii 11 18–19.
2. Philip Caraman (trans.), *Autobiography* of Weston. Jenkins, 324.
3. *Dr. John Manningham's Diary*, ed. J. Bruce.
4. G. M. Trevelyan, 63.
5. Aubrey.
6. Gardiner, I 4.
7. Edwards, II, 264.
8. 9 June 1603.
9. Thompson, 175.
10. T. N. Brushfield, *Journal of the British Archaeological Society*, ix, 35.
11. Bod Ms Carte 205. *English*
Historical Review, VIII, September 1995.
12. *op. cit.*
13. HMC Hatfield cii 77.
14. Rowse, *Throckmortons*, 236.
15. HMC Hatfield xv 208.
16. R. F. Williams, *The Court and Times of James the First*, 1, 13, 1848.
17. 27 July 1603. Transcript, orginal lost.
18. David Hume, *History of England*, 1789.
19. This theme expanded by Simon Adams, *London Review of Books*, 6 July 2000.

The Trial

1. Edwards, I, 367.
2. SP Dom II 88.
3. Stebbing, 200.
4. Stebbing, 201.
5. Edwards, I, 380.
6. 13 or 14 August 1603.
7. Document in Nicholls, 914.
8. Stebbing, 202.
9. Raleigh left the Tower on 10 November.
10. SP Dom iv 76; Edwards, I, 386.
11. Quotation from trial proceedings taken from Jardine, I. See also Cobbett, *Collection of State Trials*, ed. Thomas Howell, II, 1809.
12. Carew Raleigh, in *Observations*, says James remarked afterwards that he would be 'sorry to be tried by a Middlesex jury'.

Waiting for the End

1. Francis Osborne, *Traditional Memorials*, 1673.
2. Vol. 1, 156.
3. *England under the Stuarts*, 21.
4. Jardine, 1, 250.
5. R. F. Williams, *op. cit.*
6. BL Harleian 39.
7. R. F. Williams, *op. cit.*
8. *ibid.*
9. 27 or 28 November 1603.
10. Edwards, II, 406.
11. R. F. Williams, *op. cit.*
12. *op. cit.*, L9.
13. An amalgam of many transcripts, but chiefly BL Sloane 3250 ff 142–7.

Life in the Bloody Tower

1. Latham and Youings believe this was drafted in November at Winchester.
2. Early January 1604.
3. SP Dom Add 1580–1625, 430.
4. Peck 21. BL Cotton Titus cvi ff769–71 v. 4 July 1603.
5. Letter to Cecil, late 1604.
6. Edwards, II, 408.
7. Letter to Privy Council, end February 1604.
8. Stebbing, 246. Bayley.
9. End 1604.
10. Godfrey Goodman, *The Court of King James*, ed. J. S. Brewer, 2 vols.
11. David Green, *Sarah, Duchess of Marlborough*, London, 1967, 219.
12. Shirley, *Scientific Experiments*, BL Sloane 359 Raleigh's Chemical Notebook.
13. Nicholas Le Fèvre, *A Discourse upon Sir Walter Rawleigh's Great Cordial*, 1664.
14. Lefranc, 681.
15. SP Dom xix 2.
16. Chancery Case C24/497/107.
17. 3 August 1604.
18. Tobío, 120–23. Villa-Urrutia, *Ocios*, 31.

Friendship with the Prince

1. Raleigh to Cecil, early July 1605.
2. SP Dom xix 12.
3. HMC Hatfield Mss xvii 378.
4. SP Dom 112.
5. Letter to Privy Council, 9 November 1605.
6. Peter Hammond, in Borg.
7. Shirley, *Harriot*, 29, 21.
8. HMC Syon House 6 Report 1877 app.
9. Willson, 193–4.
10. SP Venetian 1610–13 122–3.
11. Francis Osborne, *Historical Memoirs of the Reign of Queen Elizabeth and King James*, 1658.
12. End 1607.
13. Quinn, *Raleigh and the British Empire*, Chapter VII 14.
14. Quinn, and Quinn, 349, *passim*.
15. AGS, *Estado*, 2585.
16. Purchas xvi, 2nd edn, 1614.

The Great *History*

1. HMC Hatfield fol. 139.
2. Quoted in Rowse, *Throckmortons*, 256.
3. Carew Raleigh, *Observations*.
4. Edwards, I, 624.
5. *Notes on Ben Jonson's Conversations with William Drummond of Hawthornden* (1619), 1842, 71.
6. *ibid.*
7. On Talbot's death 1618, Raleigh's *Journal* on the *Destiny*.
8. Letter to Sir Robert Cotton *c*. 1610 (Latham and Youings, 319) with list of books required.

9. 5 January 1615. McLure I, 568. SP Dom lxxi.
10. Bk II 20 b, III 1 11, II 91.14.
11. Bk II 1 13.
12. Bk II 1 12.
13. Bk IV 2 4.
14. Bk IV 2 16.
15. Bk IV 16 198.
16. Bk IV 2 7.
17. Bk V 211 18.
18. McLure I, 280.
19. Purchas xvi, 322.
20. Strachan, ch. 2, 19–35. Hakluyt, X, 441–501.

O Eloquent, Just and Mighty Death!

1. Raleigh Collection Chapel Hill NC Wm Sanderson Control Folder 4577.
2. Borg Hammond, *op. cit.*
3. 5 October 1611.
4. Thompson, 225.
5. Oldys, VIII, 237. Most extant essays by Raleigh are published in this volume.
6. PRO co 1/1 no 25. Williamson, 55–7, Harlow, *Last Voyage*, 104–5.
7. Undated.
8. 1611 undated.

9. Autumn 1611.
10. Autumn 1611.
11. McLure I, 290.
12. John Nichols, *The Progresses, Processions . . . of King James . . .*, II, 1828, 479.
13. Chamberlain to Carleton, 12 November 1612; SP Dom lxxi 32.
14. 23 November 1612; Nichols, *op. cit.*, 490.
15. V 6 12.

The Overbury Affair

1. Somerset, 126. The most recent and comprehensive book on the Overbury murder. See also Ralph Winwood, *Memorial of Affairs . . .*, 1725, and William McElwee, *The Murder of Sir Thomas Overbury*, 1952.
2. Weldon.

3. Bod Tanner, 199 fol. 198v. Somerset, 176.
4. Somerset, 204. Theodore de Mayerne, *Medicinal Counsels or Advices*, 1677 366–8; Nichols, II, *op. cit.*; Gardiner, II.
5. Winwood, *op. cit.*, III, 482.

6. Brushfield, *Trans. Devon Assoc.*, VI, 1904.
7. McLure I, 568.
8. Undated. Early 1616.
9. BP 2183 fol. 30.
10. Loomie. AGS E25 92/77 30 June 1614.
11. AGS EL5 18/5 30 August 1614.

Release

1. Bod Ms Carte 223 fol. 14/2.
2. APL 1615–10 456.
3. Maclean.
4. McLure; 27 March 1616.
5. SP Dom 1611–18 428.
6. James Spedding, *The Works of Francis Bacon*, XII 270.
7. G. J. Marcus, *Naval History of England*, 1961.
8. 1 July 1616.
9. Edwards I 566–72, II 372.
10. Raleigh's *Apologie*, written in July 1618. Harlow, 316–34.
11. Letter to Bess, 14 November 1617.
12. John Smith, *History of Virginia*, 1624.
13. Tobío, 355.
14. Tobío, 357.
15. Tobío.
16. *Apologie*. AGS 2850 fol. 28.
17. Gardiner, III, 43.
18. Personal to author.
19. BP 2168 fol. 30v. Villa-Urrutia.
20. Edwards I. Venetian Archives Consiglio Communicazioni VII, 1615–17.
21. Godfrey Goodman, *The Court of King James the First*, ed. J. S. Brewer, 2 vols., 1839.
22. Sent 10 February 1617.
23. Carew Raleigh, *Observations*.
24. English State Papers Venetian 1615–17 210.
25. *Autobiography of Phineas Pett*, ed. W. G. Perrin, 1618.
26. Maclean, *Carew*, 71.
27. Edwards, I, 475.

Aboard the *Destiny*

1. Bibl Nat Mss Dupuy 320.
2. McLure II, 64.
3. Maclean, *Carew*, 71. Williams, 236.
4. AGS 2572 fol. 257.
5. AGS 2514 fol. 86; 30 March 1617.
6. Pérez Bustamente.
7. Thompson, 277.
8. SP Dom XC 146.
9. Francisco de Jesus, *Narrative of the Spanish Marriage Treaty*, Camden Soc. 138–49, 298–313.
10. Bibl Nat Dupuy 420.
11. Thompson, 269.
12. PRO Duke of Manchester Mss Letter 219 (June 1617). HMC Comm 8th Report Part II p. 32.
13. 14 May, quoted in Gardiner III, 111; Young's translation at Simancas.
14. AGS 2598 fols. 56–64, 191 2525 fol. 6.
15. Oldys, VIII, 682–8.
16. Cal Plymouth Municipal Records, ed. R. N. Worth, Widey Court Books, 150.
17. McLure II, 850.
18. Canny in Jones, 98.
19. Raleigh's *Journal*, BL Cotton Ms Titus B VIII fl53 et seq. Reprinted in Schomburgk, Hakluyt Soc. 1848, 177–208.

Chronicle of Death

1. *Journal, op. cit.*
2. *Apologie, op. cit.*
3. Maclean, September 1617.
4. DIHE, 122, 152.
5. Maclean, *Carew*, 133.
6. APC Colonial series 1613–M18, 16.
7. Proceedings before the Privy Council, 11 January 1618. Camden Miscellany V, ed. Gardiner.
8. *Notes and Queries*, 2nd series, Vol. XI, 5 January 1861, 4.
9. 14 November 1617. Keymis's letter in Cambridge University Library Mss Ee 50–2, 3.
10. SP Dom, 1611–1618, 53.
11. APC Mss 2597 5 May 1618.

'My Brains are Broken'

1. Cayley, *Life of Raleigh*, ii, 125m, 138. Gardiner, III, 121.
2. *Apologie.*
3. Gardiner, III, 121.
4. 21 March 1618.
5. *Apologie.*
6. Hume, 358. Simón, *Setima Noticia.*
7. James's *Declaration*, drafted by Bacon.
8. *Notes and Queries, op. cit.*
9. Simón.
10. *Notes and Queries, op. cit.*
11. *Apologie.*
12. Simón.

'Piratas! Piratas!'

1. June 1618, original missing. Translated by Hume from Spanish translation AGI Seville.
2. *Notes and Queries, op. cit.*
3. A. Ballesteros, *Correspondencia Oficial de D. Diego Sármiento de Acuña*, Madrid, 1943, I, 282–7, 269. Also SP Venetian 1617–19 235, 241 (Latham and Youings, note 361).
4. Hume, 358.
5. Simón.
6. *Ho-Elianae* I, 23.
7. BL Harleian Mss 6 846 fol. 63.
8. *Ho-Elianae* I, letter 479–85 to Carew Raleigh.
9. Pérez Bustamente, 1, 99.
10. BP DIHE Gondomar to Juan de Ciriza, 5 September 1618.
11. 21 June.
12. Gardiner III 132.
13. BL Harleian Mss 7002 fol. 410.
14. BP DIHE, vol. II, 42, 15 July 1618.
15. Thompson, 314.
16. BP DIHE, II, 26 June.
17. Loomie, Gondomar to Cardinal Bellamine, 4 July 1618.
18. SP Dom xcviii 17.
19. Undated.
20. British Guiana Boundary, British Case app vol. 1 54–5.
21. ACP Colonial 1613–80 19–30.

Cold Walls Again

1. *Declaration.*
2. Sir Thomas Wilson's notes, 17 September 1618. SP Dom xcix no. 10 (continued until 96).
3. *Declaration.*
4. Oldys, I.
5. *Declaration.*
6. Wilson's notes.
7. Oldys, I, King's Narrative, 434.
8. Oldys, I, *op. cit.*
9. Edwards, I, 669.
10. Oldys, *op. cit.*
11. McLure II, 165.
12. DIHE, II 85.
13. Oldys, I.
14. 12 August 1618.
15. Thompson, 329.
16. Cayley, 2, 164.
17. PRO SP/14/103 18–20.
18. 18 September 1618.
19. SP Dom ciii no. 36.
20. BP for decision not to have Raleigh sent to Madrid, 5 September 1618.

Even Such Is Time

1. Spedding, Bacon, VI, 362–2.
2. BP 551 fol. 2.
3. Stebbing, 363–4 from Fortescue papers.
4. DIHE, I, 198.
5. *Observations, op. cit.*
6. DIHE, I, 198.
7. Undated, end October.
8. Edwards, II, 480. Birch, II, 98.
9. Edwards, I, 690, Pory to Carleton SP I vol. CIII.
10. Bod Tanner Ms 299 29.
11. SP Dom III 21a.
12. *History of England*, 388.
13. Birch, II, 97.
14. Thompson, 343.
15. Oldys, VIII, 780.
16. Edwards, II, 413.
17. Edwards, I, 698.
18. SP Dom ciii 58, Cayley II App. 78–82.
19. Monarchy of Man. BL Harleian Mss 2228.
20. *Trevelyan Papers*, III, 153.
21. Sancroft in Bod Tanner Mss, 299, fol. 29 *et seq.*
22. Lorkin to Puckering, Cayley II, 78–82.
23. Brushfield, *Trans. Devon Assoc.*, VII, 1907.
24. E. J. Sánchez Cantón, *Ejecución de Sir Walter Raleigh* in undated *Bolétin de la Real Academia de la Historia*, 126–9.

Afterwards

1. III 156 1895 ed.
2. SP Dom 588.
3. Birch, II, 104.
4. Thompson, 356.
5. BP 551 fol. 32.
6. John Pory to Carleton, 7 November 1618. SP Dom 1611–18, 588.
7. Goodman, *op. cit.*, II, 173.
8. Brushfield, VII, 1905. Rowse, *Throckmortons*, p. 319ff.

9. SP Dom 1619–23 78.
10. Gardiner, III, 154.
11. SP Dom 1611–18 589, 592.
12. SP Dom 1619–23 100.
13. APC 1619–21 177, 1619–23 428.
14. SP Dom 1619–23 297–8; personal information from Quinn.
15. SP Dom 1628–9 97, 179; APC 1627–8 473, 494, 505; Rowse, *Throckmortons*.
16. HMC App Fourth Report 286; SP Dom 1625–5 392.
17. Rowse, *Throckmortons*, 329.
18. SP Dom 1623–5 218, 247.
19. HMC App Fourth Report 294.
20. Bulstrode Whitelock, *Memorials* (1853 edn), iv, 401.
21. Brushfield, VIII, 1907.
22. G. Goodman, *The Court of King James the First*, ed. J. S. Brewer.
23. Shirley, 32.
24. DIHE 74–81. Tobío, 8.
25. Villa-Urrutia, *Lectures*.
26. Philip Edwards, 275.

Appendix

1. Brushfield, *Raleghana, Trans. Devon Assoc.*, 1896.
2. *The Raleighs take to the Sea*, M. Stanford, *Mariner's Mirror*, vol. 48, 1962.
3. Information from Charles Raleigh-Mander.

Acknowledgements

It is hard to decide in which order to list the many friends and relatives who have given up time in helping me with this book, but I must begin with my indebtedness to Raúl Balín, my companion on all my travels who has advised me on many aspects and topics, including the Spanish point of view. I must also thank his nephew José Manuel Monroy for his constant help and generosity over many years.

Perhaps I always had in mind writing about Raleigh; certainly my agent Mark Hamilton encouraged me, as has his son Bill. My interest in the world of El Dorado goes back to reading *Exploration Fawcett*, published nearly fifty years ago, and about the disappearance of Fawcett's companion Raleigh Rimell. Then I read books by Charles Waterston and Peter Fleming, and eventually Raleigh's own *Discoverie*. Stuart Proffitt finally asked me to go ahead, and my gratitude to him for his help and patience is inestimable. I am also especially grateful to Richard Ollard for invaluable advice, and to Michael Page. Cecilia Mackay has been most helpful over gathering illustrations. I am very indebted to Andrew Foot for research in Cornwall and Plymouth.

The library left me by George Eland has been important for first-hand sources. A. L. Rowse also gave me encouragement and much advice. At the end of his life I was fortunate to meet Professor David Beers Quinn, who gave useful suggestions. I am grateful to Giles FitzHerbert and his wife, Alexandra, for hospitality and assistance when he was ambassador in Venezuela. Also in Venezuela I was helped by Professor Mario Sanoja Obediente, for travel arrangements (and protection) by Enrique Lezana and his colleagues, also by Kai Rosenberg. In Colombia I had the help of Ricardo and Maria Clemencia Arango, to whom I am very grateful.

I must thank Peter Scott and Anthony Stevens for much hospitality at Fardel Manor, once the home of the Raleighs. My relatives in the United States, Jeanne Trevillian Lough and Professor Wallace Dabney Trevillian, gave me useful leads. I am also grateful to Professor Cecil Y. Lang and his wife, Violette, at Charlottesville, and to Michael Plunkett, Director of Special University Collections at the Alderman Library, the University of Virginia. My especial thanks go to Dr Robert Anthony, Curator of the Raleigh Collection, the University of North Carolina at Chapel Hill, for much assistance, and to his staff. Also in the United States I must thank Ann and David Thomas for several ideas and discoveries, and Bud Warren and Jeffrey P. Brain for information about Fort St George, Popham Beach.

In Spain my cousin Diego de Pedroso gave me valuable introductions before he died. I am also extremely grateful to his widow, Carmita, the Condesa Vda de San Esteban de Cañongo, and their daughter Luz, descendants of the great Conde de Gondomar. Isabel Aquirre Landa was very helpful at the Archivo General de Simancas, and I also thank Luis Martinez Garcia. I am grateful for the assistance at the Biblioteca de Palacio, Madrid, with the introduction from the late Ilsmo Señor Don Dalmiro de la Válgoma, and to staff at the manuscripts department at the Biblioteca Nacional, Madrid, the Archivo General de Indias, Seville, and the Escuela de Estudios Hispano-Americanos, Seville.

In Ireland I must thank another cousin, Conor MacGillycuddy, and his parents, Rose and Nicholas. I am also grateful to Michael Penruddock, agent at Lismore Castle, and Patricia McCarthy at the Cork Archives Institute. Michael MacCarthy-Morrogh's book was most useful, and I thank him for it.

Robin Harcourt Williams, Librarian and Archivist at Hatfield House, has been especially generous with help. I am also grateful to Christine North, County Archivist, Cornwall County Record Office; Angela Broome, Librarian at the Royal Institution of Cornwall; John M. Draisey, County Archivist, Devon Record Office; Hugh Jaques, County Archivist, Dorset Record Office; Jane Harris, Archivist, Hampshire Record Office; Ann Smith, Archivist, Sherborne Castle, for showing me Raleigh's will and the rooms associated with him; Sarah Barter Bailey, Librarian at the Royal Armouries at the Tower of London; and Julie Courtenay, Archivist at Lady Margaret Hall, for a copy of Mary Coate's report for the Susette Taylor Research Fellowship.

Thanks also go to Nicolas Barker, the late Edith Clay, Professor Morton N. Cohen, Roger Dean, Sarah Dick-Reade, Victor Franco de Baux, Lord Hastings, Roger Hudson, Buster Hurt, Elizabeth Jenkins, my cousin the Condesa de Madan, Henry Manisty, Bob Mann, the late Vesey Norman, Sir Richard Carew Pole, Charles Raleigh-Mander, Josephine Reid, Mary Duchess of Roxburghe, John Sandoe, Viscount Saye and Sele, the late Professor Richard N. Swift, Michael Treleaven, Angèle Vidal-Hall, Elliott Viney, and the late Alan Walker, genealogist and distant cousin.

It would be wrong if I failed to acknowledge the spadework of those biographers listed in the Bibliography. As someone who has not yet come to word processing, I am deeply grateful for all the transcribing of my handwriting over the years by Susan M. Day and Mary Turner.

Raleigh Trevelyan
June 2002

Bibliography

Primary and Essential Sources

AGI   Archivo General de Indias, Materias del Gobierno de las Indias, esp. Patronato, Santo Domingo

APC   Acts of the Privy Council, ed. J. R. Dasent, 32 vols., 1890–1907

AGS   Archivo General de Simancas: Estado

BL   British Library: Additional, Cotton, Harleian, Lansdowne, Royal, Sloane, etc.

BN   Biblioteca Nacional (Manuscritos), Madrid

BP   Biblioteca de Palacio (Manuscritos), Madrid

BOD   Bodleian Library: Carte, Clarendon, Egerton, Tanner

CSP   Calendar of State Papers: Archives of Simancas, Colonial, Domestic, Foreign, Ireland, Supplementary

DIHE   Documentos Inéditos para la Historia de España, Madrid, 1936–45, esp. at La Biblioteca de Palacio, Madrid

HMC   Historical Manuscripts Commission, esp. Calendar of Salisbury MSS at Hatfield House, 23 vols., 1883–1973

PRO   Public Record Office for State Papers Domestic etc. (SP)

Aubrey, John, *Brief Lives*, ed. Oliver Lawson Dick, London, 1949.

Bacon, Francis, *Apophthegms Old and New*, London, 1628.

Birch, Thomas, *Memoirs of the Reign of Queen Elizabeth*, 2 vols., London, 1754.

Blue Books, *British Guiana Boundary Appendix to the Case on behalf of the Government of Her Britannic Majesty*, 1898–9 (used for arbitration with Venezuela and includes translations from the Archivo General de Indias, Seville), 19 vols.

Bruce, John, *Correspondence of King James VI of Scotland*, Camden Society, London, 1861.

Brushfield, T. N., *'Raleghana'* articles between 1886 and 1909 in the *Transactions of Devonshire Association*. Bibliography 2nd ed. 1908.

Camden, William, *Britannia*, 1695.

    Annales: The True and Royal History of the Famous Empresse Elizabeth, London, 1625; ed. T. Hearne, London, 1707.

Chamberlain, John, *Letters by John Chamberlain During the Reign of Queen Elizabeth*, ed. Sarah Williams, Camden Society, London 1861.

Colección de Documentos Inéditos, para La Historia De España, esp. vols. 1–4, Madrid, 1842–95.

Collins, Arthur (ed.), *Letters and Memorials of State*, 2 vols., London, 1726.

Edwards, Edward, *The Life of Sir Walter Ralegh*, 2 vols., London, 1868.

Emden, Cecil, *Oriel Papers*, Oxford, 1948.

Fuller, Thomas, *The History of the Worthies of England*, 1662. (New edition ed. P. Austin Nuttall, 1840.)

Hailes, Lord, ed., *Secret Correspondence of Sir Robert Cecil with James VI*, London, 1766.

Hakluyt, Richard, *The Principall Navigations, Voyages and Discoveries of the English Nation*, 1589, 3 vols., 1598–1600. 12 vols., Hakluyt Society extra ser. I–XII, Glasgow, 1903–5.

Harlow, V. T., *The Discoverie of Guiana*, London, 1928.

Ralegh's Last Voyage, London, 1932.

Hariot, Thomas, *A Briefe and True Report of the New Found Land of Virginia*, 1588.

Holinshed, Raphael, *Chronicles of England, Scotland and Ireland*, augmented and continued to 1586 by John Hooker, alias Vowell, 1587; 6 vols., 1807–8.

Hooker, John, *Description of the City of Exeter*, ed. W. J. Harte, Devon and Cornwall Record Society, 1919.

Howell, James, *Epistolae Ho-Elianae*, 1645–55, ed. Joseph Jacobs, 2 vols., London, 1892.

Jardine, David, *Criminal Trials*, 1832 (selected and edited by Justin Lovill, London, 1999).

Keymis, Lawrence, *A Relation of the Second Voyage to Guiana . . . in the Year 1596*. Hakluyt, vol. X.

Latham, Agnes, ed., *The Poems of Sir Walter Raleigh*, 1929 (new edition London and Cambridge, Mass., 1962).

Latham, Agnes, and Youings, Joyce, eds., *The Letters of Sir Walter Ralegh*, Exeter, 1999.

Lee, Maurice, ed., *Dudley Carleton to John Chamberlain*, New Brunswick, 1972.

Maclean, John, ed., *Letters from Robert Cecil to Sir George Carew*, Camden Society, London, 1854.

Letters from George Lord Carew to Sir Thomas Roe, Camden Society, London, 1860.

Naunton, Sir Robert, *Fragmenta Regalia*, London, 1641.

Nicholls, Mark, *Sir Walter Ralegh's Treason: A Prosecution Document*, English Historical Review, vol. CX, September 1995.

Oldys, William, and Birch, Thomas, *Works of Sir Walter Raleigh*: Vol. I, *Life*; Vols. II–VII, *History of the World*; Vol. VIII, *Misc.*, Oxford, 1829.

Oppenheim, M., *Sir William Monson's Naval Tracts in Navy Records Society*, Vol. II, London, 1902.

Purchas, Samuel, *Haklutus Posthumus or Purchas His Pilgrimes*, 5 vols., 1625; another edition 20 vols., Glasgow, 1906.

Quinn, David Beers, *The Voyages and Colonising Expeditions of Sir Humphrey Gilbert*, Hakluyt Society, Series 2, LXXXIII–IV, 1940.
    Raleigh and The British Empire, London, 1947.
    The Roanoke Voyages 1584–1590, 2 vols., Hakluyt Society, series 2, CIV, London, 1955.
    and Ned M. Cheshire (eds.), *The New Found Land of Stephen Parmenius*, Hakluyt Society, London, 1972.
    England and the Discovery of America, 1974.
    with Alison M. Quinn, *The English New England Voyages 1602–1608*, Hakluyt Society, London, 1983.
    The Lost Colonies and their Probable Fate, Raleigh N.C., 1984.
Sanderson, William, alias Peter Heylin?, *Aulicus Coquinariae*, 1650.
    The Lives and Reigns of Mary Queen of Scotland and . . . James the Sixth, London, 1656.
Simón, Fray Pedro, *Segunda Parte, Sexta Noticia de Las Conquistas de Tierra Firme*, Bogotá, 1892.
Somers, Lord, *Tracts. Revised by Walter Scott*, vols. 2 and 3, London, 1809–10.
Stebbing, William, *Sir Walter Ralegh*, Oxford, 1891, revised 1899.
Strachey, William, *The Historie of Travell into Virginia Britannia*, ed. Lewis B. Wright and Virginia Freund, London, 1953.
Tobío Fernandez, Luis, *Gondomar y so trionfo sobre Raleigh*, Santiago, 1974.
Venezuela Boundary Dispute, see Blue Books.
Wood, Anthony à., *Athenae Oxonienses*, 1691–2.

Other Publications

Adamson, J. H., and Folland, H. F., *Shepherd of the Ocean*, London, 1969.
Andrews, Kenneth R., *English Privateering Voyages*, Cambridge, 1959.
    Elizabethan Privateering, Cambridge, 1964.
    The Last Voyage of Drake and Hawkins, Cambridge, 1972.
    Trade, Plunder and Settlement, Cambridge, 1984.
Bagwell, R., *Ireland under the Tudors*, 3 vols., 1885–90, reprinted 1962.
Bayley, John, *The History and Antiquities of The Tower of London*, vol. I, London, 1825.
Beer, Anna R., *Sir Walter Ralegh and his Readers in the Seventeenth Century*, London and New York, 1997.
Berleth, Richard, *The Twilight Lords*, New York, 1978, London 1979.
Boas, Frederick S., *Christopher Marlowe*, Oxford, 1946.
Borg, Alan *et al.*, *Strange Stories from the Tower of London*, London, 1976.
Bouillard, Patrick, *San Augustín*, Medellín, 1987.
Bray, Warwick, *The Gold of El Dorado*, Catalogue of the Royal Academy Exhibition, London, 1978.
Brigden, Susan, *New Worlds, Lost Worlds*, London, 2000.
Brooks, Eric St John, *Sir Christopher Hatton*, London, 1946.

Byrne, M. J., *Ireland under Elizabeth*, Dublin, 1903.

Caraman, Philip, *The Western Rising, 1549*, Tiverton, 1994.

Cayley, A., *Life of Sir Walter Raleigh*, 2 vols., 1806.

Cecil, Algernon, *A Life of Robert Cecil, Earl of Salisbury*, London, 1915.

Cecil, David, *The Cecils of Hatfield House*, London, 1973.

Chambers, E. K., *Sir Henry Lee*, Oxford, 1936.

Clements, H. G. J., *Local Vestiges of Sir Walter Ralegh*, Transactions of the Devonshire Association, 1873.

Coote, Stephen, *A Play of Passion: The Life of Sir Walter Ralegh*, London, 1993.

Craig, D. H., *Sir John Harington*, Boston, Mass., 1985.

Cummins, John, *Francis Drake*, London, 1995.

Dancy, John, *Walter Oakeshott*, Ipswich, 1995.

David, R. W. (ed.), *Love's Labour's Lost*, London and New York, 1990.

Devereux, W. B., *Lives and Letters of the Devereux, Earls of Essex*, 2 vols., London, 1853.

D'Ewes, Simonds, *Journals of all the Parliaments during the Reign of Queen Elizabeth*, ed. P. Bowes, London, 1682.

Duncan-Jones, Katherine, *Sir Philip Sidney*, London, 1991.
    Ungentle Shakespeare, London, 2001.

Edwards, Philip, *Sir Walter Ralegh*, London, 1953.

Elton, G. R., *England under the Tudors*, Final Edition, 1991.

Escorial, Real Monasterio de San Lorenzo de El Escorial, commemorative exhibition, *Felipe II: un Monarca y su Época*, 1998.

Falls, Cyril, *Elizabeth's Irish Wars*, London 1950.

Fenton, Edward, *The Diaries of John Dee*, Charlbury, 1998.

Firth, C. H., *Sir Walter Ralegh's History of the World* in *Essays Historical and Literary*, Oxford, 1938.

Franchetti, Ana Maria, *et al.*, *Museo del Oro*, Guide Bogotá, 1981.

Fraser, Antonia, *The Gunpowder Plot*, London, 1996.

French, Peter, *John Dee*, London, 1972.

García Oro, José, *Don Diego de Acuña, Conde de Gondomar*, Xunta de Galicia, 1997.

Gardiner, Samuel R., *History of England from the Accession of James I to the Outbreak of the Civil War*, vols. I–III, London, 1883–4.

Gil, Juan, *Mitos y Utopías del Descubrimiento*, vol. 3, *El Dorado*, Madrid, 1989.

Greenblatt, Sidney Jay, *Sir Walter Ralegh, The Renaissance Man and his Roles*, New Haven, 1973.

Grosart, A. W., *Lismore Papers*, Series 1 and 2, 10 vols., 1886–9.

Hadfield, Andrew, *Edmund Spenser's Irish Experience*, Oxford, 1997.

Hagen, Victor Wolfgang von, *The Gold of El Dorado*, London, 1974.

Halliday, F. E., *Richard Carew of Anthony*, London, 1953.
    A Cornish Chronicle, Newton Abbot, 1967.

Harington, Sir John, *Epigrams*, 1618 (Menston, 1970).
    Nugae Antiquae, 1779.

Harrison, G. B. (ed.), *Willobie His Avisa*, 1594 (Edinburgh, 1966).
    The Life and Death of Robert Devereux, Earl of Essex, London, 1937.

Hasler, P. W. (ed.), *The House of Commons 1558–1603*, 3 vols., HMSO, 1981.

Hemming, John, *The Search for El Dorado*, London, 1978.

Henley, Pauline, *Spenser in Ireland*, Cork, 1928.

Hibbard, G. A., *Thomas Nashe*, London, 1962.

Hoskins, W. G., *Devon*, London, 1954.

Howe, Bea, *A Galaxy of Governesses*, London, 1954.

Humber, John L., *Backgrounds and Preparations for the Roanoke Voyages*, Raleigh, N.C., 1986.

Hume, Martin A. S., *Sir Walter Ralegh*, London, 1897.

Hutchins, J., *History and Antiquities of the County of Dorset*, 1774 (revised edition, 4 vols., 1861–70, reprinted 1973).

Jardine, Lisa, and Stewart, Alan, *Hostage to Fortune*, London, 1998.

Jenkins, Elizabeth, *Elizabeth the Great*, London, 1958.

   Elizabeth and Leicester, London, 1961.

Jones, H. G. (ed.), *Raleigh and Quinn*, Chapel Hill, 1987.

Kamen, Henry, *Philip of Spain*, New Haven and London, 1997.

Kelsey, Harry, *Sir Francis Drake*, New Haven and London, 1998.

Klarwill, Victor von (ed.), *Queen Elizabeth and Some Foreigners*, London, 1928.

Lacey, Robert, *Sir Walter Ralegh*, London, 1973.

   Robert, Earl of Essex, London, 1971.

Lefranc, Pierre, *Sir Walter Ralegh, Écrivain*, Quebec and Paris, 1968.

Lewis, G. R., *The Stannaries*, Cambridge, Mass., 1906.

Lockyer, Roger, *The Early Stuarts*, London, 1989.

   Buckingham, London, 1981.

   James VI and I, London, 1998.

Loomie, Albert J., *Spain and the Jacobean Catholics*, vol. II, Catholic Record Society, 1978.

Lyon, F. H., *Diego de Sarmiento de Acuña, Conde de Gondomar*, London, 1916.

MacCarthy Morrogh, Michael, *The Munster Plantation*, Oxford, 1986.

McDermott, James, *Martin Frobisher*, New Haven and London, 2001.

McLure, N. E. (ed.), *The Letters of John Chamberlain*, 2 vols., Philadelphia, 1939.

Marañon, Gregorio, *Antonio Pérez*, London, 1954.

March, Rosemary, *Sherborne Castle*, Sherborne, 1979.

Martin, Colin, *Full Fathom Five*, London, 1975.

Martin, Colin, and Parker, Geoffrey, *The Spanish Armada*, London, 1988.

Mattingley, Garrett, *The Defeat of the Spanish Armada*, London, 1959.

Naipaul, V. S., *The Loss of El Dorado*, London, 1969.

   A Way in the World, London, 1994.

National Maritime Museum (Joyce Youings and others), *Royal Armada: 400 Years*, Greenwich, 1988.

Neale, J. E., *Queen Elizabeth*, London, 1934.

   Elizabeth and Her Parliaments, London, 1957.

Nicholl, Charles, *A Cup of Newes: The Life of Thomas Nashe*, London, 1984.

   The Reckoning: The Murder of Christopher Marlowe, London, 1992.

   The Creature on the Map, London, 1995.

Oakeshott, Walter, *The Queen and the Poet*, London, 1960.

Orpen, Goddard H., *Raleigh's Home at Youghal, Journal of the Society of Antiquaries of Ireland 1903*, Dublin, 1904.

Padfield, Peter, *Armada*, London, 1988.

Parker, Geoffrey, *The Grand Strategy of Philip II*, New Haven and London, 1998.

Peck, Linda Levy, *Northampton: Patronage and Policy at the Court of James I*, London, 1982.

Pérez Bustamente, C., *El Conde de Gondomar y su intervención en . . . el muerte de Sir Walter Raleigh*, Santiago, 1928.

Pope Hennessy, Sir John, *Sir Walter Raleigh in Ireland*, London, 1883.

Prince, John, *The Worthies of Devon*, Plymouth, 1710.

Quennell, Peter, *Shakespeare: The Poet and His Background*, London, 1984.

Raleigh, Carew, '*A Lover of Truth*', *Observations Upon . . . A Compleat History . . . (by William Sanderson)*, 1656.

    A Brief Relation of Sir Walter Raleigh's Troubles, Harleian Miscellany, Vol. IV, 1745.

Ramos, Demetrio, *El Mito del Dorado*, Bogotá, 1973.

Read, Conyers, *Lord Burghley and Queen Elizabeth*, London, 1960.

Rowse, A. L., *Sir Richard Grenville of the Revenge*, London, 1937.

    Tudor Cornwall, London, 1941.

    The England of Elizabeth, London, 1951.

    The Expansion of Elizabethan England, London, 1955.

    Ralegh and the Throckmortons, London, 1962.

    The Elizabethan Renaissance: The Cultural Achievement, London, 1972.

    The Tower of London, 1974.

    Court and Country, Brighton, 1987.

    (ed.), *The First Colonists*, London, 1986.

Rudick, Michael, *The Poems of Sir Walter Raleigh*, Tempe, 1999.

Sánchez Canton, Javier, Dissertation on *Conde de Gondomar* for Academia de la Historia, Madrid, 1935.

Schama, Simon, *Landscape and Memory*, London, 1995.

Schomburgk, Sir Robert H., *The Discovery of Guiana with Unpublished Documents*, London, 1848.

Shirley, John W., *Scientific Experiments of Sir W. Ralegh, The Wizard Earl, and the Three Magi in the Tower*, Ambix, 1949.

    Thomas Harriot: A Biography, Oxford, 1983.

    Sir Walter Ralegh and the New World, Chapel Hill, 1985.

    (ed.), *Thomas Harriot: Renaissance Scientist*, Oxford, 1974.

Somerset, Anne, *Unnatural Murder: Poison at the Court of James I*, London, 1997.

Sparrey, Francis, *The Description of the Isle of Trinidad, etc.*, Purchas 1906 ed., vol. XVI.

Stanford, Michael, *The Raleighs Take to the Sea*, The Mariner's Mirror, vol. 48, 1962.

Stanley, Arthur Penrhyn, *Historical Memorials of Westminster Abbey*, 6th edition, revised, 1896.

Stewart, Alan, *Philip Sidney*, London, 2000.

Strachan, Michael, *Sir Thomas Roe*, Wilton, 1989.

Strathmann, Ernest A., *Sir Walter Ralegh, A Study in Elizabethan Scepticism*, New York, 1951.

Strong, Roy, *Henry Prince of Wales*, London, 1986.

Simmons, Thomas H. B. (ed.), *Meta Incognita: A Discourse of Discovery – Martin Frobisher's Arctic Expeditions*, 2 vols., Quebec, 1999.

Thompson, Edward, *Sir Walter Raleigh*, London, 1935.

Thompson, James Westfall, *The Wars of Religion in France*, Chicago, 1909.

Thomson, Elizabeth McLure (ed.), *The Chamberlain Letters*, London, 1966.

Timbs, John, *Curiosities of London*, n.d.

Trevelyan, G. M., *England under the Stuarts*, revised edition 1946.

Trevelyan, W. C. and Trevelyan, C. E. (eds.), *The Trevelyan papers*, part I, 1857, Camden Society, Part III, 1872.

Tytler, Patrick Fraser, *Life of Sir Walter Raleigh*, Edinburgh, 1832.

Venezuela Misionera, *Veinticinco Años de Labor Misionera*, Caracas, 1949.

Villa-Urrutia, Marqués de, *Ocios Diplomaticos*, Madrid, 1927.

  La Embajada del Conde de Gondomar a Inglaterra en 1613.

  Lectures at the *Real Academia de la Historia*, Madrid, 25 May 1967.

Vivian, J. L., *Visitations of the County of Cornwall*, Exeter, 1887.

  Visitations of the County of Devon, Exeter, 1895.

Waldman, Milton, *Sir Walter Raleigh*, London, 1928.

Walker, Julia M., *Dissing Elizabeth*, Durham and London, 1998.

Wallace, Willard Mosher, *Sir Walter Raleigh*, Princeton, 1959.

Weldon, Anthony, *The Court and Character of K. James*, London, 1650.

Wernham, R. B., *Return of the Armadas*, Oxford, 1994.

White, William, *Devonshire*, 1850.

Whitehead, A. W., *Caspard de Coligny*, London, 1904.

Williams, Norman Lloyd, *Sir Walter Raleigh*, London, 1962, new edn 1988.

Williamson, James A., *The English in Guiana*, Oxford, 1923.

  Hawkins of Plymouth, London, 1949.

Willson, D. Harris, *King James VI and I*, London, 1956.

Winton, John, *Sir Walter Ralegh*, London, 1975.

Woolley, Benjamin, *The Queen's Conjuror* (Dr. Dee), London, 2001.

Yates, Frances A., *John Florio*, Cambridge, 1934.

  A Study of Love's Labour's Lost, Cambridge, 1935.

  Giordano Bruno and the Hermetic Tradition, Chicago, 1964.

  The Occult Philosophy of the Elizabethan Age, London, 1979.

Youings, Joyce (ed.), *Ralegh in Exeter*, Exeter, 1985.

  Raleigh's Country, Raleigh, N.C., 1986.

  See also Latham.

Since this book was written, Gondomar's correspondence has been published in two volumes by the Patrimonio Nacional, Madrid, and edited by M. L. López-Vidriero, including DIHE, alas too late for me to consult it.

Credits for Illustrations

Plate 1: By courtesy of the Lord Hastings, photograph J. Revell.

Plate 4: Copyright © The National Trust (Enterprises) Ltd.

Plates 5, 7, 8, 23: The National Portrait Gallery, London.

Plates 6, 25: By courtesy of the Marquess of Salisbury, Hatfield House.

Plates 10, 11: Colonial Williamsburg Foundation.

Plates 12, 13, Pages 71, 519: Copyright © The British Museum 1906-5-9-1(8), 1906-5-9-1(13), P1 216, P1 107.

Plate 19: South American Pictures, Tony Morrison.

Plates 20, 22: The British Library, Bridgeman Art Gallery 12215.

Plates 24, 28: The National Gallery of Ireland.

Plate 26: By courtesy of the Lord Egremont. Photograph: Photographic Survey, Courtauld Institute of Art.

Plate 27: Copyright © National Maritime Museum, London.

Plate 31: By courtesy of Their Graces the Duke and Duchess of Rutland.

Plate 33: Raleigh UK Limited.

Page 58: The Guildhall Museum, London; photograph Jeremy Butler.

Pages 73, 111, 228, 242 and 256: By permission of the British Library, Maps 75005 (3), G7132 sig A3V, 10003C2, 10003C32.

Page 129: Copyright © Fotomas Index.

Page 399: The Royal Armouries Museum.

Page 496: Archivo General de Simancas, 2598. Hume mss.

Page 556: By courtesy of the Condesa de San Esteban de Cañongo.

Plates 2, 3, 9, 14, 15, 16, 17, 18, 21, 29, 30, 32, 34, Pages 324, 434, 445, 471, 472: Author.

Index

Page numbers in *italics* denotes illustration